ALFRED VALDMANIS AND THE POLITICS OF SURVIVAL

Alfred Valdmanis is best known in Canada for his infamous role in Premier Joey Smallwood's scheme to industrialize Newfoundland. A Latvian immigrant, he was appointed Director General of Economic Development in 1950 with the understanding that through his connections to Europe he could entice German and Baltic industrialists to the isolated, rural island. His influence was brought to an abrupt end when, in 1954, he was charged with defrauding the government. The media, latching on to his murky past and his possible affiliation with war criminals, made him the scapegoat of Newfoundland's problems, painting him as part comedian, part sinister villain.

This was not the first time his name was connected with controversial issues. Valdmanis's wily political manoeuvring is more the stuff of fiction than history. Between 1938, at age 29, and his ironic downfall in the safe haven of Canada, he was a finance minister of pre-war Latvia, a government official during the Soviet invasion, a shrewd collaborator under the Nazi occupation, then, a friend to the Allies, a spokesman for Latvian POW and displaced persons, and an adviser to the government of Canada. In this first serious biography of Alfred Valdmanis, historian Gerhard Bassler casts the story of this political manipulator and chameleon in new terms: the often tragic consequences of the will to survive.

GERHARD BASSLER is a history professor at the Memorial University of Newfoundland.

Alfred Valdmanis and the Politics of Survival

GERHARD P. BASSLER

UNIVERSITY OF TORONTO PRESS
Toronto Buffalo London

Toronto Buffalo London

Reprinted in paperback 2017

ISBN 978-0-8020-4413-6 (cloth)
ISBN 978-1-4875-9815-0 (paper)

Printed on acid-free paper

Canadian Cataloguing in Publication Data

Bassler, Gerhard P., 1937–
Alfred Valdmanis and the politics of survival

Includes bibliographical references and index
ISBN 978-0-8020-4413-6 (bound) ISBN 978-1-4875-9815-0 (pbk.)

1. Valdmanis, Alfred, 1908–1970. 2. Latvia – History – 1918–1940. 3. Latvia – History – 1940–1991. 4. Newfoundland – Economic policy. 5. Finance ministers – Latvia – Biography. 6. Newfoundland and Labrador Corporation – Biography. 7. Latvians – Canada – Biography. I. Title.

FC601.V33B37 2000 971.063'3'092 C99-930935-8
F1034.3.V28B37 2000

University of Toronto Press acknowledges the financial assistance to its publishing program of the Canada Council for the Arts and the Ontario Arts Council.

This book has been published with the help of a grant from the Humanities and Social Sciences Federation of Canada, using funds provided by the Social Sciences and Humanities Research Council of Canada.

University of Toronto Press acknowledges the financial support for its publishing activities of the Government of Canada through the Book Publishing Industry Development Program (BPIDP).

Canadä

Contents

ACKNOWLEDGMENTS vii

NOTE ON SPELLING AND TRANSLATION xi

ABBREVIATIONS AND GLOSSARY xiii

Introduction 3

1 *Wunderkind* in Reborn Latvia: Background, Education, and Civil Service Career, 1908–1938 10

2 'The Most Active and Influential Member of the Cabinet': Minister of Finance, 1938–1939 39

3 'Better to Die Standing Up Than to Keep on Living on Your Knees': War, Resignation, and Soviet Occupation, 1939–1941 73

4 'Elected to Lead and Manage Latvian National Affairs': The Janus Face of Collaboration, July 1941 to November 1942 104

5 'Made No Bones about His Antipathy to the German Regime': The Janus Face of Resistance, November 1942 to May 1945 139

6 'I Had Committed All My Heart and My Efforts to Latvian Exiles': Refugee Politics, 1945–1948 175

7 'Starting Anew Like Our Fathers Did after the First World War': Immigrant in Canada, 1948–1950 220

8 'Develop or Perish': The Challenges of Newfoundland, 1950–1953 247

9 'The Past, Instead of Helping to Rebuild, Denies Itself': The Latvian Refugee Community and the Shadows of the Past, 1950–1954 278

10 'Only One Could Topple Him from His Height – Himself': Newfoundland's 'Economic Tsar,' 1952–1954 310

11 'Something Had Happened and a Culprit Had to Be Found': Con Man or Scapegoat? 1954–1957 328

12 'Maybe My Luck Is Used Up Already, Maybe Not': Epilogue, 1956–1970, and Conclusions 368

NOTES 391

REFERENCES 445

INDEX 457

Illustrations follow page 240

Acknowledgments

This book could not have been written without Arnis and Sofija Lucis. Natives of Latvia (Vidzeme and Zemgale provinces) and educated there as an electronics engineer and a pharmacist respectively, they became residents of St John's, Newfoundland, in 1951. Over a period of more than a decade, Arnis with the support of his wife Sofija freely gave of his time to help translate Latvian government documents, manuscripts, letters, and books. Their intimate familiarity with the Latvian cultural and social scene, along with their personal connections, refugee migration to Germany and Canada, and experience as recruitees of Valdmanis's industrialization schemes in Newfoundland helped me put the life and times of Alfred Valdmanis into context.

Invaluable reservoirs of information and inspiration, Arnis and Sofija provided essential contacts for this project. They helped arrange interviews with a number of Latvians, including Gundars and Irma Valdmanis, the latter's brother-in-law Sigurds Mikelsons, and Alfred Valdmanis's brother Osvald. Gundars kindly provided access to his father's personal papers, including very confidential notes as well as photographs in the family's possession. Arnis and Sofija also helped plan joint trips to Latvia in 1992 and 1993 – their first opportunity in almost half a century to revisit the ancestral land that had sustained them for the first twenty-four years of their lives. Their reconnection to links severed in 1944 was as exciting for me to observe as for them to experience. In particular, I benefited from generous hospitality extended in Latvia by Lilita and Madis Sīpols, Agnese and Dagnija Surgovte, Helena Ogste and Normunds Ogsts, and Stāsis Mežnieks. Thanks to Stāsis and the Latvian excursions he arranged (despite gasoline shortages) in a car lent by a relative, we were able to retrace Valdmanis's origins in Latvia – his birthplace in Ziemupe, his high school in Liepāja (Libau), the Ķegums hydropower station – and interview some of his contemporaries.

This would have been a different book without the collapse of the Soviet Union. Prior to the autumn of 1991, Soviet Latvian officials denied access to the records of the Ulmanis regime. My repeated requests to the Riga State Historical Archives remained unanswered. In late 1991 the intervention of Jean François Somcynsky of Canada's Department of External Affairs prompted the archive's director Nikolai Risov to at least acknowledge receipt of my correspondence. But on our first appearance in Riga in the summer of 1992 Risov's deputy, Beate Krajevska, still tried to withhold the hitherto classified records. She flatly refused to acknowledge a personal letter of introduction by Raimonds Pauls, Latvia's Minister of Culture. Guntis Siliņš, Consul General of Latvia in Montreal, had requested that Pauls issue the letter during his first visit to Canada. Only the diplomatic skills and persistence of Arnis Lucis and Stāsis Mežnieks prevented our return empty-handed. Once we were admitted, however, archivist Īra Zanerika went out of her way to show us as many files as time permitted.

Numerous other persons facilitated research in Latvia, Germany, and Canada. For valuable Latvian contacts I am indebted to Manfred Kerner in Berlin, Pēteris Ozoliņš and Heinrihs Strods in Riga, Kārlis Kangeris in Stockholm, and Girts Zegners in Niederkassel-Rheidt. Very helpful was Latvian information given to me by Edgars Andersons, Marģers Vestermanis, Kārlis Kangeris, Baiba Vītoliņš, Indulis Ronis, and Eriks Žagars. Archival research in Germany was eased by Maria Keipert and Lucia van der Linde of the Politisches Archiv des Auswärtigen Amts in Bonn, Wilhelm Lenz of the Bundesarchiv Koblenz, and Hubertus Herz in Kirchseeon. In Canada the assistance of Bobbie Robertson, Jack W. Pickersgill, Alberts Jekste, Günther Sann, Gordon F. Pushie, Greg Power, Fritz W. Stobbe, Herbert Matschen, Baxter Morgan, and M.F. Kuester is gratefully acknowledged.

Sincere thanks go to Arnis Dūks, Klaus Wollenweber, and Michael Wernerheim for translating documents from Latvian, Russian, and Swedish; to Melvin Baker for advice on Newfoundland aspects of the project; to Harold Pretty for research assistance; to the helpful archival staff of Memorial University's Centre for Newfoundland Studies and interlibrary loan service; to Memorial's vice-president (academic) for a subvention for the inclusion of illustrations; and to Kate Baltais for conscientious and dedicated copy-editing.

In the early 1980s I was the first researcher permitted to examine J.R. Smallwood's personal papers as they were filed by Smallwood. Some of the documents displaced in the subsequent rearrangement by the CNS archival staff are listed according to the original files in which I found them.

Last but not least, my wife, Tonya, deserves particular recognition. Without her constant prodding and editorial advice, the unanticipated massive research for this study would not have been completed.

Gerhard P. Bassler
Memorial University of Newfoundland
August 1998

Note on Spelling and Translations

All translations, unless indicated otherwise, are by the following: Arnis Lucis – Latvian; Arnis Dūks and Klaus Wollenweber – Russian; Michael Wernerheim – Swedish; and Gerhard P. Bassler – German. Latvian names and words are spelled as the authors spelled them, depending on whether the environment was Latvian-speaking or not. In Germany and North America, Latvians tend to spell their names without the Latvian-style 's' ending and without diacritical marks. For example, the Valdmanis brothers Alfreds and Osvalds identified themselves as Alfred and Osvald in Canada.

Abbreviations and Glossary

AA *Archiv des Auswärtigen Amts* (German Foreign Office Archives), Bonn
AAS *Arbetarrörelsens Arkiv*, Stockholm
Abwehr Central German military intelligence organization
Aizsargi Latvian national guard or home guard
AOP August Osis Papers, Edmonton
AVP Alfred A. Valdmanis Papers, Montreal
BA *Bundesarchiv* (German federal archives), Koblenz
BRINCO British Newfoundland Development Corporation
BSA Benno Schilde Archives, Bad Hersfeld, Germany
Cheka Extraordinary Commission to Combat Counterrevolution, Sabotage, and Speculation. Soviet political police 1917–22 (see OGPU and NKVD)
CMIC Canadian Machinery and Industry Construction Ltd (Head office: St John's, Newfoundland)
CNS Centre for Newfoundland Studies Archives at Memorial University of Newfoundland, St John's
Daugavas Vanagi Hawks of the Daugava River. Latvian legionnaires' welfare organization founded in Belgium in 1946
DP Displaced person
Einsatzgruppe Mobile armed unit of security police and SD officials assigned to kill Nazi-perceived enemies in occupied territories
Gebietskommissar District Commissar (administrative level below GK)
Generalkommissar Head of GK (administrative level below RK), e.g., for Latvia
Gestapo *Geheime Staatspolizei* (Secret State Police)

GK *Generalkommissariat* (administrative unit below RK), e.g., for Latvia
GPU See OGPU
HHA Hubertus Herz Archives, Kirchseeon, Germany
HSSPFO *Höherer SS- und Polizeiführer Ostland* (Higher SS and Police Leader for Ostland)
IMT International Military Tribunal Nuremberg – Trial of the Major War Criminals
IRO International Refugee Organization
Kalpakieši Officers who had served under Oskars Kalpaks in 1919
Landeseigene Verwaltung Latvian self-administration (1941–4)
LCK *Latviešu Centrālā Komiteja* (Latvian Central Committee)
LCP (1) *Latvijas Centrālā Padome* (Central Council of Latvia, 1943, Sweden)
(2) *Latviešu Centrālā Padome* (Latvian Central Council, 1945, Germany)
Legion *Waffen-SS Legion Lettland* (Latvian legion created in 1943 under SS auspices)
Legionnaire Latvian serving in German uniform in the Second World War
LNA *Latvijas Nacionālā Apvienība* (Latvian National Federation)
LNAK *Latviešu Nacionālā Apvienība Kānāda* (Latvian National Federation in Canada)
LNK *Latvijas Nacionālā Komiteja* (Latvian National Committee, 1945)
LNP *Latviešu Nacionālā Padome* (Latvian National Council)
LOA *Latviešu Organizāciju Apvienība* (Federation of Latvian Organizations)
LSCO *Latvijas Skautu Centrālā Organizācija (Central Organization of Latvian Scouts)*
LTA *Latvju Tautas Apvienība (Latvian People's Federation)*
LTP *Latvju Tautas Padome* (Latvian People's Council)
LVVA *Latvijas Centrālais Valsts Vēstures Arhīvs* (Central State Historical Archives of Latvia), Riga, Latvia
MIAG Mühlenbau- und Industrie-Aktiengesellschaft (Head Office: Braunschweig, Germany)
NAC National Archives of Canada, Ottawa
NALCO Newfoundland and Labrador Corporation
NKVD People's Commissariat of Internal Affairs. Soviet political police from 1934 to 1954 (1922–34 known as OGPU, sometimes also abbreviated as GPU)

OGPU State Political Administration. Soviet political police from 1922 to 1934 (renamed NKVD 1934–54, thereafter KGB)

Ostland Nazi administrative unit comprising the conquered territories of Estonia, Latvia, Lithuania, and Belorussia

Ostministerium *Reichsministerium für die besetzten Ostgebiete* (Reich Ministry for the Occupied Eastern Territories)

Outport Newfoundland fishing village

PCIRO Preparatory Commission for the IRO

Pērkonkrusts Thundercross (Latvian fascist party), suppressed by Ulmanis regime

Pērkonkrustieši Pērkonkrusts members

PRO Public Record Office, London

RK *Reichskommissar.* Head of Reich Commissariat (there were two 1941–4 – Ostland and Ukraine) in Nazi-occupied eastern Europe

RKO *Reichskommissariat Ostland*

SA *Sturmabteilung* (Storm Troopers, original Nazi paramilitary organization)

Saeima Parliament of Latvia

SC Joseph R. Smallwood Collection in the CNS

Schuma *Schutzmannschaft* (1942 Nazi designation for Latvian police in German military service)

SD *Sicherheitsdienst* (Security Service, intelligence branch of the SS)

SS *Schutzstaffel* (Nazi elite organization)

SSPFL *SS- und Polizeiführer Lettland* (SS and Police Leader for Latvia)

UNRRA United Nations Relief and Rehabilitation Administration

UTAG *Umsiedlungs-Treuhand-Aktiengesellschaft* (German resettlement and trust agency for Baltic Germans)

ALFRED VALDMANIS
AND THE POLITICS OF SURVIVAL

Introduction

In the 1950s, a one-man industry bent on lining his own pockets came to the province. The Latvian and supposed economic genius, Alfred Valdmanis, latched on to Smallwood and immediately got down to work. 'Mein premier, mein premier, you have invented a new economic theory,' Valdmanis once told Smallwood. He never did say what it was. Valdmanis is now believed to have been involved with the Nazi SS in the deportation of Jews from Latvia to the extermination camps. But he managed to steal more than $4 million in public money in today's money and stash it away before he was caught.

Bob Benson, *Evening Telegram*, 31 May 1998

To the student of mid-twentieth century Latvian and Canadian history, the name of Alfred Valdmanis evokes contradictory and ambiguous associations. Born in 1908 near Liepāja (Libau), Latvia, and killed in 1970 in a highway accident in Alberta, Canada, he lived sequentially in three countries under at least ten different political regimes, including Tsarist, Imperial German, liberal democratic, Latvian authoritarian, Soviet communist, and German National Socialist. Between 1938 and 1954 he played key roles in six of these regimes, and his name is connected with some of the period's most controversial issues. In 1954 his promising career abruptly ended with his conviction on charges of defrauding the government of Newfoundland. A political chameleon, enigmatic careerist, and charismatic manipulator, Valdmanis has left his mark on the history of Latvia, Germany, and Canada.

Yet, nearly fifty years after the end of his public career, there is no comprehensive and balanced account of Valdmanis's life, and his historical significance still awaits evaluation. Not even his record in the Latvian Ministry of Finance has been analysed. Valdmanis-related research has focused on isolated, often sensational, episodes and has tended to apply the yardstick of partisan judgment. Latvians, furthermore, are as unfamiliar with his role in Canada as Canadians are with his background in Latvia. In Canada, after unsuccessfully endeavouring to industrialize the province of Newfoundland and unlawfully enriching himself in the process, his name conjures up a spectre of negative images ranging from costly economic failure and fraud to war crimes.

Satisfactory answers to the problems posed by the controversial career and images of this Latvian require perspectives that transcend selective national perceptions of the past. Indeed, Valdmanis's biography raises questions about national historiography as well as about the morality of what biographers do. As a *Maclean's* writer wondered not long ago: 'Is it possible to write with complete accuracy about another human being? Is it fair to judge people of other eras by current moral standards? And when does a biographer's speculation cross the misty borderline into falsehood and slander?'[1] Driven by the need to make a compelling narrative, can a biographer avoid manipulating the image of the subject projected to the public?

This study has no axe to grind or vested interests – ideological or national – to defend. I have a particular interest in Canadian immigration history, but I have neither Latvian nor Baltic German personal connections nor a previous preoccupation with Baltic history. The sole reason for this study has been the challenge to disentangle the enigmatic nature, background, and contribution of the man who, as Newfoundland's senior public affairs critic Albert Perlin once put it, 'flashed like a meteor across the Newfoundland sky and became the storm centre of political controversy ... He remained all his life a man of mystery and much remains to be explained. It is doubtful whether it will ever be told.'[2]

The challenge was not just to tell the story of Valdmanis's life, but to tell it *sine ira et studio*, that is, without malice and partisan bias. Thus, first of all, cool and detached prose took precedence over sensationalist rhetoric. In addition, it necessitated sacrificing the simplifications and manipulative techniques typical of a 'fascinating story' to sometimes colourless and inconvenient detail. It meant featuring incidents and events not as ends in themselves but as threads in the web of a wider historical context. Since Valdmanis operated in diverse historical contexts, this involved, last but not least, connecting these threads into a meaningful framework, which in this case is one of survival – its requirements and consequences.

In terms of historical research, relevant documentation had to be tracked down in the public archives of Riga, Bonn, Potsdam, Koblenz, Ottawa, and St John's, and in collections of Valdmanis personal papers held in St John's, Montreal, Edmonton, and Stockholm. Primary materials in several languages – Latvian, German, English, Russian, and Swedish – needed evaluation. Printed sources had to be supplemented with testimonies obtained from interviews of contemporaries still surviving in Latvia and Canada. In short, disentangling the mystery of Valdmanis involved the examination of a wide range of primary sources. These made it possible to explain – without nationalist, ideological, or partisan blinkers – his prominence under ideologically incompatible regimes from 1934 to 1954.

The issues of the Latvian, German, and Canadian worlds interacting with Valdmanis's political career were as diverse as the scholarly literature dealing with them. Latvian historiography, with few exceptions,[3] has obscured rather than illuminated Valdmanis's historic role in Latvia. Post–Second World War Latvian historians publishing in English about the independence period not only ignore Valdmanis's term as finance minister, but also fail to evaluate critically the economic policy framework within which he worked.[4] Their rosy picture of the Ulmanis regime appears addressed to a Cold War readership in the West that needed to be reassured of Latvia's democratic credentials. Apart from studies by English and German historians,[5] only Nicholas Balabkins and Arnolds Aizsilnieks appear to have given critical attention to the direction in which the policies of the Ulmanis regime were taking Latvia.[6]

Valdmanis's roles in the Second World War have been just as difficult for Latvians and Germans to ignore as to assess. Earning him contradictory collaborationist–nationalist reputations, Valdmanis's behaviour during this period from 1940 to 1945 haunted him for the rest of his life. It found its reflection in the conflicting positions taken later by both Latvian and non-Latvian scholars. The latter include Seppo Myllyniemi, H.D. Handrack, Helmut Krausnick, Hans-Heinrich Wilhelm, Timothy Patrick Mulligan, and Romuald Misiunas and Rein Taagepera.[7] Based on the evidence manifest in German government documents, they view Valdmanis as the shrewdest, most influential defender of Latvian national interests. Meticulously researched, and generally recognized as the standard work on the German wartime occupation of Latvia, Myllyniemi's study dissects the conflicting interests within the German polycratic power structure that Valdmanis skilfully exploited for the purpose of promoting Latvian national interests.[8]

Most Latvian historians, on the other hand, whether in exile or in post-communist Latvia, have tended to ignore the jumble of overlapping jurisdictions and rivalries within the German power structure. From their perspective, the diverse agencies of the German regime – whether the army, Ostministerium, or SS – had identical interests and acted more or less in unison. The focus of this historiography is on the radical Nazi blueprints calling for germanization, colonization, and resettlement[9] – rather than on the chaotic reality of wartime occupation, which effectively nullified implementation of these blueprints.[10] By the nationalist yardstick of Latvian historiography, collaborationists of any stripe were traitors and only the pro-Allied Central Council of Latvia (LCP, founded in 1943) qualified as resistance.[11] In this undifferentiated perspective Valdmanis becomes automatically a 'quisling,'[12] 'the most prominent collaborator ... until the end ... willing to serve either Stalin or Hitler.'[13]

No doubt, collaboration and resistance appear mutually exclusive. Virtually all postwar regimes of the Nazi-occupied countries have magnified and mythologized their national resistance, while minimizing and vilifying collaboration. In reality, however, wartime behaviour often defies reduction to simple formulas and precise definition. The spectrum of Latvian resistance to German occupation, for example, ranged from the Communists to the Pērkonkrusts. In her analysis of the 1941–4 attitudes of Latvian university students and faculty, Margot Blank differentiated among four gradations of collaboration (neutral, unconditional, conditional, and tactical) as well as of resistance (symbolic, polemic, defensive, and offensive).[14]

To some it might appear that the European resistance saw its salient common denominator in undertaking action 'which you know is legally wrong, is against what the authorities tell you to do, because you know it is morally right.'[15] The morally right action might appear clear from hindsight. But how clear was it in Latvia at the time when Nazi rule was experienced as deliverance from the even worse evil of Stalinist terror? Indeed, as French President François Mitterand reaffirmed with reference to his own wartime record, the lines between resistance and collaboration were fluid.[16] Today the rehabilitation of former collaborators who defended the interests of their nations has been on the agenda all over eastern Europe: Stepan Bandera in Ukraine, Admiral Miklos von Horthy in Hungary, Ante Pavelic in Croatia, Josef Tiso in Slovakia, the

Cossacks in Russia, and, last but not least, the legionnaires in Estonia and Latvia.[17]

Virtually no scholarly literature focuses on Latvian emigrés, their experience as displaced persons, and their resettlement after the Second World War. Latvians appear only marginally in the monographs and accounts on aspects of the DP problem.[18] Aside from two articles by Edgars Andersons[19] and a statistical survey of Latvians abroad,[20] only brief sections on the Latvian refugee community appear in a few historical accounts of Latvia.[21]

The problems of Latvian immigration and adaptation in Canada are also still awaiting scholarly analysis. The most detailed account of the policy framework for Canada's admission of Waffen-SS legionnaires and potential war criminals is the unpublished report prepared for the Deschênes Commission by Alti Rodal.[22] In the debate over the identification and indictment of Latvian war criminals in Canada and Latvia, Valdmanis's name appears regularly, though he was never charged. The participation of Latvians in the destruction of the Latvian Jewish community is documented in the testimony of Latvian Holocaust survivors and the research of Krausnick and Wilhelm,[23] Marģers Vestermanis,[24] Bernhard Press,[25] and Andrew Ezergailis.[26]

The standard colourful depiction of Valdmanis's association with Newfoundland Premier J.R. Smallwood is in two chapters of Richard Gwyn's Smallwood biography. To Smallwood's and Valdmanis's quest for German industry from 1950 to 1953, G.P. Bassler devoted one scholarly article.[27] Yet, apart from brief references in memoirs by Smallwood,[28] Herbert L. Pottle,[29] Don Jamieson,[30] and William J. Browne,[31] and in the semi-autobiographical accounts of Harold Horwood[32] and Frederick C. Rowe,[33] the history of Smallwood's new industries program and Valdmanis's role in it has not yet been written.

The story of Alfred Valdmanis is, above all, the amazing odyssey of one who survived against incredible odds. In that regard, Valdmanis fits into a long line of illustrious chameleon-like survivors from the French Joseph Fouché and the Hungarian Trebitsch Lincoln to the Pole Boleslaw Piasecki, all of whom ended up hated and ostracized for compromising their ethics for the sake of survival. Fouché, a remarkably talented organizer of the espionage activities of the French police, started his political career as a Jacobin in 1792. Through shrewdness and intrigue he survived in government positions until 1815 despite revolutionary turnovers from Robespierre to Napoleon.[34] Trebitsch Lincoln, born a Hungarian

Jew, lived from 1879 to 1943 the sequential secret lives of a Christian missionary in Canada, a British MP, a spy in Berlin, and a Buddhist abbot in Shanghai.[35]

Boleslaw Piasecki was a Polish contemporary of Valdmanis. In 1935, when he was twenty-one years old, and a law student, he launched the Polish fascist and anti-Semitic paramilitary organization Falanga. He was imprisoned for six months by the Germans. Upon his release in 1940, through the intervention of influential friends, Piasecki formed the terrorist Konfederacja Narodowa that fought what he saw as Poland's arch-enemies – Germans, Russians, and Jews. Arrested again in 1945, he was set free by the Red Army in return for offering to facilitate Soviet rule over anti-communist Poland. In 1950 Piasecki acquired unique wealth and privilege in communist Poland for founding the Catholic lay organization PAX, which arranged the regime's first agreement with the Catholic Church. But blamed by Polish Catholics for the arrest of Polish Cardinal Wyszinsky in 1953, Piasecki was condemned to spend the rest of his life as a social pariah.[36]

Similarly, the enigma of Alfred Valdmanis involved his sixfold survival in situations where, judged by his past positions and associations, as well as by the fates of his contemporaries, he should not have survived: in 1940–1 he survived Soviet purges and deportations of some thirty thousand Latvians; in 1941–5 he survived Nazi occupation and then deportation by the Nazis as an unreliable collaborator; in 1945–7 he survived Allied screening for pro-Nazi collaborators; in 1949 he survived persecution by Latvian opponents in exile by his emigration to Canada; in May 1950 he survived rejection of his industrial development proposal for Nova Scotia by his appointment in Newfoundland; and in 1951–2 he survived denunciation as a war criminal. Valdmanis's luck finally ran out in 1954 when he was caught illegally diverting funds he had collected for the premier of Newfoundland into his own personal investment projects.

The twelve chapters in this book trace this miraculous string of survivals. The first half of the study covers Valdmanis's life in Europe, the second half his life in North America. His career in Latvia prior to the German occupation of 1941 is the subject of Chapters 1 to 3. Against the social, economic, and political background of Latvia between the world wars, Chapter 1 sketches Valdmanis's origins, education, and apprenticeship in the Latvian Ministry of Finance up to his appointment as finance minister. Chapter 2 analyses his policies as finance minister and his role in the Ulmanis cabinet to August 1939. Chapter 3 examines his chaotic last two months as finance minister, his resignation from the cabinet in

October 1939, and his survival in Latvia during the Soviet occupation of 1940–1.

Chapters 4 to 6 trace the ups and downs of Valdmanis's activities under German rule and in Germany. His role in German-occupied Latvia is divided into two phases: the first (1941–3), where he appeared primarily as a collaborator (Chapter 4), and the subsequent period (1943–5), where in Latvia and in Berlin Valdmanis acquired a reputation as a critic of German occupation policy and ended up interned in Germany (Chapter 5). Chapter 6 describes his rapid resurgence in the occupied western zones of Germany as a spokesman for Latvian displaced persons and legionnaires, his efforts to be recognized as their leader, and his endeavours to organize their resettlement through the International Refugee Organization (IRO).

Chapter 7 features his immigration to Canada and search for a new career – university professor, consultant for the government of Canada, or economic developer of Nova Scotia's gypsum and cement industries. The theme of Chapter 8 is his appointment and activities as director general of economic development in Newfoundland from May 1950 to February 1953. The chapter describes his efforts to recruit industries for the new industries program conceived by Premier J.R. Smallwood. Chapter 9 examines Valdmanis's involvement in the local, national, and international communities of exile Latvians and the repercussions of accusations that he was a war criminal.

Starting with the new position Valdmanis assumed as chairman of Newfoundland and Labrador Corporation (NALCO), Chapter 10 reviews the circumstances surrounding his resignation from NALCO in January 1954 and his media profile from 1950 to 1954. Chapter 11 is the story of Valdmanis's arrest and conviction, with a detailed examination of his defence, confession, and verdict, and his reflections while in prison. The concluding Chapter 12 reviews Valdmanis's discouraging efforts to rehabilitate his reputation and career, other problems of his last years, his death, and the obituaries.

chapter one

Wunderkind in Reborn Latvia: Background, Education, and Civil Service Career, 1908–1938

I met him for the first time in Canada House on the night of 23 May 1950 ... Much of what he told about himself was capable of being checked out. It had its beginning in the small Baltic state of Latvia in 1919 when Valdmanis was ten or eleven years of age. The Latvian population had been decimated in the campaigns that rolled over the Baltic region in the Great War. Having won independence, its rulers became immediately concerned about future leadership. It is here that the Valdmanis story began.

A small number of boys was selected for education by the state. Taken from their parents, brought up under Spartan conditions, trained to the limit of their talents, they were to be the elite which would ensure the continuity of expertise in Latvian government. Valdmanis, by his own tale, had an international education. He attended French and German universities, acquired five foreign languages, claimed to have learned banking under the tutelage of Dr Schacht who financed the war for Hitler, and eventually became the minister who presided over Latvia's economic progress. This was his moment of greatness.

Albert Perlin, *Daily News*, 18 August 1970

Encounters

Alfred Valdmanis struck Newfoundland Premier J.R. Smallwood 'as a Latvian, of medium height and build, with the lithe body of an athlete, a handsome and very intelligent face, and a clarity of expression in English that impressed everyone who met him.' Newfoundland broadcaster and politician Don Jamieson found 'nothing particularly striking about the man except for an almost manic intensity in the deep-set eyes of his slightly Slavic, rather handsome face.' 'The little man with the square forehead and brushed-back hair that used to be characterized as Prussian' impressed senior Newfoundland public affairs commentator Albert Perlin, however, as 'an odd person, volatile and nervous [who] talked at times like the highly practised graduate of an authoritarian school. He ... always rambled on and there was not much one could recall of his conversation after he had gone away.' To Perlin it was 'clear that he was a man in a hurry whose interest in Newfoundland development was not so great that he was averse ... to making himself a tidy fortune on the side.'[1] 'Shifty-eyed,' Newfoundland politician Baxter Morgan described him. 'Valdmanis never looked you in the eye.'[2]

On Fritz Stobbe, Newfoundland's German textile industrialist, however, Valdmanis made the impression of a 'a very, very bright, brilliant, and charming man.' Stobbe watched him talking fluently in four different languages and acting up as *the* entertainer at parties. Valdmanis 'played piano very well, he could sing, he kept the party at full speed, and I think he could have made his money just as an entertainer anytime.'[3] To Joey Smallwood, too, Valdmanis remained 'one of the most talented men I ever met, a brain, a great chess player, piano player, tennis player, a man accustomed to giving orders. As financial dictator he used to lay down the law ... In retrospect he did a magnificent job. Not willing to live on his salary, he tried to augment it illegally. I am the one who caused him to be put into jail. I never did or will forgive him. I treated him generously and that's the way he treated me.' In his memoirs Smallwood characterized his first director general of economic development as a 'brilliant and tragic man ... a product and victim of the dire events through which he lived in Latvia and war-time Germany.'[4]

From early on, Valdmanis awed his family with his drive. 'Alfred was very intelligent,' his wife Irma insisted, 'but he also worked very hard for it; this was often overlooked by many who envy his career.' 'Our father always had a presentiment that Alfred would try for the top,' Osvald Valdmanis recalled. As a child, young Osvald found it peculiar that his brother Alfred always preferred the company of influential grown-ups to friends his own age. A poem by famous Latvian poet Jānis Rainis exalts the desire to 'live fully, burn ablaze, if only for a moment, rather than smoulder under the coals for eternity. Father had become identified with that philosophy,' Alfred's son Gundars explained. 'It was a frequent toast and a continuously reaffirmed truth in his Latvian circles that death is not a deterrent in serving the cause of friends, class, tribe, or nation.'[5]

'Father earned his prestige as a result of successes in industrialization and humanitarian fields,' Gundars elaborated. 'His political power base, prestige, etc. were a result – but not the motivation. The power/prestige dimension will not explain the musician; the coach; the inhabitant of basement offices; ... the inspirational political leader; the friend of his subordinates; the writer of emotional letters; the church support; ... the personal risk taking; doing (working extra hours) rather than directing, etc. Attempting to explain a religiously idealistic act "logically" in the power/prestige/material dimension is sadly unfair – the person involved becomes either a fool or an actor.'[6]

President Kārlis Ulmanis appointed Valdmanis as his finance minister in 1938, when Valdmanis was just twenty-nine years old. Latvia's young prewar minister of finance was 'a very gifted and capable, but also a very ambitious person ... who tried to gain political influence beyond his department,' judged the German Foreign Office's Baltic expert Werner von Grundherr in 1942. Although always professing his pro-German attitude *vis-à-vis* German nationals and ethnic Germans, Valdmanis's actions did not bear out this appearance, according to von Grundherr. In reality he was a 'willing instrument of [President] Ulmanis, who appointed him finance minister to carry out his plans of de-germanization.' Samuel Levitan, in 1993 an eighty-year-old Jewish professor of history at the University of Latvia, remembered him well as 'one of the most capable members of Ulmanis's cabinet but his economic philosophy was not liberal.' Latvian Ingrid Trautmanis confirmed that Valdmanis was 'an ambitious and highly respected Latvian, who always desired only the best for Latvia.' Ulmanis's economic policies 'gave the people a lot,' and Latvians consequently 'owe a great debt' to him, concluded Riga resident Irma Losis whose husband, a forestry official, used to accompany Alfred Valdmanis on hunting trips in the 1930s.[7]

The press attaché of the German Foreign Office envoy in Riga during the German occupation was Leon von Bruemmer. In 1951 he remembered Valdmanis as an 'unusually gifted, energetic' wartime director general in Latvia: 'We were together daily for two years during the German occupation until we were both eliminated by the Gestapo as *untragbar* (unbearable) and had to leave Riga ... In the 'puppet government' he was the only national Lett who made no bones about his antipathy to the German regime and who consistently held to his position ... He was the leader of the resistance movement in word and deed.'[8]

Memories diverge sharply concerning Valdmanis's treatment of Jews. For Newfoundlanders like writer Harold Horwood, any Nazi collaborator associated with raising a Waffen-SS Legion was a traitor and a war criminal, regardless of postwar security clearance.[9] However, according to Holocaust survivor Marģers Vestermanis, Jews were not singled out for special discrimination by Valdmanis before or during the war. 'Though denounced as a quisling, Valdmanis had no connections whatever with wartime massacres of Jews,' Vestermanis has attested. 'Valdmanis collaborated only for the benefit of Latvia and not of Germany. He cannot be charged with any traitorous activity,' vouched Samuel Levitan. 'His negative image was fabricated by Latvian Social Democrats,' maintained Jānis Strādiņš, who still has vivid memories from 1941 of his own physician father hiding Valdmanis in his sanatorium from Soviet arrest.[10]

Incomplete and unconvincing as some of these reminiscences may be, concludes Smallwood biographer Richard Gwyn, 'there was never any doubt of Valdmanis' talent for survival. In occupied Europe survival was the highest virtue, achieved by alternately grovelling before Allied and Axis.' Not surprisingly, therefore, Gwyn found two versions in circulation of Valdmanis's career – the one prepared by Valdmanis and officially publicized and the other the disclosures and denunciations that emerged when he became the centre of controversy.[11]

The Rebirth of Latvia

I loved Latvia, particularly the period of reconstruction. I believed in the ideas and goals of the regime at the time and I gave all of what could be given by a young man offering his whole life for a certain goal. I was ready to give my life, and I was ready to end it when the independence of Latvia ended. For the good of Latvia, however, I was able to continue living and working in foreign countries, even when I was on a lonely island (Newfoundland), sold and buried, mainly because of the fact that something had happened and a 'culprit' had to be found. I was all alone without friends and without roots in this foreign land where I had done so much good. I saw that a human being is so little that he cannot die even if he wanted to. I have seen the sense of life collapsing.

Alfred Valdmanis in 1963[12]

Survival appears indeed as an appropriate leitmotiv characterizing not only the biography of Alfred Valdmanis, but also the history of his people. During his lifetime Latvians were alternately ruled by monarchical, democratic, fascist, communist, and Nazi military regimes. They suffered the destructive impact of two world wars and foreign occupation; they were subjected to attempts at germanization and russification; and they endured revolutionary upheavals, near-genocidal deportations to Siberia, and large-scale refugee migrations to the West. A national minority discriminated against in the Tsarist empire, virtually overnight (1918) they became the dominant nationality in the new multi-ethnic state called Latvia. They have lived in fear ever since – fear of threats to their national identity and fear of losing control over their destiny. As late as 1993, a Latvian remarked to two Canadians visiting Latvia that what identified the latter as western visitors was the absence of 'fear' in their faces.[13]

Today Latvia is known as one of the three Baltic countries whose peoples have acquired reputations not just as survivors, but as stubborn defenders of their national cultures and their right to self-determination. But the Baltic country in which Valdmanis started his political career attracted little attention in the West at the time. A contemporary British diplomat termed Latvia 'a cross between Lilliput and Utopia' whose 'plucky people hate Germany, Russia, and Poland about equally.'[14] With a small, rural-based population, it was considered prematurely born, politically unstable, belonging to the Russian sphere of influence, and diplomatically insignificant. Alfred Valdmanis claimed that Latvia's unique life force sustained his survival. But how could such a seemingly lacklustre country have aroused his passionate loyalty and devotion?

The turbulent birth of independent Latvia in 1918 left an indelible mark on the *Weltanschauung* and values of Alfred Valdmanis's generation of Latvian youth. When his parents were growing up, outsiders still perceived Latvians as a social class rather than a nationality. For centuries, speaking German and germanizing one's name had been *de rigueur* for anyone seeking upward mobility in the Latvian homelands. Numbering barely 1.5 million in 1935, but with a presence on the Baltic shores for four thousand years, Latvians had preserved their ethnic identity through centuries of German, Danish, Swedish, Polish, and Russian rule. For the previous seven centuries their local and provincial governments had been controlled by an ethnic German ruling class – a landed aristocracy of so-called Baltic barons. These, in conjunction with the stratified German urban population around them, had cultivated their own highly developed cultural and economic life. Relegated to the occupation of fishermen and peasants, the Latvian people were better known as 'an estate rather than a nation'[15] and the German ruling class equated 'Latvian' with 'peasant.'

The former duchies of Kurland (Courland) together with Livland (Livonia) form the core territories of present-day Latvia. Annexed by Russia from Poland and Sweden in the eighteenth century, they were multi-ethnic lands of stark economic and sociocultural contrasts. Latvians had to share their homeland with large, powerful minorities who in 1897 formed 31.7 per cent of the population – Russians (12 per cent), Jews (7.4 per cent), Germans (6.2 per cent), and Poles (3.4 per cent), as well as with smaller, less privileged groups of Belorussians, Lithuanians, and Estonians. These ethnic groups lived side by side without much social and cultural intermingling. Clearly defined economic, social, and political roles encouraged the preservation of distinct cultural–linguistic identities.

Change intruded in 1905 in an uprising against the russification policies of the Tsarist government and the entrenched privileges of the Baltic barons. During the stillborn Russian revolution of that year, Latvian peasants attacked 412 estates – the symbols of Baltic German landowner power – and burned many of the manorial residences. They also assassinated eighty-two Germans in Kurland and Livland. Socioeconomic change in Russia, however, opened opportunities for social mobility. Latvians increasingly desired non-agrarian careers hitherto possible only through assimilation into Baltic German culture and society. With Russia's new educational policies, agrarian reforms, and industrialization, Latvians began to acquire farms or migrate to the towns and cities, in search of work in the urban trades.

Thus, on the eve of the First World War, there were many harbingers of change in the Latvian lands. But change was tempered by continuity. In such rural areas as Ziemupe (in Kurland), the birthplace of Alfred Valdmanis, the old world lingered on. Jürgen Ernst Kroeger, a Baltic German who grew up in Kurland before the First World War, recalled that Latvian farm labourers – Germans were unavailable – on his estate lived in the most primitive shacks with clay floors and tiny windows. His Latvian playmates called Kroeger the 'young baron,' and the older Latvian employees, male and female, demonstrated their submissiveness by kissing his hand.[16]

As late as 1914 neither local and foreign politicians nor the Latvian people nor their intelligentsia had any dream of a sovereign state. Even by the beginning of 1917 cultural autonomy within the Russian Empire was the maximum goal conceivable. Spricis Paegle, minister for trade and industry in Latvia's first provisional government, later recalled that 'in the first months following the proclamation of independence, only a narrow segment of society supported the government; the masses of the people lacked the faith in the viability of an independent state of their own, as well as the will and readiness to make sacrifices for it.'[17]

External forces – Germany's war aims, the Russian Revolution, and Allied diplomacy – put Latvian independence on the agenda. Latvia owed the realization of its statehood to the historical coincidence of the simultaneous collapse of Russia and Germany.[18] Newborn Latvia, however, liked to portray independence as the fruit of a legendary struggle for national liberation. To have participated in this struggle became one of the highest national distinctions. Special attention was bestowed on the *strēlnieki* (riflemen) and *kalpakieši*. The former were the eight Latvian battalions formed in May 1915 within the Russian army to stem the German advance in the Baltic; later they were considered to have been the core of a Latvian national army. Kalpakieši were the men in a brigade of some thousand Latvian students under the command of Colonel Oskars Kalpaks (and his successor Colonel Jānis Balodis) raised in early 1919 to assist twelve thousand Baltic German and German volunteers in freeing the country from Soviet invaders.[19]

Actual sovereignty remained elusive until 1920, although the Latvian National Council had proclaimed independence on 18 November 1918 with a government headed by Kārlis Ulmanis. The economic, social, and political tasks ahead seemed awesome, in part because the myriad tasks of nation building, formidable in the best of times, came with 'ruined industries, empty coffers and plundered rural economies.'[20] Moreover, as a former gateway to the vast Russian Empire and one of its commercial and manufacturing centres, urban Latvia, especially the capital city of Riga, had inherited a comprehensive economic infrastructure, but one not geared to the needs of a small separate country. In addition, the society of the new country was divided along ethnic and religious lines as well as by political ideology and social class. The lack of democratic traditions aggravated the problems of Latvia's 1922 constitution, which vested all powers in the hands of a Saeima, a unicameral legislature based on proportional representation. Political life was at the mercy of a proliferation of political parties and changing coalition governments. Clearly, the prospects for unity, stability, and growth appeared anything but certain.

Nonetheless, despite the severity of wartime destruction and the requirements of restructuring, independent Latvia enjoyed continuous growth with a high rate of employment and a steady rise in the volume of trade. Industries relied on local resources – agricultural, wood, brick, cement, and chemical products. Latvian trade was primarily with Britain and Germany, and Latvia remained on the gold standard until the end of 1936.[21] Britain was buying much more (especially agricultural produce) than it sold, while Germany sold more than it bought. In this triangular trade the British provided the sterling reserves with which the Baltic countries could buy German products, a recent study notes. 'Among these were the capital goods with which they hoped to diversify their economies.'[22]

Recovery, growth, and prosperity can be credited to policies pursued by the parliamentary coalition governments from 1920 to 1934. Although formed from among a proliferation of between twenty and twenty-seven parties in the one-hundred-seat Saeima, these governments ably defended Latvia's domestic and foreign interests. With a voter participation rate of 75 to 82 per cent, parliamentary government successfully coped with the onslaught of the Depression and put Latvia on the road to recovery in 1933. Before the advent of the authoritarian regime in 1934, Latvian industry had weathered the worst of the Depression.[23] In 1930 Latvia could boast the highest employment rate in Europe with 71.8 per cent of the male population (compared with around 47 per cent for Switzerland, Czechoslovakia, Britain, and Italy) and 57.2 per cent of the female population (compared with 27 to 29 per cent for Italy, Britain, and Switzerland) employed.[24]

The government was deeply involved in newborn Latvia's economy through control agencies, state-run enterprises, and monopolies. Immediate postwar requirements, the weakness of the private sector, and the need to generate income deemed this involvement palatable.[25] In addition, the perceived need to protect Latvia's economy from foreign control officially justified the continued maintenance of state-run and state-owned enterprises. By 1934, 15.6 per cent of Latvia's exports came from state monopolies; by 1938 this had increased to 47.5 per cent.[26] The government, which had owned nothing in 1919, by 1930 had acquired one-third of the national wealth. One result of this policy was the creation of obstacles to the development and viability of a flourishing private sector. For example, most Latvian industrial firms were small: in 1935 the average firm employed seventeen persons.

Ethnic Latvians played only a minor role in the country's industry because they lacked either the entrepreneurial skills and experience or the necessary funds. Latvian Jews and Baltic Germans held a disproportionate 78 per cent of individually owned industrial enterprises. In the larger industries (chemical, textile, paper, wood, and metal), in 1930, foreigners had an average of 62 per cent of the shares. In Latvia's textile industry, for example, they held up to 84 per cent. Foreign textile suppliers, the Bank of Latvia explained, had conquered the market by accommodating local buyers with longer credit than Latvian manufacturers were able to provide.[27]

Educated Latvians felt strongly that political independence was incomplete as long as ethnic Latvians did not occupy a dominant position in the country's economic life. 'Every position held by a Russian or a German is subject to attacks,' reported an American visitor in 1924.[28] Taking over the numerous posts formerly occupied by Russians and Baltic Germans in the political, administrative, and cultural infrastructure, and expropriating without compensation the German- and Polish-owned estates in 1920, marked only a beginning. The sudden upward mobility of thousands fuelled a euphoria of rising expectations. Abandoning their rural lives in large numbers for urban areas, especially Riga, Latvians longed for social and economic advance.

Especially Latvia's newly educated and rapidly growing middle-class intelligentsia was anxious to assume and enjoy power in the new state. Opportunistic, desiring rapid material advance, and longing to emulate the pattern of conspicuous consumption of the prewar ruling class, they rallied behind the banner of Latvia for the Latvians, a representative of Latvia's Jewish minority noted.[29] The chief popularizer of that banner after 1930, the Latvian fascist organization Pērkonkrusts (Thunder Cross, the Latvian term for swastika), 'despite its small size, penetrated into important strata of Latvian society.'[30]

The nationally respected author, politician, and diplomat, Dr Miķelis Valters, supplied this movement for a Latvian Latvia with a comprehensive economic program. In his 1933 book, *From Collapse to Planned Economy: Problems of Latvia's Renewal, Latvia's Future,* Valters argued that the nation was not fully independent as long as its industry and commerce were in the hands of ethnic minorities. He called for ethnic Latvians to assume control of the important branches of industry and trade. This restructuring would necessitate the removal of many business elements, but it could be accomplished through government-instigated takeovers and conversions into state-owned enterprises with the help of monopolies and banks. According to Valters, national cooperation should replace the existing profit-oriented free enterprise economy, and national interests should take priority over 'narrow' class interests. Self-sufficiency was preferable to a free trade policy that meant large-scale flight of capital from Latvia. Valters saw the model for this in Mussolini's Italy with its corporate economic structure and the extraordinary powers of the government.[31]

The ethnic Latvian intelligentsia's notion of the national interest denied a separate economic role and identity to Latvia's Russian, Jewish,

German, and Polish groups, who together formed one-quarter of the population. Because these minorities astutely defended their interests through their parliamentary parties, the intelligentsia accused them of unduly benefitting from the 1922 democratic constitution. Thus, liberal democracy in general, and the Saeima in particular, were increasingly perceived as obstacles to the creation of a Latvian Latvia. The solution envisioned by the Latvian agrarian parties in alliance with the so-called Democratic Centre was to strengthen the authority of the president and reduce the rights of the ethnic minorities.[32]

The 1922 constitution of Latvia, unlike those of Estonia (1920) and Lithuania (1922), granted no special minority rights – the Saeima had failed to ratify draft Article 116 providing for cultural autonomy of ethnic minorities. Latvia also refused a League of Nations request for a declaration guaranteeing minority rights. However, a law of 6 December 1919 did allow non-Latvian minorities to establish and administer their own schools, and the government allotted public funds for these purposes. In 1931, however, the Latvian government reversed this tolerant policy. It began by closing Polish schools and cultural institutions, arbitrarily revised the German school curriculum, and eventually abolished the German educational board. Latvia's Russian and German minorities, though small, were particular concerns. For instance, their relative sizes were increasing. In the decade of 1920 to 1930, their respective percentages of the total population of Latvia grew from 8.9 to 12.5 and 3.2 to 3.7 (but by 1935 had declined to 12 and 3.2). Also, Russians and Germans were considered difficult to assimilate because they represented ruling classes only recently deposed with allegiances to powerful neighbours.[33]

Latvian ethnocentrism and anti-foreignism manifested itself sporadically throughout the 1920s. In moderation they appeared as almost necessary ingredients in the development of a new spirit of national unity. It was not until the Depression that in Latvia, as in most western countries, unprecedented mass support could be relied on for nationalist, anti-foreign, and anti-minority solutions to socioeconomic problems. Atis Ķēniņš, of the Democratic Centre and minister of education in a new right-wing coalition government, declared in 1931 that 'Latvia must have a Latvian culture. The minorities here should not believe themselves permitted to cultivate German, Russian, Polish, Jewish, and other cultures in the same way as the Latvian culture.' They were not creators of a distinct culture, Ķēniņš added, but mere consumers of a culture that had its source beyond Latvia's borders.[34]

In an atmosphere where parliament had deteriorated into an 'auction hall'[35] of narrow special interests, and international politics was being restructured by nascent fascism, a strategy focusing on the elimination of foreign influences was obviously one of the persuasive panaceas for nation building. A growing fear of Soviet and Nazi 'fifth columnism' among Latvia's Russian and German communities added even more fuel to the anti-minority sentiment. Nazi Germany became a beacon of rescue for the besieged Baltic German community, whose gradual infiltration with Nazi thought and functionaries in the 1930s provided constant pretexts for further restrictions of minority rights.[36] Latvian Jews, too, continued to be virtually excluded from the state administration, civil service, police, military, and university faculty.[37]

Under the impact of the international economic crisis, all Latvian parties except the left considered a reform of the constitution, or at least changes in the electoral law, as inevitable. Agreement about the extent and nature of reforms, nonetheless, remained elusive until Prime Minister Ulmanis's visit to National Socialist Germany in the summer of 1933. Greatly impressed by its *Ordnung*, Ulmanis threatened to override the Saeima by referendum, if necessary, to impose constitutional reforms.

In March 1934 Ulmanis toppled the existing coalition government and became premier of a new government that on 15 May 1934 declared a state of emergency. Parliament was disbanded, with the government assuming legislative functions, allegedly only until the implementation of reforms. Carried out with the support of the Minister of War General Jānis Balodis, the Home Guard (*Aizsargi*),[38] and the Latvian intelligentsia, the coup met virtually no resistance at home or from abroad. President Alberts Kviesis lent the new regime legitimacy by proclaiming its laws and remaining president until 1936.[39] At the time, Ulmanis's *coup d'état* drew media attention even from as far away as Newfoundland.[40]

The Ulmanis Regime

Kārlis Ulmanis declared his new regime to be a non-partisan triumph of the Latvian over the foreign element. He officially justified the state of emergency as a security measure against alleged threats from both the extreme right and left.[41] (The Communist party had already been outlawed in November 1933.) Some Social Democrats, leaders of fascist organizations, and local Germans accused of conspiring for Germany were arrested and imprisoned. But there seems to have been no identifiable plot by them to overthrow the government. The assumption of power by a government of national unity in alleged defence of parliamentary democracy actually turned into a rule by decree with restrictions on the freedom of speech and the elimination of political parties, including Ulmanis's own Farmers Union. Two years later Ulmanis assumed the authority of president of state, as well, and his accumulated powers enabled him to make appointments without consultation or approval.

The regime experienced no open resistance during its seven-year lifespan. The chief principled opposition came from the Social Democratic and Communist camps, although even some high-ranking Social Democrats were prepared to serve Ulmanis. Most of the members of the Saeima, including its president, accepted the change and endorsed the new government. Ulmanis, in turn, granted their request for lifetime pensions. He also arranged with the Credit Bank of Latvia to fund their personal debts. Kārlis Ulmanis later enjoyed taking credit for getting two results with one stroke: peace in the country and an opportunity to 'corrupt' the members of parliament into starting honest lives.[42]

Following a propaganda visit to Latvia in the wake of Ulmanis's assumption of power, the Italian fascist Alessandro Pavolini referred to the changes he witnessed in Latvia as exhibiting a distinct 'fascist-type orientation.'[43] But in many respects Ulmanis, who was fifty-seven years old by then, was unlike any of the other European dictators of his day. He had been, for example, the prime minister of seven democratic cabinets between 1918 and 1934. In his education, too, he was different, for he had studied in Germany, Switzerland, and America. From 1907 to 1913 Ulmanis lived in the United States, and he earned a Bachelor of Science degree in agriculture at the University of Nebraska (in 1909). 'It is obvious that Ulmanis was strongly influenced by the United States,' maintains one biographer, 'and initiated many changes, some say, to the point of "americanizing" Latvia.'[44]

Certainly, Kārlis Ulmanis distanced himself from the totalitarian methods of Hitler and Mussolini – his Minister for Public Affairs Alfreds Bērziņš observed that neither Mussolini's poses nor Hitler's martial music had struck a responsive chord in Ulmanis, who preferred to compare himself to Oliver Cromwell.[45] Ulmanis never expressed a desire to base his regime on a fascist-type party or movement. But it is equally indisputable that the Ulmanis regime absorbed Latvian right-wing radical tendencies (including those of the fascist Pērkonkrusts whose organization he had outlawed) and emulated features of European fascist states. Of course, Ulmanis could not admit to emulating Nazi Germany because it would contradict his declared strategy of eliminating the historically rooted German influences in Latvian life.

Nevertheless, historian Jürgen von Hehn was struck by the similarities to German and Italian models, in particular the structural changes of the Ulmanis regime and the means of their introduction. For example,

Ulmanis systematically set about reorganizing the government, administration, and society on the basis of the leadership principle. By the time he assumed the presidency in 1936, he was frequently referred to as *vadonis*, 'the leader.' Another example is the special interest of the régime in Latvian youth organized in the *Mazpulki.* The régime urged youth to become the mainstay of a 'renewed and united Latvia.' There were, furthermore, the endeavours to rally the workers behind the new order, to transform the trade unions into state instruments, to prevent agricultural labour from leaving the rural areas, and to introduce a rural work service for the *Mazpulki.*[46]

The Italian precedent is unmistakably reflected in the establishment of numerous economic advisory *Kameras* or chambers. As early as December 1934, a Chamber of Commerce and Industry was created, followed by a Chamber of Agriculture, a Chamber of Trades, a Chamber of Labour, a Chamber of Literature and Art, and a Chamber of Occupations. A State Economic Council and a State Cultural Council, with government-appointed members, coordinated the functions of these chambers. The proliferation of these fascistlike structures, a development incompatible with the restoration of parliamentary democracy, may help to explain why Ulmanis kept delaying the introduction of the new constitution that he had promised in 1934. There are indications that some of Ulmanis's cabinet ministers were unhappy about the postponement of the constitution, especially after Ulmanis referred to the need for a constitution in his speech of 15 May 1938.[47]

In Latvia the failure to follow the Estonian example and legitimize authoritarian rule with a referendum and a constitution was obscured by an aggressive nationalist drive against the minorities under the slogan 'a Latvian Latvia.' No longer able to represent their interests, and excluded from government and administration because of the abolition of the national and municipal parliaments, the presence of the ethnic minorities was gradually removed from all other areas of life. The government hoped to accomplish their forced assimilation into Latvian culture through the suspension of their school autonomy, the rewriting of history from a Latvian perspective, and a systematic latvianization of economic life.[48]

The ethnic Germans in Latvia were particularly severely hit by the introduction of the economic chambers. In January 1937 the German envoy in Riga, Eckhard von Schack, reported to Berlin that 'all German associations whose name might suggest occupational representations were dissolved – even if they were merely of a social nature; their assets worth millions were confiscated without compensation ... the tendency of the younger generation [of German Latvians] to depart for Germany has increased at an alarming rate.'[49] Following the agenda Miķelis Valters had publicized in 1933,[50] the regime kept up pressure to expropriate and latvianize businesses by resorting to a variety of orders, decrees, and administrative measures. The minister of finance was given special powers to investigate private companies and order their liquidation if he deemed such to be in the national interest.

The main instrument designed to accomplish this was the Credit Bank of Latvia (Latvijas Kreditbanka), founded in 1935 with the Ministry of Finance as its largest shareholder. One of its official functions was to liquidate banks and businesses having financial difficulties, especially if their shares were controlled by foreigners and members of national minorities. The influence of the Credit Bank was felt in every industrial, commercial, and agricultural activity of the country. The London *Financial Times* of 18 November 1938 viewed the bank's control of economic life as 'not always beneficial to the rest of the country's business community.' The paper charged that, though technically a private concern, the bank was in fact an instrument of government 'with very definite "totalitarian" economic notions,' and its president Andrejs Bērziņš, who was also president of the Latvian Chamber of Trade and Industry, was 'virtually the country's economic dictator.'

The elimination of 'foreign' economic influences was only one aspect of a deliberate drive to industrialize Latvia. The overall objective was nationalization of every branch of industry in combination with the establishment of new, state-owned enterprises. The government, explained Ulmanis in February 1937, has to be a party to any large-scale commercial and industrial activity, not for commercial reasons, but for long-term national–political considerations. Guided by such motives, the government began establishing so-called national enterprises, all of which were eventually supposed to revert into the hands of the people. The government was to shoulder the initial difficulties and responsibilities of these enterprises so that other countries would view Latvian enterprise more favourably and confidently.

Government propaganda hailed the formation of large state-owned industries from liquidated private enterprises as a new beginning in the economic rebirth of Latvia.[51] State interference was warranted where private initiative pursued a course 'contrary to the interests of the community,' Finance Minister Ludvigs Eķis explained to the national Congress of Merchants, Manufacturers, and House-Owners in November 1937. The system of *laissez-faire* was 'no longer acceptable in our times,' Eķis elaborated, since the 'national reformation' of 15 May 1934 had ushered in an era of planned economy in commerce and industry. Andrejs Bērziņš told the November 1937 congress even more bluntly that 'this conception of free, unhindered competition must be obliterated from our minds and from our aspirations forever. We need today some form of planned economy.'[52]

Ulmanis has left a double-edged legacy. On the one hand, most Latvians and their postwar historians have credited his economic policy in general, and that of the Credit Bank in particular, with their country's 'rapid swing away from the depression into an era of unparalleled prosperity.'[53] To make the economy more self-sufficient in an era of international economic crisis, the government promoted viable export and home production and encouraged diversification towards local industries as well as an expansion of the small industrial base. In addition to its emphasis on processed sugar and other agricultural products, manufactured building materials, and textiles, Latvia became known for its machinery and its production of sophisticated electronic, radio, photographic, and precision communications equipment. The construction in 1936 of the huge hydro-power station at the Ķegums Rapids south-east of Riga, with a capacity of 373,000 kilowatts, heralded a new era in Latvia's industrial development.

On the other hand, critics have exposed the official assertion that the coup of 1934 brought about Latvia's recovery from the Depression: they consider it one of a number of enduring myths disseminated by Ulmanis and his propaganda minister Alfreds Bērziņš. In Latvia the Depression had hit bottom in 1932, and by 1934 the economy was already showing significant improvement. Furthermore, the forced creation of national enterprises caused flight of capital and resulted in a decline in the average value of per capita industrial output during 1934–8 from 2.3 to 1.8 thousand lats.[54] Apart from creating an atmosphere in which 'no privately owned firm ever felt secure about its future,'[55] Ulmanis's restructuring, ironically, facilitated the Latvian economy's transition to the Soviet system in 1940.

The challenges of 'reborn' Latvia enabled Alfred Valdmanis to rise to the top and to claim credit for some of the alleged progress. In 1949 he boasted to an American audience that by 1939 'education, all kinds of arts, sports – were on a very high level. With university graduates reaching three per thousand of the total population we ranked second to nobody in the world ... [We had] reached the cultural standard of the best western European countries, an economic standard comparable only with that of Canada and the USA, and a social security comparable only with New Zealand. We were active in politics and in world trade, we had an active balance of trade, and an active balance of payment and still a trend upward.'[56]

Indeed, to the outside observer, Latvia did give the appearance of a prosperous and blossoming country. In July 1938 the *Münchener Neueste Nachrichten* observed that a traveller approaching Riga from the east received the impression of a well-tended, civilized, and progressive country. The writer was particularly struck by Riga's cleanliness, order, and urban renewal activity. For example, entire rows of houses were being replaced by new buildings. The new Riga was assuming the character of a modern metropolis. Its young, well-educated class did not want to lag behind their west European role models in elegance, appearance, and such urban customs as entertainment, sports, and weekend trips. 'Latvia would long have suffered from overproduction of intelligentsia,' the paper noted, 'had not the new state organism, which is deliberately adopting National Socialist and Fascist models, absorbed so many educated people in the economy and administration of cultural life.'[57]

The pre–Second World War generation of Latvians, who later endured the trauma of mass deportation, war, Soviet rule, and foreign exile, developed a deep attachment to this fairly prosperous and modern state with its advanced education, exciting cultural life, and relative personal freedom. Most of it they associated with the name and person of Kārlis Ulmanis. This was the Latvia Alfred Valdmanis longed to restore after 1941 because this was the Latvia that had shaped him and this was the Latvia that he, in turn, had helped to shape.

Alfred Valdmanis: Education and Apprenticeship, 1908–1934

Alfred Arthur Alexander Valdmanis was born on 11 September 1908 in Ziemupe, originally part of a German baronial estate named Seemuppen in the Russian province of Kurland. Located thirty kilometres north of Libau – in Latvian, Liepāja, Latvia's second largest city and seaport – Valdmanis's birthplace is a tiny, dreamy hamlet surrounded by trees, about one kilometre from the amber-rich sand dunes of the Baltic Sea. Life seems to stand still in Ziemupe. In 1993, Anna Jansone, ninety-two years old, sitting on the steps of the former local elementary school, still remembered the Valdmanis name, although the family had left after the

First World War. Even local residents less than half that age, such as Līna Iesalniece, knew that almost a century ago the Valdmanis family were fellow residents.[58]

The origin of the name Valdmanis, like many Latvian names, is Baltic German. Derived from Waldmann, which translates literally as forest man, it does not necessarily indicate German descent. In the early nineteenth century, when – with the abolition of serfdom in Russia's Baltic provinces – peasants were assigned surnames, many Latvians adopted German ones to facilitate their upward mobility. Although not claiming any German ancestry, and adopting the Latvian spelling of Alfreds Arturs Aleksandrs in his Latvian passports of 1928 and 1933, Valdmanis found it occasionally expedient to assume a German identity as Alfred Waldmann.

Alfred's father Ansis (Hans) was a teacher. Part of his education apparently had been in the obligatory three-year Russian teacher-training program introduced after 1885. While opening to Latvians new opportunities for social and economic advancement, this russification program actually fuelled the Latvian national awakening. Although compelling prospective Latvian teachers to learn Russian so they could teach it, the legislation unintentionally also spread the Latvian literary language. In addition, Latvians still needed German for virtually all professional education in the Baltic provinces. The legislation, therefore, made Ansis's student generation in effect trilingual.[59]

According to Alfred's brother Osvald, Ansis finished his education with the study of organ and violin at a specialized school. Until 1904 he taught on private estates as a live-in teacher. Then, at age forty, he made a down payment on a fairly large farm holding. He became a farmer, but also taught at a nearby school until he became incapacitated by asthma.

Alfred's son Gundars explained that his grandfather Ansis had come from a relatively well-off landowning family. Since his interests had been in academic and musical matters, however, his brother and brother's daughter managed the considerable family landholding. Later on, after he had married Lavīze Saldnieks, twenty-four years his junior, and produced children, the asthma-ridden Ansis wanted to claim his share, but his Valdmanis relatives sided with the brother and his daughter against him. According to Gundars, 'Lavīze was (correctly) portrayed as a poor uneducated wife and as having married Ansis for money and position rather than love.' When the brother and niece sued for expenses such as back wages, they were awarded the entire estate. Thus, Ansis was effectively disowned.[60]

Lavīze and the increasingly sickly Ansis raised their children without any more contact with the well-off Valdmanis clan. Instead, they social-ized in the working-class milieu of the Saldnieks who made their living operating street kiosks and selling newspapers. These connections proved beneficial to Alfred Valdmanis during the Soviet occupation of 1940–1 when some of his childhood friends and acquaintances from Liepāja achieved significant positions in the Soviet government. According to Gundars, the Saldnieks's environment was a relatively easy one to excel in, and it provided opportunity to develop leadership.[61]

Alfred, born when his mother was twenty, was the oldest of four sons among the five children. Three (Alfred, Osvald, and Emīls) earned university degrees and ended up in exile in the West, while the fourth (Frīdis) chose to stay in Soviet Latvia as a left-wing union leader. The earliest data about Alfred presage an unusual child heading for a splendid career. His brother Osvald remembered their mother saying that at a very early age Alfred used to clamber up on his father's knees asking for something to write on, and by the age of four he could read and write. Alfred's first teacher was his own father, and the family credits him with having done an excellent job. When he entered school, Alfred was already fluent in the three local languages: Latvian, German, and Russian. At elementary school (1914–20) in Liepāja, Alfred excelled in every subject except mathematics, where he was awarded only a 'C,' and in art (sketching). Telling everybody that Alfred had the qualifications to be president of the country, Alfred's father had a hunch that his eldest son would try for the very top.[62]

Liepāja in the early twentieth century was more German than Riga. Although Russian was the official language of instruction in the schools, one former resident recalled that Libau's prewar Latvian population was fluent in German.[63] The outbreak of the First World War brought increasing areas of Russia's Latvian territory under German control. The German army entered Libau, which was only thirty kilometres from the German border at that time, as early as August 1914. Although three-fifths of Kurland's population of six hundred thousand (6.5 per cent of it was ethnic German) fled from the advancing German troops who occupied most of Kurland by May 1915,[64] the Valdmanis family stayed in Libau. During the following three years the occupying forces imposed various germanization measures, especially in education. These were intended to prepare for eventual affiliation with Germany.

Thus, in his first four years of elementary schooling, Alfred Valdmanis received a German education, an experience of which he later liked to boast when trying to convince some German officials of his alleged pro-German sentiments. In Latvian circles he preferred to feature his struggles for Latvia's independence (1918–20). There he claimed to have participated in so-called student companies and to have been decorated for bravery. At that time, he asserted in 1947, 'we learned in Latvia, that men who gained high posts of state, money and honour in good times, are obliged to stay and to lead their nationals in misfortune and that they have no right to bring themselves into safety.'[65]

Osvald singled out Alfred's membership in the Latvian National Youth Organization (Latviešu Nacionālā Jauniešu Savienība), where he worked his way up from cub to leader, as another positive influence in his childhood. 'It was a great training in discipline and experience, not only to obey commands and rules, but also to be a leader and commander,' his brother Osvald recalled in 1985, and he added that Alfred had the unusual habit of seeking friends older than his age group. Indeed, most of his friends in his youth were adults, Osvald explained, and many of them held influential economic and social positions. Alfred's leadership aspirations and achievements during his high school years in Liepāja (Classic Progymnasium 1920 to 1923, Gymnasium 1923 to 1928) seem verifiable. When in March 1926 he applied for admission to a leadership training course of the LSCO youth organization in Riga, Alfred's application was approved in part because he could produce an already successful record (since May 1923) as a group leader of the Liepāja chapter of the National Youth Organization.[66]

As a student at the University of Latvia in Riga, from 1929 to 1932, Alfred completed in only three years a normally five-year course program in economics, law, and philosophy for a diploma in jurisprudence. Later, in September 1932, he was one of forty-seven graduates awarded the degree of candidate of law. For the degree he wrote an eighty-page thesis on the topic 'Compulsory Public Sale of Real Estate Seized by the Courts.' (Following a government decree of September 1939, the University of Latvia issued official certificates renaming this degree Master of Law.)[67]

The details that Alfred Valdmanis himself later released about his early years are unreliable and require verification since he tended to make his curriculum vitae fit his changing identity. For example, there is no evidence to support the boast that he had been among a select number of students given an elite education by the government to prepare them for a future leadership role in Latvia. 'In 1929 there were hardly more than a dozen of us,' Valdmanis bragged to a Standing Committee of the Canadian Senate in 1949: 'When we graduated from our universities we were sent abroad. To each one a special field was assigned. Mine was the field of economics, trade, industry, and finance. I was sent first to Germany and became special assistant to Dr Schacht, the President of the German

Reichsbank; later to France, England, Belgium, Holland – every European country. In that way we prepared our future economic, industrial, and financial leaders.'[68] A Latvian American historian, the late Edgars Andersons, concluded that Valdmanis had never worked for or under Schacht in the course of either his academic studies or professional training. Andersons had researched Valdmanis's early career, interviewed him in the 1960s, and edited his last autobiographical notes in 1983.[69]

It can, however, be ascertained that, while a university student, Valdmanis discovered that his proficiency in chess opened doors. This prowess earned him money with chess lessons and, more importantly, led the nationalist student fraternity Tālavija to offer him membership. Modelled on the German *Burschenschaften*, Latvian student fraternities were multigenerational, social networks bonded by life membership. They controlled government and civil service appointments, facilitated upward mobility, and dispensed patronage. Admittance to the civil service depended on membership in the 'right' fraternity. Tālavija was one of the most prestigious fraternities with its influence reaching deeply into the government and economy. But it was also, next to Lettonia and Selonija, one of the leading anti-Semitic fraternities and many members were affiliated with the Pērkonkrusts.[70]

While indulging in fraternity life and chess during his university days, Valdmanis managed to procure almost continuous employment in various government departments. However, the exertions must have taken their toll. Prior to graduation, he ended up in the sanatorium of Vainode to recover from the stress brought on by this routine of studying while working, 'a problem quite common with Latvian academics,' his first biographer Boriss Zemgals notes.[71] (As a former notary for the Credit Bank of Latvia, Zemgals claimed to have been privy to confidential Latvian government records. However, as indicated in Chapter 6, Zemgals's biography appears inspired, if not in fact written by Valdmanis himself.)

A turning point in Alfred's student days, according to his brother Osvald, was the election to the Saeima of Lutheran minister Dr Visvaldis Sanders on the ticket of the *Kristīga apvienība* (Christian Union), a right-wing party that for the first time captured six of the hundred seats in the (fourth) Saeima (1931–4). Acclaimed to be the most popular preacher in Liepāja, Sanders used to have Ansis and Alfred play the organ for him. Sanders started grooming Alfred early for political life, and Alfred appeared very interested. Excited at the prospects of public office, Alfred declared himself a candidate for parliament while still a university student. The minutes of a 24 January 1929 meeting of an organization calling itself the Council of the Academic Section of the Latvian National Federation (Latviešu Nacionāla Apvienība) record that Alfred Valdmanis had been accepted as a new member. Also accepted at the same meeting were Ilona Leimane and Leonīds Breikšs, two bright lights and Pērkonkrusts sympathizers among the Latvian intelligentsia of the Ulmanis era. The Latvian National Federation was the first party to advocate a reform of the Latvian constitution that would strengthen the role of the president. In the 1920s its leader Arveds Bergs was, in the words of historian Ezergailis, 'perhaps the most ominous anti-Semitic voice ... [that] made anti-Semitism in Latvia respectable.'[72]

Alfred soon realized, however, that he was not cut out for a life of public exposure and controversy, which membership in the Saeima entailed. The less conspicuous and more tangible career opportunities opening up in connection with his student employment with the government turned out to be more enticing. The official record of employment kept by the Chancellery of State in Riga shows that Alfred was employed as a messenger with the banks division of the Department of Economics from as early as October 1929. In January 1930 he was transferred to the precious metals management board of the same department's industrial division. There he was promoted to the position of deputy assistant to the metals grading inspector, and in March 1930 to the position of assistant clerk. In April 1930 he was included in the staff of the Department of Trade and Industry but terminated in November 1930 at his own request so that he could work for the District Court of Liepāja.[73] Both the departments of Economics and of Trade and Industry were within the Ministry of Finance.

According to his government record of employment, Valdmanis's professional legal career began inauspiciously in August 1932 when the director of the Department of Economics took him on as a temporary replacement for an assistant legal counsel, initially for a one-month trial period. But within the month Valdmanis was given a contractual appointment with the department's legal counselling division. In April 1934 he was promoted to legal counsel (*Juriskonsults*), and in November 1934 to senior counsel to head the joint legal office for the Department of Trade and Industry and the Department of Economics. When in April 1936 the Ministry of Finance established its own legal department, Valdmanis was invited to be its head. In June 1938 he was appointed minister of finance by directive of the president of Latvia. In step with his promotions, Valdmanis's salary increased from 200 lats in August 1932 to 592 lats in April 1936 to 1,100 lats in June 1938.[74]

Boriss Zemgals attributes the meteoric rise of Alfred Valdmanis to three factors. First, Valdmanis benefited from pure chance. Valdemārs Zāmuels, who was director of the Department of Marine Trade as well as chief legal counsel for the Ministry of Finance, needed sudden hospitalization, and his deputy Viktors Dāle, who did not take his duties seriously, was frequently absent. Second, the Ministry of Finance had an uncharacteristically high demand for legal opinions because of the recently introduced monetary restrictions. Third, Valdmanis was determined to impress his superiors with his work ethic and expertise by meeting the unusual challenges facing him. His determination was fuelled by the critical, if not outright hostile, reaction to him from members of the Riga bar association. Many of these long-term lawyers looked askance at Valdmanis, the young, inexperienced upstart and outsider from Liepāja, since they themselves had been candidates for the position of legal consultant with the Ministry of Finance and enjoyed the backing of political parties. Valdmanis was informed that he would be refused admission to the bar in Riga as long as he was employed in the Ministry of Finance. In response Valdmanis is reported to have declared that he preferred his government job over the right to practice law in Riga.[75]

At the time of Valdmanis's assistantship, requests for legal opinions were flooding the ministry, but the minister of finance would not act without the advice of his legal department, whose chief was absent for extended periods. In the absence of an experienced legal counsel, the young inexperienced assistant had the dilemma of either requesting help and thus embarrassing his supervisor or taking on the responsibilities of legal advice all by himself. He opted for the latter, staying up late and writing numerous references in various fields as well as participating in drafting statutes. In the Ministry of Finance no one seems to have been aware that for four months all those matters were attended to by a single individual, who was only twenty-four years old. This proven ability and service earned Valdmanis, in February 1933, an appointment with the Department of Marine Trade as special legal and economic consultant responsible for such matters as maritime law and the electrification of Latvia, and in April 1933, according to Zemgals, tenure as full legal counsel. The bar association was now prepared to accept him as a member.[76]

Alfred Valdmanis's growing professional contacts with the Latvian elite were cemented by his marriage, in February 1933, to Anna Irma Elvira Šlessers, daughter of a wealthy business family. They had known each other since they were fourteen and had attended high school together in Liepāja. Irma and Alfred had one daughter, Vaiva Mara, born in 1935;

two natural sons, Gundars and Videvuds, born in 1940 and 1943; and one adopted son, Agnar Johannson, born 1941. Irma's three sisters, their husbands – especially Valdis Mateus, Alfred's high school friend from Liepāja who married Katrina (Kiki) Šlessers – and her brother Jānis (John) developed close relationships with Alfred and supported him through the ups and downs of his career. Mateus was a wealthy landowner and a wholesaler for farm machinery. A prominent member of the Farmers Union, he was a popular leader in the province of Kurzeme (Kurland).

The Šlessers (the name but not necessarily the family was of Baltic German origin) were among the prominent families in Liepāja. Although their prewar fortunes derived from raw lumber exports to Britain had been decimated, they continued to be well off because Irma's father, Jānis, was a sea captain for the Red Cross during the First World War. It was Jānis who taught Alfred the rudiments of English. Jānis moved to Canada as a post–Second World War refugee and lived to be 104. The Royal Canadian Legion granted him membership because of his service as a Russian naval officer in the Russo-Japanese War of 1904–5.[77]

Apart from those with his family, Valdmanis seems to have had few intimate social relationships. Zemgals presents Valdmanis as a person shy by nature with few friends and passive when attacked. There can be little doubt that the age disparity coupled with professional envy and bitterness of colleagues limited his social contacts and reinforced certain of his personality traits. Not participating in the social life of the city or in party politics, Valdmanis preferred to immerse himself in work and study. One of his colleagues affirmed that from September 1932 to June 1938, Valdmanis authored 692 legal papers.[78] According to the character portrait drawn by Zemgals (that is, probably Valdmanis himself), Valdmanis exhibited from early on the combined traits of a loner, a climber, and a workaholic. Irma, who remembers proofreading all his legal papers, considered her husband very intelligent but emphasized that he also worked very hard, a fact often overlooked by those who envied his career. In his few spare moments he played chess and tennis. His chess proficiency won him the Latvian championship. His tennis teacher, the Baltic German entrepreneur Friedrich Kreyser, director of the Rigaer Zementfabrik C.Ch. Schmidt (after 1935 known as Rīgas Cementa Fabrikas),[79] remained one of his mentors and closest friends until 1954.

Valdmanis's ethical standards appear to have brought him lifetime enemies. In his capacity as legal counsel, he became aware of the involvement of some of the banks in unsavoury deals with politicians and parliamentarians. 'The young jurist would not accept the corrupt customs of the day. With barely concealed contempt he opposed many important men in parliament and court,' Zemgals relates. The few cases he took on as a private lawyer alongside his government duties, according to Zemgals, were usually cases of people who could not afford to pay.[80] Whether as a civil servant Valdmanis was in fact the alleged youthful idealist opposed to corrupt politicians and a champion for clean government cannot be verified.

Although projecting the image of a non-conformist, some of the key traits attributed to the young Valdmanis – quest for education, career ambition, egomania, disillusionment with liberal democracy, and espousal of ethnic nationalism – were not atypical of Latvia's young educated elite at the time. Zenta Mauriņa and Marģers Vestermanis have identified endemic 'narcissistic national pride' and exaggerated longing for upward mobility and social recognition as conspicuous features of the prewar Latvian intelligentsia. Attributed to the centuries of oppression endured by Latvians and to the strength of Latvia's German and Jewish minorities in trade, industry, and the professions, Vestermanis considers these traits the basis for ethnic Latvian germanophobic and anti-Semitic tendencies during the period 1919–41.[81]

The Youngster in the Ministry of Finance

During his term as senior legal counsel from 1934 to 1938, Alfred Valdmanis seems to have increasingly isolated himself socially. He had 'no friends in the normal sense of the word,' Zemgals reveals, and he did not talk much about his personal life. His relationships were not on a social basis or with those his own age, but on a business basis and with people of 'much higher eye-level,' such as directors of companies and departments. These more senior people continued to consider him, in the words of Zemgals, 'a youngster with some unusual characteristics such as being kind to office boys and other lower-level employees ... On a few occasions ... he confessed that once in a while he would have liked to be young. But in most instances, looking at his calendar for the next day, he realized there was no time to be young.'[82]

Zemgals attributes Valdmanis's rapid advance to senior legal counsel to the successful testing of the newly fledged junior counsel's abilities in the international arena and his subsequent increased prestige at home. Since the government lacked officials able to match Valdmanis's legal and language expertise, Zemgals maintains, Valdmanis was asked in May

1933 to present a particular Latvian case involving a long-standing trade dispute with Belgium to the court in Ghent. The Ministry of Finance had more or less given up on it as a lost cause. When in September 1933 word came of an unanticipated favourable settlement for Latvia, Valdmanis was asked to take on the defence of Latvia's territorial dispute with Estonia. The adjudication of this dispute was also favourable to Latvia.[83]

Success in Ghent, Zemgals suggests, made Valdmanis the obvious choice for the position of chief counsel as successor to Valdemārs Zāmuels, who planned to resign in favour of a newly created seat in the Senate (Latvia's highest court). Although Zāmuels did not receive the anticipated Senate seat, the Ulmanis government requested his resignation anyway in connection with a purge of senior civil service personnel. In April 1934 the minister of finance offered the position of senior counsel to Valdmanis but, so the unverifiable story goes, Valdmanis did not want to arrogate the position of his benefactor. Initially, Valdmanis agreed to take the position only on a *pro tem* basis. Only when Zāmuels insisted upon it, did Valdmanis accept a permanent appointment (in November 1934).[84]

No doubt other, perhaps more important reasons prompted Valdmanis's sudden promotion. Ulmanis, after his coup, was in dire need of dependable people, and Valdmanis, by his own admission, had made himself known as a critic of the old order and sympathizer for the aspirations of the new one. Ulmanis was faced with the job of not only consolidating his political power, but also taking inventory of the expertise available to him. Most of the people available lacked knowledge, conviction, and courage, recalled Valdmanis twenty years later. Also, at his age, Valdmanis was presumed to be still malleable. He was, to quote the metaphor Ulmanis borrowed from Mussolini, good 'clay to do the sculpturing with.'[85]

Valdmanis's rapid advance did not, understandably, endear him to his much older, more experienced colleagues. At age twenty-five he was the government's youngest senior legal counsel, and many members of the legal community were sceptical about his appointment. But from 1934 to 1939 Alfred Valdmanis did not worry about reprisals from proponents of the old regime. They had lost power, and as he saw it, offered no viable alternatives for the future. Valdmanis, on the other hand, was in a strategic position to help shape Ulmanis's new economic policy because of the role of the Ministry of Finance with its important legal consulting division and the minister's dependence on his legal counsel's advice.

The Ministry of Finance, including as it did the Department of Economics and the Department of Trade and Industry, was always more than just a treasury department. After the Ulmanis coup it became the operational centre of the new regime. Under its vast jurisdiction, Valdmanis explained (in 1963), were such domains as trade, industry, shipping, electrification, agricultural land and real estate matters (handled through the land bank and mortgage bank), the nationalization of foreign-owned companies (carried out through the Credit Bank), agreements with other countries (normally handled in the Ministry of External Affairs), agriculture (because of the subsidies and export legalities), and even the armed forces (because of the problems related to expenditures and manpower).[86]

The minister of finance from May 1934 to June 1938 was Ludvigs Eķis. Not a member of any political party, Eķis came from the Ministry of External Affairs and the diplomatic service. Although responsible for implementing the directions of Ulmanis's new economic policy and for the legal projects associated with it, he was no expert in economic matters. Reporting directly to the president, Eķis was not willing to fight his jealous colleagues in the cabinet. He demanded from Valdmanis a plan, but was allegedly unable to present and defend whatever plans Valdmanis proposed. 'It came to the point that I was called into cabinet meetings to explain Mr Eķis's proposals to the cabinet,' Valdmanis pointed out. Both Eķis and Andrejs Bērziņš, the director of the Credit Bank of Latvia, who also reported directly to the president, relied on the expertise of Valdmanis.[87]

As the head of the finance ministry's consulting division, or 'brain centre' as Zemgals terms it, Valdmanis was responsible for laying out the legal ramifications of the regime's economic policies and policy proposals. He had a hand in many if not all government contracts. Routinely asked to assist in negotiations with foreign companies, Valdmanis became involved in such issues as the settlement in July 1934 of Riga's prewar debt in London,[88] the clarification of questions concerning the Swedish match production and distribution monopoly in Latvia, and the examination of western European trade and commerce structures with the idea of selecting a suitable model for Latvia.[89] In 1935 he was assigned both the position of legal counsellor for the management of the state sugar monopoly and a seat on a commission created by the minister of finance to consider the League of Nations' imposition of economic sanctions on Italy.[90]

Alfred Valdmanis took particular pride in his proposal and draft contract with Swedish companies for the Ķegums project, signed in August 1936.[91] For more than ten years a hydroelectric deal had apparently eluded a committee of ten Latvian specialists negotiating with various countries. The loan solicited from Sweden for the construction of this power station near Riga constituted the biggest investment of foreign capital in Latvian industry.[92] In the ceremony launching the project, Valdmanis received appropriate credit and the king of Sweden bestowed on Valdmanis an honour called a commander of the Swedish Vasa Order III Rank.

In connection with the economic plans he developed for Eķis, Valdmanis took credit for having been a chief instigator in the formation of national enterprises. To guarantee their successful launching, he assumed the position of chairman of the board of each newly formed company, with the intention of resigning as soon as operations began. Since all the shares of those new companies were owned by the state, Valdmanis as chairman of the boards never owned a share in any of them. Malicious rumours planted by his detractors that he derived financial gain from these procedures were ill-founded, Valdmanis later insisted.[93] June 1938 found him chairman of the board of such different state-owned companies as Vairogs (machinery, vehicles), Aldaris (brewing), Ogle (coal), Droschiba (insurance), and Degviela (fuel). Degviela, for example, was formed by Valdmanis and four government officials in June 1937 out of the liquidated German-owned fuel- and lubricant-producing enterprise Oehlrich. It was the ninth industry reorganized as a national enterprise.[94]

Other 'daring' new projects that Valdmanis is alleged to have initiated on his own, although not all were immediately approved by President Ulmanis, include the refinancing of government employees' debts, the introduction of scholarships for qualified young people, the establishment of experimental industrial plants, the development of a rural electrification blueprint, and taxation reform. For his efforts the Latvian government in May 1937 awarded Valdmanis the Three Star Order III Rank.[95]

With the Credit Bank of Latvia, on whose board of directors he was ex officio member, Valdmanis from hindsight claims to have had more than one disagreement over economic policy. In particular, he allegedly objected to two measures. The first was the bank's interference with small projects he had planned. It converted these into large-scale ones. The second concerned interference at the new companies. In these, in addition to the professional management, the bank established committees organized and subsidized by government and staffed by non-experts. In Valdmanis's opinion, the first measure threatened the balance of Latvia's economic structure, while the second was a waste of money. That he allegedly resigned in protest from the bank's board of directors cannot be corroborated.[96]

Despite the flurry of activities and the importance of the Ministry of Finance in implementing economic changes envisioned by President Ulmanis, the ministry lacked a clear plan for restructuring Latvia's economy. Ulmanis was reportedly so busy drafting all his speeches himself that he had no time to devote to policy details. Eķis, too weak to adhere to a consistent policy, was 'juggling between the cliques, one day helping Balodis against Bērziņš and Munters, and the next day talking to Ulmanis against Balodis.' Meanwhile, the powerful Credit Bank of Latvia followed an economic rationale of its own. (Its head Andrejs Bērziņš was coincidentally also president of the influential Latvian Chamber of Commerce and Industry.) It expanded its scope from its near-monopoly in banking and its policy of liquidating foreign financial institutions into industrial restructuring. Not until mid-1937, Valdmanis revealed later, 'did we in the Ministry of Finance start getting some concrete idea about what we had, what we didn't have, and what we would have to do.'[97]

From 1934 to 1937 structural changes in the economy appear to have been propelled largely by the momentum of changes introduced in 1935. These were especially the launching of the Credit Bank and the creation of five economic chambers (the chambers of Industry and Trade, Agriculture, Trades, and Labour) as the sole representatives of occupational interests organized in local associations established and supervised by these chambers. The requirement of annual permits for commercial and industrial enterprises and the establishment of the chamber system epitomized the monopoly the regime had acquired over the economic life in Latvia.

A considerable stir was caused on 18 January 1938. On that day the government suddenly liquidated the highly successful textile syndicate Latvijas Kokvilnas Ražojumi (LKR) with its six thousand employees and an annual turnover of 30 million lats. Developed in 1929, and owned by a consortium of eleven Germans, ten Jews, two Latvians, one Russian, and one Estonian, the LKR's high profits were denounced in the press as exploitation of the Latvian people. As recently as July 1937, Andrejs Bērziņš in his capacity as president of the Latvian Chamber of Trade and Industry, however, had praised the seven cotton weaveries that formed this syndicate for their efforts to survive and succeed and for demonstrating to the government how industrial life might be revived. The official reasons given for the transformation of LKR into the state-owned joint-stock company Latvijas Kokvilna (Cotton) were (1) reduced retail prices for textiles, (2) the need for modernization, (3) product upgrading, and (4) rationalization of Latvia's entire cotton industry.[98]

The LKR takeover was made possible by a law of 17 January 1938 that gave the Credit Bank of Latvia the right to liquidate any business enterprise at its discretion and without proof of financial difficulties. On 14 December 1937 the Latvian cabinet had issued a decree requiring commercial agents of foreign-owned companies to be bona fide merchants whose rights to act as agents were subject to approval by the Department of Industry and Trade. The purpose of the decree, one official declared, was to reverse the current composition of ninety-five non-ethnic Latvian to five ethnic Latvian agents representing these companies. A further law of 11 February 1938 required the owners of companies dealing with printed materials to be Latvian citizens fluent in the Latvian language.

If there was any new policy development discernible on the eve of Valdmanis's takeover as finance minister, it was the accelerated latvianization of cultural and economic life. This was evident in President Ulmanis's introduction in May 1938 of a bicameral cultural council[99] and in the government-directed transfer of privately (and mostly non-Latvian) owned enterprises into restructured state-owned shareholding companies.

chapter two

'The Most Active and Influential Member of the Cabinet': Minister of Finance 1938–1939

Dr Valdmanis was the cleanest and hardest working minister Latvia ever had. Never has Latvia's economy been in such excellent condition as in 1938–39 under Dr Valdmanis. He cleaned out the entire state apparatus, dismissed corruptible old civil servants and replaced them by very young ones, thus generating a unique dynamic but also the animosity of seniors ... His co-workers, the factory workers, but especially the tradespeople, the progressive economic circles, and the young intelligentsia adored this barely 30-year-old person who did not belong to any party and who alone dared to defy Dr Ulmanis and to demand a new constitution and constitutional elections in Latvia. The animosity and opposition by a small group of old politicians against Dr Valdmanis was futile because Dr Valdmanis could produce results as no one before him.

Boriss Zemgals in 1947[1]

Appointment

Shortly before he resigned as minister of finance, Ludvigs Eķis made some revealing comments about his successor's agenda that may serve to put Zemgals's fulsome praises into perspective. In a confidential conversation with the German envoy Eckhard von Schack, Eķis disclosed that constant disagreements with Andrejs Bērziņš over economic policy had triggered his own resignation from the cabinet and subsequent acceptance of the post of Latvian envoy to Warsaw. The law of 17 January 1938 (which allowed the Credit Bank of Latvia to liquidate any business at its discretion), Eķis complained, had been passed over his objections and during his absence because Bērziņš had had the ear of President Ulmanis. Thanks to Andrejs Bērziņš's fiscal and economic schemes, Ekis saw Latvia heading for serious economic crisis, and he was in no mood to assume responsibility for these policies. Although Valdmanis had risen as a satellite of Andrejs Bērziņš, Ekis doubted that Valdmanis would be satisfied with the role of minister of finance in view of his 'active personality.' Both Valdmanis and Bērziņš had learned nothing from the past, Ekis feared, and would reinforce the trend towards state capitalism, a trend that would jeopardize economic relations with other countries.[2]

With his twenty-nine years Valdmanis was not eager to assume the heavy responsibilities of minister of finance, he claimed later. Nevertheless, he accepted Ulmanis's invitation on three conditions: first, he could proceed with a plan of his own design while presenting it to Ulmanis and debating it with him; second, after Ulmanis's agreement to the plan, Valdmanis would have no interference with it, not even from Ulmanis himself; and, third, Valdmanis could have complete authority to reorganize the ministry. All leading personnel were to be replaced with 'youngsters,' while the sexagenarians would be appointed as their deputies to dampen their replacements' exuberance with criticism. Ulmanis allegedly balked for six weeks before agreeing to go along with these terms. Thus, Valdmanis was not appointed until 15 June 1938, instead of as intended on 15 May, the anniversary of the Ulmanis coup.[3]

According to Zemgals, Valdmanis spelled out his conditions in a letter to the president. The pertinent government records, however, do not contain such a letter. There is only a note written to Ulmanis on 15 June 1938. In this Valdmanis accepted his appointment as minister of finance without any conditions.[4] One wonders whether someone as self-conscious about his age and still deferential to his higher-ups as Valdmanis – he used to refer to Ulmanis in contemporary fashion as 'leader' – would have mustered the audacity to extract terms at this point in his career. One may also question whether the authoritarian president of Latvia would allow a junior like Valdmanis to dictate his own terms of appointment. On the other hand, the regime's notorious shortage of dependable and qualified administrators may have left Ulmanis little choice, not only to invite Valdmanis to the cabinet but also to accept conditions. The combination of proven efficiency and competence with subservience and political reliability commended Valdmanis in this situation. 'Just look at the list of Ulmanis's cabinet,' he explained in 1963. 'How many could be classified as experts with courage and vision? ... We simply did not have the proper people. This was the reason for inviting a youngster like me to the government.'[5]

At the first cabinet meeting attended by the young minister, Ulmanis drew his attention to two immense challenges. First, to the previous duties of the finance minister had been added the responsibility for managing the many government-established enterprises. The difficulty of providing the necessary expertise to administer those enterprises was well known among government officials. Ulmanis hoped that awareness of this problem, together with the desire to do a good job, would help Valdmanis overcome those difficulties. Second, Latvia was in a general economic crisis: the sawmills had an oversupply of lumber for export, the balance of trade had been negative for months, and the reserves at the Bank of Latvia had shrunk from 46 to 40 million lats.[6]

Indeed, throughout the first half of 1938 the Latvian economy had been steadily declining. For example, public construction had virtually ceased in 1937 because it necessitated exorbitant imports, consumer sales were shrinking, and bread and meat prices were rising. Latvia's gold and foreign currency reserves were dwindling, and Latvian exports were declining even though staple exports such as lumber were trading at the lowest prices. The German legation's semi-annual review of Latvia's economy attributed this malaise in part to Latvia's continued policy of nationalization and the deterioration of conditions for private enterprise.[7]

In his inaugural address – also his first public statement – to the staff of his ministry, Alfred Valdmanis defined his agenda as being in accordance with 'the path that the leader of the people and state had shown us.' His options were of course limited by the course set by the Ulmanis regime after 1934. This meant that in putting his stamp on government policy Valdmanis had to rely on the arsenal of authoritarian and fascist economic panaceas of the time.

At the top of the agenda would be strengthening local industry, commerce, and the trades, as well as stockpiling reserves for hard times and restructuring economic ties with Latvia's neighbours. The relicensing of Latvia's joint-stock companies would progress with utmost speed and with the cooperation of the Chamber of Trade and Industry. The new order, initiated with the acquisition of national enterprises was nearing completion, but businessmen and industrialists would not have to worry since these enterprises would operate on a commercial basis; they would be no threat to any viable business venture not aiming at excessive profit. To alleviate the shortage of skilled workers in both the rural and urban areas, public construction would be cut back. The Ministry of Finance had immense responsibilities, Valdmanis continued, especially with regard to preparing the state budget and accumulating a reserve fund for old age and government pensions. Therefore all ministry employees needed to show a selfless, duty-conscious devotion to the tasks at hand, even though 'this might leave less time for our private lives.' It might even be necessary for them to put all their 'energies into the service of the Ministry of Finance.' Nonetheless, Valdmanis was convinced they would succeed if they cooperated harmoniously.[8]

In his report to Berlin, von Schack noted that Valdmanis's plan to strengthen commerce, industry, and the trades really meant further latvianization of these branches of the economy. He gave little credence to official assurances that the 'national enterprises' – because of their alleged commercial basis and non-competitive nature – would not hurt the free-enterprise sector. Von Schack claimed to have learned from reliable sources that the state enterprises did indeed threaten private enterprise because almost all were unprofitable by any commercial yardstick. This also made them a drain on the public treasury.

From his first personal meeting with Valdmanis, the German envoy came away with an ambiguous impression. On the one hand, the new finance minister wanted to promote favourable economic relations with Germany and entice German capital investment. However, he appeared embarrassed and even apologetic when asked why recently liquidated German economic interests in Latvia had not been compensated. On the other, Valdmanis refused to promise that the liquidation of German-owned insurance companies would end and that non-ethnic Latvians would not be barred from acting as agents of foreign-owned firms. To improve economic relations, Valdmanis asked that Germany stop overcharging Latvia for German exports. He conveyed to the German envoy his impression that Germany had developed a 'system' of adding 30 to 50 per cent to the price of its exports to countries with whom it had a clearing agreement. Only the future would reveal Valdmanis's hidden agenda, von Schack concluded.[9]

The New Spirit

An issue of high priority on Valdmanis's agenda as finance minister was the creation of a civil service loyal to him. A self-made man and admirer of the objectives of the coup of 15 May 1934, Valdmanis despised senior officials with a 'cloudy reputation' and those elevated to high positions on the basis of party membership. He planned to purge them and in their positions place young, like-minded co-workers who could help infuse in the government bureaucracy an enthusiastic spirit of unselfish, dedicated service.

The appointment of the new team of junior economists, legal consultants, and administrators was accomplished largely by reorganizing departments, establishing new institutes, and launching new projects. Thus, in the Ministry of Finance, Valdmanis promoted four former peers (Eduards Suksis, Augusts Celmiņš, Jānis Šakars, and E. Vilners) to be his personal aides and Anna Kunečs to be his personal secretary. To managers in the newly created Department of Foreign Trade he promoted junior barristers Aleksandrs Dinsbergs, Aleksandrs Āboliņš, Voldemārs Žagars, and Jānis Zībarts. A new Institute for the Study of Latvian Natural Resources was headed by engineer Aleksandrs Bulle and an Institute of Rationalization by professors A. Delvigs and Alfonss Eltermanis. The expansion and modernization of Latvia's commercial fleet was assigned to consul Jānis Salcmanis and shipping expert G. Krūmiņš.[10]

The creation of the Department of Foreign Trade entailed the dissolution of the Foreign Exchange Commission with its nineteen subsections composed of representatives from numerous government agencies. Within the Department of Trade and Industry the divisions in charge of commercial treaties and foreign trade were scrapped. This latter downsizing alone resulted in twenty permanent lay-offs of finance ministry staff.

Both lasting friends and lifetime enemies resulted from the numerous turnovers of government personnel. Among the latter were several directors of the Bank of Latvia, which was under the authority of the Ministry of Finance. In August 1938 Valdmanis engineered the resignation of Vilis Bandrēvičs, the director of the banks's foreign exchange department, for alleged irregularities in foreign transactions. Valdmanis had instructed the investigators to be 'strict and ruthless' even if it would hurt the department head.[11] The chair of the bank's board since 1930, Ādolfs Klīve, was the type of old-style official deeply resented by Valdmanis. He even refused to endorse Klīve for a government award requested by Ulmanis (the Cross of Achievement First Grade).[12] Klīve later retaliated by making life miserable for Valdmanis after the war.

Throughout his term of office, Valdmanis encouraged higher standards of dedication to the public service. For example, his Directive no. 375 required all his employees to submit semi-annual performance reports. The order stated that 'from these reports I would like to gain not only an evaluation of the tasks completed, but also suggestions and ideas about what changes might be desirable in the future. I would like to encourage each employee of the ministry to think about how to carry out duties better and more efficiently. This might make it possible to gradually increase the managers' decision-making powers and, in turn, require greater responsibility from them.'[13] In another directive Valdmanis addressed the long delays some divisions took to process certain inquiries and the occasional disappearance of entire files: 'For that reason I am requesting that in future all statements, opinions, references, etc. which would have required more than ten days to complete be reported to me with explanations about the reasons for the delay.'[14]

Another revealing example of Valdmanis's high expectations of civil servants are his instructions to government officials concerning trips abroad. Rather than semi-private vacations, such trips should be educational experiences, Valdmanis lectured to a meeting of department heads, directors of divisions, and managers of agencies under the Ministry of Finance on 8 July 1939. Consequently, the minutes read, 'The minister is instructing all administrators to demand from their subordinate officials sent to a foreign country, upon their return, written reports about their impressions, observations, and conclusions. Specifically, from what they had observed and experienced, they were to evaluate what could be used in Latvia. Officials on foreign visits should not content themselves with looking merely at the exhibits presented to them. They should try to familiarize themselves with actual conditions to be observed, sometimes possible in most cases, only outside the official programs.' By adhering to these guidelines, officials would not be tempted to propose the emulation of impractical, unreasonable projects, such as expensive public buildings.[15]

In his quest for ridding the public service of corruption and lethargy, Valdmanis appeared willing to raise unpopular issues in cabinet and in a less than diplomatic manner. For example, he claims to have proposed elections and restoring constitutional conditions offensive to President Ulmanis.[16] Moreover, he urged, cabinet to 'start thinking seriously' about measures to curb excessive drinking.[17] Although he believed that married women should devote themselves to their families,[18] Valdmanis supported a request for 500 lats by the National League of Latvian Women to enable them to attend the Congress of the International Women's Association in Edinburgh. The cabinet, however, rejected this motion.[19]

The available evidence suggests that Valdmanis strove to apply his personal code of ethics not only to the bureaucracy under his authority but also to Latvia's economic and social life. While his unorthodox approaches gained him more enemies than friends, they managed to generate sufficient funds for him to undertake such ambitious programs as old age pensions and student loans,[20] payment of foreign and domestic debts, and balancing Latvia's foreign trading account.

The Foreign Trade Issue

During his first half-year as minister, Valdmanis identified export trade as the key issue on his agenda because it touched on most areas of Latvia's economic life. On 7 July 1938, the occasion of his first ministerial visit to the Bank of Latvia – the state bank holding Latvia's treasury bonds, gold bullion, and coupons – Valdmanis advocated a more active export policy, both to protect the export-oriented industries from the repercussions of an international crisis and to redress Latvia's unfavourable trade arrangements with some countries. Foreign trade should be more centrally controlled by the government, he argued, and he expected the Bank of Latvia to cooperate in changing various fundamental approaches to that end.[21]

Trade with Germany was a matter of particular concern because along with Britain it was Latvia's most important foreign market. The problem for Latvia was that, unlike the British pound sterling, the German mark was not a convertible currency, and Latvia's abandonment of the gold standard in September 1936 had increased the cost of servicing her foreign debt. Germany was importing Latvian foodstuffs and raw materials – especially butter, pork, forest products, and flax – while paying with German-produced goods. The desire for a favourable balance of trade made Latvian exporters and government officials eager to export and ignore the fact that Germany did not pay its debts in money. In 1937 the proportion of Latvia's exports to Germany to imports from Germany (35.3 and 27.1 per cent respectively of the total value of Latvia's trade) was reversed for the first time since 1928.

But to balance its trade, Latvia was compelled to take German goods on Germany's terms. For Latvia this meant inflated prices, delays, and the danger of becoming an economic satellite of Germany. German manufacturers, busy filling German government orders under the Four-Year Plan to prepare Germany for war, could not meet the delivery dates promised to countries like Latvia. At the same time, Latvian exports had become a giveaway to Germany. Convinced that neither Eķis nor Ulmanis understood the clearing method devised by German Economics Minister Hjalmar Schacht, Valdmanis maintained that only he himself had been able to decipher Schacht's plan to undermine the economies of other countries. This plan required the balance of Latvian–German trade to be kept in clearing accounts at the German clearing office in Berlin. (Latvia also had clearing accounts with its third and fourth largest trading partners, the USSR and Sweden, each of whose trade was valued at 3 to 4 per cent of Latvia's total trade.) German officials, however, tended to over-value their own currency and ascribe arbitrarily low prices to imports from other countries. 'Unwittingly, unknowingly, and without realizing what was happening, we had slipped into their grip and we didn't have a single spare dollar or pound,' Valdmanis recalled.[22]

The trade issue was so important that within his first month in office Valdmanis broached it boldly not only with the German envoy in Riga but also with local representatives of large German firms. Latvia would like to increase imports from Germany, Valdmanis assured the Riga agent of the Rheinmetall-Borsig AG in mid-July 1938, but not if these had to be charged to the account of Germany's unpaid balance. The German exporters' refusal to grant the appropriate export credits and the 'completely impossible delivery terms' had created a situation for Latvia that required immediate remedy. Valdmanis even threatened to freeze Germany's outstanding balance and look for cheaper sources of supplies elsewhere. As finance minister he intended to put Latvian interests over his personal sympathy for Germany and ensure that his message was understood among all trade parties, he is reported to have insisted to the Rheinmetall-Borsig agent.[23]

Predictably the German Foreign Office refused to abandon or modify the clearing system. A frozen Latvian balance was of no use to Germany, remarked one of its spokesman laconically. He believed it would simply result in a reduction of German imports from Latvia. In dealing with German officials, Valdmanis faced the additional handicap of being known as one of the 'closest associates of the so-called dictator of Latvia's economy Andrejs Bērziņš,' who was blamed for initiating most of the anti-foreign economic measures of 1937. At an official reception in August 1938 Valdmanis had left the German envoy in Riga with the impression that he would be inclined to end what the latter termed 'the excesses of Latvian economic chauvinism' directed against German nationals and Latvians of German descent. Now Berlin decided to wait and see whether Valdmanis's alleged 'personal sympathies' for Germany were in fact strong enough to make him modify the discrimination against German-owned businesses in Latvia.[24]

As early as 15 September 1938 Valdmanis had indicated to the German trade attaché Adolf Leckzyck that he would be compelled to introduce a government monopoly of foreign trade. One of its objectives would be to redress the imbalance in German imports by imposing a reduction of Latvian exports to Germany. Latvians had noted that certain German exports were sold far more cheaply in Finland and Romania than in Latvia. The clearing system was forcing Latvia to accept Germany's unfairly high prices for its imports in Latvia while preventing the application of the surplus gained from Latvian exports. Latvia would like to improve its trade with Germany, but not at the price of destabilizing the Latvians' standard of living. When Leckzyck insinuated that a government trade monopoly was tantamount to emulating the Soviet system, Valdmanis countered that 'he had a German upbringing and his pro-German sympathies were beyond question.'[25]

Valdmanis had few illusions about his leverage in solving the trade issue in a direct way – refusing to sell or buy or changing existing contracts was only a short-term solution. The problem needed to be addressed through an integrated approach. The search for alternate markets for Latvian products drew attention to Latvia's inadequate delivery system. Although trains could deliver most Latvian exports to Germany, the Latvian merchant marine was too small for far-away markets. Success in international trade depended furthermore on improving the competitiveness of the Latvian economy on the world market; it depended on modernizing agriculture and organizing industrial production in the most efficient and economical way. Last but not least, the collapse of collective security drove home the need for an adequate defence force.

The smooth implementation of this comprehensive strategy required near-dictatorial powers. Valdmanis later claimed that President Ulmanis granted him the necessary authority. For example, no minister was permitted to submit to cabinet any proposal involving expenditures unless the proposal had been vetted by the Ministry of Finance. Until his departure on 25 October 1939, Valdmanis recalled twenty-five years later, 'I was the most active and influential member of cabinet. I could get involved and I did get involved in all matters of the government that were in any way connected with financing. I interpreted my authority in a very wide range, which included the control of student support, subsidies to farmers, old age security, and all direct and indirect import and export matters.'[26]

His special powers also gave Valdmanis 'prominence, to some extent undeserved, outside Latvia, where people quickly found out that in most matters willingly or not they would have to deal with me.'[27] 'I was well accepted outside Latvia even though in Latvia the term of "youngster" or "boy" still continued to be used. As a rule, when I was sent to other countries on special assignments, usually something had developed a kink, something had to be unravelled, had to be started up or finalized.'[28] It was virtually inevitable that the 'youngster's' surge to prominence and deep involvement in the finance-related matters of all other ministries would become a divisive issue in the cabinet.

The Integrated Strategy

Late 1938 saw the launch of the integrated strategy. The first step was the establishment on 20 September 1938 of a Department of Foreign Trade. A separate division within the Ministry of Finance, it was designed to regulate trade, payment, and foreign exchange. In addition, before the end of 1938, an Institute for the Study of Latvian Natural Resources and an Institute of Rationalization were announced. Numerous projects were soon under way – a search for alternate markets, an expansion of Latvia's merchant marine, an extension of the railway network in the countryside, a 50 per cent increase in the capacity of the Ķegums hydroelectric station, and the replacement of imported coal with hydroelectric power and peat briquets. One result of the more extensive utilization of forest products was the production of paper.

The Department of Foreign Trade with sections for trade, export, import, and foreign exchange was staffed by competent, young economists and headed by Valdmanis's friend Aleksandrs Dinsbergs. It assumed the functions of the previous Foreign Exchange Commission composed of members from the ministries of Finance, Foreign Affairs, and Agriculture, and the Bank of Latvia. According to Dinsbergs, the officials of his department had more authority than the members of the previous commission. This enabled them to effect an acceleration and rationalization of decision making in all foreign trade matters. The processing of all trade-related issues by one agency, Valdmanis explained, would facilitate a step-by-step transition to the adoption of a long-term plan in the domain of foreign trade.[29]

The German legation in Riga, while crediting Valdmanis with 'strong activity' in reforming Latvian foreign trade regulation, was not enamoured with the innovation. The regulation of foreign trade with a long-term plan was neither possible nor in the real interests of Latvian trade and industry, the legation's report to Berlin warned. It smacked of a Soviet-style trade monopoly and would open a new chapter in German–Latvian economic relations.[30] In November 1938 the German press became aware that Latvia had been deliberately curbing imports from Germany.[31] Two months later alarmed German exporters demanded a diplomatic intervention with Valdmanis. They wanted to prevent 40 per cent of a lucrative Latvian order for buses from going to Britain instead of the entire order going to Germany.[32]

By the end of June 1939 the German envoy had indications that Valdmanis was striving for an active balance of trade in order to achieve higher prices for Latvian exports to Germany. In fact, Valdmanis did manage to balance the Latvian–German clearing account.[33] The foreign trade department's manipulation of exports and imports – for example, through restricting import permits to a select group of merchants and imposing high fees for such permits – was still credited in January 1940 as an important influence on Latvian–German trade.[34]

Judged by the statistical evidence, Valdmanis succeeded in balancing the total value of Latvia's import and export trade during his term as finance minister. This is particularly evident in the trade with Germany and Britain, which together accounted for about 70 per cent of Latvia's external trade. In terms of percentages of the total value, exports to Germany declined from 35.3 per cent in 1937 to 33 per cent in 1938 and 29.5 per cent in 1939, while imports from Germany rose from 27.1 per cent in 1937 to 39 per cent in 1938 and 1939. Latvian trade with Britain manifested the opposite trend: exports increased from 38.4 per cent in 1937 to 42.5 per cent in 1938 and 41.9 per cent in 1939, while imports dropped from 21.4 per cent in 1937 to 19 per cent in 1938 and 20.8 per cent in 1939.[35]

The finance ministry's endeavours to influence the pattern of Latvia's trade were also evident in the search for alternate markets, the establishment of a transatlantic shipping line, and the modernization of Latvia's armed forces. Latvia's preferred trading partner was Britain, whose dealings were in foreign currencies. But by 1939 the discrepancy between Latvia's exports and imports with Britain had become dangerously large, and there were pressures from British manufacturers to balance the trade. Valdmanis was apprehensive of Latvia's increasing dependence on the British market where Latvian agricultural products faced competition from Scandinavian and Commonwealth countries. With 'expansion of exports to Germany absolutely impermissible and increasing exports to England likely to provoke counteraction,' Valdmanis wrote the Minister of Agriculture Jānis Birznieks in February 1939,[36] the Ministry of Finance had embarked on a scrutiny of other potential markets.

As a promising future market Valdmanis identified the United States. This market had become accessible in 1938 through Valdmanis's launching of Latvia's first shipping line to New York. In addition, this new connection opened markets in South America, especially Argentina. In one of his first acts as minister, Valdmanis created a special department, headed by Consul Jānis Salcmanis and shipping expert G. Krūmiņš, to facilitate the expansion of the Latvian commercial fleet, through construction as well as purchase. Krūmiņš – organizer of the Lithuanian commercial fleet – was put in charge of forming the government-owned shipping agency. Valdmanis arranged the purchase of the first diesel-motor ship and succeeded, through the lure of tax advantages, in inducing local shippers to purchase modern ships. By 1939 Latvia's merchant fleet consisted of 103 ships of a combined tonnage of about 200,000.[37]

Marketing was the main handicap in expanding Latvia's trade with the United States; Latvia's import–export ratio in 1937 and 1939 was 6.9 (1937) and 6.3 (1939) to 1.1 (1937) and 1.4 (1939) of the total.[38] This was despite the establishment of a Latvian–American Chamber of Commerce in New York. Valdmanis calculated that an agent working on a commission basis would take a personal interest in boosting sales. He therefore suggested to Minister for External Affairs Vilhelms Munters that a trade agent in America be appointed, instead of a trade attaché. The agent could assume responsibility for checking the credibility and credit ratings of importers and similar issues not included among the duties of a trade attaché.

To intensify trade with America, Valdmanis considered granting a concession to a joint-stock company in Riga whose shareholders would be local importers of American automobiles. The Ministry of Finance could not provide foreign currency for the import of American cars, Valdmanis stated in February 1939, but it would consider accepting a proposal by importers to set up a company promoting the export of Latvian products in America. The proceeds of those exports would finance the import of American cars. The scheme would succeed, Valdmanis believed, because 'in order to promote their products in Latvia, those large American automobile companies would promote Latvian products in America.'[39]

In the winter of 1938–9 Valdmanis explored the prospects of other new markets in negotiations with the USSR, Switzerland, Denmark, Belgium, the Netherlands, and Finland. Exports to the USSR increased in 1938, and imports from Switzerland doubled. German products in Latvia found themselves in competition with such Soviet imports as salt, fertilizers, structural iron, agricultural machinery, tools, and films, the German envoy noted. On the whole, however, Latvia found few markets in these countries or in the United States, the Balkans, and the Mediterranean, because of their similar export structure. Little Latvia lacked the population and raw materials to solve the diverse problems the government had put on its agenda, concluded the German legation's review of the Latvian economy in 1938.[40]

The Swedish Connection

A potentially expandable market for Valdmanis was Sweden, whose imports to Latvia had been around 3 per cent since 1936 but whose absorption of Latvia's exports had dropped to 2 per cent in 1938. Plans for a revival of Latvia's trade with Sweden were devised against the background of steadily deteriorating Latvian–Swedish economic relations. These started with the devaluation of the lat in September 1936, one month after the signing of the Ķegums contract, and were exacerbated by Latvia's escalating negative trade balance with Sweden. Swedish exporters had been complaining of Latvian delays of more than sixteen months in balancing accounts. As a result, private compensation deals were growing. When Valdmanis prohibited these deals in one of his first decisions as minister of finance, Sweden reacted by cancelling its clearing agreement with Latvia on 30 September 1938.[41] Valdmanis later blamed the Swedes and Munters for the breakdown in relations – the Swedes because as shrewd 'calculators' they saw no benefits in a close trade relationship with Latvia, and Munters because he had not been adept at restoring normal relations with Sweden.[42]

The cancellation of the clearing agreement endangered a loan Sweden had offered shortly before. This was in connection with the awarding of the contract for an expansion of the Ķegums hydroelectric station to Sentab, the original Swedish contractor. To reduce the import of foreign coal and other fuels and improve Latvia's balance of trade, the Latvian cabinet in July had endorsed Valdmanis's plan to enlarge Ķegums with third and fourth turbines, thereby doubling the station's output from 45,000 to 90,000 kilowatts by 1942. The Swedes offered to finance the third turbine with a loan of 2.65 million Swedish crowns, in addition to the 1936 loan of 11 million crowns. They also bid to build it faster than a competing bid by German firms and thus save Latvia 1 million lats. (Valdmanis, however, had promised the Germans to consider carefully a bid from them for the fourth turbine.) The Swedish loan still awaited official signing by the end of September 1938.[43]

Valdmanis was therefore sent to Stockholm on urgent business on 5 October 1938. On his agenda was a comprehensive review and reorganization of Latvian–Swedish economic relations. Topics included revival of trade, resumption of interest payments (discontinued in 1935) on the

Kreuger loan (that is, the loan received from the Swedish Match Trust in 1928), signing a Swedish loan and negotiating additional loans – the German envoy mentioned the sum of 18 million lats – for expansions to the Ķegums hydroelectric station.[44] The Swedes were given to understand that Valdmanis came as a special representative of the president of Latvia and as the man in charge of Latvia's economic affairs. Afterwards Valdmanis took credit for having turned an anticipated unpleasant three-day business meeting into a celebrated two-week event that opened a new chapter in Latvian–Swedish relations. The attention bestowed upon Valdmanis in Stockholm and the good time he had there made this event the high point of his ministerial career.

Despite a somewhat cool reception by the Swedish press – Valdmanis represented non-democratic Latvia in purely social-democratic Sweden – Valdmanis benefited greatly from the detailed preparations for his trip. These were made by his personal friend Friedrich Kreyser, managing director of Rigas Cementa Fabrikas, and Andrejs Bērziņš, who among the other positions that he held was also a member of this company's board of directors. To create a favourable atmosphere, Kreyser had the true purpose of the trip camouflaged publicly by arranging for the Swedish trust Skanska Cement A/B, Malmö, a shareholder of Kreyser's company, to issue invitations for a hunting excursion. At the same time, Andrejs Bērziņš had a 'Latvian Week' organized in Stockholm. Invitations to this went to Latvia's Minister for Public Affairs Alfreds Bērziņš, the rector of the University of Latvia Mārtiņš Prīmanis, as well as to a selection of high-ranking Latvian officers, civil servants, and businessmen.[45]

The itinerary for the morning of the second day scheduled Valdmanis to hold brief fifteen-minute discussions with each of three Swedish officials: Minister of the Exterior Richard Sandler (Valdmanis's personal friend in the Swedish government), Finance Minister Erik Wigforss, and Minister without Portfolio Hermann Eriksson. These were followed by an afternoon conference in the Ministry of the Exterior and an official evening dinner in Valdmanis's honour.[46] Among the guests were the head of the preceding Swedish government, Graf Helldorf; the ambassador of Sweden in Riga, B. Johansson; the ambassador of Latvia in Stockholm, Voldemars Salnais; and the mayor of Riga.[47]

Speaking in German at the banquet, Valdmanis flattered his hosts by suggesting that Latvians' historical ties with Sweden compared favourably with the ties to their former German overlords. He singled out the period of Swedish rule in Latvia (1629–1721) as a 'bright spot in the centuries-long and unchanged dark time of enslavement of the Latvian people.' Grateful for Sweden's generous economic assistance for the fledgling Latvian republic, Valdmanis promised to examine sympathetically any suggestions for promoting mutual economic relations. He acknowledged young Latvia's difficulty competing worldwide with the highly regarded Swedish products. This situation he pinpointed as causing Latvia's negative balance of trade.[48] But, Valdmanis elaborated,

> the flourishing economy of Latvia, built on firm foundations since 15 May 1934, has definite possibilities for export expansions. There are therefore no reasons a further development of mutual trade relations should not be possible ... Important are also the energy, the initiative shown by economic circles in both countries. These constitute the main basis of a favourable economic prognosis. In this situation mutual sacrifices of interests, in accordance with circumstances, would be entirely appropriate. Latvia can maintain that it has not been afraid of such sacrifices. I am all the more certain that Sweden too, will not change its favourable disposition towards the sale of our goods in its market.[49]

Latvian and Swedish newspapers were celebrating the public welcome extended to Valdmanis with extolling articles. He was greeted with 'a cordiality as has never been seen ever before,' wrote the Riga daily, *Jaunākās Ziņas* (The Latest News). The paper continued that Valdmanis's speeches were very well received and that the Swedish government had provided opportunities for personal contacts within the highest economic circles. It was in this climate that the king of Sweden had awarded Valdmanis the 'Order of the North Star – First Rank,' an honour Valdmanis often bragged about later. The entire Swedish press was taking notice of Valdmanis and other prominent Latvians arriving, including directors of Riga Cement Friedrich Kreyser and Max Braun-Wogau. Many of them were accompanied by their spouses. Even the press organ of the Swedish Social Democrats featured Valdmanis's photo and an article on the good prospects for Latvian–Swedish cooperation.[50]

On 10 October the entire party of eminent visitors was invited for an elk-hunting party that lasted several days in the Ramnesa forest.[51] As a souvenir, Kreyser presented a hunting rifle to Valdmanis. In a subsequent handwritten note Valdmanis thanked Kreyser for providing the opportunity to see the country and to meet its leaders.[52]

Upon his return to Riga, Valdmanis issued the following comments to the press:

> The negotiations ended with complete agreement on all important questions. Latvia is going to have a new trade agreement with Sweden based on the 'most favoured nation' principle. With the signing of the new agreement, the current dealings under the system of 'clearing' will be terminated and the trade accounts in the future will be settled in currency. We can anticipate a considerable increase in the export of our products to Sweden. To stimulate such an increase, a special Export Promoting Organization will be established in Sweden in which our exporters will be invited to participate. The new agreement will contain an entirely new principle: if and when our imports from Sweden should exceed our exports to Sweden, Latvia will have the right to balance the account by interrupting the 'most favoured' treatment. This clause represents an entirely new principle whose application will be very beneficial to Latvia ... I cannot emphasize enough the particular cordiality accorded not only to me but also to the whole group of Latvian visitors.

Minister of Public Affairs Bērziņš, in the same article, went so far as to maintain that 'the Swedes are now accepting the extension of western Europe to the eastern shores of the Baltic Sea ... and that economic cooperation should be as close as possible.'[53]

To expand exports in accordance with the Stockholm accord, the Credit Bank of Latvia entered into partnership with Latvijas Import Förmedling, a Stockholm company cooperating with the largest Swedish exporters to Latvia. Contacts were also established with the largest Swedish association of cooperatives, the Kooperative Förbundet, which operated four thousand stores and could easily purchase foodstuffs worth several million lats a year. Two factors, however, worked against export expansion with Sweden. One was the similarity of products exported by Latvia and Sweden. The other was political – the Swedish cooperatives were controlled by the Social Democrats, who were not interested in supporting the Ulmanis regime. Nonetheless, Valdmanis saw opportunities for export of Latvian products through the state-organized Central Association of Dairy Producers, exporters of bacon, and other firms 'in the markets not only of Sweden, but also of all other Scandinavian countries.'[54]

Since success depended on convincing the Kooperative Förbundet of the advantages of dealing with Latvia, Valdmanis requested that Birznieks's ministry of agriculture and the establishments under his supervision cooperate in the finance ministry's efforts to woo this market by providing a quick response to inquiries with precise quotations and competitive prices. 'The capture of foreign markets is an all-out effort for the Ministry of Finance,' Valdmanis declared. 'All our industrialists have been instructed to adapt their products to the preferences of their customers.'[55]

When all was said and done, however, it turned out that the Swedes were not eager for any close cooperation with Latvia. The German envoy in Riga considered this turn of events self-evident in view of the similarly structured economies of both countries. He suspected correctly that a significant discrepancy existed between the great hoopla with which the Valdmanis visit had been staged and its meagre results. Sweden and Latvia had reached only a preliminary accord to resume negotiations on a trade agreement whose outcome would also determine a loan. Characterizing the agreement as 'rather nebulous,' the envoy concluded that Valdmanis's 'entirely new principle' meant in reality the abandonment of the most favoured nation principle. The application of special duties would adversely affect the poor possibilities of developing this trade.[56]

Swedish–Latvian trade negotiations conducted in Riga during the following months extended the clearing agreement to the end of 1938 and stipulated that Swedish exports to Latvia were not to exceed the value of Latvian exports to Sweden by more than a ratio of four to three. Any Swedish exports exceeding this ratio were to be subjected to Latvian restrictions and special duties. By April 1939 Latvia had managed to reduce its negative trade balance with Sweden by 80 per cent through additional exports so that on 15 April 1939 Valdmanis was able to sign an official one-year Swedish–Latvian trade accord. According to Germany's envoy in Stockholm, Swedish observers were sceptical about Valdmanis's optimism to increase the volume of mutual trade through higher Latvian exports, as well as about Latvia's ability to pay for imports.[57]

Latvian expectations that the awarding of the third Ķegums turbine to Sweden would create a favourable atmosphere for further Swedish loans were also disappointed.[58] Sweden made further loans dependent on a resumption of Latvian interest payments (discontinued in 1935 because of a shortage of foreign currency) on the $6 million Kreuger match trust loan of 1928. Valdmanis, in turn, vetoed a Swedish plan to subcontract to a British firm a sluiceway for rafts at the Ķegums site. Instead, in mid-November 1938 he gave his blessing for the construction of this installation to the German companies MAN and Siemens.[59] 'The relationship between the Latvian builder and his Swedish contractor is anything but harmonious and will affect further loans,' reported the German envoy in Riga to Berlin on 11 January 1939.[60] His prediction was correct, for no further Swedish loans were forthcoming after Valdmanis on 11 May 1939 managed to settle the Kreuger loan dispute. The agreement saw the

Swedish match trust accepting 45 per cent of the nominal value in full payment of Latvia's obligations.[61]

Twenty-four years later Valdmanis disclosed that during his visit to Sweden in 1938 he had met a stream of representatives from government, industry, and banking. They had included the Minister of External Affairs Sandler, the Minister of Trade and Commerce Eriksson, the owner of Stockholm's Enskilda Bank Jakob Wallenberg, and the managing director of Bofors armaments. He admitted being told by all that under prevailing international conditions Sweden would not get involved with any of the Baltic states or with Finland, that the policy of expansion had died with Charles XII, and that in its place a carefully crafted defence policy combined with absolute neutrality had been established. That policy had been fully vindicated during the First World War. Valdmanis was given to understand that maybe the next generation, after the newly created Baltic states had proven that they were able to preserve their neutrality, might talk about closer Swedish–Latvian ties.[62]

Although he had reached the apogee of appreciation in a foreign land, Valdmanis realized that Swedes would be guided only by cold, nonpersonal calculations. It became clear to him that Sweden would follow a policy of the least risk and that influential Swedes were unanimous on this point. Even Valdmanis's friend Sandler was no exception. 'He was very cool when I inquired whether we could obtain some heavy armaments from Bofors and explained that this transaction would in no way be construed as involvement. He reminded me that Bofors was quite bogged down with orders, meaning that supply terms would be very long – several years.'[63] But the German envoy in Stockholm suspected that Latvia's negative balance of trade with Sweden, rather than the three-year delivery terms for Bofors's cannons, was the underlying reason for Bofors's rejection of Latvia's order.[64]

Armaments and the German Connection

Alfred Valdmanis attributed his own interest in armaments to his close association with Colonel Artūrs Dālbergs. Chairman of Vairogs and responsible for war economic planning in the Ministry of War, Dālbergs had travelled with Valdmanis to Moscow in 1937 to arrange purchases of oil and coal. Dālbergs was critical of President Ulmanis's deliberate neglect of the armed forces, blaming this on three factors: a general lack of funds, the absence of an immediate foreign threat, and Latvia's desire to steer a course of strict neutrality amid the conflicting interests of the European great powers.[65]

When Valdmanis took over the finance ministry, collective security was rapidly deteriorating. The crisis Hitler had provoked over Czechoslovakia in September 1938 brought unanticipated psychological and economic repercussions to Latvia. Ships loaded with Latvian exports for Britain waited in Latvian ports for weeks, and panicking consumers emptied their bank accounts and made a run on canned foods, goldware, silverware, and jewels.[66] The finance ministry asked textile manufacturers to obtain a four-to-six-month supply of raw cotton on consignment, and Valdmanis was considering the complete prohibition of some exports. Had the crisis continued, the Latvian government planned to proclaim a bank holiday on 30 September. Three more days of crisis, reported the German envoy to Berlin on 14 October 1938, would have forced the banks to close and the Latvian economy to shut down.[67]

The Munich Agreement (29 September), while averting economic chaos, gave rise to rumours in Latvia that Poland had secretly given up the Polish corridor to Germany in return for Lithuanian and Latvian territory. In the event of war, it was rumoured, Latvians would have less to fear from the Red Army than from German troops. Russian communism was believed to be no longer dangerous for Latvia because Ulmanis's state capitalism had prepared the country for a painless transition to the Soviet system. The Bolsheviks would also respect and make use of the Latvian intelligentsia's expertise.

In the event of German occupation, Latvians feared the worst. The German army would put in power Latvia's ethnic Germans, who would avenge their postwar discrimination. Resentment towards Latvian Germans and German nationals was reported to be at a fever pitch and von Schack had information that all Germans in Latvia would be interned in the event of mobilization.[68] A memorandum Valdmanis issued on 28 September to all directors and chiefs of administration requested them to ascertain 'in a hurry' the number and nationality of non-Latvians employed under their jurisdiction.[69]

The international crisis made clear to Latvian government officials as well as foreign observers that Latvia was woefully unprepared for armed conflict. One observer noted a severe shortage of trucks and neither air raid protection nor gas masks for the civilian population.[70] The crisis led Valdmanis to become concerned about stockpiling adequate supplies of fuel and strategic metals. Stockpiling was hampered by the limits already imposed on civilian consumption. Latvia could afford neither an unlimited import nor uncontrolled sale of oil products. At Valdmanis's urging, defence requirements received special consideration, and a reserve of strategic raw materials was accumulated to last more than a year. Valdmanis searched as far as North America for such supplies. On his instructions, for example, the managing director of the State Electro-Technical Factory (VEF), Teodors Vītols, managed to purchase two shiploads of copper in the United States in the autumn of 1939.[71]

To modernize Latvia's inadequate defences, Valdmanis found 'no money, no connections, and no knowledge of any sources of supply.'[72] Nonetheless, Minister of Defence General Jānis Balodis requested $10 million to create a small but fully motorized army. Valdmanis managed to procure the money within three months by cutting back exports to Germany, forcing active settlement of payments, and selling Latvia's useless coastal artillery to Loyalist Spain. General Balodis was so impressed with this performance, Valdmanis claimed twenty-four years later, that in the summer of 1939 he recommended to Ulmanis the appointment of Valdmanis as prime minister.

Aware of the importance of tanks in a future war, Latvia's chiefs of staff decided to make tank and anti-tank forces the core of the new army, Valdmanis recalled later. But modern arms were difficult to come by. Most of the large arms manufacturers, like Bofors in Sweden, refused to sell heavy arms to Latvia on credit. Despite his popularity in Britain, Munters was unable to purchase British-made guns, submarines, and Vickers aircraft on credit. British arms manufacturers accepted only cash orders. Moreover, Vickers aircraft had a minimum delivery date of two years.

Having been able to acquire only a few items from Britain (chiefly thirty Gloster Gladiator fighters) and tanks from Czechoslovakia, Latvia was compelled to turn to Germany for armoured cars, field howitzers, and other equipment.[73] For example, in March 1939 the Latvian war ministry negotiated the acquisition of one hundred to two hundred German armoured vehicles, 50 per cent of the cost to be financed with foreign currencies and 50 per cent through clearing. In May 1939 Latvia also ordered aircraft. Payment was to come from a clearing account (60 per cent), foreign currencies (20 per cent), and raw materials of Germany's choice (20 per cent). In these negotiations Valdmanis intervened to obtain the best possible financing arrangement, that is, by means of clearing rather than foreign exchange.[74]

Although Ulmanis had been strongly against procurement from Germany because he believed that the new weapons might be accompanied by spies masquerading as weapons' specialists,[75] only Germany could provide a solution to Latvia's perceived military needs. Germany had state-of-the-art technology, and Latvia was prepared to buy the desired arms on a swap basis. Berlin noted that the clearing system was functioning and that arms purchases helped to restore the Latvian–German balance of trade. In view of negotiations reported in June 1939 about a Latvian order of German war materiel worth 15 million Reichsmarks, the German Foreign Office expressed satisfaction about the 'increasing economic orientation of Latvia towards Germany.' German officials considered this all the more remarkable in the light of Latvian attempts to expand trade with Britain and Sweden.[76]

Trade statistics confirm that Latvian endeavours to find alternate markets for its exports to Germany were not particularly successful. Between 1937 and 1939 Latvia's exports to the United States increased only slightly, namely, from 1.1 to 1.4 per cent of the total value of exports, while imports from the United States declined from 6.9 to 6.3 per cent. In the Scandinavian markets Latvian expectations remained equally unfulfilled. The value of Latvia's trade with Sweden was even smaller than with the United States. Armaments, ironically, not only increased the volume of trade with Germany, but ultimately helped to restore Latvia's balance of payments. But armaments also tied Latvia economically more closely to Germany than Ulmanis and Valdmanis had originally desired.

Latvia's export dependence on the German market had grown acute. This became apparent as early as 1938 when Sweden cancelled its clearing agreement, and Latvia thus failed to gain better access to the Swedish market. The German envoy in Riga cabled Berlin on 31 October 1938 to 'unequivocally' threaten a visiting Latvian trade delegation under Aleksandrs Dinsbergs that Germany 'would not buy from such state enterprises as Turība, Degviela, Vairogs, Tērauds, and Latvijas Kokvilna as long as the policy of state bolshevism at the expense of local Germans and the strangling of German-owned businesses continued.'[77] The renewal of Latvia's trade agreement with Germany (now including annexed Austria and the Sudeten territories) on 12 November 1938 not only provided for a 50 per cent increase in the volume of trade, but also required Latvia to desist from further expropriation of businesses owned and operated by German nationals. From that date, the German Foreign Office remarked on 6 June 1939, 'there have been no more complaints from businesspeople who were nationals of Germany or ethnic Germans.'[78]

Endeavours to resist growing dependence on Germany became an issue that pitted the cabinet majority increasingly against a dissenting faction around Valdmanis, General Balodis, and ministers Kornēlijs Veitnieks (Veitmanis), and Bernhards Einbergs. Foreign Minister Munters tried unsuccessfully to address British complaints that Latvia discriminated against British products, whereas Valdmanis accepted the inevitability of closer relations with Germany. Ulrich von Kotze, von Schack's replacement on 19 December 1938 as German envoy in Riga, was immediately struck by the 'intimate rapport that the [Latvian] finance minister – or on the latter's behalf Director Dinsbergs – maintained with the German trade attaché in all matters concerning business deals with Germany.'[79]

In reality, the initial interpersonal relations of German trade attaché Dr Gustav Adolf Leckzyck with Latvian officials, including Valdmanis, were anything but smooth, and in November 1938 von Schack had demanded Leckzyck's removal. An economist in the Reich Ministry of Economics with expertise in northeastern Europe and the Soviet Union and a knowledge of French, Polish, Lithuanian, and Russian, Leckzyck had been appointed trade attaché for the three Baltic countries in June 1937 and was based in Riga. Von Schack's demand was ignored despite allegations that Leckzyck's arrogance, objectionable social climbing, and inferiority complex negated his usefulness. It was partly Leckzyck's fault, according to von Schack, that the volume and value of German exports to Latvia had been declining since 1937.

In April 1939 Valdmanis, too, complained to the German envoy von Kotze about Leckzyck's arrogant interference in Latvian politics, his condescending pro-German and anti-Latvian stance, and his habit of exaggerating his influence in Germany. Subsequently, Andrejs Bērziņš, Munters, and other Latvian officials also voiced dissatisfaction with Leckzyck's behaviour. During the December 1939 negotiations of the treaty regulating the 'repatriation' of Latvia's Germans, Leckzyck's anti-Latvian tone had become so offensive to Latvian foreign ministry officials that Munters identified him as a major hindrance to Latvian–German relations. Unlike von Schack, however, von Kotze defended his trade attaché repeatedly and even recommended that Leckzyck be invited to attend Latvian–German trade negotiations in Berlin. Leckzyck might have lacked tact and good manners in communicating with foreigners, von Kotze admitted to Berlin, but he must be credited with a number of business deals favourable to Germany.[80]

In contrast to Munters, however, Valdmanis overcame his original animosity to Leckzyck, and by early 1940 they had become 'good friends'[81] and apparent confidants. Valdmanis's ability to get along with this controversial German was not necessarily a manifestation of pro-German convictions. Rather, it appears to have grown out of a realistic recognition that Latvia had no alternatives to accommodating Germany. It also revealed a practical character trait that surfaced repeatedly throughout the years and enabled Valdmanis to survive almost miraculously against great odds. One German Foreign Office official astutely observed that what appeared as pro-German sympathies on the part of Valdmanis were but carefully cultivated rhetoric and appearance; they functioned to camouflage actions that proved him to be a devout Latvian nationalist and a tool of President Ulmanis.[82]

Rationalization

In contrast to his early concern for foreign trade, Alfred Valdmanis did not leave his personal stamp on the restructuring of Latvia's domestic economy until November 1938. His first domestic measures addressed complaints arising from earlier legislation, such as a minor amendment of 21 June 1938 to the joint-stock company law of December 1937.[83]

Measures like the joint-stock company law or the nationalization of foreign-owned enterprises either appeared increasingly difficult to enforce or provoked protests. Valdmanis's public and private responses imply that he, though committed to his policy objectives and the high performance standards he set in his ministry, wanted to project the image of a man opposed to bureaucratic and chauvinist extremes. The cultivation of this image was particularly useful in dealing with critics of his domestic economic policies and in his trade negotiations with Germany.

A new approach in economic policy became evident on 24 November 1938 when, in a two-hour speech, Valdmanis disclosed his blueprint for the organization of Latvian industry to the Latvian Chamber of Trade and Industry (Latvijas tirdzniecības un rūpniecības kamera, or LTRK). The key was product 'rationalization,' in other words, aiming for the best quality and most marketable product. The government wanted to strengthen industry and trade, Valdmanis stressed, but not if that strength meant only large numbers of enterprises or employees. At the same time, rationalization should not be construed as a new way of restricting private initiative and promoting nationalization.[84]

In cooperation with the LTRK, a special Institute of Rationalization was to be created within the finance ministry to work out a plan advising industrialists on rationalizing their business enterprises. Government assistance would be offered those businesses tackling this question expeditiously. Carried to its logical conclusion, this implied commercial and administrative rationalization. In other words, inefficient, ailing, or insolvent businesses would have to rely on their own regulatory associations. They would no longer be rehabilitated by administrative liquidation and transfer to state ownership.

The minister of finance would have the right to instruct the LTRK to create associations, or cartels, for certain businesses or industries within a specified period, but the LTRK would define the aims and tasks of the cartels. The cartels would, for example, regulate such matters as the process and volume of production, their respective shares of the market, prices, purchase of raw materials, and hence the number of viable businesses within their branch. This would bring about the elimination of official price controls and the lowest consumer prices. Essentially, the proposed commercial and administrative rationalization would breathe new air into Latvia's entire economy by transferring ultimate responsibility for rehabilitation from the finance ministry to the business community itself.

Cartelization would leave it up to Latvia's business leaders to suggest how economic life should be rearranged, Valdmanis explained. Their active involvement 'would make it more difficult to assume the position of an outside observer and to accuse government agencies of having liquidated a healthy enterprise in one or the other instance.' They would have to decide 'for which ones the time had arrived to exit from the stage of life.' The cartel members would also decide the fate – lease, closure, sale – of enterprises considered redundant. The solution chosen by the cartel members would be preferable to a non-renewal of licence resulting from the finance ministry's ongoing relicensing of industrial enterprises.

From the outset, Valdmanis proposed to disqualify so-called artificial industries whose poor quality and expensive products were unsuitable for export. Many of these industries had originated during the economic crisis when Latvia's export industries were in trouble and there were no funds to pay for imports. 'Natural' industries, by contrast, were those whose products were in demand and suitable for Latvia. Since Latvia was eager to export its natural resources, Valdmanis favoured healthy international interaction, not a closed national economy, as practical and desirable. That meant Latvia would be better served to import the goods demanded by Latvia's standard of living at lower prices and better quality from countries already importing Latvian products.

'Natural' industries, according to Valdmanis's definition, used raw materials found in Latvia and had large internal markets. These would be able to compete easily internationally without preferences or duties. Valdmanis maintained that their potential was far from exploited and that in many cases they constituted the least developed branches of industrial endeavour. In the lumber industry, for instance, the export of huge quantities of undressed and semi-finished lumber was attributed to the primitive state of the processing technology. Valdmanis predicted that the new industries utilizing Latvia's mineral resources were destined to become a major sector within the national industrial complex and would form a stable basis for Latvia's external trade.

Valdmanis targeted Latvia's 'splintered' production as one of the main culprits for her external trade problems: 'Instead of those splintered, separate, accidental export shipments, I wish that for once we would reach a situation where we would have some solid export companies able to maintain solid trading connections, well informed about foreign markets, taken seriously by their trading partners, and generally able to secure solid foreign trading contacts.' The government, Valdmanis said, was prepared to promote the interests of trade. As concrete examples he pointed out that already the Ministry of Finance had created a Department of Foreign Trade, the LTRK had established a division for the promotion of export trade, and in the Ministry of External Affairs a new Department of Contracts was expanding export markets by negotiating and securing trade agreements. 'The picture I am painting for you, I assure you, is not exaggerated, is not a fantasy. It is a naked reality, even if its realization depends on you.'[85]

Last but not least, Valdmanis addressed the quest for stability, particularly in light of the requirement for annual relicensing, which might not allow the development of companies capable of long-term, stable operation. He understood that the business community wanted assurances that policies and regulations would not change and that they would be permitted to enjoy the fruits of their toil. Promising to examine all rules and regulations causing uncertainty, Valdmanis pledged to revise the procedure for relicensing. In future, he declared, 'we will ask for the intended activity to be described more clearly. And then the Ministry of Finance will look at the financial strength of the company. And, third, we will demand that the companies be managed by qualified, competent people with a morally unblemished record. In regard to the annual relicensing, we shall attempt to reach as quickly as possible a modus that will allow uninterrupted operation as long as the requirements of our trade policy guidelines are met.'[86]

In an interview he granted the German envoy the next day, President Ulmanis interpreted Valdmanis's speech to mean that the development towards state monopolies and state capitalism had come to an end and that the promotion of free enterprise was now on the agenda. To Berlin, however, von Schack reported that 'the murky elaborations of the finance minister, who had little understanding of economic issues,' left the intent unclear. The envoy had reasons to assume that the trend towards latvianization in trade and industry would continue under the new slogan 'rationalization of the economy' even though it replaced the slogan 'Latvia for Latvians.'[87]

Any doubts about the direction of Latvia's economic policy were dispelled on 28 December 1938 when LTRK president Andrejs Bērziņš spoke to a group of civil servants in training. In the presence of Valdmanis he asserted that all modern economies were planned economies and that the establishment of clear guidelines was essential for successful economic planning. Thus, the intervention of the state in all production areas was both necessary and inevitable, and personal interest was subordinate to the welfare of the state and the community. Latvianization had to continue until it had completed its objectives, one of which was having the ethnic Latvian majority in the country assume control over the economy.[88]

On 8 December 1938 the laws creating the cartels and the Institute of Rationalization were passed. The first law gave all existing cartels two months to bring their operations into conformity with the legal guidelines. The leaders of the cartels were to be appointed by the finance minister on the recommendation of the LTRK. Obstruction of the cartels or refusal to join them was subject to a maximum fine of 20,000 lats. The mandate of the Institute of Rationalization was to research and define approaches to technical modernization, increased production, standardization, and efficiency. Commenting on the new laws, Valdmanis emphasized the following points: (1) the rehabilitation of Latvia's economy was still under way; (2) through more accurate calculations the operating risk of enterprises would be reduced and markets better utilized; (3) the elimination of unfair competition would guarantee consumer products of better quality; (4) rationally operating enterprises were more productive and profitable, while inefficient and non-competitive businesses had to cease operations; and (5) the above-mentioned improvements depended on coordinating and systematizing the activities of commercial and industrial enterprises.[89]

On 2 May 1939 the Rationalization Fund was established. Eligible were industrial establishments agreeing to complete rationalization before 31 December 1940. They had to borrow rationalization funds from the Bank of Latvia, the Credit Bank of Latvia, or the Mortgage Bank of Latvia; however, these loans would be interest-free if they repaid the principal before 31 December 1944.[90]

In speeches to a wide variety of groups throughout the spring and summer of 1939, Valdmanis reiterated and highlighted aspects of his industrial strategy of rationalization. For example, he addressed a gathering of mechanics and locksmiths on 5 February, the plenary meeting of the LTRK on 29 March, and the economic and cultural councils on 12 May. His favourite theme described how competition on the world market and a labour shortage at home had forced Latvia to rationalize. He also pointed out that despite unprecedented Latvian government support in agriculture every third worker was nonetheless a foreigner and an adequate supply of such foreign labour might not always be available to sustain agricultural production at the required level.[91]

Indeed, one of the government's major concerns was the rising influx of foreign labour from 41,000 in 1935 to 46,400 in 1938, partly owing to the rural vacancies created by Latvians migrating to the cities. Valdmanis told the LTRK on 29 March 1939 that he was planning to address the farm-labour problem by increasing subsidies, promoting mechanization, and raising living standards in the rural areas. The government would also promote and, if necessary, expand its policy of resettling workers from urban to rural areas. A German newspaper confirmed this government policy, adding that a plan was being implemented to bring an annual contingent of six thousand young workers to the rural areas.[92]

In industry the finance ministry's goal was to make industry stronger, more Latvian, and more competitive. Referring to 'frequent' apprehensions concerning the direction of economic policy, Valdmanis insisted that no more state-owned enterprises would be established, since 'we already have in each branch at least one financially viable national enterprise.' He was anxious to allay fears of a secret plan to introduce 'state socialism.'[93]

Since Valdmanis considered 'many' urban enterprises overstaffed, he wanted a reduction in their number of employees. But qualified and efficient employees should have priority over married female employees whose spouses held good jobs. Valdmanis elaborated on 5 February 1939: 'I must here touch on an unpopular question but one that cannot be ignored because it burdens one's sense of justice. I would therefore like to ask these women: return to your families – dedicate yourselves to the tasks you have abandoned only temporarily anyway and where you are urgently needed.'[94]

In his budget speech of 29 March 1939 Valdmanis harped on the same theme again in an even stronger tone. Here, while articulating the authoritarian state's concern for the growth of the indigenous population, Valdmanis attributed the difficulty of increasing the birth rate to the employment of women. The need for workers made it impossible to dispense with female employees entirely, 'but in reducing the number of employees in the process of rationalization, efforts should be made to liberate married women and offer them the opportunity to devote themselves more to their families. This applies not to women who have no provider or for whom insufficient income makes a job a necessity, but rather to those women who occupy paid positions in order to acquire various comforts and to eschew work at home.'[95]

On this issue Valdmanis must have struck a sensitive chord with a segment of the public, for in May 1939 he and Ulmanis received letters from ordinary people demanding action. It was a fallacy to believe that well-paid female employees would willingly quit their jobs, wrote one person. Another writer called it a 'horrible injustice and stupidity' to permit the wives of directors and upper-echelon officials to occupy highly paid positions, while veterans of the War of Independence and their families were 'suffocating' in poverty. 'Where are the limits for such shamelessness, where is the social justice, what kind of benefit is this for the country as a whole?' the writer wondered. Referring to a company director whose wife was an accountant in a government institution, one citizen wrote Valdmanis, 'Where are the limits for such impudence?'[96]

In a meeting of directors and department heads of the Ministry of Finance on 8 July 1939 Valdmanis solicited proposals for a solution to the issue of the employment of senior officials' wives. He stated categorically that it was unacceptable for such women to be employed, primarily because this interfered with their 'very important duties at home' and their 'primary obligations to their families.' Only secondarily did he consider such wives to block employment opportunities for others and to cause resentment among the lower classes. The 'key point' for Valdmanis was to 'liberate women from the overload of work,' although this might not apply to women in the professions.[97]

Valdmanis frequently drew on fascist rhetoric to vindicate the necessity of his strategy. The economic policy of the authoritarian state, he told a meeting of the economic and cultural councils on 12 May, was not centred around one individual group or class. It was the policy of the whole nation, took its energy from the people, and returned all its strength to its country and people. Because it promoted the welfare of the entire nation, the authoritarian state had the right to determine the consistency, the sequence, and the order in which this policy evolves.[98] From this vantage point, rationalization was a shrewd device to enhance state control over a growing sphere of life.

Not surprisingly, the Latvian Ministry of Finance closely monitored parallel developments in Nazi Germany.[99] There the primary intent of the emphasis on rationalization, although alleged to be the strengthening of the community spirit, was actually increased productivity.[100] Starting in January 1939, Germany was proclaiming rationalization in areas ranging from industry,[101] agriculture,[102] and retailing[103] to education.[104]

State Capitalism at a Crossroads

In public Valdmanis took credit for what he interpreted as his country's unprecedented economic growth after one year in office. As proof he referred to a budget surplus of 10 million lats, foreign currency reserves of 88.6 million lats, the highest employment rate in the world, and a rapidly rising standard of living.[105] He did not, however, dare publicize the fact that in 1938–9 the national debt was approaching Latvia's total annual revenue of 190 million lats. Latvia's monetary, credit, and fiscal situations were in reality 'anything but clear and could hardly be termed healthy in view of the material condition of the country and its productivity,' the German envoy noted in August 1939. Although taxes, fees, and duties had been raised 'to the point of exhaustion' to compensate for the loss of foreign capital, actual tax revenues had declined by 15 million lats in 1938–9 compared with 1937–8, indicating diminishing productivity. A particular feature of fiscal policy that made a clear accounting of Latvia's financial situation impossible was the ongoing Ulmanis-instigated formation of special government funds. Hidden in special budgets, these funds were not revealed to the public. By 1939 some seventy-three such special funds existed for purposes ranging from defence, reforestation, and rationalization of dairy cooperatives to old age and unemployment compensation.[106]

The maze of government regulations, takeovers, and directives dictating who would produce what and how, according to Latvian economist Arnolds Aizsilnieks, was responsible for the fact that net productivity grew more slowly than the rate of employment.[107] The acute shortage of investment capital and tax revenue was aggravated by the diversion of scarce capital and skilled labour from the producing sector into gigantic government construction projects – urban renewal, railway stations, bridges, hydroelectric power stations, and public monuments, including a massive new finance ministry building in Riga. Government promotion of industry under the auspices of latvianization, however, accelerated the migration of the rural population to the burgeoning capital city and threatened the viability of agriculture. In addition, some 5 to 6 million lats were taken out of the country annually by Polish and Lithuanian migrant workers.[108]

By mid-1939 Latvia exhibited the typical characteristics of what a British critic termed an 'authoritarian economy.'[109] Comments in the German press preferred to characterize Latvia's economic system as 'state capitalism.' (In Nazi Germany the state, apart from 'aryanizing' businesses owned by 'non-Aryans,' did not infringe on the free enterprise economy.) The trend towards compulsory cartelization of the private sector and the increase in the proportion of exports from state-owned production from 50 to 64 per cent between 1936 and 1938 indicated to one German newspaper that Latvia was moving in the direction of a planned economy.[110] To another German paper it was obvious, in view of the prominent position of state enterprises, who would have the final say within these enforced cartels.[111] A third German paper concluded that the success of all these endeavours to create a unique type of planned economy would 'very much depend on the regime's success to inspire wider public confidence in the way it proceeds.'[112]

Whether Alfred Valdmanis was able to inspire such public confidence is questionable. During the spring and summer of 1939 there is evidence of growing resistance to his strategy of continued government manipulation of the economy. Representatives of private enterprise repeatedly demanded answers to their numerous questions. They asked, for example, what benefits were gained from buying out Latvia's obligations to the Swedish match trust in May 1939 and how Latvia could afford to use its scarce reserves for this purpose? They wanted to know why industry was not being consulted about solutions to relieve the shortage of farm labour. For instance, the numerous unemployed and idle residents of small towns and more densely populated rural districts could be drafted. And why, in order to live within the limits of Latvia's possibilities and manage the economy accordingly, was it necessary to have such 'unprecedented bureaucracy'? Was such 'red tape' essential for the operation of not only foreign trade, but also private business, industrial enterprises, and state and municipal agencies?[113]

On 26 July 1939 Comptroller Jānis Kaminskis alerted Valdmanis to rackets aimed at undermining official efforts at relicensing, modernization, and enforcing price and cost reductions. In two cases racketeers contacted the targeted industries and promised in return for bribes to talk to government officials and send the appropriate references. Two individuals had already been caught in the act and imprisoned.[114] In his 12 May speech Valdmanis complained that some old industrial syndicates were refusing to dissolve and reorganize themselves into the prescribed cartels. Such syndicates were illegal, he contended, especially if their purpose was raising domestic prices. 'Their aims are different from ours; the interests of the national economy and the consumer are alien to them,' declared Valdmanis. He also reminded entrepreneurs that the law provided for 'extremely harsh' punishment in such cases.[115]

Waning public confidence in ambitious regulatory schemes was paralleled by flagging enthusiasm on the part of the government bureaucracy in implementing it. The requirement of periodic performance accounts was particularly unpopular. Shortly after Valdmanis left the cabinet, a conference of senior civil servants suspended it.[116]

Not surprisingly, Valdmanis became unusually defensive about new regulations and controls. For example, a law of 21 June 1939 requiring banks to lower the interest rate from 7 to 5.5 per cent on long-term loans and promissory notes by July 1940 threatened to trigger widespread demands for refunds instead of changeovers. This adversely affected some smaller private banks, such as the Mortgage Bank and the Land Bank because their clients were largely ethnic German citizens of Latvia. At a meeting of department heads and division directors of the finance ministry on 1 July 1939, Valdmanis went out of his way to insist that this measure was 'not directed in the slightest against any particular nationality or group of citizens'; rather, it was a matter of credit policy for the benefit of the majority and should not be interpreted in any other way. 'All officials of the ministry shall, in their explanations to others and in their conversations among themselves, keep in mind this official interpretation and reject any others.'[117]

Valdmanis expected little opposition to his takeover of the Riga stock exchange, traditionally a citadel of Baltic German merchants. In their last holdover of prewar Baltic German privilege, they had controlled access to membership by an internal vote of their association. A law of 4 July 1939 terminated this tradition of co-opting and permitted any qualified trader to be eligible for membership. Valdmanis also abolished the German spelling of Latvian names on the stock exchange's membership list.[118] 'We do not object that people who in their spirit and blood are strangers to us make a good living in our country,' Valdmanis reassured the public when addressing the newly elected board of the stock exchange on 31 July 1939, 'but only as long as they do not intend to play a dominant role. Our first consideration will always be those whose convictions and deeds speak our language, the language of this country.'[119]

To be sure, in his comments of 19 June 1939 on the 1940 budget Valdmanis kept insisting on the regime's a priori right to control the economy. For 1 April to 31 December 1940 this was to stress 'putting the brakes on the economy.' In fact, because of the acute capital shortage, Valdmanis was even prepared to jettison the policy of state investment in commercial and manufacturing enterprises.[120]

This became evident in the reversal of government plans pursued in part since early 1938 to rationalize Latvia's plywood and knitting industries. The original plan had called for liquidating a large number of allegedly unprofitable private enterprises and merging them into two government-owned cartels. Mostly owned by non-ethnic Latvians and foreigners, these enterprises stubbornly resisted. Among the fourteen firms in the plywood industry, five were Jewish-owned, four Latvian-owned, three German–British–Danish-owned, one Latvian state-owned, and one Swedish-owned. They controlled 30.4, 29.7, 30.6, 6.6, and 3.7 per cent of production respectively.[121] The knitting industry, according to a report by the Institute of Rationalization, was largely a Jewish-owned cottage industry of 1,267 businesses with some two thousand employees. Ethnic Latvians owned only 3.3 per cent of the total.[122]

In July 1939 the acute capital shortage had prompted the government to solicit private investment for manufacturing furniture and textiles. To that end Valdmanis authorized E.E. Rattermann and Brothers, a firm owned by two Baltic Germans with Valdmanis's brother-in-law Johannson as a partner, to launch two large shareholding companies with a foreign – preferably Swiss – capital of 10 million lats. Valdmanis expected Rattermann to invest 2 million lats to buy out the Jewish dwarf businesses and form one large textile trust. According to German envoy von Kotze, the idea was to 'remove the Jewish elements in this trade and free them for work in agriculture.' Von Kotze also had the impression that Valdmanis was opposed to the government's continued investment in commercial and manufacturing enterprises.[123]

Clearly, Valdmanis must have realized that Latvia's economic restructuring was not succeeding. No longer were Latvian capital and labour able to help raise the national income and standard of living. Except for the Ķegums hydro-power station, none of the 'national enterprises' was adding anything of value to existing production facilities. The government, as Latvian economist Aizsilnieks observes, had simply changed the names of the private enterprises and opened the gates to corruption and arbitrary bureaucratic action. For example, a black market flourished because of price controls, price inspectors, and fines for non-compliance.

Valdmanis justified the continuation of price fixing partly on the basis of social justice. In his 28 March 1939 speech to the Chamber of Trade and Industry, he declared that artificially high prices for agricultural products were a means to equalize incomes. But income levelling was bound to make all citizens poorer instead of more prosperous, Aizsilnieks concludes, since 'although it takes from very few quite a lot, by dividing that to very many, each gets very little.'[124]

The extent to which Valdmanis became disillusioned with the implementation of the policy framework imposed by President Ulmanis and Andrejs Bērziņš is difficult to ascertain. However, evidence testifies to the finance minister's gradual estrangement from the president. In the summer of 1939 ministers Balodis and Veidnieks are alleged to have suggested to Ulmanis that he confine himself to the decorative position of the state presidency, name Valdmanis prime minister, and hand over cabinet matters to him.[125] According to Zemgals, this caused other cabinet members to spread rumours that Valdmanis, 'overtaken by the devil of personal glory,' was trying to become prime minister and put up General Balodis as counter-candidate for president. Latvian government records, though not corroborating these rumours, confirm the insatiable appetite of Valdmanis's 'super ministry' to expand its powers and jurisdiction. In an August 1939 memorandum to Valdmanis, Ulmanis ordered finance ministry officials to confine their attention to their own sphere and not make public statements about matters that were the responsibility of other ministries.[126]

Zemgals traces the origin of Ulmanis's estrangement from Valdmanis to November 1938. At that time in recognition of the latter's achievements, Ulmanis reportedly invited Valdmanis to take over an additional portfolio, the Ministry of Justice, and in conjunction with it, the chair in the 'Little Cabinet' – a skeleton cabinet for discussing and screening all legislative acts before they were sent to the 'Big Cabinet.' According to this account, Valdmanis provisionally accepted, on two conditions: (1) several high-level, 'corrupt' officials of the Ministry of Justice would be dismissed and (2) the drafting of a new constitution would be the first task of the Ministry of Justice. The constitution, to be submitted to a plebiscite, would provide for popular election of the president and for a parliament composed of members elected by a majority of votes in the respective ridings.[127]

Ten years later, when Valdmanis was in dire need of some democratic credentials, Zemgals asserted repeatedly[128] that Valdmanis had been the only cabinet minister with the courage to raise the subject of the constitution and elections that Ulmanis had promised during his 1934 coup, but then apparently forgotten. It had shocked the idealistic young finance minister to realize that his cabinet colleagues habitually told the president only what he wanted to hear. Ministers Alfreds Bērziņš and Vilhelms Munters allegedly even flattered Ulmanis with the notion that the 'leader' was appointed by God.[129]

The claim that Valdmanis requested a constitution for Latvia cannot be substantiated. Not even his 1962–3 autobiographical notes confirm it.[130] The available evidence indicates that the question of the constitution remained anathema to Ulmanis. But whether Valdmanis actually raised the matter of the constitution or attempted to manoeuvre himself into the direction of the prime ministership, his jockeying for power marked the end of his honeymoon with Ulmanis. His 'uncontrollable desire to play the first violin' was a trait Valdmanis revealed throughout his enigmatic career, one Latvian critic concluded. Yet, he added, as finance minister, Valdmanis was undeniably 'very successful,' judged by the standards of the time and his relatively short term of sixteen months and ten days in office.[131]

chapter three

'Better to Die Standing Up Than to Keep on Living on Your Knees': War, Resignation, and Soviet Occupation, 1939–1941

Bulsons, Deputy Director of the Chancellery of State, handed over to the Soviet occupation forces all documents of his department and the personal correspondence of the president with his ministers as well ... And then it was found out that Valdmanis had been a lone wolf, an individualist who had gone his own way during the regime of President Ulmanis ... Valdmanis' letter of resignation, addressed to the president, was found among the documents of the Chancellery. It was of extremely great importance. Fervent patriotism dominates this letter, but it also expresses the sharpest possible criticism and ends with the declaration that he was unable to agree with the latest most important acts of K. Ulmanis. How then would it be possible to put Valdmanis on trial and hold him responsible for the general policy of the Ulmanis regime?

Boriss Zemgals in 1948[1]

The outbreak of the Second World War in September 1939 hurled Latvia and its Baltic neighbours from the backwaters of international politics into its maelstrom. Virtually overnight, the Ulmanis regime had to accommodate entirely unanticipated constraints on its policies. Almost immediately, Latvia was hit with disruptions of trade and acute shortages of raw materials. Then followed the imposition of Soviet bases and the exodus of Latvia's ethnic German population. The sudden realization in October 1939 that the Hitler–Stalin Pact of 23 August 1939 had doomed Latvia's freedom of movement, if not its national sovereignty, generated divisions in the cabinet and the resignation of Valdmanis. In June 1940 Soviet troops occupied the entire country and ended Latvia's national independence. To this day Latvians remember the year of Soviet rule until the German invasion in June 1941 as a nightmare. Most of Valdmanis's former cabinet colleagues disappeared in Stalin's gulags never to be seen again, but Valdmanis miraculously survived. This chapter examines his role in the unfolding demise of Latvia's independence, his timely resignation from the cabinet, and his survival under communist rule.

Latvia and the Destruction of Poland

The German invasion of Poland on 1 September 1939 had profound repercussions on the Latvian economy. The economic impact of the British and French declaration of war against Germany on 3 September forced the finance minister to suspend further latvianization initiatives. Improvising an escalating number of emergency measures became top priority for him.

Initially, the existence of Latvian non-aggression pacts with both the Soviet Union (1932) and Germany (June 1939) had lulled Latvia into a false sense of security. The full contents of the Hitler–Stalin Pact's secret protocol, which assigned the Baltic countries to the Soviet sphere of influence, were unknown in Latvia until later. Whatever early details leaked to Latvian government officials from various sources were not believed; they had been unconfirmed – German officials had repeatedly denied their validity – and treated them as rumour. Latvian foreign policy had been conducted on the assumption that the role of the Baltic countries was to maintain a balance of power in the region between Germany and Soviet Russia through a policy of non-alignment. In September 1939 Ulmanis still believed that Latvia's interests would best be protected by continued strict neutrality.[2]

The outbreak of war led to the immediate closure of the Baltic Sea to trade. This virtually strangled the commercial lifeline with Britain, one of Latvia's most important trading partners. It also seriously threatened Latvia's relations with Scandinavia. The situation left Latvia with only Germany and Soviet Russia as trading partners. They remained as the only providers of fuels and industrial raw materials, whose uninterrupted supply became a matter of great concern. For example Liepāja, which used to get its regular coal deliveries from Poland, was stranded with only one week's supply when war broke out. On 4 September Valdmanis approached the Soviet representative to Latvia, Ivan S. Zotov, with a request for an increased exchange of goods, in particular oil, coal, and metals. At the same time, Valdmanis received assurances from German trade attaché Leckzyck that Germany would be prepared to sell coal, salt, and iron to Latvia.[3]

At first the Latvian government abstained from rushing into extraordinary measures. The finance minister instructed businesses and banks not to ration the volume of deliveries to traditional customers. Notices in the press on 3 September advised the public that supplies were sufficient for normal consumption. That seemed to have delayed the onset of panic in the money and retail markets. After 4 September, however, the disruption of trade patterns could no longer be ignored and a rush on such items as sugar, salt, and flour threatened an acute shortage of staples. Salt, for example, was unavailable in Riga by 8 September.[4]

Between 4 and 19 September the finance minister issued numerous emergency measures including (1) regulations for the processing and supervision of raw materials and goods; (2) registration and distribution of stored raw materials, especially coke, naphtha, gasoline, petroleum, gas-oil, and lubricants; (3) establishment and supervision of storage depots; (4) export bans on coke, coal, iron, steel, lead, zinc, copper, brass, aluminum, wool, cotton, rubber, fuel, and lubricants; (5) sale of fuels to automobiles and motorcycles only with special permits; (6) export restrictions on foreign currency; (7) export restrictions on all goods except Latvian products; (8) registration and rationing of coke supplies for central heating requirements; and (9) requisition of Latvian merchant ships at the discretion of the minister of finance.[5]

Valdmanis publicly announced that trade by sea and land had become severely restricted. Thus, Latvian merchant vessels could be sold or leased to foreign countries only with permission of the Ministry of Finance. Despite Latvia's short-term stockpile of raw materials, a long conflict would create difficulties in obtaining raw materials for military equipment. It was therefore necessary to regulate by law the storage and distribution of vital materials. These laws, Valdmanis explained, would defuse anxieties and excitement because they would anticipate potential complications and reduce the danger of speculation. The belligerent countries as well as neutral ones already had similar laws.[6]

Valdmanis justified the introduction of some emergency measures by the need to follow the example of Latvia's neighbours. Like them, Latvia had no choice but to ration vehicle fuel. Only owners of vehicles transporting goods would be issued permits to purchase fuel. People insisting on pleasure driving would have to pay a surcharge. 'Times are very serious and require self-control and denial from all citizens.' Like other countries Latvia needed to pass neutrality laws that defined its territorial waters. Following the Scandinavian countries, Latvia planned to declare a four-mile territorial zone from its coast on, over, and under the water.[7]

To administer these measures, new duties were assigned to various departments in the Ministry of Finance. Thus, the Department of Trade and Industry was to supervise the acquisition, storage, and processing of raw materials by industries and trades, and the Department of Foreign Trade was to supervise exports, imports, and transits. The position of price inspector, first under Dinsbergs in his capacity as director of the Customs Department, then under Arnolds Elpers, was created to supervise prices and the registration of the acquisition, storage, and sale of goods by commercial enterprises.[8]

Since it appeared obvious that the loss of the British market would make the Latvian economy even more dependent on Germany, the Latvian government planned to rush a large trade delegation to Germany to discuss the expansion of German–Latvian economic relations. On 26 September, Foreign Minister Munters proposed to von Kotze that Valdmanis lead the Latvian delegation to Berlin, provided his health permitted travel. Munters also requested permission for Valdmanis to meet Walther Funk, Reich economics minister, and Hermann Goering, plenipotentiary of the Ministry of Economics. Berlin replied on 30 September that neither the appearance of Valdmanis nor a large delegation of experts was desirable. Nor was a Latvian visit possible at all until 10 October, allegedly because of negotiations with an Estonian delegation. Upon receipt of this disheartening news, Valdmanis told the German envoy, perhaps as a face-saving rejoinder, that under prevailing conditions he would not be able to leave Latvia anyway.[9]

The political situation for Latvia had, in fact, taken a dramatic turn for the worse on Saturday, 30 September, when the Soviet Union suddenly imposed itself on Latvia as the new political and economic overlord. On that day, Soviet Foreign Minister Viacheslav Molotov summoned the Latvian envoy in Moscow to demand the prompt appearance of a Latvian delegate empowered to sign a pact of mutual assistance. Aware of what was involved, since Estonia had been forced to sign such a pact on 28 September, President Ulmanis called an extraordinary cabinet meeting for Sunday, 1 October. It decided unanimously to send Foreign Minister Munters to Moscow. Munters was accompanied by Andrejs Kampe, director of the treaty department and the most capable official in the foreign ministry. A second extraordinary cabinet meeting on 3 October delegated, also unanimously, to Munters the authority to sign a treaty with terms no more severe than those imposed on Estonia. On 5 October Munters signed a pact in Moscow providing for the establishment of Soviet military bases in the country for ten years. This document in effect turned Latvia into a Soviet protectorate.[10]

The invitation to the 1 October cabinet meeting was not handled as usual through the Chancellery, but by the president's secretary, who phoned each individual minister. Attendance was obligatory,[11] but Valdmanis was absent because he was the only minister that could not be reached. Valdmanis was later to maintain that Ulmanis had deliberately excluded him. An invitation to a hunting party had been engineered by Dr Mārtiņš Prīmanis, Rector of the University of Latvia and an associate of the president, and Valdmanis had indeed been lured away from Riga for three days with the assurance that in case of an emergency cabinet meeting he would be called back.[12]

When Valdmanis was informed by his colleagues Veidnieks and Balodis on Monday, 2 October, that the cabinet had met in his absence, he broke down in complete despair, as witnessed by von Kotze. The 3 October cabinet meeting, which Valdmanis did attend confirmed his fears: the cabinet majority considered the current Soviet regime more civilized than the bloody revolutionary Bolshevism of 1917–18 and was prepared to endorse acceptance of Molotov's demands. As the chief, if not the only proponent of the idea that closer relations with Germany would best serve Latvia, Valdmanis was convinced Munters's diplomacy had betrayed Latvia's vital interests. In his vain ambition to play politics on all kinds of international stages, Munters had manoeuvred Latvia into a fatal dependence on Britain that resulted in the present collapse of Latvia's foreign policy, Valdmanis lamented to von Kotze.[13]

Valdmanis and his dissenting circle in the cabinet would have preferred someone other than Munters to be chief negotiator in a question of life and death for Latvia, especially since some considered Munters a non-Latvian, on account of his mother's German background. Valdmanis also maintained that Munters lacked instructions on how to resist Soviet demands because the Latvian government itself lacked a clear strategy for the future. It distressed Valdmanis greatly to watch what was unfolding in cabinet – from his point of view the most vociferous chauvinist demagogues were cowering in timidity and imploring Munters to procure a steamship for the flight of the government, if necessary. These were the very ones who had always advocated the slogan 'better to die standing up than to continue living on your knees.' Now was the time to demonstrate the validity of that popular slogan, Valdmanis insisted. Although the majority of the population was expected to adopt a defeatist attitude, Latvia's leaders should resist a Soviet takeover, if only as a symbolic gesture. This was the first and might be the last opportunity for Latvians to defend the independence of their country. Resistance might make the Soviets more inclined to negotiate with Latvia. Valdmanis would not entirely discount the possibility that the Soviets would not occupy Latvia if they realized that the Latvians were actually prepared to die standing up instead of lying down.[14]

The cabinet minority critical of Ulmanis's policies – War Minister Balodis, Interior Minister Veidnieks, and Transport Minister Einbergs – did not fully share these thoughts. Valdmanis was practically alone with his opinion. There was no one to whom he could entrust his bitter feelings, motivated in part by his own ambitions and envy about Munters's influence over the president. He rushed, therefore, on Monday night, 2 October, to the German envoy in Riga and, in the above-mentioned vein, vented his frustrations about the stubbornness of Ulmanis, who he believed was rejecting all reasonable advice. Deep down he hoped that Germany might still be able to save Latvia from the Soviets. On Valdmanis's initiative Ulmanis on 3 October summoned von Kotze to obtain information about the position of the German government, but von Kotze was under official instructions to sidetrack such an inquiry.[15] According to Valdmanis's autobiographical notes of 1963, however, von Kotze had informed Valdmanis on 2 October that Germany did not intend to intervene on behalf of Latvia.[16] Valdmanis failed to explain why, in view of his strong feelings about being excluded from the 1 October cabinet meeting, he helped to make the cabinet vote unanimous instead of walking out of the 3 October meeting that sealed Latvia's capitulation to the Soviets. It is quite possible that Valdmanis staged his breakdown, in part at least, to von Kotze, knowing that it would be recorded and reported to Berlin where it might serve as a credit in the future.

Although on 2 October Stalin disclosed to Munters in Moscow that Germany had recognized Latvia as part of the Soviet sphere of influence,[17] Valdmanis stayed in contact with the German envoy until the Soviet pact was signed. Through these contacts von Kotze learned on 4 October of the Soviet demand for naval bases and the intended placement of fifty thousand Soviet troops in the country.[18] By 10 October, Valdmanis had begun to plot his survival. He thought it opportune to suggest to the Soviet Chargé d'affaires Ivan A. Chichaev in Riga that he was part of a circle of influential Latvians who were accepting the pact as 'the lesser evil.' This circle reasoned, as Chichaev reported to Moscow, that under Russian influence Latvians would at least be able to preserve their national identity, whereas German occupation would most likely completely destroy it.[19]

Repatriation of the Baltic Germans

The information von Kotze received from Valdmanis had another consequence. The revelations of the Latvian government's weakness and confusion in its dealings with Moscow caused von Kotze to launch a frantic 'rescue' of Latvia's German minority. To be sure, repatriation was part of the Third Reich's racial policy and would have taken place regardless of the Valdmanis–von Kotze contacts. Also, German observers had been expressing concerns about anti-German 'rioting by the Latvian mob'[20] ever since the Soviet occupation of eastern Poland on 18 September. On 25 September Heinrich Himmler had already seized upon the idea of Baltic German repatriation and obtained Hitler's approval for it the next day, and on 28 September Molotov in a secret protocol with German Foreign Minister von Ribbentrop had agreed to Germany's transfer of the Baltic German population to Germany.[21] But Valdmanis's alarmist disclosures triggered concrete preparations for a hasty evacuation. Von Kotze's 4 October telegram to Berlin warned that once Latvia's complete capitulation to Soviet demands had become public knowledge, law and order would break down and the lives of the sixty thousand Baltic Germans and three thousand German nationals would be in imminent danger.

On 6 October von Kotze reported to the German Foreign Office that he had been conferring with leading representatives of Latvia's German community in his office for the past few days. With their help he had made numerous preparations. He had (1) created an efficient warning system based on leaders of local groups, (2) established assembly and collection points where the German colony would be protected by armed guards from 'mob rule,' (3) arranged food and medical care, and (4) provided safe conduct to arriving German transport ships. To salvage the property of evacuated Germans, von Kotze had formed a Latvian–German lawyers' committee. It was already preparing lists of properties the evacuees would have to leave behind. According to von Kotze, the measures were designed to offer the greatest protection with the smallest possible team of confidential helpers, hence causing the least danger of stirring up alarm during the coming period of uncertainty.[22]

These efforts marked the beginning of the actual process of resettling the entire Baltic German population. Announced by Adolf Hitler in a Reichstag speech on 6 October 1939, the resettlement was to proceed as a 'rescue action' in accordance with a five-point German Foreign Office draft plan based on von Kotze's measures. These included: (1) naval ships would be ready to intervene; (2) a transport ship for four thousand persons would be at the immediate disposal of the German embassy in Riga; (3) the German envoy should start immediate negotiations with the Latvian government about the voluntary departure of all ethnic Germans and German citizens and a reasonable liquidation of their property; (4) the exit, though recommended, would be voluntary; and (5) a commission, chaired by the German envoy, would arrange the technical execution of the exodus and liquidation of property.[23]

Hitler's repatriation call came like a lightning bolt and created very serious economic problems for Latvia, Valdmanis recalled. He was sure that it meant war for Latvia and proposed to the cabinet the transfer of Latvia's gold reserves to the United States.[24] But apprehensions of anti-German rioting turned out to be premature. Both the German government and President Ulmanis insisted that Hitler's call had no connection with the Latvian–Soviet mutual assistance pact. The internal security and sovereignty of Latvia were not in danger, Ulmanis publicly maintained. He pledged faithful adherence to the terms of the mutual assistance pact and looked forward to expanded Latvian–Soviet economic relations. Baltic Germans were free to leave for good, but Latvians would not be allowed to join them.[25] Since the exodus of expertise and property posed an incalculable threat to economic life, Latvia insisted that the move be regulated by a formal treaty. The Latvian government balked at a quick deal on the transfer of properties as desired by Germany. Only after several interruptions, low-level private discussions, and German concessions, was agreement reached on 30 October 1939.[26]

To the dismay of Valdmanis, Munters was Latvia's central player in these negotiations as well. According to a report of the German finance ministry's negotiator F. Litter and internal Latvian memoranda for the information of the finance minister, Munters alone negotiated the agreement's key terms with the German envoy in Riga and with Litter. Munters wanted to ensure that the German resettlement and trust agency, the Umsiedlungs-Treuhand-Aktiongesellschaft (UTAG), not become a state within the Latvian state but operate under Latvian law. The emigrants would be allowed to take their movable property with them, but cash, savings, and portfolios had to be transferred through UTAG. Property unsold upon departure had to be turned over to the UTAG, which had until the end of 1941 to dispose of real estate. The Latvian government would then acquire the remainder at a valuation to be arranged between Latvia and Germany. Industrial and commercial enterprises, as well as the properties of churches, clubs, and associations, were to be disposed of at the discretion of the Latvian government. For transferred estates the UTAG received bonds (IOUs) as acknowledgment of debt.[27]

Apart from creating complications for Munters, Valdmanis seems to have played no noticeable role in the transfer negotiations with Germany. The German trade attaché in Riga, Adolf Leckzyck, recalled in June 1941 that in 1939 Valdmanis resigned from the government because Munters foiled and the Ulmanis cabinet rejected Valdmanis's proposal to resolve the property transfer issue generously as a conciliatory gesture towards a Latvian rapprochement with Germany. However, the German Foreign Office's Baltic experts, Werner von Grundherr and Peter Kleist, maintained that the opposite was true. According to von Grundherr, Munters repeatedly complained about the difficulties Valdmanis was creating in the negotiations. Kleist remembered that Valdmanis tried to prevent the property transfer and rejected the transfer procedures for the emigrants' assets despite tedious negotiations. Valdmanis always 'affirmed his pro-German attitude and declared himself favourably disposed towards the concerns of Germans and Baltic Germans,' Kleist observed perceptively. 'In reality, there was little concrete evidence of this alleged attitude,' and Valdmanis was 'rather a willing tool of Ulmanis who appointed him finance minister to implement the regime's de-germanization plans.'[28]

The testimonies of von Grundherr and Kleist, German government records, and Ministry of Finance documentation deposited in the Latvian State Historical Archives[29] confirm in essence Zemgals's account of what happened. According to it, the finance minister agreed to let the repatriates take all personal property with them, such as art objects and jewellery, but they could not retain ownership of real estate and industrial enterprises. Although owned by the repatriates, he argued, the latter properties were also an integral part of the Latvian economy and could not be removed without serious damage to the entire system. Nor should Latvia pay compensation to former plant owners in the form of cash or increased exports to Germany. Instead, German owners would have two years to sell their holdings to Latvians with the proceeds of the sales, estimated at some 250 to 300 million lats, to be invested in the establishment of new industries for cellulose, synthetic gas, and peat products. This investment would ensure employment opportunities for several years and reduce the Soviets' appeal among Latvian workers.

Munters and Alfreds Bērziņš, however, had organized the majority of the cabinet behind their own plan to compensate the repatriates immediately in money or export goods so that the Latvian state would have no future obligations to them. Declaring this proposal detrimental to Latvian interests, Valdmanis refused to agree to it as long he was finance minister. He argued that his agreement with the president gave him sole authority for financial matters. Bērziņš and Munters countered by proposing to split Valdmanis's ministry into two and confining Valdmanis's duties either to trade and industry or to finance. They also pointed to Valdmanis's attendance at meetings in the Ministry of War and accused him of conspiring with General Jānis Balodis to prepare a coup. Not sure how seriously he should take the accusations, Ulmanis decided to reduce Valdmanis's authority within the government by giving him the option of remaining in charge of a reduced Ministry of Finance or taking over a separate Ministry of Trade and Industry.[30]

Resignation from the Cabinet

Ulmanis's decision to reduce the finance minister's powers by removing from his authority half of his 'super ministry' caused Valdmanis to submit immediately his resignation. Ulmanis is alleged at first to have refused the resignation of his finance minister. However, he had no choice when Valdmanis revealed to the upper ranks of his staff his growing differences of opinion with cabinet colleagues and the president. Valdmanis, Zemgals explains, had no desire to be part of a group who, in his opinion, were not always acting in the best interests of the country and whose mind-set he was unable to change. Since starting his career in the finance ministry in 1929 as a messenger boy, Valdmanis had worked his way up to the top without compromising his ideals of loyal service to the country, he is reported to have declared to his staff.[31]

According to a December 1939 report by a police informant, Valdmanis told a gathering of his student fraternity Tālavija that one of the reasons for his departure from the cabinet was his disagreement with the level and kind of compensation offered to departing Baltic Germans. In his opinion, it would not have been too difficult to negotiate down the value of the properties they were leaving behind in Latvia and the means of compensation. He, naively, assumed that the Soviet allies would support Latvia in this endeavour against Germany. Another reason he gave was his opposition to the creation of a Ministry of Trade to administer the increased volume of Latvian–Soviet trade resulting from the agreement signed on 18 October 1939. In Valdmanis's opinion, however, this trade should have been handled by a subdivision of the Ministry of Finance.[32]

According to Valdmanis's 1963 autobiographical notes, his opposition to the mutual assistance pact demanded by the Soviet Union marked the beginning of the train of events leading to his resignation. After discovering that the cabinet in his absence had authorized Munters to go to Moscow, Valdmanis allegedly approached the commander of the Latvian army, General Krišjānis Berķis, with a request to determine who within the general staff would be committed to 'die standing up,' as its members termed their attitude repeatedly. Valdmanis adamantly insisted (in 1963) that he had not been organizing a coup against Ulmanis; rather, he had just wanted to know the options so that the president could make an informed final decision. 'I had to know who was with us and who wasn't.' Alfreds Bērziņš immediately denounced to Ulmanis Valdmanis's meeting with Berķis as an attempt to instigate a coup. The next day Ulmanis met Valdmanis 'under very strained conditions.' They had a 'sharp exchange of words' and parted without conciliation. 'We understood that our cooperation had come to an end,' concluded Valdmanis, who claimed that two considerations had kept him from resigning immediately: the impact a cabinet crisis would have had on the negotiations in Moscow and the fear that Latvia's position would be weakened by the knowledge that Munters was not representing the entire cabinet.[33]

Government records document that Valdmanis himself initiated his resignation on 20 October, following meetings with Ulmanis that were reported in the media.[34] In a note on the finance minister's stationery and addressed to the 'very honourable Mr President,' Valdmanis scribbled that 'due to the intensive work in the Ministry of Finance I feel very tired and for that reason am obliged to kindly ask you to release me from the position I have been appointed to. With a true and deep respect, Yours, A. Valdmanis, Fin. Min.' On 24 October Ulmanis informed the cabinet that he had granted Valdmanis's request and declared him released from his duties effective 25 October. At the same time the cabinet agreed to split the finance ministry.[35] According to the official record of employment filed in the Chancellery of State, Valdmanis was released from the position of minister of finance at his own request.[36]

On the day of his departure, Valdmanis addressed his staff as follows:

> My co-workers! As of today, I am ceasing to be your head. The previous Ministry of Finance is being divided into two independent units, and I am being replaced by the new Minister of Finance, Mr J. Kaminskis, and the new Minister of Trade and Industry, Mr J. Blumbergs.

We have been united in the loyalty to our state and president. And us has united not only hard work and exemplary discipline, but also a deep friendship. Let us not attempt to evaluate the accomplished work ourselves; that should be left to others. Let us, however, thank each other for the enthusiastically and zealously accomplished common work.

Now, at the time of parting, let us promise to each other that regardless of circumstances we will not lose our real Latvian attitude: diligent work, a strong will, a courageous heart, clear thinking, and an open language.

Our thoughts and deeds to Latvia![37]

The *Wiener Neues Tagblatt* commented, based on information from its own Riga correspondent, that the resignation of Valdmanis, the appointment of former State Comptroller Kaminskis as his successor, and the creation of a new Ministry of Trade and Industry headed by the renowned economist Blumbergs, signified the resolution of a cabinet crisis that had been brewing for some time.[38]

No one doubted that the official cause Valdmanis gave for his resignation – complete physical exhaustion from overwork – was a phoney or merely a subsidiary one for weightier reasons. To be sure, work from the sudden escalation of responsibilities may have overwhelmed him. But he was only thirty-one years old, athletically built, addicted to strenuous tennis playing, and in good health. In the fall of 1939 he impressed composer Imants Sakss as a man in good physical shape and nicely suntanned, an appearance that was becoming very fashionable.[39]

After the war, Alfreds Bērziņš disseminated two conflicting versions of Valdmanis's departure. In a letter written in October 1947 to Latvian ambassador in Washington Alfred Bilmanis, Bērziņš asserted that Ulmanis actually requested Valdmanis's resignation. At first Valdmanis allegedly forwarded a memorandum to Ulmanis through the Chancellery declaring that, because he was unable to reconcile himself with the policies of the national government, especially the economic ones, he was resigning and would in future not wish to have Kārlis Ulmanis extend any favours or attention to him. (Such a memorandum has never been found among government records.) When Ulmanis then telephoned Valdmanis and asked whether 'the young man is able to write more civilized letters,' Valdmanis produced a handwritten letter asking for release from his position on grounds of poor health.

As to the 'real reasons' why Valdmanis was forced to leave the position of finance minister, Bērziņš offered a number of 'revelations' in 1947: First,

> Right after having appointed Valdmanis to the cabinet, K.U. realized that he had made a big mistake. The young man was a splendid self-promoter with absolutely limitless ambitions, but a poor minister of finance. When the war started in 1939, Latvia had practically no reserves in raw materials, not even petroleum and gasoline, although the 'energetic' young man offered the cabinet his head as a pledge that everything would be procured on time. Of course, from the beginning of the war, the Germans blockaded the sea routes. And since from the head, the one Valdmanis so heroically and daringly had pledged as security, nothing useful could be obtained, the people in the countryside were sitting in the dark for lack of petroleum, from the beginning of the wartime fall season until the first deliveries from Russia were received.

Second, with his arrogance and intrigues, 'about which a book could be written,' Valdmanis had lost all respect and trust from his cabinet colleagues. 'But he made himself completely ridiculous when he began to spread the idea that the burden of two presidencies was too heavy a load for K.U. Mr U. should take up residence as president of state in the Castle of Riga, and to the position of the president of the cabinet a "young and energetic person" should be invited. What was meant under this designation was not difficult to guess.'

Third, despite his denial, Valdmanis had received numerous financial benefits from Ulmanis for being a government minister. 'How would one characterize the 22,000 lats that Valdmanis received from the Credit Bank in addition to his salary, if not as a bonus for setting up various government-controlled industries? And how would he designate the lump-sum payment of three months salary when he left the government, despite his boasting statement to Ulmanis, not to accept anything from the hands of K.U.?'

Finally, Bērziņš even hinted at unaccounted-for sources of personal enrichment.

> Many members of the government, I would even say all of them, after six years in the cabinet left their positions just as rich as they had started out. However, 'one of the cleanest,' had managed not only to extricate himself from the debts he had been mired in before, but also to advance to ownership of a country estate in the district of Naudīte in Zemgale, of a ship named *Riga*, and membership on the board of A/S 'Raugs,' while his father-in-law, a former ship mechanic ..., had become managing director of a Jewish-owned plywood factory named 'Prima.' During a single year – not so

little! To the president, too, those achievements seemed sufficient to let V. go from the government.[40]

Any unprejudiced appreciation of these 'revelations' has to take into consideration that Alfreds Bērziņš was minister for public affairs (commonly known as 'propaganda minister') and a veteran associate and confidant of President Ulmanis. In these capacities he had looked upon the ambitions of the young upstart in the finance ministry with growing envy and apprehension. Bērziņš's own desire to succeed Ulmanis as president of state was no secret. Valdmanis, however, let it be known that he considered him totally unsuitable for such an honour. In turn, Bērziņš later had no scruples feeding Valdmanis's opponents ammunition in their political feuds after the Second World War. Since he was one of only three surviving members of Ulmanis cabinets after 1934, Bērziņš's testimony was difficult to refute. Interestingly, Bērziņš did not repeat any of these revelations in his book *1939: Lielo notikumu priekšvakarā* (1939: On the Eve of the Great Events), published in 1976. There are references to his aspiration to become prime minister. But the resignation is presented as Valdmanis's own wish in connection with the splitting of the finance ministry.[41]

Von Kotze put forward yet another interpretation of the changes in the Latvian finance ministry. His explanation resembled Leckzyck's and may have been suggested to them at the time by Valdmanis himself. The resignation was attributable, von Kotze reported to Berlin, to Foreign Minister Munters's constant encroachments on the prerogatives of the Ministry of Finance. 'As a matter of fact, Valdmanis was the one cabinet member who, from his correct appreciation of Latvian interests, always aspired to an understanding with Germany with a view particularly to future economic development. The support he had hoped to receive from military circles that reject Munters was not enough to keep him in his position.' The event was therefore a political victory for Munters. 'Not one word of recognition' had been bestowed upon the departing finance minister for his achievements, von Kotze noted.[42]

The evidence found in the now-declassified pertinent Latvian, Soviet, and German government records confirms that Valdmanis gave different explanations for his resignation to Ulmanis and his cabinet, the Latvian public, the staff of the German legation, and the Soviet envoy in Riga. The records show, for example, that German Foreign Office officials were aware that he carefully cultivated the image of a friend of Germany to German diplomats in Riga, while in the Latvian cabinet and to the

Latvian public he appeared as a staunch defender of Latvian nationalism, if necessary at the expense of German interests. This duplicitous stance, he discovered quickly, seemed conducive to both his political fortunes and his survival in times of trouble.

Contemporaries credited Valdmanis with a sharp legal mind, ambitions that reached beyond heading a government ministry, and political astuteness branded by his opponents as unprincipled opportunism. By mid-October 1939 evidence was clear to Valdmanis that timely dissociation from Ulmanis's politics might be opportune because the days of the Ulmanis regime were numbered and the future of Latvia would be determined by Soviet Russia and/or Nazi Germany. Thus, he said and did what was convenient to assure his survival on either side. He always maintained that his long-term goal was to be available to serve Latvia.

Prospective Prime Minister or Traitor?

Although no longer involved in decision making about the future of Latvia, Valdmanis retained a keen interest in these decisions and their impact on the fate of his country. Available evidence suggests that concern for the political situation, career ambition, and considerations of survival coalesced to make Valdmanis increasingly conspiratorial. He wanted Ulmanis removed as head of the cabinet and restricted to the role of president of state. This desire was reinforced by the conviction that a young, shrewd, flexible, and energetic leader like himself could somehow save the country from the annexationist designs of its Nazi and Soviet neighbours.

Valdmanis's preparations for that contingency started right after his departure from the cabinet. The sinister implications of the mutual assistance pacts signed by the Baltic countries with Stalin and the fate that might be in store for them were shockingly driven home on 30 November 1939 when Soviet forces suddenly attacked Finland. The lesson was not lost on Valdmanis, who had reason to fear that his image as a friend of Germany might seriously handicap his prospective political fortunes. On 4 December 1939 the accredited representative of the USSR in Latvia, Ivan S. Zotov, reported to Moscow the contents of a confidential conversation with Valdmanis concerning Latvian cabinet divisions over the mutual assistance pact and related matters.

According to this report, Valdmanis had revealed the contents of cabinet discussions preceding the signing of the pact. In these Ulmanis and Munters had decided to sign merely because they had had no choice;

they had wanted neither warm nor friendly relations with the Soviet Union. This position had not been shared by a group of five ministers – Balodis, Veitnieks, Volonts, Auskapš, and Valdmanis – favouring cooperation combined with friendship as the only way to secure political and economic safety for Latvia. They had rallied behind Valdmanis, Zotov related, who claimed to have been expelled from the cabinet for daring to speak up against Latvia's leader and thereby supposedly betraying his trust. Valdmanis's four sympathizers had yielded to pressures to endorse the pact because of the war situation.

No less ardently had Valdmanis vented his complaints to Zotov about the repatriation of Germans. They were treated much too softly, Valdmanis maintained, because the government had wanted to create the impression that the departing Germans should not suffer any losses. Already 20 million lats had been paid in compensation for properties left behind, and Latvians would not forgive the government for these generous payments. When Valdmanis had demanded a review of all questions concerning the settlement of repatriation accounts, Munters allegedly had taken personal offence and forced Valdmanis to resign.

However, tension in the cabinet had continued to grow, Valdmanis indicated to Zotov, in part because the resignations from cabinet had been politically inconvenient, and Valdmanis had refused to let Ulmanis persuade him to return. Balodis had allegedly kept complaining that the Latvian–Soviet pact had been unsatisfactory because it had neither defined Soviet support to the Latvian army nor addressed questions of compensation. To generate an atmosphere of peace and solidarity, Ulmanis had picked as successors for Valdmanis two faceless officials well advanced in years and with relatively limited capabilities. They had vowed to follow the instructions of Ulmanis.

In conclusion, Zotov noted that Valdmanis was now attempting to play the role of a government official forced to suffer because of his efforts on behalf of the interests of Latvians. Feeling strongly about his accusations against Munters, Valdmanis was embarking on a campaign to discredit him. Public rumours intimated that Munters's mother and sister were repatriating to Germany and that his brother was in Germany already – 'in the ranks of the Storm Troopers.' Being half-German, Munters could not represent the Latvian position and would sooner or later be removed, Valdmanis had predicted, according to Zotov. In the cabinet Munters and Alfreds Bērziņš were not loved. Around Valdmanis, however, were gathering 'strong Latvians' with their own definite ideas.[43]

Are Valdmanis's clandestine Soviet contacts in late 1939 – only recently uncovered as Soviet government records have been opened to historical research – evidence of a conversion or of hidden pro-Soviet sympathies? Was Valdmanis perhaps swayed by rumours spreading in November 1939 that the Soviets would soon occupy the country and punish those who had supported the previous regime?[44] The latter argument appears refuted by Valdmanis's revelation in 1963 that around Christmas 1939 he had a visit from the Finnish ambassador Eduard Palin. On this occasion Palin awarded him a certificate of honourary membership in the Finnish automobile association and a large silver plaque with an inscription recognizing his stand against Finland's Soviet invaders. On behalf of Palin, Valdmanis passed a message to Ulmanis and General Berķis that a planned Allied intervention in the Soviet war against Finland might also rid the Baltic countries of its Soviet bases.[45]

In view of Valdmanis's known anti-Soviet position, how is one to interpret his disclosures to Zotov? They are quite clearly a misrepresentation of the internal deliberations in the Latvian cabinet and raise questions about the reliability of Valdmanis's information, his loyalties, his goals, and his personal ethics. Recently, Latvian historian Aivars Stranga examined some of these questions. Stranga concludes that (1) Valdmanis invented his own and his group's oppositional stand in cabinet and misrepresented the views of Ulmanis and Munters to Zotov to put himself in a favourable light; (2) he was motivated by revenge for his demotion rather than by any political conviction; (3) he exhibited reprehensible disloyalty towards his government and his country; (4) his 'disclosures' amounted to near-criminal denunciation of Ulmanis and Munters; and (5) his behaviour revealed his desperate ambition to rise to the top, if necessary by conspiring with Latvia's most powerful enemies – Soviet Russia and Nazi Germany.[46]

These are valid considerations. But they tend to identify Latvia's best interests with those of the unconstitutional Ulmanis regime and its representatives and underrate the desperate quest for alternatives that might have assured survival in the ominous situation of December 1939. Even his opponents have recognized that Valdmanis had exceptional capabilities and enormous unrealized ambitions. He admitted to being a candidate for the presidency of the cabinet as early as November 1938 and again in the summer of 1939. Stranga does not doubt that the young and energetic Valdmanis could have handled the job. But Ulmanis until the end refused to relinquish any of the powers he had seized illegally.

In Estonia President Konstantin Päts broadened the base of his government by transferring power to a new prime minister to accommodate the perceived Soviet threat. To those seeking changes in the policies, structure, and composition of the Latvian government, the authoritarian regime left only the possibility of conspiracy with a foreign power. In the spring of 1940 the quest for personal survival added a powerful motive to those aspirations.

According to Valdmanis's postwar testimony, the Latvian army was the driving force for a coup against the policy of tolerating the Soviet bases and the growing Soviet influence in Latvia. Offering to procure diplomatic support and a weapons source, Valdmanis sympathized with plans by a group of officers around General Berķis (including generals Ludvigs Bolšteins, H. Rozenšteins, and Colonel Artūrs Dālbergs) to prepare an uprising with volunteer units. The generals believed that joining forces with Germany was the only realistic option in opposing the Soviets. They did not see any possibility for help from Britain. Valdmanis, Einbergs, and Veidnieks, however, though eager to accept weapons from Germany, were allegedly opposed to trading German for Soviet control of Latvia. Once properly and adequately supplied with weapons, they preferred for Latvia to defend its neutrality without foreign help.[47]

Valdmanis claimed to have approached von Kotze in early 1940 on behalf of the would-be conspirators who had believed they still had a chance to attack the Soviet bases. Von Kotze agreed to meet Valdmanis on the highway outside Riga where an engine breakdown staged by Valdmanis's driver would provide the opportunity for a brief communication. Valdmanis attributed the covertness of this meeting to the ubiquity of Soviet bases and agents in the country. The meeting turned into a failure for Valdmanis. This last request for weapons from von Kotze had met with an instant and unequivocal no.[48]

Ulmanis's alarmed and distressed radio address of 10 February 1940, according to Valdmanis, had indicated his knowledge of the planned rising against the expanding Soviet presence and his realization of the hopelessness of opposition to the Soviets. From that time on Ulmanis suppressed every idea of resistance and went out of his way to demonstrate his loyalty to Moscow. Ulmanis also imposed limits on Valdmanis's freedom of movement. Through Veidnieks, Valdmanis recalled, Ulmanis had demanded assurances that Valdmanis 'would not go anywhere and would not get involved in anything' outside his sphere as a director general of Ķegums. However, Valdmanis was permitted to continue playing tennis (on a government-owned and -controlled indoor tennis court).

As to the motives for this order, Valdmanis speculated (in 1963) that Ulmanis (1) had been afraid the Russians would learn of the planned uprising and (2) had wanted to prevent Valdmanis from getting involved with those futile ideas of resistance.[49] Possibly the main reason – not conceded by Valdmanis – for this quarantine had been Ulmanis's knowledge of conspiratorial activities initiated by Valdmanis.

This contention is supported by a 'strictly confidential' memorandum from the German legation's acting representative, G. Sthamer, of 13 March 1940 to Berlin, referring to a lengthy conversation the German trade attaché Leckzyck had with Valdmanis on 10 March. Sthamer termed Valdmanis, a man who lacked faith in England and had a very benevolent attitude towards Germany, 'one of the sharpest opponents of the Soviet Russians.' The very young and very lively Valdmanis appeared preoccupied with interfering actively in politics, Sthamer believed. Such an undertaking, however, would be in the nature of an adventure, since he and his friends had little support. Sthamer considered Valdmanis's judgment of Munters to be swayed by personal resentment. It was doubtful to Sthamer that Latvia could master the difficult situation in the country without Munters.[50]

Leckzyck's report of the conversation characterized Valdmanis as very depressed and concerned about Latvia's foreign political and economic development. The 'old man,' as Valdmanis labelled Ulmanis, had aged considerably in the last months and was rapidly losing his vigour and leadership ability. Important matters of state were being neglected in favour of trivia. Aspects of the economy, finances, and domestic politics were suffering from noticeable decay that no one dared to halt. The president was under the influence of the evil spirit of Munters, who had convinced Ulmanis that Latvia's independence needed only a British guarantee. Now Munters and Ulmanis were signing with fraudulent intentions all treaties required by Germany.

Valdmanis, Balodis, and military circles had become convinced that Munters's dishonest game was detrimental to Latvian interests, the report continued. With its record of victories, Germany was the only country able to save Latvia. Latvia's policy towards Germany during the past twenty years was no longer appropriate. Only an immediate and complete turnaround towards Germany would make sense. Latvia's policies, however, would change only if the affairs of state were transferred to a prime minister from the 'old man' and Munters. An enforced internal change would be impossible because it would give Russia a pretext for intervention.

According to Leckzyck's report, Valdmanis advised Germany to find a pretext for demanding the replacement of Munters by a man acceptable to Germany. That would entail a restructuring of the government and give General Balodis, who also had a better rapport with the Russians, a chance to become prime minister. The business of state would then be conducted by people who placed concern for the public welfare above personal interest. The outcome would also be more satisfactory for Germany.[51]

Zemgals describes, in his self-serving vein, Valdmanis's last encounter with Ulmanis. It took place in April 1940 in the president's official residence at the Castle of Riga. 'Are you still an admirer of Salazar?' Ulmanis was alleged to have asked, and he wondered whether Valdmanis still believed in an elected parliament and an elected president. 'You see my young friend,' Ulmanis told Valdmanis, 'Salazar became prime minister and leader of his country after having served as minister of finance for five years. If you had remained in the Ministry of Finance for five more years, we would have been in a position to talk about your further responsibilities. But you did not like to wait. You planned to push the president out of the way too soon.' Valdmanis denied the accusations and suggested that Ulmanis relied on whispering allegations instead of his own judgment.[52]

Valdmanis was not the only prominent Latvian whom Ulmanis suspected of conspiring against him at the time. General Balodis, who was considered to be pro-Russian, was not allowed to accept invitations from the Kremlin for fear he would plot with Soviet leaders. The deteriorating relations ended with the general's dismissal as minister of war in April 1940, followed by the removal of Transport Minister Einbergs, a Balodis sympathizer. On 24 April Munters spent three and a half hours conversing with von Kotze. On that occasion Munters disclosed the reasons for firing Balodis: he had made unauthorized decisions, instigated increasingly violent controversies in the cabinet, refused to attend cabinet meetings, and taken personal offence at Ulmanis's attempts to muzzle him.[53] The replacements for Balodis and Einbergs, just as for Valdmanis earlier, were non-controversial old men who kept the cabinet a pliable instrument for Ulmanis.

Twenty-five years later Valdmanis labelled his conspiratorial activity in the spring of 1940 'legitimate resistance.' Ulmanis's unconstitutional dictatorship, instead of uniting the country, left Latvia internally weak and divided on the eve of the Soviet occupation. The conspirator acted from the belief that time was running out. 'If we had had five more years,' Valdmanis lamented in 1963, a new generation would have taken over the country. It would have been more open and more internationally oriented:

> Ulmanis's job was to secure the 'house.' He had to build with what clay he had on hand. He was working mostly with the same assistants as in parliamentary Latvia. What else could he do? My generation was already different. We had a different understanding of problems. We had different relations and we had a wider perspective. Admittedly, Ulmanis had already started to make use of us, assigned us difficult jobs. Given five more years and youngsters like me would have been leaders in all the other sectors of government. For us, the young generation, it was not an empty phrase when we claimed that it is better to die standing up than to keep on living on your knees.[54]

Director General of Ķegums

Although Valdmanis stayed out of the political limelight after his exit from the cabinet, he continued to be prominent in Latvia's economic life. In addition to his chairmanship of the Riga stock exchange, he devoted himself to industrial projects ranging from the electrification of the railway system to the production of artificial nitrogen fertilizer. In December 1939 the leaders of the various commercial, industrial, and shipping trades elected Valdmanis over the government candidate as the head of their organization. His chief ambition, however, was to accelerate the country's electrification. It would, Valdmanis argued, provide the basis for rapid industrialization and for a general increase in the standard of living.[55]

In December 1939 the hydro-power station at Ķegums, with whose construction Valdmanis had long been associated, was put into service. By far Latvia's largest industrial project, it had started operations with one turbine. Of its initial annual output of 160 million kilowatt hours, 140 million were designated for Riga. Valdmanis eagerly accepted on 21 December 1939 the cabinet's appointment of himself as director general of the state electrical enterprise Ķegums, as recommended by Finance Minister Kaminskis. Kaminskis also recommended to cabinet that the director general receive a salary of 1,600 lats per month, a free apartment including heating and lighting, and 6,000 lats per year for unitemized expenses. That amounted to a considerable increase of 1,100 lats above his minister's salary.[56] It also indicated that Ulmanis had not rejected Valdmanis completely.

The new job involved more than the engineering, planning, and installing of high voltage lines and of high and low voltage distributors over the entire country that Zemgals describes.[57] As director general of Ķegums, Valdmanis was also invited to participate in biweekly meetings of department heads within the Ministry of Finance. The minutes of these meetings reveal that this forum discussed all kinds of acute policy issues related to Latvia's growing economic difficulties and the urgency of reducing government expenditures. One of the issues addressed at the 2 March 1940 meeting was the utilization of capital by government-supported shareholding companies. Valdmanis exposed some 'very clever' examples of how government-supported shareholding companies were writing off lats (A/S Kiegelmeier 1.5 million and A/S Kudra 2 million). Valdmanis also drew attention to another new joint-stock company. It had spent 700,000 lats to build a new factory at the seaside and then asked the government to fund the construction of harbour facilities and a railway connection.

Recurring items on the agenda were the retirement of redundant officials and the need to identify superfluous government employees who could be allocated to compulsory farm work. At the 2 March 1940 meeting Valdmanis was very critical of the government scheme of forced leaves and retirements. He doubted whether the workload of essential employees would permit additional leaves. Most of the senior officials could not even take their full annual vacations. Furthermore, replacements for retirees would work with dedication only when they had job security. Few institutions were still reducing their operations and redundant parallelism in the state bureaucracy, far from being eliminated, was in some cases even being created. It would be more appropriate to recruit farm labourers from employees identified as redundant when new enterprises were formed from old ones. Especially discriminatory, in Valdmanis's opinion, was the practice of classifying private property owners as more eligible than others for unpaid leave (a euphemism for farm work).[58]

During the 10 May 1940 meeting the department heads considered new guidelines for the Ministry of Finance. Not afraid to raise controversial issues, Valdmanis moved that the minister have certain supervisory rights over the big state banks and that his veto rights be more clearly defined. Valdmanis had raised a very valid point, the minister and deputy minister conceded, but a change would be very difficult to implement. For twenty years the board of the Bank of Latvia had been independent in its decisions and directly subordinated to the president, they explained. But Valdmanis insisted that this matter, never before raised in the cabinet, was important enough to be raised now. Kaminskis responded that this would be done 'if and when it should become necessary. There are questions that should not be asked without consideration of the consequences.' After that 'friendly' advice Valdmanis withdrew from any further discussions of that agenda item.[59]

The 30 May 1940 meeting dealt with whether special leave without pay to perform farm work should be required of government employees and to what farms they would be sent. This measure, intended to address a shortage of funds and of agricultural labour, was loaded with problems. For example, the manager of the sugar monopoly questioned the suitability of white-collar workers for farm work, while Valdmanis drew attention to the controversial fact that some farmers, particular in Zemgale, were such harsh employers that they found it difficult to get farm labourers. 'Would such employers now be rewarded with replacement office workers?'

Those to be considered first for the proposed two-month leave without pay were civil servants owning farms or urban rental property that could give them sufficient income during the leave. Valdmanis proposed that not only the lower ranks of the civil service be considered for the assigned leave, but also 'the highest echelons,' that is, ministers and department directors. The cabinet should take up the matter of designating some ministers and department directors for agricultural leave: 'I personally believe that the heads of government establishments with competent deputies should have no difficulty taking such short-term leave,' Valdmanis urged. Government employees on such leave should be required to obtain performance certificates from the local agricultural association and if their performance was judged too weak should not be allowed to return to their government job.[60]

The last recorded meeting of department heads in the Ministry of Finance was on Monday, 17 June 1940. On this day the Latvian government resigned in compliance with an ultimatum from Soviet Foreign Minister Molotov, and Soviet forces started to take control of Latvia. The meeting was called by Minister Blumbergs to inform staff that the government had accepted all Soviet demands and resigned. Unlike President Smetona of Lithuania, whose flight from his country had left a very negative impression on his countrymen, President Ulmanis had definitely decided not to leave Riga. He would continue to carry out his obligations as president of state, while a separate president of the cabinet of ministers would be appointed, Blumbergs stated.

Valdmanis was the only one of twenty-nine participants to ask for clarification: 'The cabinet of ministers has resigned today, but the president of state, Mr Ulmanis, has not resigned?' Blumbergs replied that the Soviet leaders had demanded the formation of a new government in which they could have more confidence. 'How about freedom of movement – will it be restricted as troops arrive?' Valdmanis wondered aloud. The minister had no knowledge of any restrictions or any plans by Soviet forces to interfere in the internal affairs of Latvia.[61]

The Red Nightmare, 17 June 1940 to 1 July 1941

Between 17 June and 5 August 1940 the Soviet Union annexed Latvia in three stages: First, Andrei Vyshinskii, deputy chairman of the Soviet Council of People's Commissars, arrived in Riga on 20 June to install a pro-Communist government under Professor Augusts Kirchenšteins and to free the members of Latvia's socialist parties imprisoned by Ulmanis. The next step was the organization of rigged parliamentary elections on 14–15 July, allegedly based on Latvia's 1922 constitution. The last step was the proclamation of the Latvian Socialist Soviet Republic as part of the USSR on 21 July 1940 and the resignation of Ulmanis as president of state. Sovietization proceeded immediately and had transformed all levels of state, society, and the economy by the time German troops arrived in Riga on 1 July 1941.

Shortly before the takeover in 1940, Valdmanis had arranged with the Ministry of Agriculture for his country property to be transferred to the state for use as a school of agriculture on condition that the state guarantee sustenance for his mother, sister, and brother. After the takeover Valdmanis retained his position as director general of Ķegums until 30 September 1940. He surrendered his passport to the new administration because, claims Zemgals, he had decided to stay at his post just as Ulmanis had pledged in his radio address of 18 June 1940 not to leave his post. Putting faith in the new government's promise that parliamentary elections on 14 July would be based on the 1922 constitution, Valdmanis together with General Balodis, former minister of education Atis Ķēniņš, and others compiled a list of candidates under the heading 'the call of democratic Latvians,' although he did not stand for election himself.[62]

Whatever hopes Valdmanis may have had of improving his political fortunes under the new regime evaporated quickly because Soviet officials permitted only the 'working people's block' to field candidates' lists. At the same time NKVD agents began to round up prominent Latvians and attempted to extort political confessions from associates and supporters of Ulmanis. On 22 July Ulmanis was deported to the Soviet Union, followed by Munters and most other members of the former government. In despair, thousands of ethnic Latvians – one source mentions more than 10,000 – approached UTAG officials requesting to join the last transport of Baltic German repatriates to depart for Germany in early 1941.[63] But only 1,821 Latvians managed to join the last contingent of 10,500 ethnic Germans leaving Latvia.[64] One of the applicants was former propaganda minister Alfreds Bērziņš. As early as 1 July 1940 von Kotze cabled to Berlin that Bērziņš, pressured by Soviet secret agents to denounce Ulmanis and Munters, had 'begged urgently' for a German passport or help to arrange his escape to Germany.[65] Von Kotze turned him down, but Bērziņš managed to reach Germany nonetheless by way of Finland and Sweden.

Two other applicants for resettlement were Valdmanis and his secretary, Anna Kunetz (in Latvian 'Kunečs'). According to German Foreign Office officials von Grundherr and Kleist, Valdmanis expressed his request to von Kotze through an ethnic German intermediary. While Ms Kunetz was resettled, Valdmanis was rejected because the German envoy anticipated the Soviet authorities would refuse the resettlement of a former member of the Ulmanis government. In addition, von Grundherr and Kleist considered Valdmanis politically undesirable because his actions had been dictated by Latvian interests detrimental to German interests.[66]

There is no reference to this attempted escape in Zemgals's book. According to Valdmanis's 1963 recollections, however, the idea of resettlement to Germany was initiated by the German envoy when he found out that Valdmanis was to be arrested. Von Kotze offered to issue the required papers to Valdmanis and his family, as well as sanctuary in the premises of the German legation until his departure. Although prepared to register his family as Germans in order to save them, as for himself Valdmanis 'decided to remain and if necessary to die in Latvia where I had been born, grown up, and involved with the government to the best of my ability.' This was in compliance with Ulmanis's request not to escape and if necessary to sacrifice one's life, so that the people as a whole would get off more easily, Valdmanis claimed. His alleged refusal to be repatriated was one of those issues raised repeatedly afterwards, stated Valdmanis, sometimes as incrimination, and sometimes as proof of his strength of character.[67]

Valdmanis expected his own arrest to be only a matter of time when he learned that Ulmanis, Munters, Apsītis, and Veidnieks had been deported and Bērziņš had escaped. Nonetheless, despite the threat of arrest, Zemgals contends, Valdmanis was prepared to defend his record as a minister. He deliberately did not change his lifestyle: as usual he arose at 7 a.m., played tennis for an hour, and by 9 a.m. arrived in his limousine at his office, where Commissar Pāvels Vītols functioned as a watchdog. Dressed and awake during most of the nights in the summer of 1940, Valdmanis awaited his arrest. When in September he was arrested in his office, he allegedly left in style – 'properly dressed, gloves on, a gentleman as always' – and instructed his chauffeur to drive him and his guards to prison in his limousine.

Detained in the Riga Central Prison for four weeks, most of the time in isolation, his health deteriorated rapidly. His wife recalls that Valdmanis was tortured there, came back in pain, had sleepless nights, and used to curl up asking, 'Did I tell them anything, Irma?'[68] Upon his release on 2 October, Valdmanis entered a medical clinic, where he stayed until Christmas 1940. Meanwhile his apartment had been confiscated, his family evicted and moved to a very small flat in Riga, and family friends had become reluctant to maintain contact. Looking for a source of income, Valdmanis found work in January 1941 as chief of the planning section in the silk and knitting trust. Following a brief rearrest and release, Valdmanis had himself declared seriously ill, first with heart trouble, then with tuberculosis, and transferred from one clinic to another. There he felt safe enough to play his daily match of tennis and volleyball games with the medical staff. During the mass arrests of 13–14 June 1941 Valdmanis hid on the dunes of Riga and afterwards in the Cēsis tuberculosis sanatorium. News of the German invasion of the Soviet Union on 22 June 1941 prompted him to flee from his sanatorium into the forests of Vidzeme in northern Latvia where he joined others awaiting the arrival of German forces in July 1941.[69]

The main evidence for Valdmanis's behaviour under the communist regime is Zemgals's account. Valdmanis's elusively shrewd dealings with the authorities, however, are confirmed by one piece of supplementary evidence, namely, the chairman's handwritten draft report of a speech by citizen Valdmanis to a meeting of the managers of the knitting industry in January 1941. Discovered in July 1941, after German troops had occupied Riga, the report opened with the observation that the speech was very clever and diplomatic, and it was impossible to describe it accurately. The industry faced catastrophe because of a shortage of raw materials, a shortage of silk in the Soviet Union, and an unprofessional approach by the party and administrators, Valdmanis pointed out. To prevent lay-offs, the managers should compile a collective report showing the reality of the situation and try to get the Communist party to act.

To achieve results, the former operators should get the managers to lobby those with political influence, Valdmanis suggested. To lobby the party was a somewhat unusual approach, the reporter noted, and wondered whether Valdmanis himself should not approach the party leadership and do the lobbying. Valdmanis explained that he had already talked to party leaders and was advised that any submission should follow proper channels and go through its own commissariat. He had no other place to turn and had no access to the state plan in Moscow. In the discussion, the painful truth became evident that the appointed supervisors were a serious hindrance to the operation. In a roundabout way Valdmanis pointed to the need to get rid of them and to the incompetence of the party and the various branches of the administration under its control in economic matters. Despite his awareness that he could be prosecuted for this speech, Valdmanis concluded, he was speaking openly and stated the situation as it really was.[70] The next day he was indeed rearrested at his place of work.

The Valdmanis family narrowly escaped the sweeping round-up and deportation to Siberia of some sixteen thousand Latvians on 13–14 June 1941. While Valdmanis, after warnings that he might be arrested, sought refuge on the dunes near Riga, his old chauffeur spirited the family away to a tiny cottage near the Lithuanian border. Valdmanis was reunited with his family only in early July when they moved back to their Riga apartment after German troops had occupied Latvia.

As a result of the harrowing mass deportations in mid-June 1941, Alfred and Irma Valdmanis added to their family a deportee's child miraculously snatched from the claws of death. It was three-month-old baby Agnar, son of Irma's married oldest sister Elizabeth Johannson, a concert pianist. Arrested with her two children and separated from her husband, she was locked into one of the 490 boxcars packed with arrested Latvians waiting to be sent eastward. Since the infant's chances of surviving the trip were slim, she had decided to wrap him in newspaper and leave him behind. She bribed a soldier with her watch to give the bundle to a strange woman among the bystanders with the request to deliver it to Irma's mother in Riga. The Valdmanises raised Agnar with their own three children and legally adopted him at the end of the war to thwart Soviet attempts at repatriation. After seventeen years in Siberia, 'Aunt Lissy' was allowed to return to Latvia and from there join the Valdmanis family in Montreal. Lissy's daughter, however, who had survived Siberia with her mother, was not allowed to emigrate. As late as 1986 the Valdmanis family feared that publication of Lissy's ordeal might subject her daughter in Soviet Latvia to reprisals.[71]

Since suspect Latvians were arrested and deported at the rate of some three hundred a month, starting in July 1940,[72] the survival of Valdmanis seemed a miracle. German intelligence verified his imprisonment,[73] and Latvian witnesses have attested to his subsequent refuge in clinics[74] and employment with the knitting industry.[75] However, the evidence about the reasons for his release from prison, his failure to be deported like other former ministers, and his ability to survive in Latvia the entire year of Red Terror, is contradictory. Zemgals provides the most detailed account of his imprisonment and gives the following unverifiable reasons for Valdmanis's release. First, his brave attitude in jail – in contrast to the 'not so heroic behaviour' of other arrested former high officials – gained him the respect of his jailers. Second, the records of the previous government proved to the new regime that Valdmanis was not a yes-man in the cabinet.

Furthermore, according to Zemgals, official records revealed that under Ulmanis millions of lats had gone into the pockets of such high officials as Bērziņš, Klīve, Rancāns, Karčevskis, Fridrichsons, and Eķis, but none to Valdmanis, whose records instead showed debts. Ulmanis had allegedly instructed the Credit Bank in November 1939 to forgive Valdmanis's debts, but Valdmanis had rejected the offer. Zemgals maintains that the only transaction involving 12,000 lats to Valdmanis had been allocated to fifty poor families, to cover the costs of funerals, and to prevent the bankruptcies of small farmers. Despite its diligent efforts, Zemgals claims, the prosecution uncovered nothing in Valdmanis's past of which to accuse him, so a public trial under these circumstances would have hurt their very unpopular regime.

Last but not least, Zemgals attributes Valdmanis's relative freedom and survival under 'the red nightmare' to the intervention of a number of friends and associates. People's Commissar of Justice Andrejs Jablonskis received representations for Valdmanis's release from prison from five different committees of workers from various government departments. Five former co-workers from his ministry – Jagars, Suksis, Šakars, Mednis, and Kārkliņš – even volunteered to vouch for Valdmanis's promise not to flee to Germany. Valdmanis owed his release from custody to the intervention of physician Dr Marta Vīgants. She had successfully treated high Communist party officials who owed her favours. The person who offered Valdmanis a job in the textile industry in January 1941 was a former school friend of his.

To prevent Valdmanis's rearrest, Vīgants and two colleagues diagnosed him as having life-threatening heart trouble and admitted him to the cardiac department of the university clinic. These doctors and the entire class of fifty to sixty medical students protected Valdmanis. When the hospital was to be inspected by trustees of the Communist party, Vīgants declared Valdmanis sick with tuberculosis and arranged his transfer to the TB sanatorium. Valdmanis survived in communist Latvia not only because he was popular or had a large circle of friends. Rather, the help he received was typical of the spirit of Latvians cooperating with Latvians in those days, Zemgals points out.[76]

Alfreds Bērziņš, whom Valdmanis publicly identified as his chief opponent in the cabinet and the beneficiary of large gifts of money from Ulmanis, later took revenge with shocking allegations of why Valdmanis survived the red nightmare. Absent from Latvia at the time and admitting that his information was based on hearsay and logic, Bērziņš nonetheless doubted that honesty and popularity and the guarantee of three individuals could explain the survival of Valdmanis. For what reason should Valdmanis have been excepted when, starting with Ulmanis, everything was weeded out that could be, roots and all, and tens of thousands were being banished to Siberia or executed on the spot? Bērziņš wondered. Popularity and respect by the population, instead of saving Valdmanis, should actually have made him a target for merciless persecution because the Soviets tried to destroy the Baltic intelligentsia. How could anyone believe Zemgals's naive affirmation that for fear of harming their already unpopular regime, the Bolsheviks with the support of 150,000 Red Army troops would let Valdmanis go free?

As far as was known to Bērziņš, not a single member of the intelligentsia was released from custody without having first agreed to accept 'certain obligations.' Bērziņš had no official proof of Valdmanis's cooperation with the NKVD. But from others Alfreds Bērziņš claimed to have heard that the wife of the former director of the Credit Bank, Andrejs Bērziņš, had a message from her husband, who was detained in the Central Prison, indicating that his fate would not have turned out to be that tragic had Valdmanis not made it so. Could this note from prison not have indicated something, even if firsthand evidence was missing?

Furthermore, if all the students of the medical and dental faculties were involved in protecting and hiding Valdmanis, how could the Bolsheviks with their system of informers not have heard or seen anything of those efforts? Among the numerous Latvian refugees in postwar Germany, Bērziņš had not found anyone boasting of participating in 'save Valdmanis' activities.[77] But neither have researchers scrutinizing Soviet government and KGB records for confirmation of Bērziņš's 'revelations,' found any evidence incriminating Valdmanis as an NKVD informer.[78]

A third explanation for Valdmanis's survival during the 'red nightmare' was based on intelligence that trade attaché Leckzyck had received in Germany in mid-June 1941. It had come from repatriates and refugees, especially from Valdmanis's secretary Ms Kunetz who was among the last batch of repatriates in the spring of 1941. Leckzyck concluded that Valdmanis had great influence among Latvians and had 'manoeuvred himself through' (*durchlaviert*) under the Bolsheviks because the records of the old Latvian secret police depicted him as an opponent of the Ulmanis regime.

In reality, Leckzyck believed, Valdmanis was preparing the ground for Germany, as if he had a premonition of Hitler's long-range plans for eastern Europe. Upon Leckzyck's departure from Riga, on 14 September 1940, Valdmanis had allegedly confided that guns and ammunition from old Latvian army supplies had been secured. In May 1941, according to intelligence Leckzyck received in Germany through Kunetz, Valdmanis together with others had secretly organized a network of eighty thousand old national guardsmen (*Aizsargi*). He wanted Leckzyck to know that when 'the time arrives' (*die Dinge soweit sind*), the Lithuanians and Latvians should be incorporated into the Reich as members of the Prussian family of peoples and Valdmanis would make himself available for the implementation of this idea.[79]

The available evidence does not corroborate Valdmanis's involvement in underground activities of any kind during the Soviet occupation or knowledge of an impending German invasion. It does indicate, however, his desire to keep his options open for the future. Indeed, as far back as October 1939, Valdmanis had put several irons in the fire, that is, he had through clandestine contacts with German and Soviet diplomats systematically laid the groundwork for alternate career options under German or Soviet rule. He could then, as circumstances required, play either his Soviet or his German card. His uncanny survival instinct and career ambition were two sides of the same coin.

For survival in Soviet Latvia, Gundars believed, his father Alfred benefited greatly from his acquaintance with some of the higher officials in the new Soviet regime, whom he had known since childhood days in Liepāja. He was alleged to have been in secret contact with them and helped them draft speeches in favour of less repressive policies.[80] In the final analysis, however, the pro-Soviet image Valdmanis had managed to convey of himself to Moscow in 1939 may well have been crucial, just as his pro-German image with Leckzyck and von Kotze formed the basis for his political resurgence in July 1941. Significantly, all references to Valdmanis in the recently published reports by Latvia's Soviet envoys to Moscow (August to December 1939) present him as friend of the people, critic of Ulmanis's associates and policies, and a genuine or potential sympathizer of the Soviet Union.[81]

chapter four

'Elected to Lead and Manage Latvian National Affairs': The Janus Face of Collaboration, July 1941 to November 1942

I was elected on 11 July 1941 in a secret assembly of representatives of all Latvian national organizations ... to lead and manage Latvian national affairs until the restoration of Latvia's sovereignty. This amounted to the creation of what came to be known after the war as a 'resistance movement.' With much pride and courage I established the network of Latvian patriots.

Alfred Valdmanis, AVP, 1947

By the time Alfred Valdmanis left his hiding place in the woods and reappeared in Riga on 4 July 1941, three days after the arrival of German troops, the atmosphere had changed radically. Stalin's devious and brutal regime had smothered any potential resistance against the German invaders and had reversed long-standing attitudes. The general mood had suddenly turned pro-German and anti-Jewish, although prior to 1940 Latvians had harboured neither feelings of friendship for Germans nor active anti-Semitic sentiments. Indeed, the new occupiers were being welcomed as liberators and expected to facilitate the restoration of national independence. Meanwhile Jews were being associated with Soviet rule.

Against this background, several reasons suggested collaboration with Germany as a viable approach to pursue Latvian national interests. At first, German military supremacy left no other option for regaining some form of national autonomy. But even as Germany retreated and resentment grew against its oppressive occupation, most Latvians dreaded Soviet 'liberation' as the greater evil. Latvian collaborative initiatives were also encouraged by the obvious lack of coherent political goals and structures on the German side. Latvians along with the other Baltic peoples ranked high on the Nazi racial scale in comparison with other east European peoples under German occupation. The Balts were treated more humanely by the Germans, invited to collaborate, and granted so-called benefits and privileges unavailable to, for example, Russians. But this was offset by the much higher threshold of expectations of the Baltic peoples.

Valdmanis's strategy exemplifies how collaboration became increasingly indistinguishable from resistance. This chapter examines the evolution of the Latvian collaborationist agenda and Valdmanis's prominent role in it, in particular (1) endeavours to form a provisional government, (2) the fate of Latvia's Jews, and (3) the quest for as much de facto autonomy as possible.

Liberation

The search for post-Soviet leadership in Latvia began immediately after Germany's invasion of Soviet territory on 22 June 1941. Inspired by Lithuanian radio broadcasts of 23 June announcing the formation of a provisional Lithuanian government under Colonel Kazys Skirpa, Latvian insurgents on 28 June temporarily captured the Riga radio station, where they proclaimed the liberation of Latvia and the formation of a provisional government.[1] On 1 July, in accordance with a prewar contingency plan, senior Latvian army officers under Colonel Ernests Kreišmanis together with leading kalpakieši set up a so-called Latvijas Organizācijas Centrs or Organizational Centre of Latvia (LOC). It invited former Minister of Transport Bernhards Einbergs to form a provisional national government representing LOC, Pērkonkrusts, and student fraternities. However, Einsatzgruppe A Commander, SS-Brigadeführer (SS Major General) Walter Stahlecker, refused to recognize Einbergs.

The result was a power struggle between Einbergs and Kreišmanis, who was already assigning former Ulmanis administrators as directors to the various departments of the national self-administration. The situation was chaotic. In the words of an anonymous contemporary analyst, it was 'a time of terrible denunciations and in-fighting which reached such proportions that complaints were directed at the highest level of the German army.' The appointed directors were reported to be less concerned with their duties than with 'stuffing their stomachs' and undermining each other's power.[2]

The chaos was worsened by the wild sprouting of Latvian self-defence units. Before the last Red Army units had left Riga, a Health Department official by the name of Malmanis on his own initiative began organizing a police service with as many as five thousand former Latvian army members, policemen, Aizsargi, and students.[3] In addition, several other self-defence organizations vied for the right to wear Latvian uniforms, bear arms, and carry out police duties. Einsatzgruppe A empowered the execution commando launched by Viktors Arājs and auxiliary police units (Polizeihilfsdienst or PHD) that included members of the former police, Latvian army, and Aizsargi.[4] Latvians were volunteering in such numbers for self-defence and security duties, Stahlecker reported, that 150 of them could be sent to Belorussia on duty.[5] By October 1941 Latvia's 8,218 auxiliary police outnumbered German police in Latvia 45 to 1.[6]

On 5 July the Abwehr brought former Latvian military attachés in Berlin and Kaunas, Colonel Aleksandrs Plensners and Lieutenant Colonel Viktors Deglavs, to Riga[7] with the authority to organize Latvian self-defence units in 'free corps fashion.' Plensners told the LOC that he had come to take over as commander-in-chief of the Latvian armed forces, and Deglavs would act as his chief of staff. The German army would support the restoration of Latvian sovereignty in return for a few divisions of Latvian volunteers.[8]

Hopes of national independence, however, were soon dampened. On 6 July the German army in Riga announced that Plensners and Deglavs were merely members of an advisory council of six Latvians whose leader, General Oskars Dankers, would arrive shortly from Berlin. The next day Stahlecker appointed the pro-German Latvian Lieutenant Colonel Voldemārs Veiss, who had just arrived from his German exile, as commander of all police units in Latvia.[9] On 8 July, when the Red Army had retreated beyond the Latvian border, Germans disarmed existing Latvian defence units and forbade Latvians to wear uniforms or carry arms. The German army halted any political–military centralization tendencies among Latvians by putting Veiss in charge of forming, under SS auspices, a 3,000-man auxiliary police (*Hilfsordnungspolizei*, after November 1941 renamed *Schutzmannschaft* or *Schuma* for short). Members were nonetheless issued the uniforms of the former Latvian national army. By 22 October 1941 some of these units were the first Latvians sent to the Russian front to serve at the discretion of the German army.[10]

Throughout July, according to secret SD (SS Security Service) reports, officials, Farmers Union followers, Pērkonkrustieši, student fraternities, and officers were jockeying for positions of power. Officers and civil servants of the former Ulmanis regime formed a noticeable circle of 'post hunters' eager to restore pre-Soviet conditions. Pērkonkrustieši, on the other hand, were fighting for a new fascist Latvia. They were divided between a majority advocating the old goal of a Latvia for Latvians and a minority seeking Latvia's salvation under Nazi Germany's new order. Pērkonkrusts leaders were 'very disappointed,' SD intelligence reported, to see the German civil administration destroy their hopes for a Slovakian type of autonomy for Latvia.[11] In the view of SD officials, they were suitable collaborators only 'if adroitly directed and supervised.'[12] On the Pērkonkrusts agenda was a final reckoning with Latvia's Jews.[13] Indeed, Pērkonkrusts activists were 'reliable and indispensable' only as 'exterminators' of Jews and Bolsheviks, according to Friedrich Trampedach, the civil administration's chief political adviser.[14]

The most notorious killer in Pērkonkrusts was Viktors Arājs, a thirty-one-year-old law graduate, and member of the prestigious nationalist student fraternity Lettonia, from the University of Latvia. With SD blessing he began on 1 July 1941 recruiting volunteers from eminent Latvian student fraternities and Pērkonkrusts. Their commando, which grew from five hundred men in July 1941 to several companies comprising some twelve hundred men by 1943, marked the origin of a systematic campaign of sadistic killing of Latvian Jews. Aided by denunciations from the population, various Latvian SD commandos and SD-authorized self-defence units composed of Aizsargi, students, and former police vied through the summer of 1941 to make Latvian towns *judenfrei* or assist German commandos in this task. Without willing Latvian help, Holocaust survivors emphasize, thirty thousand Latvian Jews could not have been killed in one month by the German Einsatzkommando of 160 men.[15] At the hands of Arājs's squad alone was the 'sadistic'[16] murder of 26,000 Latvian Jews, including three-quarters of the Jewish population of rural Latvia – fifteen thousand by the late summer of 1941. The total count of victims attributed to Arājs's men in Latvia and Belorussia is estimated to possibly be as high as 120,000.[17]

What motivated Latvians to become willing executors of the genocidal designs of their German 'liberators'? Their involvement cannot be attributed solely to Nazi instigations and Hitler's order.[18] The available evidence suggests the need for a scapegoat for the disappearance of thirty-five thousand Latvians during the one year of Soviet rule. Jews, barred from public service prior to 1940, were noted in conspicuous positions in the Soviet regime of 1940–1.[19] Although suffering disproportionate persecution under the Soviet occupation of Latvia in 1940–1, Latvian Jews were believed to have welcomed the Russians and served as guides and interpreters for the Russian officers who had carried out the mass arrests and deportations of sixteen thousand Latvians in the night of 13–14 June 1941.[20] (As late as 1948 Latvian exile groups in the West publicly blamed 'Jewish communists' for the crimes of the Soviet regime of 1940–1.[21]) The discovery in July 1941 of Soviet plans for even more arrests and deportations fuelled the desire for revenge.[22] Attacks against local Jews started as soon as the Soviets were withdrawing from the invading Germans,[23] 'before any SD had arrived and were able to tolerate, promote, or direct it.'[24]

Two incidents occurring in Riga on 1 July 1941, witnessed by Latvians whom Valdmanis later resettled in Newfoundland, are typical of the anti-Semitic mood greeting the Germans. The first incident concerns the Riga Film Studio group's broadcasting of the liberation of Latvia shortly before the entry of German forces. On the seized radio transmitter, group leader Alberts Jekste announced the 'end to Communists and Jewry.'[25] The second incident was witnessed by a pharmacist in a Riga hospital. One of her co-workers was a pre-1940 Latvian police officer who had found work as an orderly after the Soviet takeover and whose wife and children had been deported to Siberia on 14 June. 'I will kill every Jew in sight,' he announced as he appeared in the hospital in his former police uniform on 1 July 1941 to quit his job as an orderly.[26] By mid-August 1941 Latvian self-defence and police commandos containing a high percentage of university students and former police had done Germany's Nazi rulers the 'favour' of massacring half the total number of thirty-two thousand Latvian Jews killed in SD-organized operations.[27]

Structure and Goals of the Occupation Regime

Although by the fall of 1941 Germans had assumed total control of the killing operations, German rule in Latvia was anything but monolithic. The peculiarities of the German power structure and the confusion caused by changing objectives were major factors for collaborationists to consider. Sharing responsibility for administering occupation policy in Ostland – the administrative unit comprising the Baltic lands and Belorussia – but often competing, were four overlapping authorities. These were in particular the army, the SS, the Wirtschaftsstab Ost (Hermann Göring's economic agency of Germany's Four-Year Plan), and the Ostministerium with its three sometimes divisive levels of administration located in Riga: on top the Reichskommissariat Ostland (RKO), below it a Generalkommissariat (GK) for each of the three Baltic lands and Belorussia, and at the bottom district commissariats (Gebietskommissariate) – six for Latvia including one for Riga.

From the beginning, the commander of the German army stationed in Latvia, General Karl von Roques and his chief of staff Arno Kriegsheim were openly sympathetic to Latvian national aspirations.[28] They were very critical of the conduct and aims of Germany's war in the east and the Einsatzgruppen's massacres of Jews.[29] They were given a free hand by their superior, Quartermaster General Eduard Wagner, whose staff refused to implement many of Hitler's directives.[30] Even the position of the SS, whose influence expanded from security, intelligence, and racial questions to political, economic, and military spheres, appeared contradictory and ambivalent. SS General Stahlecker's Einsatzgruppe A engaged in systematic massacres, with the help of local security forces. The SD alerted higher-ups of any disloyal stirrings to Germany's official aims and carried out arrests. Nevertheless, in 1943 the senior SS commander, Friedrich Jeckeln, raised the possibility of national independence to entice Latvian cooperation in recruiting a Latvian SS legion.

An initial blueprint of 8 May 1941 envisaged full incorporation of the Baltic states into the Reich 'through germanization of racially suitable elements, colonization by Germanic peoples, and resettlement of undesirable elements.'[31] But not even the head of the so-called Ostministerium in Berlin (mandated to administer the occupied eastern territories), Baltic German Alfred Rosenberg, had a clear idea of what he should and would be able to accomplish. Born in 1893 in Reval, Rosenberg had studied in Riga and emigrated to Germany in November 1918. Rosenberg was the 'philosopher' of Nazism but a weak minister inept at organizing and retaining power.[32] He and his Baltic German adviser Werner Hasselblatt singled out the Latvian intelligentsia among the unassimilable elements. They proposed deporting this group to Russia.[33] On 25 June 1941, however, Rosenberg revised his instructions and stressed the need to win the sympathy of the population. To achieve this, he now favoured 'a treatment that suits the country and its population ... The conquered territory as a whole must not be viewed as a land of exploitation.' He talked of supporting the cultural autonomy and separatist aspirations of the Baltic peoples to 'turn them into a shield against Muscovy.'[34]

No wonder the chiefs of the three levels of the Ostland civil administration based in Riga could not agree on the expediency of accommodating Latvian aspirations for autonomy and self-government. Ostland targeted the Baltic peoples for privileged treatment in contrast to their

Slavic neighbours. Its head was Reichskommissar Hinrich Lohse, described as 'the very essence of a Nazi small-town big shot, a gross, vain, silly man, whose walrus-like appearance explained what he was at first sight.'[35] Suffering from delusions of personal grandeur, he intended to make his 'ducal' position hereditary.[36] As a rule, Lohse opposed challenges to his position and to the integrity of his Reichskommissariat; however, after late 1943 he became more tolerant of demands for Baltic autonomy.

The level below the RKO was the Generalkommissariat (GK). Head for the GK in Riga, covering the territory of Latvia, was Otto Heinrich Drechsler. A dentist and former mayor of Lübeck who had lost one leg in the First World War, Generalkommissar Drechsler was from the outset critical of the hypocrisy of German policy and more receptive to Latvian interests. For example, Drechsler endeavoured to make economic and political concessions to Latvians, and he favoured the appointment of Latvians to responsible posts.[37] Riga district commissar and major Hugo Wittrock, however, considered Riga a German city and vetoed the interference of any Latvian authority in its affairs.[38] No wonder, Rosenberg's Ostministerium became known in Berlin as 'Chaostministerium,' that is, 'Chaos East Ministry.'[39]

The administrative turmoil among the occupiers was worsened by the input of even more players. Wirtschaftsinspektion Nord with its Wirtschaftskommando Riga (subdivisions of Wirtschaftsstab Ost) were authorized to exploit economic resources for the benefit of the German war effort. In addition, the German Foreign Office representative in Riga, Adolf von Windecker, as well as the Abwehr manoeuvred in favour of Baltic autonomy.[40]

Independent SS actions affected all levels of the Ostland administration. But even within the SS hierarchy flourished more or less open rivalries and conflicts. The SS and Police Leader for Latvia SS Major General Dr Walther Schröder was known as a sociable official well informed about and benevolently inclined towards Latvian national aspirations. However, his superior, Higher SS and Police Leader Ostland (HSSPFO) Friedrich Jeckeln, had the reputation of a fanatical, stubborn, cruel, and extremely ambitious National Socialist. According to a contemporary Latvian officer, Jeckeln was greatly disliked, not only by the Latvians, but also by many German officials, including Drechsler and SS Chief Schröder.[41]

Riga was de jure and de facto under provisional German military administration from the arrival of German troops on 1 July 1941 until a German civil administration was extended over all of Latvia on 1 September 1941.[42] The Ostministerium was not even created until 17 July. On 25 July it was given control over Lithuania and Latvian territory south of Riga and the river Daugava (Dvina, also Düna). But by then the army was reluctant to relinquish its power. As late as mid-August 1941 the army firmly refused to allow Lohse, head of the Ostland civil administration, to enter Riga on the grounds that he had no permit. Lohse documented this action in a complaint to Rosenberg.[43]

This meant that for two months after German troops entered Riga on 1 July they lacked clear directives concerning the future of Latvia. They did not seem aware of any secret blueprints for the political future of the so-called Ostland. Hitler himself in his proclamation of war on Soviet Russia declared that he did not recognize the Soviet annexation of the Baltic states. Few, therefore, had reason to doubt the sincerity of Field Marshall Georg von Küchler's radio declaration on 1 July 1941 that the Baltic states had been liberated. In Riga the German army commander permitted the playing of the Latvian national anthem and the hoisting of the Latvian red-white-red flag until mid-August 1941. But, beyond that, he was not prepared to make political decisions without instructions from Berlin. Similarly, the commander of Einsatzgruppe A, arriving on the heels of the German army, complained about the absence of any comprehensive political directives. The very informative periodic SD intelligence reports highlight the political confusion on the German side.

Confusion also prevailed within Wirtschaftsinspektion Nord and Wirtschaftskommando Riga. They both followed the invading German army but had their assignments directly from Hermann Göring's Wirtschaftsstab Ost. Their so-called *Grüne Mappe*, a blueprint from Göring to restore food and oil production solely for the benefit of the German war effort, turned out to be unworkable in Latvia because it was designed chiefly for Russian conditions.[44] Peter Kleist, attached to the army as Rosenberg's representative, warned Berlin on 30 July 1941 that 'Latvians are watching with amazement this senseless political chaos on the German side. They believe that the Reich ... has the intention to restore Latvian independence.'[45]

Formation of a Latvian Self-Administration

Indeed, the jumble of overlapping jurisdictions and resulting rivalries within the German power structure drew ambitious and shrewd Latvian nationalists like Alfred Valdmanis into collaboration with pragmatic and sympathetic German officials. Despairing over the German army commanders' refusal to legalize a provisional government, the LOC turned to Valdmanis. On 6 July he accepted the challenge. On that day Plensners and Deglavs sought out the cooperation of Valdmanis in restoring order and economic life. But instead of being able to recruit Valdmanis for their mandate, they ended up authorizing his. Within one week Valdmanis managed to rally the sparring Latvian factions behind a new strategy – to defer the formation of an official government and concentrate on restoring the pre-1940 personnel and technical apparatus of the government departments.

On 8 July Valdmanis convened a meeting of sixty representatives of former departments in the Ministry of Finance. Announcing the news he had learned from Plensners and Deglavs, that a Latvian puppet government (officially called *Vertrauensrat*) formed in Berlin would arrive shortly in Riga, he appointed a Latvian self-administration of eight departments. Within the following week he added two more departments. He called their heads directors general. Most of these had been senior administrators under President Ulmanis. Although taking responsibility for everything, Valdmanis himself assumed no official position. This stance would enable him to become official head later on or, at the very least, to survive. He justified his actions with the argument that 'if a true national government arrives, it will find us having completed important and necessary preparations; if, on the other hand, the government turns out to be a fake ... it will find a ready and operating state apparatus of our own.'[46]

To elect a body representing the interests of Latvia *vis-à-vis* Germany, LOC on 11 July 1941 gathered an assembly of fifty-one representatives from government, political parties, the resurrected departments, veterans' organizations, student bodies, and such non-political bodies as the Lutheran church (represented by Archbishop Teodors Gruenbergs), the university, and the Association of Industrialists. According to a secret German summary of the proceedings, Valdmanis asked the representatives of all groups present to state their specific aims and to see if all could not present a united front behind one or several spokespersons for the Latvian nation.[47]

The meeting saw the election of a delegation of leaders from three dominant political forces at the time – Valdmanis, Pērkonkrusts leader Gustavs Celmiņš, and Deglavs. Valdmanis was elected leader of the delegation. Their top priority was to be recognized by Berlin and be invited to visit there. As a basis for negotiations with Hitler, according to one source,[48] the meeting adopted a Pērkonkrusts memorandum offering to free Latvia of Jews, Russians, and Poles. Although Berlin issued no invitation, Celmiņš, against the wishes of Valdmanis and Deglavs, decided to go there anyway. Meanwhile, a telegram Valdmanis, Celmiņš, and Plensners sent Hitler on 13 July 1941 declaring loyalty and assurances of cooperation appears never to have reached its destination.[49]

After Celmiņš's departure for Berlin and Deglavs's alleged suicide on 18 July 1941,[50] Valdmanis remained the sole spokesperson of the LOC-sponsored mandate. With this authority he continued to make appointments to reconstruct a functioning government apparatus. As a rule, he selected directors and civil servants with proven skills from the administration of independent Latvia and, at the same time, kept out Pērkonkrusts members. Not wanting to provoke the occupation powers, he assumed no official office himself but remained available in a private city apartment – not his home – for consultation by the directors general and the coordination of their work.[51]

Historian Agnis Balodis concluded (in 1991) that Valdmanis had formed a de facto government of Latvia in all but name. Without German consent, Valdmanis had successfully carried out the adjustments necessary for a changeover from the preceding Soviet administration. Not trusted in Berlin, Valdmanis's Latvian nationalist administration was set on a collision course with the SD and Rosenberg, who was planning to impose his own subservient self-administration of Latvian expatriates.[52]

Quest for 'Normalization'

In the spectrum of political groups vying for leadership under German occupation, Valdmanis promoted the quest of the Ulmanis followers for 'normalization,' that is, the continuity of the pre-1940 state of Latvia. In the Latvians' frantic efforts to restore the functioning of national institutions and form a de facto government, Valdmanis quickly emerged as the key Latvian figure in the eyes of official German observers.[53] Although he 'remained shrewdly in the background,' he is credited in Kleist's reports to Berlin with influencing the Latvian press, theatre, and economic policy 'decisively.' During a four-day absence of Kleist, Valdmanis reportedly 'tricked' (*überrumpelt*) the local German authorities into approving a performance in the National Opera of a Latvian concert sponsored by a Valdmanis-organized department for arts and public affairs. The National Opera in Riga was thus able to resume a program of Latvian concerts, plays, and operas, 'although the normal season had not yet begun.'[54]

Valdmanis's tactics also managed to present the Ostministerium with the *fait accompli* of a reopened university. Thanks to the quick action of the reconstituted departments of finance and state control, the university could recruit additional faculty and prepare a program of courses within two to three weeks. To Latvian morale the functioning opera and the university were important symbols of a normalized cultural life. The Ostministerium's original plans had destined both for replacement by German institutions.[55]

Did Valdmanis have a secret formula for his success? Although initially seeking the cooperation of all political factions and groups, including leading Saeima politicians and pērkonkrustieši, he soon acted 'completely independently and tried to push aside Colonel Kreišmanis,' a German memorandum revealed.[56] This is confirmed by Pērkonkrusts leader Celmiņš, who disclosed in 1944 that in early July 1941 Valdmanis had sought his cooperation. After leaving Riga in mid-July 1941, however, Celmiņš was excluded from power by Valdmanis, who 'entered various connections that brought him very far ahead.'[57] The latter seems to have owed much of his leverage over competing Latvian factions to the authority he derived from his German contacts and their need to rely on Latvian administrators. The head of Wehrwirtschaftskommando Nord sent for Valdmanis as early as 8 July 1941, ostensibly in order to claim the modern finance ministry building for his Wirtschaftsstab, and General von Roques asked for a meeting with Valdmanis the day he arrived in Riga on 10 July.[58]

Apart from the usefulness of his economic expertise, Valdmanis possessed credentials as a more trustworthy collaborator in the eyes of the German army than other prominent Latvians; namely, he had influential German acquaintances from prewar days. One was Adolf Leckzyck, former trade attaché of the German legation in Riga. Shortly after the German attack on the Soviet Union, Leckzyck applied in vain for an assignment to RK Ostland in Riga to help 'the coming man in Latvia ... Alfred Waldmann' take over. But Leckzyck nevertheless managed to arrive in Riga with the German army, seconded to the German Supreme Commander Ostland as economic adviser.[59] Plensners and Deglavs sent Valdmanis on 7 July written authorization to undertake measures to address economic problems. Valdmanis was also endorsed by men like Viktors Arājs for whom, as one contemporary analyst put it, 'many doors stood open.'[60] However, although Valdmanis is alleged to have made anti-Semitic statements in 1941,[61] no available evidence links him to Arājs's massacres or any other murder of Latvian Jews.[62]

An anonymous but well-informed German source – possibly Leckzyck – suggested in 1941 that Valdmanis had been preselected in Berlin as the Germans' designated director of economic affairs in Latvia. Leckzyck had advised Rosenberg's office as early as 25 June 1941 that Valdmanis was Germany's best choice because he enjoyed enormous influence among Latvians, whereas Latvians who had moved to Germany in 1940 would be unacceptable as leaders in a liberated Latvia. Valdmanis's stature received additional support from information transmitted by his former secretary Anna Kunetz that he had allegedly organized a secret anti-Soviet resistance movement and had committed himself to integrate Latvia into the Reich's 'Prussian family of peoples.'[63]

German government records of 1941 refer to Valdmanis as an employee of the Wirtschaftsinspektion Nord.[64] Arājs had allegedly initiated the contact between Valdmanis and Colonel Nagel, commanding officer of Wehrwirtschaftskommando Nord. Valdmanis's mandate was to assist in the restoration of economic life by the German army, which expected to be headquartered in Riga for a while. To this end, the German army command authorized all of Valdmanis's departmental appointments, enabling him to prevail over his opponents in the LOC.[65]

'Valdmanis acquired the confidence of the highest military authority, General von Roques, and cultivated this contact for some time,' reported the above-mentioned anonymous 1941 source.[66] In fact, from the outset, Valdmanis appears to have been the German military administration's trusted Latvian expert in economic matters, while colonels Plensners and Deglavs were the trusted advisers in political–military matters, and Professor W. Klumberg (director of the former Herder Institute in Riga) in cultural matters. Plensners, Deglavs, and Klumberg had arrived in Riga with the German army. According to Kleist, it was on the advice of Klumberg that von Roques decided to cooperate with the self-administration appointed by Valdmanis.[67]

Whatever his real motives or later assertions, during July 1941 Valdmanis furnished sufficient proof to the occupying powers that he was a valuable collaborator. A summary of his 11 July telegram to 'the Führer of Grossdeutschland and of all indogermanic peoples' was published in the Riga newspaper *Tēvija* (Fatherland) of 16 July 1941. It expressed the Latvians' hope 'to be able to participate in the war for the liberation of Europe and put the fate of the Latvian people in the hands of Adolf Hitler. We are waiting in trust and confidence.'

Two articles Valdmanis wrote for *Tēvija* of 16 and 26 July castigated Latvians for having applauded the prewar exodus of Latvia's Germans and for having opened the country to the 'red monster' without a fight, even though Latvia's troops were itching to face the Russians. 'We wanted to die standing upright and capitulated nonetheless without a shot – that was even more bitter.' Now, the only option left for Latvians was coexistence with the German people under Nazi Germany's new order: 'Another way we do not have, and after so many errors we can say with confidence but also with fervour – another way we no longer desire and shall also never again desire.'[68]

In July 1941, when a German final victory seemed all but certain and Nazi Germany's ultimate plans for Latvia were unclear, such submissiveness appeared both honest and tactically expedient. It was necessary in order to retain German army support for Valdmanis's administration and to ward off ongoing schemes by Rosenberg and the SS to impose on the Latvian departments a subservient Vertrauensrat or Generalrat (as Rosenberg named it in early July 1941[69]). Rosenberg had already selected General Oskars Dankers as the leader of such a body. Arriving in Riga on 18 July 1941, this retired Latvian general had left for Germany with the exodus in June 1940, where he had claimed to be a German-born repatriate. (Despite applying for German citizenship there, he had not received it.)[70]

Some other parts of the German power structure were also not charmed by Valdmanis. An SD report warned of the unwelcome implications of the joint message of loyalty from Valdmanis, Celmiņš, and Plensners and their desire to be received in Berlin. Such a united Latvian national front among hitherto disparate factions might very soon produce 'undesirable aims.'[71] Similar alarming reports from Kleist in Riga reveal that Valdmanis was, despite his protestations of loyalty to Hitler, playing a shrewd double game and that Rosenberg's Ostministerium – not permitted to extend its civil administration to Riga until 1 September 1941 – was unable to see eye-to-eye with the German military on the issue of Latvian self-government. Not only had 'Valdmanis appointed a circle of Latvians in the form of a complete cabinet,' complained Kleist to Berlin on 30 July 1941, without any German investigation of their background. On top of that, Valdmanis had audaciously told Kleist that he considered Dankers and his Vertrauensrat as 'people to whom one may give money but not the hand, for they were bought by Germany.'[72]

In the eyes of the SD, Valdmanis and his team were serving as front men for the 'Ulmanis clique.'[73] As early as 14 July, an SD reporter had noted angrily that in light of the 'resurrection' of the 'Ulmanis clique' the planned Vertrauensrat had become obsolete.[74] By 19 August 1941 the SD foresaw great difficulties for the policies Rosenberg and his administration were planning to introduce shortly in Latvia. The economic exploitation and germanization of Latvians would be as much resisted as the imposition of the Latvian Vertrauensrat appointed in Berlin.[75] On 22 August Kleist reported that Alfred Valdmanis, though controlling economic policy as well as the press and the theatre, was cleverly hiding in the background. Unfavourable evidence against Valdmanis was accumulating to the point, Kleist warned, where his removal from Latvia must be considered. 'If he is not removed, it will be impossible for me to shape Latvia's political development.'[76]

From Directorate General to *Landeseigene Verwaltung*

Valdmanis had clearly become *persona non grata* for the Ostministerium already by the time its jurisdiction was extended over all of Latvia (September 1941). Yet instead of being removed, as Kleist had demanded, he survived and prevailed over his opponents. The administrative changes he had engineered in July 1941 could not be undone without inviting chaos. Through 1942 Valdmanis helped shape Latvia's political development in his various capacities as official collaborationist, director general of justice, and unofficial guardian of the Latvian national interest, a mandate (received at the 11 July assembly) enabling him to develop secret networks of contacts among Latvians and ultimately openly challenge German occupation policy.

During late August and September 1941, when the German army had to relinquish most of its political authority in Latvia to Rosenberg's civil regime, Valdmanis again benefited from the lack of clear German policies and the poor coordination among German agencies in Riga. While Rosenberg was trying to install his Vertrauensrat in Latvia, Lohse's chief political adviser Trampedach urged in a report of 16 August:

> Any central Latvian leadership arising in any form from the Latvian urban intelligentsia must be ousted. There is no need for a collective body or individual to represent the entire Latvian people at the Generalkommissariat level. German rule interacts with the regionally divided local population only through the Gebietskommissar. Above the district chiefs there are no Latvian agencies. The toleration of ministries in Kaunas and directories general in Riga by the supreme commander of the occupation army is an unforgivable mistake ... There should be no [Latvian] agency communicating with the Generalkommissariat, and the highest court in the General-

> kommissariat should be occupied by German judges. Finally, there should be no central leadership of the Latvian defence force and other Latvian associations ... Under no circumstances should the university be permitted to reopen.

Lohse adorned the advice with marginal concurring comments like '*richtig,*' '*sehr richtig,*' and '*ausgezeichnet*' and ordered it brought to the attention of Rosenberg and the Generalkommissare.[77] 'Clear guidelines and plans apparently do not exist,' warned SD reports of 15 and 19 August 1941 with regard to Lohse's newly established Reichskommissariat Ostland.[78]

According to SD intelligence on 15 August, Kleist was to ensure that the Latvian individuals handpicked by Rosenberg actually took over as Vertrauensrat. They were apparently biding their time in Riga with no influence on the ongoing political power game. Part of the problem was Hitler's refusal until September 1941 to sanction the existence of national self-administrations. Thus, the directors general, despite their de facto recognition by the army, as well as the Vertrauensrat preselected in Berlin, had no legal existence.[79] To ease the Generalkommissariat's impending takeover in Riga, Kleist negotiated at length with von Roques. He convinced von Roques on 21 August to appoint General Dankers to the key position of director general of the Interior, where he would be responsible for all personnel matters. Kleist assumed this would bring Dankers's associates into the directorate and remove undesirable Valdmanis appointments.[80]

This manoeuvre had, however, an unanticipated outcome. In an open letter to the German authorities, Valdmanis refused to recognize the appointment of Dankers. He also asked his directors general to ignore the announcement that Colonel Freimanis, Colonel Veiss, Dr Sanders, and Evalds Andersons would take over the directorates of trade and industry, police and armed forces, education and culture, and finance and comptroller respectively. When Dankers published his dismissal of Valdmanis-appointed comptroller Pēteris Vanags and his replacement by A. Melliņš (like Andersons a leading Pērkonkrusts member) in the press, Vanags, on instructions from Valdmanis, had Latvian guards posted at the doors to his office building and kept Melliņš from entering. Since Dankers did not want to call in German police, his associates had to set up office in the building of the Latvian Association and content themselves with positions as deputy directors in Dankers's department. The stand-off between the two competing directorates general lasted for more than six weeks while Drechsler, Generalkommissar for Latvia, was in a quandary.[81]

The tug-of-war was eventually ended by Egon Bönner, chief of the GK's political department and deputy Generalkommissar. Bönner summoned Dankers on 2 October 1941 to question the need for four deputy directors in the latter's department. Dankers denied responsibility for these appointments and declared that Rosenberg had instructed him to act as the trusted representative (*Vertrauensmann*) of the Latvian people and ensure a smooth transfer from the Latvian to the German administration. Sanders, Freimanis, and Andersons had been forced on him as deputy directors by Kleist and the SD against his will, Dankers complained, and he would have preferred better men for this office. Andersons and Melliņš were unacceptable to the German administration, Bönner declared, and Dankers had no right to dismiss Vanags without the authority of the Generalkommissar.[82] Bönner resolved the stand-off by refusing appointments to Dankers's associates.

Alfred Valdmanis could not have found a more sympathetic German official. In the German civil administration of Latvia, Bönner was most critical of German policies and tactics. This former mayor of the German city of Essen believed that German rule should be exercised in a realistic and cooperative spirit, with Latvians assuming as much responsibility for the administration of their country as possible.[83] He therefore opposed Wittrock's stubborn efforts to force a German municipal administration on Riga. Sympathetic to the Latvian national cause, Bönner lobbied to allow Latvians as much freedom as possible to celebrate their Independence Day on 18 November 1942.[84] Until Bönner's removal from Riga, at the end of 1942, Valdmanis owed his survival and continued political prominence largely to Bönner, who was in turn backed by Drechsler.[85]

Having prevailed over Dankers in the autumn of 1941, Valdmanis then tried to create a united Latvian front by having Dankers dissociate himself from his Berlin appointees and join Valdmanis's team. Within his own directorate, however, Dankers had to accept a department of internal security headed by Colonel Veiss, an action probably instigated by SS chief Schröder. (The Latvian Veiss had been chief of the Auxiliary Police and in charge of organizing the first Latvian military units for service at the Russian front.) General Dankers did agree to work with Valdmanis's team provided he become the official head of the directors general and that Drechsler approve of the changes. According to Zemgals, Valdmanis's group accepted Dankers's terms on condition that the new head would be the one to present to the Generalkommissariat the decisions and proposals arrived at by majority vote of the modified directorate general.[86]

To counter the influence of Dankers and Veiss, the directors general invited Valdmanis to come on board as well. On 12 November 1941 he assumed the position of director general of justice or, more correctly, legal administration.[87] Prior to that he had served as chairman of the Latvian Civil Court and, for two months, as acting chief public prosecutor in the Latvian Senate (the country's highest court) from 2 September 1941 until that body was dissolved on 1 November 1941.[88] Drechsler endorsed the reorganization of the Latvian self-administration, but refused to officially recognize it as a collegial body. Of the directors general he would consider only Dankers as the spokesman of the Latvian people. Dankers thus bestowed legitimacy upon Valdmanis's nationalist bloc and, as spokesman of the directors general, was doing their bidding with the occupation regime.

Shortly after Valdmanis's appointment as a director general, rumours spread that an impending decree from Berlin would restrict the German civil administration to a mere supervisory agency and restore most government functions to Latvians. These rumours galvanized Latvian politics and divided the camp of Ulmanis sympathizers and members of his Farmers Union. While playing into the hand of the faction around Valdmanis and former President Kviesis, who both viewed collaboration as a sine qua non for any defence of Latvian interests, it caused Ulmanis associates like Ādolfs Klīve, former president of the Bank of Latvia, to distance themselves from this pro-German group. The realization in intelligentsia circles that a restoration of Latvia's independence was not within foreseeable reach deepened the division, especially following the announcement that the traditional celebrations on 18 November, the anniversary of Latvia's independence, were to be prohibited.[89]

Drechsler's de facto recognition of the directors general was not legalized in Berlin until 19 March 1942. The directors general officially assumed their offices, now collectively named *landeseigene Verwaltung* – self-administration – on 7 May. The delays reflected the serious differences within the Ostministerium over the composition of self-administrations and their responsibilities in the four Ostland general commissariats. Special complications were caused by Latvia where, in contrast with Lithuania and Estonia, no obvious pro-German group could be identified. A particularly contentious issue among Drechsler, Lohse, and the SD was the personality of Alfred Valdmanis and the role he should play.

The pro-Latvian attitude of Drechsler is confirmed by Latvian contemporaries[90] and documented in a number of memoranda Drechsler sent to his superiors. From the outset he believed that the occupation regime could only benefit from allowing Latvians to administer their own affairs and reducing the role of the German civil administration to a mere controlling function. 'It was unthinkable for me,' Drechsler wrote Rosenberg in 1942, 'to fill the key posts of the self-administration with mere "straw puppets."' Such straw puppets, apart from being unsuitable for effective work, he believed, would have been despised by the local population.[91]

Drechsler encouraged his Latvian directors general to be open with him and assured them of equally honest responses on his part. He viewed the use and advocacy of indiscriminate force by victory-intoxicated Germans as a bad omen. Aware that he was unable to change the course of events – Drechsler considered himself only a 'marionette [*Hampelmann*] with little real power' – he saw no point in sacrificing himself with futile resistance. By staying at his post, he believed, he might at least be able to protect like-minded colleagues and avert a worse evil. Drechsler shared Bönner's view that much was to be gained by trying to cooperate with Latvians and backed Bönner's handling of the Valdmanis–Dankers dispute.[92]

In March 1942 Drechsler had gone even further. Around March–April 1942, Valdmanis recalled in 1947, Drechsler authorized Bönner to offer Valdmanis the position of first director general. Valdmanis declined, but Bönner asked him to reconsider, reminding him of the recognition and honour implicit in this promotion. Since he could be more open with Bönner, Valdmanis allegedly replied that he would consider it a disgrace rather than an honour to play the first fiddle in the self-administration when he knew that in reality a foreign occupation power was in charge. 'I believe the time will come when Latvia will need men like you' was Bönner's response as remembered by Valdmanis, and he warned Valdmanis to beware of the SD, which was keeping a close watch on him.[93]

An SD report of 24 April 1942, however, gives a slightly different account of this incident. It noted that the day after the decree legalizing Latvia's self-administration was published (19 March 1942), all the directors general except General Dankers submitted their resignations. The resignations were instigated by Valdmanis in the expectation of further administrative concessions, or even the proclamation of a Latvian national government.[94] Drechsler asked the directors to remain in office, but offered Dankers's position to Valdmanis. The latter, with some reservations, accepted. But the SD pressured Drechsler to withdraw the offer at once, and Valdmanis was left with his justice portfolio.[95]

Drechsler wrote Lohse on 25 March 1942 that he had decided to leave Dankers in his previous position, although in his opinion Dankers lacked the intellectual and personal capabilities required for this office. 'Dankers shows little initiative, little judgment of his own, and little understanding of administrative matters.' Valdmanis would be fully up to the challenges of the position and no serious political objections, Drechsler believed, could be raised against him. 'But in order to completely clear the charges against him, most of which have already been cleared up, I consider it opportune to leave him in his previous post for further observation,' Drechsler concluded.[96]

The strongest and most serious opposition to Drechsler's handling of the Valdmanis case came from the SD, for whom Valdmanis was already too influential as director general of justice. As director general of the interior, with his position equivalent to that of prime minister, he would be even stronger, the SD warned. At the Generalkommissariat meeting on 20 March 1942, the commander of the security police Rudolf Lange objected not only to a promotion of Valdmanis to director general of the interior, but also to his continued presence in the self-administration as such. The SD chief argued that Valdmanis's record while director general of justice, as well as at the time of Latvian independence, had not furnished any proof that he was honestly supporting the policies of the Reich. More specifically, Valdmanis did not participate in any of the causes whereby the Latvian population had manifested its pro-German attitude, such as the struggle against the Red Army, the removal of the Jews, recruitment for the Reichsarbeitsdienst (RAD), collection of winter clothing for the front, volunteering for Schutzmannschaften, and promoting Latvian appreciation of National Socialism and the German role in the restructuring of Europe.

Kleist, now chief of the Ostministerium's Ostland Department, raised similar concerns. Always highly critical of Valdmanis's appointment as director general in November 1941, Kleist demanded that Valdmanis be replaced. Valdmanis had acquired his position through 'shrewd tactics,' Kleist charged. Aided and abetted by a Generalkommissar who refused to receive Dankers, Valdmanis had managed to outmanoeuvre the associates of Dankers and 'dump' them as directors general, including the chief of the Latvian police Veiss.

As proof that Valdmanis was an unreliable character with a dubious record, Kleist drew attention to the following incidents: Valdmanis's attempt as minister of finance to prevent the transfer of part of the assets of the Baltic Germans resettled in 1939–40; his futile endeavour in 1940 to be resettled to Germany; his negative attitude towards Latvian recruitment drives for Schutzmannschaften and the RAD; his suspicious interest in Latvian youth organizations; and his ostentatious display to leading personalities of scars allegedly acquired as a result of Bolshevik torture but in reality stemming from a medical operation.[97]

To deprive Valdmanis of his German army backing in Riga, Kleist tried repeatedly to engineer Leckzyck's dismissal as adviser to the army's chief commander in Ostland. Kleist's allies in the SD, Ostministerium, and Foreign Office depicted Leckzyck as a notorious rumour-monger with a Social Democratic past. He was the main source for the propagation of Valdmanis's pro-German image, they charged, when in reality the young finance minister had distinguished himself as 'one of the most prominent racketeers' willingly executing Ulmanis's policy of de-germanizing Latvia. It is typical of the rifts in the German occupation regime that despite such serious accusations, Kleist and his allies were unable to dislodge Leckzyck from his post in Riga until the end of 1943.[98]

Critical reports about Valdmanis came even from district commissars like Hermann Hansen in Valmiera (Wolmar) who had repeatedly heard that Valdmanis's political past was unacceptable. Particularly sharp attacks were aimed against several directors general by Valmiera's district administrator Winter. He rejected the directors general and stated firmly that 'the most successful work can be accomplished only in cooperation with us. Personnel policy matters should be entirely in the hands of the Generalkommissar,' reported Hansen.[99]

At the level of the Reichskommissariat Ostland, the de facto recognition of a Latvian self-administration was viewed as an unfortunate turn of events. Latvia, unlike Slovakia, was historically destined for germanization, insisted Trampedach. He wanted this objective to be taken into account in the creation of a local administration and argued as follows: Unlike the rural population, the political leaders of independent Latvia, especially under Ulmanis, were so hostile to everything German that they preferred to throw themselves into the arms of Bolshevism instead of seeking Germany's support. Anti-germanism was still prevalent among members of the Latvian civil service and intellectual professions, despite the shock effect of Bolshevism. To allow this group to regain influence over the country through a virtually independent Latvian administration would amount to 'organizing your opponent yourself.'

Trampedach saw this as a particular dilemma for Latvia, where truly pro-German administrators could not be found. There, directors general like Valdmanis spared no effort to strengthen Latvian unity and national consciousness in order to make it a factor shaping the future, regardless of how the war would end. Trampedach concluded from this that the Latvian leadership and administration ought to be decentralized and any Latvian self-government confined to the district level. Latvians should be treated well economically and personally, and matters of insignificance could be left to a Latvian administration. But important affairs should be administered by Germans directly and not left to Latvian directors general.[100]

Nonetheless, the only change in the Latvian self-administration the Reichskommissariat was able to effect was a reduction in the number of directors general from nine to six, ostensibly to simplify the administration. Credit for this idea was claimed by the head of Lohse's central department, Wilhelm Burmeister, who, contrary to Trampedach's premises, was in favour of cultural autonomy for the Baltic peoples. Burmeister recommended the reappointment of Valdmanis as one of the six directors general because Valdmanis enjoyed the confidence of Latvians and accepted Latvia's attachment to Germany as an unalterable fact. However, it was prudent not to entrust Valdmanis with the office of first director general for the time being because there would be 'danger in conceding too much influence to Valdmanis. Such a man may not have an appropriate counterpart on the German side and would try to play out the different German authorities (civil administration, army, police) against each other.'[101]

In the end, the Ostministerium ignored the objections of Trampedach and the SD. The decree of March 1942 legalized the existence of the so-called landeseigene Verwaltung, defined its place in the administrative hierarchy, and thereby simply confirmed the ambiguous status quo. German rule, Rosenberg decreed, 'is principally confined to control [*Aufsichtsverwaltung*] in the technical sense, while the actual administrative work is left to the self-administration.' German administrators were to interfere only when immediate German interests were at stake. 'The native population has proven its pro-German attitude and desire to cooperate in so many ways from the beginning of the occupation, that the granting of far-reaching self-administration is in order,' the decree stated. The directors general, however, were not to be considered a collegial body – the term 'directorate general' was to be avoided – but individually responsible to the Generalkommissar. They had no head or presidium, but for the purpose of facilitating German control the director general of the interior would have a somewhat elevated position.[102]

On 25 April 1942 Rosenberg approved the list of directors general submitted by the Reichskommissariat Ostland and originally drawn up by the Generalkommissariat. He endorsed Drechsler's criteria for the selection – professional qualifications, political reliability, and respect among the Latvian population – so that they would 'not be considered paid agents of the Reich.' Drechsler had justified his selection with the argument that he knew these men because he had worked with them before and that his effort to find men who had not been in public life before had failed. Valdmanis, Drechsler's memorandum observed, 'had proven himself very well' in his previous position as director general of justice.

Rosenberg, however, singled out the case of Valdmanis as problematic in view of Kleist's report and asked that Kleist's charges be re-examined. 'As improbable as the Valdmanis display of alleged Bolshevik torture scars would seem in view of the presumed intelligence of Valdmanis,' Rosenberg noted, 'his behaviour cannot be entirely discounted.' Whether Valdmanis ought to be seen as the driving force behind attempts by the Ulmanis circle to bring about a nationalist consolidation of Riga with the rural population, Rosenberg was unable to judge. However, Valdmanis would under no circumstances be allowed to assume any functions other than head of the Directorate General of Justice. Should complications arise instigated by Valdmanis, Rosenberg warned, the Generalkommissar in Riga must take the responsibility.[103]

Director General of Justice

According to his record of employment issued by the Directorate General of Justice on 17 May 1944, Valdmanis was head of that department from 16 November 1941 to 16 April 1943. The German name of his portfolio translates as civil justice or court administration (*Gerichtswesen*). In this capacity his responsibility was confined to the organization and management of Latvian courts and their application of Latvian law.[104] By the end of August 1941 Latvians had restored most of their judicial institutions from the time of independence, including the Senate as the highest court of the land. But these were not officially recognized until a 15 March 1942 decree confirmed the applicability of Latvian law for all Latvian agencies of justice.[105]

Although the German authorities did not revoke the validity of Latvian law and its enforcement agencies, their jurisdiction was in danger of progressive erosion. Latvian institutions had no right of legislation, no authority over Germans and Jews, and no authority over German courts. Established on 6 October 1941 and staffed by German judges and lawyers, the so-called German courts (including a High Court) had jurisdiction in criminal matters and civil actions affecting Germans in Latvia. In addition, they could take on any legal matter the Reichskommissariat Ostland might withdraw from Latvian courts. A decree of 15 March 1942 abolished the Senate and provided that (1) the local legal authorities base their activity on the laws valid on 17 June 1940 and on the decrees issued since the arrival of the German army, (2) the jurisdiction of local courts be restricted by the authority assigned to the German judiciary in accordance with the decree of 19 December 1941 (concerning the Introduction and Organization of German Judiciary in the Occupied Eastern Territories), (3) the Generalkommissar confirm the judges, attorneys, magistrates, heads of penitentiaries, notaries, barristers, and solicitors proposed by the director general of justice, and (4) Jews, *Mischlinge* (people of mixed race), spouses of Jews, relatives of Jews, and Freemasons be excluded from any function in the administration of justice. In addition, Latvian jurisdiction was restricted by German Courts Martial and special German non-military courts meting out instant justice for all sorts of transgressions.[106]

When Valdmanis took over the Directorate General of Justice, located in the former Ministry of Justice, it consisted of only a small office for civil proceedings. Since the Germans set up their own higher and lower courts, they initially left to Latvians only divorce cases. Then they gave the Latvians a few categories of civil cases, and in 1943 virtually all affairs of ordinary justice. Valdmanis was not shy in claiming credit for the expansion of the jurisdiction of his office and the establishment of an independent Directorate of Justice. He considered himself 'overwhelmingly more capable and intelligent' than the rarely seen German magistrate ordered to supervise the activities in his directorate. His was the only department that tried to avoid posting German or bilingual signs.

For more than one reason, the Directorate General of Justice was ideally suited as an instrument of resistance against German occupation policy. In selecting his departmental personnel – chairman of the bar, president of the notaries public, presiding judges, and government attorneys – Valdmanis took care to ensure they were reliable as well as patriotic. (Only the president of the Supreme Court of Jelgava proved a disappointment, for he did not mind taking orders from District Commissar Walther von Medem.) The privilege of inspection trips throughout the country to attend regional court sessions and supervise the administration of Latvian law afforded Valdmanis additional opportunities to meet people from all walks of life, spread his views, and build networks of contacts.[107]

During his stint as a director general, Valdmanis engaged not only in regular official communications with the Generalkommissar, as defined by the terms of his office. He was also deeply involved in conspiratorial activities fuelled by his desire for the restoration of national autonomy. For example, Valdmanis helped build and joined patriotic networks of teachers, officers, and youth. No document has yet surfaced indicating his unconditional agreement with any of the occupation regime's objectives, policies, or administrative structures. On the contrary, from the beginning virtually all his officially documented dealings with the Generalkommissariat show that he habitually raised issues transcending the authority of his department, boldly addressed sensitive political matters, and was prepared to represent concerns of the entire body of directors general with frankness.

Most revealing in this respect is an unsigned fifteen-page 'Memorandum on Acute Questions in Latvia' filed among the papers of his directorate general. Dated November 1941, it was presented to the Generalkommissar on behalf of the directors of all the departments of the self-administration. Judging by its style and content, the author was almost certainly Valdmanis. The memorandum shows an impressive grasp of Latvia's economic and financial situation and highlights the problems of internal administration, integration into the Ostland region, reprivatization, financial matters, cultural questions, and pensions. It is quite critical of the German administration's refusal to tackle any of the pressing problems in these areas. Expecting a standard of living comparable to that of Denmark (where the allowable wartime butter consumption exceeded Germany's) and a cultural life befitting one of the oldest North European cultures, the memo warned that apathy, failure, fear, and unrest were rapidly increasing among the Latvian people.[108]

Within his own directorate Valdmanis himself not only defied the German decree prescribing the Nazi salute (raised arm) for everyone in Latvia. According to the testimony of contemporaries, he also requested that his subordinates refrain from adopting the salute and from dealing with members of the German police and SD.[109] When the SD demanded an investigation of this matter, Bönner, who chaired the inquiry, refused to force the issue by concluding that Latvians could not be compelled to copy the German salute.[110]

Zemgals relates one particular incident that occurred in Jelgava (Mitau). While visiting a session of the High Court, Valdmanis allegedly openly criticized the Nazi salute and urged adherence to the Latvian tradition of lifting one's hat or salute by standing still at attention. He also questioned the validity of German orders and decrees in the realm of civil law where Latvian legal traditions were supposed to prevail. This particular incident, according to Zemgals, triggered a complaint from the German district commissar to Rosenberg.[111]

Petty obstructionism was among Valdmanis's routine tactics. For instance, he directed Latvian judges not to visit SD offices but have the SD come to them.[112] In February 1942 the Generalkommissariat demanded a review of youth legislation passed in prewar Latvia. Valdmanis first sent his detailed reply in Latvian – although German was the prescribed language of communication between Latvian and German administrative agencies – and forwarded a German translation only four weeks later in response to a request from Drechsler's office.[113]

How shrewdly Valdmanis proceeded in expanding the authority of his department is indicated in the documented request by the Directorate General of Justice in February 1943 for permission to appoint the chairpersons of the municipal *Waisengerichte*, that is, the courts dealing with orphans and their guardianship. Previously Valdmanis's department had had only the right to *confirm* the appointment of chairpersons appointed to these orphans' courts by the municipal government. In the case of Riga, the right to appoint was exercised by the bureaucracy of District Commissar Wittrock, who considered it a valuable instrument of germanization. To make his claim to this right palatable to the order-loving German authorities, Valdmanis argued that the current arrangement was an anomaly from an administrative, legal, and economic point of view. Integration into the Latvian court administration would save municipal expenditures and rationalize overall activity.[114]

The fate of defunct Latvian government departments was also of concern to Valdmanis. On 19 November 1942 he informed the German director of the Latvian State Archives that the Council of the Directors General had authorized him to clarify the state of affairs of those departments not reactivated after 1 July 1941, that is, the ministries of the Exterior, War, and Public Affairs. To that end he requested permission for his representative, retired General Rūdolfs Bangerskis, to examine the relevant records in the archive. This request violated two official prohibitions – reference to the directors general as a collegial body with the right to make collective decisions, and perusal by Latvians of Latvian government records in the state archives. After considering the matter for almost six weeks, the Generalkommissariat decided to permit specifically requested records to be accessed in Bönner's office.[115]

A potentially serious provocation was Valdmanis's open obstruction of German decrees. In one instance he allegedly instructed Latvian courts not to enforce a strict German order treating the requisitioning of food beyond allowable quotas as a criminal offence. Throughout 1942 food shortages were a cause of strong discontent among Latvians. Even such basic items as potatoes and cabbage were in short supply.[116] The resentment was exacerbated by much higher food allowances for resident German nationals. In view also of the close social links between the urban and rural segments of the population, Latvian courts considered the German order unjust and applicable only to commercially operating food speculators.[117] The matter was referred to the Reichskommissariat Ostland, where top officials including Burmeister sympathized with the plight of Latvians and advised ignoring Valdmanis's obstructions.[118]

SD records confirm the responsibility of Valdmanis for the determination with which Latvian legal circles maintained the validity of Latvian legal norms and resisted the introduction of German law. By shrewdly exploiting his privileged position in the self-administration, Valdmanis had allegedly managed to win over 'the widest circles' of the legal profession for his political objectives. 'The oral and written guidelines he issued to Latvian courts were of an explicitly nationalist Latvian character,' reported an SD analyst, 'and resulted in a negative attitude of the civil servants and clerks employed in the administration of justice towards legal innovations introduced by Germans.'[119]

German sources acknowledge that Valdmanis used to have the final say on Latvian appointments, both within his directorate and to other top Latvian offices. At the end of February 1942 that 'influence and predominance of Valdmanis in personnel matters was broken for the first time,' SD intelligence gloated: Drechsler had appointed former Pērkonkrusts member Adolfs Šilde over Valdmanis's objections to manage Volkshilfe (People's Help), a powerful charitable organization with branches all over Latvia supporting Latvians suffering war-related losses and injuries.[120] In early December 1942 Valdmanis failed again, this time in his endeavours to have Colonel Plensners fill the vacant post of director general of culture and public affairs. Plensners was considered too anti-German by some officials in the Generalkommissariat, despite the assurances of Valdmanis to the contrary.[121]

Numerous documents in the records of the occupation regime point to approval from fellow directors general for Valdmanis's tactic of collaboration. The extent of their trust in his determination to defend Latvian national interests is manifested in their unanimous resolution in late 1942 to transfer to him all interdepartmental matters transcending the jurisdiction of the directors general. Drechsler was forced to void this resolution because it violated the decree of 7 March 1942 legalizing the directorates general and appointing the director general of the interior to be their spokesman *vis-à-vis* the Generalkommissar. Although Drechsler believed that Latvian affairs should be administered as much as possible by Latvians, he could not allow the directors general to elevate Valdmanis to a *primus inter pares* and vest him with the rights of a government head.[122]

In June 1942 a visiting delegation of pro-German Dutch bankers, businesspeople, and administrators under Dutch fascist leader Rost van Tonningen saw Valdmanis's role in Latvia's self-administration in an unrefracted light. Examining ways the Netherlands might cooperate in the reconstruction of the occupied eastern territories, they were the first foreign visitors the Latvian directors general were asked to host. The impressions of the Dutch, summarized in four points in a confidential political report, minced no words. The visitors noted, first, a uniform chauvinist national consciousness permeated all layers of the Latvian population; second, all Latvians stood in a clear front against *Deutschtum* (Germanism) and differed only in the degree to which they camouflaged their views *vis-à-vis* the Germans; third, in Latvia more than elsewhere in Ostland, the Generalkommissariat had largely lost control to the Latvian administration; and finally, the constant expansion and strengthening of the self-administration indicated that it was systematically preparing for an impending confrontation with the German leadership. The report stressed that germanization could be carried out only with the most brutal means.[123]

Organizing Latvian Youth

Valdmanis's difficulty of protecting Latvian nationalist pursuits with a legitimate pro-German appearance is even more evident in his ongoing preoccupation with youth questions. His endeavours in the spring of 1942 to crown conspiratorial preparations with the creation of an officially sanctioned Latvian youth organization, added fuel to the controversy about the nature of his collaboration and his role as a director general.

According to Zemgals, Valdmanis's involvement in illegal activities originated with a teachers' network Valdmanis helped develop by appointing Jānis Celms as director general of education in mid-July 1941 and by successfully recommending Mārtiņš Prīmanis to succeed Celms in April 1942. Celms, a fervent nationalist and former director of the Department of Education commissioned the like-minded young superintendent of primary schools, Arvīds Dravnieks, as director of elementary education to create a net of reliable patriotic teachers across the country. Drāvnieks used the appointment of suitable public school inspectors to further his cause. Behind the screen of legal school work, illegal activities were organized with teachers as intermediaries. Although in 1942 one school inspector was investigated and in 1943 two school inspectors were arrested, the network was not uncovered until early in 1944.[124]

A. Nepārts, one of the activists of the teachers' network, traced its origins to 2 October 1940, when a group of students from the Teachers Institute met in Jelgava and agreed on the necessity for military and ideological resistance to the communist regime. Calling themselves *Latviešu Nacionālā partija* (Latvian National party), the unit was well enough organized by June 1941 to cooperate with such illegal groups as Jaunlatvieši (Young Latvians) and anti-communist partisans, take over temporary authority in Jelgava when the Soviet police left, and continue conspiratorial activities under the German regime. Their leaders besides Nepārts were D. Raudziņš, Eriks Pārups (both were arrested at the end of 1942), and Viktors Dāniels.

Repelled by the partisan fighting between Pērkonkrusts and the Farmers Union (Ulmanis's party) and by the low morale of the Aizsargi, Nepārts's group decided to create a non-partisan movement to generate national self-confidence and act as a harbinger for the idea of a renewal of national independence. Networks among teachers, former military officers, and youth would coordinate the movement. Contact was made in September 1941 with teachers through Dravnieks, with young officers through Lieutenant Endziņš, and with the illegal paper *Tautas Balss* (The People's Voice) through P. Vīksna. In September 1941 sixty graduates of the Teachers Institute were the first Latvians won over for the cause.

Several links were established with Valdmanis, who supplied guidelines and advice. His perceived stand above parties appealed to Nepārts's co-conspirators. Information and advice from Valdmanis, who was in contact with Pārups, was particularly welcome when in September 1941 battalions of Latvian volunteers were recruited for service at the Russian front. Similarly, directives came from Valdmanis through Dāniels and Dravnieks in December 1941. At that time, all young Latvians were declared subject to mobilization for the Reich labour service. Seen as a means to convert Latvian youth to National Socialism, this one-year work term in Germany became a prerequisite for university admission. Valdmanis counselled a wait-and-see tactic combined with cautious passive resistance to both German policies. His rationale was to concede small matters in order to save the principle of 'no Latvian blood for a foreign cause.' Secret SD reports in the spring of 1942 confirm the success of Valdmanis's tactics. Both German recruiting campaigns generated considerable underground activity, such as the increased appearance of illegal anti-German literature, and the recruiting efforts fell below expectations.[125]

During early 1942 Dāniels and Nepārts worked out the program and structure for a youth organization as part of their movement's expansion of its network of military and general communications within Latvia (with some extensions to Estonia and Lithuania). Because of the anticipated difficulty to influence the organizational development, three leaders were selected to take on separate responsibilities: Dāniels as idea man, Olģerts Šteinbriks as manager of personnel and headquarters, and Šteinhards as supervisor of practical matters. Young former military officers were chosen for district leadership, and teachers for direct work with young people. Nepārts stated that his organization supported Valdmanis's struggle against the draft, of Latvian recruits 'with all the means at our disposal.' In early 1943 these youth leaders were arrested and some, including Neparts, spent the rest of the war in concentration camps.[126]

Paralleling these conspiratorial efforts, initiatives were under way to revive Mazpulki, the official youth organization of the Ulmanis regime. In the turbulent days of July 1941 Valdmanis was dismayed to watch the Latvian youth drawn to Pērkonkrusts, local fascists he tried to keep from gaining power. One of its former leaders (Lūsis) recalls that in the early weeks of German occupation Valdmanis had come to him seeking his support to restore Mazpulki. They both examined the matter with former Mazpulki inspector Ķirš, who apparently felt he could not cooperate because Valdmanis, as participant of the assembly of 11 July, had sent a letter of gratitude to Hitler. It was implied that representatives of Mazpulki had not been invited because, as one source put it, 'Ulmanis and the communists were bedfellows and Mazpulki are the children of Ulmanis. Also, information about the burning of synagogues and the execution of Jews was brought up.'[127]

In the autumn of 1941 a report by Einsatzgruppe A commander Stahlecker proposed the creation of youth organizations under camouflaged German control. The purpose was to educate Latvian youth ideologically.[128] An SS private named Laurson discussed plans with Latvian youth representatives about future youth work and prepared lists of names of prospective youth leaders for the creation of a Latvian state youth organization. But the Reichskommissariat Ostland refused to authorize such efforts before the related issues of labour service, voluntary associations, and sports organizations had been decided and the new civil administration had been stabilized.[129]

It is possible that this proposal for a Latvian state youth organization was inspired by Valdmanis, for in mid-January 1942 he presented to Leckzyck a similar grand scheme for uniting the seventeen Latvian youth associations into one centralized organization with the mandate to infuse Latvian youth with National Socialist spirit. Such an organization could re-educate the working class as well as the 'mistrustful' urban educated class, the proposal claimed. Their aspirations disappointed by the regimes of Ulmanis, the Soviets, and the German occupiers, Latvian workers might be attracted to National Socialism through the organizations joined by their children. Because of the widespread mistrust of Latvians and their apprehensions about the future, Valdmanis stressed, the National Socialist spirit had to be disseminated adroitly.

To press his point, Valdmanis wanted to leave no doubt that he shared Nazi racial distinctions between Latvians and Latgallians. The latter, he noted uncritically, had been objects of executions by shooting under German occupation. In independent Latvia, he contended, Latgallians had had the greatest difficulties getting along with Latvians. An 'unhappy mixture of Poles, Lithuanians, Russians, and Latvians,' Latgallians had never really identified as Latvians, according to Valdmanis.

In the report Valdmanis stressed the following points. The Latvian people were not interested in independence, because they knew an Allied victory would assure the return of the Bolsheviks who would destroy the Baltic peoples. Even a non-communist victorious Russia would re-annex the Baltic states, russify them, and reduce them to Asiatic barbarism. Should, as in the First World War, Russia and Germany collapse simultaneously, Poland would extend its boundaries from Narva to Odessa. Latvians, with their mental alertness and intelligence, appreciated the protection they were getting from the German army. But more inducements were necessary to win Latvians over to National Socialism. For example, in addition to the proposed organization of youth, food rations and wages for workers had to be raised. Formerly active Latvian servicemen should not be reduced to performing only police duties because these duties were still associated with their poor reputation from Tsarist times. Rather, they should be allowed to fight Bolshevism at the front. Also, administrative measures should consider the Latvian mentality.

Leckzyck prepared a four-page transcript of these elaborations for the army commander for Ostland, who forwarded copies to Rosenberg and Lohse. Their political advisers Benninghaus and Trampedach were immediately suspicious of Valdmanis's real intentions. 'It is not in our interest to promote measures in the most diverse areas whose sole objective is to provide Latvians and Latvia with a centralized authoritarian structure,' commented Benninghaus. And Trampedach judged Latvian National Socialism to be an inappropriate tool to germanize the Latvian people. 'It will, on the contrary, strengthen the notion of independence among the Latvian people.' Leckzyck came under particular fire from Benninghaus for his uncritical presentation of Valdmanis's ideas. Benninghaus considered this sufficient cause to demand Leckzyck's immediate dismissal as adviser to the army commander for Ostland.[130]

Mazpulki or Hitler Youth?

Valdmanis, however, was not to be deterred. In early 1942 he and Drechsler reportedly discussed, in the presence of former Mazpulki leader Lūsis, the creation of a youth organization based on Mazpulki cadres. At that meeting Drechsler asked Valdmanis to prepare a draft constitution for it. Rumours subsequently circulated that he had been installed as 'chief of the Mazpulki.'[131] On 10 February 1942 Trampedach referred to Valdmanis's draft constitution and a *Tēvija* article promoting it. They were, Trampedach argued, typical examples of the Latvian intelligentsia's objectionable urge to propagate the need for Latvian unity and national consciousness so they could be utilized as a political lever later, whatever the outcome of the war.[132]

The final youth organizational initiative came from the Generalkommissariat, which was under instructions from higher-ups to establish an organization modelled on the Hitler Youth. A *Tēvija* article of 15 June 1942, perhaps written by Valdmanis, informed Latvians that the Generalkommissar had consented to the foundations for a Latvian youth organization. Henceforth, Latvian youngsters aged ten to thirteen could be 'faithful to their families and homeland, their *völkisch* uniqueness and culture,' and 'shake off all the disgraceful doctrines communist rule had tried to inject into them.' Under the guidance of the German Führer, Latvian youth could now prepare themselves for the struggle against the 'blood enemy of our people: Bolshevism and Judaism.'[133] Clearly, the idea was to organize Latvian youth under German control, thereby creating a vehicle for the germanization of Latvians.

On 8 July 1942 Captain Aleksandrs Mateass was received by Drechsler as the prospective chief of the Generalkommissariat's leadership and advisory staff for Latvian youth. Mateass had returned from the front freshly decorated with the Iron Cross, Second Class (EKII), the first Latvian to receive that award for bravery.[134] His installation was to be a low-key affair with little or no publicity, but the publisher of *Tēvija* sabotaged that strategy when he publicized the event in its 9 July issue.[135] Mateass quickly made contact with other leaders of the Latvian Youth Organization and formed an effective centre of Latvian youth leadership. He cooperated with the Latvian national underground until his replacement in 1943 by the pro-German former scout leader Rullis.[136]

According to the original German plan, there was to be no central Latvian youth leadership. The Latvian district leaders would be appointed by and subordinated to their respective district commissariat. But to Latvian spokespersons this attempt to 'organize Latvian youth' was an unacceptable substitute for a 'Latvian youth organization.' When Valdmanis protested about the original plan, Drechsler amended it so that the chief of the Latvian youth leadership staff would compile a list of district youth leaders and present it for approval to the Generalkommissar. Munske, the German youth leader seconded to the GK, however, considered this a preposterous arrangement pregnant with far-reaching psychological consequences for the Latvian youth leaders. Wondering 'what the Latvian director general of justice has to do with the youth question,' Munske is reported to have registered objections with Drechsler's adviser Simm, who nonetheless defended the arrangement. Surely, Munske charged, Valdmanis must have brainwashed Simm during their daily tennis matches. Thanks to meddling by Valdmanis, the report concluded, the Latvian youth leadership had been revived, more centralized and unified than it had ever been in the days of independent Latvia.[137]

Other disgruntled Baltic German officials in Latvia were also apprehensive about Valdmanis's perceived hostile tactics, his alleged anti-German conspiracy with Pērkonkrusts leaders, and the 'lettophilism' of Drechsler's office. One disgruntled former adviser of Lohse was so concerned about Valdmanis's intimate relationship with Drechsler's adviser Simm that he alarmed his superiors about it. The resulting conflict between the adviser and Simm had be settled in court.[138]

Anonymous complaints received by the youth division of the Reichskommissariat Ostland indicated Valdmanis's commitment to ensuring his vision of the youth organization. For instance, after the end of the training course for the first Latvian youth leaders selected in Jelgava, Valdmanis reportedly contacted several of the participants and questioned them about aspects of that course. He was especially interested in who had been the instructors and what had been discussed. Another complaint noted that Latvian uniforms had been permitted, as well as the Latvian national colours on the armbands, and the Latvian national crest on the badges. The anonymous source, suspected to have been District Commissar von Medem, complained that the Latvian Youth Organization relied on Valdmanis[139] instead of interacting with the Hitler Youth, as had been recommended by Lohse in March 1942.[140]

By 30 October 1942 SD intelligence concluded that the efforts to develop a Latvian youth organization had fizzled out.[141] Meanwhile, in that month news reached Rosenberg of Valdmanis's 'active involvement' in restructuring the youth organization's leadership. Rosenberg reacted on 18 October 1942 with an indignant protest to Lohse. Valdmanis had previously been accused of promoting the politicization of the national consciousness in Latvia, particularly of Latvian youth, and now he was violating the Generalkommissar's promise to confine himself to questions of civil justice, Rosenberg protested. 'The leadership of youth is a highly political matter that cannot be placed on the same level with ordinary administration.' Valdmanis's opposition to the appointment of district youth leaders by the district commissar was unacceptable to Rosenberg, and he asked Lohse to arrange an inquiry into the entire matter.[142] Whether any inquiry was held at all, or the result of one is unknown.

In a December 1942 memorandum to Rosenberg, Drechsler defended his approach to the organization of the Latvian youth as entirely in accordance with his policy towards the Latvian self-administration. Based on the premise that granting Latvians more freedom and responsibility would induce them to cooperate more readily, Drechsler found Valdmanis's interest in youth issues not at all alarming. To refuse the directors general the right to be informed about such issues would reduce their incentive to cooperate. At any rate, since Drechsler appointed the head of the youth organization and the installation of district youth leaders required the consent of the district commissar, the independence of the Latvian youth organization was so narrowly circumscribed that there was nothing to be alarmed about, in his opinion.[143]

But a confidential German report about a training course in Riga for Latvian youth leaders in February 1943 concluded that despite the acceptance of coexistence with Germany, any admiration of Adolf Hitler and identification with his way of thinking were non-existent among Latvians.

'Twenty years of democratic government and previous national independence had made young Latvians very sensitive.' The report blamed Alfred Valdmanis and his circles for doing everything to alienate the new Latvian youth leadership from the National Socialist spirit and demanded that 'Mr Valdmanis and the wire-pullers behind him must be silenced as soon as possible.'[144]

Two secret collaborators with Valdmanis on the youth movement were Dāniels and Šteinbriks. In late 1942 German sources identified Dāniels as a trustworthy young idealist and 'valuable' youth leader, and Šteinbriks as a well-mannered, 'enthusiastic' youth leader, 'politically very deft,' very intelligent, interested in everything, and 'constantly trying to cover himself in all directions.'[145] Typical for Šteinbriks defiant mood before his arrest in early 1943 is the following incident. As head of the organizational and personnel department of the Latvian Youth Organization, Šteinbriks was told by Rosenberg's youth expert Nickel that all Latvian aspirations directed against the German Reich had to be eradicated and their carriers had to be hanged. Šteinbriks is reported to have replied that, in turn, numerous Germans responsible for disturbing good Latvian–German relations also needed to be hanged, for example, the railway official who wanted to introduce corporal punishment for Latvian railway employees.[146]

What may have delayed the dismissal of Valdmanis as director general in 1942, and saved his credibility in the eyes of the German authorities, were occasional denunciations of his collaboration in anonymous underground leaflets, such as the article in issue number 7 of *Tautas Balss,* entitled 'Real Politics!' and put out by the Association of Latvian Nationalists on 15 July 1942. It attacked Valdmanis as

> the former finance minister who in the critical days before the arrival of the Bolsheviks resigned from the government in order to be free of responsibility and now hypocritically begged and grovelled for the benevolence of the German 'masters.'
>
> While his fellow countrymen shed their blood at the front, this 'representative of the Latvian people' abandons himself to living high on the hog and holds one party after another! With what right does such a person call himself a representative of the people? With what right does he do it? Perhaps because before the war he already received large sums of money from the German embassy!?
>
> Where was this 'representative of the Latvian people' on the evening and in the night of 1–2 July, when the people celebrated the anniversary of their liberation? While many Latvian workers could not leave their jobs and par-

ticipate in the festivities, this lecher with like-minded drinking pals and lechers took part in a 'festivity' that deteriorated in the morning into a veritable orgy!!

How long will the people be kept in the dark? Why is the truth not known about these men who then as now care only for their personal welfare, but present themselves to the public as the true representatives of the people's interests? In times when our people participate in the struggle against Bolshevism, we cannot let these men go unpunished. They have to assume responsibility for all that before the entire people!

The Germans could not identify the group behind this leaflet and suspected Pērkonkrusts. Trampedach speculated that it may have been produced in the office of a German agency, camouflaged as an illegal paper, to confuse Latvian oppositional circles.[147]

chapter five

'Make No Bones about His Antipathy to the German Regime': The Janus Face of Resistance, November 1942 to May 1945

Mystery surrounds his next experience. It is said that he had accepted a commission from the Germans to recruit a Latvian legion to fight the Russians. Later he found himself in a German prison where he said he was again marked out for execution, but was saved because he held the Swedish Order of the Pole [sic] *Star founded in 1748 to reward civil merit, and this placed him under the protection of the King of Sweden. Next he found himself a senior administrator of wartime production of cement and gypsum. He told me that he had no choice and was always under the eyes of a guard.*

Albert Perlin, *Daily News*, 18 August 1970

The resistance record of Alfred Valdmanis after January 1943 defies belief. However, his experience was not as unique as it appears at first glance. Collaboration and resistance, far from representing fixed positions, frequently marked opposite poles of a continuum of changing wartime attitudes everywhere towards the occupiers. David Littlejohn uses the metaphor of an hourglass, with collaboration the sand in the upper bulb, to illustrate this change. At first 'collaboration predominated and resistance was negligible. As the war progressed, however, and the prospects of German victory receded, the sands of collaboration began to run out while those of resistance multiplied.'[1]

Not infrequently, collaborators resorted to resistance when collaboration failed. In France, for example, the lines between resistance and collaboration were fluid and there were abrupt crossovers in both directions, former French President François Mitterand disclosed as he revealed his own past role as both a collaborator and a resistance fighter.[2] This chapter examines what skills or strategies helped Valdmanis survive his repeated crossovers to the end of the Second World War.

The Genesis of the Waffen-SS Legion Lettland

The relentless German need for troops, even foreign ones, culminated for Latvians in the creation of a Latvian Waffen-SS Legion in early 1943. This opened the final act in Valdmanis's career as an official wartime collaborator. As Germany's inability to gain a decisive victory in Russia became manifest in the winter of 1942–3, Valdmanis's tactic of marking time by neither supporting nor openly resisting German recruiting efforts became obsolete. The SS leaders' insistence on a larger Latvian military contribution called the bluff of Valdmanis's balancing act between collaboration and resistance and forced him to show his colours.

Valdmanis had hoped that mobilization of a Latvian army could be delayed until the last stages of the war. Then, as in the First World War, such troops might become of crucial advantage in gaining national independence. However, under the pressures of the changing situation, the tenuous accord among Latvia's collaborating leadership began to break down. For a growing faction the time seemed opportune to demand the formation of Latvian regiments commanded by Latvian officers, with or without German concessions regarding Latvian autonomy. Since service in the German army was restricted to German nationals, a Latvian legion had to be formed under the auspices of the Waffen-SS. Valdmanis now took upon himself the dual challenge of averting an open split in the Latvian self-administration while preventing the SS from exploiting the rifts among Latvians. Furthermore, in a confrontation with the SS over the issue of mandatory military service, he could not count on any German ally. In such a scenario, no German army commander or civil administrator would dare to take his side.

Although Hitler still objected as late as April 1942 to arming the conquered peoples of the east, SS chief Heinrich Himmler, while opposing the formation of SS legions in Ostland, favoured the creation of as many small units of Schutzmannschaften (Schuma) as possible.[3] Latvian Schuma battalions had been formed since October 1941 – fourteen by July 1942 and forty by 1944 – for instant dispatch to the eastern front. They were organized under the command of the SSPFL Walther Schröder, whose superior was the HSSPFO Friedrich Jeckeln. In February 1942 Schröder transferred recruitment to a Latvian committee under Gustavs Celmiņš and the formation of military units to Latvian Lieutenant Colonel Roberts Osis. Both were attached to General Dankers's directorate general of the interior.[4] The recruiting campaigns for volunteers were backed by a rather persuasive German propaganda offensive maintaining that the Latvians' only viable future lay with Germany because the Allies had sold out the Baltic countries to Stalin.[5]

The formation of small Latvian units, dispersed among the German army, dispatched to battles far from Latvia's borders, and lacking a Latvian command, caused considerable dissatisfaction among Latvians. To address these problems, some Latvian officers and Celmiņš wanted the creation of a Latvian Legion, that is, a Latvian army under whose umbrella all Latvian fighting units would be integrated. In late August 1942 Hitler gave his blessing to the formation of an Estonian but not a Latvian Waffen-SS Legion, although Latvians had rendered the same war service and furnished more recruits than Estonia. The necessity for Latvians to have their own army of a hundred thousand men was on the agenda of the self-administration repeatedly, but nothing was decided. Zemgals claims, and the records of the occupation authorities confirm, that Valdmanis consistently opposed proposals to call Latvians to arms without prior agreement on a worthy national purpose and appropriate political concessions from the Germans.[6]

In the second half of 1942, the number of Schuma volunteers declined drastically, so the SS began to form new Schuma units from members serving in the auxiliary police and home guard. These were promised to be released after six weeks of Schuma service. The promise, however, was not kept and the supply of volunteers dried up completely in late 1942. At the same time, intensified Russian partisan activities required the assignment of more and more troops to security duties in the rear of the front lines because the battles to conquer and relieve Stalingrad severely drained the manpower reserves available to the German command.[7]

In this situation, according to Dankers's recollections, Schröder on 3 November 1942 invited Dankers and the Latvian colonels Veiss, Osis, and Kripēns to request permission from Jeckeln for the formation of a Latvian Legion. According to Zemgals, Dankers, Veiss, Osis, and Celmiņš had for some time been approaching Jeckeln behind Valdmanis's back. Meanwhile, Valdmanis apparently tried but failed to obtain the endorsement of his fellow directors general for a draft letter to Drechsler demanding political concessions in return for Latvian troops. 'If you want to be sent to a German prison, why do you want to take us with you?'

Director General of Education Prīmanis is quoted to have replied to Valdmanis.[8] On 4 November 1942 Valdmanis decided to give his letter to Generalkommissar Drechsler with the comment that it was not an official statement, but merely contained some personal thoughts.[9]

The Latvian Problem

Entitled 'The Latvian Problem' and purporting to serve merely as a basis for informal discussions, the letter spoke a daringly blunt language. It was, in fact, a brilliantly crafted eleven-page memorandum highlighting the bitter disappointment among Latvians over their experience of seventeen months of German occupation. After sketching German–Latvian relations as a long history of conflict, Valdmanis justified Latvians' yearning for national self-determination. Following the ordeals of Bolshevik rule, Latvians had pinned all their hopes on Germany: 'With what love the German soldiers were received and guided on in Latvia cannot be put in words here ... It is impossible to describe in this brief memorandum the extent of the endeavours to obtain German permission to sacrifice Latvian resources and Latvian blood in order to assist in the struggle for a new Europe. But everything has turned out to be different, quite different.'

Latvians, Valdmanis stated bluntly, had 'received only insults from their liberators, friends, and leaders' in the joint struggle against Bolshevism. 'Every Latvian, including those who have never been politically motivated, will ask what is actually going on here? Have the Germans really come as liberators – or as conquerors?' Although repeating his desire to avoid excessive criticism, Valdmanis could not restrain himself from terming the situation 'unbearable.'

The greatest desire of all Latvians was the return of national independence, Valdmanis maintained, an independence acknowledged in 1941 by General von Roques. From the standpoint of international law, Latvia had never lost it. Latvians would never make good German citizens for this reason and for linguistic ones. They would be better served with the status of a free state to be guaranteed by Germany for a specified time, as in the case of Slovakia. An autonomous Latvia could participate in the ongoing war as an ally of Germany under German supreme command. During the guarantee period an appropriate educational policy in Latvia could promote a further rapprochement. Valdmanis was confident that Latvians would ratify such a solution in a plebiscite, but its realization depended entirely on the goodwill of Germany. The alternative would be an impoverished Latvia so hostile to Germany that it would be incapable of participating in the rebuilding of the new Europe.[10]

Instead of taking up the issues raised by Valdmanis, the Germans rejected Valdmanis's memorandum out of hand as an unacceptable provocation. Drechsler informed Valdmanis that this kind of submission was 'highly undesirable,' could not be discussed by him, and was not suitable to be forwarded to Berlin. Reichskommissar Lohse summoned General Dankers to inform him that the Germans had never recognized Valdmanis as a spokesman and that they would not react to any memorandum written by him. Within two weeks, Valdmanis's memorandum had gained additional significance because during that time the Allies had landed in North Africa and at Stalingrad the defeat of the German forces had become obvious. Latvians wondered whether the final stage of the war had begun. At the end of November 1942, two Latvian officers (Plensners and Silgailis) impressed on Valdmanis the need to drop his opposition to mobilization and negotiate with the Germans the formation of a Latvian army trained and commanded by Latvians.[11]

With data supplied by Silgailis, and based on calculations of the former chiefs of staff of Latvia, Valdmanis sent Drechsler a stiffly worded supplementary memorandum on 1 December 1942. It spelled out the requirements for successful Latvian mobilization, namely, (1) the restoration of Latvian autonomy guaranteed by Germany to take place at a specified time, (2) an officers' training school, (3) a three-month training period, (4) the availability of German army units as substitutes for missing specialized Latvian units, and (5) assignment to a front sector near the borders of Latvia. Under these conditions an army of at least a hundred thousand men could be raised plus a force of twenty-five thousand senior recruits for service in the rear.[12] To himself Valdmanis reasoned that 'we could gain freedom only by fighting, and the conditions of independence were meant to prevent the Germans from trying to enlist Latvian soldiers into German units and throw them prematurely into battle.'[13]

Drechsler returned the memorandum the following day at a meeting to which he had invited all the Latvian directors general. Again he declared that it contained inappropriate political demands. Drechsler also noted that it was signed only by Valdmanis who was not authorized to speak on behalf of Latvians. At this point, Valdmanis immediately rewrote the memorandum in a more diplomatic language and had it signed by all the directors general. It was handed to Drechsler with the assertion that its contents, and that of Valdmanis's memorandum 'The Latvian Problem,' reflected the unanimous view of the self-administration.[14]

Events now developed quickly and dramatically. Drechsler forwarded Valdmanis's memoranda to Lohse, who on 22 December 1942 summoned Dankers to tell him that the Germans did not wish to be confronted with conditions and were sure of final victory without Latvian military assistance. From Lohse, the bureaucracy of the Ostministerium received word of 'The Latvian Problem,' and Kleist commented that mobilization could be carried out only with German help, but, 'if the directors general demand a kind of Slovakia, then this has to be resolutely rejected at the present. Since, furthermore, the directors general do not meet the political requirements of the Reich, it is proposed that they be removed from their positions while simultaneously the healthy ingredients of their memorandum be implemented by unquestionably pro-German personalities.'[15]

Meanwhile, copies of 'The Latvian Problem' were uncovered circulating among the public. Although the SD could not find the distribution source, Valdmanis was a prime suspect. He, however, denied any involvement.[16] Valdmanis's memoranda also reached Himmler and Rosenberg. Both of them, for different reasons, agreed on the desirability of a statute of autonomy for the Baltic states. Rosenberg proceeded to prepare several options for Baltic autonomy and discussed them with Hitler on 2 February 1943. On 8 March 1943 word reached Rosenberg that Hitler had rejected the idea of autonomy. Earlier, however, on 24 January 1943, Hitler had agreed to Himmler's request and ordered the formation of a 'Latvian SS volunteer legion.'[17]

The self-administration learned about the latter decision on 27 January, when Schröder invited the Director General of Education and Chancellor of the University at Riga Mārtiņš Prīmanis, Deputy Director General of the Interior Voldemārs Veiss, Director of Personnel Affairs at the Directorate General of the Interior Arturs Silgailis, and Manager of Latvian Sports Roberts Plūme to meet with him. A sociable person, who often met with Latvians privately and was favourably inclined towards their national aspirations, Walther Schröder cheerfully announced that Hitler had granted the Latvians' wish for a volunteer legion to be named Waffen-SS Legion Lettland and that assembling it would be a mere police matter. To show Hitler their appreciation, Schröder suggested that Latvians could easily recruit a regiment within two days from university students and athletes. The Latvian representatives, however, declared themselves unable to go ahead without political authorization.[18]

The Valdmanis Protocols

Later on the same day, Schröder invited the same group of Latvians to a meeting with the directors general, including Valdmanis. Schröder wanted to know what should go in the report he would be sending Jeckeln, his superior. Schröder enticed them with the bait that by supplying a large number of volunteers (he would be counting on five or six thousand men from the ranks of student and sports enthusiasts), Latvia would gain prominence among the peoples of the Reich and eventually merit a 'Latvia for Latvians.' The directors general expressed their good intentions but felt that cooperation on such short notice was a practical impossibility.

Valdmanis took the offensive and explained to Schröder, 'A man being sent to war, must know what he is going to fight, and perhaps die, for.' The combat enthusiasm that Latvians had once shown had greatly declined because the Germans had created unfavourable circumstances:

> We do not have private ownership of the soil today which might be a cause worth fighting for, because the Bolshevik 'nationalization' was left in force; one cannot even fight for the future of one's people because one does not even know if one is allowed to mention it; those who do, are put behind bars by the German police ... All of Latvia – and it is necessary to say this openly – is in the grip of a sullen paralysis. Many don't seem to care whether they are swallowed by the Bolsheviks or sucked up by the Germans; a possibility to go on living cannot be discerned with either of them. Whose fault is this, Mr General? From where shall we procure the volunteers?

On behalf of the self-administration Valdmanis demanded the creation of a more suitable climate to inspire Latvians to volunteer. This would not necessarily mean putting Latvia's independence on the agenda, but it would at least mean an amnesty for the arrested patriots; equality of Latvians and Germans with regard to wages, pensions, and food rations; and the right to defend only the Latvian people and the boundaries of Latvia.[19] Schröder promised to forward the points stressed by Valdmanis to his superiors and, in return, requested a definitive response from the directors general as soon as possible. According to Zemgals, Valdmanis also turned down 'in a sharp, rather rude, manner' Schröder's invitation to continue discussions in a more informal atmosphere over dinner.[20]

Two days later, on 29 January 1943, Drechsler convened the directors general in a conference attended by Schröder and Drechsler's advisers Simm and von Borcke. Before the conference, the directors general met in Valdmanis's office and agreed that General Dankers would present their collective position, since Valdmanis had already had too much exposure. Dankers, however, turned in a weak performance, and no one could tell whether he had said 'yes' or 'no' to the German demands. Then, as Zemgals relates in his gushing style,

> Valdmanis, sitting next to Dankers, turned to him and in Latvian requested that he speak once more and end with a clear 'no.' Seeing it, the Germans called upon Valdmanis himself to say frankly what he felt should be said. Valdmanis could not retreat, nor did he intend to retreat. Realizing that it would be his last speech, deeply appreciating the tragic position of the Latvian nation, and clearly visualizing his own fate, he felt that the time had come to sacrifice himself ... The Germans demanded Latvian youth for war and the reply could be but 'yes' or 'no.' It had become imperative to show the Latvian nation a way, it had become imperative to attract the attention of the world to the tragedy of the Baltic nations, it had become imperative to leave a testimony for future times and for history.

The original German-language version of the conference transcripts (produced by Valdmanis for official German consumption), indicate a less dramatic scenario and a few minor differences from the text published by Zemgals. But it leaves little doubt that on this occasion Valdmanis took his most outspoken stand to date. Had Hitler permitted or ordered a Latvian SS voluntary legion? Valdmanis wondered. In the first case it would be important to know who had asked for it, in the second case to whom the order had been directed. This time Valdmanis decided to be entirely candid about the state of mind of the 'so-called directors general, those seven rotten pillars who have lost their good name and are already eyeing each other disparagingly':

> All of us have but one common and one only ideal, our only desire: the restoration of an independent Republic of Latvia. Whatever we do and say, this dream is with us from seven in the morning until the late evening. In the presence of all seven, I am repeating here again that none of us thinks differently. We hope to reach our goal one day. But we would prefer to receive our Latvian independence from Germany instead of from other powers ... otherwise we would have to fear that after 15 or 20 years this new

> privilege would be terminated again. Therefore we would like to be allied with you and join you. But do not dare to repulse us and guide us into a different direction ... We admire your Führer and know that he is the Führer of the German people, but we are Latvians ... Do not impose on our small people tests which go beyond our strength.

With the Bolsheviks approaching Latvia's borders, Valdmanis warned that the country was lapsing into a gloomy and hopeless silence. Unlike the Germans, 'we see nothing on which to pin our hopes ... What should Latvians fight for? What should they be told other than to oppose Bolshevism?' Valdmanis compared the dilemma of Latvians with someone asked to attack unarmed with their bare hands a bear or with a forest worker ordered to cut wood without an axe. Success in recruiting volunteers could not be expected without German concessions and incentives. Valdmanis proposed, and the conference participants agreed, not to proceed with the campaign for volunteers. In the absence of volunteers, Drechsler and Schröder proposed to consider Dankers's suggestion to issue an authorization for conscription.

Drechsler is reported to have likened Valdmanis's speech to a 'good piano improvisation' that contained themes about philosophy, politics, and life. Admitting that he was well aware of Latvians' plight and problems, he promised to do what he could to improve the situation. An amnesty for young patriots, the reprivatization of property nationalized by the Soviets during their occupation, and the matters of pensions and higher food rations were being seriously considered, but the independence of Latvia could be granted only by Hitler. Drechsler shared the concern about the mood of Latvia's self-administration articulated by Prīmanis, who let it be known that the directors general had repeatedly considered resigning. Their position was, 'in fact, very bad,' their competencies needed to be clarified, and among the public they were 'gradually losing their good name,' Prīmanis complained. Drechsler indicated that this question would also soon be decided, but for the time being he had to rule out of order Valdmanis's repeated references to Dankers as 'my chief.' The Latvian self-administration was not a collegial body headed by a president, Drechsler declared, and he did not want to give anyone reasons to assume that he was indirectly recognizing a Latvian government.[21]

Valdmanis's performances in the meetings with Schröder and Drechsler became known in their mimeographed forms as Protocol no. 1 and Protocol no. 2, or simply the 'Valdmanis Protocols.' Most likely written by Valdmanis himself immediately after the respective events, the conference transcripts were reproduced in Latvian and German and distributed by Dāniels's and Nepārts's underground networks.[22] References to the 'Valdmanis Protocols' and 'The Latvian Problem' in SD reports and in the correspondence between the four levels of German civil administration confirm that Valdmanis was a more provocative and courageous defender of the Latvian national interest than any of his colleagues and that he was the only director general with clearly articulated political views. Even historians who depict Valdmanis as a subservient German quisling concede that each of these statements was a 'masterpiece,' spoke an 'unbelievably open language,' and 'offered the nation exactly what it wanted: namely, to create and administer its own independent country.'[23]

Resignation and Aftermath

An SD investigation could neither uncover the distribution network nor prove the participation of Valdmanis. No doubt, Valdmanis had become *persona non grata* with the SD and an embarrassment even to Drechsler. But the true story of his departure from office is difficult to reconstruct. Zemgals claims that the Gestapo decided to liquidate Valdmanis and that he barely escaped an assassination attempt. His life was allegedly saved, according to Zemgals, by the chief of the Abwehr, Colonel Kurt Graebe, the Foreign Office representative in Riga Adolf Windecker, and Drechsler with the argument that Valdmanis had not betrayed any German authority because he had always refused a declaration of loyalty.[24]

Valdmanis himself stated in 1946 and 1947 that it was impossible to liquidate him because he was too well known – his many high and highest decorations from foreign governments compelled Germans to persecute him with caution. The Germans, therefore, chose to dismiss him on the grounds of 'bad health,' he claimed, and Drechsler gave him the option of being turned over to the Gestapo or choosing honourable death (*Ehrentod*) as a volunteer at the eastern front. Valdmanis went on to disclose 'openly and honestly that I would have chosen the "Ehrentod." But I had to fear, that this action would be interpreted as a contradiction to my protocols which were a signal for all Balts to resist mobilization. Therefore I refused the "Ehrentod."'[25]

According to Wittrock, it was Drechsler who tried to 'remove' the rebellious director general from Riga when his submissions became too arrogant. However, Drechsler succeeded only with the help of the SD.[26] None of these stories can be entirely corroborated, but all seem to contain some part of the truth.

The actual course of events may not have been quite so dramatic. As in October 1939, Valdmanis's sense of survival told him when it was time to get out. In early 1943 the SD began to crack down on illegal nationalist activities. Between 26 January and 4 February 1943 it uncovered the illegal student organization Brīvā Latvija (Free Latvia) and arrested more than twenty students distributing the illegal paper *Tā Zeme ir Mūsu* (This Land Is Ours). The usually reliable SD intelligence service reported that the arrest had caused a great sensation in social circles because the arrested students belonged to prominent families of Riga's intelligentsia. In March 1943 Nepārts and two of his fellow conspirators were arrested and interrogated about their contacts with Pārups, Raudziņš, and Valdmanis. They spent the rest of the war in concentration camps, an ordeal which one of them (J. Krāstiņš) did not survive.[27]

At the same time, Latvians were receiving firsthand information about the German defeat at the Volga and northern Caucasus front. Sicherheitsdienst intelligence indicated that the German retreat formed the frightened Latvians' main topic of conversation. Rumours spread that German troops were about to withdraw from Latvia, allow the Bolsheviks to liquidate nationalist-minded Latvians, and then reoccupy the country purged of its nationalist elements.[28] Clearly, the writing was on the wall. For Valdmanis, who had tried to achieve his political objective – a measure of Latvian independence – with the help of the Germans, the game seemed up. Realizing that he had outlived his usefulness in the self-administration, Valdmanis resigned.

Both Drechsler and Windecker went on record in April 1943 to state that Valdmanis had initiated his departure himself.[29] And in his first comment on the event, Alfred Rosenberg confirmed that 'the resignation of Valdmanis, despite all efforts to retain him, could no longer be avoided.'[30] Placed under SD house arrest, Valdmanis was given the option of leaving Latvia.[31] The Directorate General of Justice recorded 16 April 1943 as the official date of his retirement from office.[32] Valdmanis, however, always maintained that he had resigned right after the 29 January 1943 meeting and departed from Latvia in March 1943. SD Commander Rudolf Lange, in a report of January 1944 (concerning the arrest of Celmiņš for anti-German propaganda), remarked that Valdmanis, unlike Celmiņš, had willingly accepted an offer to take up a well-paid position in Germany.[33] According to one Baltic German contemporary, Valdmanis was offered this option because he was considered potentially useful in future.[34]

When Alfred Valdmanis resigned as director general, developments were rapidly making his political strategy obsolete. In disregard of the self-administration's objections of January 1943, conscription for the Latvian Legion had started on 26 February 1943. To camouflage this violation of the Hague Convention of 1907, the Germans decreed obligatory labour service in the Ostland territories and used the self-administration's Department of Labour as the conscription agency. Upon registering and being found medically fit for military service, Latvians in the age groups born from 1919 to 1924 were required to choose military or labour service and to sign that they had selected military service voluntarily.

In light of the German determination to proceed and with the Red Army advancing, the directors general abandoned their insistence on political concessions in favour of assurances concerning the training, command, and deployment of the legion. In a letter of 23 February 1943 to Lohse, Jeckeln, Drechsler, and the German army commander in the Ostland General Wolfsberger, General Dankers made the recruitment cooperation of the Latvian self-administration conditional upon German acceptance of the following minimal demands: Latvian officers would be in command, every Latvian to be conscripted would have the right to join the legion and would not be pressured in his choice of service, and Latvian legionnaires would be treated in every respect like members of the German army. Furthermore, the legion would be trained in Latvia and would be deployed near Latvia.[35]

The Germans promised to accept Dankers's minimal demands, but in practice reneged on some of them. Although 67,584 Latvians, that is, over 85 per cent of those called up, registered for service, only eighteen thousand were allowed to join the Legion; eleven thousand were attached as auxiliary volunteers (Hilfswillige or Hiwi) to the German army, and twenty-seven thousand to labour units.[36] According to the Riga recruiting office, however, some four thousand of the eighteen thousand registered did not comply with their call-up and 'a fairly large number' simply deserted. In Riga, 34 per cent of the seven thousand inspected for military service by the end of April 1943 tried to have their registration reversed. 'Had we become soft,' the recruiting officer declared, 'not even 1,500 recruits would have been available for military service in this district.'[37]

Trampedach, however, maintained that the surprisingly high percentage of initial 'voluntary' registration in Latvia – which in contrast to the boycott in Lithuania was on a level with that in the Reich – amounted to the people's rejection of the negative propaganda spread by its intelligentsia and to a refutation of the stand taken by the directors general.

Assuming that Valdmanis was still in office and claiming to have proof that he had authored the draft of Dankers's letter, Trampedach viewed Valdmanis and Dankers as the chief political troublemakers and demanded that they be replaced by more cooperative directors general. He argued that Latvians should be rewarded for cooperation with the official renunciation of any resettlement plan and compensated for the lack of political autonomy by abolishing the different treatment of Latvians from Germans, including the discriminatory differential in prices and wages. The intelligentsia should be given the opportunity to earn well in German service and thus, 'in view of the materialist attitude of these circles, tie them to our leadership.' The sympathies of a people cannot be won, Trampedach conceded in March 1943, if they are treated only as an object of economic exploitation.[38]

While wages, working conditions, and the food supply improved somewhat in April 1943,[39] the general mood remained depressed as further mobilizations were demanded in October and November 1943. Again, the Latvian self-administration and General Bangerskis demanded restoration of national sovereignty as a prerequisite. Again, Drechsler ignored the demand and mobilization went ahead anyway. The dilemma of the Latvians was, as Visvaldis Mangulis summarized poignantly: 'If they did not mobilize and the Germans won the war, then the Latvians would have a weak claim to independence because freedom from Soviet rule would have been won by the Germans. If they did not mobilize and the Germans lost the war, then surely Latvia would be occupied by the Reds once more and the "Ghastly Year" would be repeated again and again. Thus the only choice was to mobilize and fight for independence, hoping for ultimate help from the Western Allies.'[40]

In the controversy among Latvia's political and military leaders over which strategy would best achieve political concessions leading to national independence – more recruits as a price for concessions, or concessions as the reward for more recruits and for combat action[41] – the latter won out. Once the go-ahead for the legion had been given, its command became the legal centre of Latvian resistance to German rule as officers and ranks reared in the traditions of the Latvian army ensured that a Latvian spirit prevailed in the legion from the outset. For example, orders were given in Latvian, the ranks, roll-calls, and prayer hymn were the same as in the old Latvian army, and legionnaires wore arm badges with the Latvian colours and the inscription 'Latvija.' In addition, the Latvian national anthem was played regularly, and Latvian National Day was observed on 18 November 1943 for the first time since 1939 with a parade in Riga.[42] Latvians noted with amazement the divided German responses – members of the German army, including generals, joined Latvians in saluting the Latvian national anthem and flag, whereas German civil administrators offered no gestures of respect.[43]

The Shadow of Valdmanis in Latvia

After Alfred Valdmanis left the political stage, German officials saw in the surge of Latvian nationalism the fruition of his work. An SD report of 2 April 1943 attributed difficulties in mobilizing Latvian troops to the general acceptance of Valdmanis's request for a prior clarification of Latvia's status in international law. The report refers to Valdmanis as if he were still in office.[44] Three weeks later, SD intelligence credited the 'former' director general of justice and the circulation of his protocols with the drastic reversal of a hitherto pro-German public opinion: 'During the recent weeks these protocols have been the chief topic of conversation of the Latvian population. The discussions were particularly lively in circles of the Latvian intelligentsia. As a result of the circulation of the protocols and the simultaneous crushing of the hopes for Latvian independence, an intensified anti-German attitude has been observed among the Latvian population, especially in circles of the chauvinist-minded intelligentsia.'

Conscription for the Latvian Legion was perceived as a sacrifice of the Latvian people, the SD report noted, for which it expected to be rewarded with autonomy: 'The Valdmanis Protocols, by articulating these demands in the form of an ultimatum, have done much to promote this almost unanimous point of view. A large proportion of the population, especially in the cities, is taking part in the discussion of these questions. The rural population is more interested in the practical implications autonomy would have for their own economy.'[45]

Valdmanis's provocative arguments stirred up the officialdom of the Reichskommissariat Ostland just as their first attempts to meet some key nationalist demands had failed. A decree of 18 February 1943 on the reprivatization of property permitted the restitution of rural and urban real estate to applicants of 'proven political and economic reliability,' that is, those supporting the German war effort.[46] Latvians did not consider the decree a concession but rather an overdue measure, too little too late, and conditioned by the military situation.[47] Military requirements also generated a simultaneous consensus among Drechsler, Lohse, Rosenberg, Schröder, Jeckeln, and Himmler that a Slovakia-type autonomy should be granted to the Baltic peoples, but Hitler in early March 1943 vetoed its implementation.[48]

Not surprisingly, Valdmanis's ghost continued to haunt all four levels of the Ostland administrative hierarchy until the end. At the lowest level, most of the district commissars shared the view of their colleague von Medem, the resolute advocate of germanization in Jelgava (Mitau). He denounced the author of 'The Latvian Problem' as 'the Riga lawyer with the prehistoric way of thinking.'[49] Von Medem viewed the escalating demands for autonomy as the work of anti-German forces dominating the self-administration and local police and also influencing the legion. In his opinion only a radical change of personnel could remedy that problem.[50]

Riga's German mayor Hugo Wittrock had a habit of referring to the self-administration and its supporters as the 'Latvian clique.' That their appetites would get bigger and bigger was predictable, he wrote Rosenberg in February 1943: 'First Volkshilfe, then directorate general, now protectorate, then "à la Slovakia," and finally merely a loose treaty with the Reich. The end – I don't want to spell out! The arrogance of these well-known gentlemen, as you may have learned, has now reached its peak. But once kicked in the teeth [*einmal kräftig übers Maul geschlagen*], that gang takes cover quickly, which is what actually happened.'

To Wittrock the 'increasingly arrogant tone' of Valdmanis's submissions was proof of irreparable damage done. And since Valdmanis had already been permitted too much interference in the administration of the Generalkommissariat, Wittrock mused in retrospect, prudence dictated that he be politely ushered out of Latvia.[51]

Typical of the mind-set of Baltic Germans like Wittrock and von Medem are two Baltic German rejoinders to Valdmanis's memorandum 'The Latvian Problem.' One is an undated anonymous twenty-three-page typescript entitled 'Reply to "The Latvian Problem."' The other is authored by Wilhelm von Rüdiger, president of the German Baltic People's Association from 1923 to 1935, and entitled 'My Reply.'

The first 'Reply,' apparently from the pen of one of Wittrock's Baltic German acquaintances, is laced with lengthy excerpts of historical reflections by Alfred Rosenberg. Its author may have lived in Latvia prior to 1939 and after July 1941 and is familiar with the details of Baltic history. Ridiculing the allegedly flawed anti-German historical perspective of 'The Latvian Problem,' the typescript attempts to refute it point by point from a pro-German perspective. It advances the hypothesis that claims to Latvian independence have no basis in history or recent political developments, that all of Latvia's real culture is without exception the result of centuries of German *Kulturarbeit* (cultural work), and that as soon as Latvia lost its Germans in 1939, Latvians surrendered themselves and their state without resistance to the Soviets.

The author of the 'Reply' reserved particularly harsh judgment for the period of Latvian independence. Starting with a breach of faith towards the German troops liberating Latvia from the Bolsheviks, independent Latvia refused these troops the homestead land promised them and destroyed their memorial cemetery in Riga. The alleged economic prosperity was phoney because it was based almost exclusively on the uncompensated confiscation of German landholdings and German industrial enterprises. The Ulmanis regime abolished the cultural autonomy of the ethnic minorities and forced everyone to speak Latvian. Germans were systematically removed from all public, economic, and cultural positions in the country. The 'Reply' characterized Latvians as indulging in a mad euphoria of sovereignty (*Souveränitätsrausch*), accompanied by a craze for education (*Bildungsrausch*) 'producing an urban proletariat of semi-educated intellectuals,' all of which assumed very unhealthy proportions and was bound to lead to disaster.

The 'Reply' wondered whether Latvians really believed 'that with the arrival of the German troops their independent state would fall into their lap, exactly as in 1918, without any contribution or struggle of their own?' The allegedly strong Latvian yearning for independence, the 'Reply' contends, is typical of only a small part of the population, namely, the intelligentsia with its materialist longing for a smug and comfortable civil service existence. In contrast, the majority of the population, especially in the rural areas, opposed a resurrection of the Latvian state. It must be kept in mind, the 'Reply' continued, that Latvian independence lasted a mere twenty-two years against the background of 711 years of German rule. Independence was not the result of any Latvian achievement, and its demise has passed just as ingloriously into history without any struggle. In reality, the 'Reply' concluded, it was not Latvia that was liberated, but the freedom of the Germans to shape the future of this land.[52]

Wilhelm von Rüdiger countered 'The Latvian Problem' in a similar vein but not quite as arrogantly. Submitted in Berlin in February 1943, allegedly at the request of a group of friends, von Rüdiger's response set out to refute Valdmanis's 'wrong account' of Latvian–German relations. Latvians had to become a unified people only under the beneficial rule of the Germans protecting them from destruction and absorption by the

Russians, von Rüdiger maintained. As in 1941, German troops had liberated Latvia from Bolshevism in 1919 – the Latvian battalion under Colonel Kalpaks had numbered no more than six hundred men. Repeating the thesis of the Baltic Germans' historic achievements and the ingratitude of the Baltic peoples, von Rüdiger concluded that Latvia's independence was a 'bad dream' for the Germans in Latvia. The Latvian intelligentsia's obsession with independence was neither warranted nor shared by the rural population. Latvia's future should be determined by the interests of the Reich and not the wishes of Latvians.[53]

Not all German responses were as belligerent as these four. At the Generalkommissariat level, Drechsler's comments on Valdmanis's legacy amounted essentially to damage control. For example, not until 20 April 1943 did he forward copies of 'The Latvian Problem' and the protocols to Lohse. These he accompanied with rather weak protestations that he considered the first submission highly undesirable and the tone – but not the contents – of the protocols inaccurate. The protocols incorrectly created the impression that 'Valdmanis had told me off in unmistakable words and that I had only answered hesitatingly and in an easy-going manner.' It was essentially for that reason, Drechsler contended, that he accepted Valdmanis request to resign. He always encouraged the members of the Latvian self-administration to talk to him openly, Drechsler claimed, rather than have him find out their opinions from third parties.[54]

In August 1943 Drechsler tried to explain to Rosenberg that his prime objective in Latvia had been the pacification of the country for the benefit of the German war effort. He could best achieve this, he believed, in cooperation with leading representatives of the local population. In this endeavour Valdmanis had accommodated him. With regard to the organization of youth, Valdmanis had initiated nothing Drechsler had not already declared to be his own view. Nor was Valdmanis's involvement more active than Drechsler had permitted. On the contrary, Valdmanis originally opposed the appointment of Mateass as youth leader, Drechsler claimed. To reinforce his point, Drechsler quoted Leckzyck attesting to Valdmanis's alleged intentions to create a Latvian youth organization that would allow training in a National Socialist spirit.

To appease Rosenberg, Drechsler repeated his earlier contention that, from the outset, he had viewed 'The Latvian Problem' as a private affair of Valdmanis, never treated its contents as the subject of official communications from the self-administration, and rejected it along with the protocols. Drechsler doubted that Valdmanis had built any special network. On the contrary, Valdmanis's following among the population was so small that his resignation caused no commotion whatsoever. The Valdmanis case should therefore be treated as an episode rather than a symptom, Drechsler concluded.[55]

In a confidential memorandum to Lohse, dated 19 June 1943, Drechsler explained the problems of his administration and the wider context in which the Valdmanis episode had become possible. Although guided by the desire to make German rule palatable to the Latvian people, Drechsler claimed that he had to live with the mistakes of other German agencies without being able to correct them. For example, he had inherited the consequences of serious blunders made by the military administration prior to his takeover on 1 September 1941 that had soured the political mood of the country. Foremost among these was the immediate disarming of Latvians who had fought the retreating Bolsheviks before the arrival of the German army. Even after assuming office, Drechsler had no control over German rejections of Latvian requests to fight the Red Army, the refusal to award Schuma volunteers deserved German decorations for bravery, and the rebuffing of Valdmanis's proposal to mobilize an army of a hundred thousand men. Drechsler was convinced the proposal would have been viable, judged by the successful conscription campaign of March 1943.

Drechsler, furthermore, lamented the lack of a Latvian central political organization and the failure to proclaim a clear political goal, even if that goal were annexation to Germany. 'Honest politics will always get us further in Latvia than an unworthy hide-and-seek,' was his motto. When he took over on 1 September 1941 Drechsler 'faced a body of so-called directors general whose legal and factual authority was in no way defined.' On the other hand, the new German civil administration, before its functions were clearly established, assumed many petty tasks that should have been left to the Latvians. With the city of Riga and the Latvian economy placed entirely under German control, the self-administration was deprived of any initiative. Not only was the Bolshevik economic system maintained in defiance of Drechsler's repeated protests, the nationalized enterprises – even if not essential for the war effort – were also placed in the hands of German trustees. Also, despite Drechsler's urgent requests, food rations for Latvians were not put on a par with those of Germans until 1943.

Finally, there was the endemic conflict of competencies between the German civil and police administrations, on the one hand, and between the heads of the Generalkommissariat and the Reichskommissariat, on the other. The police, particularly its SD branch, had acquired influence that seriously impeded the routine work of the civil administration. Drechsler was unable to counter the extraordinarily negative effects on the public mood of executions and mass arrests, as well as the continuous conflicts this system generated. Even within the small preserve left to Drechsler's administration, initiatives were bound to be paralyzed by the authority of the RKO to make decisions affecting the lower administrative level and to approve every measure from below. As a remedy, Drechsler proposed a clear separation of functions between the two levels of government and the introduction of a mixed German–Latvian administration (*Mischverwaltung*), that is, a German deputy for each Latvian director general. The deputy would simultaneously head a GK department. Such a structure could easily be transformed into a purely Latvian or purely German administration, depending on future developments.[56]

The Shadow of Valdmanis in Berlin

At the Reichskommissariat Ostland level, Hinrich Lohse was originally a strong critic of Alfred Valdmanis. When the Latvian self-administration endorsed 'The Latvian Problem' in December 1942 and offered to mobilize a Latvian army of a hundred thousand men in return for Slovakia-type autonomy, Lohse rejected the proposal as utopian. Most Latvians were employed in war-essential production, he maintained, and autonomy for Latvia would set a precedent for Belgium and Estonia, among others. He declared the Latvian attitude anti-German and intolerable and threatened to change it with force.[57] Until March 1943 Lohse endorsed the argument of his adviser Trampedach that the recognition of the self-administration had been a mistake rectifiable now only by replacing uncooperative directors general with reliable Latvians and Germans. In a 15 March 1943 memorandum to Rosenberg, Trampedach proposed removing Dankers and Valdmanis for opposing mobilization. After Valdmanis's departure, Lohse and Burmeister endorsed Drechsler's blueprint of a *Mischverwaltung* modelled on the Nazi regime in Bohemia and Moravia.[58]

As the Valdmanis case escalated, Lohse became caught between Drechsler's defensive stance and Rosenberg's quest for a scapegoat. Constant barrages by Rosenberg coupled with his plans for Baltic autonomy that would make the Reichskommissariat Ostland, and therefore Lohse redundant, turned Lohse into an ally of Drechsler by October 1943. Latvia's undeniable achievements in agricultural and industrial production and in mobilizing a legion were proof of Drechsler's successful approaches, Lohse informed Rosenberg on 4 October 1943, and he emphatically rejected allegations that Drechsler had violated directives from above in his dealings with Valdmanis. Lohse shared Drechsler's view that Valdmanis must not be treated as a symptom of a general situation but rather as an isolated case, and he served notice on Rosenberg that 'I must place myself as a protector in front of Generalkommissar Staatsrat Dr Drechsler ... and declare that in executing his official duties he is enjoying my full confidence.'[59]

At the Ostministerium level, the official records leave no doubt that Rosenberg was the main catalyst in the escalation of the Valdmanis spectre in 1943. By July 1943 Rosenberg had concluded that this matter was serious because it represented more widespread developments. In late July 1943 Kleist acknowledged that Rosenberg had asked him to prepare a memorandum about the Valdmanis case and identify the 'culprits' in this development. Kleist replied that he no longer considered the Valdmanis episode in a negative light. He did not believe that the political and economic situation in Latvia was as unfavourable as in Lithuania, and he found it futile to search for a culprit when no problem – and hence no culprit – existed.[60]

A review of Latvian developments from Rosenberg's perspective revealed that German policy towards the Baltic peoples had been generous from the outset. This generosity expressed itself above all in the installation of self-administrations, the acceptance of Reich labour service volunteers, the launch of a youth organization, the toleration of cultural freedom, the revival of the prewar school system, and the restoration of Latvian law, Rosenberg lectured to Lohse on 23 July 1943. More could not reasonably be expected in wartime. Indeed, the general public accepted this situation. The only ones objecting were the formerly influential circles in Riga, that is, those previously occupying leading positions in the military, civil service, or economy. Alfred Valdmanis was a case in point. Rosenberg reminded Lohse that trouble had been anticipated already in April 1942. Drechsler had been warned then to reconsider Valdmanis's appointment or assume responsibility for the complications arising.

Rosenberg was particularly upset that Valdmanis had interfered openly in the organization of Latvian youth despite the clear terms of his April 1942 appointment confining him to the administration of civil justice. Instead of stopping Valdmanis, Rosenberg charged, Drechsler and his adviser Simm had cooperated with Valdmanis in structuring the youth movement on the Mazpulki model and even allowed Valdmanis to select its leadership. A regrettable consequence of this development was the inclusion of 'openly inflammatory' articles in the training manual, an example of which Wittrock had forwarded to him in April 1943.[61]

A matter of considerable irritation for Rosenberg was 'The Latvian Problem.' Only 'very late' had he received a copy, he complained, and then not through the official Drechsler–Lohse channel, but from 'another source' – presumably Wittrock. Its contents, to which Valdmanis had committed the entire self-administration, should have been rejected on no uncertain terms, Rosenberg maintained. He singled out Valdmanis's 'arrogant' references to the agrarian reform of 1920, the foundation of Latvian statehood, the current yearning for independence, the allegedly insulting treatment of Latvians after July 1941, the claim that Latvia never lost its sovereignty from the viewpoint of international law, and the proposal for Latvian autonomy on the model of Slovakia. To Rosenberg all this manifested a frame of mind that saw the German army existing for only three reasons: 'to liberate a country that had surrendered itself to Bolshevism without resistance, to reinstate the old "leaders" of the indigenous population, and to continue to defend that government with German blood!'

Protocol no. 2, which Rosenberg had also received late and through unofficial channels, was the final proof to him that Valdmanis 'tried to virtually force' the other directors general to recognize his demand for an independent Latvian state. Rosenberg was dismayed that, according to the protocol, Drechsler had called Valdmanis's attacks 'a good piano improvisation,' instead of interrupting him and repudiating them. With this manoeuvre 'he has decisively promoted the very development of which I had warned you and the Generalkommissar in Riga from the first day,' Rosenberg berated Lohse in July 1943, and warned that henceforth Drechsler had to repudiate unequivocally all those endeavours on which Valdmanis had embarked, unimpeded, for eighteen months: 'Although he has personally vanished, the course of political development pursued by him will undoubtedly be continued by his friends and by the apparatus created by him. His agents in the cooperatives are still active today – the consequences of his impact on Latvian youth have already become manifest and will not disappear with the departure of a few people.'

The success with recruitment, however, had convinced Rosenberg that ordinary people did not instinctively react the way Valdmanis and his associates preferred. Reviewing the entire development that led to 'so many challenges and disturbances,' Rosenberg concluded, 'it was a serious political mistake to install such a controversial personality and to retain him for such a long time, particularly after the nature of his activity had become progressively clearer.' Step-by-step all the identifiable friends of Valdmanis must be replaced by other personalities, Rosenberg demanded, and Drechsler must suppress all aspirations of the kind reflected by Valdmanis in the memorandum and the protocols.[62]

In a follow-up letter of 9 September 1943 Rosenberg vented his anger at Lohse for talking back to him instead of complying. If the protocol was incorrect, as Drechsler claimed, why had he tolerated the disparagement of his own personality without a clear response, thus damaging his authority? Rosenberg wondered. And he snapped: 'I have not received a message from the Generalkommissar that the co-workers of Valdmanis have been dismissed. This should have been a self-evident measure with regard to a kind of behaviour amounting to high treason.' Rosenberg found it most regrettable that such an obvious major political mistake as the installation and toleration of Valdmanis, although recommended by an 'obscure' member (Leckzyck) of Germany's prewar legation in Riga, was still being defended.[63]

In subsequent correspondence, discussions, and memoranda dealing with administrative or constitutional reforms for the Baltic lands, Rosenberg continued to refer to the lessons to be learned from the Valdmanis case. In one such memorandum (to Hitler on 23 November 1943), Rosenberg reviewed the Valdmanis case in considerable detail in connection with problems arising from supplementary mobilizations of Latvians for the Waffen-SS Legion. Devoting two pages of his seven-page text to the description of the Valdmanis case, he treated it as an important lesson for two reasons – countering renewed Latvian requests for autonomy[64] and justifying their suppression. 'The [Latvian] desire to view the conscription of Latvians into the German army as the first act of a newly arising sovereign national state has always existed and repeatedly expressed itself,' Rosenberg argued, but the generous concessions made by the Ostministerium had gone a long way to meeting justifiable aspirations. Rosenberg regretted that the self-administrations had trivialized these concessions to the point that, as the Valdmanis experience demonstrated, nothing less than the proclamation of a free Latvian state was considered satisfactory. The memorandum concluded with Rosenberg's threat to arrest the directors general should they attempt blackmail by collectively resigning.[65]

On 17 December 1943 Rosenberg informed Himmler that, as part of a plan to enlarge the functions of the self-administration, all incumbent

Latvian directors general would be dismissed and replaced by politically, professionally, and personally more suitable men. A few days earlier Drechsler and Lohse had cautioned Rosenberg, however, that finding suitable replacements would not be easy. They knew from experience that no 'halfway qualified Latvian' would offer himself for this position. As an example, Drechsler had referred to the current deputy director general of justice, the former president of Latvia, Alberts Kviesis who, although reliable and suitable, had been using all kinds of excuses to refuse assuming responsibility as director general and successor to Valdmanis.[66] Failure to grant Latvia the expected autonomy had 'caused Latvians to lose all respect for Germans,' Abwehr intelligence meanwhile ascertained. It confirmed that 'the German is today viewed as incompetent, corrupt, selfish, narrow-minded, conceited, and uncultured.'[67]

Rosenberg was still citing the lessons of the Valdmanis case as late as 31 May 1944, when he referred to it in connection with two events. The Latvian directors general and the Latvian youth leadership had refused to supply anti-aircraft gun helpers for deployment in Germany coincidentally as 160 prominent Latvians had signed a memorandum demanding national sovereignty. Behind this memorandum was the Central Council of Latvia founded in August 1943 and chaired by Konstantīns Čakste who, as Rosenberg noted, had already been arrested. Certain Latvian circles had never appreciated the generous treatment accorded to Latvia under German occupation, Rosenberg told General Dankers, whom he had summoned to Berlin: 'I am drawing attention to the memorandum of the former Director General Valdmanis that contained an unacceptable critique of the German administration, furthermore to the minutes of a meeting with the Generalkommissar, which were widely distributed by a person that has not been identified to this day.' Rosenberg tried to convince Dankers that Drechsler and Lohse had shown extreme generosity. Dankers should appreciate that the Germans could also have adopted a totally different attitude. In the end Dankers repeated what he had already told Drechsler in the 29 January 1943 meeting, namely, that forcible conscription might be the only way to obtain the desired result.[68]

The Shadow of Valdmanis outside Latvia and Germany

Valdmanis's activity in the Latvian self-administration cast its shadows not only among the Ostministerium officialdom, but also beyond the borders of Latvia and Germany. Through underground channels the message of 'The Latvian Problem' and the protocols reached Estonia,

Lithuania, and Finland,[69] and appeared to have galvanized resistance to German rule there. In Estonia a similar memorandum of 15 March 1943 by Oscar Angelus, a member of the Estonian self-administration, to his Generalkommissariat, echoed Valdmanis's open challenges.[70] In Lithuania the content of the Valdmanis protocols was passed on by word of mouth, fuelling a campaign of anti-German leaflets. It helped to inspire, according to S. Suziedelis (dean of the philosophical faculty of the university in Kaunas at the time), widespread resistance against military conscription of Lithuanian youth.[71]

Reports from Finland in March 1943, however, painted a radically different picture and referred to Valdmanis for the first time as a 'quisling.' Unidentified sources characterized him as 'offering' to create a Latvian army a hundred thousand strong, provided the Germans changed Latvia's administrative–political status to resemble that of Slovakia and that this army be used only to protect Latvia. To one Finnish source it appeared 'evident' that the Nazi commissar general was instrumental in 'suggesting' this offer; Latvians demanded full independence and could not be bribed by the promise of a status like Slovakia's – only 'quislings' could be. Nor would the demand of the quislings for a national army have any brighter prospects, the source contended.[72]

The theme of Valdmanis as a quisling is developed in more detail in Gregory Meiksins's book *The Baltic Riddle*, published in English in New York in October 1943. The author, despite his obvious pro-communist leanings,[73] is identified as 'neither a Russian nor a Communist but a young Latvian lawyer and economist whose democratic views compelled him in 1937 to become a refugee from the pro-Nazi regime of Ulmanis.'[74] By 1941 Meiksins had arrived in the United States where he joined the U.S. Navy. Until 1939 he edited the illegal Latvian paper *Brīvība* (Freedom), which was forwarded through Sweden for clandestine circulation in Latvia. He collaborated with former Latvian foreign minister Feliks Cielēns and was in contact with the democratic opposition movement organizing in August 1943 under the name of Central Council of Latvia (LCP). Maintaining in his book, *The Baltic Riddle*, that the Germans failed to win the support of any single public group in the Baltics, Meiksins rails: 'Their sole support is a gang of Fascist collaborators, who were thrown out of office in the Baltic Soviet republics and thereafter conspired against the governments. Representing only themselves and upheld by German bayonets alone, these Nazi henchmen live in constant dread, fearing the hate of the patriotic citizens ... They are also inclined to forgive and forget the Nazi crimes while raising a clamour about

Bolshevik transgressions.' In *The Baltic Riddle* the directors general are denounced as 'self-governing quislings' appointed by the occupation authorities, and Alfred Valdmanis as one of the assistants of quisling Oskars Dankers, whom the Germans 'hand picked' long before they occupied Riga. In a second, abbreviated version entitled *The Baltic Soviet Republics* (New York, 1944), Meiksins repeats this denunciation.

Meiksins's ideological bias and factual errors – for example the 'disclosure,' reiterated in the 1944 edition, that Lohse was killed by 'fearless' Belorussian partisans – are obvious. But *The Baltic Riddle* also contains one of the first detailed and amazingly accurate reports prepared by American Jewish organizations about conditions in the Riga ghetto and the dreadful massacring of twenty-six thousand Latvian Jewish men, women, and children in the nearby forest of Bickern (Biķernieki) in November and December 1941.[75] He exposed the ruthless local 'henchmen' of the Nazis 'whom the population hates worse than Germans' and wondered why Baltic ex-diplomats in the West promoting the restoration of their country maintained silence about these activities. Promoting the return of the Baltics to the Soviet Union, *The Baltic Riddle* wondered why certain Baltic emigrants in the West continued to prefer German control to union with Russia, even as Germany's defeat was in sight.[76] Sooner or later such Latvian residents in America as Alfred Bilmanis would manifest their solidarity with quislings like Valdmanis, Meiksins predicted in 1944. 'Ask these gentlemen who the Hitler quislings are today and you would be speaking to them of their own intimate, trusted friends.'[77]

Alfred Bilmanis, author and Latvian envoy at that time still officially serving in Washington – because the United States refused to recognize Stalin's and Hitler's annexation of the Baltic states – did not, however, fulfil Meiksins's prophesy. Almost simultaneously with the appearance of *The Baltic Riddle*, Bilmanis's office issued two publications on conditions in Latvia under German occupation. Compiled in June 1943 under the title *Latvia under German Occupation 1941–1943* and revised in February 1944 as *Latvia under German Occupation in 1943*, each of these publications portrayed Valdmanis in a different light: first as member of a body of 'despicable quislings' and then – after Valdmanis's resignation – as a courageous advocate of Latvia's national independence. Reviewing Latvia's administrative system, economic order, and cultural life under German rule, the 1943 publication highlighted the impotence of the Latvian self-administration. Allegedly created so the Germans could delegate 'quislinglike' tasks, this body became 'actually a Nazi stooge institution to deceive the population.' This depiction was in line with Bilmanis's declaration on 28 July 1942 that the Latvian self-administration was 'illegal, null, and void.' Valdmanis was one of those characterized as 'willing tools and stooges, imposed on the Baltic peoples by the Nazis.' A footnote informs that Valdmanis had just resigned 'because of ill health.'[78]

Bilmanis's 1944 publication, on the other hand, depicts Valdmanis as a nationalist demanding more rights for Latvians. Based on information received from Sweden, it focuses on the mobilization of Latvian 'volunteers' in 1943 and the role of the Latvian self-administration. Here Valdmanis is presented as author of a November 1942 memorandum endorsed by all the directors general demanding the independence of Latvia. A victim of his courage, Valdmanis was reportedly 'placed under house arrest for a few weeks, but was then sent to Germany, where he must remain as a "pensioner."' It was understood in the Allied camp, Bilmanis suggested, that high officials in Latvia, like ordinary Latvians, had to play a double role and that resigning from an official position was by no means an easy matter. To underline his point, Bilmanis quoted a Latvian refugee who upon arriving in Sweden in 1943 explained the moral dilemma of his people: 'The general attitude is now quite different to that existing in the summer of 1941 ... We received the Germans with flowers in honest trust and without hypocrisy. Today the life of every Latvian is a continual round of hypocrisy. Deep in our souls we hate the Germans, but at the same time we must deal with them with a smile, for we understand that we dare not yet revolt against them, no matter how deep our hatred may be. They still help us to keep the Bolsheviks from crossing our borders.'[79]

A key problem with American reporting about conditions in wartime Latvia was lack of reliable information, even for Latvian diplomats. From Latvia 'very little news has seeped abroad' acknowledged Bilmanis's 1944 publication in its opening paragraphs. Delivery to Sweden of the newspaper *Tēvija* ended in November 1942 and of the *Deutsche Zeitung im Ostland* in February 1943. Finally, in July 1943 all mail contacts terminated. Practically the only source of information was the growing number of Latvian refugees in Stockholm. However, included in Bilmanis's 1944 publication is a four-page manifesto of February 1944 by the Central Council of Latvia (LCP), a pro-Allied underground organization founded on 13 August 1943 in Riga. It indicated the existence of an illegal network of nationalists. The manifesto denounced the self-administration headed by General Dankers and Professor Prīmanis as an unconstitutional and illegal body with no right to speak in the name of the Latvian people.

The LCP, founded by members of the four largest Saeima parties, not surprisingly also denounced Valdmanis as a quisling and traitor. LCP member Ādolfs Klīve called his former adversary the main driving force behind the mobilization of Latvians. But popular support in Latvia for the LCP brand of pro-Allied resistance had been virtually non-existent in 1941–2. Their star began to rise only with the prospects of Germany's defeat and the need to plan for Latvia's independence under Allied auspices. In February 1944 LCP leader Konstantīns Čakste conveyed rumours circulating in Riga to Voldemars Salnais, the Latvian envoy in Sweden, suggesting that when the Red Army crossed into Latvian territory, Germany would restore the sovereignty of Latvia. According to these rumours, Valdmanis was earmarked to enter a government that would include mostly repatriates.[80]

Exiled to Germany

If the Sicherheitsdienst had decided to liquidate Alfred Valdmanis in February or March 1943, as Zemgals claims, how could one explain his seemingly privileged and comfortable exile in Germany from the spring of 1943 until the end of the war? 'Persons persecuted by the Gestapo could only dream about such conditions,' commented a recent critic who discarded as fabrication Zemgals's entire story about Valdmanis's continued police surveillance, persecutions, and suffering in Germany.[81] And Valdmanis's postwar opponents were only too happy to question his entire record and credentials of wartime resistance. They particularly noted that, unlike Valdmanis, other leading Latvians such as Čakste, Einbergs, Alfreds Bērziņš, and even Celmiņš were sent to concentration camps.

What these critics have failed to acknowledge were Valdmanis's shrewd survival skills, especially his uncanny ability to cultivate important contacts and leave a positive impression of himself. Some of his protectors admired his seemingly boundless energy, some his courage to speak out, some his diplomatic skills, and some the charisma he exuded. 'From the first day of our acquaintance he appeared to me as the cleverest, most courageous, and perhaps also the most cunning representative of the Latvian intelligentsia,' testified Windecker. And his Riga press attaché, Leon von Bruemmer, remembered Valdmanis as an 'unusually gifted, energetic' director general with whom he was in contact 'daily' for two years during the occupation until they were both removed as 'untragbar' (unacceptable) and had to leave Riga. Von Bruemmer insisted that in the Latvian self-administration Valdmanis 'was the only national Lett who made no bones about his antipathy to the German regime and who consistently held to his position. All the others and the "Premier," General Dankers, prostrated themselves before the German Nazis ... He was the leader of the resistance movement in word and deed.'[82]

When German Foreign Office representative Windecker arrived in Riga in January 1942, he was an outspoken but powerless advocate of Latvian independence. Although explicitly ordered by his boss, Reich Foreign Minister Joachim von Ribbentrop, to abstain from any interference in Generalkommissariat politics and from advancing any political views of his own, Windecker nonetheless did offer advice and help to Latvian patriots until he was recalled in April 1944 following a conflict with Lohse. What drew Windecker to Valdmanis was the 'baffling openness with which Valdmanis criticized the policies of the Ostministerium.'[83]

The chief of the Abwehr in Riga, Lieutenant Colonel Kurt Graebe was equally impressed with Valdmanis for his stance as a 'one-hundred-percent patriot' not willing 'to trade the Bolshevik yoke for National Socialist domination.' Graebe, who was not a member of the Nazi Party, had arrived in Riga on 12 August 1941 assigned to monitor public opinion and maintain contact with the local population. He recalled in 1947 that his higher-ups in the Abwehr had instructed him to press for the restoration of Latvian independence. Knowledge of this encouraged Valdmanis to devote himself to the Latvian self-administration as a temporary expedient. However, Valdmanis exposed himself to grave personal danger, according to Graebe, because German occupation policy drove Valdmanis first into secret and then into open opposition.[84]

An old acquaintance who held Valdmanis in high esteem was Dr Karl Rasche. A director of the Dresdner Bank, he had considerable influence and important connections. The bank rose from near bankruptcy in 1932 to become Germany's second largest after 1934. This success it owed to Rasche's zealous support of Hitler's policies of 'aryanization' of Jewish property, rearmament and autarky, preparation for wars of aggression, and exploitation of occupied territories. An inveterate Nazi and high-ranking SS officer (Obersturmbannführer since 1938), Rasche was tried at Nuremberg and sentenced in 1948 to a seven-year prison term. (He was released early, in part because of favourable testimony by such friends as Swiss banker Rudolf Speich whose Schweizerische Bankenverein had wartime dealings with the Dresdner Bank.) Rasche's eagerness to maximize profits from Nazi military conquests was well known and prompted circulation of the following rhyme among his colleagues in 1943: 'Who is marching behind the first [German] tank? It is Dr Rasche from the Dresdner Bank!'[85]

As a prewar director on the Riga board of the Libauer Bank, Rasche had known Valdmanis since 1935 and in 1939 hosted his visit to Germany. In July 1941 Rasche's aim was to 'reactivate old personal connections' for the new tasks of exploiting local resources in cooperation with the Reichskommissariat Ostland. To this end he created the Deutsche Ostland-Bank AG in Riga in August 1941. One of his objects was integrating the Riga cement works into a German cement trust managed by Friedrich Kreyser. Set up as a prospective shareholders' society with the name Rigaer Vereinigte Portland-Zementwerke und Baustoff GmbH, its mandate was to double output. By 1943 the Dresdner Bank had become the central economic force in the entire Ostland.[86]

The testimonials of these persons supplement Valdmanis's own account and help to solve the mystery of his relocation in the spring of 1943. Shortly after Valdmanis had tendered his resignation as director general, Graebe warned him of his impending arrest by the SD. Together with Windecker, Graebe went to 'a lot of trouble' to prevent Valdmanis's arrest and assignment to a concentration camp. They solicited support, for example, from former German envoy to Latvia, Ulrich von Kotze. He sent an affidavit recommending Valdmanis to the commander of the German army in Riga. In it von Kotze stated he knew Valdmanis as a politician and an honourable man, as the kind of person German officials would like to see in Latvia.[87]

The most crucial and dramatic player in the rescue operation, however, was Rasche. Claus Borries, an employee of the German military administration in Riga, knew of the long acquaintance between Rasche and Valdmanis. It was Borries who brought Valdmanis's plight to the attention of Rasche in Berlin. On Easter morning 1943, when Graebe received information that Valdmanis's 'final liquidation was only a matter of hours,' Windecker and Rasche made a surprise visit to Valdmanis's residence to warn him that under no circumstances should he leave his quarters and step outside. The next morning an RKO car would arrive with two men well known to Valdmanis. These would take him directly to Berlin. There he would remain under the protection and supervision of Rasche and be offered a job with the Dresdner Bank. Rasche, he learned, had made a commitment that Valdmanis would not flee and would refrain from political activities until the end of the war. The SD, Valdmanis was made to understand, had nothing good in store for him. Valdmanis later explained that he had had no choice but to comply. 'There was nothing else I could do but to be thankful and agree to those conditions.' Otherwise he would have endangered himself and his family.[88]

The reasons for his stay of execution were never quite clear to Valdmanis. 'I know only that I had some sympathizers, some known, some unknown to me.' Rasche testified in 1947 that he had intervened with a number of authorities and party offices, either personally or through Borries and the Chief of Military Administration in Riga, Mr Fromme, to get Valdmanis out of Riga. Borries and Fromme continued to assist Rasche in dealing with recurring problems that Valdmanis encountered with the police and Ostministerium in Berlin. Valdmanis kept inviting political trouble, Rasche explained, because he was a well-known Latvian nationalist and 'rather careless in voicing his opinion in political matters.'[89] The personal safety of Valdmanis's family was also looked after by this supportive network. Irma Valdmanis and the children stayed in Riga until 1944 when Windecker helped arrange for them to leave Latvia. They found temporary refuge in Dobshichovic near Prague, an arrangement provided by Baltic German industrialist Wickert.[90]

By November 1943 Valdmanis knew that he could also count on the support of Lohse who, as explained above, had parted ways with Rosenberg over the lessons to be learned from Valdmanis's open resistance to mobilization. Valdmanis learned of Lohse's sympathetic attitude in the summer of 1943. At that time he applied to have his law degree from the University of Latvia, which on 28 August 1940 had been officially renamed Magister juris, recognized in Germany as the equivalent of a doctoral degree. In support of the application, Valdmanis's prewar associate Jānis Šakars, in his new capacity as head of the judicial department in the Directorate General of Justice, issued a certificate attesting to the scholarly qualifications of the applicant. In the period from September 1932 to June 1938, the certificate stated, Valdmanis had authored 692 discourses on matters of civil and commercial law, at least 10 per cent of which constituted comprehensive scholarly studies.[91]

A German decree of December 1940 permitted routine upgrading of master's degrees awarded by the universities of Riga and Tartu (Estonia) to German doctoral degrees. However, cases of political internees required the additional approval of the Reichscommissariat Ostland. Lohse and Burmeister approved Valdmanis's application on 18 November 1943.[92] Shortly thereafter they granted Valdmanis's request for a one-month visit to his family at their country place in Latvia.

Upon arriving in Riga for the visit, Valdmanis, according to a 1947 affidavit for Lohse, was whisked to Burmeister's house and apprised of

Burmeister's own and Lohse's attitude. The date of 18 November 1943 – Latvia's Independence Day – on Valdmanis's doctoral certificate was no coincidence, Burmeister pointed out, but deliberately chosen in appreciation of, 'and even admiration for,' Valdmanis's patriotic, though hopeless, struggle. Burmeister allegedly disclosed that Lohse and his closest advisers had considered collective resignation because they had gradually been deprived of all real influence by Himmler and Rosenberg. However, then they decided to stay on and make common cause with the German army, which had a reputation for being as anti-communist as it was anti-Gestapo and anti-SD. Their plan was to beat the Soviets, carry out a purge of the Nazi regime, restore a state of law, renew Baltic independence, and initiate a policy of peace, cooperation, and friendship. All European countries would be invited to consider establishing a United States of Europe. Because Valdmanis would be needed to help implement this plan, Lohse and Burmeister had decided to save his life.

This account of Lohse's regard for Valdmanis raises more than one question. Apart from the inflated political role assigned to Valdmanis, it conflicts with the views Lohse expressed in his memorandum to Hitler submitted behind Rosenberg's back in November 1943. In that memorandum Lohse questioned the political reliability of Latvia's 'politicizing intelligentsia who would never be satisfied with any kind of autonomy status.' Especially in times of increased danger from the east, Lohse maintained, it would be imperative for Germany to hold on tightly to the reins of power.[93] On the other hand, Lohse was known to have become an inveterate opponent of Rosenberg and the SS[94] and, because of that, a supporter of Drechsler's attitude towards Valdmanis. The latter's visit to Riga and the conferral of his doctoral degree on 18 November 1943 is also documented. The known breakdown of relations between Lohse and Rosenberg in 1944 is further evidence supporting the essence of Valdmanis's testimony.

Mindful of the value of personal contacts for survival, Alfred Valdmanis in 1947 willingly repaid the debt he owed Lohse for rescuing him from the clutches of the SD. Although never a personal friend of this high-ranking and veteran member of the Nazi Party, Valdmanis supported Lohse under oath against charges of war crimes. Lohse was a German patriot who carried out orders, but humanely and with the greatest respect for honesty and justice, swore Valdmanis. Thus, he credited Lohse, despite Lohse's admittedly undeniable Nazi convictions and loyal service to the Third Reich, not only with the salvation of Baltic patriots like himself, but also with futile attempts to prevent the killing of Jews.[95] However, with his irksome, uninhibited habitual bragging, Valdmanis played into the hands of critics and political opponents eager to discard his entire testimony. For example, in testifying for Lohse and others, Valdmanis never forgot to emphasize and elevate his own historic role: 'In July 1941, I assumed unofficially, but clearly, the leadership of the Latvian patriotic movement. I fought for Latvia's liberty and independence honestly, and more openly than secretly.'[96]

Political Internment or Privileged Exile?

Some Latvian politicians have had considerable difficulties coming to grips with the miraculous survival of Valdmanis, especially if they themselves had experienced detention in German concentration camps. One of these was Valdmanis's former cabinet colleague and foe Alfreds Bērziņš. Prohibited from returning to Latvia after twenty-seven months of imprisonment in Sachsenhausen concentration camp and assigned a job in Berlin, Bērziņš came across Valdmanis there in late 1943. Valdmanis invited him for a chat at the Adlon Hotel, where he was staying. Built in 1907 directly by the Brandenburg Gate to accommodate the most prominent visitors of Kaiser William II and the German government, the Adlon remained Berlin's most elegant and modern hotel until its destruction in 1945. In his memoirs, published in 1971, Bērziņš recalls that Valdmanis

> led me up to a room on the second floor, which was nicely decorated and fitted out with a bathroom and many other facilities. The room was even equipped with a bookcase full of books ... At some point in the conversation Valdmanis mentioned that, in a way, we had become colleagues again because, as he said, he also had suffered from Gestapo persecution. I couldn't understand how anybody persecuted by the Gestapo could live in Berlin under such conditions. To my undiplomatic question where he got the necessary means, Valdmanis replied that he was receiving a salary or a grant from the Dresdner Bank.

In subsequent get-togethers Bērziņš found out that Valdmanis's family were living near Prague and that Valdmanis was flying there regularly to visit them. To alleviate Bērziņš's problem with wartime shortages in Berlin, Valdmanis had offered to bring him anything available in Prague. However, Bērziņš had to refuse the offer because his monthly income covered only absolute essentials. Instead, he availed himself of the generosity of Latvian VEF technician Blumbergs, who made regular visits to Latvia from where he brought back ham, sausages, butter, and other food items already in short supply in Germany. Blumbergs had an apartment in Berlin in which Bērziņš also used to meet Valdmanis.[97]

Why, commented Bērziņš to Bilmanis in October 1947, 'did residing in one of Berlin's most expensive hotels and using wartime air transport not present any difficulties for somebody like Valdmanis, who was hated for participation in the resistance movement and designated for destruction by the all-powerful Gestapo?' In that letter Bērziņš also contended that Valdmanis enjoyed the privilege of air transportation on trips between Berlin and Riga, a claim he did not repeat in his memoirs of 1971.[98] All these 'special privileges' proved to Bērziņš that, in reality, Valdmanis was considered harmless by the Gestapo and that his portrayal by Zemgals as 'the most daring of the active fighters for Latvian independence' was a distortion of the truth.

Bērziņš's reaction is understandable. In view of his own experience, he saw arrest, imprisonment, or execution as the only legitimate indications of resistance. For him the ability to survive by evading arrest was evidence of treason. The truth, however, was not that clear-cut. Valdmanis may well have accepted Rasche's or Borries's offers to accompany them on flights to Prague or Riga – the contention cannot be corroborated – but that does not constitute conclusive evidence that he was a quisling or a traitor. Nor did the comparatively comfortable existence Valdmanis enjoyed, thanks to his influential protectors in Germany, have to mean that the SD and the Ostministerium were no longer anxious to have him arrested. No evidence refutes Burmeister's testimony that the SD was constantly on Valdmanis's heels and 'had he offered continued reason for suspicion, would have delivered him immediately to a concentration camp.'[99] Indeed, Valdmanis's protectors could not prevent obtrusive SD surveillance during his visit to Latvia for his degree. Nevertheless, endeavours by the local Gestapo of Jelgava to arrest Valdmanis on charges of anti-German activities foundered on the refusal of local residents to sign a prepared statement of accusation.[100]

Correspondence with the Dutch industrialist Joan Münninghoff, deposited in the Valdmanis Family Papers, illustrates the kinds of difficulties Valdmanis experienced with the Ostministerium and the SD. Valdmanis's connections with Münninghoff go back to the 1930s when the latter was a close friend of Ulmanis and his right hand in many foreign dealings and contacts. Throughout the war he offered funding and support for the Valdmanis family, if needed. Irma Valdmanis was instructed to carry his name and phone number on her so she could contact him if she or any of the family were in danger.[101] In July 1943

Münninghoff requested permission from senior Ostministerium officials Dr Runte and Malletke to appoint Valdmanis as the Berlin agent of the Dutch firm Poorthsdyk. Runte was prepared to give his permission on the grounds that it would simplify Valdmanis's supervision. Malletke, however, wanted the matter referred to Herr Baumgärtner, director of the political department. Quite familiar with the case, Baumgärtner, as paraphrased in Münninghoff's letter to Valdmanis, left no doubt that

> it was war now and there was a 'terrible decimation [*Verschleiß*] of people' going on. You should have bitten the dust, too, as one among the many thousands whose liberty and life had to be sacrificed as enemies of the Third Reich. It was completely incomprehensible to him, the director of the political department, how some could have intervened to have you banished to Berlin and kept under surveillance to avoid unnecessary fuss. You ought to be considered and treated as an enemy of the Germans. Never would the Ostministerium permit you to obtain employment where you would come into contact with government agencies.

Münninghoff's retort was to ask whether there was any work in Germany that would not entail contact with government agencies. Baumgärtner suggested Münninghoff better be quiet or otherwise the fate Valdmanis should have deserved some time ago would catch up with him.[102]

In March 1944 Münninghoff undertook a second initiative, this time to engage Valdmanis for the Sarnate-Moor works in the Netherlands, where no contact with government agencies would be involved. Dr Runte was prepared to recommend a six-month residence permit, to be approved by the SD headquarters in Berlin. Münninghoff was disappointed that the officials there were furious about the request. They allegedly stated, 'Herr Valdmanis seems to hope for an invasion in the West. Getting now to the West would suit someone like him just fine! We do not want to waste another word on this! He knows exactly that he is not banished to Holland but to Berlin. Berlin is not Riga and, should he try to play his Riga game in Berlin, he will have an experience that will take care of his desire once and for all! Tell him that!' Münninghoff regretted that all the plans he had forged for Valdmanis and his family had collapsed.[103]

Late in 1943 Valdmanis was the alleged centre of a harrowing experience. During the first heavy British fire bombing of Berlin in the night of 22–3 November, he credited 'God and a lucky fate' for saving his life. Together with some seven or eight hundred Berliners he had sought refuge in the cellars of the Albert Speer ministry, but bombs struck, turning it into a burning tomb. Although injured himself, according to testimony given in 1954, 'Valdmanis calmed the panicky crowd and found a way out for the entombed men and women. He guided them to safety and was the last to leave the burning building. His eyes were damaged by the fire and, although an operation saved his sight, he still suffers from the effects when over-tired. The day following the bombing the Berlin newspapers were still looking for the unknown hero who had saved the 800 people.'[104]

Until the end of the war, Valdmaņis's life consisted of a near inexplicable sequence of conspiratorial acts, police harassments, favours from high-level protectors, and miraculous survivals. In June 1944 new threats of arrest faced Valdmanis when the Gestapo in Königsberg intercepted two letters he had addressed to the Inspector-General of the Latvian Legion, General Rūdolfs Bangerskis, and State Comptroller Vanags. Valdmanis refused to plead guilty to charges of conspiring and inciting the Latvian people against the Germans and maintained that he had only informed the Latvian self-administration of his views. Again he was saved by Rasche, who arranged in July 1944 for Valdmanis to be transferred further west. There he was to work as a cement production planner for the Dyckerhoff Cement Works in Biebrich on the Rhine and in Wiesbaden.[105]

In February 1944 rumours were circulating in Riga that Berlin was about to restore the autonomy of Latvia and Estonia, and Valdmanis was among those mentioned – the others were Roberts Liepiņš, attorneys Voits and Rūsis, and Arnolds Kviesis – to form the new Latvian government.[106] In 1963 Valdmanis recalled that sometime in 1944 he was approached unexpectedly by a high-ranking SS officer who asked if he would object to being proposed to Hitler as a future leader of Latvians after the war. Valdmanis allegedly rejected the favour of being appointed in Berlin as an *Unterhäuptling* of the Führer.[107] This story cannot be corroborated. In March 1947, however, Valdmanis's political opponents made a similar allegation, which Valdmanis rejected then as a fabrication and a joke. Referring to a 13 February 1947 speech by Colonel Roberts Osis, they asserted that in the last days of the war the German occupation authorities of Kurland had declared Valdmanis to be the top candidate for the post of 'Duke of Kurland.' Osis was in the Kurland bridgehead, which German and Latvian troops successfully defended until the armistice. In early May 1945 Osis made a last desperate attempt there to launch a provisional government of Latvia, with himself as temporary president, after General Bangerskis's initiative of February 1945 had failed.[108]

In January 1945 Valdmanis escaped from Gestapo surveillance in western Germany to live with his family near Prague. In May, after Germany's surrender, he relocated to Schmorda in the nearby German state of Thuringia, then occupied by American troops. From there he moved first to Eisenach, and next to Gotha, before returning to Schmorda later in the summer of 1945.[109] Throughout the war he had faced great odds, but 'I survived,' is how Alfred Valdmanis summed up his wartime exploits to Canadian senators in 1949.[110]

chapter six

'I Had Committed All My Heart and My Efforts to Latvian Exiles': Refugee Politics, 1945–1948

There was a time when I had committed all I had – my heart, my mind, my thoughts, and my efforts to the Latvian people and to Latvian exiles in foreign lands. I thought that I knew the way we would have to go if we intended to avoid our extinction. But I didn't know how to convince others that my motives were clean and my ideas not selfish. I didn't know how to conquer doubts, mistrust, jealousy, possibly even hatred which had built up against me.

Alfred Valdmanis, 'Reflections of an Exile,' 1949

At the end of the Second World War close to one-quarter of the entire population of Germany was displaced persons (DP) and refugees. Half of these (some eight to ten million) were displaced Europeans of non-German background, eight million of whom were repatriated during 1945–46, leaving a 'hard core' of about one million by 1947. Valdmanis estimated that some 265,000 Latvians (that is 19 per cent of the population remaining in Latvia in 1945) found themselves as displaced persons in occupied Germany. Of these, 45,000 had come as contract and forced labourers, 30,000 as soldiers, and 190,000 as refugees.[1] Virtually all of the last two categories had sought the protection of the zones controlled by the western Allies. They were torn between the hope of returning soon to a free and independent homeland and the fear that they might be forcibly repatriated and punished by Latvia's resurrected Soviet regime.

For displaced East Europeans dreading Soviet retaliation and surviving the defeat of Nazi Germany in western Europe, the end of the fighting thus marked the beginning of a new round of survival challenges. For refugees this meant gathering in DP camps under United Nations (UNRRA and later IRO) auspices for shelter, food, and possible repatriation; endeavouring to preserve their national and cultural identities, planning resettlement, and finally dealing with charges of collaboration and participation in war crimes. For soldiers it meant release from POW camps, security screening, and the threat of forcible repatriation. Refugee politics during 1945–8 thus involved diverse challenges in defence of displaced national and religious groups' struggles for survival – physical, political, and cultural. For refugee leaders, like Valdmanis, with political ambitions, the need to vindicate their own discredited past turned refugee politics also into a quest for personal survival.

Advising the U.S. Army on Refugees

At the Yalta Conference, on 11 February 1945, the western Allies had agreed to repatriate Soviet POWs and civilians. Stalin's definition of these included all East Europeans whose homelands he claimed as part of the Soviet Union. Repatriation commenced on 22 May at a daily rate of twenty thousand and reached more than fifty thousand in June. By September 1945, two million Soviet nationals from the western zones of Germany and Austria had been repatriated along with three million from the Soviet-occupied area.[2] Fear gripped displaced East Europeans stranded in the American-occupied Saxony and Thuringia when they learned, in June 1945, that Americans would shortly relinquish control to the Soviets in exchange for Allied rights in Berlin. Word spread in May and June that American commanders were proposing to collect Balts in camps and hand them over to Soviet authorities for repatriation.[3]

While in Thuringia with his family, Valdmanis was approached by Latvian, Estonian, and Lithuanian refugees imploring him to defend their interests. Almost simultaneously, the Americans also wanted to meet with refugee representatives to inform them of American withdrawal from Thuringia and Saxony during the first week of July 1945. Initially the Americans dealt with a so-called Baltic Central Committee, established in Gotha at the time of the American troops' arrival and headed by Valdmanis's former underground contact Arvīds Dravnieks and by Lithuanian Professor Suziedelis. On 12 June 1945 Dravnieks visited Valdmanis in the company of an American officer who invited the two Latvians to American Headquarters in Frankfurt am Main. There they learned that the withdrawing Americans were willing to evacuate all of the Baltic displaced persons to the west with up to 40 kilograms of goods per person. General Lucius Clay, deputy American supreme commander to General Dwight D. Eisenhower, gave orders to the American forces to take all the displaced persons who desired to move, other than Soviet citizens. But Clay also made it clear that the U.S. did not apply the term 'Soviet citizen' to citizens of the Baltic states.[4]

Since it was doubtful that all the American local commanders would receive that directive in time, Valdmanis in two days of consultations with Colonel S.R. Mickelsen, chief of the Civil Affairs Division of the U.S. Army Command, European Theater (Hqs USFET/EUCOM), agreed to assume responsibility for informing his countrymen and thus spare them the fate of forcible repatriation to the Soviet Union. With a few assistants and the cooperation of American commanders in Gotha, Saalfeld, and other places, he organized the successful transfer of his countrymen to the west.[5] Only one case became known of refugees falling into Soviet hands. In this instance, one of Valdmanis's assistants was accused of having botched the evacuation of several hundred refugees from one Thuringian city.[6] The Allies now had an estimated 250,000 Latvians under their protection. Some fifteen thousand Latvians had remained in the Soviet zone, either to return home voluntarily or to be forcibly repatriated.[7]

The delivery of Latvians into Soviet hands was a genuine, ever-present nightmare for Valdmanis in 1945. He did not share the assumption, widespread in Baltic refugee circles, that the defeat of Germany would be followed by a confrontation between the Soviet Union and the United States. Instead, he maintained, it would take years before the western Allies and the Soviets would become enemies, and the anticipation of an early return home was a pipedream. The liberation of the Baltic countries would not happen automatically, he believed, and the Baltic peoples had to put pressure on the Allies to force the Soviets out. In occupied Germany, however, displaced persons encountered great difficulties in dealing with the Allies. Their best hope was to move quickly further west, for example to the Netherlands or England. It was imperative, Valdmanis believed, to move as long as Eisenhower was supreme commander and before occupied countries had reasserted their full sovereignty.[8]

In early July 1945 the Baltic Central Committee appointed Valdmanis, without his knowledge, as official representative for all Baltic refugees. Before it disbanded following internal squabbles, the committee informed the U.S. State Department and the envoys of the Baltic states of this assignment. On 6 July 1945 the Americans invited Valdmanis to stay at American headquarters as assistant to Major A. Kramer, chief of the Displaced Persons Branch of the U.S. general staff.[9]

Although not considering himself authorized to act on behalf of anyone but Latvians, Valdmanis was not unhappy with his new assignment with the U.S. general staff. He considered this an important step towards resuming high office back home. He also hoped that his appointment would facilitate his endeavours to detach the case of Latvian legionnaires from that of the German POWs. But realizing that his privileged position might be controversial among the refugees, he refused to assume responsibility for representing Lithuanians and Estonians.[10]

By mid-July 1945, Valdmanis's activities had become known well enough in the American zone for him to receive increasing requests from individuals and groups of Latvian displaced persons to represent their interests *vis-à-vis* the Allied military government of Germany. For example, on 9 July he was visited by several prominent Latvians, including former parliamentarians and representatives of DP camps, such as Arvīds Dravnieks, A. Dancauskis, A. Laiviņš, J. Lejiņš, and Dr Kīsle. They represented nine Latvian committees formed by some fifteen thousand Latvians living in the area between Mannheim, Würzburg, Nuremberg, and Innsbruck.[11] They reported facing a bleak, unknown future. Their camps were overcrowded and operated at the whim of officers of the United Nations Relief and Rehabilitation Administration(UNRRA), who were not hiding their opinion that only war criminals would refuse repatriation. Merely talking about the possibility of war between Soviet and western forces was punishable by military courts with a five-year jail term. All kinds of absurd and contradictory tales thrived in this atmosphere. For example, it was rumoured that such high-ranking Latvian officers as Colonel Arvīds Kripēns were under British orders to form Latvian battle divisions and that Colonel Roberts Osis had been proclaimed President of Latvia.[12]

The Creation of the Latvian Central Committee

To ensure the effective launching of a refugee organization, Valdmanis travelled to Lübeck in the British zone of Germany to see what, if any, organizations existed there. He wanted to take a team of ten delegates, but trains were not in operation, so he had to find and repair three dilapidated cars, two of which made it to Lübeck in July 1945. There he discovered the existence of a Latvian National Committee (LNK), founded with German consent in Potsdam in February 1945. It was headed by General Bangerskis until he was arrested by the Allies. Bangerkis's position was then assumed by Professor Fricis Gulbis with assistance by Colonel A. Plensners and J. Miezis. Gulbis's and Valdmanis's delegation agreed on 13 July 1945 to create a single Latvian central representation in exile, pending ratification by members in the American zone.[13]

Called the Latvian Central Committee (LCK), the new organization replaced the Latvian National Committee (LNK). Its 14 July 1945 founding conference in Lübeck was attended by the Gulbis and Valdmanis groups and also former cabinet minister Alfreds Bērziņš, former Saeima member J. Lejiņš, former director of public schools Arvīds Dravnieks, and president of the Latvian Red Cross Dr N. Vētra. With Gulbis and Valdmanis chairing, its mandate was to prepare elections for a Latvian Central Council (LCP), to convene in Detmold in the British zone. From the British occupation authorities Valdmanis was able to pry office facilities for LCK and a room accommodating up to one hundred occupants in a building called *Frische Quelle* (Fresh Spring) in Detmold.[14]

In order to make LCK and LCP as representative as possible of Latvians in Germany, during August 1945 Valdmanis travelled all over southern and northern Germany visiting DP camps and meeting prominent Latvians. He was hoping to garner as LCK members persons with a high profile in community work, especially former faculty of the University of Latvia. They would serve until elections for a legally constituted and permanent Latvian leadership could be held. His endeavours, however, were only partially successful. Some did promise support, but others were lukewarm or even opposed. A number of renowned academics responded favourably; for example, Professor Arveds Švābe promised to relocate with his family from Munich, and Professor Kārlis Kundziņš from Flensburg to Detmold. On 7 August 1945 Valdmanis, identifying himself as 'Former Latvian minister of finances 1938–39,' asked the Latvian envoys in London and Washington, Kārlis Zariņš and Alfreds Bilmanis, for help. He informed them about the 'Latvian Supreme [*sic*] Committee' formed in Germany to address the refugees' needs for food, clothing, and schools, and treatment in POW camps. Intended to function as a mere 'aid organization,' the committee promised not to disturb the work of the ambassadors. Zariņš immediately offered his support, but Bilmanis did not reply.[15]

Valdmanis's encounter with the group of Dr Pauls Kalniņš, Ādolfs Klīve, Voldemārs Bastjānis, and Roman Catholic Bishop Jāzeps Rancāns, however, resulted in serious disagreement. As Zemgals reports, the group refused to buy Valdmanis's argument that LCK should operate in a spirit of national solidarity and not allow divisions along the lines of the former political parties. A Social Democrat and Saeima president from 1925 to its end in 1934, Kalniņš claimed the constitutional authority of president of the cabinet by virtue of his Saeima position, an authority he had delegated to Mintauts Čakste. He had not come to visit a president, Valdmanis explained, but rather a respectable senior Latvian who in independent Latvia had held high honours and a well-paid position. Would Kalniņš be prepared to lead the refugee community, if necessary with a committee composed of fellow socialists? At their final central committee meeting in Liepāja, Social Democrats had resolved not to participate in any refugee committee, Kalniņš declared. He denounced Valdmanis as an opportunist soliciting votes for his candidacy for president. The Ulmanis regime was criminal, he continued, and the participants in the coup would be punished after the return to Latvia.

From Klīve and Rancāns, Valdmanis received a similar message: all rights to the leadership of Latvia belonged to the original Central Council of Latvia (Latvijas Centrālā Padome, or LCP) formed in 1943. It claimed to have been the vanguard of resistance in German-occupied Latvia. Since the names and addresses of its members could not be revealed for the time being, the director of the Latvian Red Cross, Roberts Liepiņš, would act on their behalf and look after the interests of the refugees and POWs in Germany. In the British zone, where the Latvian Red Cross was not recognized, Valdmanis noted, Bishop Rancāns advised Latvian POWs 'to rely on the wisdom of God'; God would not subject them to an ordeal too heavy to bear. Klīve vented his group's true apprehensions more frankly. 'Chief,' Klīve is reported to have addressed Valdmanis, 'I have always called you my "chief," since you, as minister of finance, were also the chief of the Bank of Latvia. The bank never had a chief like you before. I do not intend to hide that. But, chief, if here in exile you try to take advantage of the fact that you are younger, more active, and better than we seniors at speaking one or the other language, and attempt to get a metre or two ahead of us and be the first one in the chair of the president of Latvia, then our ways will part.'[16]

Valdmanis found it very discouraging, he lamented to his brother-in-law Valdis Mateus, that now he had to deal again with the same old Saeima representatives who had been his opponents at the time of his rise in the 1930s. In those days he 'knew very well what had to be done,' while now he was less sure. Although he was 'the only one trying to do at least something,' Valdmanis clearly recognized 'lots of manoeuvring' against him behind his back.[17] To Latvia's extraordinary envoy in Britain, Kārlis Zariņš, who had lived in London since 1933, Valdmanis elaborated in October 1945 that Latvia's 1922 constitution had proven itself totally unsuitable. He believed that the Ulmanis regime had represented 'the highest pinnacles our nation ever achieved' and forced Latvians to accept two important lessons – the need for strong and stable leadership and the benefits of harmony between the leadership and the people. Although he contended that he himself got along quite well with the group around Kalniņš from July 1941 until his deportation in March 1943, Valdmanis concluded that he had to pay the price for Ulmanis's neglect to prepare a new constitution.

In October 1945 Valdmanis defined the LCK position as follows: (1) the suspension of the 1922 constitution had been accepted by the nation; (2) patriotic activities during the period of German occupation, whether open or secret, should not constitute criteria for future rights of leadership; (3) the Ulmanis regime was legal – its acts were recognized domestically and internationally; (4) the special authority to defend the interests of Latvia that Ulmanis on 18 May 1940 had assigned to Zariņš, and in case of Zariņš's disability to Bilmanis, cannot be challenged by people with 'mouldy titles' but only by legally elected representatives of the nation; (5) immediately after the liberation of Latvia, the nation would elect a temporary president instructed to form a temporary government to present a new constitution for approval; and (6) the committee appointed to prepare this constitution would be directed to change the principle of proportional representation to one of representation by districts and to replace the indirect by a direct election of the president. Individuals could thus be held responsible for the actions and promises of parliamentarians to the electorate. Valdmanis believed that since these changes would be beneficial for democracy and the people elected, a large majority would support them.[18]

Although clearly the chief driving force behind the creation of the LCK, Valdmanis's recruiting efforts were beset by serious setbacks. To his disappointment, none of the persons promising to relocate to Detmold before 25 August had arrived there by the end of August. Some had lost faith in the viability of the LCK; others viewed it suspiciously as an instrument of Valdmanis's ambition. Professor Gulbis did not cooperate as planned and alleged that Valdmanis had visited General Eisenhower for selfish motives, or, to quote Valdmanis's angry denial, 'only for the purpose of clearing my way for the future.' Valdmanis admitted that 'very many' viewed the decision to create the LCK as nothing but a 'means of self-promotion.' But he questioned whether this justified 'destroying the whole thing' when so much needed to be rescued.[19]

Nonetheless, thanks to Valdmanis's tireless efforts, the first official convention got under way on 18 November 1945 in Detmold. The delegates to this and future sessions were divided into such factions as

Ulmanites, Valdmanites, and Parliamentarians, with little comradeship and friendship among them.[20] In several stages of voting – one delegate from each five hundred, one elector for each five thousand Latvians, all by secret ballot – Professor K. Kundziņš was chosen chairman of LCK and, with a large majority, Valdmanis president of LCP. Elected from all areas in Germany where Latvian DPs lived, Valdmanis now had a legal mandate from Latvians displaced in western Europe to speak on their behalf. On 30 October 1945 he had passed the last potentially serious hurdle to act as their representative when he received his first security clearance from the U.S. Military Government. The certificate issued by Public Safety Officer Gerald Ziskind stated that 'Dr Waldmanis, former Latvian minister of finance ... has never participated in politics and his character and background are excellent.'[21] The formal launching of the new organization was timely and his elevation to its leadership appropriate and well deserved, Valdmanis confided to Zariņš, who was rapidly becoming the sounding board for his thoughts and feelings:

> With the best of my conscience I can say to myself and to others that the work I carried out in Germany under unimaginably difficult circumstances all this time was demanding very heavy sacrifices from me. But on the other hand, I have been successful in getting some kind of a handle on all the problems that are so painful to us in our exile ... I cannot predict and I cannot visualize what would happen if suddenly I would turn my back on all those matters. The worries and the trust I feel the large majority of our people, in particular the legionnaires and their relatives, have placed in me, as well as the noisy reaction I got whenever I left my position or when I expressed a wish to do so, have at all times forced me to forge ahead. This has been the case although trying personal experiences, almost continuous since 1940, as well as serious damages to my health, have been draining my energy.[22]

The Legionnaires

The fate of the legionnaires (Latvians fighting in German uniform) captured by the Allies at the end of the war was a priority for Valdmanis. In fact, it was one of his main arguments for a strong and unified central organization, with authority to speak on behalf of all Latvian exiles. Their problem was complicated by the fact that the majority of legionnaires were nominally members of the Waffen-SS. As such, they were initially treated like German SS. In the first months after the war, the Allies were unable to understand the different structures and functions of the SS and unwilling to distinguish between the German and non-German Waffen-SS. Consequently, some Latvian legionnaires were kept in POW camps together with German SS.

The legionnaires interpreted their initial treatment as a bad omen. The largest contingent of non-German enemy personnel in Allied captivity were the fifteen thousand Latvians in German uniform who had surrendered to the British in May 1945. These included the remainders of 15th Waffen-Grenadier Division of the SS, with its regimental commanders Colonels Vilis Janums, Arvīds Kripēns, and Voldemars Skaistlauks. Created from scratch in 1943, the division had taken part in the Battle of Berlin. Pending investigations into their backgrounds, most of them were transferred to Camp Zedelghem in Belgium by September 1945. This led to a rumour in Latvian DP camps that Colonel Janums's troops had been declared war criminals and sent to forced labour in Belgian coal mines.[23] In July 1945 the British arrested General Bangerskis, who was released in December 1945, and word spread that the French were repatriating Baltic POWs. Fears that the worst was yet to come were not unfounded – during 1945 Sweden actually delivered 2,370 Baltic legionnaires, despite self-mutilations and other manifestations of desperate resistance, from the presumed haven of Swedish internment to the Soviets.[24]

Considerable confusion reigned in Allied circles about the identity and history of Balts in Waffen-SS uniforms and the treatment they deserved. This was not surprising because their circumstances were complicated. To Allied officials in Germany, these Balts were authentic collaborators and not eligible for UNRRA assistance. Under the constitution of UNRRA, bona fide DP status was denied to war criminals, quislings, collaborators, traitors, and ex-Wehrmacht personnel. According to Thomas Brimelow, the British Foreign Office Soviet expert, the Balts were to be kept 'as long as possible, and as quietly as possible, in the status of POW.' His dilemma was that the British were 'highly sympathetic' towards the Balts, while they had evidence incriminating some of them – Latvian colonels Janums and Kripēns had commanded units that contained men who had earlier been in the Arājs commando and in police units participating in atrocities against Jews, communists, and others.[25]

Memoranda explaining the background of Latvian Waffen-SS to the Allies had been prepared by Bangerskis, Gulbis, Dr Vētra, and other Latvians to little avail. In September 1945 Zariņš presented two appeals to the British minister of the exterior requesting the release of Latvian POWs from British captivity as victims of circumstance. Valdmanis, too, since June 1945 had been trying to convince the Allies that the Latvian legionnaires did not serve as regular parts of either the Waffen-SS or the German armed forces. They were mobilized under duress, he argued, with the promise that they would be defending their own country from the Soviets.

At the end of August, finally, the mediation of the British Red Cross enabled Valdmanis to contact Field Marshal Sir Harold Alexander. Awarded the rank of a Latvian colonel and Latvia's highest military decorations for his important role in the struggle for Latvia's independence in 1919, Alexander was expected to help Latvian soldiers in distress. Valdmanis implored him on 30 August 1945 to separate Latvian from German POWs and to improve their living conditions. Latvian legionnaires were not a part of the regular German Waffen-SS, he pleaded, and should be treated as a distinct entity. Valdmanis's 'chief point' is, summarized Brimelow in London, 'that the Latvians who were captured in German uniform did not deserve the fate that has befallen them of being imprisoned in German SS pens. It is not a very strong point. The Latvians as a whole were not SS-minded, but some of them were and it may well be that at least a proportion of the prisoners richly merited what has happened to them.'[26]

Alexander replied to Valdmanis that he had instructed the chief of staff of Field Marshal Sir Bernard Montgomery's British Army of the Rhine (BAOR) to investigate the origin and legal status of the Latvian Legion and report on his findings. Subsequently, Valdmanis was invited to join the staff of British headquarters in Kassel as an adviser on Baltic POWs.[27] However, the clarification of the Latvian POW matter proceeded very slowly and the nature of improvements differed from camp to camp. Without official position or clear title Valdmanis had little leverage to lobby for changes. Only after his security clearance in October was LCK able to appoint him its representative for Latvian legionnaire matters in Belgium and in the British zone of Germany. POW representation for the American zone, however, was delegated to Roberts Liepiņš, a member of LCK from the Esslingen DP camp.[28]

To Valdmanis this division of responsibilities was crippling at that crucial time. The operation of the International Red Cross (IRC) and the delivery of CARE packages to DPs in the American zone was being obstructed to the point where shipment of Red Cross Aid had to be suspended, as a Latvian Red Cross report of 17 January 1946 revealed. It was also impossible to search and care for Latvian POWs in American camps in France and Italy, since even as late as January 1946 the IRC received virtually no information about these camps. A contentious issue was, finally, the disbursement of the $100,000 Latvian Red Cross fund deposited in Geneva. Bilmanis planned to assign $10,000 of it to the Swedish Red Cross and $5,000 to the Danish Red Cross for the care of Latvian refugees.[29]

By October 1945 all Latvian POW camps in the British zone had sent Valdmanis pleas and authorizations to represent them and, as he informed Zariņš, 'to try to rescue them, because still today in any matter concerning the SS, the talk is about rescuing.'[30] As late as 28 November 1945, for example, Soviet officers entered Zedelghem Camp and with British consent tried to arrest Colonel Kripēns, commander of the 32nd Regiment of the 15th Waffen-Grenadier Division of the SS. He resisted by attempting suicide and had to be taken to a British hospital, thus giving Zariņš time to intervene with the Foreign Office. The outcome of Kripēns's case remained in suspense, with the Foreign Office prepared to hand him over to the Soviets in January 1946, provided they supplied evidence that he was a war criminal. The Soviets, however, could only prove that he was a member of the Waffen-SS. For the Soviets this was by definition a criminal organization and it was about to be declared as such by the International Military Tribunal at Nuremberg in 1946.[31]

In late 1945 Valdmanis made repeated attempts to visit Zedelghem Camp and ascertain the state of its Latvian POWs. On 14 October he asked Zariņš to assure the POWs of Valdmanis's efforts on their behalf through the Latvian representative in Belgium, Miķelis Valters. The latter's wife, however, voiced serious concerns about Valdmanis's credentials for the job, as her widely circulated letter of November 1945 to Zariņš revealed. Data gathered by the local representative of the International Red Cross indicated, she wrote, that 'not only Latvian legionnaires, but also Latvian immigrants as a whole have been accused of pro-Nazi sympathies. The spirit of National Socialism is allegedly stronger in some Latvians than in most Germans.' She went on to imply that Valdmanis should be suspect because of his Nazi connections and his identification with prewar Latvia's fascist dictatorship.[32] One week later he applied unsuccessfully for British permission to have one of Zariņš's secretaries accompany him to visit the camp.[33]

At the beginning of January 1946 an LCK delegation was finally able to reach the camp in a roundabout way and negotiate an improvement of POW conditions.[34] Valdmanis met with colonels Janums and Kripēns to inform them that their units' legal position had been cleared with the staff of Montgomery and that the appropriate instructions for bringing their treatment in line with that of the legionnaires in Germany were being awaited.[35]

How had their status been cleared? On 20 December 1945 the senior Soviet commander, Marshall V. Zhukov, demanded that Montgomery either repatriate the Baltic POWs or disband and discharge them. The Foreign Office, having a choice of moving them out of the British zone or discharging them into civilian DP camps, opted for the latter.[36] As told by Zemgals and A. Dancauskis, one last crisis arose before they were released from captivity. In the last days of December 1945, Colonel R. Osis brought the alarming message that, according to the British military commander in Westerburg, some four thousand Latvian POWs would be repatriated to the Soviets. Osis's panic-stricken men urged LCK to intervene. LCK deputy Professor Kundziņš, fearing to expose himself to danger, turned in desperation to Valdmanis who had just resigned as LCP president. On 30 December 1945 Valdmanis drafted a plea to the British pointing out why Latvian POWs should not be delivered to the Soviets against their will and warning of mass suicides in face of any such repatriation. The next day he personally delivered the plea, signed by himself as president of LCP, to British headquarters.[37]

It seems likely that the entire crisis was triggered by a false alarm, for in January 1946 the British conferred DP status on 16,500 Baltic Waffen-SS veterans in their zone and released them from custody in a steady flow through 1946. Even the assurance given by British military headquarters in Germany, that the POWs would be carefully screened before being released into privileged DP status, was largely ignored. Zariņš' persistent and systematic undermining of the Soviet ideological definition of 'war crimes' found increasing sympathy in the Foreign Office. By the beginning of 1947, the British government accepted Zariņš's defence of even notorious mass murderers identified in the Soviet press as war criminals. Latvians such as Viktors Arājs, Zariņš argued on 21 January 1947, 'were great national patriots, men of quite modest means; anti-Bolshevik, of course, but certainly not to be described as fascists. I should feel very relieved if His Majesty's Government would allow them to come to the safety of this country.'[38]

The 90,000 Baltic POWs in the American zone were subjected to a more scrupulous investigation to separate imposters from those deserving preferential DP treatment. Screenings already completed had indicated to the Americans by February 1946 that as many as 40 per cent of

Baltic POWs were true volunteers and active military collaborators with the Germans. In contrast to the British approach of declaring all Baltic POWs eligible for DP status, American screening was more in line with UNRRA policy. This placed the onus of proof of conscription on each POW himself. Since a relatively high proportion of Balts were subsequently declared ineligible for UNRRA care, it is not surprising that their advocates lobbied heavily to undermine the rationale for screening.[39] In a memorandum drafted in Weilburg in February 1946, prominently highlighting his own role as a resistance leader, Valdmanis tried to refute the charge that a high percentage of Latvians were active collaborators.

In his memorandum 'Latvians in the Ranks of the German Army,' Valdmanis argued that Latvians were first disarmed under German occupation, then rearmed by the SS into voluntary police battalions, and finally baited into the legion with increasing pressure, yielding about thirty thousand troops by 1944. He conceded that in 1941 a few thousand might have been real 'volunteers.' These included the members of the so-called Arājs group – maybe a few hundred – and the recruits for the police battalions. The purpose and aims of the Arājs group were unknown, Valdmanis contended. 'It has nothing to do with Latvian soldiers, Latvian officers, and Latvian army. Not one of the Latvian officers has entered this unit.' Volunteers for police battalions were usually motivated by a 'burning desire to avenge' the fate of relatives and friends victimized by the Soviets. It may have been a mistake to support mobilization in 1944, Valdmanis concluded, because there were no chances to defend Latvia's borders. He put some blame on the foolishness and weakness of General Bangerskis, an old servant of the nation who could never be a traitor. Bangerskis believed in the imprudent but proud principle that 'only after we have obtained arms, can we obtain freedom, not otherwise.'[40]

In March 1946 Valdmanis passed a second security screening by the U.S. Military Government. The certificate signed by Gerald Ziskind listed the following points:

> (1) It is apparent that Dr Valdmanis possesses the traits and conviction of a person believing in democratic ideals, that he is an extremely self-sacrificing individual interested in serving his fellow-people. (2) Screening by CIC reveals that Dr Valdmanis is categorized as having shown strong evidence of anti-Nazi activity. (3) Dr Valdmanis ... has amply demonstrated his ability to handle large financial responsibilities. (4) Dr Valdmanis's wife ... is also declared politically clear as well as his four children. (5) The Military Gov-

> ernment desires to extend strong favorable recommendation in behalf of the background and capabilities of Dr Valdmanis and his family.[41]

Quisling

On 3 December 1945, two weeks after Valdmanis's election as president of LCP, Bishop Rancāns showed up at an LCK meeting from which Valdmanis happened to be absent. He came to distribute copies of Bilmanis's 1943 brochure *Latvia under German Occupation 1941–1943* labelling Valdmanis a quisling and to suggest that LCK should oust Valdmanis. Three delegates from the Esslingen DP Camp – Ādolfs Klīve, Voldemārs Bastjānis, and A. Kācens – arrived at the meeting and in the name of the camp's 5,570 members reiterated the demand for the immediate resignation of Alfred Valdmanis;[42] otherwise they would have him removed by the occupation authorities. The members of the LCK executive disagreed with Bilmanis's judgment and were at a loss to explain it, but they agreed that Bilmanis and Valdmanis could not both represent the Latvian cause. One of them had to resign, preferably Valdmanis, since Bilmanis could not be dismissed. Disappointed that none of his LCK executive was prepared to defend him, Valdmanis subsequently offered to resign unless his name was cleared.[43]

Zariņš was now his last hope. On 14 December 1945 Valdmanis poured out his heart to him lamenting how Bilmanis, whom Valdmanis had never met, could call him a traitor on the basis of mere rumours from Finland in 1943. How could Bilmanis use the resources of the Latvian state to attack him from the safety of far away? Valdmanis asked indignantly: 'If I were a private person I would know what to do without hesitation about this crazy accusation. However, I am now the head of the highest organization of Latvian exiles. If I'd leave, the organization would either disintegrate or at least for a while be unable to carry out its mandate. Of course, that is exactly what several people with the old party membership cards in their pockets are expecting to happen.' Valdmanis implored Zariņš to help rehabilitate his reputation. Otherwise Valdmanis would have to publicize Bilmanis's publicly funded denunciation campaign, Zariņš's refusal to rehabilitate him, and his own inability to continue in office while fighting off personal accusations.[44]

On 22 December 1945 the LCK executive came to Valdmanis's defence by challenging the mandate of the Esslingen delegation and its right to demand the removal of elected LCP officers without due process. Where does one draw the line? the executive wondered. If exclusions are to be considered on the grounds of official positions held during the German occupation period, LCK chairman Kundziņš and secretary Gulbis declared, then such exclusion should also be applicable to persons having held positions under the Soviet occupation. From this category should also be excluded all those who, for reasons of political unreliability, had been removed from their posts by the occupation authorities and those who acted to the best of their ability in the interest of the Latvian nation. Since during the occupation period many institutions continued to operate, including the university, fine arts academy, and music conservatory, and many Latvians returned from fleeing the Bolsheviks, should all those people be treated as collaborators and excluded from work for the refugees and POWs?

In any case, Kundziņš and Gulbis maintained, it was not the position as such that should determine whether that person's record was detrimental or not, but what a person did for or against the vital interests of the nation, regardless of the positions held. The LCK could not objectively investigate and condemn anybody without documentation supporting accusations. If the Esslingen colony had any concrete evidence, they should submit it to the internal court of the LCK. It was not the duty of the LCK to divide and weaken the refugee community and its organization by splitting it. If Latvian organizations without any authorization would join the search for war criminals started by the occupation powers, such behaviour would be immediately exploited to the detriment of Latvians. The only proper way to change the leadership of LCK and LCP was by electing candidates with an immaculate past. 'It was illogical and undemocratic,' Kundziņš and Gulbis concluded, 'to demand the removal of members legally elected, people who have worked very hard, particularly for the legionnaires' interests, and to whom the electors have given their trust.'[45]

Shortly after that statement had been sent to Esslingen and before a reply from Zariņš arrived, Valdmanis quit as LCP president. When he resumed office at the end of December 1945 in response to Colonel Osis's plea for intervention in the POW crisis recounted above, more bad news awaited him: first, a disappointing response from Zariņš; then, another attack from Esslingen. Zariņš replied that he was 'not only a little, but quite a bit surprised about the tone of the letter.' Refusing to speak in the name of Bilmanis, he suggested that Valdmanis should address his objections directly to the author. Valdmanis should understand that 'in the days when the Anglo-Saxon countries put all their effort into defeating Nazi aggression ... the feeling of the time was that anyone who in any way was cooperating with Germany was an enemy of England and the United States.' There was no way of knowing whether the very little information about conditions in Latvia during the war was objective. But the 'fact that the Anglo-Saxon democracies wanted to know whether we were for or against the Germans' must be recognized, Zariņš explained. As for rumoured intrigues by Klīve, Bastjānis, and others, Zariņš wondered why Valdmanis as a lawyer and democratically elected representative enjoying the confidence of Latvians was paying any serious attention. Zariņš was convinced none of those alleged enemies of Valdmanis had any serious intention to denounce him.[46]

Kārlis Zariņš was not far off the mark. The response from Esslingen to the LCK insisted that their objective was not any personal vendetta against Valdmanis; they did not want to judge him or destroy him. Nor did they want a split among Latvians. But they believed that Latvians should be concerned with denazification: 'Our opinion is that Latvian organizations should dissociate themselves not only from proven National Socialist elements, but also those who the western democracies, for various reasons, would consider as such. Ignoring such a reality could lead us to unforeseeable "catastrophe." We should not cover them, defend them, or even elect them to very visible positions ... not a personal career or high position is important, but the interests of the whole nation should be put first.'[47]

In support of their argument the Esslingen group quoted the November 1945 letter from the wife of Miķelis Valters, Latvian envoy to Belgium, alleging that the British authorities viewed Latvian refugees and POWs as still imbued with a stronger pro-Nazi spirit than most of the Germans. Was not that view confirmed by 'very visible representatives of that regime continuing quite openly to represent Latvian emigrants and by those emigrants not objecting to their presence?' the Esslingen critics wondered. Should one thus be surprised at the harsh treatment of the Baltic POWs in Zedelghem?

The Esslingen group made it clear that they were more concerned with 'political correctness' than with production of evidence that Valdmanis was a quisling. For them, the question was not whether the past actions of persons like Valdmanis were right or wrong, but 'whether the presence of such persons in leading positions of emigrant organizations would or could be beneficial to our situation as viewed from the perspective of the western democracies.' It meant that once Valdmanis had been stigmatized as a quisling in 1943 by Bilmanis and Meiksins, whether rightly or wrongly, he would automatically continue to be perceived as such after the war. Against this self-fulfilling prophesy there was no defence.[48]

On 7 February 1946 Valdmanis drafted a declaration of resignation, addressed to 'compatriots' and to be announced at the second LCP session on 23 February in Hanau, near Frankfurt. Although still supported by a majority, Valdmanis wrote, that was insufficient because he wanted unity among Latvians. 'And that I will be unable to achieve as long as there are persons trying to reintroduce into our life in exile the old spirit of partocracy and infighting.' He could not work with one hand, he declared, while fighting off his opponents with the other. The only reason for his departure was absolute refusal 'to lower myself to a level at which some people are using their God-given capabilities not to create and help, but to destroy.' If the LCK should ever find itself in difficulties and call for his help, he would serve again.[49]

An adulating article titled 'Was all that really necessary?' in the paper *Tēvzeme* (Fatherland) deplored Valdmanis's departure and reflected the charisma Alfred Valdmanis exuded on many of his contemporaries. The author of the article reviewed Valdmanis's achievements, lamenting that it would be very difficult to find someone with such an excellent record, understanding of the issues, mastery of many languages, and fearless stand for a just cause:

> We, his friends and admirers, cannot find words to describe his self-denying efforts. We will simply say 'thank you' because he appreciated simplicity and clarity. And to his non-friends we are issuing a challenge to name any other Latvian who can pride himself on having successfully defended the interests and honour of the Latvian nation under such dreadful conditions, starting with the time of occupations in Latvia ... Are we really going to keep on pretending that we do not know what the population's feeling has been all along, and are we going to keep throwing accusations at one of our best?[50]

Despite the pleas of eighteen of LCK's twenty-four members, Valdmanis refused to take back his resignation as LCP president. (His successor, Judge P. Sterste, was elected unanimously.)[51] He realized that he was not ready to tackle his opponents for two reasons: he believed their instigating centre to be in Sweden, and he was still awaiting his final security clearance from the British and American authorities. In Sweden, Valdmanis found, many Latvian politicians, dismissed and silenced after Ulmanis's coup, rallied behind the so-called Central Council of Latvia (LCP) advocating the revival of the old political parties. They argued that Latvians needed to be trained in the proper exercise of democracy and promoted their cause by claiming to have been the leaders of the national resistance against the German occupation of Latvia. Among their agents and allies were the Esslingen group, Bilmanis, and even the Communist party-controlled Latvian-language paper *Amerikas Latvietis* (The American Latvian). Copies of this paper circulated in the refugee camps in Germany disseminating derogatory articles originating in Sweden about Valdmanis as an alleged fascist and quisling. Against this international network Valdmanis saw little chance of defending himself effectively without clarification of his personal status and his historical record.[52]

To cover himself against denunciations to British and American authorities, Valdmanis approached the headquarters of BAOR and the U.S. Army Command, European Theater, requesting an inquiry. He wanted to know whether there was any document in British hands unfavourable to him and whether there would be any reservations to his continued activity on behalf of Latvians. In response the British cleared Valdmanis fully with regard to the period of Soviet and German occupations of Latvia, attesting to his past courage and honour. The Americans, as indicated above, acknowledged the 'strong evidence' of his anti-Nazi activity, his democratic convictions, and his record as an 'extremely self-sacrificing individual interested in serving his fellow-people.' BAOR officials transmitted their brief to Zariņš in London.[53]

Probably as a basis for these inquiries, Valdmanis prepared a review of his wartime activities. In this he outlined his role as leader of Latvia's national resistance movement from July 1941 to March 1943. As highlights of his activity, Valdmanis singled out his election on 11 July 1941 by various groups and institutions as Latvia's spokesman, his designation the following day as interim 'chief director' for the most important ministries, his refusal to be ousted by the Dankers repatriates, his leadership of a number of small underground groups as well as of large networks of youth, girls, officers, and other associations, his efforts as director general of justice to maintain Latvian institutions and customs, and his consistent opposition to mobilization without a prospect of national independence. Having given the signal for open resistance in early 1943, Valdmanis claimed that he was exiled to Germany rather than liquidated, because he was known too well.[54]

Valdmanis's departure from the LCP did not reconcile the Esslingen group with the LCK. Instead, Klīve and Bastjānis approached Sterste in July 1946 with the proposal to create a Latvian umbrella organization expressing the will of Latvians everywhere, including those in Latvia, and coordinating their activities. The chair of its coordinating centre would alternate between the LCK of Detmold and the LCK committee of Esslingen.[55] The Esslingen committee terminated its cooperation when the LCK executive refused to act on this quest for the formation of a provisional government in exile.

An unsigned letter of November 1946 from Sweden suggested that the formation of a provisional government was indeed on the agenda, but the Latvian groups in Sweden were too splintered to proceed with it. However, Valdmanis's organization in Germany could well be the core of such a government, ready to move in and take over control in Latvia when the situation arose. The letter proposed that the key positions should be assigned well in advance, with some vacancies left for the opposition when they would be ready to switch sides. Following the precedent of 1917, the letter urged, a pre-declaration should be made now: 'At least one side has to be completely ready before the hour of liberation. History shows that when decisive action occurs, clever people will join.' The letter did not consider the opposition to Valdmanis, which though united in opposing him, was prepared to act in the event of liberation.[56]

The correspondence of Zariņš with Klīve and Bastjānis reveals that the latter two, while refusing to submit their ideas to the democratic test of elections, accused the LCK of splitting the Latvian community. They were apparently supported by Valters who denounced Zariņš's credentials for being 'as important and as useless as a used streetcar ticket.' Valters's use of 'poison gas' prompted Zariņš, as he put it, to hit back with 'heavy artillery.' He questioned the claims of the LCP in Sweden to represent the national resistance movement in Latvia as well as the standing and privileges of the former Latvian parliament. He found it completely unacceptable for Klīve and Bastjānis to declare that they would never sit at the same table with Valdmanis. As a democratically elected person, Valdmanis must not be ignored. Zariņš demanded that 'if there are serious objections against him, those ought to be presented for investigation. If there are no serious objections, then there should be silence.' Zariņš realized his own constant harping on the idea of unity was counterproductive, he conceded to Klīve and Bastjānis, as long as the members of one group did not have the will to unite.[57] And to Valdmanis, Zariņš confessed that their recent correspondence had revealed a surprising 'kind of understanding and a parallelism of ideas.'[58]

In 1947 Valdmanis had regained enough confidence and enthusiasm to immerse himself again in refugee politics. At the LCK meeting of 14 February 1947 he offered his candidacy as president of LCP and was elected with the bare majority of fifteen to fourteen votes. He thanked the delegates for their trust but admitted that with such a small majority it was impossible to act effectively. For that reason he asked for the support of at least two-thirds of the delegates at the next session and promised to resign if he did not obtain it. Until then, that is, for the following three months, he promised to work as hard as he usually did. 'I have learned to do both, to take orders and to lead, and for the next three months I intend to lead. In order to get a job done, it is important to know where one stands and what one wants to do.'[59]

After thus accepting his election, Valdmanis inaugurated his presidency with a major speech outlining the current state of affairs and his plans for the future. Entitled 'Not to Split and to Destroy, but to Unite and Create,' the speech focused on the main problems affecting the Latvian displaced persons community. First was the moral duty of LCK, as the only representation of free Latvians, to speak on behalf of the people left in Latvia as well. Second was the need to convince the world that Latvians had actually lost their independence and freedom in 1940 rather than earlier in 1934. 'We cannot state that we were liberated and made happy again in 1940.' Latvians in exile should trust the LCK that somehow it would find a way back for them to their homeland. For the time being, survival of the Latvian community had top priority.

Emigration from Germany might become necessary to preserve the life and morale of the community in exile. It would be important that the entire community migrate together, and that they find a country willing to take them, no matter how far away. 'We should not repeat the tragic errors of the Russian emigrés [of the First World War] who remained on the spot until they lost their ability to survive and ended in total disintegration.' However, steps to emigrate could not be considered until the threat of the never-ending security screenings, 'the purpose of which I haven't been able to figure out,' were guided into more reasonable channels. Those who were screened out still needed to be looked after. With the discontinuation of the relief organizations, employment and education would become top concerns.

The LCP and the LCK would continue to refuse to engage in any kind of politics for the sake of politics. Constitutional questions should be decided by all Latvians after the liberation of Latvia. 'While having to concentrate on rescue, we should not waste time creating a table of ranks.' Outside Germany, all work was being coordinated by special envoy Zariņš in accordance with the extraordinary authority conferred on him by the last legitimate government of Latvia in 1940. Latvians should not look for deficiencies in this arrangement, but support Mr Zariņš.

Latvians also had a duty to support the LCK and LCP. Since these organizations had no coercive powers, their authority would be easy to destroy by irresponsible criticism.

Valdmanis extended a special invitation to the 'small group of so-called politicians' to refrain from irresponsible talk and to do some concrete work. He praised mothers, teachers, and soldiers for the sacrifices they had made under unimaginable difficulties. He was happy to note that Latvians in Denmark and Austria had joined the LCK, although it could not do much for them. He hoped that LCK would also be joined by the small group of Latvian exiles in Sweden, 'a group that unfortunately up to now has caused irritation and sadness.' Then, Valdmanis concluded, 'the Almighty will not deny his blessings to our much suffering nation. Bless, dear Lord, our work, give us power, courage, and unity. Bless our nation and bless our country Latvia.'[60]

The speech impressed Zariņš – both with its content and its bluntness. It was painful, he wrote Valdmanis in April 1947, 'to see that our compatriots don't want to get on a friendly and cooperative track.' Too bad that Valdmanis had only a 'single vote' majority in his election to LCP president. Under those circumstances it would have been smarter for Valdmanis to withdraw his candidacy. 'You might have gained more authority that way ... With your intelligence and ability to work, it might have been more beneficial to be in the opposition – of course, in a constructive way.' That way Valdmanis might have prepared for his eventual comeback with a majority of three-quarters or even higher. Now he should announce that, as a matter of trust, he would resign if he could not get a three-quarters support in the next election. For Zariņš, this seemed the only way out of the escalating squabbles between the Detmold and Esslingen parties and their requests for support in the name of unity: One party wanted Zariņš to speak out in favour of the election of former government ministers Valdmanis and Bērziņš, and the other party indicated that without Valdmanis in a leading position they would get along very well with the LCK.[61]

Following his election as LCP president, the Americans appointed Valdmanis officially Foreign Liaison Officer Serving the U.S. Armed Forces, European Theater.[62] As such, he was the representative of Latvian displaced persons as well as a counsel and adviser in matters of all Baltic refugees. He also received an army post Exchange ration card, allowing him access to American cigarettes and coffee, and a casino mess card, entitling him to the privileges of all Frankfurt Military Post Type 'B' messes and clubs in accordance with his status as 'Consultant, HQ Eucom,

Civil Affairs Division.' On 30 July 1947 the Military Government in the U.S. zone issued him a passport for stateless persons. It was valid for all European countries.[63]

Taking advantage of the security provided by his privileged status, Valdmanis forged ahead with his program regardless of opposition. He ignored challenges from Professor A. Švābe, chairman of the LCK, referring to him as a 'relic' of the authoritarian regime of the past with no right to act for all Latvians in exile. He even felt secure enough to prevent a harsh resolution proposed by Colonel Janums against Bilmanis being brought to a vote. But Bilmanis nonetheless continued his denunciation of Valdmanis as a quisling and demanded his resignation. He was worried that Valdmanis might declare himself provisional president of Latvia and remove him from his post. At the following LCK meeting, thirty-six of the forty-five delegates present voted for Valdmanis, nine abstained, and no votes were cast against him, giving him a two-thirds majority.[64]

Valdmanis's initiatives as LCP president, instead of silencing his opposition, made them redouble their efforts to get rid of him. They bombarded Zariņš, the LCK executive, and the Allied authorities with petitions demanding his removal. Three weeks after the election of Valdmanis, their offensive started with a seven-page, single-spaced, typed message to Zariņš and an open letter to the members of LCP and LCK. The message to Zariņš reiterated their standard allegations that Valdmanis was a quisling because Bilmanis said so in his 1943 publication. The only evidence they offered to support this allegation was the observation that Valdmanis 'by means of his activities during both occupations has compromised himself to the highest degree and as a leader of the refugees is threatening the best interests of all Latvians in exile.' They argued that if they accepted Valdmanis as leader, the Allies would be left with the impression that all Latvians in exile are pro-Nazis.

The Esslingen committee wanted to play a significant role in the restoration of national independence and democracy as they had seen happen in Austria in 1945. The Esslingen committee considered it obvious from a legal and constitutional point of view that the Saeima elected in 1931 and suspended by Ulmanis continued to be a de jure authority. Currently, this authority was represented by the Swedish-based LCP founded in August 1943 that now coordinated and directed all organized resistance in Latvia. This LCP included two-thirds of the former parliamentarians. After the death in 1946 of the former Saeima president, Pauls Kalniņš, the committee expected the highest ranking official of democratic Latvia to be his deputy, Bishop V. Rancāns. According to the 1922 constitution, Rancāns should now become the acting president of Latvia. Who else should represent the Latvian nation today, the Esslingen committee wondered, when even Zariņš was no longer recognized by the British government as a properly accredited ambassador? An amalgamation of the LCP in Detmold with the Swedish-based LCP was unacceptable, because the Detmold LCP as a non-political refugee organization would weaken the political authority necessary for the defence of the interests of Latvia.[65]

In an open letter to LCP and LCK of March 1947, thirty-four members of the council of the Esslingen colony did not bother to present a reasoned statement of their position and resorted directly to polemics. After due reference to Bilmanis's publication of 1943 as the authority on Valdmanis's record as a quisling, the letter quoted out of context various statements made by Valdmanis during the war. According to these quotations, Valdmanis offered the Germans an army of a hundred thousand Latvians with no conditions attached, he placed his entire trust in the Germans, he asked for German permission to allow him to sacrifice Latvian resources and blood for a new Nazi Europe, he was guided by the will of the *Führer*, he was prepared to surrender vital sovereign Latvian rights in return for a mere Slovakia-type of autonomy, he offered a far-reaching German–Latvian understanding, he guaranteed a German–Latvian community of fate and brotherhood in arms (*Waffenbrüderschaft*), and so on.

The letter claimed to have allowed the documents to speak for themselves and that not all the documents available had been presented yet. To the authors' knowledge, 'Valdmanis had never offered any opposition.' They alleged that Valdmanis, while claiming to have been deported to Germany, actually visited Riga several times, including at least one trip by airplane.' The authors claimed that they did not intend to conduct a trial but to show that such compromising facts existed and that Latvians could not afford to let their most vital interests be subject to the 'megalomania of a single person.'[66]

Upset by this letter, Alfred Valdmanis did not confine his response to a refutation of the polemics from Esslingen. Recalling the tenet that only he who is without sin should cast the first stone, Valdmanis proceeded with his own disclosures of some compromising wartime details concerning his chief adversaries Brūno Kalniņš, Voldemārs Bastjānis, A. Kācens, and Roberts Liepiņš. In the case of Bastjānis, for example, Valdmanis recalled his promotion to head of the central financial administration at the end of 1942 when it became evident that Latvia's fate was annexation and many Latvians were arrested and sent to concentration camps. In his new position Bastjānis earned exactly twice as much as Valdmanis and, as Valdmanis sarcastically put it,

> was no doubt leading a fierce underground fight and did it, of course, much smarter than I because his underground activities were the reason why German occupation authorities paid him that well. I was brought to Germany with my old Latvian passport in the company of two SS officers in their police vehicle. Mr Bastjānis left in a heavy truck containing his possessions and with certificates in his pockets praising his cooperation and requesting all possible help to him in Germany. In none of the CIC screenings have I hidden anything about my past, while Mr Bastjānis in his declarations had forgotten quite a lot.

The authors of the polemical letter, Valdmanis charged, had created a crude forgery – a distortion even of Bilmanis's 1943 text. Their intent was to convert a clearly patriotic intention into its exact opposite and 'filth.' Valdmanis acknowledged he felt deeply hurt by Bilmanis's careless use of the term 'quisling': 'Every one of you knows that I am not deserving it.' For the sake of truth, Valdmanis expected the resistance fighters in Esslingen to inform Bilmanis objectively about conditions in Latvia at the time and his actions there. Bilmanis himself had admitted in his publication that he was relying on rumours from Finland. Why would the Esslingen people try to destroy an innocent individual with fabrications, Valdmanis wondered aloud, when deep in their hearts they 'all know very well that I have always attempted to go the road of righteousness and to speak the truth?' Maybe they were mere agents of has-beens, he concluded, who did not know how to leave the stage with honour.[67]

In an attempt to clear the air and explore the chances of cooperation, Valdmanis sought a personal encounter with opposition spokesman Bishop Rancāns. However, Valdmanis doomed those chances because he insisted on his indispensability and their acknowledgment of his (1) record as a fighter against Russian communism and German Nazism and (2) refusal to recognize the validity of the 1922 constitution. To Bishop Rancāns, the main obstacle to cooperation was the conspicuous participation in refugee organizations of people with prominent roles under the occupying powers. These people were 'hampering the efforts of the representatives of old democratic Latvia to defend the vital interests of the Latvian nation.' The only organization qualified to speak on behalf of all Latvians was the Swedish-based LCP, according to Bishop Rancāns. The council elected by the refugees ought to cooperate in every way with the leadership of this LCP. Rancāns saw no shortage among the refugees of politically untainted persons with the experience and authority to take care of DP needs and problems. He cited Professor Kundziņš as an example.[68]

Alfreds Bilmanis and Alfreds Bērziņš Enter the Fray

Rumours that he had rehabilitated Valdmanis caused Bilmanis to enter the fray personally in June 1947 with an elaborate public denial. Bilmanis declared that he had never written a letter to Valdmanis, although Valdmanis had written several letters to him. In fact, Bilmanis insisted, he had never met Valdmanis and had distanced himself from him and his colleagues in the Ostland administration long ago. Regardless of their motives, Bilmanis claimed to have expressed distaste about any Latvian willing to cooperate with German aggressors. The ultimate judge of those actions would have to be the courts of independent Latvia. Bilmanis revealed that he had received copies of presentations submitted to the British security officials who had cleared Valdmanis. The presentations[69] contained, in Bilmanis's opinion, many unproven self-promotions that were unacceptable without corroboration considering Valdmanis's 1942 memorandum offering close cooperation with Germany and the conversion of Latvia into a protectorate similar to that of Slovakia.

For this reason Valdmanis – as well as Latvians who had served under the Bolshevik occupation – was not suitable to lead refugee organizations, but legally elected former parliamentarians would be the ideal representatives of Latvian interests. All Latvians should stand behind their flag and 1922 constitution. Criticizing this constitution as possibly useless should be out of the question, for it was 'the best we had from our past.' The constitution defined Latvia as a sovereign, independent, democratic republic with a territory and a flag. All Latvians should carry this message in their hearts.

Luckily, Bilmanis concluded, God had preserved for Latvians in exile not only a number of former members of Latvia's parliament but also the deputy president of that parliament, Bishop Rancāns. The bishop was and, with God's help, would remain 'a living embodiment of our state tradition.' Attached to the published version of this declaration was the verbatim copy of a July 1942 statement, allegedly made by Bilmanis, concerning the official installation of the directorate general of Latvia. It identified Valdmanis as 'the former Latvian Minister of Finance, dismissed in 1939 by the President,' and the directors general as 'a puppet regime' designed to 'camouflage the real purposes of Nazi Germany – the perpetual enslavement, the oppression and exploitation of Latvia.'[70]

In a follow-up letter on 8 July 1947 Bilmanis reaffirmed his position to Latvia's United Nations envoy in Geneva, Jūlijs Feldmanis. Although Valdmanis had called him 'insane' and now threatened to remove him from his post, Bilmanis categorically rejected the legitimacy of any action of those 'Nazi-appointed directors general, regardless of what kinds of motives they might have had.' According to this letter, it was well known that Valdmanis – in his desire to be washed clean and escape punishment – 'fabricated' his election to the LCP presidency and tried several times to get an affidavit of rehabilitation from Bilmanis. The American agencies and the International Red Cross should be properly informed about Valdmanis. That would be neither 'mudslinging' nor 'self-screening,' nor denunciation.

Bilmanis also rejected the right of Valdmanis, who considered himself 'virtually the head of the Latvian government,' to require from the International Red Cross accountability for $85,000 spent from the frozen assets of the Latvian Red Cross. Only Feldmanis, as a member of the board of the Latvian Red Cross had that right. Bilmanis disputed the right of the LCP or LCK to absorb the functions of the Latvian Red Cross withheld in the British zone of Germany. Although Valdmanis allegedly claimed that as minister of finance he had transferred state funds to the United States for Red Cross purposes, Bilmanis wanted it to be known that 'Valdmanis had been dismissed from his position by the President of State Ulmanis for certain important reasons best known to Valdmanis himself. But I also do know why.' The apparatus of the Latvian state continued to exist through its legally appointed ambassadors, members of the board of the Latvian Red Cross, and delegates from the Latvian to the International Red Cross. That apparatus, Bilmanis concluded, could not be replaced by an 'accidentally elected LCP by some accidental refugees.'[71]

In July 1947 Bilmanis planned to raise the issue of the recognition of Latvian sovereignty at the United Nations in Geneva. He planned to form a delegation including the Latvian envoys and Bishop Rancāns because, as he cabled them, 'I am continuing to consider him [Rancāns] as the highest-ranking representative of the Latvian government in exile.' Rancāns would be invited as an extraordinary envoy of Latvia and not of the Detmold LCP. There would be no hope to obtain funding for an LCP delegation. The Detmold LCP would have to cease functioning as an organization of activists, Bilmanis maintained: 'Some time ago I proposed to Bishop Rancāns the creation of an organization of the former members of parliament now in exile. From this organization Zariņš as the extraordinary envoy of Latvia would be able to select delegates for the various conferences. It is evident that the LCP would have to dissolve itself to be replaced by merely apolitical committees of refugees. My initiative was either ignored or rejected by some. The members of the LCP cannot represent the Latvian nation.'[72]

To promote the cause of Bishop Rancāns and expose 'the activities of former Director General Alfreds Valdmanis,' the Stockholm LCP in August 1947 copied Bilmanis's letter to Feldmanis and circulated it widely.[73] 'Thousands' of copies inviting denunciations of Valdmanis had been found in Geneva, wrote Boriss Zemgals, identifying himself as former notary public for the Credit Bank of Latvia, to his prewar acquaintance Bilmanis on 23 September 1947, but 'we are not prepared to accept these as being written by you because it would mean that you have stooped to the level of a Moscow agent.' Claiming to have no specific political ambitions or associations, Zemgals wanted to express his disappointment that, based on wrong information, an envoy of Latvians was trying to ruin rather than support one of the few remaining leading patriots. Ordinary Latvians would let Bilmanis know one way or the other, Zemgals concluded, that 'you, our glorious ambassador, who have been reading about our fate in foreign newspapers from a safe distance, and we, namely, the part of our people who themselves had to wade through the hell of torture and swamps of blood, have nothing in common any more except the language.'[74]

Within a week Bilmanis responded to Zemgals, signalling the inauguration of a revealing exchange of views between Valdmanis's most formidable opponent and his alleged closest confidant. Right now the Latvian cause would be best served, Bilmanis replied, if those who had been very visible during the Bolshevik and German occupations would not become so visible again as Latvia's representatives, 'not because of what Latvians might think of them, but because of how the foreigner evaluates them.' To this he added allegations of unethical behaviour, even though he admitted not knowing Valdmanis personally. Specifically, Bilmanis claimed to have information that Valdmanis (1) had to resign as minister of finance because he mixed personal financial matters with official duties, (2) transferred the title of his country property for the establishment of a collective farm (kolkhoz) to ingratiate himself with the Soviet regime, and (3) paid a visit, with Gustavs Celmiņš, as early as 11 July 1941 to the German authorities without having been invited.

Bilmanis, on the other hand, claimed to have (1) condemned the actions of the pro-Soviet Kirchenšteins government as early as 13 July 1940, (2) distanced himself from the German–Soviet agreement of 12 January 1941, and (3) completely dissociated himself from all German policy and the directors general as not representing the will of the Latvian nation. None of the Latvian exiles would now have the benefit of asylum in the British or American zones if he as their ambassador would not have taken such a position against the directors general and Valdmanis's proposal for a Latvian–German military alliance and a Latvian protectorate à la Slovakia.

The war crimes trials, revealing Nazi plans to colonize and germanize Latvia, confirmed to Bilmanis the correctness of his course of action. 'Even you, my dear Mr Zemgals, would not be able to sit now in Geneva and have under your discretion properties, including $1,000 notes which, as Feldmanis told me, were deposited in the account of the Geneva legation. Those properties would have been confiscated either by Hitler or by the now victorious Allied forces. That would have been the result if I had supported Valdmanis's position.' In Bilmanis's judgment, there were two sides to Valdmanis. 'On the one side, great activity, ability, and ambition to be a leader. But unfortunately there are other facts, heavy ones, that are pulling him down.' It may be just as opportune, Bilmanis maintained, to dissociate oneself as much from people who held glorious positions during the German occupation as during the Bolshevik takeover.[75]

Responding, on 6 October 1947, Zemgals lost no time refuting Bilmanis's charges point by point and acquainting him with what he claimed to be the views of 95 per cent of Latvian exiles. Valdmanis, to begin with, was not forced to resign but, on the contrary, in October 1939 Ulmanis had tried very hard to prevent his resignation, Zemgals insisted. 'Many of us are well aware of the Balodis–Valdmanis–Veidnieks–Einbergs fight for the creation of a new constitution; we know it because we were very close to that project.' On the issue of mixing matters of state with personal affairs, Zemgals wondered whether one of the cleanest ministers during the time of Latvian independence could be accused of not knowing how to separate the two?

After the Bolshevik takeover, Zemgals continued, Valdmanis was arrested to be sentenced in a show trial. But it became apparent that he was virtually the only high official of the Ulmanis regime who had not appropriated anything that he had not actually earned. In fact, he had refused the gifts generously dispersed by Ulmanis through the Credit Bank of Latvia, a claim that Zemgals as former notary of that bank would be able to document in detail. Concerned that proceedings against Valdmanis would hurt their very unpopular regime, Zemgals stated, the Bolsheviks released Valdmanis from jail until the day of the trial. Engineer A. Jagars (whose son was now in Germany), magistrate A. Ungurs (in Germany), and economist E. Suksis (in Sweden) co-signed a guarantee to the special investigator and people's prosecutor V. Blāzma that Valdmanis would not escape.

At the beginning of 1941, Zemgals went on, Valdmanis worked for about two weeks in the silk and knitting trust under engineer N. Dambergs (now in Germany). Dambergs with the help of Professor Miķelsons, Dr Marta Vīgants, and Dr Feliks Staks (all now in Germany) arranged Valdmanis's admittance to the cardiac wing of the university clinic to protect him from arrest until the night of mass deportations, when together with his guarantors Valdmanis disappeared into the forests of Latvia.

Concerning the German occupation Zemgals could testify, as vice chairman of the association of notaries public at the time, that the Directorate General of Justice under Valdmanis became the first centre for Latvian patriots. Hundreds of Latvian judges, lawyers, and notaries now living in Germany were able to witness Valdmanis's stance:

> It is possible that you, dear Ambassador, do not know what in Latvia was known to everybody, that following the German occupation of Riga, the internal matters of Latvia were taken over by the staff of the former Latvian army, calling themselves the organizational centre, and looking for and appointing Valdmanis as their spokesman. He, as it later became evident, opposed German policies more than any other of the former high officials had ever done. From day to day we were very concerned about Valdmanis's safety and life.

Zemgals suggested that Bilmanis was being manipulated by people like Bishop Rancāns, Klīve, and Bastjānis who were afraid to operate openly and with factual information. The insinuation that Valdmanis intended to liquidate Bilmanis was proof of their desperation to get Bilmanis on their side after their failure to win Zariņš over. In view of Bilmanis's partisan public statements and his invitation to Feldmanis to denounce

Valdmanis, Zemgals wondered how far Bilmanis intended to let his friends use him. Bilmanis had made serious mistakes in the past, for example, when he claimed in a press release of 1940 that the Kirchenšteins regime was not communist. The information Bilmanis was relying on now was in part unreliable wartime information, in part a deliberate distortion of the truth, Zemgals reiterated. The badly hurt nation of Latvia did not deserve to be wounded even more by its own ambassadors promoting partisan interests from a safe distance, concluded Zemgals. As Bilmanis 'waded with increased enthusiasm further and deeper' into the quicksand of self-destructive controversy, Zemgals wondered 'how that will end for all of us.'[76]

Bilmanis's reply of 10 October is not available. Judged by Zemgals next letter of 20 October 1947 to Bilmanis, it continued to focus on Valdmanis's alleged record as a traitor based on information supplied by former ministers of government, deputy presidents of the Saeima, and high-ranking army officers. A notary of the Credit Bank of Latvia and a trusted associate of its director Andrejs Bērziņš, Zemgals claimed to have evidence refuting allegations that Valdmanis caused Bērziņš's arrest. 'There was no opportunity to denounce Andrejs Bērziņš,' insisted Zemgals: 'He was fired in the first hour of Kirchenšteins's regime; Klavs Lorencs was instructed to collect all his keys (assuming that the safes of the bank contained documentary evidence against the Ulmanis regime). It happened so suddenly that A.B. did not even have a chance to collect the salary due him. Referring to his contract with Ulmanis, A.B. requested from the Kirchenšteins regime his backpay, reimbursement for his legitimate expenses, and the three-year salary due him in case of lay-off, in total a considerable amount. The result was his immediate arrest.'

Concerning Valdmanis's alleged treasonous collaboration with the German occupation powers, Zemgals wondered why Bilmanis refused to apply the same label to former President Arnolds Kviesis. Succeeding Valdmanis as director general of justice in 1943, he had obediently carried out German orders, instead of opposing them as Valdmanis had done. 'As you have stated yourself, you do not know Valdmanis, and I am saying you did not know and you do not know the conditions we all were in,' Zemgals protested. The crux of the problem was, Zemgals summed up, that 'having made a mistake you are refusing to admit it, that you continue stubbornly in the same direction while desperately looking for anything you could accuse Valdmanis of.'

All the high-ranking officials on whom Bilmanis relied for information, Zemgals pointed out, belonged to the same small group Latvians in exile had heard about only very recently. Calling itself LCP, this group had 'created only evil.' It had done very little for Latvian displaced persons and was held in low esteem by Latvian legionnaires, Zemgals stressed. 'Don't you remember our good old politicians and their ways of doing things? But their time has passed by now, and you should not let yourself be hitched to their wagon.'[77]

Thereafter the exchange of views between Zemgals and Bilmanis ended abruptly. On 28 October 1947 Ulmanis's former propaganda minister Alfreds Bērziņš sent Bilmanis a five-page comment on Zemgals's 6 October letter, which Bilmanis had circulated among his friends. Behind the identity of Zemgals 'who at no time was a person of significance in social or political life' was very likely Valdmanis himself, Bērziņš warned. Apart from his naive rushing to the defence of Valdmanis, how would Zemgals know about all the goings-on in the national cabinet, behind the scenes in the GPU [NKVD], and in the German occupational establishment? Zemgals even knew why the Bolsheviks had not proceeded with their trial against Valdmanis and why they let him – the only member of the Ulmanis cabinet in Soviet custody – go free. Bērziņš was probably correct. The available evidence does suggest that behind the alias of Boriss Zemgals hid Alfred Valdmanis, whose ruse had succeeded in drawing out Bilmanis and engaging him into the kind of dialogue that he had publicly pledged to refuse.

Maintaining that Valdmanis was distorting the truth, Bērziņš then set out to present the facts as he knew and remembered them, 'all revealing a series of dirty tricks designed to grab power and control the government.' To begin with, Valdmanis resigned in October 1939 at the request and not against the will of Ulmanis. The constitution was never a contentious issue, Bērziņš insisted. During Valdmanis's term as finance minister, cabinet did not even discuss it. Instead, Ulmanis allegedly regretted the appointment of the young and 'splendid self-promoter with absolutely limitless ambitions' who turned out to be a poor finance minister.

According to Bērziņš, Valdmanis lost his credibility completely when he promoted the idea that Ulmanis should confine his role to president of state and allow a 'young and energetic person' to become prime minister. Concerning corruption, Bērziņš remembered that Valdmanis certainly received his share of grants and subsidies from Ulmanis. While most ministers retired only as wealthy as they had started out, Bērziņš alleged, Valdmanis had managed to rid himself of his debts and acquire a country estate, a ship, and membership on the board of A/S Raugs, and make his father-in-law manager of a plywood factory. Such 'achievements' within one year, Bērziņš claimed, prompted Ulmanis to let Valdmanis go.

Most disturbing, however, was Bērziņš's explanation of Valdmanis's miraculous survival after the Soviet takeover when the Bolsheviks attempted to weed out 'root and branch' anything even potentially detrimental to their future plans. Valdmanis's alleged popularity should have been all the more reason to persecute him, since the entire national leadership of Latvia was being deported. Citing hearsay, Bērziņš alleged that Valdmanis had obtained his release from custody in return for agreeing to cooperate with the Soviet secret police (see chapter 3).

Bērziņš ventured on even more slippery ground with his contention that in July 1941 former Latvian army staff had made no efforts to establish a functioning administration. Valdmanis's authority, Bērziņš insisted, was derived solely from the German army through the mediation of Colonel Plensners. The claim that Valdmanis had been in the forefront of the resistance was simply an insult to all who had suffered in German prisons and concentration camps, as well as to the few who knew about Valdmanis's allegedly 'harmful and treasonous' petitions of July 1941 and December 1942.

How else can it be explained, asked Bērziņš, that the NKVD and Gestapo, both known for their cruelty to opposition, did not even restrict the freedom of Valdmanis? His privileged circumstances in Berlin in early 1944, which Bērziņš himself had seen, were sufficient to refute any claims of participation in the resistance. Some future time, 'when we will not have to be ashamed of quarrelling in front of strangers,' would expose 'the habitual lies, the self-promoting games in which he is playing the martyr and the hero at the same time, and the many foul machinations during the time of both occupations as well as the intrigues of the present.' All this evidence about Valdmanis's so-called depravity enabled Bērziņš to endorse the stance of Bilmanis and question how 'honourable' persons with 'such an outstanding record of public service' as Bishop Rancāns, Klīve, Liepiņš, and Bastjānis could be considered capable of cheating and lying.

To give Bilmanis 'a glimpse of Valdmanis's methods,' Bērziņš proceeded to reveal how he himself was allegedly victimized in the contest for leadership at the February 1946 LCP session in Hanau. After having announced his intention to challenge Valdmanis on the first day of the gathering, Bērziņš recounted, he was arrested by an American secret service officer on a charge of having collaborated with the Gestapo and the Japanese secret service. From an unidentified informer Bērziņš claimed to have learned that Valdmanis and his co-conspirators had offered themselves as witnesses, one of whom is supposed to have gloated that the last member of Latvia's 'black government' had been removed. Kept in custody for seventeen days, Bērziņš never doubted for one moment that it was Alfred Valdmanis who had caused his detention to eliminate him from the race for LCP leadership.

That argument might be compelling had Bērziņš not overlooked the fact that at the Hanau meeting in February 1946, as related above, Valdmanis was not even in the leadership race but instead reconfirmed his resignation as LCP president. In the concluding remarks of his long letter to Bilmanis, Bērziņš himself suggested a possible motive for these potentially devastating 'revelations.' With DP life drab and the prospects dim, Bērziņš lamented, 'I am looking everywhere for some kind of saviour.'[78] At the time, Bērziņš is reported to have offered the following justification for his damning exposure of Valdmanis: 'In the political arena it is quite common to throw mud, and a very thick skin is needed to survive there; anybody who is attacked has a right to fight back and if he is unable or doesn't know how to, he should get out.'[79]

Not surprisingly, in his memoirs published twenty-four years later, Alfred Bērziņš presented an altered version of the circumstances surrounding his February 1946 episode. This very detailed 1971 account reduced the period of Bērziņš's arrest to two weeks from seventeen days and failed to mention the Japanese secret service. Especially striking is the absence of any reference to Valdmanis as the culprit and cause of Bērziņš's arrest. In fact, in 1971 Bērziņš recalled that when he was released from detention at the end of the February 1946 LCP meeting, 'my former colleague Alfred Valdmanis offered to do all he could to help me. He said that he was having difficulties of his own and was also being accused of collaboration with the Nazis during the occupation. This LCP session was the last time I saw Valdmanis.'[80]

By the fall of 1947 the Latvian exile community had become saturated with unverified 'fairy tales about the heroic deeds' of Bishop Rancāns and his friends, and their Stockholm-centred umbrella organization. The real underground activists during the German occupation, LCP secretary J. Arājs (not to be confused with Viktors Arājs!) contended, had never heard of the alleged resistance record of the parliamentarians that even Bilmanis was unable to verify. According to Arājs, Bishop Rancāns could find only one witness, Latvia's former envoy to Sweden Voldemars Salnais, 'unfortunately a person not in Latvia during the occupation.' That witness claimed 3,500 of the 4,500 Latvians fleeing to Sweden would not have made it without the LCP.[81]

Why would Latvians under the hard blows of foreign exile be so eager to attack one of their most dedicated, competent, and self-sacrificing leaders, who had defended Latvian interests under German occupation, who had saved Latvian refugees in Thuringia from forcible repatriation, and who had fought for the release of Latvian legionnaires from unjustified imprisonment? Was this self-destructive impulse perhaps a trait inherited from the foreign rulers over Latvia, wondered pastor Alfreds Gulbis in an article written for the Latvian press. Gulbis reminded his readers that in past difficult times, less competent functionaries had often tried to diminish the reputations of achievement-oriented patriots by accusing them of germanophilism, russophilism, or anglophilism. These aspersions also became instruments of purge, for example, under the 1940–41 Soviet regime, when the attribution of anglophilism or americanism resulted in deportation, or under German occupation, when the charge of russophilism brought confinement in a concentration camp, or after 1945, when the imputation of germanism was the signal for special Cheka treatment.

Gulbis suggested that Latvians in exile let a cult of worshipping titles and positions blind them instead of examining the persons occupying these. 'We no longer look for the most decent, most honest, most courageous, or most nationalistically oriented candidates, but instead accept the bearers of high-sounding former or current titles. The shadow of the grand-sounding title can completely hide a little man.' Articulating the sentiments of Valdmanis's rank-and-file admirers and supporters, Gulbis declared that now 'it matters more than ever that the leadership of our people is in the hands of the very best men of our nation.'[82]

With the International Refugee Organization

Valdmanis's political fortunes in Latvian refugee organizations began to plunge in the face of the denunciatory campaign waged by Bilmanis, Alfreds Bērziņš, Bishop Rancāns, and their political friends. In September 1947 Valdmanis decided to resign permanently as LCP president right after having accepted a position offered by the Preparatory Commission for the International Refugee Organization (PCIRO) in Geneva. In terms of his work for refugees, the change actually amounted to a promotion. Now he was at the headquarters of the organization that decided the fate of all refugees. The LCP mandate was confined to the representation of refugee interests with Allied agencies in occupied Germany.[83]

Although the United Nations mandate did not permit the IRO to employ refugees or displaced persons, the U.S. armed forces pressured IRO headquarters to avail itself of Valdmanis's services. Appointed assistant chief of the Division of Planning and Field Services, Valdmanis became operational head of department in October 1947 owing to the extended absence of his superior. He was the only DP given a position of this seniority and importance by the IRO.[84] During his one-year term with the IRO, Valdmanis took credit for pursuing three objectives: (1) official IRO recognition of Baltic national DP organizations, (2) provision of employment for refugees who could neither emigrate nor return to Latvia, and (3) termination of screening former Latvian legionnaires out of DP camps and IRO acceptance of Latvian legionnaires and civilian refugees as bona fide DPs.

Valdmanis claimed success in all these pursuits. By December 1947 the IRO accepted Valdmanis's proposal for recognition of the Baltic refugees' national central committees. This was particularly important for Latvians unable or unwilling to emigrate from Germany. The legionnaires, too, benefited from his intercession. Alfred Valdmanis claimed credit for convincing the IRO in October 1947 to reconsider its opposition to rehabilitate Latvians who had fought in Waffen-SS uniform against Bolshevism. Especially critical in this case was the evidence of Valdmanis's opposition on 27 and 29 January 1943 to the mobilization of Latvians. This persuaded the IRO to adopt the ruling that Baltic nationals, who from 1943 on had 'volunteered' for service in the German armed forces, be considered mobilized by force. Valdmanis also took credit for having helped draw up a new IRO screening directive released in March 1948: these Baltic legionnaires were allowed a change in status to become bona fide displaced persons. The administrative skills Valdmanis demonstrated throughout earned him a promotion to IRO negotiator with prospective immigrant-receiving countries, including Canada, in matters of resettling Latvian and other bona fide displaced persons.[85]

Meanwhile Roberts Liepiņš (a former president of the Latvian Red Cross), on behalf of Bishop Rancāns, had been attempting to induce Latvia's envoy in Geneva, Jānis Feldmanis, to denounce Valdmanis to the IRO directorate from the day Valdmanis joined the IRO. Feldmanis refused to cooperate with Liepiņš, whereupon anonymous letters from Germany denounced Valdmanis at IRO headquarters. The denunciations triggered a wide-ranging investigation by the American secret service, the U.S. Department of Defense, the U.S. Department of State, the American embassy in London, the British secret service, and the British Ministry of External Affairs.[86] On 16 November 1947 his peace had been shattered, Valdmanis informed his brother-in-law Valdis Mateus, when news reached him of a wide-ranging investigation in process in Esslingen, Nuremberg, and Frankfurt. In Nuremberg, Valdmanis wrote Mateus, 'A new investigator interviewed the accused German industrialists active in the territory of Latvia and quizzed them in particular about me. The answer in general seems to have been that German authorities thought I would be useful in implementing their programs. But subsequently it was revealed that I was one of the worst kind of chauvinists deserving liquidation, and that I was saved by the intervention of some influential German friends.'[87]

From London, Kārlis Zariņš tried to assure Valdmanis as early as 19 November 1947 that the attempt of the Esslingen group 'to empty a bucket of dishwater over your head' was about to backfire. From an agent in the investigation, Zariņš had just received a report 'full of the most complimentary references and a very beneficial evaluation' of Valdmanis. Zariņš was very pleased that in a country where investigations are on a much higher level than anywhere else, 'one of our countrymen has been granted such highly favourable recognition. I am congratulating you on this matter. You can now relax and continue to work for the benefit of our country and our countrymen.'[88]

Valdmanis, however, was unable to relax until after he had made his final plea to the U.S. Intelligence Division in Frankfurt on 26 December 1947. According to the transcripts, he argued that Rancāns, Klīve, Bastjānis, Liepiņš, Kalniņš, Krūka, and Slakāns had denounced him three times. They had done this out of self-interest, jealousy, and fear of never getting higher governmental positions. These men tried to convince Latvians, that Valdmanis's election as the representative of all Latvian refugees would show that Latvians remained fascists and that the British and Americans did not want to have anything to do with him. At the same time, Valdmanis testified, these men 'were insisting to you that the Latvians did not want me, that I was a quisling, and that I was never properly elected and only pretending to my elected status.' Bilmanis, he concluded, had been maliciously taken advantage of in this ploy. A sick, old person, Alfred Bilmanis had never met Valdmanis, did not know about conditions in Latvia and about Latvian conditions in Germany, and, considering these circumstances, had acted in good faith.[89]

The official verdict issued on 3 January 1948 cleared Valdmanis of all war crimes and quisling charges. 'The verdict was extremely favourable to me,' he told friends in Germany on 10 January 1948. 'I really don't know how I obtained that complete clearance, because my mighty adversaries had prepared their noose very expertly. They attacked me all at once and from all sides in Germany, in Washington, and here in Geneva. It was no joke any more. From now on it will no longer be possible for them to talk about my alleged war crimes. The only place left for the small circle in Esslingen to turn to would be Moscow. Thus, until we return to Latvia there will be peace.'[90]

The details and extent of the conspiracy to silence Valdmanis once and for all emerged only gradually. 'Only now I begin to see,' he wrote Mateus on 24 January 1948, 'how strong a net had been woven to catch and drown me. That was a matter going way beyond the boundaries of the [DP] camps or the [occupation] zones.'[91] He found himself caught in a truly kafkaesque dilemma. As in Kafka's novel fragment *The Trial,* Valdmanis could no longer identify all of his accusers, their charges, the courts at which these might be tried, and the possible outcome. And against the known charges and innuendos, mostly based on incomplete or false evidence and motivated by fear of his allegedly insatiable ambitions, Valdmanis was unable to defend himself.

Among the affidavits exonerating Valdmanis and his political record was a five-page, typed statement signed by Latvian Lutheran Archbishop T. Grīnbergs (Teodors Gruenbergs), his secretary E. Rozītis, and current LCP chairman Lavenieks. They wondered how a man who had always been visible to the Latvian people, remained in close touch with the community of Latvian refugees, and earned their almost undivided confidence, could be called a collaborator or quisling.[92] There were also depositions by former German Foreign Office envoy in Riga, Dr Adolf Windecker, and Colonel K. Graebe of the Abwehr. (Windecker was returning a favour for the supportive testimony Valdmanis had offered at Windecker's denazification trial on 26 August 1947.) He and Graebe attested to Valdmanis's resistance credentials and recalled that Valdmanis collaborated only to promote Latvian sovereignty.[93] And there was finally a certified affidavit signed by Boriss Zemgals, but likely written by Valdmanis himself. It featured the transformation of 'the cleanest and most hard-working finance minister Latvia ever had' into 'the most dedicated leader of the national resistance to German occupation.' In the vein of his forthcoming Valdmanis biography, Zemgals's affidavit portrayed the young heroic genius as 'unquestionably one of the most gifted, bravest, and honest men Latvia ever had.' He would 'rather die standing upright than live on in slavery' and was 'sacrificing his life to his unhappy compatriots.'[94]

Support must also have come from Zariņš, judged by the sympathy he voiced on 10 March 1948 for Valdmanis's shrewd dealing with Germany's occupation powers. As a small nation, 'we should agree that we have to be as sly as snakes' and avoid suicidal open resistance, Zariņš remarked, and he recalled a conversation he had had with an important member of Churchill's cabinet coincidentally sitting next to Zariņš at a wartime banquet. This British cabinet member had allegedly said to Zariņš: 'You are a small nation – only two million. Each intelligent person is worth gold. Therefore do not waste any with sabotage. The reprisals can create a loss which you will not be able to replace. Your intelligentsia will be greatly needed later on. Do not copy the Poles. Their population was 35 million. If in underground activities they lose 10 or 15 million, that would be tragic but still leave them 20 million to survive as a nation. You simply don't have such reserves.'[95]

What should now happen to the denouncers? Valdmanis asked his friends. They must not be allowed to get by with merely a public denial of their manoeuvres. 'Liepiņš and Rancāns are in our hands,' he rejoiced. 'If we are going to deliver a punch, it must be a knockout.' Otherwise 'we might as well volunteer to become beet harvesters in Canada; that would then be the proper place for us.'[96] Before this option became an unexpected reality, however, Valdmanis and his friends agreed on a two-pronged offensive. They would request punitive American action while publicly exposing the denunciation. The request to the Intelligence Division of U.S. Army HQ in Frankfurt stated that 'because we have no court now where we could punish the above-mentioned denouncers ourselves and because we want to avoid any kind of "lynch-justice," we do request you, Americans, in the name of justice: *to bring Rancāns, Klīve, Liepiņš, and Bastjānis before an American Military Court or to treat them as security suspects'* (emphasis in the original).

According to the attached rationale, these men had betrayed the American government and tried to 'exterminate' a man who was supported by 99 per cent of all Latvians and 'who is our onliest [*sic*] hope as well as the onliest [*sic*] hope of our oppressed compatriots in Latvia.' His disappearance would mean the loss of a leader 'miles and miles ahead and above of any Latvian.' Likely drafted by Valdmanis himself, as the boastful style suggests, the request was allegedly not motivated by revenge. At stake was the defence of the Latvian nation and prevention of another unmerited attack against Valdmanis, a man 'too busy and too proud to defend himself.'[97] At the end of February 1948 a public statement was drafted for dissemination, using the legionnaires' welfare organization Daugavas Vanagi (Hawks of the Daugava, founded in Belgium in 1946) as a forum declaring Rancāns, Liepiņš, Klīve, and Bastjānis to be dishonourable men.[98]

The mere fact that Valdmanis was accused of war crimes, even though judged innocent, severely shook his position with the IRO. At the beginning of January 1948 IRO underwent a draconian budget cut and personnel reduction. Cancelled was the 6 January 1948 assignment given Valdmanis by PCIRO Executive Secretary H.W. Tuck to travel to Canada, approach all provincial governments, and negotiate an agreement on behalf of IRO about large-scale DP resettlement. In March those negotiations were conducted by Wing Commander Robert Innes.[99] By the end of January Valdmanis did not know whether he would have to return to Germany or 'whether in the very near future I will go across the great waters.'[100] As of February 1948 he found himself outside the new budget. He had helped draft the new IRO screening directive to extend bona fide DP status to Latvian legionnaires, but its implementation was delayed because several IRO officials opposed the eligibility of Baltic Waffen-SS. Starting in March 1948, however, IRO decided to renew his employment, and by mid-April Valdmanis reported being busy 'doing all I can to arrange opportunities for emigration of large and small groups.'[101]

Withdrawal from Refugee Politics

Despite his resignation as LCP president in September 1947, Valdmanis had retained his membership in the LCK. Following his clearance of all war crimes and quisling charges, he planned to stage a political comeback from this base. 'The time had come for LCP to decide on the creation of the LTP for the purpose of rescuing Latvia as a nation and state and that decision should be made at the next LCP session,' he wrote Mateus (who was also an LCK member) on 21 February 1948. The strategy would be first to elect a new LCP and LCK executive (where the pro-Valdmanis faction was anticipated to obtain a majority) and then to have the executive approve the launching of a new organization called Latvian People's Council (Latvju Tautas Padome, or LTP).[102]

According to the draft constitution, the LTP represented all citizens of Latvia, regardless of current residence. The *raison d'être* of the LTP was restoration of Latvian independence, to be achieved through a unified effort, such as the intervention of Latvian ambassadors appointed to the

United Nations and other international bodies, the implementation of binding instructions issued to all Latvian organizations by the ambassadors, and the adoption of whatever other measures might be necessary. Defining itself as non-political, the LTP was to be composed of experienced former government officials, judges, church leaders, personalities of high social standing, diplomats, as well as leaders of refugee organizations. The LTP chairperson was to be elected by a two-thirds majority, the remaining nine-member executive by a simple majority of the members. The responsibilities of the executive would be divided into eight sections, each specializing in the area of a major government department.

Until the liberation of Latvia from foreign rule, and until a democratically elected constituent assembly could decide the constitution of free Latvia, the LTP was to function as the highest advisory Latvian organization. Immediately upon the liberation of Latvia, the LTP would assume government duties. Under special circumstances, the LTP could take over the functions and duties of a provisional government even before the liberation of Latvia. The chairman of the LTP would become minister president.[103]

As early as February 1948, the Latvian paper *Latvju Ziņas* (Latvian News) appearing in Sweden carried an anonymous attack on the LTP project as unconstitutional and undemocratic. It charged that the LTP was ignoring the 1922 constitution and tried to recreate Latvia, when all that was needed for the restoration of sovereignty was to remove some obstacles. The article went on to accuse the founders of the LTP of setting themselves up to assume control over Latvia like eastern dictators and without consideration for the values of western democracy. Only association with the political ideas of the West would produce a free Latvia in a world of free countries, and hence guarantee freedom for every citizen in the state. How were the undemocratic ideas of the LTP to be reconciled with the Human Rights Charter of the United Nations that upheld such individual rights as freedom of speech, association, and political parties? Western democracy could not be imagined without political parties as agents of political life, the article maintained.[104]

The LTP, however, instead of becoming the launching pad for a government-in-exile, was destined to remain a pipedream. At the Würzburg meeting of the LCK in early April 1948, Valdmanis was outmanoeuvred by his unexpectedly well-organized opponents. They managed to pass a resolution creating a new Latvian National Federation (LNA) and a Latvian National Council (LNP) as part of a new umbrella organization called Federation of Latvian Organizations (LOA). In the LNA and LNP, membership would be confined to those recognizing the 1922 constitution. Many delegates voted for this clause without thinking much about it,[105] commented Valdmanis afterwards, but he was unable to do so. 'I cannot defame the period after 15 May [1934] and ... I cannot imagine a greater disaster than a return to the corrupt system created by the 1922 constitution. The people aware of my attitude and forcing this clause knew that they are excluding me from further participation.'

In regard to the LNA, Valdmanis confided to Mateus, 'I am not only free, but actually rejected.' Contrary to Valdmanis's policy not to discriminate on the basis of political convictions, the LNA statutes were pushing away all those who wanted to work for Latvia without accepting the 1922 constitution. 'I have been excluded and rejected, and consequently the only thing left for me to do is to collect my family and get lost.' Valdmanis doubted whether 'much would be gained by emigration, except losing some friends or possibly enemies.' But in exchange for relinquishing his LCK membership, Valdmanis informed Mateus, he would now fully associate himself with the Latvian People's Federation (LTA). This organization counted seven members, according to Mateus. Established in Esslingen in early January 1947, and closely associated with Daugavas Vanagi,[106] the LTA was prepared to go with Valdmanis 'through fire and water.' Of course, in order to become a mass party, Valdmanis continued, it would be necessary to have a broader membership base, trust in the leader with all his bad characteristics, an LTA council, an ideological platform, and so on.[107]

The crumpling of his political ambitions sent Valdmanis into a severe soul-searching depression. To an unidentified 'dear, old, good friend' Valdmanis confessed that he did not have many friends, and the ones he did have, he did not know how to keep. 'For deserved and undeserved reasons,' they sooner or later turned away from him. His greatest handicap was 'that I do not know how to talk, that is, how to "open up," and how to "explain myself." In countless cases in my life, I have felt that only a few words would have sufficed to prevent me from losing a dear and intimate person. But never before, not even once in my previous life, have I been able to find and say them. That is the greatest tragedy in my life and one day it is going to break me.' Reviewing the beginnings of his career, this 'unbelievably gifted individual,' as Valdmanis called himself, bemoaned the misfortune that he was 'jerked up too early and quickly.' He whined, 'my career advanced, so to speak, in jumps and, believe me, against my will. How very much at that time did I not want to be a minister; I had the premonition that I would be "chewed up there." And so it was. At least that was the time when it started.'

He had no opportunity to develop hate and envy, Valdmanis claimed. His meteoric rise gave him no occasion to envy anybody. Since hate and envy were therefore incomprehensible to him, he did not know how to fight them. Valdmanis candidly admitted that he had enemies and understood their right to hate him. Nonetheless, he added, 'In my heart I have always wanted only good, I am also just a human being and I have done many things I should not have done.' Latvians had many decent and wise men with whom he would not dare to compare himself, but they had become invisible, probably because at a time like this it was nearly impossible to present oneself. 'God knows that I have not wanted to impose myself as a kind of "leader." From head to foot I am already covered with scars that have demanded nearly superhuman strength. But now I am physically and mentally exhausted because for resting I have had no time.'

Whether he was good or bad, whether people loved or hated him, Valdmanis considered himself always willing and able to do something beneficial for Latvians. 'I did not mind being used,' he assured that friend. And he insisted that all that was necessary to promote the common good was to control or suppress one's anger and hate. The tragedy of Latvian refugees was that they did not know how to separate personal from community matters and that, with great enthusiasm, they cultivated 'disassociation.' If separation into sectarian divisions was what Latvians wanted, they could do that later. Right now, in Valdmanis's opinion, they have only one valid question. 'Can you do something useful, do you want to do it, do you have the necessary support, and do you believe that you have the authority? Nothing else.'[108]

Days of Happiness and Distress

The printed word was now the only weapon left to challenge the perceptions and politics of Alfred Valdmanis's opponents and to set the record straight. Now, more than ever, would it be necessary to present to them and to posterity a historical account of Valdmanis record, just as it was 'important to state the truth about anybody who had acted with the best intentions for his country,' as the preface to the book *Dienas baltas nebaltas* put it. Completed in May 1948, though not published until one year later in Geneva, its full title reads in translation: *Days of Happiness and Distress: A report about the work of Alfred Valdmanis on behalf of his country and countrymen.* Though crediting others, including Valdmanis, for their input, Boriss Zemgals presented himself as the author of the book. The nephew of former Latvian state president Gustāvs Zemgals and official notary of the Credit Bank of Latvia, Boriss Zemgals claimed to have been caretaker and keeper of a great part of the documents and secrets of the government.

The book is divided into four parts: (1) Flag Waving (1932–39), (2) The Red Nightmare (1940–41), (3) Under the Swastika (1941–45), and (4) In Exile (1945–48). The apologetic tendency and the inclination to boast clearly indicate a style characteristic of Valdmanis. Also, passages depicting his mind-set, confidential conversations, rationale for political manoeuvres, and behind-the-scenes politicking point to Valdmanis's authorship. Questions about the credibility of certain assertions in parts 1 and 2 arise from the desire to overcompensate for his opponents' alleged distortion of his political record and the belittling of his achievements. Quite obvious is the endeavour to enhance Valdmanis's democratic, anti-German, and patriotic credentials. Valdmanis's autobiographical notes of 1962–3, edited posthumously by Edgars Andersons in 1983, attempt to correct some of these deficiencies.[109] The reliability of parts 3 and 4 of *Dienas baltas nebaltas* is corroborated by the records of the German occupation authorities and the availability of numerous contemporary witnesses.

Kārlis Zariņš knew Boriss Zemgals personally and portrayed him as a stubborn and quarrelsome fighter for Valdmanis's cause.[110] These traits are reaffirmed in a May 1949 letter Boriss Zemgals's son, Leonīds Zemgals, addressed to Aleksandrs Āboliņš. It authorized Āboliņš to use the letter, two copies of which are deposited in the Valdmanis Family Papers, 'for any purpose you would see fit.' In it the younger Zemgals confirmed that 'my untimely departed father was an extraordinary admirer of Mr Valdmanis, mainly because of his abilities and his courage.' The son also revealed that, when around the turn of 1947–8 Valdmanis was under a heavy burden of work and stress caused by the investigations, 'my father took care of all of his personal business.'

Leonīds Zemgals recounted that in Geneva his father argued a lot with Valdmanis about the latter's habit of not defending himself against unjustified attacks. 'In time the truth always becomes apparent by itself,' Valdmanis used to maintain according to Leonīds Zemgals, and Boriss Zemgals used to retort that 'even Christ was crucified by means of false accusations and that continuous systematic accusations can muddy up a lot.' At Valdmanis's suggestion that he would simply get out if he could not take the accusations any longer, Leonīds Zemgals's father would get very angry and reply, 'You belong to your country, the country which has given you all your opportunities, and there is no place where you can disappear.' For these reasons but triggered by his lengthy correspondence with Bilmanis, Leonīds Zemgals disclosed, his father started work on the manuscript.

Unfortunately, the younger Zemgals explained, financial exigencies permitted the publication of only an abridged version of the manuscript. Allegedly missing and never printed were chapters about Valdmanis's youth, about Alfreds Bērziņš's activities against Valdmanis in the cabinet, and about the conspiracy in Esslingen where on the initiative of the former Latvian Red Cross Director Liepiņš and with the assistance of Bastjānis and Klīve, the denunciation of Valdmanis was hatched and subsequently forwarded to Washington. The sudden death of Boriss Zemgals when the manuscript was at the printer's caused a delay in the book's publication.

The book was also intended to present the truth about the creation of the Latvian Legion and the patriotic roles played by colonels Plensners and Silgailis, according to Leonīds Zemgals. His father was opposed to the idea of military officers meddling in politics and particularly unhappy about the officers' initiatives in the formation of police battalions. He was concerned that some irresponsible officers would start recruiting Latvians too early and throw them into battles where they would perish without benefit to Latvian independence. 'My father was convinced that anybody had the right to do with his own life what he wanted, but others could be drawn into a war only on the basis of the proper authorization.'[111]

Clearly, all these were concerns dear to the heart of Valdmanis, but whether he drafted Leonīds Zemgals's letter himself can be neither corroborated nor refuted. A large number of the documents on which *Dienas baltas nebaltas* is based are still in the possession of the Valdmanis family. Valdmanis was unable to write that book himself, the Preface explains, because

> he himself keeps silent. During the occupation period he fought for the very existence of the Latvian people and I could appreciate his silence. When he was deported to Germany in the course of the war, he was forbidden to speak. After the collapse of Germany he was flooded with work and did not have time to speak. After he was elected one of the highest representatives of Latvians in exile he refused to speak about himself because he was too proud and did not want to cheapen himself. When subsequently suffering some of the most undeserved attacks, he continued to be silent. It was his conviction that a leader of exiles should stay above internal conflicts

> and has no right to plunge into controversies on personal matters. And he obstinately continues to keep silent, saying 'What shall I speak about? I only did what I felt I had to do under those circumstances, no more.'

Alfred Valdmanis's associates, according to the book's introduction, disagreed and felt that his record should be publicized by Zemgals. Opponents, however, have contended that Zemgals was a mere alias for Valdmanis, who had reasons for concealing his authorship. 'I know that Valdmanis had written *Dienas baltas nebaltas*,' acknowledged his Edmonton friend August J. Osis seven years after Valdmanis's death.[112] Most likely, Zemgals allowed Valdmanis to write most or all of the book and use Zemgals's name to promote a common cause – surviving the challenges ahead.

chapter seven

'Starting Anew Like Our Fathers Did after the First World War': Immigrant in Canada, 1948–1950

It is my belief that these people [the Baltic Waffen-SS] are the ones you want from the standpoint of the Canadian immigration policy. They are almost all single; they are young and physically strong. They are strongly anti-communist ... They are much like myself. Their past has been crushed, their former lives smashed. They have to start anew much like our fathers did after the First World War.

Alfred Valdmanis to Canadian Senators, 1949

Immigration to Canada

Alfred Valdmanis immigrated to Canada on 13 October 1948 accompanied by his wife Irma and their four children. They came to stay. Disembarking at Quebec City from the SS *Empress of Canada,* they entered Canada with a minimum of bureaucratic red tape, a balance of U.S.$10,000 in Valdmanis's American Express account in New York,[1] and a professorship in economics for him at McGill University in Montreal. For Irma, the cross on Mount Royal was a good omen; it gave reassurance that Canada would be good to her and her family.[2] For many, if not the majority, of Valdmanis's fellow countrymen in exile, Canada had been the preferred country of resettlement. Most of them, however, did not on arrival have the relatively trouble-free immigration and settling-in experience of the Valdmanis family.

Indeed, Canada must have been a most desirable destination for Latvian refugees, judging by the pleas for admission Ottawa received at the end of the Second World War. As early as August 1945, a Canadian major in

Germany requested the admission of twenty-five Latvians known to him personally. He found them to be 'scrupulously honest, industrious and law-abiding' and added that 'it is astonishing to note that the wishes of so many of these people are to immigrate to Canada if they cannot return to their native countries.'

Many Latvians in Europe believed that Canada's new governor general would intercede on their behalf because he had sided with them in the First World War. In a typical petition of May 1946, forty-three Latvians from the Esslingen DP camp reminded Field Marshal Viscount Harold Alexander of Tunis that 'the Latvians, a small nation from the Baltic state of Latvia, have not forgotten, that after the First World War your Excellency helped them to secure their freedom and independence, being then the commander of the united forces which fought against the invading enemies of Latvia.' Starting in May 1946, requests arrived from thousands in groups of up to 437 and 450 Latvians petitioning Lord Alexander and Canadian government officials for admission. Among these groups were such illustrious Latvian legionnaires as colonels J. Priede and Voldemars Skaistlauks from the Esslingen camp. At the time, all groups were declared non-admissible as immigrants or referred to United Nations agencies.[3]

The first Latvian DPs, among a transport of 832 DPs, arrived in Canada – to work in lumber camps – in October 1947. The RCMP found SS tattoo marks on three of the Latvian arrivals, indicating they had been recruited for the Latvian Waffen-SS Legion, probably in 1943. The three men denied that they had served in the German armed forces, and were admitted without further screening. Security guidelines in 1948 formally barred bearers of SS tattoos from Canada. Until 1949 Canadian security officers exercised a high degree of personal discretion in admitting immigrants, relying almost totally on interviews with applicants for information about their background. Subjective screening procedures and preoccupation with communist infiltration thus conspired to facilitate the admission of possible Nazi war criminals.[4]

Most Latvians involved in war crimes bore no SS tattoos, so they could evade probing immigration screening altogether. The auxiliary police units for which they had volunteered in 1941 were integrated automatically into the newly created Waffen-SS Legion in 1943 or continued as local police. One such war criminal, Haralds Puntulis, arrived in Canada on 13 October 1948. Police chief in the Rēzekne district from July 1941 to 1944, Puntulis ordered several local killing operations. In the summer of 1941, for example, he and his men rounded up all the Jews in the villages of Ribiena and Malta and shot them, some in a nearby forest and some in a cellar. (Puntulis died in his Canadian home in 1982 without ever having been charged in Canada for his wartime crimes.)[5]

As the Cold War assumed more ominous dimensions in connection with the Berlin Blockade, Latvians resorted to desperate ways to leave Europe. One Latvian group actually sailed their own vessel to Boston. The Latvian honourary consul in Toronto informed Deputy Minister of Mines and Resources and head of the immigration branch, Hugh Keenleyside, in August 1948, of the event and urged him to permit their immigration to Canada because 'no decision has been made as to allowing them to enter the United States. They would like to come to Canada but as you know they ran out of resources which forced them to land at Boston ... they would like to proceed to Toronto and I have been assured by the Lutheran group at Kitchener that suitable accommodation can be secured. I think you will agree with me that any group that has the courage to sail the Atlantic under such strong physical handicaps – they will undoubtedly make good Canadian citizens.' Keenleyside refused to give preferential consideration to the request of 'any group of political refugees who may have succeeded in reaching Canadian shores at whatever great personal risk.'[6]

Considerable debate developed during 1948 in the Latvian DP community over the merits of emigrating from Germany, and over the question of whether and how it should be organized. The Latvian Central Committee (like the Lithuanian and Estonian central committees) and refugee community spokespersons would have preferred cohesive group settlement, enabling Latvians to retain their ethnocultural identity as well as the ability and desire to return to their homeland. Many Latvians, on the other hand, were eager to resettle under any conditions. In November 1947 Latvian London envoy Kārlis Zariņš was worried that Latvians had no 'well-founded reason' for their excessive enthusiasm about the idea of emigration to Canada, when that country would not even consider group settlement and care for invalids.[7]

By the spring of 1948 Zariņš and Valdmanis agreed that the threatening international situation dictated that Latvians get out of Germany. Zariņš preferred for Latvians to stay in western Europe. Valdmanis, however, through the International Refugee Organization, was working on arrangements for migration to overseas destinations such as Abyssinia and Venezuela. With group resettlement impossible, Valdmanis proposed that contact be maintained through a central registry, a practice that Zariņš said had proven a failure in England.[8] At the 5 March 1948 session of LCP, it was noted with apprehension that emigration was scattering the community of Latvian exiles and that to channel the movement to Canada care centres would have to be set up there.[9] Then on 30 March 1948 Valdmanis learned from Robert Innes, IRO director of resettlement, that Canada would not allow large-scale immigration.[10]

Throughout the summer and autumn of 1948 LCP and LCK vainly persisted with their request that holding camps be established in Canada for Latvian families admitted as immigrants. The Baltic national committees in Germany protested jointly, on 9 September 1948, to J. Allison Glen, the Canadian minister responsible for immigration: 'The general situation in realizing the resettlement programme of IRO has not undergone any favourable change of late. Governments of receiving countries have not adopted the IRO proposed principles of admission as reiterated by Mr H.W. Tuck, Executive Secretary of IRO ... providing (1) acceptance of family groups without qualification, [and] (2) the acceptance of DPs on an across-the-board basis, rather than merely on a labour-recruitment basis.' The memorandum complained that Canada was considering only families with no more than two children, so other dependents had to be split from these families and left 'upon the mercy of the anti-DP-minded German authorities.'[11]

'In the matter of admissions Canada is most petty,' concluded the minutes of an LCP meeting. 'Although it would be logistically easy to return from Canada to Latvia, this is a prospect Canadians are absolutely unhappy with.'[12] Canada was delaying admission, while Brazil had offered to accept 5,000 and Argentina had opened its doors to 2,900 Latvian applicants in the summer of 1948.[13] By November 1948 some 16,000 Latvians had emigrated from Germany and Austria. At that time, the Latvian Central Committee (LCK) listed 90,500 Latvians as still resident in western Europe (88,500 in Germany and 2,000 in Austria), 50 per cent of whom were aged seventeen to forty-one. Canada recorded 877 Latvian DP admissions in 1947–8 and 3,331 in 1948–9 (for the year ending 31 March 1949).[14]

In response to an urgent LCK appeal that Canada admit more Latvian refugees with families or allow the establishment of holding camps in Canada to be maintained by Latvians, Keenleyside reiterated:

> Past experience has shown that settlement in racial groups or colonies is not in the best interests of Canada or of the people concerned ... The existing policy for the reception of displaced persons in Canada is based upon applications from legal residents of this Dominion (relatives, friends or

employers) who are able and willing to guarantee suitable settlement arrangements. In the case of workers brought forward under the group labour plan, the employer usually requests single or unattached persons, or those who are willing to come forward alone, leaving their families to follow at a later date after the family head has become established and can provide suitable accommodation. Where the employer signifies his willingness to receive a family, the dependents may come forward at the same time. The possibility of establishing holding camps for dependents has been under consideration but, for various reasons, it has not been practicable to establish such camps.[15]

A New Life

As early as 1947 Valdmanis had toyed with the idea of moving to Canada. It was, however, not until after his opponents in April 1948 had excluded him from Latvian refugee politics in Germany that the decision to emigrate matured. Also, the planned closure of IRO in 1949 was to terminate his assignment in Geneva and leave him unemployed. Valdmanis did not consider resettlement in Canada, however, as the end of his involvement in Latvian politics. On the contrary. While out of range of the attacks by his opponents, he hoped to promote the cause of Latvian independence more effectively than he had been able to in western Europe. Above all, at age forty, Valdmanis looked forward to starting a new life and career in Canada, leaving behind the hopelessly entrenched old-world hatreds and the burden of painful and embarrassing political legacies.

Rudyard Kipling's poem 'If' so inspired him for a new beginning that he kept copies on himself and in his personal files:

If you can keep your head when all about you
Are losing theirs and blaming it on you;
If you can trust yourself when all men doubt you,
But make allowance for their doubting too:
If you can wait and not be tired by waiting,
Or being lied about, don't deal in lies
Or being hated don't give away to hating,
And yet don't look too good nor talk too wise;

If you can dream – and not make dreams your master;
If you can think – and not make thoughts your aim,

If you can meet with Triumph and Disaster
  And treat those two impostors just the same
If you can bear to hear the truth you've spoken
  Twisted by knaves to make a trap for fools,
Or watch the things you gave your life to, broken,
  And stoop and build'em up with worn-out tools;

If you can make one heap of all your winnings
  And risk it on one turn of pitch and toss,
And lose, and start again at your beginnings
  And never breathe a word about your loss:
If you can force your heart and nerve and sinew
  To serve your turn long after they are gone,
And so hold on when there is nothing in you
  Except the will which says to them: 'Hold on!'

If you can talk with crowds and keep your virtue
  Or walk with Kings – nor lose the common touch,
If neither foes nor loving friends can hurt you,
  If all men court with you, but none too much:
If you can fill the unforgiving minute
  With sixty seconds worth of distance run,
Yours is the Earth and everything that's in it,
  And – which is more – you'll be a Man, my son!

A revealing glimpse of how Valdmanis intended to dispose of his political past, and prepare the ground for a new future, can be gleaned from the curriculum vitae he submitted to the Canadian immigration authorities on 8 August 1948. Most striking is the omission of any reference to his role as a director general during the German occupation of Latvia. The chronology jumps from his imprisonment in 1940 by the Russians as a 'foe of the Nations' to his imprisonment in 1943 by the Germans as an 'anti-Nazi.' Valdmanis described his position in the Ulmanis cabinet as a 'a non-political expert on European economy.' As the institution awarding his doctor of jurisprudence degree, he picked the University of Frankfurt an der Oder. No one could evaluate this claim because this city, in the Soviet zone of Germany, had been almost completely destroyed in 1945. In reality, his doctoral degree had been converted in November 1943 from a magister of jurisprudence (which, in turn, had been converted in 1940 from his degree of candidate of law awarded in

1932) and did not involve the University of Frankfurt an der Oder at all (see Chapter 5). On this particular résumé Valdmanis listed proficiency in seven languages, but three (Polish, Czech, and Bulgarian) did not reappear in any of his previous or later résumés.

In Geneva Valdmanis had managed to establish a good reputation at IRO and cultivate close contacts with influential Canadians, such as Wing Commander Robert Innes and Hugh Keenleyside, deputy minister of mines and resources in charge of the immigration branch. Keenleyside had probably first met Valdmanis on the former's tour of Canada's European immigration facilities in the summer of 1948. Having accepted into his home in Canada an Estonian DP, who became his daughter-in-law and for whom he procured employment with IRO, Keenleyside was known to be sympathetic to the plight of Baltic displaced persons.[16]

For DPs who were academics, an opportunity to cut through the red tape of Canada's entry restrictions suddenly presented itself, in 1948, in the form of the Lady Davis Foundation. It was established in March that year by Sir Mortimer Davis to enrich Canadian universities by sponsoring outstanding European refugee scholars. The Lady Davis Foundation advertised its fellowship program widely among various DP and refugee agencies, including the IRO Resettlement Division, headed by Innes. The foundation paid a very generous, one-year salary ($5,000 to $10,000) to a fellow, advanced or reimbursed travel expenses, and procured accommodation. Most importantly, for DP professionals and intellectuals, it helped clear their nearly insurmountable immigration hurdles. Among the first four hundred applicants, one hundred were rejected outright, but the remaining three hundred were adjudicated by a committee of Canadian university presidents. By September 1949 the first thirty-two fellows had arrived in Canada, including one other Latvian besides Alfred Valdmanis.[17]

The media greeted their arrival as a welcome deviation from existing entry restrictions that permitted displaced persons to enter Canada only as bulk contract labour for lumber camps, mines, and farms. Weighted against the admission of professionals, because these were supposedly 'hard to place,' existing immigration policy took no advantage of 'brains and talents going to waste in European DP camps,' charged the *Winnipeg Free Press.* With the professions such as dentistry and medicine tightly controlling admission to practice, immigration officials were granting entry to DP professionals only under exceptional circumstances. The addition to the McGill University faculty of the first two Lady Davis fellows – Latvian Alfred Tauriņš and Hungarian Istvan Anhalt – with expertise in chemistry and music respectively proved to the *Free Press* that Canada was 'just as much in need of brains as brawn.' The least likely to become a burden on the country in the long run, professionals instead would 'bring ideas, inventiveness, and talents' with 'immeasurable benefit' to Canada, the paper contended.[18]

On 30 June 1948 Valdmanis was informed that he had been awarded a one-year $3,000 fellowship plus travel expenses. Soon afterwards, on 30 July by Order-in-Council PC 3395, the foundation's application for Valdmanis's admission to Canada was approved.[19] As his research project, Valdmanis had proposed 'Canada's Foreign Trade,' to be pursued originally as a member of the department of economics at McGill University.[20] But Valdmanis never did make it to McGill. After a talk with Keenleyside and Senator Wilson, he joined, instead, the faculty at Carleton College in Ottawa as a professor of economics and political science. Meanwhile, for his family residence he chose first Aylmer, Quebec, and from 1950, Montreal. Valdmanis took up his academic position on 1 December 1948. From then on, he presented himself to the public as doctor of jurisprudence from the University of Frankfurt and former Latvian minister of economics, finance, trade, and industry who had been imprisoned during the war – first by the Russians and then by the Germans.[21]

Among Valdmanis's personal papers are notes for an economics lecture he presented at Carleton. These seem to consist, by and large, of excerpts from Harold Macmillan's 1938 publication *The Middle Way* and Valdmanis's occasional summary reflections on them. Focusing on what Macmillan termed 'industrial reconstruction' that 'borrows both from capitalist and socialist schools of thought,' the excerpts hark back to the restructuring policies Valdmanis had embraced under Kārlis Ulmanis. If the object of economic effort is to increase the production of wealth for the benefit of all, the notes postulate, then the analysis of what people want should turn the focus on social services, the machinery of distribution, the organization of ownership, and industrial reconstruction.

The need for industrial reconstruction, for example, is derived from the realization that efficiency does not necessarily follow from the maintenance of competition. 'You are led, in fact, however unwillingly, to quite the opposite view, that the most efficient industries are the most highly organized and integrated industries and that competition is quite as often an obstacle as a spur to efficiency.' Industrial reconstruction is summarized as an appreciation of the fact that certain industries and services are of 'key importance to the vigorous economic life of the community.' Once these have reached 'the stage of development when their conduct requires to be governed by much wider social considerations than the profit-making incentive alone will provide, [they] should be brought under either some suitable form of public ownership and management or, in certain cases, a form of statutory control or supervision.'[22]

Politics as an academic subject must have been as dear to Valdmanis's heart as economics. On 10 February 1949, identifying himself as a professor of political economy, he announced a series of seminars on European government and politics sponsored by Carleton's department of political science. This seminar course included ten lectures, to be offered every Thursday at 4 p.m., beginning 10 February. The topic he chose was the government and politics of European countries, beginning with 'The Overthrow of Tsardom and the Stabilizing of Communism in Russia.'[23]

The week he presented his last lecture in that series, Valdmanis was invited to appear before the Standing Committee on Immigration and Labour of the Senate of Canada and speak about conditions in the Baltic countries during the war, his own experiences, and the immigration of Balts from the DP camps. The committee had a mandate to examine the operation and administration of the Immigration Act and report on the desirability of facilitating the entry of displaced persons from Europe. The Senate's invitation to Valdmanis was prompted by his employment in Ottawa as a consultant on immigration by the Immigration Branch and by the ongoing review of immigration policy in view of petitions requesting Canada to relax existing restrictions on the admission of Baltic displaced persons.

DP Politics in Ottawa and the Waffen-SS Issue

The arrangement to employ Alfred Valdmanis as a government consultant on immigration matters had been initiated only six weeks after his arrival, when Keenleyside submitted a recommendation to council that the services of Valdmanis be utilized on a part-time advisory basis. The proposal aimed at a 'rather loose' arrangement under which Valdmanis would serve as a consultant on DP immigration for a twelve-month period at a monthly fee of $100. 'Dr Valdmanis knows seven languages (his English is practically perfect),' and he would know the background of many of the refugees, noted Keenleyside. He added that Valdmanis had come with recommendations from the head of IRO and others 'who spoke most eulogistically of his qualifications and character' and had allegedly been offered posts in 'several leading United States universities and by, among others, the Ford Motor Company in Detroit.' In view of his exceptional record, it would be 'most desirable' to encourage Valdmanis to make Canada his new home. According to the recommendation, Valdmanis could be of great assistance since Canada was facing emergency problems, such as that created by the expected arrival of 261 Estonian and Latvian refugees who had crossed the North Atlantic in a corvette.[24]

In the spring of 1949 the alleged harsh treatment of Latvian legionnaires in security screenings was the issue of particular concern to Latvian refugees and their representatives. Kārlis Zariņš, in London, wanted the Canadian government to know that 'there was a very great interest among our people [in Germany] for emigration to Canada.' Canada was the country to which they felt most drawn because, among other things, of the similar climate. However, emigration was severely restricted by the great reluctance of Canada to accept men from the Latvian Legion. These soldiers had been forcibly mobilized, Zariņš pointed out emphatically, 'and when they fought it was not for the German cause, but in the hope of keeping out of our native land the communists who had made the year 1940–1 one of horror for as long as Latvian history lasts.' Britain had already admitted ten thousand former Latvian legionnaires and was 'very satisfied' with them – they formed the 'soundest elements,' worked well, and were 'steady and well disciplined.' Zariņš also expected IRO to reverse its official attitude towards them.[25]

Zariņš based his expectation on a detailed 24 February 1949 memorandum by Jūlijs Feldmanis, the Latvian representative in Geneva. Ottawa also received a copy of this nineteen-page memorandum. It deplored that Baltic displaced persons in Germany and Austria were undergoing their sixth or seventh screening, a process 'particularly merciless for ex-soldiers who were forcibly mobilized by the German occupying authorities in violation of the Hague Convention.' The western Allies had released all mobilized Latvian soldiers from POW camps in August 1946 'on the same grounds as soldiers from Alsace-Lorraine, Luxemburg, Eupen and Malmedy.' However, IRO (and hence countries, such as Canada, admitting DPs screened for resettlement) had not accepted this rationale. IRO had been guided by directive PO No. 42, Article 5, Paragraph 4, which stated: 'Baltic nationals who started military service before the first compulsory conscription in January 1943 should be regarded as volunteers, ineligible unless they give proof to the contrary.' IRO also excluded from its care 'any person who can be shown to have voluntarily assisted the enemy forces ... against the United Nations.' Feldmanis's memorandum was designed to convince IRO officials that Latvian ex-POWs without exception should be treated as bona fide DPs.

The memorandum recapitulated the standard arguments in support of the contention that the members of the so-called Latvian Volunteer Waffen-SS Legion were neither volunteers nor in any way comparable to the German SS but, in reality, victims of circumstance. It vehemently denied that Latvian volunteer police units forming the early core of the legion were accomplices in serious war crimes. The only Latvians actually volunteering for German military service in July 1941 were 'hot-headed' youths, motivated by hatred of the Bolshevik aggressors or fear of judicial inquiries, Feldmanis contended. 'Official evidence indicates that none of them came back from the front.' Starting in December 1941, 'people were simply put on the train and wakened up next morning in front of the trenches in the Leningrad areas.' Feldmanis insisted that Hitler's Germany must be held fully responsible for any war crimes, even if Nazi records seem to accuse Baltic nationals, since Nazi documents would naturally support Nazi arguments.

Latvians might actually be victims of a Jewish conspiracy, Feldmanis insinuated. Whereas Balts were being screened six times or more, IRO had not bothered to screen any 'of the hundreds of thousands of Jewish refugees' from eastern Europe, many of whom were presumed to have been communist agents. To the knowledge of Feldmanis and his friends, 'not one Jew has been declared ineligible' by IRO. It looked to him as if the IRO constitution was being applied severely only to some of the refugees. The majority of the eligibility officers in the IRO Baltic section, 'or so it is said, happen to belong to the national group of refugees which has so far been spared in screening operations.' Does their Jewishness, Feldmanis wondered, account for their 'excessive zeal' in screening Latvians? And he added that some American journalists were reinforcing this discrimination by accusing all non-Jewish refugees of collaboration with the Nazis and criticizing the alleged leniency of IRO authorities. IRO should live up to its symbol of a lifebuoy, Feldmanis insisted, and acknowledge that 'the Balts have as much a right as the Jews to the understanding, sympathy and consideration of IRO officials.'[26]

The pressures in support of Latvian legionnaires, generated by Valdmanis's former associates Feldmanis in Geneva and Zariņš in London as spokesmen for the Latvian Central Committee in Germany, formed the immediate background to the questions Valdmanis expected to be asked on 27 April 1949 by the thirty-three members of the Standing Committee on Immigration and Labour of the Senate of Canada. This was his first major opportunity in Canada to draw on his experience and display his expertise on displaced persons and refugees as an adviser to the immigration branch. Arriving without a prepared statement, Valdmanis was asked to describe his background and associations. As on two known previous occasions since his emigration from Europe, Valdmanis claimed to have been imprisoned by the Russians in 1940, freed by the German invasion in July 1941, and arrested by the Germans in 1943, as the leader of an anti-German resistance movement. Once again, he omitted his role as director general of justice.

This time Valdmanis presented a fantastic new version of how he had survived an alleged SS trial and certain execution. He claimed that the Swedish ambassador in Berlin had intervened on his behalf because he possessed the highest decoration Sweden could give to anyone – the Grand Commander of the Stella Polaris, and this was only one of the orders he had received from a number of European countries. This decoration was supposed to be returned to the Swedish king upon the awardee's death. At first the intervention was repulsed by German Foreign Minister von Ribbentrop with the argument, according to Valdmanis, that Latvia was under German jurisdiction and that therefore this was a German affair. Fortunately, Hitler was extremely anxious to be on good terms with Sweden, 'so my execution was postponed for a week, then two weeks; and at that time postponement of an execution was almost sure to mean that you saved your life. So I survived.' Valdmanis did not indicate how he happened to be privy to von Ribbentrop's communications and Hitler's motives. How he survived, he told the senators, was hard for him to explain.[27]

It is equally hard to comprehend the strange ending to this miraculous escape: 'I was ordered by the Germans to make economic planning for them. I was taken to Biberich am Rhein ... not far from Wiesbaden ... I had to do planning work for the Germans on cement, gypsum, lime, limestone and alabaster. Indirectly it was economic planning for war.' He was ordered to do this work because the Germans knew he was a Latvian government trainee. That meant, Valdmanis explained, that he had been among a small group of boys selected by the Latvian government as the country's future leaders. His training was in economics, trade, industry, and finance. In the course of his apprenticeship he had been sent to many European countries where he had made valuable contacts. In Germany, in the early 1930s, for example, he claimed to have worked as a special assistant to Reichsbank President Dr Hjalmar Schacht.

Valdmanis told the Senate committee that his preoccupation with matters related to refugees and Baltic legionnaires in exile developed in 1945. Thanks to the good offices of Field Marshal Alexander at that time, he was able to join and advise the staffs of Field Marshal Montgomery and General Eisenhower. In 1947, on the recmmendation of the U.S. Army, he became a senior staff member of IRO. From experience, Valdmanis knew Balts to be the most freedom-loving, anti-communist, highly skilled, and enterprising people imaginable. In the words of Valdmanis these people 'know how to build up a country because every twenty or twenty-five years they have been involved in a major war and have had to start from scratch again.' There were four types of Baltic displaced persons, Valdmanis explained: (1) those sent as forced labourers to Germany, (2) those taken prisoners by Germans, (3) the Baltic Waffen-SS, and (4) those who retreated with the Germans before the Red Army advance. All of them preferred to settle in Canada, a country much like their own.

Of particular concern to Valdmanis was the undeserved fate of the twenty thousand or so Baltic Waffen-SS veterans in Germany and Austria. They had had a choice only between the two evils of Russian and German occupation. Valdmanis, to be 'absolutely frank' with the senators, conceded that Latvians considered German occupation the lesser evil. When a second Russian invasion threatened in 1944, they let themselves be mobilized and put in uniforms that looked like SS uniforms, but with significant differences – for example, the SS letters were replaced by the national colours of their own country. More than half of these men died in action. Less than half of those who survived the end of the war managed to break through the German lines and surrender to the forces of Eisenhower and Montgomery. In January 1946 many of them were released from POW camps to DP camps because the Allied forces realized that these Balts 'had nothing to do with the SS.'

Having recognized their rehabilitation, the United States, Britain, and Australia were admitting them as immigrants. He himself, Valdmanis liked to stress, had helped draw up the IRO screening directives recognizing these people as bona fide DPs. But Canada was still excluding these 'extremely fine' and most desirable immigrants – almost all were single, young, and physically strong, easily adaptable, God-fearing, and 'strongly' anti-communist. 'They are much like myself,' Valdmanis declared. 'Their past has been crushed, their former lives smashed. They have to start anew much like our fathers did after the First World War.' In conclusion, Valdmanis tried to assure the senators that Latvians had enjoyed political liberty up to 1940. Only Russians and those misled by them, referred to the government of Latvia after 1934 as a dictatorship. In reality, Valdmanis contended, 'our new constitution was prepared but not introduced in conjunction with a military treaty which Russia forced on the Baltic States in October 1939.'[28]

Since the proceedings of this hearing appeared in print and were open to public scrutiny, Valdmanis's testimony became one of the few frequently quoted bits of biographical information about him and a favourite subject of satire by some journalists. The published proceedings thus contributed much to the genesis of the subsequent legend of Valdmanis as an enigma. Critical reaction to his Senate testimony came immediately from the Polish pro-communist ethnic press; it considered the alleged adviser to Hitler's Reichsbank president to be 'infected with Nazism.'[29]

A more serious attack was launched in early 1950 by the communist-oriented, Russian-language paper *Vestnik* (Messenger), published in Toronto. The paper castigated Valdmanis for 'lecturing' to the Senate of Canada about the illegal dictatorship of the communists and the misery it brought to Latvian fascists, while not mentioning with a single word the mass murder of people in his homeland during the time of Nazi occupation. 'He did not reveal to Canadian Senators the well-known fact, a fact confirmed by the DPs themselves, that the Hitlerites did not have a shortage of executioners for their great death camp in Riga – there were always enough Latvian volunteers. The same abundance of killers was found in all other cities and populated areas.' Canadian senators should have asked Valdmanis where those murderers were today, the paper protested, for it would be hard to believe that 'the professor' knew nothing about that. 'He was the one who, while in Germany, settled those monsters in the DP camps and subsequently transferred them to Canada,' *Vestnik* maintained, and concluded that 'none of those criminals did he deliver into the hands of justice.'[30]

Reflections of an Exile

Preoccupation with the legacy of his political past prompted Valdmanis in the autumn of 1949 to undertake a final review of his battles to liberate, organize, and lead the postwar Latvian DP community in European exile. Starting with 'Reflections of an Exile,' in a series of seven articles,[31] he reappraised from his new Canadian perspective the self-destructive ambitions of exile politics. There was a time, Valdmanis recalled, 'when I had committed all I had – my heart, my mind, my thoughts, and my efforts to the Latvian people and to Latvian exiles in foreign lands. I thought that I knew the way we would have to go if we intended to avoid our elimination. But I didn't know how to convince people that my motives were clean and my ideas not selfish.' By resigning from exile politics, Valdmanis was hoping to achieve a cooling effect in the senseless fights among personalities and facilitate the restoration of unity and concentration on common challenges and goals. He was not ashamed to admit that this had been a painful decision at the time.

One year later in Canada, however, it had become clear to him that nothing had improved. In fact, he saw Latvian refugees destined to suffer the fate of all emigrés in modern history, as the experience of refugees from the French and Russian revolutions had shown. These passed through two painful stages – first, loss of the fatherland and then disintegration of the emigrés' community. The belief by Russian refugee politicians that they would be the true liberators of Russia, delivering the passive majority of the population, and prosecuting the collaborators, caused arguments about the future constitution and splintering of the refugee groups. 'The devil himself could not have invented a more grandiose way to rip apart and destroy' their foundation and goals.

With hindsight, Valdmanis saw the Latvian refugee community disintegrate in a similar way, namely, when 'a group of Latvian political activists in an unfortunate dark night came upon the idea to recreate the former Latvian political parties in exile.' For Valdmanis, splitting up into parties in times of national disaster was the 'most irresponsible and awful division of effort that any group of people can experience.' The smaller the support for any particular party, the more that party resorted to questionable modes of justifying its organization. The best way to silence opponents was to pronounce them fascists, because at the end of the war such a label was a dangerous accusation. The definition of fascist could be stretched to include all officials in the Ulmanis regime.

Pretending to defend democracy, continued Valdmanis, they started to denounce non-conforming Latvian national leaders in Sweden and Germany to the security organs and were ready to deliver Latvian legionnaires to the Soviets. Valdmanis drew attention to the fact that, even as he was writing this article, the same dishonest campaign of intimidation was being conducted against the current LCP and LNP chairman, Colonel Janums, whose only sin appeared to have been his competence as an officer and his popularity with the legionnaires. A plan of attack had allegedly also been worked out against Zariņš. As a result, Latvians in exile were now divided into two basic groups: the so-called patriots, who opposed division into parties, and the party activists, for whom fighting for the type of freedom prescribed by their party was more important than liberation of the nation. While the energy of the leaders was taken up fighting off all kinds of accusations, the members of the refugee organizations lost interest in the issues. This was exactly what the party enthusiasts wished.

In 1945 Valdmanis had envisioned 'a single organization' comprising all Latvian exiles to ensure the survival of the group and to coordinate its efforts towards the liberation of Latvia. In those critical days, as the Soviets demanded repatriation and the western powers wanted to relinquish responsibility for the refugees, 'several' of the Latvian party leaders, according to Valdmanis, favoured 'sacrificing thousands of Latvian fighting men in order to avoid having all 300,000 Latvian refugees branded as fascists.' On one occasion in 1945 Valdmanis found himself denounced as 'a dangerous fascist' simultaneously to British as well as to U.S. authorities by the same Latvian party activists, Valdmanis recalled. This happened after he participated in negotiations to ameliorate the lot of Latvian legionnaires in POW camps in Belgium. 'These denunciations just didn't stop, only each next one was better prepared and nastier until finally I had to admit that I couldn't continue, had to give up and get out ... I decided to emigrate.'

Valdmanis claimed that, as LCP chairman, he had made several futile efforts to appease the party people because he wanted to create a unified national front and stop the campaign of denunciations. For example, he would not object to any titles they wished to assign to themselves nor to any propaganda about their preferred type of constitution. But they demanded exactly what he was not able to deliver, namely, official 'recognition of their constitution, parliament, and functionaries, in other words, their dictatorship.' That would not only have been a denial of Valdmanis's conviction, but creation of a government-in-exile whose recognition would have terminated the position of Zariņš and other Latvian envoys in western capitals. The requirement to recognize the 1922 constitution meant, in effect, that those unwilling to do so would not be recognized as Latvians.

Not surprising to Valdmanis, the imposition of this requirement in April 1948, in combination with the statutory right of one-third of the members present at any meeting to veto any decision, had brought about the bankruptcy of the organization based on it. Latvians were left now with a large proliferation of parties, groups, and associations created in exile, each barely able to support itself. As long as the party men would not permit the LNP to operate or liquidate itself, in order 'to hold on to their dream of grabbing power in new Latvia,' emigration seemed to be the only way out for ordinary Latvian exiles. From the perspective of North America, the goings-on in and with these organizations were incomprehensible to Latvian emigrants. Undeniably, 'dissociation had started and can end only in a permanent loss of identity.'

What next? wondered Valdmanis. 'If we could only reconcile our idealism with realities,' the 'big miracle' might actually happen. A war might start soon, and God 'may take us by our hand and lead us back to the land of our fathers.' But, prophetically, he predicted Latvians would more likely have to remain in foreign lands for at least five, ten, or more years. During this time they would need some political guidance to coordinate preparations for their eventual return to Latvia. Guidance in future could be delegated to the seventy-year-old Extraordinary Ambassador Zariņš or, if he refused, to Daugavas Vanagi. It was the largest association of Latvian exiles and an 'umbrella organization for all the idealistic and dependable elements of our society, including fighting patriots.'

It would be a big step forward, Valdmanis believed, if such a centre could induce Latvian local organizations to stop issuing contradictory declarations to the United Nations. Local organizations would be left in charge of economic and cultural matters and would no longer be expected to heed such well-meant advice as: (1) Latvians should seek to remain poor; (2) those with special talents should make a living by day and sacrifice their nights for the national cause; (3) to keep them from losing their ethnicity, Latvian girls should under no circumstances learn English; and (4) children should not attend local schools, so as not to be alienated from Latvian culture. Such suggestions were, in Valdmanis's opinion, absolutely unrealistic.

The time had come for Latvians to start a new life from the bottom up, but hopefully only on a temporary basis. To be sure, grave concerns continued to require attention – 'what to do for our bleeding country,' what to do for Latvians still in various camps and expecting help, and to what degree Latvians in those foreign lands could and should dare to expect help from each other. But Latvians abroad should attempt to leave a positive mark wherever they were: 'We should never let our brains go rusty. Let's do something. Let's create our national groups. Let's organize Latvian clubs and associations. Let's help each other as much as possible to establish ourselves. Let's do anything we can for the spirit of national pride and national ambition. Let's create many small Latvias in foreign countries. Let's not worry about launching a national umbrella organization, because it has become apparent that this meant building a home from the roof down.'

The Valdmanis family tried to translate the lesson of these articles into practice and make a major effort to adjust to the North American environment. While Alfred Valdmanis stayed in Ottawa, Irma and the four children aged thirteen, eight, seven, and five years, were spending the summer of 1949 in Madison, Wisconsin. There they were hosted by three families, one of whom had 'met' them by correspondence while they were living in a DP camp in Germany. This American family had sent packages to the camp when they learned of the plight of Baltic refugees. In Madison the Valdmanis children were deliberately put into three different homes so they would be forced to use English exclusively. Apparently, Valdmanis had hoped earlier that local playmates would teach his youngsters English. Instead, he observed the playmates going home chattering in Latvian.[32]

To bring his family back at the end of August that first summer, Valdmanis was granted a two-week business leave to visit Washington. While in the United States, he gave a speech before an American audience, in which he reviewed the history of the Latvian people from AD 400 to 1949 and its significance in the context of the Cold War. Europe owed a great debt to the Baltic countries because they stopped the westward march of communism after the First World War, he claimed, and saved the West from 'the most terrible tyranny ever met with in our times.' To counter Latvia's long-existing brain drain, mostly to Russia and Germany, the new government of independent Latvia had selected able and promising schoolboys and given them the best education available, including studies in foreign countries, so that they could eventually improve life in Latvia and unite the people in opposition to the destructive faith of communism. According to Valdmanis, Latvia had had the second highest proportion of university graduates in the world and a standard of living comparable only to that of Canada and the United States. Emphasizing quality of life, Latvia had had one of the most advanced insurance, pension, medicare, maternity, and disability schemes of its day.

Alfred Valdmanis was eager to let his audience know that, in October 1939, the Latvian cabinet had yielded to the Soviet demand for military bases – with only himself abstaining. The other cabinet members wanted to believe Stalin's solemn 'Bolshevik word of honour' and that the Soviets would respect the sovereign rights of the Baltic countries. Their reward was a reign of terror inflicted on Latvia by the Soviet invaders including the arrest and deportation to Siberia of three-quarters of 1 per cent of the total population. Step by step the Kremlin had taken over half of Europe. Where would it stop? America was a strong country but, Valdmanis cautioned, 'you lack some of our experience.' The United States should learn from Latvia's mistakes and be ready to make sacrifices. Doing his best to help America learn and realize this, Valdmanis concluded, was the only way he could also help the Latvian nation.[33]

The Nova Scotia Research Foundation Project

By August 1949 Valdmanis had added an appointment as a consultant on industrial development with the federal Department of Trade and Commerce to his one-year employment with the immigration branch in Ottawa. He had no academic responsibilities that autumn, and his association with Carleton College apparently terminated after the expiration of his one-year Lady Davis fellowship. With his new appointment Valdmanis now had his own government office, Room 2180, in the Department of Trade and Commerce Temporary Building No. 2 in Ottawa. This he used as the main address for his official mail from other departments.[34]

Not long after, G.D. Mallory, this department's director of industrial development, informed Valdmanis of Nova Scotia's long-standing interest in a gypsum industry. Valdmanis claimed expertise in this area, and so Mallory arranged to have Robert Howland, vice-president of the Nova Scotia Research Foundation, a provincial government agency, invite the Latvian to be a temporary consultant. This foundation was backed by a group of Nova Scotian investors whose principals were Colonel J.C. MacKeen (vice-president, Royal Securities Corporation Ltd), J.M. Stewart, KC, and Colonel Roy Jodrey. It was exploring ways to establish a 50 per cent government-owned plant to manufacture plaster, wallboard, and plaster lath.

The government of Nova Scotia was promoting the idea of a 50 per cent provincially owned gypsum industry utilizing the rich local deposits of high-quality gypsum. From these deposits, two and a half million tons were already being exported annually to the United States and Montreal. Eager to turn the project from a pipedream into a realizable proposition, the trio of investors welcomed the prospect of assistance from Valdmanis. He had on hand a team of specialists – engineers, technicians, and skilled workers experienced in gypsum production. They were prepared to form the nucleus of the new industry, namely, a firm of consulting engineers coordinating the purchase and erection of a plant utilizing state-of-the-art technology at competitive prices. They also would have liked to invest some equity funds in the new enterprise.[35]

The team of specialists Valdmanis had available were Latvians in Germany assembled by chief engineer Ernest Leja, production director of the gypsum works Stadtoldendorf and Ellrich. In contrast to Valdmanis with his 'fiery' temper, Leja was a cool, rational, meticulously conscientious professional engineer. Twelve years older than Valdmanis, Leja specialized in the technology of gypsum, cement, and lime production. In 1937, he had become managing director of AG Schieferis, Latvia, whose quality gypsum products were in great demand in Europe. From 1939 to 1944 Leja and his team of experts had to work first for Latvia's Soviet regime, then for the German war effort.[36] Although eligible as bona fide displaced persons under UNRRA and IRO care after 1945, they preferred being involved in the challenges of postwar reconstruction to idling in the relative comfort of DP camp life.

With the support of Valdmanis (whom they called their former 'supreme chief') and the British military authorities, they were permitted to restart gypsum production under the name Schieferit Plattenwerk in Bodenwerder in the British zone of Germany in 1946. Their products quickly established themselves in the German and world markets under the brand name 'Rigips,' and the plant they built in Bodenwerder is known today as Rigips-Baustoffwerke.[37] To the Canadian commercial representative in Frankfurt am Main, Leja elaborated in January 1950: 'Out of almost nothing we rebuilt the outdated German plants in Stadtoldendorf and built and equipped a new quarry, introducing the modern "air lift" system, built a new plaster plant and a new wallboard plant in Bodenwerder, the latter being finished as recently as the spring of 1949. We have established a new method in plaster production – the "pneumatic" plant – which is very little known in the world and gives a better and cheaper product; and we have risen from next to zero to the greatest gypsum producers in the British zone.'[38]

Leja had additional, very personal reasons for wanting to emigrate. His first wife and two sons had been deported to Siberia by the Soviets in June 1940. He had remarried and had a child with his second wife. After the war he worried that his first wife might return and charge him with bigamy, according to Valdmanis. Too old for eligibility in any of the Canadian immigration schemes, Leja had to look for a special scheme, such as the recruitment of a group of experts for a specific, difficult project in Canada.[39]

The man to whose efforts Leja's takeover of the Bodenwerder gypsum plant and Valdmanis's proposals to the Nova Scotia Research Foundation were most indebted was the Baltic German Friedrich Kreyser. Director general of C.C. Schmidt (before 1940 Latvia's only cement company; in 1941 renamed Rigaer Vereinigte Portlandzement- und Baustoffwerke), Kreyser had been the foremost cement industrialist in Latvia from the 1920s to 1945.[40] A model of decency, honesty, and modesty, Kreyser enjoyed wide respect among Latvians and Germans as well as close contact with Ulmanis. Thanks to him, Latvia had retained its reputation as a pioneer in the manufacture of cement and gypsum products.

The original incentive for the production of cement in Latvia had been provided by the huge slag heaps of limestone brought as ballast by British sailing vessels that loaded Russian export goods at the port of Riga. Schmidt successfully increased demand in Latvia with its monopoly on cement production. By sending instructors with presses for cement tile throughout the country, Schmidt popularized the use of these materials in rural construction. In 1944–5 Latvia's uniquely trained and coordinated team of cement and gypsum specialists did not become scattered, but thanks to the personal efforts of Leja, reassembled in Germany at Bodenwerder on the Weser.[41]

In 1945 Kreyser, appointed director of Vereinigte Baustoffwerke Bodenwerder, was put in charge of rebuilding the entire cement and gypsum industry in the British zone of Germany with plans and specialists he had saved from Riga. After erecting several modern plants, including the largest gypsum wallboard factory in Germany[42] 'with immense pains' and 'from nothing,' as he wrote Valdmanis, Kreyser and his longtime assistant manager Max Braun-Wogau resigned from Vereinigte Baustoffwerke rather than take orders from a newly appointed chairman of the board. In April 1950 Kreyser and Braun-Wogau started from scratch again by launching their own enterprise called Neue Technik GmbH, Consulting Engineers. The firm advertised as its specialty the erection and operation of entire industrial installations and entire mills processing gypsum, cement, and limestone.[43]

Kreyser's experience and connections as a gypsum and cement industrialist, combined with the expertise of Leja's team, enabled Valdmanis to prepare a viable and competitive proposal for the Nova Scotia Research Foundation and to promote it aggressively. Leja and his Latvian team saw this as providing Valdmanis with the opportunity to arrange for

ATPUHTA

Redakcija un ekspedīcija: Rīgā, Kalēju ielā 29.   Par redakciju atbild: izdevēja Emilija Benjamiņa.

JAUNIECELTAIS FINANČU MINISTRS ALFRĒDS VALDMANIS
AR KUNDZI IRMU UN MEITU VAIVU.

Latvia's newly appointed finance minister, Alfred Valdmanis, with his wife, Irma, and daughter, Vaiva Mara, featured on the cover of *Atpuhta* (Leisure) magazine. (Source: Irma Valdmanis)

Alfred Valdmanis with wife, Irma, after his award of the Order of the North-Star, October 1938. (Source: Irma Valdmanis)

The Valdmanis family after their arrival in Montreal, 1948. Centre row from left: Gundars, Mara, Irma; front: Videvuds, Agnar (adopted). (Source: Irma Valdmanis)

Premier J.R. Smallwood found a soulmate, Alfred Valdmanis, about 1950. (Source: Irma Valdmanis)

West German economics minister Ludwig Erhard (centre) entertaining Smallwood's party during their first visit to Germany in September 1950. Smallwood was the first foreign government head officially hosted by the West German government. (Source: Irma Valdmanis)

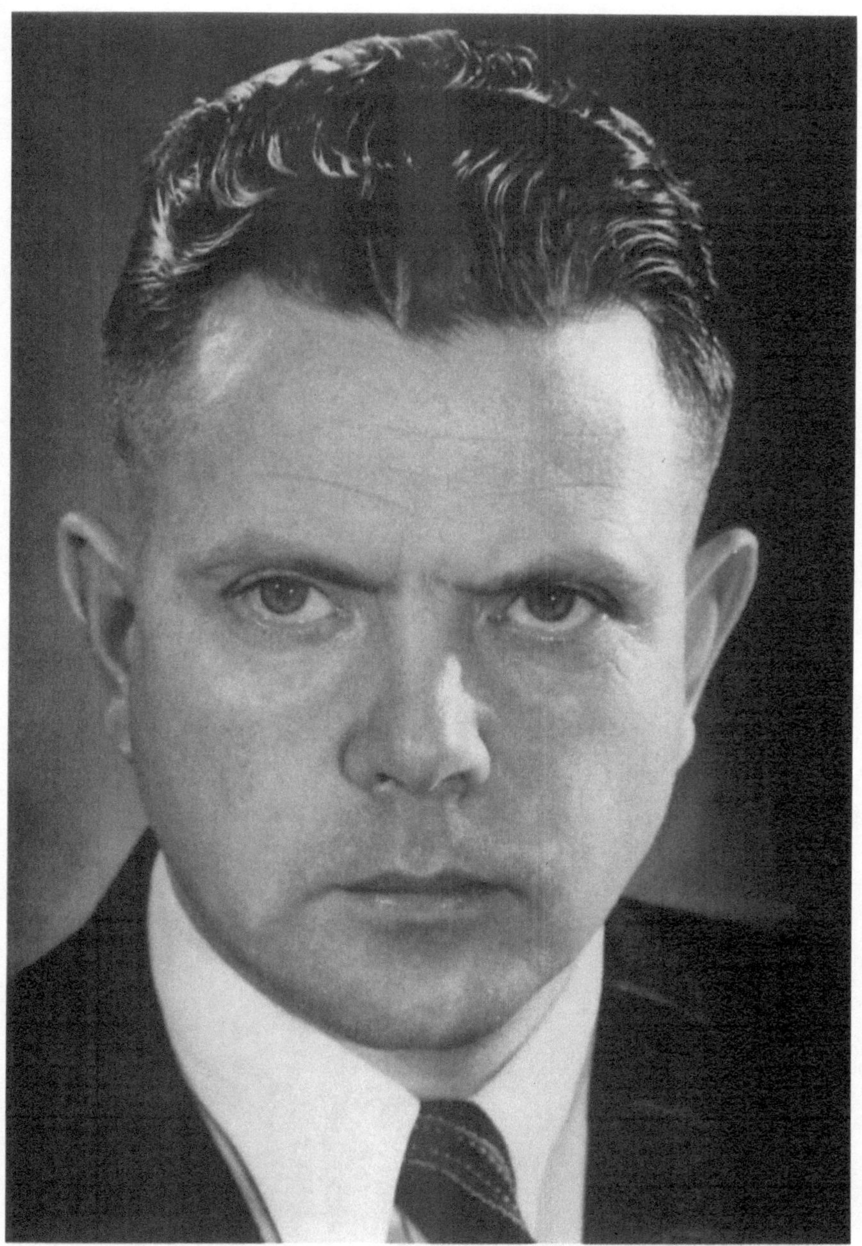

A. Valdmanis (about 1950–2), the 'little man with the square forehead and brushed-back hair that used to be characterized as Prussian' (Albert Perlin). There was an 'almost manic intensity in the deep-set eyes of his slightly Slavic, rather handsome face' (Don Jamieson). (Source: CNS)

Benno Schilde representative August Roemer signing the gypsum plant contract with J.R. Smallwood and members of his cabinet at the Colonial Building in St John's, 9 September 1950. On the far left: Hubertus Herz of Benno Schilde. (Source: Hubertus Herz)

Members of the New York group inspecting the site for a marine oil hardening plant in Harbour Grace, 15 November 1951. From left: Alf Simmons and John Sheppard (Harbour Grace), G.M. Mackintosh, H. Ripley, Valdmanis, Minister J. Chalker, and R. Sheppard of Harbour Grace. (Source: CNS)

Plotting NALCO strategy with William Stephenson, May 1952. (Source: CNS)

Smallwood delegation inspecting MIAG plant in Braunschweig while on an industrial tour in Germany, September 1951. (Source: Irma Valdmanis)

For five days MIAG owner Dr Johannes Lerch wined and dined the Smallwood party like royalty in his palatial residence in Garmisch-Partenkirchen, Germany, September 1951. (Facing from left: J. Lerch, Ms Marx (?), Valdmanis, and M. Braun-Wogau.) The festivities culminated in a toast by Lerch promising to build a machinery plant in St John's ... (Source: L.R. Curtis estate)

... and a toast by Smallwood declaring Lerch a consultant on economic development to the Newfoundland government. (Facing from left: E.H. Roethe, Ms Roethe, L.R. Curtis, Ms Lerch, and Smallwood.) (Source: L.R. Curtis estate)

Valdmanis, Mrs Lerch, and Smallwood celebrating in Garmisch, September 1951. (Source: L.R. Curtis estate)

Partying in Garmisch, September 1951. Mrs Lerch, Valdmanis, Smallwood (kissing waitress), and Friedrich Kreyser looking on. (Source: Irma Valdmanis)

Dinner at the Mount Royal Hotel, Montreal, 4 January 1954, following Herz's last commission payment to Valdmanis. From left: Irma Valdmanis, Hubertus Herz, Mara Valdmanis, Alfred Valdmanis, Ernest Leja. (Source: CNS)

With Irma, who visited Newfoundland only twice, at St John's airport. With 'tears in his eyes' he was reported saying goodbye to the industrialists he had brought here and the members of his staff. (Source: Irma Valdmanis)

Taken to the St John's Court House under RCMP escort, April 1954. 'He remained ramrod stiff and looking straight ahead ... crowds lined part of Duckworth and Water Streets.' (Source: *Evening Telegram*)

Leaving the St John's Court House, April 1954. 'Crowds blocked the court room, people stared in what courthouse windows provided vantage points.' (Source: *Evening Telegram*)

Tennis champion in Edmonton, 1965. (Source: Irma Valdmanis)

their emigration. Although well established in Germany, Leja informed Canada's commercial representative in Frankfurt am Main, 'We are not Germans and Germany is not our native country.' By the end of 1949 they were ready and eager to rise to the challenge posed by Valdmanis to 'help build up Canada's gypsum industry.'[44]

Leja received his initial request for information from Valdmanis at the end of October 1949. He responded quickly by forwarding his first calculations and proposals on 9 November. Arguing that a plant of the large size he had built in Germany (with a production capacity of 45,000 square feet per eight-hour shift) could not be justified for the Canadian market, Leja outlined options for two smaller (2,400 square feet per shift and 7,000 square feet per shift) gypsum wallboard plants supplied entirely from Germany. The dilemma was that the smaller the plant, the less mechanized it could be and the less revenue the invested capital could produce. So Leja urged that to avoid disappointing the investors, and endangering the chances for future projects, it would be advisable for him to come on a ten-day trip to Canada and evaluate the situation on the spot before entering into any final agreement. Concerning financing, Leja would be able to raise DM60,000 to be used for the purchase of equipment in Germany and enable the fund-raisers to become partners in the new enterprise.[45]

In less than a month in Canada, Valdmanis and Leja hammered out a preliminary proposal. Every aspect of the project was covered – from the plant's products, personnel, location, and capacity to calculations of markets, prices, freight rates, required capital, revenues, and expenses. The plant size and technology (traditional kettle or new pneumatic process) would depend on the location (proximity to the gypsum rock quarry), markets, and financing. Leaving nothing to chance, Valdmanis took up temporary residence in Halifax on 20 November 1949 and prepared, with data supplied by Leja, the foundation's 'First Memorandum for Discussion' of 28 November, and the more comprehensive 'Second Memorandum for Discussion' of 21 December 1949 for the gypsum project.

Based on revised higher market estimates, the second memorandum proposed a huge 200-ton per twenty-four-hour pneumatic process plaster plant in combination with a 90,000 square foot per twenty-four-hour or a 150,000 square foot per twenty-four hours wallboard plant. Located near a gypsum rock quarry, the plant would cost $1.5 million and yield net earnings of 13.8 per cent on capital employed. Its chief markets for wallboard would be in the Maritimes and Quebec (about 7,500 square feet each), while Valdmanis estimated the Newfoundland market would absorb an additional 8,000 square feet and exports to Latin America about 10,000 square feet of wallboard. The plant would be operated by a group of ten to eighteen Latvian specialists, together with Canadian sales and accounting personnel. The memorandum warned that 'the essential personnel are still available, but may cease to be available within a matter of weeks.' As explained by the research foundation:

> This team developed a special technique of calcining gypsum in Latvia and operated a plant of this nature from 1936 to 1944. During the latter part of 1948 they began construction of an improved version of the Latvian plant in British-occupied Germany. This plant has been operating since its completion in the first half of 1949. The claim for the process is that operating costs are lower and that quality is more readily controlled due to the continuous nature of the operation. The method is considered secret in view of the impossibility in recent years of establishing patents in Germany.[46]

Valdmanis conceded to Dr Howland, vice-president of the Nova Scotia Research Foundation, that the proposal was based on a perception of need or unsupplied demand and, hence, on 'a reasonable guess' about markets to be 'captured,' an estimate that might be questioned. But he insisted that 'once an assumption is made we must logically stick to it.' The plant he proposed 'would set the *quality standards* [emphasis in the original] for Canadian gypsum products; I believe that cost per ton gypsum in powder form ... is lower than the same grade produced elsewhere in Canada, and I believe that cost per 1000 sq. ft. wall board is not higher – and, after introducing higher production capacity, should drop below – the production cost of any other wallboard producer in Canada. The plant price is exceptionally low.'[47]

To finalize the project, Colonel MacKeen and Dr H.D. Smith, president of the Nova Scotia Research Foundation, toured Leja's plant with Valdmanis in Germany at the end of January 1950. While in Germany, Valdmanis signed a 'gentleman's agreement' with Kreyser, to expire by 15 April 1950, in recognition of 'their friendship of long years standing' and in order to settle former business relations and enable Valdmanis to start a business in Canada. The agreement guaranteed the delivery of a pneumatic plaster plant and a wallboard plant at the exceptionally low prices of $114,500 and $286,000 respectively and provided that Neue Technik would not supply a pneumatic plaster plant to anyone else for a period of five years, except with Valdmanis's written permission. Because there was no patent protection for German inventions, Valdmanis was given personal responsibility for protecting the secrets of the new technology. If the process required a patent, 92.5 per cent of the revenue from the patent would go to Neue Technik. The agreement offered warranties for machinery, workmanship, and performance of the plants and provided for a one-third down payment within ten days of signing the contract, one-third after the equipment had been loaded on board at a German seaport, and the remainder thirty days after receipt of shipment in Canada. The terms were backed by bank guarantees from a Canadian bank.[48]

By early 1950 Valdmanis thought he had a deal that would put Kreyser in business overseas, enable Leja and his team to emigrate to Canada, and leave him as president of the new company at an annual salary of $25,000 to $30,000. In March 1950 Leja with some members of his team visited Canada and the United States as the guests of the research foundation. They were to advise regarding raw materials and plant site and to get acquainted with practices of the American industry. Upon Leja's departure, however, a number of unresolved contentious issues left Valdmanis's Canadian group of investors with second thoughts about rushing into 'our Haligonian project.' They appeared particularly concerned about the terms of the deal, Valdmanis's role in it, and the financing.

The investors were concerned about Valdmanis's insistence that the more expensive pneumatic plaster plant had become 'mandatory' because he had acquired a special option on this new system. Did Valdmanis have any personal material motive for excluding from consideration a competitive bid by an American manufacturer for cheaper technologies? they wondered. Local specialists hesitated to pass judgment on a system they did not know. If the pneumatic process would not work as cheaply and efficiently as promised, who would pay for a changeover to the proven kettle process? In such an event, how serious would be the hold-up in the manufacture of wallboard?[49]

Concerning the set-up of capital, Colonel MacKeen appeared apprehensive about Valdmanis's request for the controlling majority of the escrow, the acquisition of $75,000 in shares for himself, and some more shares for the 'group.' MacKeen found Valdmanis's desire to be slated for president of the new company inopportune. At the very most, MacKeen would consider Valdmanis becoming chairman of the board, or vice-president and technical adviser at a salary of $10,000 to $12,000. But

Valdmanis demanded a minimum $15,000 salary and wanted the board of directors to make an adjustment after each year, the final salary not to exceed $25,000. Other outstanding problems were the railway freight rates and how to raise the capital.[50]

Between 22 and 24 March 1950 the fate of the project was to be decided. If he won, Valdmanis wrote his brother-in-law Valdis Mateus, 'then we will be in a position to start a Latvian colony.' Two American syndicates seemed to feel threatened enough to direct a fact-finding mission to New York in order to prove errors in Valdmanis's calculations. They succeeded in excluding him from the mission, claiming that he was 'a difficult man to talk to.' Disturbed about his exclusion, Valdmanis did not think that he himself could be replaced, although engineer Leja did arrive from Germany to replace him.[51]

By the middle of April 1950 Leja became impatient with the never-ending demands for clarification. He knew that revealing the layout before the final contract was signed would expose the secrets of the production process and give competitors an advantage. Leja expressed even more doubts to Valdmanis: 'The Nova Scotia investors are looking for a 10 percent annual return from you; they are squeezing every penny out of you. Somewhere that blackmail has to stop, the point has been reached where we should walk away from the negotiations. Our company, Neue Technik, feels insulted by such methods.' Leja looked with disdain at the low bid from Fibre Engineering and Machinery Company in New York because it was merely an estimate leaving out all kinds of expenses, and not a final quotation. With the present deal, Neue Technik could not make any profit, and it also had to worry about unforeseen expenses because of the commitment to build and supply a factory in a foreign country.

Leja advised that some of his people should move to Canada immediately to set up a group of consulting engineers. 'Even if we would not succeed [this time] to break into the Canadian market with German machinery, it will be much easier next time, and you would have on hand a group of technical people familiar with the state of the art in Germany. In the beginning that group could be very small. Single-handedly you cannot last long. Just being able to discuss problems with someone else can be a great relief,' Leja suggested. Leja proposed to salvage what could be salvaged and prepare a retreat from the current project. As a possible alternative project, a takeover of the Windsor Plaster Company might be considered. This would mean slow progress, but at least a beginning.[52] Leja was obviously still interested in emigrating to Canada.

Setback

When a two-week extension of the gentleman's agreement had expired at the end of April 1950, the project was still awaiting funding from the prospective investors. Not until mid-June did Colonel MacKeen confirm the investors' inability 'to raise the required capital in the intermediate stage, that is $550,000 Preferred stock which was necessary to complete the financing.' Approaches had been made to three of the leading banking houses, MacKeen explained, but financing for new ventures of this type was difficult to obtain. In June 1950, Building Products Ltd, a large Canadian concern distributing nearly every line of building material except plaster and gypsum, revived its interest in the project and inquired about obtaining the terms and guarantees offered by Neue Technik, the expertise of Leja's team, and the rights to the process. By then, however, Valdmanis and Leja had moved on to more challenging tasks in Newfoundland.[53]

By the beginning of May 1950 Valdmanis and Leja had had to reconcile themselves to the painful fact that the Nova Scotia gypsum project was as good as dead. Valdmanis wanted no further discussions about what had gone wrong. Nevertheless, Leja, in the interest of their mutual plans for the future, 'which are and remain the *suprema lex*,' insisted on a post-mortem. Errors were made in negotiating, Leja admitted, but the blame for the failure to close the deal had to be placed squarely on the syndicate of gypsum producers in Canada and their friends in the American industry: 'Just look at your and Howland's calculations worked out over Easter – an investment of $1.5 million to produce $650,000 profit in a single year! What more enticing proposition could be imagined – a uranium mine? And the result – still no financing. It should be quite evident that this is not the way to do it.'

What lessons could be learned for the future? Leja thought it had been a mistake to present the project without any options for changes. 'Our approach amounted to a *va banque*, a take-it-or-leave-it attitude, which is a very dangerous strategy.' This was a lesson to remember at the start of any new venture, he admonished. Contrary to Valdmanis's belief, the problems with the gypsum project were not the result of misfortune, namely – suddenly no financing. They were actually just a step in a natural sequence of events stemming from the Canadian gypsum producers' lack of interest in having a plant in Nova Scotia.

With the project's failure, future ventures were uncertain. Leja's Latvian team in Germany was in danger of disintegrating and thus becoming unavailable. 'They do not consider Germany safe for permanent residence and are thinking about settling someplace else,' Leja apprised Valdmanis. Since IRO was scheduled to close down by 30 June 1950, funding for emigration would be available only to those registered before that date. Some had a choice of going to Australia, some to the United States, and some to Norway. At the same time, with the deregulation of the German economy, Germany's export business was booming again, and all the major firms were fully booked with orders. The big German companies were no longer interested in export for the sake of exporting. In future, Leja predicted, 'we should be realistic and count on export deals to Canada only if they can show profit for the suppliers.'[54]

Kreyser, too, rejected Valdmanis's insinuation that Neue Technik could have saved the project by lowering the price for the wallboard plant. 'Our price package for the machinery was lowered to a point which, in view of the fact that neither we nor you would have been able to add anything to it, could be considered almost foolhardy.' Characterizing Leja as one of his 'best and most mature men,' Kreyser agreed with Leja that there was no point in looking for scapegoats and engaging in mutual recriminations. Valdmanis must realize that 'each project entails the possibility of failures. What matters is how one bears them and that one learns from them.'[55]

At Easter 1950 Valdmanis's future appeared grim. Looking out of an eighth-storey window in Halifax that day, he recalled in August 1954, he had resolved that at the next opportunity, he would look out first for himself and his family. Ultimately, this fateful decision to improve his economic fortunes – by hook or by crook, if need be – became his master and led him to his doom.[56]

chapter eight

'Develop or Perish': The Challenges of Newfoundland, 1950–1953

On the eve of Empire Day in 1950 I had a telephone call from the Premier. He invited me to his office in Canada House ... A few people were coming and going and each time someone new came he was introduced to Dr Alfred Valdmanis who was then exhorted to tell once more the extraordinary story of his life. He was a small, volatile, dynamic person with a square, Teutonic head, topped by a brush-cut, a curious mixture of anxiety and arrogance. His tale was fantastic but was told with so much earnestness that it was credible ... That night he told how he had seen the dumping of slag from the steel mills at North Sydney and had learned that ships plied between that port and Aguathuna in Newfoundland to fetch limestone. Here was the basis for a first new industry – blast-furnace cement. So the Valdmanis era began.

Albert Perlin, *Daily News*, 24 September 1969

The anxieties that Alfred Valdmanis suffered as a result of the collapse of the Nova Scotia gypsum project were short-lived. In May 1950, almost at the same time that the Nova Scotia deal was falling through and not the least owing to the reputation Valdmanis had acquired in connection with that project, even greater career opportunities opened up. The call came from the former British dominion of Newfoundland. Having chosen the benefits of union with Canada in a 1948 referendum, Newfoundland was now looking for an economist to direct the diversification and modernization of its backward fishery-centred economy.

Union with Canada since 1949 had triggered a social, cultural, and psychological revolution of unparalleled dimensions in Newfoundland.

A closed, rural, backward, and ethnically homogeneous society of fishermen with virtually no urban middle class and a ruling elite of some two dozen fish merchants, the people of Newfoundland were no longer satisfied with life based around outport fishing. They were abandoning hundreds of secluded settlements and moving to the larger urban centres for the amenities of 'schools, roads, electric lights, water and sewer facilities, and for social life and entertainment.'[1] They were also migrating in large numbers to other parts of Canada in search of jobs, prompted in part by a marketing crisis of the Newfoundland salt fish industry and adjustment difficulties of hitherto sheltered local secondary industries.[2] A wide consensus existed across the dividing lines of political parties, economic interest, social class, and competing media that Newfoundland needed industrial development in order to provide a higher standard of living.[3]

For Joseph R. Smallwood, the province's first premier, Confederation was a challenge as well as an opportunity. Eager to realize his old dream of a new Newfoundland built on land-based industries, he had at his disposal a budget surplus of $40 million inherited from Newfoundland's pre-1948 government. 'Premier Smallwood has a great sense of urgency about economic development,' remarked an American development consultant contracted by Smallwood in February 1950. Smallwood was convinced that Newfoundland '"must develop or perish." Because of the union of Newfoundland–Labrador with Canada, allowing free migration of the island's people to the mainland; and because of the accumulated surplus from the war, certain to be dissipated and unlikely to be re-established in the normal course of affairs, Premier Smallwood feels that it is "now or never." He begrudges every week that passes without constructive action.'[4]

Since 'the levels and patterns of North American consumption were the goal,' it has been argued, 'it is not surprising that development strategies to achieve it were imported as well.'[5] At first, Smallwood had been dealing with such big names in the world of North American business, investment banking and industrial development as Nelson Rockefeller and his International Basic Economy Corporation (IBEC), and Sir William Stephenson, head of World Enterprises. None of these had new ideas or concrete proposals. Most discouraging was the lack of interest shown by Canadian, American, and British industrialists in risking investment in this remote island–province with its rural lifestyle, preindustrial fishing economy, and small population of around 360,000, mostly scattered in some thirteen hundred virtually inaccessible outports along the coast.

Having fought to bring Newfoundland into Canada, Joey Smallwood was now worried about the consequences. Although wielding near-absolute power in Newfoundland, Smallwood could not divorce economic development from politics; his government, he maintained, had to stand or fall on economic development. Temperament, conviction, and circumstance prompted him to consider taking greater risks. On the eve of Valdmanis's arrival he summed up his strategy in such slogans as 'develop or perish,' 'make or break,' and 'gamble.'[6]

Lacking training and experience in economics and business administration, Smallwood turned to his friend from high school days, Albert Perlin, a newspaper editor and eminent public affairs critic whose unconventional views he had always respected. 'We have to start almost from scratch,' Perlin advised. 'First, get the right man as technical director of the development operation.' That man should be 'young enough to have plenty of drive' and 'imaginative enough to see the woods as well as the trees.' Such a man would not be easy to find, Perlin admitted, and suggested that he be hired for a year or two from a top-notch industrial engineering firm with experience in rehabilitating the economies of underdeveloped countries.[7] Smallwood forwarded Perlin's ideas to C.D. Howe, federal minister of trade and commerce, who agreed in writing to help search for a man with the appropriate qualifications. After Donald Nelson, chairman of the U.S. War Production Board, and George Cadbury had declined the honour, Howe through his officials and Newfoundland Senator Ray Petten 'highly recommended' Alfred Valdmanis.[8]

Director General of Economic Development

On his 10 May 1950 trip to Ottawa, Smallwood asked Alfred Valdmanis for a meeting at the Chateau Laurier hotel.[9] Smallwood left the hotel convinced he had found a saviour for Newfoundland. Reports about this meeting leave little doubt that Smallwood was overawed by this Latvian's life and international connections. He was particularly impressed that the young Valdmanis, who claimed to have been among a small elite group of youths specially selected and trained to serve their country, had been groomed to become the 'economic czar' of Latvia, responsible for industrial and economic development. His political credentials during the Soviet and Nazi occupations of Latvia seemed impeccable, as attested to by an abridged translation of Zemgals's *Dienas baltas nebaltas* that Valdmanis had brought along and given to Smallwood. (Chapter 6 discusses the likelihood that Valdmanis, not Zemgals, authored this work.)

To dispel any doubts, Valdmanis removed his shirt to show off the alleged torture scars on his back[10] – scars he had also presented to Latvia's German occupation authorities as alleged proof of Soviet torture, but which the German official Peter Kleist attributed to a childhood operation. Valdmanis's act and story appeared to be 'straightforward terms and tones' to Smallwood. After all, Valdmanis had been 'highly recommended,' appeared 'brilliant and knowledgeable,' with a 'handsome and very intelligent face' and an amazing 'clarity of expression in English.'[11]

The interview lasted all day and well into the night – largely because of Smallwood's fascination with Valdmanis's story – and ultimately zoomed in, as Valdmanis reported to Leja and Kreyser, on the expediency of cement production.[12] Cement was needed for practically every aspect of economic development, including the building of roads and bridges. However, there was a great cement shortage in Canada. The shortage was especially great in eastern Canada. In Newfoundland, for instance, nobody knew when cement orders would be filled. At the Dosco plant in Sydney, Nova Scotia, Valdmanis had noted 'that the slag which was the waste from the furnaces of the steel mill was being dumped. He knew also that ships sailed to Aguathuna [in Newfoundland] in ballast to take on limestone for the Sydney mills ... Why not, he asked, bring the slag from Sydney to Aguathuna and start a cement plant? It seemed natural and right. Then and there a new industry was born.'[13]

As early as 1947 Smallwood had been entranced with the idea of a Newfoundland-based cement industry because all the ingredients were available on the island. But local businessmen on the Newfoundland Industrial Development Board had rejected it.[14] Excited about launching the industrialization drive with a cement plant, Smallwood visited Valdmanis in his Montreal apartment, where they discussed the terms of his position.[15] Smallwood hired him on the spot with a $10,000 annual salary. The appointment was to take effect on 23 May 1950, subject to provincial cabinet approval. For his title Valdmanis chose 'director general' because in Europe a director general was 'considered a very rare bird, a person required to have exceptional abilities, trustworthiness, the talent to direct matters and people, and the capability of research and administration (execution).'[16] Smallwood decided that the new director general was to serve directly under him. 'I was no civil servant. There were no rules, no regulations, no contracts. I had to make a fast start, and together we would succeed,' Valdmanis recalled.[17]

Upon his arrival in St John's, on 23 May 1950, Valdmanis was first introduced to the eight cabinet members and then to such close friends of Smallwood as Albert Perlin and Don Jamieson. The cabinet minutes record that Valdmanis submitted character references from highly reputable sources and that 'he felt confident that there was larger scope for his talents in the field of industrial development in this Province than on the Mainland.' Appointed adviser on economic development on a contractual basis, the continuance of Valdmanis's services was to be reviewed after one year 'in the light of the tangible results he had been able to accomplish.'[18] The Newfoundland representative of the federal Department of Trade and Commerce, Bobbie Robertson, had been instructed by C.D. Howe to look after Valdmanis. She remembered Valdmanis telling her shortly after his arrival in St John's that he would not be a 'yes-man' and that he considered the members of Smallwood's cabinet 'a bunch of nincompoops.'[19]

Perlin found Valdmanis 'a small, volatile, dynamic person with a square, Teutonic head, topped by a brushcut, a curious mixture of anxiety and arrogance.' His tale appeared 'fantastic' to Perlin, but 'was told with so much earnestness that it was credible.' According to broadcaster–politician Don Jamieson, nothing was particularly striking about Valdmanis's appearance. However, his behaviour, when addressing Smallwood, was like that of 'a musical comedy count, bowing, clicking his heels' and referring to his host as 'my Premier.' Beyond such theatrics, Valdmanis remained silent as Joey Smallwood extolled the virtues of this 'gifted superman whose naturally brilliant mind had been honed to a fine edge by constant study, and whose body had been steeled by spartan exercise and discipline.' Valdmanis, by contrast, sounded 'downright cautious and conventional' as he argued for resource-based industries and conveyed an impression of competence.[20]

Other Newfoundlanders instinctively disliked this enigmatic foreigner who liked to be addressed as 'Doctor.' As Smallwood's friend and later critic, writer Harold Horwood, put it, Valdmanis 'looked, dressed, and acted like an undersized storm trooper. He was arrogant and he was an obvious phoney, a *poseur.*'[21] It was evident from the beginning, Smallwood explained, that 'his imperious manner and rather obviously insincere flattery of my colleagues, each of whom he called "Your Excellency"' led to his being 'hated by some, tolerated by others, and greatly liked by only a few; but he was respected for his brains and talents by all.'[22]

There was no dearth of unsolicited advice from friends and strangers. 'Read well our history,' warned a resident of Harbour Breton. Newfoundlanders 'will expect you to do miracles.'[23] From Corner Brook fellow Latvian refugee immigrant Alex Berzinsh – since 1948 head of Bowater's development and research division and provincial vice-consul of Free Latvia – offered this guidance (in Latvian) to Valdmanis:

> You have been appointed to the biggest and most difficult job in Canada today. It will not be easy to improve conditions on this island with its low level of development and ongoing depression. Only with great energy and adaptability in thinking will it be possible to influence the people's slow-working minds. They have to be convinced that they are capable of doing something ... We do have one enthusiast – our Premier Smallwood. While he is not blessed with knowledge in economics, he knows how to influence and motivate his people. In economic matters you will have to be his hitherto missing right hand. You will have to ensure that things will not get out of control, that efforts are concentrated on practical projects capable of successful development and with future potential.[24]

Similar counsel came from Germany. Valdmanis's friends there, still smarting from the blow to their fortunes in Nova Scotia, greeted the unexpected news of the Newfoundland appointment with cautious optimism. They warned that this time the first project must be one that could be carried out quickly and successfully. The government and population must also view it as beneficial to the economy. 'It must be sure to succeed,' insisted Ernest Leja, and 'must not be a washout.' Friedrich Kreyser was even more concerned: 'The new tasks may become the beginning of a great career for you, if you are able to solve them successfully. A failure, however, will block your way for a long time.'[25]

Cement and Gypsum

Valdmanis had already decided to start with a Portland cement plant with a production capacity of 100,000 tons per annum. That was the minimum capacity needed to produce cement competitively. Newfoundland could not absorb more than 40,000 to 50,000 tons, therefore markets for the rest had to be found on the mainland. Looking for prospective investors for the plant, Valdmanis approached the same brokers that had been involved in the stillborn Nova Scotia project, that is, the New York group of Michael Lewin, T. Reed Vreeland, and Thomas W. Hill – the latter two in their respective capacities as president and vice-president of the Cement and General Development Corporation of New York.

Later Valdmanis claimed that initially he had tried to convince Joey Smallwood of the benefits of proceeding slowly and systematically with industrial development. Allegedly proposing to set $3 million aside in a revolving fund to launch at least one new industry a year, Valdmanis visualized depositing the proceeds from the sale of this industry upon its completion into the revolving fund to start another industry. This approach would have allowed for sufficient time to study the feasibilities of other industries; however, it would have taken ten years for results to be seen.

In accordance with this approach – whether Valdmanis in fact recommended it in May 1950 cannot be confirmed – he proposed building a slag cement grinding mill at Aguathuna, using slag from the Dosco steel mill in North Sydney and clinker imported from Europe. Machinery producing clinker could be installed later, and then Newfoundland would have a full-fledged cement industry. The alleged motive was to keep the price of the envisioned first industry below $1 million, so that it could be sold to private interests at cost. But why bother with a slag cement factory, Howe and Leja are said to have wondered, since the money and raw materials for a Portland cement factory were available? Although such a plant, according to Dosco calculations, necessitated the construction of a $500,000 pier at Aguathuna – a large dead investment Valdmanis claimed – Smallwood was prepared to throw in the extra money and write it off.[26]

From the start, the decision seems to have been to go for a Portland cement factory. It was certainly the preferred choice of Valdmanis, despite his later denial, because it enabled him to play up his strongest drawing card: his connections with Kreyser and Leja. Valdmanis was not interested in calling for tenders, and Smallwood was impatient and wanted the fastest deal. The choice of a German-built mill was thus a foregone conclusion. Through Valdmanis's connections Newfoundland was to get a cement mill on better terms, at a lower price, and in half the time one would be available elsewhere in North America.[27] Expecting to profit from Valdmanis's work in Newfoundland, Kreyser and his firm Neue Technik promised to supply all the necessary experts and contacts. As a basis for Valdmanis's calculations, Kreyser forwarded detailed prewar and wartime records of cement production in Riga, Kattowitz, and some German cement plants. Leja, designated to become chief engineer on his arrival in late June 1950, planned to 'work out not only a specific project, but some kind of a general plan for the future.'[28]

Kreyser arranged for the German machinery manufacturer MIAG to bid for the construction of the cement plant. In the negotiations for the contract, Valdmanis reduced the price until MIAG was left with virtually no profit. He refused the MIAG demand for an escalator clause (that is, if their wages or prices for materials went up, the Newfoundland government would pay more) and obtained the cement factory at some $2.8 million. The price included a secret contribution to the Liberal party of $300,000, but payable to a New York account specified by Valdmanis. The only witness to this arrangement was Ernest Leja, who at the request of Valdmanis finalized the deal with the manager of MIAG's cement machinery department, Kurt Steinbrück, at the beginning of August 1950.[29] The cabinet's reservations about the deal as a government enterprise were summed up in Finance Minister H.W. Quinton's remark to Valdmanis: 'Surely you can build the plant, but how are you going to get rid of it?'[30]

From the beginning, then, Valdmanis was involved in negotiations with the New York group about the terms of their purchase of the cement mill. In return, the group wanted a Labrador timber concession. In hectic negotiations Valdmanis tried to finalize the sale at cost ($3 million) before the mill was constructed and obtain a cash down payment. However, after the group had entered into a gentleman's agreement on 19 July 1950, the decision was announced, on 2 August 1950, to start construction entirely with public funds. In October Valdmanis wrote from New York that the group would be prepared to spend money to fight the Canada Cement Company competition, but would ask the government for a three-year credit instead of the cash down payment.[31] On 1 November 1950 the group signed a preliminary contract for a joint-stock company to be organized by the end of February 1951. This company was to buy the plant.[32]

Confident that the cement plant would be sold, Valdmanis boasted to Smallwood in December 1950 that he had gone 'straight out for results' instead of doing 'what all so-called "advisors" do: sit down and study ... for a year.'[33] Yet, through early 1951 Valdmanis continued to explore prospects of selling the mill for $4 million cash to Belgian cement industrialist Baron Paul Kronacker or Texas oil millionaire Rogers, or of vesting it into a Newfoundland development corporation funded by Harriman-Ripley of New York.[34] On the recommendation of Valdmanis, the cement mill was incorporated in August 1951 as a 100 per cent government-owned company. It was named North Star Cement Ltd – after Valdmanis's prewar decoration from Sweden.[35] In August 1952, finally, the plant was sold for $4 million to MIAG's Canadian Machinery Holding Trust, a subsidiary of the same company that built it. The terms were a $200,000 down payment and a government loan equal to the purchase price.[36] To avoid charges for reneging on the contract of November 1950, Valdmanis,

Smallwood, and Attorney General Leslie R. Curtis agreed for Newfoundland to pay a $50,000 penalty to the group for breach of good faith.[37]

It did not take Valdmanis long to convince Smallwood of the desirability of a gypsum industry on the same terms. It would be built by the German machinery manufacturer Benno Schilde and consist of a plaster and wallboard plant of larger capacity than Valdmanis had proposed earlier for Nova Scotia. Meanwhile, by July 1950 the prospects for a new gypsum plant in Nova Scotia had suddenly improved.[38] Valdmanis's previous market studies had left little doubt that no more than one gypsum products industry could be viable in the Atlantic provinces and either Newfoundland or Nova Scotia would have it. Nova Scotia had earlier hesitated to proceed with the project because of estimates submitted by the American-owned gypsum syndicate in Canada. They suggested that, instead of Valdmanis's calculation of $1.5 million, a capital investment far in excess of $3 million would be required.

These 'American figures,' Valdmanis pointed out to Smallwood, were correct only if the routine 'American way' was chosen – 'piecemeal' deals – placing orders here and there, and nobody responsible for the different machinery pieces 'clicking as a unit' and for strict times for delivery and construction. 'There are many industries which cannot succeed in Newfoundland if the "normal" (American) price is to be paid for their establishment; but, on the other hand, several new industries will survive and become a success in this country, if we can build them at say, 70% of the normal cost, and if we can secure the necessary specialists presently so badly lacking not only in Newfoundland, but in all Maritime provinces.'[39]

The cabinet approved the gypsum project on 9 September 1950. Through Kreyser's contacts and Valdmanis's shrewd bargaining in St John's with the representatives of the German machinery manufacturers, Newfoundland obtained such low tenders on its cement and gypsum plants that the German suppliers allegedly actually lost money on these deals. 'The fact of the matter is we were half ashamed at what Dr Valdmanis and Mr Ernest Leja screwed the price down to,' Smallwood stated in the Newfoundland House of Assembly on 16 March 1951. The firms of MIAG and Benno Schilde signed the contracts mainly because they were led to believe that more business would follow. Leja became supervising engineer and then general manager of both plants.[40]

The price for the gypsum industry contracted with Benno Schilde was $2 million. It included the customary 5 per cent commission for Kreyser's firm Neue Technik and what Benno Schilde thought to be a legitimate commission of $200,000 to the premier of Newfoundland, payable to Valdmanis. In reality, the final price of the gypsum as well as the cement plant was about one-third more than anticipated, and the plants took almost twice the stipulated time to go into full production. Still, they turned out to be cheaper than plants of comparable capacity, as pointed out in an audit by a New York consulting engineering firm in 1952.[41] They were two of three completely government-funded industries started in Newfoundland in 1950. Valdmanis is often erroneously associated with the third one, a birch products or hardwoods industry. Launched in December 1950, it was initiated entirely by local building contractor Chester Dawe with a $2.84 million government loan.[42]

The Price Tag of Economic Development

The launching of the cement and gypsum plants was accomplished at the price of a hectic work pace characterizing the approach to economic development in the years to come. Valdmanis had found no opportunity to sleep for five days, he wrote his brother-in-law Valdis Mateus on 9 August 1950. He had to carry out negotiations for plant construction and financing simultaneously, while also shaking up the bureaucracy of five ministries to meet the agreed-upon deadlines so the offers would not become void. It was a 'hard and tough fight' because 'my bureaucrats simply could not understand that.' Then, in this pre-jet age era, the first three weeks of September would see him commuting constantly between St John's, New York, Washington, and Europe. For Valdmanis work was '99 per cent of life,' though he had doubts about the physical toll: 'I definitely believe that brains should not be permitted to rust, that something has to be created every day, every minute, and regardless where a person lives. Still, somehow I have the feeling that I am doing something exceeding my normal capabilities and that I am "eating away" not only the interests of what God has given me but also squandering the basic capital itself.'[43]

Construction of the cement and gypsum plants were heralds of more industries to come – now, however, in increasingly helter-skelter fashion. As early as 11 June 1950 Valdmanis raised the matter of funding the development of fishing, timber, mining, and manufacturing industries, as well as of agricultural resources and transport facilities proposed by Smallwood with the New York group on a visit to New York. Strategic enterprises, such as a military road from the south coast to Gander, a refinery, and hydro-power plant even justified outright grants, he suggested.[44]

'There is no single cement project alone. There is to be a chain of industrial development in Newfoundland, of which the cement project is to be only the first link,' Valdmanis told Michael Lewin of the group on 16 August 1950. The group would be invited to secure all the capital required for this development. In addition to the above-mentioned projects, Valdmanis foresaw a flour mill, a whale, seal, cod liver oil hardening plant, and a fur tannery for a total of $10 million. There would be a $10 million reorganization of the fishing industry (including drying, freezing fish, and processing plants), a $45 million third pulp and paper mill with housing and town facilities (in Bay D'Espoir, based on Labrador timber), plus a $10 million smelter (in Bay D'Espoir) and an oil refinery (in Placentia Bay), for a total capital investment of $80 million. After the gypsum factory, priority was to be given to the flour mill ($1.5 million), oil hardening plant ($1 million), fur tannery ($0.5 million), and pulp and paper mill ($45 million). Apart from the cement and gypsum plants, these were essentially Smallwood's priorities. Realizing that all these plans were 'somewhat vague,' Valdmanis asked Michael Lewin 'to undertake all steps necessary to show the Premier a clear picture of all the problems involved so that he can make up his mind.' Newfoundland needed 'action now,' Valdmanis urged, 'a plan and a clear agreement.'[45]

From New York Valdmanis informed Deputy Minister N. Short in September 1950 that he was 'pretty far advanced in a terrific struggle the outcome of which may "make" Newfoundland,' a deliberate reference to the premier's declared intention to 'make or break Newfoundland.' Lewin was driving hard to get a third pulp and paper mill established in connection with plans to incorporate a new crown company and the granting of some thirty-five million cords of timber. That was 'a tempo' Valdmanis liked 'very much,' and he issued a flood of requests to Short from preparing surveys, estimates, and meetings to arranging travel and receptions in his absence. Worried that Short would balk and spoil his game plan, Valdmanis pleaded: 'Please don't mind me "pushing." It is not for me but for you. I am very tired, but I am keeping going ... until we decide to halt this terrific pace and have some rest. I'm afraid such time may come. But until then – let's keep going.'[46]

The massive development program envisioned, Valdmanis and the group agreed, could be undertaken only by a development corporation operating entirely as a business proposition and with extensive mining and cutting rights granted to it. It would have to be created by charter at the next session of the Newfoundland legislature.[47] Under the auspices of this corporation, wholly owned subsidiaries could be formed to operate cement, mining, and pulp and paper projects. To raise the necessary capital, more powerful Wall Street financiers and Canadian investment bankers, such as Harriman-Ripley of New York and Wood Gundy of Toronto, were added to the group as shareholders of the corporation. In June 1951 it came to be incorporated as NALCO (Newfoundland and Labrador Corporation). Valdmanis claimed that he had originally conceived of the idea of this development corporation, 'as a strictly businesslike organization with participation of private capital but also with strong Government interest in it.'[48]

Simultaneously, Valdmanis approached German contacts with similar requests for far-reaching and fast development in Newfoundland. In October 1950 Kreyser arranged for Valdmanis to lead Smallwood and two of his cabinet ministers (James Chalker and Herman Quinton) through Germany for two weeks on a 2,200-mile tour to inspect industries and meet business leaders. This was the first of three trips through Germany arranged for Smallwood by Valdmanis. They visited chemical, flour, cement, fish and fish meal, machine, and wood products plants, including those of IG Farben, Krupp, MIAG, Benno Schilde, and Claudius Peters. The Newfoundland party was captivated by the respectful welcome and generous treatment accorded them everywhere. To Chalker, the accomplished heel clicking and bowing between Valdmanis and the company directors they met was like having 'hinges on your arse.'[49] In Bad Hersfeld Smallwood was so impressed with his tour of the Benno Schilde machinery plant that he proposed to move the entire operation to Newfoundland.[50]

In Bonn the German vice-chancellor entertained Smallwood's party, and Minister of Economics Ludwig Erhard (later chancellor) held a dinner in their honour. On the latter occasion Smallwood expressed his preference for plants and machinery from Germany, Newfoundland's chief customer of Bell Island iron ore until 1939.[51] German newspapers and radio stations featured Smallwood's invitation to Germans, issued at a Bonn press conference attended by eighty correspondents, to come to Newfoundland.[52] In Hamburg Smallwood declared that he foresaw great prospects for German workers in Newfoundland and that he was preparing plans for a mass immigration.[53] Back home the premier disclosed that he 'talked with many industrialists and financial magnates who are most anxious to establish a stake for themselves on this side of the water.' His target was '10,000 new jobs for Newfoundlanders in the next two or three years.' He had also placed machinery orders in Germany, Smallwood explained, because he had obtained better prices, and the faster delivery promised meant that plant production would begin in half the time.[54]

With the level of expectations reaching new heights, would Valdmanis be able to deliver? In December 1950 he approached Kreyser's friend Arthur Siegheim, a German pulp and paper magnate whom Smallwood had met in Germany, with what he called a 'dream' of his. 'I am dreaming of two pulp and paper mills in Newfoundland' – one in Labrador, the other in the Bay D'Espoir area of Newfoundland, Valdmanis pleaded. The inaccessibility of Labrador would be compensated for by the availability of 'incredibly' cheap power from the Hamilton River and abundant timber stands. 'Can you and are you willing, through your good and powerful connections, to help me to arrange this paper mill being built within a, say, "impossibly" short period of time?' What he meant was 'having it ready and in production within a year and half to two years.' Valdmanis visualized such an 'exceptional deal being executed with payments made by us, not only in hard cash, dollars, but also in kind,' such as timber, cellulose, or both. 'I repeat, my dear Dr Siegheim, this is a "dream." I visualize a great and flourishing business springing out of this "dream," a business as real and as hard as cement.'[55]

He had approached machine manufacturers in Sweden and Switzerland with similar letters, Valdmanis advised Smallwood. The idea was 'to get many groups interested for the purpose of obtaining quick delivery and – possibly – long-term credits. I believe in this. A new town in Labrador ... immediately *plus* another mill in the South and a chemical or steel industry there. It's *not* [emphasis in the original] a dream only!'[56] From Stahlbau Rheinhausen (formerly Krupp), with whom Smallwood's delegation had made inquiries while in Germany, Valdmanis had received confirmation in October 1950 that a steel mill based on Krupp's Renn patent could be delivered on short order, in sixteen to twenty-four months.[57] By the beginning of December 1950, Krupp also had the firm of Siemens-Schuckert lined up as builders of the required hydro-electric power stations.[58]

Siegheim thought it 'entirely possible' to realize this 'dream' of Valdmanis and Smallwood. 'I love such ideas and I believe to have learnt from my 44-year practical experience that the dear Lord has endowed me with the very capabilities of solving such difficult problems,' Siegheim gushed.[59] Although the dream got nowhere, for a number of reasons, its escalating dimensions kept Newfoundland in suspense throughout 1951.

As outlined in the media and the Newfoundland legislature, Siegheim founded a Swiss-registered Labrador Timber Utilization Company

(LATUCO) to launch a colossal enterprise in Labrador with the assistance of several hundred Finnish, Swedish, and German forest and timber specialists. His prime incentive was the exploitation of pulpwood to meet chronic shortages in the German pulp and paper industry. In June 1951 Valdmanis procured for him a special government concession to harvest 200,000 cords of pulpwood annually for ten years at $5 per cord, a price three to ten times above that of other Canadian provinces. Siegheim agreed to pay $1 million annually for this concession, regardless of how much he exported. In addition, he promised to introduce in Labrador a modern forest economy with a forestry school, a professor's chair in forestry at Memorial University of Newfoundland in St John's, modern forest laws, model farms and settlements, and, last but not least, a pulp and paper mill.[60]

From the outset Valdmanis was so fixated on the Siegheim project that he regretted the extent to which he had committed himself and Smallwood, 'at least morally,' to Wall Street financial groups in connection with the establishment of a development corporation. By June 1951, as the Siegheim deal was firmed up, Valdmanis was prepared to dump Harriman-Ripley, Wood Gundy, and the New York group. In the legislature Smallwood promoted the enigmatic Siegheim as 'a man of great wealth, who, if it is of any interest to the House, lives in a castle which is well known.'[61] 'If ever there was a Santa Claus, he was one,' Liberal backbencher Samuel Drover mocked in October 1951 when the great Siegheim failed to deliver.[62]

Not surprisingly, the host of development projects that Valdmanis was juggling by the end of 1950 increased Smallwood's dependence on him. So, the moment seemed opportune for Valdmanis to raise the issues of a salary increase and a long-term contract. He had had an offer from a New York firm to become vice-president and general manager at $50,000 a year, plus some shares, he informed Smallwood on 12 December 1950, and it had hurt him very much that the cabinet had refused to recognize his work and thought he was 'just good enough for being kept on a "try-out" basis at $714 per month.' His small and dedicated staff, too, had been underpaid and overworked. Since he had the highest regard for Smallwood – after President Ulmanis he had not met any man whom he respected more – he would be prepared to stay on at half the salary that he could get elsewhere: 'I do it because I like this country, and because I like this particular type of work for which I may have been born. I do not want to bargain, but I am not out for money.' Should the 'big Corporation' come into being, and should it be necessary that Valdmanis take over some responsibilities with it, 'I shall not fail to voluntarily ask for a reduction in my salary I am to draw from the Government.'[63]

By organizing Smallwood's economic development and by proving his expertise at those 'special themes' he proved capable of, he was easily repaying the money his office received every year, Valdmanis continued. Smallwood should always keep in mind that something much more than German machinery had led to the contracts already signed or in preparation. This 'something' was 'the knowledge, the trained brain, the skill to master the subject plus commanding impression plus world-wide connections with the best firms in the world. I think I have all this. But, nevertheless, it imposes a gigantic task on me. Does anyone suppose I can carry it with one assistant, one private secretary and one typist? And being supported actively *only* by the Premier?' Valdmanis took credit for 'the great American names' he had managed to associate with the projected development corporation. These names alone would assure Smallwood 'infallible success' in his self-imposed mission to 'make Newfoundland' and 'the materializing of Newfoundland's wildest dreams so far as sound development goes.' Surely Smallwood would appreciate that 'all this was *my* dream supported by your vision; it was *my* work done in tiresome, sleepless nights although I need sleep as everyone else, since I am not the "superman" some people refer to in fun.'[64]

As a condition for staying, Valdmanis made several demands, to be effective 1 January 1951. He wanted a four-year contract, an annual salary of $25,000 (provided his salary would always be $5,000 higher than any other salary paid out of public funds), and a budget of $25,000 for creating and maintaining an adequate staff. He wanted the right to select his staff, appoint them on a contract basis, and determine their salaries. According to Harold Horwood, Valdmanis could not endure the slight of having discovered that Clive Planta, another outside expert Smallwood had hired as deputy minister of fisheries, was to start work in January 1951 at a salary of $15,000. On top of that, it was Smallwood's idea to offer Planta such an unheard-of salary. (In 1954 Horwood discovered three other Newfoundland government experts, 'all collecting $25,000 a year or better.')[65]

In return for his increased salary, Valdmanis would undertake to eliminate unemployment by 1952 by establishing within his four-year term *at least* the following industries: a flour mill, a feed mill, a fur-processing plant, a leather tannery, a marine-oil-processing plant, a fish cannery, two 500-ton paper mills (one in Labrador and one in Bay D'Espoir with the latter depending on availability of a reliable survey, cost of hydroelectricity, and U.S. special financing), U.S.$25 million 'special financing' for new industrial areas in Labrador and on the south coast, a steel or chemical industry (depending on availability of hydro-power), and at least four additional unspecified industries.[66]

Smallwood, then earning $7,000 as premier, granted Valdmanis's demands without reservations. 'Please do not even think of leaving us,' he cabled to Valdmanis in New York. 'We will hold you whatever the cost.'[67] The salary increase reinforced Valdmanis's already controversial public image. How could Newfoundland afford such a man? members of the Opposition wondered, if 'the Prime Minister of Canada only gets $18,000 a year. The Chief Justice gets $25,000 a year, the highest man in Canada. The Governor of the Royal Bank gets $30,000.' Smallwood's standard reply was that 'in the few months he had been with the Government, [Valdmanis] has earned for Newfoundland several times his total salary for the whole period of his contract.'[68]

In Valdmanis's dedication to new industries, workaholic style, and enthusiasm for grand schemes, Smallwood had found a soulmate. 'It is difficult to say where the work of one ends and the effort of the other one starts. All that is achieved is a joint effort of both of us,' Joey Smallwood explained from the vantage point of March 1953.[69] He never lost his awe for the Latvian's seemingly unlimited skills: 'He was one of the best tennis players we ever saw in Newfoundland; he was a superb dancer, had a glorious singing voice, was an accomplished musician, spoke half a dozen languages ... He was a walking encyclopedia on many of the countries of Europe; he knew every industrialist of importance in Western Germany ... he was a superior chess player, so some of my chess-playing friends told me; and generally he was one of the most talented men I have ever known.'[70]

Time was running out for Smallwood. In May 1950 he had realized that the $40 million surplus bequeathed by Newfoundland's pre-1948 Commission of Government had shrunk dramatically to less than $10 million. By December 1950 he had developed boundless faith in his Latvian wizard's ability to produce results, in part because he refused to consider any alternatives to rapid industrial development. 'Always and always,' he repeated in desperation to Valdmanis that he had no choice, 'there would be no room for long planning, sitting and debating while the most daring and best Newfoundlanders would migrate to the Mainland.'[71]

Valdmanis, grateful that Smallwood liked him, had in turn come to like Smallwood and his 'wild enthusiasm.' The only frightening thing was

Smallwood's 'switching mind.' According to Valdmanis, 'there was no night' when he was in St John's when he had not spent four or five hours with Smallwood 'discussing and talking about his dreams and trying to give some practical shape to them.' Smallwood had 'no practical grasp whatever as far as industrialization was concerned; on the other hand, his enthusiasm and the way he talked had a strong appeal.' Smallwood's expertise was in talking and making propaganda, but success required at least some factual work, 'certainly the more the better.' And 'that was my job,' Valdmanis recalled.[72]

Did Valdmanis have a theory of economic development or an overall vision of his own? In an article published in the spring of 1951 he argued that Newfoundland needed a 'Five Year Plan' in order to catch up with Canada. Underdeveloped areas could not attain the economic standard of the highly developed ones by a policy of gradual change while competing against great odds. 'As a rule, the poor are bound to remain the underdogs, until and unless a combination of tremendous effort plus some lucky break elevates them.' Newfoundland had the resources, the people, and the will to catch up with the mainland, Valdmanis believed. Her limestone and gypsum rock, for example, had proven to be the best in the Western Hemisphere, and the industries processing these minerals were already generating secondary industries. Even more promising were the untapped resources of Labrador. If the exploitation of the millions of cords of Labrador pulpwood could be combined with the development of its vast hydro-power potential, the economics of Newfoundland would be changed drastically. A newsprint mill in Labrador timber could provide some six to eight thousand jobs and become the embryo of a new town. And there was pulpwood in the province for more than one paper mill. The goal would be a Newfoundland with industry in sound balance to fisheries, with gradually developing farming and gardening. This would not be just a pipedream – 'if many will help and nobody blocks the way.' The idea advanced by some of converting Newfoundland into a 'National Park' with a limited population of 250,000 and the emigration of the surplus population was absurd and cruel because such a situation would make Newfoundlanders unhappy. Valdmanis knew from experience that for emigrants 'it takes a whole generation to become "acclimatized" socially, politically, even physically.'[73]

In a follow-up comment, journalist Rupert Jackson suggested that Valdmanis was now putting into operation some of his boyhood dreams about social and economic development. He set a hard-working pace almost impossible to match; he shunned publicity, never talked about himself, did not smoke, and did not like hard liquor. Occasionally he would relax by playing tennis or the piano. 'Otherwise he leads a very lonely life in a world of his own. His most devoted subordinates as well as his very few true friends refer to him always as "The Doctor": calling him "Alf" would be near blasphemy to them.' There were many reasons why profound admiration and inevitable jealousies were focused around 'this immensely intense, very unusual man,' who looked like and moved with 'the ease of a well-trained sportsman, but whose eyes – perhaps the most impressive part of this young-looking newcomer to Newfoundland – have the unforgettable light of a fanatic or a man of destiny.'[74]

Fishing in Troubled Waters

Valdmanis started his new term with 'the greatest possible freedom of action for the benefit of Newfoundland,' as he told an acquaintance.[75] He was also in a tight spot to deliver the thirteen industries that he had promised to launch in 1951. To do so, he concentrated increasingly on his German contacts. German entrepreneurs were interested in Newfoundland for several reasons that Smallwood eagerly exploited as 'fishing in troubled waters.' They were anxious to regain a foothold anywhere in North America to rebuild their prewar markets, they were looking for an 'escape hatch' (as Smallwood put it[76]) from the acute Soviet threat in Europe, and some wanted to re-establish in North America their enterprises destroyed or expropriated in eastern Europe. Although Newfoundland was little known in German-speaking Europe, Canada had acquired a reputation as 'the land of the future' and, as the leading Swiss financial paper noted in May 1952, 'economically and politically Newfoundland is Canada.'[77]

While central Europe was completely ignorant about general conditions in Newfoundland, Newfoundland had also serious impediments to relying on Germans. To begin with, war-ravaged Europe had an acute dollar shortage. In addition, the Allies had imposed foreign exchange controls until January 1952. To redress the enormous dollar gap in West Germany's trade after 1949, German exports to the dollar markets were officially promoted. At the same time, the export of German capital investment was virtually prohibited. Valdmanis, therefore, had to devise a clever policy specifically geared to the participation of German interests. To conserve Newfoundland funds, no more industries would be built entirely from public funds until private interests could be found to take over the cement and gypsum plants. In February 1951 a policy was adopted for German participation to 'take the form of bringing (a) their machinery and (b) their know-how into the new joint companies, and such German capital would form a partnership with local (Newfoundland) private capital and/or, if necessary and desired, also Newfoundland government capital would participate.'[78]

In practice this meant that investment by private interests would be 'matched dollar for dollar by the Newfoundland government,' as Valdmanis liked to put it.[79] The government's contribution would consist of loan guarantees or direct loans for a ten-year period at 4.5 to 5 per cent interest equal to the investment of the company or individual setting up the industry. The government loan would be secured by a mortgage on the assets of the company to be incorporated in Newfoundland. The declared purpose of the loans was to enable private companies outside the dollar area 'to procure the necessary dollars, to pay customs duties, erect a building, install machinery, and operate the plant for a few months until returns would begin to come in.'[80] Without these inducements, Smallwood admitted, 'we could not have persuaded one company to come here.'[81]

The search for suitable investors was conducted through Valdmanis's close acquaintance and mentor Friedrich Kreyser and his consulting engineering firm Neue Technik in Stadtoldendorf, Germany. Kreyser mobilized his business contacts in Germany, Austria, Switzerland, Belgium, and Scandinavia. During Smallwood's visit to Germany in October 1950, Valdmanis met shipowner Walter J. Hinneberg and his lawyer-father Werner in Hamburg. Werner with the occasional assistance of Walter agreed to act as a clearing-house in the recruitment of 'serious and reliable' entrepreneurs and projects.[82] The prospective investors in Germany were to reimburse Werner for his expenses and pay him a commission for his services. In practice, he occasionally relied on sub-agents to whom he paid a finder's fee.

The plan was for Valdmanis to travel to Germany to size up the projects whenever Hinneberg or Kreyser had lined up a number of interested parties. There he would, if possible, sign a 'gentleman's agreement' to be reviewed and confirmed after his return to St John's. From prospective investors Valdmanis's office would require detailed information about the type and value of machinery to be imported, the capacity and size of the proposed plant, its requirements of water, fuel, electric power, and raw materials, its output and production costs, and the anticipated markets. Based on this information, Valdmanis's staff of six – one assistant director, one researcher, one engineer, one special assistant, one private secretary and one typist – would prepare a comprehensive report for cabinet and legislative approval.

Hinneberg's first detailed proposal, a lead industry, was presented in October 1950 while Smallwood and Valdmanis were visiting Hamburg. Although on 29 May 1950 Valdmanis signed a gentleman's agreement with the firm Bleiindustrie Jung und Lindig in Hamburg for a branch manufacturing plant, the negotiations to complete the deal dragged on until November 1952, and finally died.[83] Other projects discussed in Hamburg were a bread industry producing crisp bread (Knaeckebrot), Zwieback, and wafers; a tannery; a marine oil hardening plant processing the oil of whales and seals caught by ships owned by Hinneberg's shipping company, 'Nordmeer,' or sold by it to a Newfoundland subsidiary; a flour mill; and a fish canning factory. It was understood that the projects had to be brought to fruition on short order. By the beginning of January 1951 Hinneberg presented builders of two enterprises – for a flour mill Georg E.R. Plange of Düsseldorf in association with his architect William Jenny and for a tannery W. Dorn from Elmshorn or A.C. Hoffmann from Hamburg. Dorn promised to unload his machinery in St John's as early as March 1951 and start tanning operations two months later.[84]

In February 1951 the Hinnebergs visited St John's. Indicative of the temper of the times were their worries about the 'very unfortunate political situation' prompting their wish not to be separated from their families. They therefore had requested travel documents for their wives, grandmother, sister and brother-in-law, a three-year-old child and a baby, as well as permission to send several crates of valuables for storage.[85] In St John's, Werner Hinneberg discussed the feasibility of the following projects with Valdmanis: fish meal, fish canning, clothing, paint, lead, optical goods, gloves, and a leather factory.[86] Hinneberg returned to Germany 'deeply impressed' and more than ever committed to help solve Newfoundland's problems.

Valdmanis now advised that any new European industries would be financed by bank loans 'on the strength of a Newfoundland guarantee and not through a direct cash advance.' However, an international bank to assume such financing still had to be found. In the meantime, as Newfoundland's financial position needed consolidation, 'we have slowed down a bit our former really hectic pace,' he explained on 3 March 1951.[87] In fact what had happened was that Newfoundland's pre-Confederation surplus was spent. There was no more spare cash to hand out.

By April 1951 Hinneberg had numerous new propositions lined up – machinery plant, cotton mill, shoe factory, furniture factory, sawmill, fur dressing and dyeing factory, fish tannery, fish filleting and fish meal plant, construction industry, fountain pen production, and electrical appliances, as well as chipboard, cardboard, and liner board industries.[88] Now even Valdmanis became impatient and he decided to 'earnestly and sincerely' urge Hinneberg 'to prepare *only one* [emphasis in the original] scheme, and let's start executing it, and executing it soon. If that one scheme will work out, the Newfoundland people and their Government will know you from your deeds, and we may be able to consider the next step. But unless we can have in the bag at least one good scheme with you – perhaps Dr Dorn's leather factory – we shall be afraid we, and particularly you, are losing much time and effort.' The federal Department of Defence Production would be prepared to place some substantial orders with the new leather factory.[89]

Despite Hinneberg's endeavours, a group of Latvian refugees in Germany proposing a film industry managed to score the first commitment from Valdmanis. Albert Jekste and his Riga Film unit, who had somehow salvaged their technologically highly advanced sound film equipment from Latvia to Germany were wartime acquaintances of Valdmanis. On his first visit to Germany in October 1950, Smallwood and Valdmanis had inspected their Hamburg studio and immediately recognized their potential significance. In Newfoundland, Smallwood wanted them to produce documentary films for his government, demonstrating the success of its economic policy. Valdmanis agreed to act as guarantor for the obligations Jekste had incurred in Germany because they formed a lien on the investment he wanted to bring to Newfoundland.[90]

The deal with Dorn was finalized during Valdmanis's two-week stay at Hotel Goldene Krone in Jugendheim, Germany, in May 1951. There Valdmanis conferred with Hinneberg, Kreyser, Siegheim, Hugo Stinnes, and representatives of MIAG and Benno Schilde. Dorn, eager to emigrate to Canada, would have the Hamburg construction firm of Werner Suerbier build his tannery in the small town of Carbonear 100 kilometres from St John's. Suerbier would ship all the required building materials (including cement and nails) and equipment from Germany by August 1951 and would, as well, build facilities for other new industries expected to come.[91]

The day after his return to St John's, Valdmanis proudly announced to Smallwood that an additional eleven new industries were in the pipeline.[92] Among the projects receiving preliminary approval in Jugendheim were a machine manufacturing plant (E.H. Roethe and Paul Hagenbach), a leather goods industry (Anton Schaefers), a fur (dressing, dyeing, and treatment) plant to be in operation by July 1952 (Dr Michael Mertens, Julius Landau, and Johannes Schulze), and an optical industry manufacturing eyeglasses (Professor Lothar Sennewald). In June and July 1951 these promoters, together with Suerbier and Dorn, were invited to Newfoundland to discuss their undertakings with the cabinet. It then approved loans ranging from $50,000 repayable in three years for Schaefers to $750,000 repayable in ten years for Mertens.[93] The Sennewald agreement was put on hold until Leitz, the world-renowned German optical manufacturer, had considered and rejected the idea of a branch plant in Newfoundland. Knowing that a Leitz move to Ontario was also under consideration, Valdmanis had offered in vain 'to provide, on a long-term loan basis, practically the whole capital required.' Newfoundland was 'not afraid of lending *your* Canadian Company, incorporated in Newfoundland, *any* [emphasis in the original] amount of money you might reasonably need.'[94]

At Jugendheim, the central event was the signing of the vaunted Siegheim deal – logging and timber management by LATUCO plus a paper mill at Bay D'Espoir. The building of a cellulose mill at Lake Melville in Labrador had now been assigned to Hugo Stinnes. The pulpwood required by these plants would yield an additional $2 million to Newfoundland, Valdmanis fantasized to Smallwood from Germany. 'Of course these are plans or may-be dreams for the future, but this "future" may not exceed a few years only, and in the meantime or rather immediately, you will have the assured income of one million dollars per annum for the pulpwood sold to Dr Siegheim's Swiss company.' From MIAG Valdmanis held out hope of bringing home a project 'no Newfoundlander has ever dreamed of, except, perhaps, you.' Thereafter, the main challenge left would be the envisaged development corporation, into which the cement and gypsum mills and the discussed timber and mining areas could be vested and through which the budget deficit could be eliminated.

Exuberant about the prospect of being able 'to produce things in Newfoundland which will be next to impossible,' Valdmanis urged Smallwood to make no more concessions to Harriman-Ripley, Wood Gundy, and the New York group. 'If they come on very humble terms, let's accept them, just to honour our previous discussions, talks, and terms. But do not yield even a little bit, please! We can do very well without them.' Naively assuming that he could manipulate German business tycoons and Wall Street bankers, Valdmanis gloated to Smallwood: 'Let's remember that once you told me you trust me so much, that you would be ready to go with me through hell, if necessary. I remember, and I remember that you and your Government trusted me and risked to plunge with me into some multimillion dollar ventures in the very beginning of our collaboration, when you knew very little of what I actually know and can do for you. Now you know much more and your colleagues feel with some confidence that you can trust me.'[95]

The high point of this fishing venture in troubled waters was Smallwood's second tour of Europe from 4 to 30 September 1951. Accompanied by Attorney General, Leslie Curtis and Curtis's daughter and guided by Valdmanis, who also functioned as interpreter, the chief destination was again Germany with business excursions to England, Switzerland, the Netherlands, Denmark, and Sweden. In Frankfurt they met Hinneberg, then were guests of Siegheim for three days at his castle in Staffelstein, where they were treated to an open-air ballet and to fireworks. For five days MIAG owner Dr Johannes Lerch wined and dined them like royalty in his plush, palatial residence in Garmisch. The festivities culminated in a toast by Lerch promising to build a machinery plant in St John's and a toast by Smallwood declaring Lerch a consultant on economic development to the Newfoundland government.

The Smallwood delegation also visited Heidelberg, Bonn, and the Ruhr Valley, touring furniture and shoe factories and the industrial facilities of Leitz, Krupp, Hoechst, IG Farben, Benno Schilde, and MIAG. The red carpet was rolled out wherever they appeared. Smallwood and Curtis were impressed that Valdmanis appeared to be known and respected everywhere. On the last day of their visit, Smallwood hosted a reception at Hinneberg's Hamburg residence for some forty representatives of fifteen industries. In all, thirteen projects were negotiated, including a hydro-power station, steel mill, and production facilities for matches, oil hardening, tiles, leather goods, machinery, shoes, chipboard, textiles, and wools. Only the last five of these came to be realized.[96]

Upon his return, Smallwood announced a provincial election for 26 November 1951 on his record of economic development. He boasted that on his trip to Europe he had secured fifteen new industries, topped by a steel mill to process Bell Island iron ore. These, together with eight new industries acquired before that trip, would give nearly eight thousand full-time jobs by the end of 1952 and fifteen thousand new jobs before the end of 1953. Newfoundland would not have these industries without Dr Valdmanis, and to hire him was one of the smartest things he ever did, Smallwood declared in a CBC radio broadcast. Wherever they travelled in Europe, be it England, Holland, Germany, Switzerland, Denmark, or Sweden, Smallwood found that Valdmanis knew everyone and everyone knew Valdmanis. It was apparent that he was respected and trusted in the highest circles in all those countries. Thanking God for the day when he had discovered Valdmanis and taken him away from Carleton College and from the government of Canada to work for the people of Newfoundland, Smallwood went on to confess: 'And now that I know what a man of honour he is, what a man of remarkable ability and brains he is; now that I know that he toils day and night for Newfoundland; now that I know what he has done for Newfoundland, and what he will do, I say solemnly to my fellow citizens tonight that I would not want to be Premier of Newfoundland if I lost him.'[97]

Smallwood's second trip to Germany generated considerable publicity for Newfoundland and numerous new propositions were forwarded by Hinneberg. Although most of the industries about which Smallwood boasted did not materialize, Valdmanis and Smallwood managed in the following year to commit seven major German industrial concerns to establish eight branch plants in Newfoundland between 1952 and 1954: MIAG of Brunswick with a heavy machinery plant near St John's; Rawe and Company of Nordhorn with a cotton and textile mill in St John's; G. Hahlbrock of Hamelin with a glove factory in Carbonear; Moser and Sons of Schramberg with a chipboard factory in Donovans; Haguma of Hanover with a rubber plant in Holyrood; Hanning and Kahl of Bielefeld with a car battery plant in Topsail; and Eckart Strickwarenfabrik of Vocklabruck, Austria, with a knitting mill in Brigus. One of Germany's largest shoe manufacturers, Roland Rieker of Tuttlingen, was prepared in November 1951 to build a branch plant in St John's. However, he backed out when Smallwood decided this factory had to be near the new tannery in the small town of Harbour Grace, ninety kilometres from St John's.[98]

In the autumn of 1951 Hinneberg's and Kreyser's solicitation of German industries developed such momentum and German response appeared so promising that Smallwood's cabinet agreed to appoint as special assistants to the director general of economic development Kreyser's friends Max Braun-Wogau and Dr Herbert Kaulbach (a senior German civil servant in the West German Department of Economics) with his secretary Hanna Hilpert.[99] 'Canadian Promoting and Trading Ltd' with headquarters in St John's was to be launched by Valdmanis, Kreyser, and Braun-Wogau to cultivate the new ties and coordinate German and Newfoundland interests.[100] German–Newfoundland trade was expected to increase with the steady influx of German machinery and settlers, and a proposal was entertained for a loan to a Düsseldorf promoter so he could open a direct Hamburg–Newfoundland shipping line to eliminate the traditional detour via Liverpool and Rotterdam.[101] Because of Valdmanis's strategy, German economics minister Ludwig Erhard singled out Newfoundland as one of the most accessible areas of the dollar market, deserving the special attention of German business.[102]

Unholy Dash for New Industries

In reality, however, fishing in troubled waters turned out to be more problematic than Smallwood and Valdmanis dared to admit. As early as mid-October 1951, as Smallwood was praising Valdmanis to the skies, the Siegheim deal began to unravel. After investing $100,000 in his Labrador project and incurring debts in St John's he could not pay, Siegheim's experts concluded that Lake Melville was navigable only ninety days annually. To ship out the contracted 200,000 cords of pulpwood, seven to eight ships would have to be loaded simultaneously (since loading of one ship would take fourteen days), but there were not enough timber yards and docking places for loading eight ships simultaneously. Siegheim also wondered how he could obtain at least six hundred Newfoundlanders willing to work in the Labrador forest or, alternatively, permission to import the lacking men. Unless he could prove the technical feasibility of his plan, the German government would not release the necessary dollars.[103] In early 1952, however, Siegheim's inability to procure the 3.8 million dollars necessary for purchasing, cutting, and shipping 100,000 cords of wood emerged as his core problem.[104]

Siegheim's failure to deliver gave Valdmanis his first great scare. 'Should you fail, for reasons of being double-crossed by your own Government officials or other German companies, or any other reason whatsoever,' he warned Siegheim, 'it would cause great inconvenience, and, certainly, some political unpleasantness too.' If that should happen, no more Newfoundland and Labrador pulpwood would go to Germany in future. 'Rightly or wrongly, your failure would be regarded as a *German* failure,' Valdmanis wanted to make emphatically clear to Siegheim and the German officials involved, 'and we won't be dealing with any more German interests thereafter.'[105]

A serious problem delaying the launching of some and deterring other industries was caused by the difficulty of equipping German-owned plants in Newfoundland with new machinery. Items manufactured in Germany needed a special permit before they could be exported as investment. Also, normally their equivalent in foreign currency had to be returned to the German treasury for conversion into German currency. Such special permits were extremely hard to procure. In 1951 Germans planning to start manufacturing in Newfoundland had to go to great lengths to camouflage their intentions of starting a new enterprise abroad. To do this they had to declare to German authorities that they would (1) export used machinery, (2) rent it to a Newfoundland firm, and (3) return rental income to Germany.[106] Some tried to circumvent the restrictions by dealing through Swiss business and banking connections.[107] Others were hatching complicated schemes of circumventing the foreign exchange controls, such as inducing Smallwood to acquire blocked Deutschmarks, paid as West German indemnity to victims of Nazi persecution.[108]

Indeed, German foreign exchange and capital export controls made industrialization on a fifty–fifty basis in Newfoundland almost impossible. The German promoters' difficulty in investing had two adverse effects. First, it caused Smallwood to raise most or all of the financing with loans. He would decide this 'without any advice or technical help from anybody.' As Valdmanis explained in retrospect, the German party could just 'pretend' to invest, and the Newfoundland government, granting loans to establish new industries, could just 'pretend' that it was a fifty–fifty deal. To be sure, some companies made real investments, but the new industries relied increasingly on Newfoundland money only. The entire set-up conspired to encourage foreign promoters to defraud the Newfoundland government.[109]

Second, the Germans found themselves 'caught between two fires.' If they invested in Newfoundland, they broke German regulations and risked severe penalties in Germany. If they made no investments, they cheated the Newfoundland government, which, as Valdmanis candidly observed, 'in the person of Mr Smallwood would willingly allow itself to be cheated.' Always quite proud of his fishing in troubled waters, Smallwood was in effect 'helping, and even inviting, German subjects to break German law.'[110] Not surprisingly, in 1953 the West German government began to investigate the German firms and individuals investing in Newfoundland for suspected illegal foreign exchange manipulations and flight of capital. This resulted in the arrest of MIAG director Herbert Marx in October 1953 and Haguma director Ludwig Grube in early 1954. Lerch eluded the authorities by taking up residence in Montreal.[111]

To attain Smallwood's goal of launching as many new industries as possible in the shortest possible time, Valdmanis had to relax screening procedures, disregard negative evidence, and increase government assistance. MIAG's decision to build a machinery plant near St John's, for instance, was hastened by playing up the prospects for defence contracts (which never materialized) and by dispensing with the usual requirement that the German investor first prove the objectives and economics of the proposed operation. The extent to which Smallwood was prepared to gamble became evident in December 1951 when his cabinet approved a ten-year loan of $150,000 to Lothar Sennewald, an East German refugee practising ophthalmology in Saarbrücken.[112]

In June 1951 Sennewald had signed a preliminary agreement that within one month after his machinery arrived he would start producing frames for eyeglasses, employing fifty to a hundred workers. His optical industry would then expand step by step first to lens grinding, then to the production of optical equipment, and ultimately to a full-fledged eyeglass industry. Valdmanis at first supported the proposal. But he changed his mind after he had determined that its quarrelsome promoter lacked knowledge of the economics and functioning of an optical industry. Intelligence Hinneberg had gathered in Germany confirmed this negative impression.[113] Sennewald, however, refused to disappear and continued to bombard Valdmanis and Smallwood with threats demanding the promised loan while they were trying to attract Leitz.[114] Ample data existed on which a decision could be intelligently based, Valdmanis argued and begged Smallwood 'to take the case out of my hands.' Valdmanis conceded that he may have been too harsh because 'I have been aware of the old truth that one may risk his own money at will but must think twice when the people's money is involved.'[115]

On 24 November 1951 Sennewald suddenly arrived in Newfoundland at the invitation of the leader of the Opposition. The plan was for him to 'expose' Smallwood on the eve of the provincial election. Smallwood, however, had him intercepted and silenced by asking him whether he was interested in politics or in getting an industry established. Two weeks later the cabinet approved Sennewald's loan. 'My feeling was,' Smallwood explained to the House of Assembly, 'the poor devil, he is an able man, and this is his chance to get his family out and to give us an industry ... He can make in his factory in St John's for 70 cents an eyeglass frame which sells retail in St John's for $8.00, which sells wholesale for $2.63 ... This is a sound little industry.'[116] The 'sound little industry' never got off the ground. Instead, Sennewald unsuccessfully tried to defraud the government by transferring the government loans to his personal account while sending as collateral from Germany crates with scrap iron that he kept sealed and in storage for two years.[117]

In an effort to reach agreements with Moser, Hahlbrock, and Rieker in December 1951 for chipboard, glove, and shoe factories, drastic deviations were made from the strategy adopted in February 1951. Valdmanis recommended that these proposed industries should receive government assistance to the tune of 62, 64, and 66 per cent respectively of the total capital investment required. He argued that, since other Canadian provinces had learned from Newfoundland how to attract German industries, Newfoundland would now have to compete with Quebec and Ontario: 'The traditional desire of establishing an industry close to market will detract many interests from Newfoundland.' Valdmanis warned that Newfoundland would soon have to look for industries in countries less eager to establish factories abroad, such as England, Sweden, Switzerland, the United States, and mainland Canada.[118]

From visits to Ottawa in late 1951 and early 1952 Valdmanis returned with the impression of a growing suspicion there 'that we may handle some things in too quick, even a wild manner.' He became concerned about allegations that he was establishing 'an industry a month,' and leading 'a steady stream of Germans into Newfoundland.'[119] The extent of Ottawa's misgivings became apparent in its refusal to assist Newfoundland's fledgling industrialization efforts, either by renewing the premium granted in 1949 to Newfoundland manufacturers when bidding on federal contracts or by procuring defence contracts for the new industries.[120] By the end of June 1952 prospects were anything but rosy. 'Clouds are gathering over our three government industries,' Valdmanis wrote Kreyser in mid-1952. 'They have cost considerably more than planned and anticipated.' Some technical defects and unforeseen marketing problems worried him as much as the inability to sell the cement and gypsum plants.[121]

Hinneberg's voluminous correspondence, and with it his services, abruptly ceased in September 1952. His honorarium from German promoters was based on the economic success of their enterprise in Newfoundland. In 1951 he had suffered a net loss of DM2,800 with the Newfoundland dealings. Having conducted a successful solicitor's practice for thirty years, Hinneberg wrote Valdmanis, German auditors would not understand how he could continuously operate with a loss when processing large projects that absorbed almost his entire energy. From the Newfoundland government he received no remuneration. Valdmanis had cleverly exacted a sworn commitment from Hinneberg that he make no claims against any Newfoundland officials or involve them in any compensation contracted between himself and his clients. 'We must be sure that ... no shadow of a doubt could ever arise here or in Germany, as to the absolute honesty and integrity of Newfoundland officials who deal and will deal with your clients,' Valdmanis stressed. 'Any suspicion is and would be simply fantastic and impossible and below our dignity.'[122]

On 10 August 1952 Valdmanis accompanied Smallwood for the third and last time on a major industrial tour of Europe. In the company of cabinet ministers Leslie Curtis, Edward Spencer, and Gregory Power, they spent almost seven weeks travelling in England, Germany, Switzerland, Holland, Belgium, and Italy. In London Smallwood laid the foundations for the British Newfoundland Corporation (BRINCO, incorporated in March 1953) by offering a reluctant Anthony de Rothschild exclusive exploration rights for natural resources on most uncommitted land in Newfoundland and Labrador. In return Rothschild was to form a syndicate to develop any natural resources found, including the hydropower of Hamilton Falls (renamed Churchill Falls in 1965) in Labrador. Although Valdmanis was not consulted on the offer, Smallwood used Valdmanis's reputation and connections to obtain a deal. He would be 'off to Germany right away to offer his concession to companies there,' Smallwood threatened the reluctant Rothschild negotiators in September 1952. 'No doubt he would get a better reception there than he had in London.'[123]

At the papal summer residence of Castel Gandolfo, Valdmanis's connections managed to secure a private audience with Pope Pius XII for Smallwood and Power on 22 September. At the request of constituents they carried with them a supply of rosaries and other objects for papal blessing. According to a Latvian press report, the Pope told Valdmanis that 'he thought very often about the unfortunate Latvian people and was praying that God would help them in their distress.'[124] Years later Greg Power recalled that the pontiff had greeted Valdmanis warmly like an old acquaintance with 'Alfred, how are you?' but made 'short shrift' of their packages of cheap trinkets for Roman Catholic voters. Still, Smallwood felt justified to cable back home on the eve of polling day in Ferryland (a heavily Roman Catholic district held by the Opposition) that the Pope's blessing had been received.[125]

Among the industries they visited in Germany were the battery plant of Hanning and Kahl in Bielefeld and Ludwig Grube's Haguma rubber works in Hanover. With their owners, and with tax consultant Egon Koch of Hanover, deals were struck about battery, rubber, and shoe production in Newfoundland. This time Valdmanis's name was not featured prominently in connection with the trip. Because Valdmanis had reservations about the deals with Grube, Hanning, and Koch, he did not attend the signing of these agreements. Contact with Grube had come about when Smallwood met him at the Canadian National Exhibition in Toronto in May 1952, and Grube expressed interest in building a rubber plant in Newfoundland. Valdmanis questioned its viability but Smallwood had already endorsed the request in principle. On 14 October 1952 cabinet agreed to loan Grube $1 million so he could launch his Superior Rubber company in Newfoundland. Grube, whose war-damaged Hanover factory had been completely rebuilt, sent his obsolete machinery to Newfoundland and then transferred Newfoundland government loan funds to Germany and the United States. Completed in 1954, the rubber plant always malfunctioned, was found to have no proper bookkeeping, and turned into the most conspicuous scandal of Smallwood's new industries program. However, rumours that it was so inept that it produced boots for only one foot have not been confirmed.[126]

Withdrawal from the New Industries Program

It was his experience with Grube and Sennewald that prompted Valdmanis's resolve that 'this unholy dash for new industries, whether they had a chance or not, had to be stopped.' A moratorium on additional industries was necessary because most of the new industries launched, although promising, needed some attention. Smallwood, however, could not be restrained. He kept on looking for more industries and promised whatever funds were required to sign a contract.[127]

By 5 February 1953 Valdmanis wanted no more part of this. On that date he asked Smallwood to relieve him of his duties as director general of economic development effective 1 March. The full-time responsibilities of that position and the NALCO presidency had acquired proportions 'which no one man could conscientiously plan, direct, and supervise any more.' He explained that 'for the consolidation period now coming, I am not indispensable as full-time director general.' In addition, Valdmanis stated, he had been offered a senior position with a great industrial concern.[128]

To Friedrich Kreyser he confided that with great care he had managed to accomplish the changeover in an atmosphere of friendship. He had relinquished his post primarily out of the conviction 'that the brakes had to be put on further new industries in order to consolidate the ones brought here and because I was unable to convince my great "small man" that my view was correct.'[129] That made Kreyser wonder whether the road travelled under the pain of so many worries and labours was the right one: 'An endless chain of sorrows and almost superhuman work and what is the result? Does it correspond to the labours invested or have you and we misused and wasted much energy and effort? ... What has been accomplished? How about the material results and advantages? Or have you on the basis of your previous activity become such a famous man that your fame is sufficient to secure you an equivalent position in a different area?'

Valdmanis had, in fact, no fallback position apart from his presidency of NALCO for another year, he revealed to Kreyser. Having no contract and unsure about his salary, he was prepared to 'let everything float for a while.' A possibility to become chairman of an IG Farben subsidiary in Newfoundland seemed to 'drift away' with the corporation's decision not to come to the province. In the final analysis, Valdmanis concluded, he and Kreyser had created something positive but individual persons had failed them: 'One after the other abandoned the "team spirit" and the need to stick together "for better or worse." From the results of this we are all suffering now.' Kreyser, who knew Latvian, wrapped up his reply in one of Valdmanis's favourite quotes from Ulmanis: '*Ar tiem mãliem kas ir, jãmũrẽ*' (you've got to build with what you've got).[130]

chapter nine

'The Past, Instead of Helping to Rebuild, Denies Itself': The Latvian Refugee Community and the Shadows of the Past, 1950–1954

I do not know of anybody in the history of our people who has been attacked that much, slandered that much, and has been the target of so many attempts at destruction.

Aleksandrs Osītis to Alfred Valdmanis, 27 August 1950

In despair, and partially also in disgust, I had turned away from the past that, instead of helping to rebuild, denies itself and tears itself to pieces.

Alfred Valdmanis to Leon von Bruemmer, May 1953

From the day of his arrival in Canada, Alfred Valdmanis took pains to project an identity guaranteeing not just survival but resurgence to prominence. He had ensured his survival under communism, National Socialism, and postwar Allied security screening, thanks to an uncanny talent to cultivate vital personal contacts. In the openness of New World democracy, however, his networks of contacts became obsolete. Wanting to rely increasingly on his revised image, Valdmanis found his Old World images resurfacing to hound him everywhere.

Indeed, as this chapter illustrates, the past adhered to him like a shadow: It coloured the news about his rise to prominence in Newfoundland. It was the basis for the esteem in which he was held by the local Latvian community. It was the point of reference for much of the Latvian mail that flooded his St John's mailbox from Latvian exiles all over the world. Ultimately, it imposed itself on his new identity and corrupted its credibility.

The Local Latvian Community

Valdmanis's first Latvian contacts in Newfoundland were Wolf Grobins and Alex Berzinsh. Grobins was a Latvian Jew who had arrived in 1938 with U.K.-certified qualifications as a physician and had a practice in St John's by the time of Valdmanis's arrival.[1] Berzinsh was an engineer with Bowater's Pulp and Paper Mill at Corner Brook and Newfoundland consul of free Latvia. Manager before the Second World War of the British-owned Baltic Wood Pulp Mills at Sloka near Riga, he arrived in Corner Brook in February 1948. Had the government accepted his 1949 proposal to attach the faculty and equipment of the Latvian Navigation School to Memorial University College of Newfoundland, Berzinsh instead of Valdmanis would have founded Newfoundland's first Latvian community. Evacuated in 1944 from Riga to Flensburg, Germany, this navigation school was now looking for a new permanent host institution in the West.[2] In late 1949 Berzinsh had also supplied market calculations concerning cement and gypsum for Valdmanis's Nova Scotia project. After May 1950, though, Valdmanis resented his interference and the credit Berzinsh claimed for his advice. It was Valdmanis who rejected Berzinsh's plans and loan applications for a $3.5 million wallboard mill.[3]

Following Smallwood's appointment of Valdmanis, however, the local Latvian community began to grow in leaps and bounds. Most settled in the centres of industrial development – in the Corner Brook area (where cement and gypsum plants were being built) and in St John's. In Corner Brook Ernest Leja, former director of Latvia's state-owned gypsum industry, was to supervise the construction of cement and gypsum plants. With the help of Neue Technik and former co-workers, Leja reassembled in Newfoundland virtually his entire former team of specialists – a mixture of Baltic Germans and ethnic Latvians who had found refuge in the western zones of Germany in 1945. In 1951 Corner Brook's community of approximately a hundred newcomer families from Germany contained one-quarter ethnic Latvian and thirteen Baltic German families from Latvia. The remainder were mostly German nationals, two-thirds of whom stayed in Newfoundland only briefly.[4]

The Newfoundland Latvian community owed its beginnings to Valdmanis because he systematically recruited Latvian office staff, experts for various government departments, professionals, technicians, and businessmen. In early July 1950 he hired, on a mutual friend's recommendation, Olga Leikucs as his personal assistant and multilingual secretary at an annual salary of $1,800 (raised to $4,560 by 1953). She came to him from employment with a chartered bank after having worked in Canada for one year as a domestic servant.[5] Fluent in Latvian, German, French, Danish, and English, this attractive, young, and single Latvian refugee took care of Valdmanis's extensive foreign-language correspondence, especially during his absences. 'She is young and just a little girl, but she is intelligent, knows a great deal about my plans, and, presently, is my best – and, indeed, only – helper,' Valdmanis wrote Deputy Minister of Economic Development N. Short in September 1950, as he sent for her to assist in negotiations in Toronto and Ottawa.[6] Leikucs's occasional accompaniment of Valdmanis in his travels generated rumours about their degree of intimacy. Of these '50 percent were true,' according to his brother-in-law Sigurds Mikelsons.[7]

In August 1950 Valdmanis requested and received permission to bring his old acquaintance Arnolds L. Graudins from New York for the position of assistant director general of economic development. An experienced economist and loyal assistant of Valdmanis, he began at a salary of $4,800. Of the same age and a fellow graduate in economics from the University of Latvia, Graudins owed his release from Soviet arrest in 1940 to Valdmanis's testimony.[8] As manager of the Riga municipal board from 1934 to 1940, chief analyst of the Latvian Department of Industry during the war, and assistant camp leader of two IRO DP camps after the war, Graudins had shadowed most of Valdmanis's life and activities closely. In December 1951 Valdmanis added Karl Lapins as research engineer to his office staff, and in June 1952 Jekabs T. Arajs as assistant to Leikucs.[9]

Of twelve Latvian families Valdmanis was prepared to sponsor personally in 1951, five (the Saulite, Mikelsons, Jacobsons, Straus, and Krumins families) arrived. The family heads were offered Newfoundland government jobs as physician, architect, draughtsman, bridge engineer, and road engineer.[10] In 1952 Valdmanis and Jacobsons jointly sponsored the resettlement of a forty-nine-year-old Latvian widow, Anna Dzinejs de Raimonds, from Venezuela to Newfoundland.[11] Valdmanis also helped bring to St John's his one-year-older acquaintance from school days in Liepāja, Alberts Jekste, a broadcaster, film producer, and Minox project supervisor with Latvia's government-owned electro-technical industry (VEF). Like Valdmanis, a survivor with a chequered past, Jekste had collaborated with the Soviets in 1940, in part to save his friends from arrest. Before the Soviets' retreat from Riga, Jekste had bravely broadcast a call in June 1941 for the liberation of Latvia. As a radio operator in 1944–5 he had defied Red Army assaults on 'Fortress Kurland.' Jekste also had a long-time connection with Leja. He had known him since

1922 and had recommended him in 1937 as director of the state-owned gypsum industry. In April 1941, claimed Jekste, he was able to procure a flight for Leja to Moscow in a vain attempt to obtain the return of the latter's wife and eighteen-year-old son who had been arrested. Both remained detained for fifteen years in Siberia.[12]

In 1951, to enable Jekste to purchase part of his investment in a new firm named Atlantic Films and Electronics Ltd, Valdmanis personally guaranteed a $20,000 loan.[13] Of the thirteen members of Jekste's Riga Film team, however, Canada admitted only Ralph Balodis and Arnis Lucis and their families (in 1951). When Canada refused Jekste entry on charges of war crimes, Valdmanis and Smallwood travelled to Ottawa personally to demand a review of the evidence by the minister of citizenship and immigration.[14] Smallwood maintained that Jekste was wrongly accused of having been a member of the Nazi Party and of having filmed the processes of killing the inmates at Buchenwald concentration camp.[15] In reality, Jekste had been an inmate of Salaspils concentration camp (near Riga) for eighteen months (as an alleged Soviet collaborator). He had managed to obtain his release by joining the Latvian Legion. Admitted as a sponsored immigrant to the United States in 1951, he had entered Canada as a visitor.[16]

These pioneer immigrants from Latvia attracted others. Atlantic Films, once in operation, provided employment for thirteen Latvians, two Baltic Germans, and four Germans. By the end of 1952 there were two Latvian dentists (Junija Langins and Ruta Snikeris) and four Latvian physicians (Velta Mikelsons, Janis Krumins, Janis Maurins, and Wolf Grobins) in Newfoundland. Both dentists obtained permission to practice through the intervention of Valdmanis and Smallwood with the dental association.[17] Dr Krumins joined the medical staff of the Sanatorium in St John's. In Corner Brook, Bowater added Latvians E. Langins and Karlis Bulins as laboratory engineers to Alex Berzinsh. By 1954 Newfoundland's Latvian community had grown to some two hundred souls. Latvians held highly respectable, skilled positions in the province's economic life and did not take away jobs from the native-born.

Jekste's endeavours in St John's and Leja's in Corner Brook to reassemble their skilled prewar teams from Latvia meant that Baltic Germans ended up working with Latvians. Jekste and Leja were interested solely in the qualifications of their skilled workers and avoided any ethnic favouritism. Leja's hiring practices, however, irritated some Latvians who demanded that Valdmanis demonstrate his patriotism by giving preference to ethnic Latvians.[18] Baltic Germans, in turn, charged ethnic Latvians with forming 'cliques among themselves' and preferring a 'Latvian ghetto.'[19]

What helped Latvians and Baltic Germans forge one more or less harmonious community were the benefits derived from the presence of Alfred Valdmanis. They also shared the experience of newcomers in a closed society that had had virtually no immigrants for more than a century and tended to view foreigners with suspicion. 'They sat, so to speak, in the same boat,' remarked one Baltic German in Corner Brook.[20] Latvians were frequently confused with Germans – a stereotype derived from wartime fears of submarines and sabotage – and in Corner Brook Valdmanis was considered a German as late as the 1980s.[21] Valdmanis also arranged for the Reverend Alfreds Skrodelis, representative of the Latvian Lutheran Archbishop in Canada to visit in January 1953 and organize a local congregation.[22]

Typical of the ambiguous relationship between the two groups is the story circulating among Canada's Baltic Germans about how in 1948 Valdmanis allegedly foiled early Baltic German admission to Canada. 'I know the Baltic Germans well,' Valdmanis is said to have responded to a prominent Canadian promoter of the Canadian Baltic Aid Committee travelling to Geneva to inquire with Valdmanis (who was IRO's Baltic expert at the time) about the desirability of admitting these 'Balts' to Canada as refugees. Baltic Germans, Valdmanis allegedly snapped, were the worst of all the Hitler followers. Out of 'love to their Führer' they had relocated from Latvia to Germany in 1939, joined the party, and remained loyal to the Führer. If Canada was looking for Nazis, that would be the surest way to get them. Valdmanis claimed to have known them for years and would be able to mention names. Of course, he admitted, there were also decent Baltic Germans, such as Baron Hahn, Prince Lieven, and Count Robert W. von Keyserlingk (who was among those recommending that Valdmanis be sponsored by the Lady Davis Foundation). 'But the others are impossible,' he is reported to have asserted.[23]

Post–Second World War Latvian refugee immigrants have been noted for their national pride and desire to return to their homeland once it was liberated.[24] While in Canada most preferred, like Valdmanis, the metropolitan ambience where they could coalesce into larger communities of Latvians, like in Toronto or Montreal. Latvians in Newfoundland had difficulty adjusting to the assimilationist pressures in their host society and considered living in its 'village environment' as a sort of 'punishment.'[25] Their sole reason for being there was Valdmanis. He was the community builder, gave them a sense of importance, and made them feel 'as one family.'[26] And they were proud of him. This is why they noticed his weaknesses with dismay – in particular, at Latvian parties in late 1953 his high-strung behaviour and display of a curious urge to prove his worth and wealth to junior Latvians.[27]

In the Newfoundland legislature, Valdmanis was controversial from the beginning. His salary, credentials, and achievements were constantly being questioned. Members of the Opposition considered him a 'great actor' who was 'in velvet' and 'away three parts of his time,' but who could not be trusted 'with a hot stove.'[28] Why was the government bringing in so many Latvians who were taking away jobs from Newfoundlanders? the Opposition kept asking. Joey Smallwood's standard reply was that these people had qualifications that were in great demand but unavailable in Newfoundland at the time, for example, as road engineers, bridge designers, and draughtsmen. In a population of 350,000 souls 'we will not be too contaminated by bringing in twenty or thirty Latvians,' Smallwood once retorted.[29]

On their first trip to Germany, in October 1950, the entire Smallwood party met in Wiesbaden with the chairman of the Latvian Central Committee (LCK), Colonel Vilis Janums, and his executive board to discuss emigration and job opportunities for Latvians in Newfoundland. Immediately after the meeting several specialists were offered job contracts, a Latvian paper in Germany reported, and more openings were to be made available for silversmiths, woodcutters, leather craftsmen, technicians, agriculturists, medical doctors, engineers, and others.[30]

Although the local Latvian community remained small, Smallwood noted in a 1952 statement to the press, its members held highly responsible positions in the province's economic life. In part because of his admiration for Alfred Valdmanis's achievements, Smallwood counted Latvians to be among his 'worthiest and most respected citizens' and did not hesitate to express his public desire for more Latvians to come and help in the development effort. Aware that he would lose Valdmanis one day – the day Latvia would regain its freedom – Smallwood claimed to be satisfied that Newfoundland's loss would be Latvia's gain. Back in Latvia Valdmanis would be able to utilize the experience gained here. Based on his own experience and travels through Europe and North America, Smallwood could not think of anybody 'as capable of making friends for Latvia as Valdmanis.'[31]

Through his exposure in the media, involvement in Latvian organizations, and speaking engagements, Valdmanis remained a leading representative of exiled Latvians and a symbol of hope and pride as far away as Australia and New Zealand.[32] Speeches of his were broadcast on national radio, for example, his forty-five-minute address of October 1950 to the Canadian Council of Laymen in Toronto.[33] Smallwood acknowledged the importance of this aspect by allowing himself to be drawn into some of these activities. For example, in the autumn of 1952 Valdmanis was one of the initiators of a new organization called the Latvian National Centre (Latviešu nacionālais centrs). Its declared purpose was to direct the efforts of Latvians in exile away from splintering and in-fighting and towards the liberation of Latvia. At the official launching on 14 December 1952 in the Stadtler Hotel of New York, Congressman O.K. Armstrong, Premier Smallwood, and Alfred Valdmanis were featured as honorary members. (Among the members elected to the executive board was Valdis Mateus, Valdmanis's brother-in-law.)[34] Also, on the fourth anniversary of Newfoundland's confederation with Canada, various Latvian organizations in North America sent Joey Smallwood messages of support and 'loyal' devotion.

Smallwood so highly regarded work done by Dr Alfred Valdmanis within the past two and a half years that the former had 'more than once' officially declared that Newfoundland would erect a monument in gratitude to this Latvian director general,' reported the paper *Latvija* on 4 April 1953 to highlight the benefits of four years of confederation with Canada. 'When Latvia will be free would you visit us?' the Reverend Skrodelis wondered in an interview with Smallwood in March 1953. 'That is my dream,' Smallwood reportedly replied. 'I want to see Latvians in their own country, these people, who after the First World War with hard will and tough work built up their destroyed country into a flourishing state both economically and culturally.'[35]

Assorted Pleas for Help

Thanks to his retention of influential positions through almost two decades of changing environments, Alfred Valdmanis was able to acquire a diverse network of personal connections. Some of these dated to his student days, some to his prewar years with the Latvian finance ministry, some to wartime activities, some to his postwar roles in Latvian refugee organizations and in IRO, and still others to more recent North American government, business, ethnic, and church contacts. The voluminous personal correspondence that Valdmanis conducted from his St John's office indicates the extent of his connections. It throws light on the nature of his appeal among the dispersed Latvian diaspora in the West. And it shows a dark side to his fame – the temptation of some to exploit his past for the purpose of blackmail and the tenacious determination of others to destroy his credibility.

Under the heading *Dažāda veida palīdzības lūgumi* (Various Types of Appeals for Assistance), Valdmanis filed a collection of letters from Latvians all over the world. These letters show him to be leading actor in dramas running on two stages simultaneously. One stage features his workaholic preoccupation with Newfoundland's economic development. The other reveals his image, role, social connections, and political aspirations in the globally dispersed community of Latvian exiles.

The correspondence came from friends offering expertise and contacts, Latvians soliciting his endorsement of various causes, and refugees appealing for assistance for anything from letters of reference or help with immigration to employment and outright charity. Valdmanis was not able to do much for most of them. He had no leverage with officials in the federal government, the jobs he could procure in the Newfoundland Department of Economic Development and with NALCO were limited in number, the Conservative opposition was ready to jump on him for any cause, and the Newfoundland public was suspicious of foreigners in influential positions. Valdmanis was only too aware that public opinion resented what seemed to be favours extended to foreigners of non-British origin in general, and to Germans and their associates in particular.

A wide range of supplications from Latvians in Argentina, Sweden, the United States, Canada, and Germany arrived in St John's as early as the autumn of 1950. For example, one Aleksandrs Osītis, a former DP acquaintance, lamented the dispersal of his family – one brother and a sister in Canada, another brother in the United States, and himself in Argentina. He professed not to know any other Latvian who, after having been attacked, slandered, and targeted for destruction as much as Valdmanis, was able to secure a position so befitting his capabilities. 'I can now imagine the long faces of some of your so-called friends,' wrote Osītis. From Stamford, Connecticut, Ed Strazdiņš sought advice on how to bring the family of his brother-in-law from Denmark 'somehow' to Canada. Fate, he remarked, had designated Valdmanis to be a benefactor to many directly and indirectly.[36]

From Sweden, Lote Švābe, a former political or personal adversary, was prepared to swallow her pride for the sake of her children and solicit Valdmanis's help in procuring a Canadian education for them. From DP camp Augustdorf (near Detmold) in Germany, former film producer and director as well as entrepreneur Vilis Lapenieks inquired whether Newfoundland would be interested in helping him start manufacturing typewriter ribbons and carbon paper, processing forest products, or opening a modern photography studio. Ernests Ķerve from England wanted a job in Corner Brook and pointed out that he hoped Valdmanis would live up to the expectations he had generated in several recent speeches that he was working for the benefit of his countrymen and their future.[37] In none of these cases was Valdmanis willing or able to help.

Business offers received more serious attention. In July 1950, already, one Rittmeister Mikelis Puhris informed Valdmanis that as secretary of an association of contractors and industrialists interested in relocating from Germany to 'safe' countries, he could offer complete production facilities for brickyards, cement plants, oil refineries, and chemical distilleries. All they needed were visas, reimbursement of shipping costs, and the work orders. As the Canadian representative of this group, Valdmanis's share would be 1 per cent of the profits, that is, 'at least ten times the salary of a professor at any Canadian university.' 'With open arms,' Valdmanis replied, he would welcome such installations as an oil refinery, hydro-electric station, tannery, fish-oil, floating fish-processing, and seafood plants, lumber processor, and a pulp and paper mill. But knowing that they cost millions, he wondered how Puhris would get the permits to take them out of Germany.

Valdmanis met Puhris during his first tour of Germany with Smallwood, in October 1950, and authorized him to coordinate the necessary preparations. These would enable Latvian and other displaced persons in Germany to emigrate. Puhris, who claimed to have devoted a whole chapter in a book of his to Valdmanis, was particularly interested in obtaining visas for former Latvian legionnaires. 'They are actually *your* soldiers and potentially *your future palace guards* [underlining, possibly by Valdmanis, in the original],' he flattered Valdmanis. It eventually appeared that the only entrepreneur ready to come to Newfoundland was a building contractor interested in his own personal emigration. In February 1951 Valdmanis revoked Puhris's authorization.[38]

From Brazil, Luiz Ansis Dārziņš proposed to arrange a Brazil-Newfoundland trade contract for large-scale export of codfish to Brazil with payment in Brazilian currency or some compensation business.[39] From Copenhagen, Aleksandrs Bankiņš offered his expertise in operating cement-mixing machinery, crushing graphite slabs, and cheese processing. In view of Premier Smallwood's widely advertised attitude towards Latvians, Bankiņš hoped to be invited to help industrialize Newfoundland.[40] Jānis

Brežinskis wondered, from Toronto, whether it would be practical to start the production of prefabricated buildings in Newfoundland,[41] and an unidentified promoter offered to organize a department in charge of photographic documentation of construction projects.[42] Johans Dombrovskis in Freiburg, Germany, offered to develop facilities utilizing wood waste for the production of wood gas or chipboard in return for Valdmanis's assistance in his emigration to Canada. Primitive living and working conditions would not deter him, Dombrovskis wrote, since he already had experience living in self-constructed barracks in the forests of Kurzeme and in southwest Germany. Valdmanis had no use for any of these proposals.[43]

A pleasant surprise offer came in July 1951 from Dr Miķelis Valters, who was representing chemical firms in France, Belgium, and Switzerland. Valdmanis welcomed the opportunity to resume contacts with this respected former government minister, ambassador, and author who had already attained his place in history when Valdmanis was still a child. Despite their disagreements, Valdmanis conceded that 'you have been my mentor and protector (like a father) from my very early youth,' an experience he would remember with gratitude forever. Concerning business possibilities, Valters should know that Newfoundland's development was based strictly on private initiative and capitalist principles. No more raw materials, at the most semi-finished products, would be exported. Valdmanis had also considered borrowing some $10 to $20 million for direct financing of some of the industrialization projects. He had been thinking of ten to fifteen-year loans, which should be possible since Newfoundland had no debts and was realizing a small annual surplus. To discuss these and related matters, Valdmanis said he was eager to meet Valters in Basel.

As far as his own historical role was concerned, Valdmanis 'attempted to do whatever seemed to be the best for that particular problem at that particular time.' Rather than dwell on past differences, Valdmanis wanted to focus on the present. The question was 'Who can do it?' not 'Who is authorized?' The Latvians' tragedy, in Valdmanis's opinion, was that 'too many of us with some rights or authorizations – legal or illegal, factual or imagined – sit on them, talk about them but do not do anything for the common good.'[44]

Sundry other pleas to Valdmanis ranged from finding a position in a Canadian symphony orchestra for conductor Teodors Reiters, who was unemployed in Stockholm at the time,[45] to helping the two sons of J. Inveiss in Milwaukee find refuge in Canada from the American draft.

Inveiss felt that 'we should spill our blood only for our country but certainly not in a ridiculous place like Korea.' In this case, Valdmanis advised his secretary, 'No action.' [46] Ruta Viskers, who had recently arrived from Denmark to continue her studies in Toronto, wanted help in February 1952 in procuring a scholarship. She was encouraged by a cousin of one Mr Zemgalis and several former high-ranking officers of the Latvian army to approach Valdmanis as a man who could find solutions to all kinds of problems and who would be 'the most likely future leader of our country after its liberation from the communist oppression.'[47] To requests by Professor Pēteris Ķikauka for an immigration visa for the daughter of friends in Venezuela, Valdmanis replied that his stock in Ottawa was too low.[48]

Writing from Buenos Aires, and reminding Valdmanis of their prewar encounters in the Riga tennis club, attorney Welta Neimanis was trying to reclaim from the British Ministry of Transport the Latvian steamer *Spīdola* formerly owned by the P. Dannenbergs Steamship Company. Neimanis wondered whether this vessel could be temporarily registered in Newfoundland and then licensed in Canada. 'Please file away,' Valdmanis instructed Leikucs.[49] In Toronto, V. Muskats needed capital to start a candy factory. For $600 he offered Valdmanis a painting he had saved from Riga, entitled *Armour Helmet,* by the well-known Baltic artist Karl Huhn. Muskats was looking for a buyer among 'well-established Latvians' and recalled, in vain, his support for Valdmanis in Riga during the German occupation.[50] Nor was Valdmanis prepared to loan $500 or $600 for a poultry operation to Žanis Leimanis, a former employee in the Directorate General of Justice who had suffered one medical and business misfortune after another since his arrival in Brazil in 1948.[51] Writing from Washington, Vilis Vuškalns offered Valdmanis a franchise on a patented electrolytic plating process designed to increase the durability of steel and the strength of soft metals. Toronto bookstore owner P. Avotiņš requested a subsidy for the production of low-priced Latvian books. Along the margin of this letter Valdmanis scribbled: 'No – I really cannot afford to support all those very good and beneficial ideas.'[52]

As a rule, Valdmanis complied without hesitation to requests for affidavits and letters of recommendation from wartime and prewar political friends and associates. Among these were Viktors Dāle and Jānis Celms. Valdmanis attested that in his capacity as 'elected Latvian leader (wartime resistance movement),' he had 'appointed Dāle president of the District Court of Riga in 1942' and that Dāle belonged 'both to the anti-Soviet as well as anti-Nazi movements' during the period 1940–4.[53] In the case of Celms, who feared that political enemies would try to prevent his emigration from his German DP camp to North America, Valdmanis certified:

> In July 1941, I, acting on behalf of the Latvian Nation in an emergency situation, directed you to recreate the Latvian national school system which had been destroyed during the Soviet regime. Your principle task, however, was to create a reliable patriotic movement comprising mainly the directors and the principals of colleges, high and elementary schools, for the purpose of obstructing and resisting Nazi Germany's tendency to absorb the Baltic countries and people. Your activities were discovered, and in early 1942 you were dismissed by German occupation powers from the position of director of national education, which position *I* [emphasis in the original] had assigned to you.[54]

Valdmanis's statement for Edgars Ozols, chauffeur to the Latvian finance ministry in the 1930s, helped Ozols find employment as the personal driver for the French ambassador to the United Nations. Pēteris Ozols was a doorman in a New York office building but wanted to find a more suitable job. To help Ozols, Valdmanis issued a certificate verifying that Ozols had been employed with Ķegums from 1940 to 1944 as bookkeeper, accountant, and personnel manager. Karlis Bulins supported his employment application at Bowater in Corner Brook with a statement from Valdmanis that attested that Bulins had been the manager of the Jelgava hydro-power facilities from 1937 to 1944 and supervising engineer of the Ķegums expansion program there.[55] Aleksandrs Stīpnieks wanted a reference stating that he was 'a person of substance,' and Alfred Valdmanis certified that Stīpnieks had held a senior position with the Bank of Latvia from 1922 to 1943.[56] In February 1952 Valdmanis promised to support the applications of Bruno Bērziņš and Klandis Treilons, two senior Latvian marine biologists living in Sweden, for the vacant position of senior biologist with the Newfoundland Fisheries Research Station.[57]

Near-intractable problems were posed by former legionnaires. In July 1950 E. Pērkons, officer in a Latvian police battalion from March to October 1942 and in the legion from June 1943 to July 1944, requested advice on how he could join his son who had been admitted to Canada in February 1948. The Canadian Immigration Commission had turned down and IRO had blocked visas for Pērkons, his wife, and second son. Valdmanis refused to issue an affidavit since he did not know Pērkons, and for clearance of his status referred him to Colonel Janums, Chairman of the LCK in Detmold, and to the minister of citizenship and immigration in Ottawa.[58]

Equally futile was the quest for help in June 1952 by legionnaire ex-officer Nikolājs Zvirbulis from Copenhagen, whose visa application had been inexplicably turned down by both the American and the Canadian screening teams, although he had a job lined up in Ottawa and family in the United States. His last hope was Valdmanis, who during a brief visit to Denmark in the summer of 1951 had allegedly offered to help former legionnaires in trouble. After waiting two months in vain for a reply, Zvirbulis tried to reach Valdmanis through Alexander Āboliņš in Toronto. The latter begged help for this 'very dependable supporter,' who placed esteem for Valdmanis next to that for President Ulmanis: 'That would strengthen our wing and renew the old faith in V's ability to help people in need of help.' Even Olga Leikucs asked to be added to those wanting to help when she discovered that 'Z.' was the brother of one of her best friends. Finally, after three and a half months, Leikucs's assistant Jekabs Arajs delivered this final 'very heavy blow': Valdmanis had no leverage in Denmark, his job kept him continuously on the road, and the few days spent in St John's left no time for personal matters. With no time to write personal letters, he had even less time to go to Ottawa on behalf of personal problems, 'even if he wanted to.'[59]

To straightforward supplications for 'a few dollars' from the sixty-six-year-old destitute, though formerly well-to-do, M. Seja in Chicago Valdmanis responded with a $10 donation.[60] At the request of Ansis Jansons, who was the editor of the Toronto newspaper *Latvija*, Valdmanis also sent personal cheques as Christmas gifts to two needy Latvian women in Toronto, each with two children. The recipients were Ingrīda Vīksne (a writer) and Tonīja Krūka (wife of the commanding officer of Jansons's company). An alleged admirer of Valdmanis and member of the Latvian National Federation in Canada (LNAK) council, Krūka's unselfish dedication had helped numerous war invalids and tuberculosis-afflicted legionnaires. 'How could you, with all your workload, worries, and problems, find the time to remember the smallest of your children?' she wondered gratefully: 'I felt as if God himself had lifted the load of worries and problems from our shoulders.'[61] To editor Ernests Gūnars Grīnbergs of *Ulubele, Rašu jauniešu žurnāls*, a magazine dedicated to the next generation of Latvians, Valdmanis donated $50 to enable the publication of the next issue.[62]

The request of fifty-six-year-old Jānis Siliņš, however, for funding from the 'rich ones' of DM300 worth of dental work backfired. Siliņš, a former receptionist for Latvia's Minister of Trade and Industry, J. Blumbergs, claimed to be an admirer and supporter of Valdmanis and a friend of his father-in-law. Blaming the rejection of his American visa application on denunciations, Siliņš was disappointed with life in general and Latvians in particular. In America life was nothing but parties, drinking, and carefree relaxing, Siliņš complained, and attributed his continued misery in Germany in part to the insulting interception of his letters by Valdmanis' secretary. An indignant Olga Leikucs decided, apparently without Valdmanis's input but with the approval of his wife, to straighten Siliņš out.[63] Her six-page, single-spaced lecture in the spring of 1953 provides a revealing glimpse of Valdmanis, his situation in Newfoundland, and her feelings and devotion to her boss.

Siliņš's problems had nothing to do with exile but were a manifestation of human nature, Leikucs suggested. 'You need a set of dentures, Mr Valdmanis needs new lungs, my sister a new eye ... Should they not also have a feeling of injustice and offence?' What if, like Valdmanis, Siliņš for years had been denounced at least once a year? Would it not have been easier for Valdmanis to flee the country in 1940 than to face torture by the NKVD and to be held responsible for the actions of the Ulmanis regime; or after 1941 to acquiesce in the formation of the Latvian Legion without demanding independence as the price; or after 1945 not to fight for the release of Latvian legionnaires from POW camps and threatened repatriation? Valdmanis had been denounced numerous times and suffered greatly because of his love for his people. He did not deserve to be bombarded with undeserved accusations. 'But have you heard Mr Valdmanis complain? Has he ever responded in kind? No! He remains silent. I think that many of us who are demanding justice and compensation could learn from his example.'

Life in America was not as Latvians had heard twenty years ago, Leikucs continued. All immigrants had to start from the bottom and Latvians, many of them professionals with unrecognized university degrees, had few immediately marketable skills – physicians worked as cleaners, lawyers as janitors, and engineers as draftsmen. 'In this land nobody will take care of you. You have to get your own bowl as well as something to put into it.' But how about Valdmanis? Would one not expect a man in his position to have a staff of several hundred, a comfortable suite of offices, and – apart from signing a few documents and attending boring board meetings – enjoying life in high society?

Life and work in Newfoundland were anything but normal, Leikucs reminded Siliņš. 'Before the arrival of Valdmanis, Newfoundland was known only as a remote, poor, undeveloped, windswept, foggy island inhabited by several thousand tuberculosis-infected fishermen ... When I arrived I found Valdmanis in a smallish dim basement office, where besides a local stenographer–typist his company consisted of a dozen mice.' But it would not be fair to criticize locals because they offered the best they had and, 'not having seen much of the civilized world and not knowing what to do and how to convert their poor island into a province of Canada,' this set-up seemed satisfactory to them. Valdmanis had no data of any value to work with, except the knowledge that the island produced only dried cod, anything needed for existence had to be imported, and past efforts to bring about changes had failed. 'Valdmanis himself, with some engineers, had to trek through bush and swamp looking for sites suitable for the factories. He himself had to negotiate the financing and construction of the new plants. And while at the same time he had to prepare surveys and evaluate natural resources for further development, his 'most difficult problem was to get foreign capital interested in a poor island which had nothing concrete to offer in return.' Selling something that really did not exist was not easy.

Thanks to this 'super-human effort,' Leikucs went on, Newfoundland now had six operational factories, six under construction, and just as many on the planning board – just three years after Valdmanis's arrival. Then, there was NALCO, formed with the participation of American capital and dedicated to the exploration of natural resources. His achievements, while bringing recognition and fame to Valdmanis, had exacted their toll on his health and quality of life. He had no time for family and friends or the large number of personal letters arriving daily begging for jobs, money, and assistance with immigration. There were 'hundreds and hundreds of them.' How could anyone help these hundreds if there was serious and difficult work to be done? When could or should it be done?

Awareness of these limitations meant for Valdmanis giving up his hopes and dreams to help his people, Leikucs concluded. What would be the point of bothering him with all those letters full of despair, fear, and misfortune? 'If I wished his early death I would keep on adding to his already heavy load. But I do not. I would like to see him able to continue because it is possible there will be a day when Latvians will need his services again.' In his reply addressed 'to the Guard,' Siliņš considered Leikucs's 'sermon' and her non-delivery of his letters to Valdmanis an insult not only to him personally, but also to other Latvian veterans, because he was convinced that Valdmanis himself would not refuse him anything.[64]

The last pleas for help, received in the spring and summer of 1953, all requested either a job or assistance in finding one. They came from

Latvians such as Augusts Lūkiņš, who for three years had been toiling as a gardener and occasional worker in the dirty milling plant of the gold mines in Duparquet, Quebec; from Jānis Roziņš, who lived with his miner son in Sudbury, Ontario, unemployed, in a 'little house on wheels'; from F. Richters in New Jersey, who begged for a job offer contract in Canada for his daughter and son-in-law still living in Germany; and from Arvīds Immers, who had to hear that he was 'an undesirable foreigner here in Germany because they have to take care of their own refugees and their unemployed ones.' Olga Leikucs's standard reply to all these requests was that jobs were scarce in Newfoundland and that they should apply directly to one of the eight new industries that had recently been established there.[65]

Members of Valdmanis's former student fraternity Tālavija, usually expected special consideration. Eriks Ritums in Detroit wanted help to relocate his brother and his family from Belgium to Canada.[66] Jānis Pusbarņieks wrote from Sweden asking whether he could organize a plywood industry or expand an existing one.[67] Armands Pētersons in Arvida, Quebec, offered for sale new floating cranes from Germany. As the only Latvian employed at the Aluminum Company of Canada, with its French workers and conservative English management, Pētersons felt looked down upon because no one knew anything about Latvia. A *Maclean's* article in July 1952 featuring a story on Alfred Valdmanis changed all that. Suddenly Pētersons's associates became interested in him, his ideas and designs were appreciated, and he was 'really pleased that I could claim to know a Latvian like you.'[68] From the DP camp in Neustadt, which in November 1952 still had about two hundred Latvians, fraternity brother Hermans Luters, who was living 'deeply in debt,' begged for a package with foodstuffs or 'some dollars.' Leikucs treated him to what had become the standard reply by mid-1952 – that Valdmanis was nearly constantly absent and that for private correspondence there was 'simply no time.'[69]

Fraternity brother Jānis Radziņš from Detroit was so offended at not receiving a personal reply from Valdmanis that he resorted to blackmail. Saeima member A. Gailītis of the Farmers Union had documentation, Radziņš threatened, 'to prove both that you and Karčevskis sneaked to Vyshinskii to crucify the good old man K.U. [Kārlis Ulmanis] and succeeded just like the Jews with Jesus Christ! Tell me, can you prove that you are no Judas? If you can, send me exonerating documentation or name witnesses, but if you cannot – tell me immediately whether you can get me a well-paid job as an engineer in Canada. Yes or No? I have been fighting long and hard to save your reputation. I am expecting gratitude and compensation.' On the file Valdmanis scribbled: 'received 29 January 1952.'[70] His response is unknown.

From another fraternity brother in Detroit, Arturs Mednis, Valdmanis learned that he was 'the only member of the Ulmanis government about whom legends are being told today.' It was amazing what variety of accomplishments were being attributed to him and how many admirers he had among the younger Tālavija members, wrote Mednis. However, the editors of the Latvian American paper *Laiks* (Time), he confided, wanted to embarrass Valdmanis by focusing on his efforts on behalf of Latvian legionnaires and by hoping that Premier Smallwood would lose the next election. Mednis warned Valdmanis to beware of the relatively short life of a regime in democratic countries. Taking the time for a personal reply, Valdmanis reminisced about the old days together with their student friends Ungurs, Eltermans, and Suks, 'all youngsters who had managed "somehow" to get into very important positions. We all were convinced that we had the potential to show "the old ones" what the "youngsters" were capable of doing – and then everything suddenly collapsed.' He was counting on all of them meeting again back in Riga, but then another generation of 'young ones' may be in a position of influence 'in a land saturated with the spirit of the "Old."'[71]

In August 1951 Tālavija fraternity archivist Albiņš Sietiņsons in Bay City, Michigan, sent Valdmanis a questionnaire to complete. It requested information about the education and career of fraternity members since 1926. Alfred Valdmanis had returned a previous questionnaire with no data on his life prior to his arrival in Canada, causing Sietiņsons to complain that too many questions had been answered with 'information submitted previously and can be found in the [1925 anniversary] album.' In particular, the archivist asked for the names of universities and faculties attended, period of attendance, list of fraternity brothers, degrees completed, and 'if not completed, why not.' Valdmanis refused to comply and directed Olga Leikucs to 'file away please. Personal matter.' A year later Valdmanis ignored a second reminder to complete and return the questionnaire despite the threat that fraternity brothers not complying would be brought before the internal court of the fraternity. A final request, arriving in March 1953, asked specifically: 'At which university and for what subject did you receive your doctoral degree in law?' This time Valdmanis disposed of the matter by instructing his secretary: 'for my next trip to Nfld please.'[72]

Revealing how he had obtained his doctoral degree would have compelled Valdmanis to twist the truth again or disclose a potentially embarrassing aspect of his past. Either outcome would have jeopardized the carefully cultivated new image alluded to in the following Latvian poem published in the Tālavija newsletter *Runcis* (Tom Cat) of 14 December 1951:

Like mushrooms after a rain
Grow factory structures,
Their smokestacks supporting the clouds.
Around Alfred the aura of success is glowing
Creating a heaven on earth.
No longer is Valdmanis using his feet,
Up in the air in flying machines is he rushing
With ideas like thunderbolts flashing
When New York or Europe is calling.
To get a good hold on all of the world,
Like lava his projects are spreading;
Looking for places to fill
But mountains still remain standing still.

War Criminal?

The new image Valdmanis was cultivating was precarious indeed. How easily it could be shattered and attention turn to the mysteries of his past became apparent on 18 August 1951. That day the New York Jewish paper *Der Tag* carried a special dispatch from Toronto under the headline 'Alfred Valdmanis, Latvian Nazi and Mass Murderer of Jews Conducting Rabble-rousing Propaganda in Canada.' The article was occasioned by a speech Valdmanis was to give in Toronto to Daugavas Vanagi, the welfare society created in 1946 by former legionnaires. The dispatch asserted that many of the members of this society had taken part in the mass murder of Latvian Jews and that it was closely allied with Ukrainians who had collaborated with the Nazis in the mass murder of Jews in Ukrainian cities and villages. A 'guest' such as Valdmanis meant 'terrible anti-Jewish hate' in Canada. Valdmanis, who had allegedly visited Hitler in 1941, 1942, and 1943 and had demanded that the Jews in Latvia and in the Riga ghetto be liquidated, was given a free hand by Hitler to do just that. This 'mass murderer and war criminal' who occupied a top post in Newfoundland was now travelling through Canada spreading his anti-Semitic hate propaganda.

In its issue of 18 October 1951 the Canadian Jewish weekly *Vochenblatt* repeated the war crimes charges under the heading: 'Fascists Pour into Province.' The article maintained that the arrival of the 'Latvian Fascist and Hitlerite' Alfred Valdmanis, who was allegedly instrumental in killing Jews in Latvia, had aroused apprehension in the local Jewish community. The leaders of that community, concerned over the influx of German and Latvian immigrants, blamed the lack of screening for the entry of 'a considerable number of Nazis' who settled down to carry out their hate propaganda. Riga-born Robert W. Keyserlingk, publisher of *The Ensign: Canada's National News Weekly* and a prominent member of Canada's Baltic German community, warned Valdmanis confidentially that these accusations were appearing in the press and that they were known to the Opposition in the Newfoundland legislature.[73]

Smallwood and Valdmanis were in Germany when news of the accusations broke. In Newfoundland rumours, as well as copies, began to circulate of the translated *Vochenblatt* piece. (Considerable liberties had been taken with the translation.) The local press, however, refrained from commenting because it was impossible to obtain the facts in the premier's absence. On 8 October, in his first public statement on the issue, Joey Smallwood struck back terming the accusation a gross lie. Far from being a war criminal, Valdmanis had been the number one Latvian on the communist's wanted list and had been in a concentration camp for a year after the communists overran Latvia. When the Germans occupied the country, Valdmanis was briefly given a government post but within a few weeks incurred Nazi disfavour and was back in a concentration camp. One of the reasons for this, Smallwood maintained, was Valdmanis's insistence on better treatment for Latvian Jews, by whom he was held in high regard.[74]

In subsequent comments to the press and to the House of Assembly, Smallwood emphasized that Valdmanis's war record had been investigated by British and American intelligence, as well as the German investigation courts, and he could not have become a valuable member of General Eisenhower's headquarters in Frankfurt had his record not been spotless. In the midst of an election campaign, Smallwood lost no time to denounce the 'foul, malicious and utterly false attack' against Valdmanis. 'No government was served by a man more loyal and with greater effect and efficiency,' Premier Smallwood told the legislature on 25 October 1951, and someday the people of Newfoundland would 'erect a monument to this architect of the economic development plan.'[75]

A few days later Smallwood tabled in the legislature his own statement in reply to the editor of *Der Tag*, accompanied by a letter from Elja Lurje, New York lawyer, investment broker, and executive of the Zionist Federation of Latvia. Lurje's letter, dated 9 October 1951, attested to Valdmanis's 'unimpeachable' character and integrity. A Latvian citizen of Jewish extraction who had lived in Riga since 1924, knew Valdmanis since 1927, and was in concentration camps in Riga in 1941 and Stuthoff (Germany) in 1944, Lurje termed the charges appearing in *Der Tag* 'a gross and malicious lie.' He vouched for Valdmanis as a just and fair man, practising and advocating a democratic way of life, at all times ready to help people, and never exhibiting any racial prejudice or bigotry.[76]

In his statement published in *Der Tag*, on 27 October 1951, Smallwood vindicated himself as 'strongly pro-Jewish' and 'a Zionist long before Jews who now favour Zionism were willing to say so.' He also vindicated Valdmanis whose conduct towards Jews was honourable and thoroughly fair while minister in the government of Latvia. The attack reflected gravely upon the U.S. army for appointing him to IRO, the Canadian government for admitting him to Canada, and the Newfoundland government for employing him. In reality, according to the investigations by the British, American, and Canadian security services, 'not a single blemish can truthfully attach to his name.' The circulation of the unfounded accusations had caused the gravest possible injury to Dr Valdmanis and the government of Newfoundland where Jews were given the highest respect. An editorial comment attached to Smallwood's letter stated that *Der Tag*'s investigations in private and official quarters, including documents from the Latvian Refugee Committee and the American occupation authorities, had shown the dispatch from Toronto to be a false accusation drummed up by Valdmanis's enemies.[77]

Once aroused, however, the ghosts of Valdmanis's past would not disappear. In Ottawa, Newfoundland Progressive Conservative MP for St John's East Gordon Higgins read the Jewish article to the entire Parliament and gave notice of the following seven questions: (1) When was Valdmanis admitted to Canada? (2) Had he become a naturalized citizen? (3) Under whose sponsorship did he enter? (4) What was his history prior to entering Canada? (5) Was he employed by the government of Canada? (6) If yes, in what positions and at what salaries? and (7) By whom was he recommended to the government of Newfoundland? An apprehensive Smallwood, who with Valdmanis had just returned from a meeting with Minister of Citizenship and Immigration Walter E. Harris to discuss the Jekste case, cabled Harris: 'We never had a man of greater loyalty and ability, we stand by him, and we ask you please to take a firm stand and declare that according to your data and information he has met immigration requirements, is a bona fide immigrant, and has served this country well.'[78]

Valdmanis, too, communicated to Harris his embarrassment that he should receive 'such' public gratitude for his work from a Newfoundlander. Just in case Harris had no complete dossier on him, Valdmanis forwarded copies of relevant certificates and affidavits; he had already sent copies to the prime minister and the deputy chief commissioner of the RCMP. He also sent copies of the Lurje letter and telegram exchanges with Arthur Slavitt, a prominent New York lawyer of Jewish extraction and attorney for Texas oil millionaire, Rogers (in May 1951 Rogers was interested in buying the cement plant in Corner Brook). Through Slavitt, Valdmanis initiated legal action and would only give release to *Der Tag* pending the publication of a retraction.[79] Slavitt also learned from the publisher of *Der Tag* that the article had first appeared in the Toronto communist newspaper the *Canada Jewish Weekly* or *Canada Yiddish Folkenblatt.*[80]

Harris received information from Newfoundland Senator Ray Petten that C.D. Howe had introduced Valdmanis to him and through him Smallwood had met Valdmanis. In addition, Petten had been assured from a former citizen of Latvia, who knew Valdmanis, that he was one of the 'patriots' who fled from the Russians into the forests and later returned when the Germans arrived.[81] On 31 October 1951 Harris gave only the barest answers to Higgins's questions, based on information Valdmanis had provided prior to entering Canada. He referred to Valdmanis's doctoral degree awarded by the University of Frankfurt and to his imprisonment under Russian and German occupations in 1940 and from 1943 to 1945. Question (1) he answered with the date only, question (5) with 'yes,' and question (7) with 'no information.'

But, to Premier Smallwood's chagrin, more was to come. On 7 November 1951 W.J. Browne, PC member for St John's West, decided to use the stage of Parliament to make Newfoundland's 'brilliant economic advisor' a political issue in Ottawa and St John's. Although worth only $100 a month to the Department of Trade and Commerce in Ottawa, Browne remarked, Valdmanis was engaged by Smallwood at the 'modest' salary of $25,000 a year to initiate one industry per month. Indeed, he mocked, Valdmanis had already exceeded that quota, judged by Smallwood's recent announcement of twenty-five industries started or conceived. All the plants were to be 50 per cent government-funded, operated by Germans, and supplied with German machinery. Such methods of industrialization would not appeal to everybody, and Browne was sure that with its government industries this province would become a socialist paradise. Browne recalled that eight years ago Gregory Meiksins had termed Valdmanis 'the Quisling of Latvia and a Nazi collaborator.' With Valdmanis's assistance, Browne warned, 'we are having national socialism in Canada today.' Smallwood was calling an election, Browne concluded, because he did not want to disclose any unsavoury particulars about his new industries. Valdmanis would 'have to bear the responsibility for the ruin which he may be bringing upon this country by this mad venture into national socialism.'[82]

The *Globe and Mail* and Montreal *Gazette* reported Browne's speech the following day under the headlines 'Ace Director a Quisling, MP Claims,' and 'Feeling Runs High over Latvian Who Steers Economics of Newfie.' Both articles linked Browne's 'revelations' and the information Higgins had extracted from W.E. Harris with the public record of Valdmanis's appearance in April 1949 before the Senate Committee on Immigration. The resulting image of Valdmanis was rather contradictory and raised more questions than it answered. The Montreal *Gazette*, for example, featured Valdmanis's training under the 'German economic wizard' Dr Schacht, his alleged role as economic planner in Germany in the Second World War, and his plea to admit some twenty thousand Baltic Waffen-SS members to Canada. His own account the *Gazette* found incredible – anti-German resistance, rescue through Swedish intervention from SS trial and near execution. 'It was hard to explain ... but here it was,' the correspondent quoted Valdmanis and noted that his story 'leaps abruptly from 1941 to 1943.'

An article in *Newsweek* magazine, on 19 November 1951 and entitled 'Savior or Quisling?' suggested a similar credibility gap. Reviewing the story Valdmanis had told the Senate committee in 1949, the article expressed wonder at how in little more than a year of his arrival in Canada, Valdmanis could hold jobs with two universities and three government departments. He had, stated the writer, quoting a former employer of Valdmanis, 'a definite totalitarian streak of mind. We just couldn't keep him.'

In a letter to the editor of *Newsweek*, Leon von Bruemmer, a wartime German Foreign Office employee stationed in Riga who had been in close contact with the Latvian 'puppet government,' countered that Valdmanis had 'made no bones about his antipathy to the German regime.' Far from having been a quisling, he was 'the leader of the resistance movement in word and deed. Like all others, including many German officials, he had no occasion to know about the shooting of Jews, since that was kept strictly within the province of the SD.'[83] More support came from the national director of the Canadian Anti-Communist League. Smallwood should not be intimidated by those who charged Valdmanis with being 'anti-Semitic,' advised Ron Gostick. In communist double-talk the term 'anti-Semitic' was usually substituted for 'anti-Communist' in order 'to smear those who are admittedly anti-Communist,' Gostick explained.[84]

The sensational exposures in parliament and in the media had local, national, and international repercussions. They ensured that, in time for the Newfoundland snap election of 26 November 1951, and for ever thereafter, Valdmanis would be an issue of political controversy and that the Pandora's box of his past, once opened, would continue to yield ammunition to his and Smallwood's opponents. It was not fair to make Valdmanis the butt of censure for the problems of Newfoundland's industrial development program, the St John's *Evening Telegram* exhorted its readers on 6 December 1951. He was merely doing his job as the agent of the cabinet and the legislature. To the *Sunday Herald*, on 23 December 1951, Valdmanis expressed his fear that potential development schemes might be endangered by the 'tremendous amount of loose talk that has been going the rounds lately regarding the Government program.' The paper's editor agreed that, while the public has a right to be fully informed about all the development deals, it was not necessary 'to lash out brutally at the personalities involved.' George McNamara of St John's implored Valdmanis not to take too seriously what had been said and written during the heat of the election campaign. 'Our Newfoundland people – and doubtless you have observed this – are eminently fair and tolerant. Racial prejudice is unknown here ... In time you will find it so.'[85]

Latvian responses were especially strong. The Boston branch of Daugavas Vanagi begged Valdmanis not to refuse the offer of an honourary membership 'for your heroic action on behalf of Latvian legionnaires as POWs and thereafter.' To Smallwood the same organization as well as the Council of American Latvian Organizations in Boston expressed their admiration for his support of Valdmanis 'even when his own compatriots were not quick enough to respond to the malevolent or misinformed attackers.' The president of the Latvian Society of Tennessee offered Premier Smallwood any information he needed, since its members knew Valdmanis quite well as 'a man of high ideals and a fighter for democracy and freedom, against oppression and dictatorship.' The executive of the Latvian National Federation in Canada (LNAK), the official voice of the community, too, expressed solidarity with Valdmanis in his defence against his detractors. They thought that the accusations were drummed up by existing businesses to prevent Valdmanis from creating competition. A Latvian member of the executive of the Toronto YMCA offered to issue affidavits to Valdmanis or act as a witness, if necessary.[86]

The New York Latvian paper *Laiks*, on 24 November 1951, voiced concern about the way the English-language press in Canada and the United States was covering the Valdmanis affair. It reprinted the Montreal *Gazette* article in Latvian translation and expressed the hope that Valdmanis would know how to not only refute the accusations against him personally but also dispel negative perceptions of Latvian legionnaires. Such perceptions had been conveyed in the Canadian press in connection with the campaign against Valdmanis. *Laiks* reported that the LNAK had decided to let Valdmanis choose his own method of defence.

The harshest Latvian review came, not surprisingly, from the Latvian Social Democratic paper *Latvijas Ziņas* (News of Latvia), published in Sweden. This was the mouthpiece of the Stockholm Committee of the Latvian Social Democratic Workers Party, which in June 1952 had sent incriminating information about Valdmanis's past to its Canadian fellow Social Democratic Party, the Co-operative Commonwealth Federation (CCF), with a request to have him removed from his post in Newfoundland.[87] Having risen steeply in Canada, the paper noted on 22 November 1952, Valdmanis 'landed smack in the middle of the squabbles of Canadian politics.' In his position his activities were bound to draw attention to his chequered personality and past – and the various autobiographical stories he had broadcast 'with his particular customary lack of modesty,' were bound to catch up with him. Since the publication of *Dienas baltas* and his famous speeches at Latvian meetings in North America, these stories were no longer a secret to most Latvians.

There was, *Latvijas Ziņas* elaborated, his claim to have been a Latvian resistance leader at the invitation of Churchill and Roosevelt. There was his story of salvation from sure death in 1943 by the intercession of the king of Sweden. Most unbelievable was the claim that the Germans, after having nearly executed him, engaged him in their wartime economic planning. Latvians also had to worry that Valdmanis's involvement on behalf of Latvian legionnaires might have done them more harm than good. The latter were still not being admitted to Canada and were now being saddled with the stigma that they had been supporters of National Socialism and its regime. 'We should keep in mind that the real anti-Nazi fighters landed up in prison or ended their lives in concentration camps, but definitely not in the planning offices of Nazi Germany.'

The standard rejoinder to this type of attack appeared in the Toronto paper *Latvija* on 19 November 1952. Entitled 'The sunny and shadowy side of exile: why was all that necessary?' and signed anonymously 'Saturns,' the article exhibits the style and reasoning typical of Valdmanis and may indeed have been written by him. Of all Latvians in exile, it remarked, Valdmanis had no doubt achieved the most notable reputation internationally. Even in non-Latvian circles he was recognized as an exceptionally bright economist who had experience with leading financiers and statesmen and had established useful contacts for a liberated Latvia. While Latvians could only wish to have more such men, some Latvian cliques and individuals were going out of their way to hurt him. These were primarily the former party politicians who, implacably opposed and motivated by hate towards Valdmanis, had launched several 'grand offensives' to destroy him. First they denounced him as a collaborator to the occupation authorities in Germany. These acquitted him of all charges and revealed the names of the instigators. The second offensive took place during the November 1951 Newfoundland provincial election, with the aim to destroy his reputation and cause the defeat of Premier Smallwood. This attack, although launched at an international level, also disintegrated.

The fight over and around Valdmanis would not die down, *Latvija* lamented. Alfred Valdmanis had repeatedly declared – again on 31 October 1952 in New York – that, far from aiming for the position of president or prime minister in a liberated Latvia, he would simply be happy to be able to devote all his energy, experience, and expertise to his country. He was also reported as opposing the resurrection of authoritarianism in Latvia and advocating a democratic constitution guaranteeing the widest possible freedom of expression for the people. But no matter what he would say or do, he continued to be denounced as a fascist. Consequently, the non-Latvian public and press had a much higher opinion of Valdmanis than many Latvians themselves had.

Quest for Personal Vindication

Characteristic of Valdmanis's roundabout handling of questions about his past was his exchange of letters with Saul Hayes, National Executive Director of the Canadian Jewish Congress. The exchange was started in late October 1951 by Valdmanis to find the source behind the attack and obtain an exonerating statement. Hayes replied in mid-November with two questions: (1) Was Valdmanis part of the Ulmanis government and did he manifest approval of its policies? and (2) What were Valdmanis's activities during the two-year gap 1941–3 left blank in Harris's answer to Higgins's questions? Hayes did not want this to be interpreted as any board of inquiry, or any desire to take political sides, but merely as a matter of ethics and self-protection. After a month-long delay, Valdmanis responded that on the advice of Smallwood he would not answer these questions personally. Instead, Smallwood would convey authentic statements from unimpeachable British sources, as well as from his knowledge of Latvian history and facts, during his forthcoming visit to Montreal in early January. Valdmanis would also forward extracts of the book *Days of Happiness and Distress* detailing his former activities. Hayes returned the extracts on 21 January 1952 with the comment that 'it proved interesting reading.'[88]

Six months later Valdmanis would publicly pride himself on knowing Mr and Mrs Hayes personally and encourage his old Latvian Jewish acquaintance in Munich, lawyer Dr Jeannot Levenson, to 'feel free to use our old and good friendship' in his efforts to emigrate. Levenson, who was sent in 1944 to Stutthof concentration camp, had 'learned to respect very highly the professional as well as human qualities of Dr Valdmanis' and spontaneously attested to his 'very good and high reputation among colleagues in *all* [emphasis in the original] circles of the population in pre-war Latvia.'[89] Other correspondence with Latvians reveals how shaken Valdmanis was by the publicity of the accusations levelled in *Der Tag*. He could not offer much help, he wrote a Latvian stranger requesting assistance with a Canadian visa for friends in Venezuela, because of a 'completely lunatic accusation attempting to make me responsible for the extermination of Jews in Latvia.' His stock in Ottawa had dropped drastically. The minister of immigration was himself in need to justify letting Valdmanis into Canada. Harris worried 'also about the fact that I have been permitted to achieve what some people call a high position.'[90]

Only his friends in Germany were fully aware of the state of his dejection over the *Der Tag* affair and the dimensions it was assuming. 'I must get rid of my "Jewish murders" and stupid, but dangerous, stuff like that,' he confessed to Friedrich Kreyser, his quasi-father-confessor, on 12 December 1951. No Christmas candles would be burning for him this year. During the coming month he would have to suffer a subjectively very difficult ordeal because he was no good at self-defence. He foresaw the need for a lot more fighting and suffering in order to create something and to help. Help was the purpose of life; not 'happiness': 'To help – the smaller, the weaker, the poorer one. To stretch out your arms, to cast your eyes forward, to fan the fire in the soul again and again so that it burns – without worrying that it burns down – if only a little brother feels a bit of the warmth. And there are so many little brothers, there are millions. Dear Lord, why didn't he send us a few centuries ago, why were we born into this incredulous, small, weak, and unfaithful world?'

Kreyser, from the vantage point of being a generation older, wished that Valdmanis would recognize the relative value of all actions and happenings, and that true happiness cannot be found outside, but inside oneself. This wisdom of old age had always been a good compass for the future. It was futile to allow oneself to be consumed by the past. One should enjoy the beauty of life as it appeared with its thousands of riddles and questions. Valdmanis replied that he had read Kreyser's words slowly and given much thought to them. Still he believed that man was sent into the world to carry out a God-ordained task. Those who had recognized their mission were usually driven to carry it out: 'They follow their dream like madmen.' Such human beings could never be entirely happy, they were consumed by their own inner fire. 'Why should anyone be "happy"? Or why should "happiness" be what most people mean by it?' Valdmanis believed that one had to follow one's 'star' on a path increasingly lonely and psychologically painful. Regardless of the obstacles, the bottom line remained accountability to one's conscience.[91]

The concrete question of what witnesses could be approached to testify on behalf of Valdmanis posed a major problem. Valdmanis was still cultivating personal contacts with such *alte Kameraden* as Adolf Windecker, Wilhelm Burmeister, Harald Seehusen, Karl Rasche, and even Hinrich Lohse, with whom he arranged meetings on his European visits as late as 1953.[92] Any testimonials from these former Nazi officials, apart from lacking credibility, might have been counterproductive because the majority of Newfoundland's Jews originated in Latvia and adjoining Baltic regions. On his first visit to Newfoundland for the official signing, on 23 November 1950, of the gypsum plant contract, Kreyser had noticed many stores in downtown St John's and Corner Brook in the hands of Jews, some of them 'old acquaintances from Daugavpils, Riga, and Kaunas who had emigrated after the First World War.'[93] These Jews had every reason to be alarmed about the accusations against Valdmanis and might have taken indications of his association with officials of the former German occupation regime in Latvia as proof of his complicity.

Meanwhile Max Braun-Wogau, their mutual Baltic German friend and deputy director of Kreyser's Neue Technik, was pursuing a three-pronged course of action to obtain some active support for Valdmanis from Swedish or Jewish circles in Europe. In Stockholm he approached Dr Ernst Wehtje, a director of Skanska Cement and member of the Riksdag, and requested a letter to the premier of Newfoundland corroborating the wartime Swedish intervention. Wehtje tried but failed to obtain confirmation from former Ambassador Rickert to Berlin. Rickert could not remember any details – so much had happened in those days – and recommended two senior officials associated with the Swedish foreign ministry at the time.[94]

A second avenue to be pursued originated with Braun-Wogau's Baltic German friend Fritz Koch in Stockholm. It targeted Gillel Storch, a member of the executive of the World Jewish Congress and its representative for Scandinavia who had enabled sixty thousand Jews to emigrate from the Baltic states. Storch was to be approached through the mediation of his old Jewish friend Fritz Berend, a former businessman from Liepāja, who remembered Valdmanis's reputation as an 'anti-vācietis' (anti-German). A declaration from Storch would, as Braun-Wogau put it, be 'the sort of proof in our hands that could not be more compelling.' For the Berend–Storch meeting a detailed chronological listing of all the positions occupied by Valdmanis from July 1941 to 1945 was required.

Should 'Action I and II' produce no results, Koch would be prepared to start a third action through his friend Lennard Nylander, now Swedish consul general in New York, but stationed in Berlin during the war. All that would be required was for Valdmanis to write to Koch, as a former acquaintance associated with the Latvian enterprise Lenta, and ask him to have the desired statement issued. Koch would then write Nylander requesting him to 'state the commonly known facts.' Or Valdmanis could personally get in touch with Nylander in New York. Braun-Wogau, however, hoped that 'Action III' would not be necessary.[95]

Valdmanis, concerned about some aspects of these schemes, urged Braun-Wogau to use only personal diplomacy and refer to Zemgals's book as authority. He could not afford trouble with the World Jewish Congress, and a negative report by Storch, 'though undeserved,' would have serious consequences. In fact, as Berend found out, the congress had already commissioned a report from Storch. According to Storch, it was going to be negative because of 'incriminating newspaper articles with anti-[Semitic] tendency' authored by Valdmanis in 1941. Berend refused to believe this and, sure of the untenability of the accusations, tried to convince Storch of the need to prevent an injustice. Although Storch offered to show the incriminating materials, Berend was able to talk Storch into withholding his report from the congress for the time being. Storch was indebted to Berend for guaranteeing his credits before the war. Berend was expecting return favours for himself from Valdmanis in the form of drilling concessions granted to the Swedish mining syndicate Svenska Diamantberg-Borrings A/B, and perhaps other possibilities.[96]

Since a positive declaration from Storch seemed unlikely (the only concession that could be extracted from him would be neutrality), Berend proposed yet another move: to seek the support of Mrs Siegrid Kalniņš in Sweden. From August 1941 to July 1942, Kalniņš had been attached to the Nachrichtendienst Nord (Intelligence Staff North) in Riga and had participated in actions by the Canaris group against the shooting of Jews. Mrs Kalniņš considered the accusations made against Valdmanis complete nonsense. Braun-Wogau suggested that her testimony, together with that of Berend could be useful. Berend himself attributed the denunciation to a personal vendetta by L. Breikšs, chairman of the Latvian Committee in Stockholm.[97]

As early as the end of January 1952 Valdmanis, apparently anticipating the futility of these actions, was prepared 'quietly to resign himself to fate,' instead of pressing charges. Kreyser, however, was sure that anyone living in Latvia at the time could refute the accusations against Valdmanis. They were so absurd that they would be an interesting challenge to a politically astute lawyer. The wartime directors general had wielded no actual power and influence on events; they had not been involved with the horrors of that time, nor had they had the ability to prevent them, Kreyser reasoned. Credible witnesses willing to attest to this fact would be pastors Bernewitz and Osoling, Wilhelm von Rüdiger, Oberlandesrichter Noltein, Riga mayor Wittrock, Gustav Leckzyck, possibly General Bremer (Braemer), Dr E. Schwartz, Westermann, and others. Kreyser urged Valdmanis to entrust the entire matter to a competent attorney and not allow himself to become diverted from his other duties.[98]

These duties appeared to be in a state of dangerous disarray, Kreyser cautioned in February 1951. The disarray had reached such proportions that people returned from visits to St John's with the impression that a distracted Valdmanis was nearly at the end of his rope. 'You have to understand how strongly these people, who have been inspired in their decision in part by personal trust in you, are affected by such apprehensions,' Kreyser warned him. He was sick and tired of repeatedly hearing the word 'hurry' from Valdmanis, who seemed to be 'the type of person able to learn only from damages incurred by their mistakes.' What was the point of all this slaving, hurrying, and worrying if there was no sense that what was being created had stability and if it was constantly at the mercy of political intrigues and accidents? Kreyser wondered.[99]

On top of apprehensions concerning his personal reputation, occupational responsibilities, and relationships with friends and acquaintances, Valdmanis worried about his rapport with Premier Smallwood. In view of obvious attempts by the Opposition in Ottawa and St John's to drive a wedge between them, poison the minds of Newfoundlanders with 'Jewish murder stories,' and play on Newfoundlanders' 'natural susceptibility towards the seed of suspicion,' one question began to loom increasingly larger in Valdmanis's mind: 'Will the Premier become suspicious of me ... Will he be *made* suspicious by some of his friends who may, in good *or* in bad faith, have become suspicious?' Valdmanis decided to face the problem head-on and address a four-part 'Memorandum about Loyalty,' dated 10 March 1952, to Smallwood.

In Part A, entitled 'Personal Loyalty,' Valdmanis argued that he could never refer to Smallwood in anything but the most complimentary terms. Having never made a single speech since his arrival and having had no occasion to refer publicly to Smallwood, he could not understand how 'honest' suspicion could start growing. In Part B, entitled 'Political Loyalty,' Valdmanis suggested that no gossip about opposing or 'double-crossing' government policy could gain ground since his very presence in Newfoundland was because of the government's economic development policy and only as long as the government continued that policy. According to Part C, entitled 'Announcements, Speeches, Interviews,' Smallwood could publicize his own ideas while Valdmanis had to 'remain in the realm of accomplished facts.'

The event that the memorandum tried to address in particular is described in Part C. In November 1951 Wall Street bankers J.P. Ripley and George M. Mackintosh had arrived alarmed at rumours that Valdmanis and Smallwood were 'driving at high speed which, if not checked, must end in a crash.' Ripley, according to Valdmanis, had asked at least ten times about the '25 industries' and wondered how he had established their economic feasibility in such a short time. Valdmanis explained that first they had visions, or dreams, 50 per cent of which remained as ideas to be investigated, and not more than 25 per cent of these would be narrowed down to negotiable projects. More than 50 per cent of the negotiable projects would be dropped during the negotiation stage lasting several months so that in the end only 5 per cent of the dreams would become final propositions. Ripley and Mackintosh also wanted to see the files showing the investigations of the economic feasibility of projects at various stages. They took some of the files with them, and later the Opposition quoted some of the data from them.

In Part D, entitled 'Wanting Things Done *My* Way,' Valdmanis offered to resign as director, if the cabinet objected to his way of doing things and preferred to have him merely as a consultant at a considerably lower salary. He advised, however, they should carefully compare the cost and results of his directorship with the cost of some mainland experts engaged before 1950 and their results. Regarding his present job as 'man-killing' anyway, he had done all he did 'less for money than out of admiration for an honest Newfoundlander who is devoting his life to raising his undernourished and underdeveloped people, and who obviously cannot perform that miracle alone.' Anyone who thought he could do Valdmanis's job in a more agreeable way could gladly have it. In the margin Olga Leikucs noted: 'Chapter D was not attached to the Memo forwarded to Premier Smallwood.'[100]

Smallwood was far from questioning these pleas of loyalty, as his spirited defence of the director general in the March 1952 session of the House of Assembly suggests. If anything, Smallwood continued to be as much taken in by Valdmanis's competence and presumed integrity as in October 1951, when he declared that 'if Dr Valdmanis has to go, I go too.'[101] Why not openly acknowledge that Valdmanis, though not a Canadian citizen, was already an outstanding political figure in Canada? Smallwood asked a staff reporter of the paper *Latvija* in October 1952. Voters satisfied with Valdmanis's economic program were voting for Smallwood's administration and those who were against this program were voting against the government. Rarely could a man be credited with such 'tremendous' achievements as Valdmanis had accomplished for Newfoundland, Smallwood maintained. Only three years earlier Newfoundland was unheard of and, if known, then only as a backward, underdeveloped island. Today it was well known among financiers and industrialists on both sides of the Atlantic.[102]

For Valdmanis, however, the scars inflicted by the public denunciations would not heal. His 'painfully rebuilt new life' was shattered, he confessed to Leon von Bruemmer. To this 'noble' wartime friend, who in the 19 November 1951 issue of *Newsweek* had depicted Valdmanis as a courageous anti-German resistance leader, Valdmanis confided in May 1953: 'In despair, and partially also in disgust, I had turned away from the past which, instead of helping to rebuild, denies itself and tears itself to pieces. From the appalling denunciation that hit me in October–

November 1951, I have never been able to recuperate fully. Again and again the questions kept creeping up: who did it, why was it done, why did no one stand up for the truth?'[103]

chapter ten

'Only One Could Topple Him from His Height – Himself': Newfoundland's 'Economic Tsar,' 1952–1954

The team of Smallwood and Valdmanis was terrific although slower thinkers felt that it ought to have been held in check by a third member who would urge caution and a slower approach ... In a sense he [Valdmanis] flashed like a meteor across the Newfoundland sky but the industries he helped to establish are here and he is likely in the long run to be remembered by what happened to them.

Albert Perlin, *Evening Telegram*, 11 February 1954

By 1953 it was obvious to critical observers that Newfoundland Premier Joey Smallwood's industrialization scheme was in trouble. To this day most Newfoundlanders regard Alfred Valdmanis as the chief culprit and a con man – some even contend that he accepted the assignment knowing that failure was certain – whereas Smallwood's economic strategy was allegedly based on sound growth-centre theory, that is, establishing industries that create spin-off products and employment.[1] The history of Smallwood's so-called new industries program and its ultimate failure transcends the scope of this study and remains to be written. Nevertheless, the available evidence identifies Smallwood's imposition of political priorities as a key factor. Between 1950 and 1953 political expediency increasingly dictated Smallwood's choice of remote industrial sites, unsound funding arrangements, dubious promoters, and ill-suited industries – against the advice of his director general of economic development.

Valdmanis had accepted his Newfoundland assignment confident of success. After all, he had his extensive Latvian and German connections plus Smallwood's enthusiastic support. Indeed, he regarded the launching of viable new industries essential for his immediate career survival in the New World and a vital stepping stone for more momentous career moves to come. Determined to be a success, Valdmanis knew he would be judged by the viability of the industries launched under his auspices. When he realized as early as 1952, however, that his efforts were doomed for reasons beyond his control, his survival instinct sought out greener pastures. The evidence presented in this chapter suggests that through association with NALCO Alfred Valdmanis hoped to survive – bolster his reputation, remove himself from the limelight of Newfoundland politics, and use his international connections for a more promising career move. It also suggests that Premier Joey Smallwood, under growing attack for the problems his new industries program was incurring, and concerned about his own political survival, deeply resented Valdmanis's use of NALCO for the purpose of salvaging his own career.

Chairman of the Newfoundland and Labrador Corporation

The media accurately presented Valdmanis's retirement as director of economic development on 1 March 1953 as a reassignment, if not a promotion, to chairman of NALCO.[2] The post had been vacant since Sir William Stephenson's resignation the previous November. In his new position, Valdmanis disclosed to a business acquaintance in Germany, 'I have become much more independent, hope to be out of the political limelight, and may also be able to transfer half of my activities to the mainland, as I have always wanted to do.'[3] The transfer also meant that, as chairman of NALCO, Valdmanis would now relinquish his unpaid role as president of NALCO to local businessman Chesley A. Pippy and earn a salary of $30,000 retroactive to 1 January 1953. The next highest salaries on the NALCO payroll in 1952 and 1953 were paid to the director of mining ($14,000), the president and vice-president ($10,000 each). In fact, his salary made Valdmanis one of the highest paid officials in Canada and the envy of all but the tiniest handful of public servants.[4]

As chairman of NALCO, Valdmanis reached the pinnacle of his career. Latvian friends jokingly cautioned him that the only one who could topple him from the soaring heights to which he had risen was himself.[5] Portrayed by journalists and foreign observers as 'Newfoundland's economic czar,'[6] Alfred Valdmanis enjoyed identifying with his prominent public image. For the *Canadian Who's Who* he drafted the following biographical entry of himself:

> Before the war, rose high in Latvian and European economics and politics; at the age of twenty-nine became Cabinet Minister of Finance, Trade and Industry of the Republic of Latvia, 1938–39; received a great number of official recognitions (decorations) from European governments for outstanding achievements in general economics and industrial development. Since his arrival in Canada in 1948 has been professor of economics, advisor to the Federal Government and in 1951 became Director General of Economic Development of the Government of Newfoundland. With Premier Smallwood, Dr Valdmanis is credited with the great strides by which Newfoundland has been catching up economically with the mainland of Canada. As one of the leading economists of this country, Dr Valdmanis has not been content with a government position and, as the newly elected Chairman (for five years) of the Newfoundland and Labrador Corporation, has returned to business life.[7]

As indicated in Chapter 8, NALCO was a joint brainchild of Smallwood and Valdmanis. It took on shape as part of their endeavours to sell the new cement plant to the New York group (consisting primarily of the Cement and General Development Corporation of New York, with which William Stephenson was associated) and to secure funding for an escalating array of new industries. Its core idea was a government–business partnership to develop Newfoundland's resources and keep them under Newfoundland control. Especially the form in which NALCO was set up and incorporated was indebted to Valdmanis's genius, despite Smallwood's later claims. It was Valdmanis who pursued Harriman-Ripley of New York and Wood Gundy of Toronto to become its chief private investors, insisted that it be more than 50 per cent government-owned, devised its management structure, and selected its capable staff. From the outset Valdmanis was slated to be both president of NALCO and a member of its board of directors. The famous Sir William Stephenson agreed to be chairman of the board effective March 1952. A Manitoban, who had made a fortune from his invention of the wireless transmission of pictures, Stephenson had been a secret service liaison between the United States and Britain during the Second World War and was associated with a number of big business enterprises in Jamaica.[8]

It was Valdmanis's idea to have NALCO float a loan so it could buy the government-owned cement, gypsum, and hardwood industries. In the spring of 1951 he came to view the 'celebrated' corporation as a panacea for the inability to sell these industries as well as for other intractable financial and economic development problems. The corporation offered a variety of benefits to the government, Valdmanis reminded Smallwood on the eve of its establishment, in June 1951, as a Crown corporation with an authorized capital of three million non-par value shares: 'We need the corporation as a medium, into which the cement-mill, the gypsum-mill, the Labrador timber areas and the discussed mining areas can be vested. We need the corporation for you and your Government because through this corporation (by deliberately declining and/or withholding payments of dividends) you can make your Government budget work without deficit; you can just regulate your Government budget by paying or not paying into the treasury the corporation's profits before the end of a certain budget year.'

Shortly before the NALCO Act was passed in the Newfoundland legislature, on 22 June 1951, Valdmanis cabled Smallwood from Germany detailing his last urgent request for changes. These included vesting specific timber and mining grants into the corporation and deleting references to founders and to special rights of the minority group. This would relieve Valdmanis from the 'terrific pressure, under which I am presently working in Germany.' Otherwise, the 'excellent schemes' he was pursuing in Germany might be refused by an 'uncontrolled' corporation, 'in which case my prestige in Europe would be killed and I would be made useless to you and to Newfoundland.' The creation of a corporation, as defined by Valdmanis, would give Smallwood an 'instrument through which to negotiate and conduct business in a business-like manner and on a business-like basis.' While being formally independent, NALCO would function as the government's 'economic arm.'[9]

During Stephenson's seven months in office, NALCO failed to raise a necessary $10 million bond issue to acquire the government-owned cement, gypsum, and birch plants and provide it with a source of income. Stephenson's apparent prestige and connections in international investment banking had not managed to finalize a single sale in New York or Canada. He allegedly tore up a cheque for a $10-million loan he had raised in New York and subsequently resigned when he realized that Smallwood, on the advice of Valdmanis, kept making loans behind his back to American entrepreneur Walter E. Siebert and others. It did not take long for Stephenson's disagreement with Valdmanis over policy to become an open secret.[10]

'Staring payment bankruptcy squarely into the eyes,' Valdmanis confided to Friedrich Kreyser in June 1952, 'I did the only thing left to do. I negotiated a loan directly for the province. I had no authority – nor does the government – to do that, only the legislature could take such a step

... That this was the only salvation from a terrible crash, the Premier would not dare reveal.' The loan was subsequently approved in a special session of the House of Assembly, but Alfred Valdmanis had no illusion that the government had suffered a terrible loss of prestige. Smallwood, 'who had always promised money to others, now himself had to borrow money hastily.' It was also a heavy blow for the corporation which had proven itself not to be worth $10 million. Smallwood could not ignore the undeniable fact that 'credit was granted to the government when it was denied the corporation.' Valdmanis believed that the weight would now shift back to the government.[11]

Valdmanis was right for more than one reason. For example, the idea that NALCO should take the government out of business never even had a chance to be tried because Smallwood would not relinquish economic development and his financing of it. On the contrary, Valdmanis found that Smallwood gradually assumed more and more direct personal control.[12] Moreover, when Valdmanis took over as chairman, Smallwood was in the process of restructuring NALCO – 'denationalizing' it and turning it into a 'mineral and forest company'[13] divested of its industrial development function and emasculated by concessions to BRINCO and Canadian Javelin. 'My Premier is ceding whatever is still available in Newfoundland and Labrador to the Rothschild group' except what had been promised to other interests, Valdmanis lamented to Kreyser and declared that he was not participating in this deal.[14] He endorsed the warning by NALCO director George M. Mackintosh, who represented the minority (Harriman-Ripley and Wood Gundy) shareholders' interests, that the government's transfer of the Hamilton River grant from NALCO to BRINCO would 'cause very much trouble to the Province, and could certainly jeopardize the position of NALCO.'[15] As soon as he could see NALCO put on the right track, Valdmanis wrote Michael Lewin in New York, he would be 'able to retire more or less' from his present 'very active duties on this Island' and go into some private business with Lewin.[16]

By an amendment on 20 May 1953 to the NALCO Act, Joey Smallwood ended government majority ownership – 'denationalized' NALCO as he put it. When by September 1953 John C. Doyle's syndicate Canadian Javelin Foundries and Machine Works Ltd offered to buy 1.5 million newly issued NALCO shares at $5 a share, Valdmanis thought NALCO's future was assured. Initially, the financial arrangement appeared sound. According to an agreement of 3 September 1953, Doyle paid $650,000 down in cash, promised to pay $1 million by the end of 1953, and another $6.5 million within five years. Doyle's offer – prompted by the discovery of iron near Wabush Lake in Labrador – by far exceeded anything NALCO had received to date. On the eleven-member NALCO board, six seats – a majority – went to Doyle. To friends Valdmanis announced that he had no intention of giving up as chairman.[17] In October 1953 he opened a NALCO office in Montreal with a four-person staff: a clerk (his associate Alexander Āboliņš), driver, stenographer, and 'personal assistant to the chairman.'[18] The German consul general in Montreal, Adolph Reifferscheidt, who visited St John's in mid-August 1953, reported to Bonn that Valdmanis, whose position seemed temporarily weakened, had 'unmistakably regained greater influence on the entire economic policy of the government of Newfoundland.' Valdmanis had told Reifferscheidt that he was 'on the verge of new decisions concerning his future activity.'[19]

Valdmanis, who for some time had been visiting Newfoundland only in 'whirlwind visits (*Sturzflügen*),' as he wrote an old German acquaintance,[20] was now absent for months at a time. In Premier Smallwood's words, he would 'come down here for maybe three days. There would be a mad rush for three or four days, night and day, and then he would be off again ... He travelled all over the continent of North America – that was when we were promoting NALCO.'[21] NALCO president, from July 1954, Victor Geffine, who was also vice-president of Canadian Javelin, refused to reside in Newfoundland; his predecessor, local businessman Ches Pippy, had also been constantly absent. As a result, conflicts developed among senior NALCO staff in St John's, especially vice-president Cedric Wallis, secretary-treasurer Ronald Turta (both recruited by Valdmanis), and chief geologist R.J. MacNeill. 'Many problems are stored up by our staff for discussion with the President, whom they keep expecting,' Wallis complained to Valdmanis on 14 January 1954. 'The children must see their father pretty regularly or discipline will suffer.'[22]

One of the problems was Turta's handling of salary increases and his questioning of MacNeill's field expenses following instructions by Valdmanis that the treasurer must assume full responsibility for all expenditures. The older Wallis and MacNeill resented the assertion of authority by 'young fellows' like Turta. In particular, Wallis resented what he called Valdmanis's duplicity. On the one hand Valdmanis instructed NALCO staff that he would no longer deal with managerial matters that were now Geffine's responsibility, on the other hand without consulting Wallis he issued new powers to officers such as Turta. To resolve the crisis, Wallis, who was de facto president without having the proper authority and salary for the job, demanded his promotion to full president, as apparently had been promised by Valdmanis repeatedly. Wallis was unable to discuss these issues with Valdmanis in Montreal on 26 December 1953, as planned, because of the NALCO crisis with Doyle.[23] In January 1954 Wallis and Turta took their dispute directly to Smallwood.

By December 1953 Valdmanis had reconsidered the wisdom of selling NALCO to Javelin and tried desperately to block the sale. His efforts were aided by John Doyle's financial difficulties and the delisting of Canadian Javelin from the Montreal stock exchange. Meanwhile, Doyle sought Valdmanis's agreement for the following plan, as Valdmanis summarized it:

> Javelin would sell to NALCO for approximately $7 million the Wabush concession which had been granted to Javelin by NALCO only in July ... So NALCO would purchase back its own concession for $7 million. Immediately, Javelin, to which NALCO would owe $7 million, would purchase all those NALCO shares which Javelin had agreed to purchase and would not pay over the five-year period but right away, full cash. In such a way Javelin would own control of NALCO, and through NALCO indirectly the Wabush concession *without paying one red cent in cash* [emphasis in the original].[24]

Valdmanis claimed that he was deeply shocked and warned Smallwood. To thwart Doyle, Valdmanis, in his capacity as chairman of NALCO, decided to get tough. He aborted a special board meeting called by the Javelin directors for 30 December 1953, caused Doyle to default on his unpaid shares the next day, and on 4 January unsuccessfully demanded the resignation of all the Javelin directors from the NALCO board since they were no longer qualified to serve. When behind his back Doyle attempted to extract a deal from the premier, Valdmanis even tried to rein in Smallwood. Through Attorney General Curtis he let Smallwood know that, although the government was the largest shareholder, the premier had no authority to negotiate with Doyle on behalf of NALCO since he was not its chief executive officer. The 'conflict of top leadership in NALCO between Mr Doyle and Dr Valdmanis' had deteriorated to the point, NALCO President Geffine acknowledged in March 1954, that 'for the past few months ... no constructive program could be worked out.'[25]

This turned out to be a Pyrrhic victory for Valdmanis. On 12 February 1954 Premier Smallwood pulled the rug from under his feet by announcing Valdmanis's departure as chairman of NALCO. A month later, Doyle was granted rights to 2,400 square miles of prime NALCO holdings in Labrador, although Javelin shares had fallen back to half their value of October 1953.[26]

Until his last day in office, Alfred Valdmanis had tried to bring together a group that could raise a minimum of $500,000 to market Labrador pulpwood. It was a partial revival of the Siegheim proposition that Valdmanis had pursued through 1953. Swiss sawmill owner Rudolf Hanhart was to put up one-third, and Ewald Zippmann and John Murdock the rest. Zippmann was a tile manufacturer and shipowner from Wermelskirchen, Germany, and Murdock a wealthy Quebec timber entrepreneur and member of the Canadian Javelin syndicate. The master plan, of 29 January 1954, called for Hanhart to market the pulpwood in Europe, Zippmann to take care of shipping from Lake Melville to Europe, and Murdock to cut the timber in Labrador. However, minimum funding was not assured, Smallwood was unwilling to kick in government funds, and the financially powerful Murdock had ambitions to buy out Hanhart and Valdmanis from the expected lucrative business.

The deal with Murdock was also designed to make Doyle pliant. In the struggle over control of NALCO, Murdock promised to support Smallwood. Valdmanis was counting on an internal revolt in Canadian Javelin against Doyle and for Murdock and Geffine to take over the syndicate. With time running out in January, and the annual NALCO meeting planned for the end of February 1954, Valdmanis tightened the pressure on Hanhart, wondering what it would take to launch a company ready to start in 1954: 'We cannot afford a setback that could become fatal.' The matter was so important to Valdmanis that he decided to bother Smallwood with it in a lengthy letter two weeks after his resignation.[27]

Departure from NALCO

Local Latvians knew Alfred Valdmanis to be businesslike and aloof when they first met him in 1950–1. In late 1953 they saw him transformed into 'a restless man who couldn't sit down for five minutes. He made incoherent and weird remarks as if he were on drugs.'[28] Broadcaster Don Jamieson found him 'tense,' undergoing 'pronounced changes in mood during a single conversation,' and exhibiting the 'disorientation symptoms of a drunk.'[29] On his last visit to the Canadian embassy in Germany, in 1953, Valdmanis is reported to have been arrogant and to have left an 'extremely unfavourable impression.'[30]

The underlying reasons for Valdmanis's departure, Jamieson recalled, were the irritations that his increasing independence caused Premier Smallwood. It had always bothered Smallwood that Valdmanis never took up residence in St John's – Irma had visited Newfoundland only twice – and now he was even transferring the operation of NALCO to Montreal. Increasingly, Valdmanis spoke of differences of opinion with Smallwood. The tenor of his complaints, as witnessed by Jamieson, was 'Smallwood did not pay enough attention to his advice':

> The breaking point was Valdmanis's actions as head of NALCO. But the erosion of Smallwood's confidence had begun even earlier ... Quite simply, Valdmanis had become too big for his boots. While Smallwood had been sincere about giving his carte blanche, the dispensation did not extend to actions designed to keep Smallwood ignorant of Valdmanis's plans. Those around the Premier who resented and mistrusted the Latvian were legion. It was only a matter of time, therefore, before their constant stories about Valdmanis's indiscretions began to fuel Smallwood's sense of betrayal.[31]

Valdmanis's departure as NALCO chairman was not voluntary. He arrived in St John's on 31 January 1954 and, as he wrote a friend, planned to stay until the next NALCO board meeting in March when he would present his so-called Murdock proposition.[32] But Smallwood fired him on 7 February. According to Smallwood, the dismissal was triggered by a visit of NALCO officers Cedric Wallis and Ronald Turta who brought certain 'astonishing' facts to Smallwood's attention. One of these was the unauthorized establishment of a NALCO office in Montreal. Another was the luxurious office furnishings acquired in Montreal at NALCO expense, including a 'magnificent' antique clock ordered from Toronto.[33] Smallwood may also have been alerted to the fact that Valdmanis used to drive the NALCO car from Montreal to New York to visit his relatives Valdis and Katrina Mateus. Canadian and American customs allegedly never stopped the official government vehicle. (The Mateus family had migrated in late 1949 to New York, one of the largest centres of Latvian exile activity, where Valdis had accepted work as manager of various buildings. In New York Valdis was also looking after Alfred's personal business and Latvian political interests.)[34]

Smallwood accused Valdmanis of receiving for two months his old director general's salary along with his new salary as NALCO chairman and padding one or two of his travel expense accounts.[35] Considering Valdmanis's constant travelling on behalf of NALCO, and his relationship with and importance to Smallwood, these irregularities would seem trivial. Valdmanis promptly refunded the salary overpayment[36] but Smallwood, only prepared to offer exemption from prosecution,[37] demanded his formal letter of resignation. Curiously, Valdmanis was allowed to remain a NALCO director at $7,500 annually until after the NALCO annual meeting of 8 March 1954.[38]

In his official letter, dated 8 February 1954 and released by Smallwood, Valdmanis suggested three reasons for resigning. He fully appreciated the necessity of NALCO's chairman having his main residence in St John's, he was about to accept a job which would keep him very busy on the Canadian mainland and in the United States, and he asked for forgiveness where he had failed in his pursuit of economic development.[39] They were, after all, 'two men from two different worlds, very different worlds, neither of them easy to deal with,' as Valdmanis reminded Smallwood in his parting remarks.[40] An additional irritant, identified in Valdmanis's farewell notes to Smallwood, was the ongoing investigation by West German authorities into a suspected breach of foreign exchange control regulations and illegal export of capital by German investors to Newfoundland. Smallwood was worried that political opponents might exploit this as an indirect investigation into the execution of contracts Smallwood had signed as minister of economic development.

The issue flared up when Mrs Trudi Braun-Wogau (whose husband Max, vice-president of Superior Rubber Ltd, lay sick in a Swiss hospital) suddenly arrived on 7 February 1954 in St John's begging Smallwood and Valdmanis for help to have Ludwig Grube, president of Superior Rubber, released from a German prison. Grube had been arrested in Germany when an unreported $80,000 in cash, whose origin he could not explain, was found in his possession. To get him released, she needed an affidavit stating that Grube held the dollars in trust for a Canadian personality. But the premier and his director general of economic development Gordon Pushie refused to endorse such a statement and tangle with German courts. As with the preceding German investigation of MIAG director Herbert Marx, Smallwood feared that the Opposition would seize upon these irregularities and accuse him of offering a haven for illegal German capital exports and for Nazis. In addition, a Newfoundland government-ordered audit of Superior Rubber brought to light irregular bookkeeping, a transfer of $200,000 to New York, and an unexplained cash payment of $40,000 to Max Braun-Wogau. However, to get his friend Braun-Wogau off the hook and Grube out of jail, Valdmanis furnished the desired affidavit the day before he sent Smallwood his resignation as NALCO chairman.[41]

As a reminder of his continued usefulness, Valdmanis warned Smallwood, on 26 February 1954, that he had learned from his recent discussions with Consul General Reifferscheidt in Montreal that 'practically all Germans who had been connected with Newfoundland, are, or will be under investigation and that, indirectly but clearly this is an investigation directed *directly* against those German citizens who signed the contracts with you, but indirectly it is also an investigation into the execution of contracts which have been signed by the Premier in his capacity as Minister of Economic Development.' In his next meeting with the German consul general, Smallwood should point out, as Valdmanis had done, that it was natural for the German export value of exported machinery to differ from the fair value the Newfoundland government had placed on it. Smallwood should stress that 'there are two entirely different approaches – the Germans' approach, who are interested in receiving the export dollars for value shipped out of the country, and, a completely different standpoint, namely the value the Minister of Economic Development has placed upon the ready-made factories in Newfoundland.'

Reifferscheidt, Valdmanis asserted, would be willing to help on that basis. He would certainly want Smallwood to meet Chancellor Adenauer because Germans had not forgotten that Smallwood was the first Canadian statesman to call on them in 1950 while they were technically still at war with Canada. But Valdmanis shrewdly cautioned Smallwood that Reifferscheidt would not recommend the premier visit Adenauer 'as long as these little unpleasant incidents have not been cleared up.' Meanwhile, he had assured Reifferscheidt, Valdmanis indicated, that he was still a director of NALCO, that nothing had changed in his 'mutual and deep friendship' with Smallwood, and that his resignation had been entirely based on family reasons and his intentions to go into private business.[42]

Reifferscheidt, however, reported a different version to Bonn. Valdmanis had revealed to him confidentially that his resignation resulted from severe disagreements with Smallwood and Curtis over the consequences to be drawn from Canadian Javelin's non-fulfilment of its obligations. For economic and legal reasons Valdmanis had demanded NALCO's divorce from Canadian Javelin, while Smallwood for political reasons wanted to avoid a public scandal. In connection with the return of NALCO to government control, Smallwood allegedly demanded that Valdmanis move his residence to St John's, accept a civil service type of contract, and be readily available. Valdmanis had rejected this request for family and career reasons. It would, for instance, have prevented him from pursuing other business interests, such as his involvement in the North

Star Development Corporation, founded by him and linked to a south German commercial agency. According to Reifferscheidt's report, Valdmanis nonetheless claimed that as NALCO board member he promised Smallwood to see the German industries through their current problems until they were 'over the hill.'[43]

In support of his arguments Valdmanis handed the consul general five recent NALCO documents which Reifferscheidt attached to his report to Bonn. They were (1) the text of the agreement between NALCO and Canadian Javelin of 3 September 1953, (2) a letter by NALCO secretary-treasurer Ronald Turta of 4 January 1954 declaring that Canadian Javelin had defaulted on the agreement of 3 September 1953, (3) Valdmanis's request of 6 January 1954 that the Canadian Javelin directors confirm their resignation from NALCO, (4) Valdmanis's draft annual report as Chairman of NALCO, and (5) a memorandum drafted 17 February 1954 by Valdmanis entitled 'How Should NALCO Carry On?'

In this draft annual report, Valdmanis referred to NALCO as 'a completely new approach to the problem of rapid development of an underdeveloped country' but always in danger of becoming just another government department. Had it retained its original character as a Crown corporation, it would have generated slow development and low income and would have had to be subsidized by the government. However, to fulfil its mission as visualized by its founders, NALCO had to aim at the following: (1) expedite development by accepting calculated risks; (2) if necessary, go into development alone or with other companies, or sell their discoveries at a sound price; and (3) raise working and risk capital from people willing to take a calculated risk and share in its results. For its shares to be saleable, NALCO needed a solid administration and top scientists. These objectives had been fully accomplished in 1953. For NALCO this was the first 'exceedingly happy and successful year' in its forestry, mineral exploration, and financial aspects. With 'our little branch office in Montreal,' as Valdmanis termed it, enabling him to start recruiting field personnel early and by personal contacts on the mainland, he felt able to plan for 1954 with confidence.

The memorandum 'How Should NALCO Carry On?' elaborated on the central ideas of the draft annual report, namely, that NALCO 'represents a unique economic idea,' had 'outstanding success in 1953,' cannot go back without 'committing suicide,' and had to 'break into the mainland' economically by climbing 'on the stock market as the first Newfoundland company in history.' Instead of reducing its staff and 'farming out' its areas, like the Department of Mines and Resources, NALCO as befits 'a true business organization standing on its own feet and responsible to its shareholders only' must begin selling its voting stock to the public at large. Because NALCO could present a sound, capable, firmly established management together with areas and rights irrevocably granted, it could now dare to approach risk-takers, and would thus raise its own risk capital. This represented Valdmanis's last thoughts on making NALCO 'a unique and great success.'

The last time Valdmanis was in St John's in an official capacity was to take part in the annual meeting of NALCO from 8 to 10 April 1954 as a member of its board of directors. Smallwood needed his vote to finalize the purchase of a smaller block of NALCO shares by the Javelin group than originally planned, obtain the resignation of most of the Javelin group of directors, and revert control of NALCO to nominees of the Newfoundland government. At the end of this meeting, Valdmanis tendered his resignation from the NALCO board, noted the *Evening Telegram* inconspicuously on 12 April 1954, thus terminating all connection with the corporation. Shortly before, on 5 March, Alfred and Irma Valdmanis had become Canadian citizens. It was hard to abandon allegiance to their beloved Latvia, they wrote Smallwood, but because he had sponsored them he would always live in their memory as '*our*' (emphasis in the original) premier, 'in good as well as in bad times.'[44]

Valdmanis's last official presence in St John's went virtually unnoticed. Earlier, on Thursday, 11 February 1954, he had bid his public farewell. On that day St John's airport had been 'jammed' with friends and representatives of the new industries to see Valdmanis and his wife off. With 'tears in his eyes' he was reported saying 'goodbye to the industrialists he had brought here and the members of his staff.' Mrs Valdmanis was presented with a bouquet of roses. 'I did not expect you to come to say goodbye,' her husband had modestly responded. 'People have seemed more afraid of me than anything else.' A combination of business and family interests was taking him to Montreal, he explained, because 'we are Montrealers,' although he left a great part of himself in Newfoundland.[45] Representatives of the government were conspicuously absent.

'Dr Valdmanis severs his last connection with Newfoundland ... and is not likely to return here again except possibly as a visitor or on purely private business,' reported a news release by Premier Smallwood. The statement concluded with 'Newfoundland will not soon again see so remarkable a man as Alfred Valdmanis.'[46] The Latvian and the reasons for his departure remained a mystery to Newfoundlanders.

Media Perspectives

In the media speculation was rife about the exit of the 'enigmatic little man who caused more controversy in his four years with us than most public figures cause in a lifetime.' Could Premier Smallwood afford to jettison his 'right arm' just when his fledgling new industries needed expert guidance? In March rumours swept St John's that Smallwood was about to appropriate funds to have a statue erected in Bannerman Park to Dr Valdmanis. To public affairs critic Harold Horwood this was just malicious gossip, like the charge that Valdmanis was anti-Jewish or a German sympathizer during the Second World War. 'Gazing into our crystal ball we see a great blank where that statue ought to be.' Fuelled by enough evidence indicating a 'deep and irreparable rift between himself and his former employers,' the intriguing question persisted, 'Has the Doctor walked out or has he been relieved of his duties?'[47]

The sudden disappearance of the enigmatic Latvian from the Newfoundland stage put the question of his legacy to the province on the agenda. Albert Perlin wondered whether Valdmanis and Smallwood were not 'too much alike to pull too well together in harness for a long drive.' The Smallwood–Valdmanis team was terrific in its energy and dynamism, but ought to have been held in check by a third member urging caution and slowing down. Valdmanis, who 'flashed like a meteor across the Newfoundland sky,' would be remembered by what happened to the industries he helped to establish.[48] Perlin had speculated earlier that Valdmanis's resignation as director general signalled the beginning of his departure. As the 'galvanizing influence' on industrial development since 1950, Valdmanis had set a 'terrific' working pace and could even 'outvie Premier Smallwood in sustained ceaseless effort when a job is to be done.' As chairman of NALCO his presence in Newfoundland was not required, and he was free to accept other engagements on the mainland.[49]

On the whole, the North American media projected a very flattering image of Valdmanis's four years of achievements in Newfoundland. As recently as October 1953, *Business Week* had credited his 'expert professional advice' with helping to lay the groundwork for Newfoundland's development. After dipping into the treasury to point the way with 'three small sample industries,' Valdmanis had now placed this development 'safely in the hands of private enterprise.' His contacts abroad, the paper suggested, had 'tended to give Newfoundland's development program something of a continental flavor.'

Under the heading 'Newfoundland Looks to the Future,' the October 1952 issue of *G.M. Topics* depicted Smallwood's gamble as one of 'staggering proportions.' Its success was owed to his 'brilliant' young Latvian economist, who had been an inmate during part of the war years in German and Russian concentration camps. The cement and gypsum plants built by Valdmanis at almost half the price estimated by engineers, pushed Newfoundland's development towards bigger and better things. An article in *Time* magazine, on 22 September 1952, quoted Valdmanis as strongly disliking government-owned enterprise. But, the initial 'three sample plants' were working models of diversified industry needed to show to outside investors. In *Maclean's* magazine, on 30 August 1952, Gordon Pushie similarly credited Valdmanis with creating a booming atmosphere through initial, though subsequently undesirable, prime pumping.

To Harold Horwood, an astute news commentator for the *Evening Telegram*, however, the new industries program was regarded outside Newfoundland with too much admiration. He wrote, on 11 October 1952, that Newfoundlanders themselves were divided in their feelings towards the policy: 'Some think it is a miracle of progress, others think it is tens of millions of public money down the drain.' The local attitude was one 'either of cheers or sneers.' With the prospect of twenty-five industries following the 1951 Smallwood–Valdmanis trip to Germany, publicity became both lavish and consistently favourable, Horwood observed. No one expected the program to assume the scope it did. Horwood speculated that in retrospect this era might be looked upon as Newfoundland's great awakening.

The foreign-language press shared this optimistic note. The German Canadian weekly *Der Courier*, on 16 July 1952, attributed 'the miracle of Newfoundland' almost entirely to Valdmanis. It was Valdmanis who had brought Smallwood to Bonn where eighty reporters took note of Newfoundland's quest for German specialists and industries; he had prepared the financial arrangements enabling Germans to invest in Newfoundland; and he had been working on the exploration of Labrador's resources. In an article of 2 May 1952 entitled 'Newfoundland – Land of the Future,' Switzerland's leading financial paper *Der Bund* portrayed Valdmanis as the experienced professional, guiding Newfoundland's development with care, foresight, and forcefulness. 'His presence alone guarantees to a European that in Newfoundland he is in a country of friends.' Although economically and politically Newfoundland was Canada, it was for the Swiss the nearest and most European country across the ocean.

On the occasion of his visit to Sweden, in the company of Smallwood in October 1951, the Swedish press lavished nothing but praise on Valdmanis. Without critical editorial comments, right- and left-wing papers reproduced Smallwood's attribution of credit to Valdmanis for launching Newfoundland on the road to industrial development 'after a 400-year sleep.' This was the same Valdmanis, *Dagens Nyheter, Socialins Tidungen,* and *Sanska Dagbladet* reminded their readers on 3 October 1951, who had caused a sensation before the war when at the age of twenty-nine he had become Europe's youngest finance minister.

For reporter James Montagnes, writing for the *Memphis Press – Scimitar* and the *Quebec Chronicle Telegraph,* on 19 and 25 January 1952, Valdmanis was an important figure in the North American economy. 'He used his knowledge of economics and industrial development in northeastern Europe to develop Newfoundland's economy, where he found similar natural resources, only more of them, than in his native land.' About his background the paper incorrectly stated that he was thrown into a prison camp in 1941 by the Russians and left there by the Germans after they had driven out the Russians, and that he was not released until 1945.

Many Canadians read Ian Sclanders's 'They're Betting Newfoundland's Bankroll,' in *Maclean's* magazine of 1 July 1952. The subtitle neatly wraps up its thesis: 'Premier Joey Smallwood, with a refugee expert named Alfred Valdmanis calling the shots, is gambling millions on an industrial revolution that is already changing Canada's newest province.' Even Smallwood's worst political enemies had to admit that Newfoundland was booming as never before in history and that Valdmanis deserved much of the credit. An American steel corporation, watching his handling of the cement project, had allegedly offered him a job at $50,000 a year. The article characterized Valdmanis as a pleasant-looking man of forty-three, who 'works as hard as the cod fishermen. He reaches his office sharp at nine every morning, including Sundays, and seldom quits before nine at night.'

Earlier major feature articles, both appearing in April 1951, were similarly preoccupied with Valdmanis's unconventional appearance and habits. Robert Johnson, in 'Valdmanis: A Latvian in Newfoundland,' published in *Canadian Business* (and repeated as 'The Life Story of Alfred Valdmanis' in the St John's *Daily News,* 1 May 1951), described Valdmanis as a man who would not talk about himself, shunned publicity, did not smoke nor drink hard liquor, led a lonely life in a world of his own, played piano and tennis, and set a working pace almost impossible to match. While putting into operation some of his boyhood dreams about social and economic development, Valdmanis is perceptively quoted arguing to the builders of the cement and gypsum plants: 'Gentlemen, you must not have any profit this time, but there is more business here for you. Why not forego short-term gain for future profits?' Rupert Jackson's 'Industry Builder' in *Atlantic Guardian* repeated the same personal characteristics almost literally and commented on the penetrating light in Valdmanis's eyes. Media attention focused on even such minor details as Valdmanis's habit of taking off his shoes while flying.[50]

On 9 November 1950 Rupert Jackson introduced the director general in the Windsor *Morning Star* as part of a trio from Latvia – together with Olga Leikucs and Arnolds Graudins – giving 'dynamic' leadership to the development of Newfoundland. Valdmanis, although only 42 then, was 'a man of rare talents.' Starting on his second career after having already 'packed a long career into his lifetime,' his credentials were alleged to have included special leadership training in his native land and a 'string of degrees' from master of economics and philosophy to doctor of jurisprudence from Frankfurt University. His record also included initiating research industries and directing several industrial developments. He had also been held a political prisoner at various times by the Russians and Germans.

On the occasion of his appointment in Newfoundland, a local paper had featured this exotic and – for North Americans – enigmatic career in front-page exposure 'like something out of a story-book': he was one of seven hundred boys who had been specially selected to be trained for leadership in Latvia, at age twenty-three he was a doctor of jurisprudence at the University of Frankfurt, as a 'foe of the nation' he had endured severe ordeals under Soviet and Nazi occupation but the king of Sweden had intervened to save him; he had saved eight hundred people from death in the bombing of a Berlin public building and thus was a sure bet for a high decoration for bravery, he was a top planner with IRO in Geneva, he was in high demand in Ottawa when Smallwood hired him, and so on.[51] Following this first major portrayal, the repetition of the embellished highlights of Valdmanis's fantastic career (as originally presented to the Canadian Senate in 1949) became a regular identification mark. It accompanied, with minor variations, press comments on his subsequent achievements in Newfoundland.

Valdmanis was not always highlighted in reviews of Newfoundland's economic development. For example, major articles in the *Times Weekly Review* and the *Financial Post*[52] ignored him completely in the summer of 1953. Outright negative comments, however, were rare before 1954. The *Times Weekly Review* of August 1953, for instance, attributed the strengths and weaknesses of Newfoundland's industrial progress entirely to Premier Smallwood who 'almost single-handed[ly]' had brought Newfoundland to outside notice 'in a way no one else has ever succeeded in doing.'[53]

In the spring of 1954, by contrast, press comments began to take their cue from the political opposition which, in the absence of positive information on the progress of the new industries and their financial condition, resorted to wholesale condemnation. Thirty million dollars had been poured into projects backed by the 'sinister' Valdmanis who 'packed his bag and left Newfoundland with his loot,' Opposition leader Malcolm Hollet charged. Moreover, his friends from all over the world had proceeded to clean up on the surplus bequeathed by the pre-Confederation government. According to Hollet, Valdmanis had become a director of the American firm Douay Import and Export and, during his term as director general of economic development, invested heavily in such companies as a fish plant near St Andrews, New Brunswick. Were the stone blocks outside the government Colonial Building intended for a statue of Dr Valdmanis or as tombstones for his new industries? Hollet wondered.[54]

In his 'Notebook' column of 13 March 1954 Harold Horwood speculated that Valdmanis had arranged the deal, never made public, by which Javelin would buy NALCO for $7,500,000. Valdmanis must have left under a cloud of government disapproval, he suspected, because during the storm of Opposition abuse the premier 'sat in stony silence' uttering not a word in defence of his former paladin. Horwood insinuated that the arrangements with the European industrialists were murky. He 'gravely' doubted that all of them invested their 50 per cent share into the enterprise. 'Certainly there was opportunity,' he concluded prophetically, 'for financial manipulation and misappropriation of funds.' Whether anyone had taken advantage of that opportunity, he claimed not to know yet.[55]

chapter eleven

'Something Had Happened and a Culprit Had to Be Found': Con Man or Scapegoat? 1954–1957

I was on a lonely island (Newfoundland), sold and buried, mainly because of the fact that something had happened and a culprit had to be found. I was all alone without friends and without roots in a foreign land where I had done so much good. I saw that a human being is so little that he cannot die even if he wanted to. I have seen the sense of life collapsing.

Alfred Valdmanis in 1963[1]

Arrest

Two weeks after Alfred Valdmanis had terminated all official connections with Newfoundland, Premier Joey Smallwood opened the final round in the enigmatic Latvian's career. It was a bombshell. At 5 a.m. on 23 April 1954 Smallwood called the Canadian Press representative in St John's to tell him that Valdmanis had just been arrested in New Brunswick on criminal charges of extortion. He was accused of pocketing large sums of money from various firms he had been dealing with on behalf of the government of Newfoundland. Apparently Smallwood had not suspected any personal dishonesty when he had demanded Valdmanis's resignation from NALCO. Requesting the arrest of a person with such great talents, Smallwood now confessed, was the most unpleasant duty he had ever had to perform. It came after growing suspicions and quiet investigations following Valdmanis's departure.[2]

Smallwood disclosed, a year later in a long night session of the Newfoundland legislature, that sometime in March 1954 a mutual acquaintance had drawn his attention to a 10 per cent commission for the premier's party and received by Valdmanis from Benno Schilde on the price contracted for the gypsum plant in 1950. At the time Valdmanis had insisted that the premier must not be involved in the deal. Also, as construction proceeded, payments were to be made to the American Express Company in New York City into an account of Katrina Mateus, the sister of Valdmanis's wife. The informant identified Benno Schilde director Dr Hubertus Herz as a witness to the transactions. Anxious to get to the bottom of the matter before someone else would expose it, Smallwood asked Herz to confirm the allegations in writing. From Herz, Smallwood learned that the German foreign exchange control authority had approved the dollar transactions of Schilde on the ground that the firm of MIAG had shortly before been granted a similar request to remit commission payments to New York. Armed with this evidence, Smallwood had called the superintendent of the RCMP at midnight and demanded that he immediately trace the payments in New York, recover the money, and have Valdmanis arrested and charged. Smallwood was anxious to take full and sole credit for the prosecution of his former 'close friend and collaborator ... who had been closer to me than any other man.'[3]

The main points of Smallwood's account are confirmed by Herz. From 5 to 21 April 1954 Herz was in Newfoundland to resolve the fate of an additional $150,000 Smallwood had agreed in 1952 to pay Benno Schilde towards an unexpected increase of $200,000 in expenses incurred during construction of the gypsum plant. Benno Schilde wanted the money released without further obligations. But Smallwood always insisted that this ex gratia payment must be invested in Eastern Machinery and Engineering Company (EMENCO), a Benno Schilde subsidiary, which was to manufacture industrial equipment in Bay Roberts. In negotiations with Schilde directors in March 1953 in St John's, Premier Smallwood had signed a memorandum of agreement setting up the company with a capital of $200,000. According to the deed, three shares of $100 each had been issued to its nominal founders: solicitor Donald W.K. Dawe, his sister M.M. Dawe, and engineer Ernest Leja.[4]

Herz, however, continued to look for ways to get out of the EMENCO commitment because Benno Schilde had lost money on the gypsum plant deal. In December 1953 Valdmanis seemed to be offering a solution when he pressured Herz to remit the last instalment of $40,000 of the secret $200,000 commission as a quid pro quo for giving notice that Benno Schilde had abandoned the EMENCO plan. Under the impression from Valdmanis that the commission was intended for the Liberal party, Herz travelled to Canada in January 1954, borrowed the money from the Canadian account Smallwood had set up for EMENCO, and wanted to deliver it personally to the Liberal party treasurer in Ottawa. But Valdmanis insisted that the payment had to be made through him and led Leja to believe that this had been demanded by Smallwood, then vacationing in Jamaica. In February, Smallwood was back, and, to the surprise of Leja and Herz, was angrily insisting that Benno Schilde honour its commitment to EMENCO. Leja now had to reassure Smallwood that although Benno Schilde had no intention to renege on EMENCO, its hands were tied by current German government investigations threatening a heavy tax on the $150,000 refund. Leja became increasingly suspicious when Valdmanis unexpectedly resigned from NALCO that same month and, in March, immediately repaid into the EMENCO account the $40,000 Herz had borrowed from it for the 'commission.'[5]

What put Smallwood on the track of secret kickbacks to Valdmanis, according to a confidential memorandum to Smallwood by Herz of 22 April 1954, was Leja's worry about his own innocent involvement in the scheme of collecting commissions allegedly for the Liberal party. Since Leja had witnessed this and previous transactions, he was unwittingly an accomplice in the extraction of commission payments, and he began to question whether the money had actually been going to the Liberal party. Leja decided he would inquire with the party's treasurer Senator Ray Petten in Ottawa – and found that none of the new industries had made any financial contributions.

Petten then informed Smallwood of Leja's inquiry and suspicions and prompted the premier to press Leja and Herz for full details of Valdmanis's financial manipulations. They willingly supplied the evidence Smallwood requested, namely, that Valdmanis had demanded and received payments to Katrina Mateus of $50,000 each in January and June 1951, $25,000 each in September and October 1951, and $10,000 in March 1953. Initially Smallwood indicated he wanted to refund everything to the original donors. If Leja could persuade Smallwood to return some of the money, Herz was prepared to offer Leja rewards ranging from $10,000 for the return of $20,000, to $30,000 for the return of the full amount of $160,000 to Benno Schilde.[6]

From Leja, Herz also learned that, apparently unknown to Smallwood, Valdmanis was a major shareholder in several of the new industries he had brought to Newfoundland, in particular the Canadian Industries Construction Holding Trust which was the umbrella organization of the MIAG subsidiary in Newfoundland. From its head, Johannes Lerch,

Valdmanis was alleged to have received large sums of money – Leja had seen a MIAG cheque for $60,000 issued to Katrina Mateus in Valdmanis's office. Leja suspected that Valdmanis was also involved in the schemes of Max Braun-Wogau and the fraud of Lothar Sennewald. The latter was the scoundrel whom Smallwood was forcing to work in the St John's General Hospital to repay the money he had diverted from a $150,000 government credit (see Chapter 8). Smallwood had always wondered, Leja recalled, why Valdmanis suddenly turned white when told how the RCMP had uncovered Sennewald's fraudulent financial transactions.[7]

The *Ottawa Evening Journal* was the first Canadian paper to break the story of Valdmanis's arrest. The following was on its front page on 23 April 1954: 'Ex-economic chief of Newfoundland arrested by RCMP on extortion charge. Very large sums allegedly taken in official deals.' Referring to Valdmanis as the 'economic mystery man who came to Canada as a displaced person,' the paper devoted a whole page to the details of Valdmanis's arrest, his role as 'probably one of the highest paid civil servants in Canada,' and his 'story-book career' as presented in 1949 to the Senate Labour and Immigration Committee.

The next day, numerous other Canadian papers featured the story. The *Ottawa Journal* suggested that a guilty verdict might bring considerable political fallout. The Montreal *Gazette* thought that 'the resignation of the whole Smallwood Liberal cabinet must automatically follow a conviction.' The St John's *Evening Telegram* of 24 April carried the front-page headline: 'Latvian must be "innocent." Valdmanis brother taken by surprise, knew nothing.' Canada's national German-language paper *Der Nordwesten*, on 28 April 1954, wondered whether there was a factual basis for all the accusations levelled against 'the Latvian Schacht,' who had pledged to turn the fishermen's province of Newfoundland into a German-type of Ruhr area.

The Public, the Media, and the Trial

Alfred Valdmanis was arrested on 23 April 1954 at 2 a.m. at his brother Osvald's home in St Andrews, New Brunswick, where Alfred had bought a fish-processing plant that January. Given twenty minutes to dress, he was taken to the Saint John (New Brunswick) County Jail to be sent for trial to Newfoundland.

In Newfoundland, with its 96 per cent homogeneous population of British origin, historic lack of steady immigration, and latent suspicion of 'foreigners,' the arrest and trial of the controversial Latvian wizard was a public sensation of the first order to be remembered for decades. Valdmanis arrived in St John's on a heavy North Star aircraft from Saint John on Saturday, 25 April, at 3:55 p.m. As reported in the *Daily News*, 'The airport was crowded with hordes of curious citizens, and the approaches were lined with hundreds of vehicles.' At the ramp, Valdmanis, under police escort, was whisked into a black RCMP car, and taken to the court-house where again large crowds were waiting for him. He was charged, upon the complaint of Joseph R. Smallwood, with having defrauded the government of Newfoundland of $150,000 in the period January to October 1951. When ordered remanded in custody without bail for eight days, 'he remained ramrod stiff and looking straight ahead.'[8]

On Sunday the papers were full of news that appeared to promise sensational disclosures in upcoming court appearances. The hottest item was that a leading member of the political Opposition, former Progressive Conservative Member of Parliament for St John's East Gordon F. Higgins, was assuming the defence of Valdmanis. (The public did not learn that Valdmanis had first approached Donald W.K. Dawe, partner in a law firm with Attorney-General Curtis, to defend him.[9]) When the Lady Davis Foundation publicly denied retaining Higgins, Higgins was only too happy to supply the media with certified copies of telegrams confirming that Irma Valdmanis had sought legal counsel from the Lady Davis Foundation in Montreal whose solicitors, Messrs Phillips, Bloomfield, Vineberg, and Goodman recommended their St John's correspondents Messrs Hunt, Emerson, Stirling, and Higgins.[10] This was ironically the same Higgins who had earlier raised questions about Valdmanis in Parliament.

Valdmanis made a number of requests to speak to Premier Smallwood about his arrest. Smallwood would not talk to him. Confined in the St John's Penitentiary, Valdmanis was reported as refusing to mix with other prisoners, accept the services of a chaplain, or ask for any extra tobacco rations as was the habit of many prisoners. The premier, meanwhile, announced his intention to allow no privileges over those of other prisoners and to lay additional charges upon completion of the current investigation. On 1 May the public learned of an additional criminal charge against Valdmanis for defrauding MIAG of $360,000. This amount was reduced to $270,000 two days later. Smallwood was determined to steal the thunder from under both the political Opposition and the media with their demands for a royal commission of inquiry into the extent of mismanagement of the new industries as well as secret kickbacks from them.[11]

Surprisingly, the media initially portrayed Valdmanis's plight in a sympathetic light. Eating and sleeping very little since his arrest, he was reported to be incapable of preparing instructions for his defence. The trial would be a farce, Higgins kept arguing in court, unless his client was freed on bail for four to six weeks. St John's psychiatrist Dr E.L. Sharpe had given Valdmanis sedatives and testified that his patient had memory problems, blackouts, and all the symptoms of one on the verge of a breakdown. Court-appointed Dr W. Black, psychiatrist at St John's Hospital for Mental and Nervous Diseases, considered Valdmanis mentally sound, although he did complain of heart pains, headaches, and a night-time feeling of claustrophobia. On 1 May Higgins announced that he would seek a writ of habeas corpus should bail again be denied.[12]

Finally, Valdmanis was freed on 7 May after bail had been set at $100,000. Valdmanis put up $50,000 of his own money and Margaret Kavanagh, wife of a St John's dentist, and Mary Higgins, mother of the defence lawyer, each arranged an additional $25,000. For the first time in memory, women stood as 'bondsmen' in Newfoundland, the *Evening Telegram* noted. When Valdmanis was freed on bail, 'crowds blocked the court room, people stared in what courthouse windows provided vantage points [and] more crowds lined part of Duckworth and Water Streets.' However, two days later, on 9 May, Valdmanis was rearrested at his lawyer's residence. This arrest arose from a civil action taken by the government of Newfoundland for the recovery of $270,000, allegedly received by Valdmanis from the German firm of MIAG. In the House of Assembly Opposition member W.J. Browne wondered why the government was involved in a suit that should properly by brought by the German firm in question.[13]

During his brief two-day release on bail, Valdmanis visited his aged mother who was staying with his sister-in-law Dr Velta Mikelsons in St John's. When they learned Valdmanis was to be rearrested, Mikelsons accompanied him to the residence of Higgins.[14] The press did not seem to be aware that before his rearrest he also went to Holyrood to visit his friend Max Braun-Wogau, vice-president of Superior Rubber.[15] Alfred Valdmanis was determined that his wife Irma not see him in prison, a situation she could never have imagined 'in her wildest dreams,' he told a reporter before his rearrest. Devoted to raising their four children, Irma had stayed out of politics and out of her husband's work. Nevertheless, she did visit him and stayed in St John's until the end of June accompanied by her Toronto lawyer Joseph Sedgwick. On 11 June Olga Leikucs, who had resigned as Valdmanis's assistant on 31 August 1953, arrived for one-and a-half days. During this surprise meeting 'she was wearing a smart blue coat and white hat,' the press noted, but the purpose of her visit remained unknown.[16]

Newfoundland Attorney General L.R. Curtis's intent with the warrant of arrest was to prevent Valdmanis from escaping or disposing of any of his property.[17] After his rearrest, Valdmanis was not jailed, but kept under custody in the Newfoundland Hotel. On 7 June he was moved to the cheaper Cochrane Hotel. In the legislature the Opposition accused the government of treating the Latvian as if he were behind the Iron Curtain. Attorney General Curtis deplored the 'veritable campaign of propaganda inspired by those responsible for his defence,' whose alleged objective was to arouse public sympathy for the accused. Curtis explained that a person out on bail was permitted to leave the province and the country. The same people now making propaganda in favour of Valdmanis, Curtis retorted, would have blamed the government if Valdmanis vanished.[18]

The extensive publicity and political flavour given to the case became a matter of considerable concern even to the Supreme Court of Newfoundland during the summer of 1954. Chief Justice Sir Albert Walsh chastised the media in particular on a number of issues. These included (1) the publication of both a statement of claim by the government and abstracts of affidavits filed to support the order for rearrest on civil charges, (2) the reference to the trial as a 'farce,' (3) the suggestion that certain court action may amount to 'persecution rather than prosecution,' and (4) the 'very unfortunate' ongoing 'trial by newspaper and trial by radio' instead of trial on the evidence produced in court. The affidavits in question were by MIAG officials Heinz-Joachim Wilke and Erich Kirmse confirming the transfer to Valdmanis of $270,000, and by Joey Smallwood denying that authority had been given to collect these commissions. The judges felt compelled to issue a 'clear warning' that they would not tolerate anything prejudicing a fair trial or anyone transgressing proper principles of common law.[19]

The preliminary inquiry, originally scheduled for 5 June, but postponed several times to await the arrival of witnesses, finally got under way on 2 August. It lasted one week. Eleven witnesses, including six from Germany, testified in closed hearings. 'Quite calm and collected on entering and leaving the court,' Valdmanis told newsmen he was eager to start fighting the revised charges of unlawfully defrauding the government of Newfoundland of $270,000 between August 1950 and 31 October 1951, and of $200,000 between 2 January 1951 and 24 February 1954.

On 9 August he was committed for trial on 21 September, and returned to jail because bail was refused.[20]

In a dramatic and surprise courtroom move on 15 September 1954, one day before the date set for a bail request, Alfred Valdmanis abruptly changed his plea to guilty on the second charge. He had decided 'to ask for a light sentence rather than fight to its bitter end a case that promised the ultimate in sensational revelations.' He turned over all his assets – valued at $568,750.80, and, one would have thought, more than enough to make restitution. It was not revealed until March 1957 that subsequent sales of these assets netted only $13,450. Since few were aware of the 15 September hearing, only lawyers, police, and reporters occupied the benches. Looking tired, the defendant was reported standing 'at attention between two red-coated Mounties,' while his lawyer Higgins pleaded for over half an hour with the court to exercise the greatest clemency possible.[21]

In his plea Higgins reviewed the 'extraordinary' career of his client and quoted Smallwood's widely broadcasted public tributes of October and November 1951 to Valdmanis's work. If the new industries turned out to be as successful as the premier believed, Higgins asserted, 'we must give credit to the prisoner for bringing them about.' Doing everything possible to arouse the court's sympathy for his client, Higgins credited Valdmanis even with bravery. Higgins recounted that during an air raid on Berlin his client had risked his own life to calm eight hundred people caught under a burning public building and guide them to safety. The last one to leave the burning site, he suffered irreparable damage to his eyes. Now his career was finished. His admission of fraud was already a severe punishment for him. Moreover, he would lose his Canadian citizenship and Canada would deport him if the Department of National Revenue pursued criminal proceedings against him, as was likely.

Chief Justice Sir Albert Walsh reserved sentencing for two days while considering the clemency plea. On 17 September the courtroom was so packed that several lawyers and reporters had to sit in the vacant jury box, reported the *Montreal Star*. Several hundred people crowded around the old stone court-house to gawk at 'the neatly dressed prisoner who had been the centre of political controversies in Newfoundland.' To their disappointment, the proceedings took less than five minutes. The sentence for the charge to which he had pleaded guilty was four years at hard labour to be served at St John's. (Hard labour, St John's penitentiary Superintendent Case explained to the media the next day, meant any work assigned to prisoners.[22]) On motion of Solicitor General Myles

Murray, the first charge was suspended *sine die*, that is, postponed indefinitely at the prosecution's discretion. The civil action was also dropped, since Valdmanis agreed to turn over all his assets, except for his home in Montreal which was mortgaged in his wife's name. When Walsh pronounced the severe sentence – five years was the maximum penalty under the charge – 'the prisoner's head sagged, his eyes blinked, and he swallowed hard. Then he was led off by two Mounties.'[23]

The sensational case was over. It ended abruptly with no evidence heard, and the long-expected trial, set for 21 September with a double-panel jury, never took place. Inevitably, rumours of a cover-up began to circulate. In March 1955 Attorney General Curtis disclosed that three reasons had led to acceptance the 'guilty' plea which was made at the earnest request of Valdmanis's counsel in Montreal and to dropping the other charges. First, what would a trial accomplish? There was no use 'whipping a dead horse.' Second, the case would be very expensive to prosecute. The needed witnesses from Germany might not even come. Finally, it was not in Newfoundland's interest to proceed since it showed every indication of developing into a 'purely political trial.'[24] To this day, the 'inside' story of the Valdmanis trial remains unknown. This despite periodic media reviews of contradictory, incredible episodes of his 'storybook career.'

What the *Evening Telegram*, (on 15 September 1954) characterized as 'the Valdmanis economic era' had now become history. It had been

> a fantastic epoch in which he brought 13 industries to Newfoundland, all of them still controversial, none of them yet a certain financial success, some of them apparently headed for receivership ... It was an era labelled by the political Opposition 'the Smallwood–Valdmanis Government.' For at least part of this period the dark little Doctor from the Baltic was Premier Smallwood's only real advisor, and pulled far more weight in shaping Government policy than did any Member of the Cabinet. The Premier called him 'the greatest man ever to come to Newfoundland,' and declared, 'No Government is served by a man more loyal, or with greater effect and efficiency.'

Widely respected Newfoundland current affairs commentator Albert Perlin summed up the public's disappointment over the absence of evidence and the mysteriousness of the whole business. He wondered, 'How, for example, was it first discovered that Valdmanis was getting money from German industrialists? Why did he not realize that some of the large investments he was making would cause suspicion? Why did he linger for five months in prison, waiting until three or four days before his trial, before he pleaded guilty to one of the charges? These and many other questions remain unanswered to make Valdmanis hardly less mysterious after sentence than he was at any time before.' Perlin, who had met Valdmanis quite a few times, was left with the impression of an 'odd person, volatile and nervous,' who appeared like the 'highly-practised graduate of an authoritarian school.' Perlin could not recall much of his 'rambling' conversations, but often suspected him to be a 'man in a hurry,' whose concern for Newfoundland's development was no greater than his desire to enrich himself on the side. 'The mystery that has surrounded Valdmanis from the beginning,' Perlin concluded, 'has stayed with him to the end.'[25]

Outright damning was the information gathered by columnist Harold Horwood, a former Smallwood associate and friend-turned-critic. By September 1954 Horwood had come to consider the Valdmanis story a systematically cultivated legend, 'sufficiently fantastic even in its factual outline ... like something out of Arabian Nights.' Bothered by the constant reappearance of bits and pieces of this legend as 'cold, hard fact,' Horwood set about separating 'proven fact' from fiction. Accordingly, he concluded that Valdmanis was (1) a powerful member of a pro-fascist government in Latvia from 1938 to 1940 and 'virtual Tsar of his country's finance and industry,' (2) a recipient of the Swedish order of Stella Polaris, an honour 'passed out wholesale' to European bureaucrats to build goodwill for Sweden, (3) in important positions for Hitler's Nazis during the Second World War, (4) a friend of many Prussian industrialist top brass, (5) a displaced persons adviser for the Americans after the war, (6) a refugee immigrant to Canada, and (7) a Department of Immigration adviser promoting the Baltic Waffen-SS – despite their deserved 'reputation second to none for war crimes and atrocities against humanity' – as desirable citizens.

Horwood found no evidence to support Valdmanis's claims that (1) he was condemned to be shot by the Russians and the Germans (how could someone escaping an SS firing squad by the skin of his teeth end up with an executive job in the German war effort? Horwood wondered), (2) the king of Sweden intervened with Hitler to save his life, (3) the Bolsheviks imprisoned and tortured him, (4) he rose to prominence in Latvia because the Latvian government sponsored a competitive education scheme that selected the smartest of the smartest for top government positions, and (5) he fathered NALCO, the brainchild of Smallwood.[26]

As his source for debunking the Valdmanis legend, Harold Horwood credits Latvians in Canada. It is not known whether any of Horwood's informers lived in Newfoundland. Intelligence critical of Valdmanis's past, however, was not difficult to come by. The Stockholm Committee of the Latvian Social Democratic Workers Party, for example, had for years spared no effort to defame Valdmanis as a 'Latvian traitor' and 'quisling.' After the news of Valdmanis's arrest broke on 23 April 1954, the secretary of the Stockholm committee, Laimonis Esenvalds, sent letters to such newspapers as the *New York Times* refuting the claim that Valdmanis was imprisoned in a concentration camp. Instead, he termed Valdmanis a prominent collaborator until 1945, who subsequently 'has always been an intercessor for pro-fascist ideas.'[27]

Esenvalds also asked his fellow Social Democrats in the Cooperative Commonwealth Federation (CCF) in Ottawa to inform the Canadian press, members of Parliament, and the public about the following 'true facts': Valdmanis was neither imprisoned by the Nazis, nor released by a personal intervention of the Swedish king; he was not active among any of the resistance groups in Latvia but was a 'high Nazi official' during the war, planning the mobilization of Latvian youth into the German army; and instead of suffering under the Russian and German occupations, he ended up 'comfortably situated in Berlin drawing a two thousand Reichsmark salary monthly.' With the extorted money, according to the Stockholm committee, Valdmanis supported such Latvian fascist newspapers as *Latvija Amērikā* (Toronto), *Ceļa Zīmes* (Signposts, London), and *Latvju Vārds* (The Word of Latvians, Stockholm), anti-democratic groups, and an anti-democratic Latvian world organization.[28]

Who is this Valdmanis, wondered Canada's national German-language paper *Der Nordwesten*, on 22 September 1954, who arrived as a penniless DP in Canada yet was not satisfied with a salary exceeding that of the prime minister? His true character as a carpetbagger who always managed to land on his feet had been recognized long before. It was no accident that the Germany of the early postwar years, 'this most lucrative fishing ground of all charlatans,' was especially close to his heart. England had refused to fall for his sweet talk. It would be the ultimate irony if he were deported back to the Germany he had denounced, although it had freed him from the claws of the Bolsheviks in 1941 and offered him asylum in 1945.

The Defence

Because Valdmanis never took the stand in his defence, lurking suspicions remain. Did he plead guilty under duress? Was he framed? Was a backstage deal struck to prevent his side of the story from being publicized? Even such a relatively prominent person as Bobbie Robertson, St John's representative of the federal Department of Trade and Commerce, considered the outsider and foreigner Valdmanis to have been a scapegoat in an environment of crooked local politicians. She believed at least one of Premier Smallwood's close associates in the cabinet to have been in cahoots with Valdmanis on some of the deals of which the latter was accused.[29]

Feelings ran especially high among Latvians. The Very Reverend Alfreds Skrodelis, Dean and Representative of the Latvian Lutheran Archbishop in Canada, who on 12 June 1954 held a service at St Thomas Church for the apprehensive local Latvian community, sent Gordon Higgins a character reference of 'Dr Alfred Waldmanis' whom he had known since 1938 as a person of honesty and 'ethical purity.' Skrodelis found it hard to imagine that the accused could have deliberately wronged the interests of Newfoundland.[30] Ojārs Gobiņš, in New York, expressed the sentiment of many Latvians to whom the charges against Valdmanis seemed 'completely unbelievable.' He reminded Smallwood that it was not easy to find another man of such unusual devotion to his duty, who in Latvia had 'worked nights and days to carry out the plans of the Latvian Government, disregarding his health and refusing any extra compensation' and who after the war had devoted all his energies to help displaced persons. Valdmanis's manner may seem strange, maintained Gobins, for he is 'the kind of person who does rather than talks' and whose chief weakness was that 'he never defends himself, for he believes that what he does is right.'[31]

Alfred's brother Emils believed that Alfred was being victimized by his former political enemies. From Stockholm he advised using the trial to unmask the denouncers, 'whether they come from our own people or from the ranks of foreigners and regardless how high the status they are occupying.' According to Emils, the prosecution was being interpreted in loyal Latvian circles as follows: (1) Latvian opponents of Valdmanis were convinced that, despite his public disclaimer, he still had ambitions in Latvian politics; (2) they had snooped out each of Valdmanis's moves and actions in New York, looking for evidence they could use against him; (3) Alfreds Bērziņš was the head of the anti-Valdmanis faction in New York, which had secretly swayed Ernest Leja and his associates to act; and (4) Valdmanis had no trusted persons to warn him in time of those 'scoundrels.' Emils reported that leading Latvians in Sweden had been collecting signatures as an expression of loyalty and support, all hoping that Valdmanis would be able to fight off the accusations.[32]

With what evidence or arguments had Valdmanis planned to plead his innocence? Even the prosecution did not appear to have been privy to most of the details and overall strategy of the defence. In March 1955 Attorney General Curtis speculated in the Newfoundland legislature about four arguments Valdmanis could have raised on his own behalf. First, he could have denied the payments. This tactic might have been successful had the witnesses refused either to come from Germany or to testify. Second, he could have admitted that he received the money and repaid it to the premier. Third, with the cooperation of the MIAG and Benno Schilde management, he might have argued that he had received the funds to hold in trust for them. Finally, he might have argued that he received and invested the money for the Liberal party or the premier. Knowing Valdmanis to be resourceful and capable, Solicitor General Myles Murray recalled later, Smallwood was clearly worried what the accused might say or do if the money were never found.[33]

While in prison and awaiting his trial Valdmanis had in fact prepared for Higgins an elaborate defence consisting of some twenty-six statements on various aspects of his activities from May 1950 to May 1954. These were drafted from memory because in April 1954 the RCMP had raided Valdmanis's home in Montreal and confiscated all his personal papers and correspondence.[34] Concerning questions about his doctoral degree, Higgins was able to refer to two testimonies of July 1954. One was from Wilhelm Burmeister, a retired official of the former Reich Ministry of Science and Education, and the other from Janis Krumins, a St John's physician. These certified that in 1943 Valdmanis had been granted special permission in Germany to use the title of doctor on the grounds of having earned a master's degree at the University of Latvia.[35]

Central to Valdmanis's argument is his acknowledgment that he collected commission payments from MIAG and Benno Schilde and invested them, but he identified Premier Smallwood as the mastermind of the plot. Smallwood, he claimed, wanted him to do this for the needs of his Liberal party, for the premier allegedly saw government bribes as the only way to fund his party; a party in power always needed money, especially Newfoundland's Liberals, who could depend on neither federal

Liberal charity nor local business support. Smallwood, known for saying, 'Water Street would raise half a million of dollars against him within a week, but not for him,' supposedly considered foreign contracts the best source of party funds.[36]

Smallwood's political role model in Newfoundland, claimed defence statements, was Richard Squires, reputed to be a politically astute scoundrel. Pursuing a policy of economic diversification and development, Squires had finished his two terms of office as prime minister of Newfoundland (1921–3 and 1928–32) in a morass of corruption and scandals that ended with Newfoundland bankrupt. According to Valdmanis, Smallwood used to say, 'Sir Richard Squires did one very foolish thing. He, himself, used to be a collector of money for his Party Fund. That finally broke him ... they will never catch me like that.' To realize his dreams, 'by hook or by crook,' as Smallwood put it, he needed to be financially able to spring an election at any time. A 10 per cent commission was the rule on government contracts, Smallwood allegedly told Valdmanis, a practice every child knew was the only way to acquire some slush funds. The premier emphasized that this 'was the accepted thing everywhere, everybody knew it.' Smallwood insisted, however, that he must be kept entirely out of these deals: 'I know nothing and will never know anything. But I will be right there with you.'[37]

Smallwood's main desire was to stay in power, Valdmanis submitted, especially to ensure the success of his economic development program. He needed Valdmanis to produce immediate results. There was no time for long planning, sitting, and debating while the most daring and best Newfoundlanders migrated to the mainland. Valdmanis came to like Smallwood and his 'wild enthusiasm.' After some hesitation, therefore, he had promised not to let him down and agreed to take charge of the whole business – both new industries and Liberal party commissions. Smallwood would pilot the deals through the institutions so Valdmanis was not to worry about anything, and he assured his Latvian friend that 'I will always hold my protecting hand over you.' Valdmanis termed this 'my education on Newfoundland matters.'[38]

The Valdmanis version of events saw the first commission of $300,000 on the $2.8 million cement mill contract as actually negotiated by Ernest Leja at the request of Valdmanis. Leja had a good rapport with the MIAG representative and thus became unwittingly drawn in as a witness to Smallwood's alleged secret. Valdmanis took credit for securing the cheapest cement mill in North America, a financial deal that left MIAG with no more profit than the satisfaction of being one of the first German firms to obtain a foothold in the overseas export market. By the autumn of 1951, after having paid secret commissions of $220,000US to New York and $55,000Can to St John's, MIAG claimed a loss on the cement deal. During his 1951 visit to Germany, Smallwood promised MIAG an *ex gratia* payment of $261,590 in return for building a machinery plant at Octagon Pond near St John's. The amount of this payment was virtually identical to the sum of MIAG's commission payments, and Valdmanis contended that Smallwood had decided to refund from government money what MIAG had 'secretly' paid the Liberal party.[39]

In Valdmanis's version of the case of Benno Schilde, the commission process differed from that in the MIAG case. Valdmanis did not support the claim that the $150,000 *ex gratia* payment promised the firm in Germany in 1951 was a refund on a $200,000 commission the firm had paid up to that time. Instead, he argued that Smallwood was indignant that $50,000 of the commission remained unpaid when the gypsum plant was finished and that Benno Schilde delayed erecting the agreed-upon EMENCO plant in Bay Roberts. Smallwood allegedly (1) became increasingly impatient with Valdmanis for bungling the deal, (2) demanded that he clear up the mess with Hubertus Herz by the end of 1953, and (3) agreed that the remaining secret funds be put in a holding company that Valdmanis on several occasions had suggested be set up in St John's.

Valdmanis asserted that he had been too preoccupied with the escalating NALCO crisis to devote the required attention to these matters. To bridge his deepening rift with Smallwood, Valdmanis contended that he had demanded the immediate presence of Herz, who proposed to see Smallwood directly about the outstanding secret payments. But Valdmanis insisted that Leja and Herz withdraw $40,000 from the $150,000 EMENCO account Smallwood had established for the *ex gratia* payment. They were to deposit the withdrawal into Valdmanis's personal account in the Bank of Montreal, allegedly to be held 'in trust' until a final settlement was reached. In retrospect, Valdmanis claimed that he had thus foolishly manoeuvred Smallwood into a position vulnerable to blackmail by Benno Schilde or Leja. According to Valdmanis, Smallwood 'exploded' when he realized that Leja knew everything about payments to the party.[40]

Far-fetched as this line of reasoning may appear, Valdmanis in his defence went even further. He claimed that Smallwood had proposed the creation in New York of a revolving party fund that would be self-supporting. That is, the money paid into it was to be invested into profit-making ventures. However, the New York broker and attorney, Elja Lurje, who had been entrusted with this matter, had unwisely invested the money in unprofitable businesses. Valdmanis explained that Lurje, whom he maintained to have known by reputation already before the war, was introduced to him sometime in November 1950 and also recommended by Friedrich Kreyser. Valdmanis said that Smallwood had agreed that Lurje be authorized to manage the secret party fund. A copy of the official power-of-attorney issued to Lurje for managing the account, and notarized by L.R. Curtis as attorney general, was in fact still in Valdmanis's possession. Dated 9 June 1951, this document was to have been used to support the defence's claim that the commission payments were held in trust for the Liberal party.[41]

Lurje disliked investing in small companies and steered Valdmanis first towards a fifty–fifty partnership with fish industrialist (specialized in sardine and herring packing) Samuel Zwecker of Brooklyn. 'There was a big plan to go into three fish industries,' but then the so-called party fund became a one-third partner in Zwecker's Port Clyde Packing Company in Maine with Valdmanis a non-paid member of the board. Another person said to be involved was bank agent Dr Leon Viasmensky, who had undertaken to investigate the soundness of these propositions. In July 1951 they 'plunged' into control of Duane Import and Export Corporation, and in July 1952 they acquired the bankrupt fish-processing enterprise St Andrews Packers Ltd in New Brunswick for $35,000. Valdmanis started out with a 55 per cent share of this enterprise and co-ownership with Elja Lurje, Arthur Slavitt, a Mr Jackson, and Duane Import and Export Corporation. In 1953 Valdmanis bought Slavitt's share for $12,500. In January 1954 Valdmanis acquired all the shares along with an old $300,000 claim against St Andrew's Packers and became president of the corporation and chairman of its board of directors. In New York, St Andrews Packers acquired an independently registered sales agency staffed by Joseph H. Hahn as sales agent and Valdis Mateus as treasurer. Directors of operation in St Andrews were Valdmanis's long-time Latvian associate Alexander Āboliņš and his brother Osvald Valdmanis.

The St Andrews plant lay idle through 1953, and Valdmanis was looking for a $100,000 to $150,000 cash infusion to get it going. He stated that in 1952 Joey Smallwood had agreed to take over the plant eventually and establish an agency for it in the United States. However, in 1953 there was only $10,000 left in the revolving fund of the New York account of Katrina Mateus. The additional funds Smallwood allegedly intended to invest were Benno Schilde's $40,000 and two reclaimed loans to prospective industrialists. One was a $10,000 loan to United Cotton Mills in St John's, which was repaid in the form of ten thousand shares issued to Valdmanis but immediately purchased for $10,000 by John Cabot Textiles, the United Cotton Mill's Montreal affiliate. A refund for $50,000 came from German ceramics industrialist Ewald Zippmann. In November 1951 Valdmanis had arranged a $50,000 loan for Zippmann to be paid out in Switzerland. In return Valdmanis had been promised a share (20 to 25 per cent) in Zippmann's planned $1 million brick and tile industry in Clarenville, Newfoundland. When Zippmann subsequently lost interest in the project, Valdmanis requested a refund of the money in early 1954 to the New York account of Katrina Mateus.

Valdmanis claimed that it had been decided, in January 1954, to put the Liberal party's Canadian assets into a Montreal-incorporated holding company called North Star Development Corporation. Its president would be Valdmanis, while his brother-in-law Valdis Mateus and Atlantic Hardboard Industries chief Gustav Karl Weis would be directors. Among the assets vested into this holding company were the shares of the so-called Atlantic Jewellery and Watch Company in Montreal, launched in 1952 with a $7,000 transfer from Lurje. Although originally set up as a jewellery business under Latvian immigrant Zitmans, this company became a mainland sales organization for Valdmanis's holding company when Zitmans transferred his half of the shares to Valdmanis. All this happened, Valdmanis maintained, with the knowledge and at times on the initiative of Joey Smallwood.

Concerning the genesis of the St Andrews project, Valdmanis's personal papers (confiscated by the RCMP and subsequently turned over to Smallwood) document his contact with Lurje from August 1950. This contact had been established on the recommendation of Friedrich Kreyser with whom Lurje claimed to have enjoyed many years of 'mutually satisfactory cooperation.' Kreyser appears to have intended for Lurje in New York to play a role comparable to that of Hinneberg in Germany, in other words, to help Valdmanis recruit American investors, for example, to establish or purchase a Newfoundland fish-processing plant that would export its products to the United States. When Lurje turned this assignment over to Viasmensky after three months, Valdmanis showed increasing interest in the investment opportunities. For example, in November 1950 Valdmanis was ready to personally invest 3 million dollars in a $6 million cement plant to be built in either Mexico, Panama, Cuba, Haiti, or Brazil.[42]

Valdmanis's correspondence shows that the St Andrews project was first offered to Valdmanis in February 1952 by Boston attorney Alfred Malagodi as a complete company town – consisting of two hotels and housing for some five hundred people – with a fish plant that had been defunct since 1948. The asking price was $475,000 for what Malagodi described as 'one of the greatest industrial set-ups that I know of that is readily available and in good condition for immediate operation.' With its docking facilities for deep ship and rail connections, it could be operated for any type of industry or manufacturing. Malagodi was sure that Valdmanis would come up with an industrial use that could very well be tied in with its fishing and canning operations. Interestingly, Valdmanis replied in March 1952 that he considered Malagodi's project a poor investment because of the acute shortage of labour in the entire St Andrews area and the competition of Connors Brothers, the biggest fish-packing company in the British Empire. At that time Valdmanis did 'not see any possibility of getting anybody in Newfoundland – and within the circles I might know outside Newfoundland – interested in this venture.'[43]

The German firm Hochseefischerei Kiel AG, however, prepared a report in January 1953, explaining that an American group had purchased the St Andrews factory premises for the purpose of establishing, with German specialists, a food-processing plant using the most modern technology. The German group would supply, besides expert personnel, all the necessary machines and take over the management. Apart from a limited number of experts, all labour would be drawn from Canadian sources. The contracting of a factory-controlled fishing fleet and the possible participation of German fishermen was being contemplated.[44]

This American group was St Andrews Packers Ltd, as revealed by documents in Valdmanis's possession. Elja Lurje had been elected its president, Arthur Slavitt secretary, and Alfred Valdmanis a director. On 9 January 1954 Lurje and Slavitt had resigned and transferred all rights to Alfred A. Valdmanis as president, Osvald Valdmanis as secretary, and Valdis Mateus as treasurer. In a 'statement and designation' notarized two days later in New York, the seat of the company was declared to be New York City, its business within the state of New York to include wholesale and retail dealership in food items (fish, meat, fruit, vegetables, etc.), manufacturing and producing goods and commodities of all kinds, and owning and operating ships and vessels.[45] At the end of February 1954, Valdmanis as president of St Andrews Packers Ltd, wrote to a

Newfoundland supplier that 'we own a huge plant and premises in St Andrews, NB' and 'we are interested in any kind of seafood, inasmuch as it can be safely delivered to Rockland, Boston, New York or Philadelphia, and we are also interested in blueberries, raspberries and strawberries at competitive prices.'[46]

More credible than Valdmanis's claim that Smallwood was knowingly involved in all of this, might be Valdmanis's allegations of rampant graft. In 1953 Smallwood allegedly asked the manager of Canadian Machinery and Industry Construction Ltd (CMIC) to assemble a new Jeep from two old ones for his son Ramsay. Even though this work cost more than a new Jeep, CMIC manager Dr Eberhard Hermann Roethe was urged to send a token bill only. Valdmanis also confirmed rumours that the managers of United Cotton Mills and of Superior Rubber bribed Smallwood with prefabricated hen-house barracks for his farm. 'No barracks – no loan,' Smallwood was quoted as having told the Cotton Mills manager. In March 1954 Valdmanis claimed to have learned from an upset Smallwood that auditors of Ludwig Grube's books had found the hen-house deal recorded.[47]

As a return favour Superior Rubber president Grube allegedly expected Smallwood's help when he was jailed in Germany in early 1954 for illegally possessing $80,000. Grube had declared that the money had been transferred from the Newfoundland government and in order to be released from prison he needed official confirmation from Newfoundland. That was the reason for Trudi Braun-Wogau's personal appearance in St John's in February 1954. According to Valdmanis, Smallwood was afraid to sign such a statement and assigned the task to solicitor Donald W.K. Dawe and Valdmanis. They drew up a note stating that as director general Valdmanis had requested his deputy Gordon Pushie to arrange a $100,000 loan to be sent to Grube. That note got Grube out of jail. After his arrest, however, it got Valdmanis in more trouble when Smallwood began to suggest that Valdmanis had owed Grube favours. When Valdmanis was temporarily released on bail, in May 1954, he visited his friend Max Braun-Wogau, vice-president of Superior Rubber in Holyrood, who assured him that he and Grube would not allow Valdmanis to be harmed for this.[48]

In September 1953, when NALCO was sold to John Doyle and its fortunes suddenly seemed to soar to unprecedented heights, Valdmanis claimed that he had been offered as NALCO chairman an option for fifty thousand NALCO shares at $5 a share. During a boat trip on the St Lawrence River with Doyle and Smallwood, Valdmanis recalled, Curtis had asked to come in on the deal, and Smallwood wanted Greg Power to be added as a silent partner. Valdmanis had had no choice but to agree. His $30,000 salary as NALCO chairman, Valdmanis disclosed, was first proposed by Chesley Pippy in recognition of Valdmanis's invaluable connections with some of Europe's greatest industrialists who had prepared a royal reception for Premier Smallwood's party wherever they went on their first trip to Germany.[49]

The statements of defence that Valdmanis drew up were not confined to refuting the charges of the prosecution and illuminating specific incidents embarrassing to Smallwood. They also highlighted the problematic nature of the entire new industries program. Valdmanis stressed that he would have preferred to have taken more time to study the province's needs, resources, and potential resources when he was appointed director general. His idea had been to start with the creation of a $3 million revolving fund, he contended, and this would have sufficed to build at least one new industry. The next industry would not have been built until the first one was sold to private interests, and the fund filled up again. The interval would also have provided sufficient time to study the economic feasibility of other industries. The revolving fund would have been self-supporting, free of political interference, and subject only to government control. This had been the original concept of NALCO.

Valdmanis put the entire blame on Smallwood for the new industries 'whirlwind' with its hasty decisions and wasteful ventures. Smallwood deserved credit for vision and enthusiasm, but he 'had no practical grasp whatever as far as industrialization was concerned.' Desperate 'to make or to break' his new Canadian province, Smallwood encouraged deception and corruption. In fact, Smallwood himself had ended up 'helping, and even inviting, German subjects to break German law,' Valdmanis maintained. He found it impossible to pursue any other course because Smallwood would not allow politics to be removed from business. On the contrary, 'he gradually assumed full and personal control.' The financially irresponsible, 'unholy dash for new industries, whether they had a chance or not,' Valdmanis concluded, had ultimately forced his own withdrawal from the directorship of Newfoundland's economic development.[50]

The Evidence for Indictment

Caught between a rock and a hard place, Premier Smallwood had had his case carefully prepared. On the one hand he had to produce irrefutable proof that the money was not collected on his orders and did not end up in his pockets. On the other, he had to ensure that the trial would not deteriorate into a general debate over the merits of his approach to economic development and thus vindicate the Opposition's persistent call for a royal commission of inquiry into the new industries program. 'In ordering the arrest of the man who had been closer to me than any other man – I took my political life in my hands,' Smallwood admitted to the legislature in March 1955.

The Crown's key evidence was produced in the preliminary inquiry from 2 to 9 August 1954 in the form of depositions from eleven witnesses: six from Germany (Herbert Marx, Heinz-Joachim Wilke, and Erich Kirmse of MIAG, Hubertus Herz and August Roemer of Benno Schilde, and Friedrich Kreyser of Neue Technik), three RCMP officers, one American Express Company official, and J.R. Smallwood. The prosecution had no power to call witnesses from Germany without their consent. Therefore, relying on the excellent rapport established with MIAG head Johannes Lerch in Garmisch in September 1951, Premier Smallwood cabled him in July 1954 that 'it is very important that Marx and Steinbruck both come here in addition to the other men. I would regard it as a personal favour from you to me if you would instruct both these gentleman to arrive at the same time with the others. Kindest regards.'[51] Steinbrück was too sick to travel, but the other representatives of the three German firms who were asked by both Smallwood and Leja to testify did come. They wanted to clear their names, protect their business interests, and defend themselves against a simultaneous West German indictment for alleged foreign currency exchange fraud. They knew that the West German government and its diplomatic and consular representatives in Canada were watching the case carefully for revelations of German activities considered illegal under German law.

The German embassy in Ottawa and consulate general in Montreal had long been suspicious of the secrecy surrounding the establishment of German industries in Newfoundland and Valdmanis's failure to communicate with the German ambassador. Not until March 1954 had the German consul general discovered that Valdmanis was a major shareholder in several of the new industries, for example, Valdmanis revealed to him that he had personally financed 25 per cent of the $400,000 capital of Atlantic Hardboard Industries. Now, German officials were scrutinizing the transactions of Benno Schilde and, in particular, MIAG whose president Johannes Lerch, had sought refuge in Montreal from indictment in Germany for flight of capital.[52]

The first three witnesses at the preliminary inquiry were MIAG officials chief engineer Erich Kirmse, sales manager Herbert Marx, and his assistant Heinz-Joachim Wilke. They testified that when the original contract for the construction of the cement mill was signed, in August 1950, Marx had entered upon a second agreement with Valdmanis providing for MIAG to pay a commission of $300,000. The first payment of $50,000 was to be delivered in cash to Valdmanis and the remaining ones were to be deposited in the account of Katrina Mateus at the American Express Company in New York.

Marx testified that Valdmanis had demanded the money for the Liberal party, but warned him not to mention it to Smallwood. Wilke affirmed that he had arranged the transfers from Germany to Newfoundland and New York, and Kirmse verified that he personally had delivered to Valdmanis the first $50,000 payment in five-, ten-, and twenty-dollar bills. He described how the money had been taken from the first instalment of the Newfoundland government's advance to MIAG, deposited in its account at the Canadian Bank of Commerce branch in Corner Brook. The bank manager had found withdrawal of such an amount in cash so unusual that he had needed two days to get the money ready and insisted that Kirmse pick it up with a witness. Accompanied by Ernest Leja, Kirmse had carried the money away in a black briefcase lent by the bank manager. Kirmse had then taken the money to St John's, where Valdmanis had refused to issue a receipt; he had merely made a mark on a bank slip which Kirmse had then taken to Wilke in Germany.

Perhaps the most incriminating evidence for the prosecution came from Benno Schilde's export business manager, Hubertus Herz, and from Friedrich Kreyser, director of the consulting engineering firm Neue Technik. As chief negotiator of the gypsum mill contract, Herz testified that Valdmanis had bargained down Benno Schilde's bid from $1.8 to $1.35 million and then taken Herz aside to request that $200,000 be directed to the Liberal party for an election fund. Valdmanis had demanded a timetable showing a breakdown of the payments. He had then handed to Herz a slip from a calendar pad with the account of Katrina Mateus to which the payments were to be made. Herz had kept it in a safe. Herz swore that he himself had given Valdmanis the first $25,000 in cash, but Valdmanis had refused to provide the requested receipt.

Forty thousand dollars of this fund was still outstanding by the end of 1953. An impatient Valdmanis had cabled Herz to rush to Montreal with it. To satisfy Valdmanis, Herz and Leja had taken the money from Premier Smallwood's $150,000 EMENCO account. Soon, however, instead of releasing Benno Schilde, as Valdmanis had promised, from the obligation to erect the EMENCO plant in Bay Roberts, Smallwood had demanded that Benno Schilde refund the $150,000 reserved for EMENCO. Valdmanis, who had by now resigned as chairman of NALCO, had quickly repaid the $40,000 into the EMENCO account and asked Benno Schilde to retain him as attorney in the dispute over the $150,000. Suspicious of these moves, Herz and Leja had finally decided to clear up the entire matter with Smallwood.

Herz hit the defence with a bombshell. In the preliminary inquiry he admitted that he had given the St John's police a letter that Valdmanis had written from jail to Kreyser in Germany. Partly in German and partly in Latvian, the letter asked Kreyser to prevail upon MIAG and Benno Schilde officials to testify that the money they had sent to Katrina Mateus had not been intended as a commission: in other words, Valdmanis asked them to commit perjury. He wanted them to say these had been funds to be held in trust for these companies so that they would accumulate dollars to their credit in North America. They should testify that the payments were termed a commission merely to conceal from the German currency control authority their transfer abroad for other purposes. For any friend in distress, Valdmanis begged, he would have done the same. He asked that the reply be sent to his lawyer.

Kreyser testified that he had received this letter from Valdmanis in April 1954. He had passed it to Herz on condition that Herz would use it only to defend himself in Germany against the charge of having illegally sent money out of Germany as a means of converting it into dollars.[53] Kreyser's personal correspondence with Herz confirms the grave reservations with which Kreyser surrendered Valdmanis's letter. 'Is my behaviour, in the final analysis, not a breach of trust towards one who is despairing, if not guilty?' Kreyser had worried and wondered whether passing on this letter to Newfoundland might not lead to 'exactly the kind of situation we tried to avoid and draw more people into the affair. It is now only too likely that Mr Higgins and V. will resort to any imaginable length to incriminate and discredit through whatever statements, whether true or false, the persons testifying against them. It could be that in connection with these developments even I may have to appear over there. Only with a heavy heart can I imagine what might happen then.'[54]

Herz insisted that his company, too, was not in the least interested in playing the role of accuser. Benno Schilde was only interested in protecting itself from unfair attacks and suspicions. From Attorney General Curtis, Herz had learned that Valdmanis had approached Dr E. Roethe, vice-president of CMIC in St John's in a similar way he had approached Kreyser. For that reason Herz had considered it essential to turn over the letter to the police in St John's. Leja had first pressured Herz to report its existence to the RCMP. When Herz had complied, the RCMP then demanded the original. In view of Kreyser's reservations, however, Herz had decided to forward the letter to Leja, whose integrity they both wanted to protect. He alone was to decide whether and when he would make use of Valdmanis's incriminating letter.[55]

On the witness stand in St John's, Kreyser stated that when he initiated the contacts with MIAG and Benno Schilde, Valdmanis informed him that 10 per cent of any estimates would have to be set aside. It was not until Smallwood's first visit to Germany that Valdmanis had revealed that the 10 per cent was destined for the Liberal party's election fund and was to be kept an absolute secret. For arranging the deals with MIAG and Benno Schilde, Kreyser declared, Neue Technik had made a legal profit of $40,000, which he and Valdmanis had earlier agreed to share. This is the only amount that Kreyser, on instructions from Valdmanis, had sent to Elja Lurje in New York. There had been no other financial transactions between Kreyser and Lurje.

The flow of U.S. dollar payments into and out of the account of Katrina Mateus was detailed in the deposition of American Express Company agent C.H. Weltner. He showed that in the twenty-two transactions from October 1950 to 24 February 1954, $450,000 was deposited and $465,000 was drawn, and by June 1954 the account had a balance of $850. Six cheques had been issued to Elja Lurje for a total of $230,000, two to Samuel Zwecker totalling $165,000, and two for $60,000 together, to Valdis Mateus and one to Ewald Zippmann for $50,000.

The remaining evidence for indictment came from three RCMP officers who had searched Valdmanis's premises in St Andrews and Montreal, where they had confiscated and identified incriminating letters. One of these letters, Smallwood later revealed to the Newfoundland legislature, was to Valdmanis's wife Irma about money he had sent her: '"Now dear, I am sending you this parcel." At one time he sent $25,000 in bank notes to her, and insured it for $50, sent it parcel post through the mail from St John's to Montreal – $50,000 – or sent it by express and insured it for $50. "... and dear don't forget this money is for you. This is your money. If anything happens to me don't let Katrina ... claim it. Don't forget if anything happens to me this is your money."'[56]

Smallwood's deposition in the preliminary inquiry denied that Valdmanis had been given any authority to collect contributions for the

Liberal party and that the premier had any knowledge of agreements concerning such commissions or payments from German firms. The evidence paraded in court made Smallwood's charges against Valdmanis appear irrefutable. 'We not only had the witnesses who paid him the money but we had the records of the payments and we could trace the money from the time he got it until it went out the window or wherever else he threw it,' Attorney General Curtis summed up after the trial. The only unresolved mystery is the fate of the money. Did Valdmanis lose the money to the bad management of his investment broker,[57] or was he blackmailed by his countrymen, as some insiders suspected at the time?[58]

The Verdict

Despite the overwhelming evidence of the prosecution, the consensus after the preliminary inquiry had been that Valdmanis was prepared to fight to the end. His choice of trial by jury rather than by judge and the scanty cross-examination of the witnesses by the defence counsel had seemed to indicate that he might not bother to refute the evidence of the prosecution. (Beginning with the testimony of Hubertus Herz on 3 August, Noel Goodrich assumed the defence from Gordon Higgins, who had fallen ill.) Rather, as Adolph Reifferscheidt, the German consul general in Montreal reported to Bonn, Valdmanis's tactic might be to argue that he had bargained down the price for the industries he had contracted by a significantly larger amount than he had pocketed in commissions. The suggestion that his negotiating skills actually benefited the province might win over one or the other juror and create a hung jury.[59] By 1954 Smallwood's 'make-or-break' approach to industrialization had generated enough discontent in the province to make the outcome of a trial by jury anything but predictable.

Valdmanis's sudden plea of guilty on 15 September – on one of Smallwood's two charges – therefore came as a complete surprise. In his reports to Bonn, Reifferscheidt noted that the final charges differed from earlier ones by not involving the two German firms in any claims or actions. Also, Valdmanis was not asked to plead with regard to the MIAG-related charge, which was kept in abeyance. Since five years would have been the maximum sentence for one charge, observers were surprised that the verdict – four years at hard labour – was not more lenient. It was believed that Valdmanis had agreed to plead guilty under duress and because he was assured of a milder sentence. Gordon Pushie, however, the new director general of economic development, let Reifferscheidt know that the verdict was the best possible deal Valdmanis's Montreal solicitor had been able to arrange in tedious negotiations with the Newfoundland government.[60]

Valdmanis himself, judging by his confidential messages from prison, seems to have thrown in the towel. Officially he was not permitted to write more than one letter per week, and this on a Sunday and in English. It then had to pass the censor. But friends, in particular Dr Janis Maurins, smuggled his secret notes in Latvian to family members. Full of lamentations over his fate, these notes reveal that the out-of-court settlement was a last resort after his defence had foundered at the preliminary inquiry. The court was not an arena for a fight, he wrote his brother-in-law Valdis on 30 July, but made up of people who would break him to a point where he would not recognize himself any more. Nobody could help him after his physical and mental powers had been sapped during his long confinement in a small, hot room comparable to a cage:

> My brain is overheated, I have headaches, it is difficult for me to formulate even the simplest idea in words. With what is left of my mental ability, I realize that I am no adversary to anybody. And the fact that the government had engaged a second prosecutor is just an unneeded compliment to me because I am no longer the man I have been, a man who, maybe in his last half-crazy flare-up of activity, had started a new era on this island. From me, you can expect anything during the court process. Whatever I have done or still may do, please try with time passing to forgive me. My dear ones, all please forgive me.[61]

On 8 August Valdmanis confided to friends that Higgins had collapsed on the second day of the hearing and so for four days he had had no competent defence attorney. It all happened after an argument between them concerning the authenticity of a letter of 1950. Attributed to Valdmanis, it discredited his entire theory regarding the party funds. After the letter was added to the evidence against him, he had decided to relinquish his rights to call witnesses on his behalf, to cross examine the prosecution's witnesses, and to implicate Bērziņš, Jekste, or Leja. 'I am taking today all the load on myself and only myself. I know that under such circumstances I have to plead guilty,' he scribbled to Valdis on 9 August, and 'that my sentence will not be five years but ten instead, which means that my life will end with that.' This would be his last message from outside jail, he sobbed.[62]

The follow-up note to Valdis, dated 'in jail, 14 August 1954,' was more explicit. It acknowledged that the defence was weak anyway and suddenly collapsed completely when the police presented three letters allegedly written by Valdmanis in September and October 1950. In these he told his wife Irma that the money in the account of Katrina Mateus would belong to her should anything happen to him. Valdmanis admitted that he was finished by the prosecution's documents and witnesses alone and that the appearance of the letters spared only Leja, Braun-Wogau, and others from needing to give 'very unpleasant' testimony. The letters proved that Irma and Katrina were innocent but for the accused 'an abyss opened up.'

From that moment on Valdmanis had envisaged two equally detestable alternatives. First, to go through the procedural commotions of the trial, 'silent, with clenched teeth and Higgins beating the drums, and facing the clearly visible desire of the prosecutor to get even by giving me ten years (five plus five, five for each of the two transgressions and not permitting the sentences to run concurrently).' The other alternative was an admission of guilt. 'It is a direction into which I am pushed from all sides as the only practical solution,' Valdmanis disclosed in a long note that he labelled 'absolutely confidential.' Pressure came from Higgins, the prosecution, and his Montreal solicitor Major Louis M. Bloomfield, QC.[63]

Valdmanis himself had diagnosed his mental condition as half-consciousness, unsure whether all of this was not a horrible nightmare. He might not survive his jail term and might die within the next two years, he speculated, quoting Latvian physician Dr J. Maurins, and if he would survive where would he go and what could he do? 'Where would I go to start a new life? My dear good innocent Irma and children, today I am writing to them informing them that all they own will be taken from them, that the boys will be permitted to hate me, and that they should find a way to change their surname in anticipation of the difficulties awaiting them in the future.'

Since Higgins was washing his hands in innocence by conveniently checking into a hospital in the middle of the preliminaries and staying there, Valdmanis claimed, the main representation of Valdmanis's interests rested with Bloomfield. Renowned for having drafted the U.N. resolution leading to the creation of the state of Israel, Bloomfield was also the personal lawyer of Lady Davis. He had agreed to negotiate with Smallwood on behalf of Valdmanis.[64] His assistant, Hyman Baker, met Attorney General Curtis to determine whether, in return for accepting sole responsibility for all the offences charged, it would be possible to limit Valdmanis's sentence to three or four years.

Valdmanis had been prepared to accept whatever advice Bloomfield would offer. But he worried about whether Bloomfield and Lady Davis would want to be associated with a criminal and his family. Moreover, after his confession, he feared, no Latvian would offer a helping hand, his mother would not survive very long, and his daughter Mara and the boys would have to grow up as the children of a con man. The assumption that Smallwood would be 'bloodthirsty' after he was filled up with information from Bērziņš, Jekste, Leja, and an unidentified individual named Springers left little hope that a deal was possible involving a confession. On the contrary, Smallwood would probably consider the total destruction of his prisoner a good deed. Valdmanis intimated that something tragic and irrevocable might happen by the time those lines reached their destiny. He had 'no energy left, none. I am near collapse, apathy, and insanity.'[65]

When he was a child, Valdmanis recalled, a gypsy had prophesied his tragic end. An end in jail and the destruction of an entire family, however, he had not been able to imagine. But 'the seed of death I myself planted in August 1950, four years ago. O my God.' In the event of a trial (he called the trial 'that insanity and case of self-destruction'), he begged his relatives and friends, not to come and witness that act of shame:

> All my abilities, all my mind, I have given to this country. With a broken soul, but nevertheless with superhuman effort I ripped open this land to civilization. I created a foundation for further peaceful development. When Mara asked whether I intended to tell the court that I had also done something *good*, I had to tell my dear proud daughter that the answer is no. My share will be only the bad and only that. But so it is in this world, and now I have to give away my life. I could have taken two million, and I believe that God would pardon me. What all I have not suffered since 1950: Lurje's and Jak's blackmail etc., as in a spider web, and now disaster ... I think that I know life even though I have not known how to live it.

The gloomy message of despair and doom concluded with a plea to Valdis to forgive him and to stand by Irma. The upcoming tragedy in St John's would be great, but the tragedy in Montreal would be even greater. A postscript assured Valdmanis's family that suicide was out of reach: 'I am guarded too well.'[66]

On 24 August 1954 Valdmanis had started to accept reality. 'I, your beloved, admired, and respected Alfred, I whom you all knew from way back in childhood, I am the one who has destroyed you all, me,' he began his letter to Valdis and Kiki warning them not to lose their minds but to save his wife and children from committing suicide. 'I am guilty. I have to confess now but I have nothing to say.' He had learned that the prosecution had finally formulated the accusation against him as two separate charges of fraud (in the amounts of $270,000 and $200,000) against the government. The maximum sentence for each charge was a five-year prison term for a total prison sentence of ten years plus confiscation of all his assets. Despairing over how he would survive a ten-year sentence, he confessed to Valdis and Kiki that his poor wife Irma

> did not know anything, regardless of my letters of September and October 1950. She was so trusting in the honesty of her Alfred, just as all of you, and up to August 1950 I had never touched a single cent not earned by myself ... What a terrible power overcame me in 1950. At Easter (in Halifax) I stood for a long time in front of my eighth-floor window and I was thinking. I had in me a seed of a tragedy and in Newfoundland that power took control of me. In August (when Leja on my instructions demanded from MIAG $300,000) I was not really aware of what I was doing. I was in a sort of a trance. But I repeated it in November (Benno Schilde $200,000). Later I actually did not remember the details about exactly how the money was requested, how it was given and how it was received. All that I heard and saw only during the (confidential) preliminary inquiry and I could not believe that I would actually have been able to do it ... With a broken heart and soul I still managed to perform miracles in Newfoundland. I lived only for that. I never counted that money of misfortune. Now I understand it had come to *destroy me.*[67]

The remorseful perpetrator traced the seeds of his tragedy to 1940 when his soul was broken, and to 1943–5 when his will power and mind were shaken. Further damage he attributed to the continued denunciations after the war, 'a damage from which I really never recovered.' Valdmanis found it tragic that his destruction came for a crime from which, in his mind, he felt very detached. Also heart wrenching was that he had completely destroyed not only himself but also his innocent family. Nonetheless, his wife had reassured him that she would continue to love him and wait for him. 'Isn't all that an insanity and maybe I am insane? No, I *was.*' During the summer of 1954 Valdmanis had a chance to look at himself and could not believe that he had actually done what he had done. Prophetically, he foresaw, nobody would ever completely know and understand this tragedy. 'Please save Mulitis [nickname for Irma] and the children,' a grief-stricken Valdmanis again begged Valdis and Kiki. 'They are all so innocent. Too late, much too late to think about why. Dear Lord, what a horrible ending, and the river of mud that is to follow.'[68]

On 25 August Valdmanis reported that he had the first indications of a deal involving an admission of guilt. It was developing 'at high speed' between the government and his attorneys in Montreal and St John's. The 'horror' of what to tell the children, relatives, and friends was fast approaching. It was no longer possible to qualify his responsibility. Since he had to cede all his rights to the St Andrews property, he asked his wife to forward all relevant documents – the balance sheet, Valdis's claim, and Abolins's shares destined for a person or firm called Benton. Furthermore, he asked that an attempt be made to recover Lurje's $30,000 promissory notes. Valdmanis doubted that Abolins and Lurje would comply or hold the assets for Irma. Āboliņš was still in possession of the power of attorney issued by Valdmanis, so he expected Āboliņš to 'try some dirty trick for himself and Lurje,' such as cashing in the paid-up amount of Valdmanis's life insurance. Lurje had been entrusted with $5,000 cash to pay that life insurance policy but now it appeared he had kept the money for himself.[69]

By 3 September Valdmanis knew what kind of a deal his lawyers Bloomfield and Baker had been able to strike in Montreal with Newfoundland's minister of justice. In court, on 21 September, 'I'll admit that I am the single and only one culprit in the crime I am accused of.' For him it represented a simple act of survival so that he would not be condemned to die a slow death in jail. The plea bargain saw Valdmanis pleading guilty to defrauding the Newfoundland government of $470,000. In return, the government would terminate one of the criminal proceedings. For the other charge the prosecution would demand the smallest possible sentence – around three years, and not all of this would be served. All property anywhere in Valdmanis's name had to be turned over to the government. The alternative, he revealed to Valdis Mateus, was a ten-year conviction, a civil case and taxes pending, and the likelihood that he would not leave Newfoundland alive.

The news of the settlement drove home to Valdmanis the realization that relatives, friends – and everything – was lost, 'even the children.' To Valdis Mateus, Valdmanis acknowledged that this sentence after the horrible degradation would haunt him for life. 'I'll have no place to go, job opportunities for a former convict sentenced for fraud will be non-existent ... For me that means destruction and the same for the children ... For the boys it would be best if they were adopted by other people.' In time they would hate him, he thought. His sense of loss was aggravated by the assumption that several local Latvians – Leja, Jekste, Langins, Jacobsons – who presumably knew as early as the end of February that Smallwood was planning his arrest, had failed to warn him. It was impossible to imagine how his poor family would survive in shame and poverty. 'What insane act have I committed? What had taken possession of me? Who can forgive me? It is impossible!! Possibly only God. Yes.'[70]

Two weeks after his guilty plea, Valdmanis had come to terms with his fate. He could sleep again at night, he wrote Valdis, and for the first time after many years of sickness he felt well again. His spirit was broken from his horrible past experiences, and now he was on the road to disaster which could end in a mental institution. It was ironic that in his sick state of mind he stumbled in a money matter – precisely his area of expertise all his life. He had gradually come to view what actually happened not as a crime but a deep, horrible tragedy that could not be comprehended by outsiders: 'The day when in court I took all the blame on myself, in my mind I was very far from the place. I was in the Latvian forest and visualized myself following a trail on a sunny autumn day together with my wife. I can remember seeing it clearly and then I suddenly heard Higgins say he was finished. Then I realized that Higgins was talking to the judge and I returned to reality.'[71]

Usually, Alfred Valdmanis's mind turned to the immediate future. 'Please help my poor wife bring up our children,' was a standard plea to Valdis. Maybe Valdis could move with his family from New York to Montreal? As far as his own redemption was concerned, Valdmanis believed he could cleanse himself only by returning to work, maybe not again in Canada, possible in Africa: 'If only I could remain alive without losing my mind and somehow regain my freedom, I would then once again try to prove myself and my efforts might gain forgiveness.'[72]

The notion of salvation through hard work became a recurrent wish. In his 9 October note to Valdis, Valdmanis accepted his punishment as God-ordained in order to salvage his soul and save his mind from darkness. He had given up his death wish and knew that he wanted to live. Once released, he would be in a better position to know his obligations and try to correct the wrong he had caused. 'If after one year I could get out again by means of parole, I will still be unbroken. I have already had many deep thoughts ... hoping that possibly we all together could establish in Canada or the United States a Latvian enterprise in some field, maybe a cooperative. I know that only with work can I regain my name and reputation.' On 31 October he declared to Valdis his willingness 'to go to Africa, Australia, New Zealand, or any one of the South American countries where I could somehow get started.' This depended, of course, on his friends' success in getting him released from prison and helping him find a job.[73]

Finding out what friends were left and willing to help loomed as growing concerns in the confidential messages to Valdis towards the end of 1954. However, early release was another nagging worry. Most disconcerting in his 31 October message was the lack of progress towards this. The second charge involving $270,000, to which Valdmanis pleaded not guilty, was still not formally terminated.

Fearing that it was kept open as a threat against him, Valdmanis still was not sure whether he would get out alive and with a sane mind. In his opinion Gordon Higgins was partly to blame for this. Valdmanis had earlier accused him of heavy drinking, breaking down in the preliminary inquiry, and then leaving him without a defender against a well-organized prosecution. 'That man actually hates me, and on his own he will never do anything to help me.' There was no point starting a fight in Newfoundland. Under no circumstances should anybody dare to accuse Smallwood openly, because Valdmanis would be the one to suffer the consequences. He expected only Bloomfield could manage to achieve early parole, possibly sooner than the two years considered normal in Canada.[74]

All the more important, therefore, was the loyalty of old friends. The support of people who remembered that Valdmanis had done much good in the past and who wanted to see him free and back to work would be particularly important for Bloomfield. Valdmanis was especially grateful that the Latvian National Committee (LNC) refused to join the effort of others to 'liquidate' him. Despite their bickering, Latvians actually had a compassionate organization to 'follow the heart,' he was surprised to discover. The attitude of LNC reminded him of the way the Finns treated their President Väinö Tanner imprisoned at Soviet insistence from 1944 to 1948.[75]

Valdmanis hoped that Bloomfield, despite actually knowing little about his client and being underpaid for his services, would be satisfied to be rewarded with moral gratitude and popularity. Valdmanis thought it would flatter Bloomfield's self-esteem to be approached by such persons as the LNC board members, Dean Skrodelis, Captain Kruger's wife in Toronto, and Beland Honderich, financial editor of the *Toronto Star,* Canada's largest newspaper. Bloomfield's help would also be needed for his client's rehabilitation.[76]

By December 1954 Valdmanis's optimistic mood of October began to evaporate. He warned Valdis that their secret correspondence through Dr Maurins might come to an abrupt end. An ill omen concerned five registered letters to Valdmanis from Tonija Krūka in Toronto. They had apparently been redirected to the RCMP in Ottawa for translation and censorship. Furthermore, parole proceedings could not begin because the charges arising from the second accusation had not been formally terminated. This delay occurred despite written assurances to Bloomfield by the minister of justice. Valdmanis clung to the possibility of parole as his last hope because 'it will be difficult for me to hold on longer than the year 1955.'[77]

The matter of parole would be decided in Ottawa, but the determining factor would be references from the prison superintendent, the solicitor general, and the trial judge. Parole, Valdmanis insisted, was not a trial based on the question of guilt or innocence. According to him, parole should be granted on the following grounds: (1) his unblemished past, (2) his valuable contribution to society through his life's work, (3) his suffering during the war and during the time he was a refugee in Europe, (4) his good deeds done in Newfoundland, (5) affidavits that he would not associate with criminals of any kind, and (6) a guarantee that he would have employment.[78]

An unanswered question for Valdmanis was whether Louis Bloomfield would take on the matter of parole. So far he had not committed himself, nor had he promised to find a job for Valdmanis. Suggestions to start an import–export business made little sense to Valdmanis since he did 'not have anything anymore and without money nothing can be started.' And the LNC could be of no help. Unfortunately, Bērziņš and Springers had worked Valdmanis over quite thoroughly, and no one would be eager to help a convicted criminal. Perhaps, Valdmanis mused, a short letter to Bloomfield wishing him a happy New Year would remind Bloomfield that there was still something good and valuable left in Valdmanis. Mrs Kruger, a family friend in Toronto, had already written Bloomfield and planned to meet him personally. Maybe someone could get the LNC to thank Bloomfield for his past efforts and express hope for his success in obtaining Valdmanis's release in 1955.[79]

In more than one respect, Bloomfield seemed to be the last resort for the Valdmanis family in Montreal. Their financial situation caused by his conviction was severe. The hope that friends would intercede with Bloomfield to find relief is manifest in a confidential supplication from Valdmanis to an unidentified member of the LNC. Irma should not know about this, Valdmanis requested, 'because she would be very hurt and ashamed.' Although she had a MA in mathematics and was fluent in English, German, and Danish, she was working in a small insurance company, quite a distance from home, for $140 a month. She found it so difficult to make ends meet that she would continue to work during her lunch break instead of having something to eat somewhere. She was aware that because of her age she did not have many choices. 'But in our desperate situation she is grateful for what she has now,' explained Valdmanis and pleaded that his friend approach Major Bloomfield to help his wife find a better job closer to home. Maybe she could find better working conditions with Imperial Tobacco where Bloomfield had some influence because Lady Davis was a major shareholder.[80]

Upcoming expenses for the house mortgage, taxes, and clothing for spring and fall would require even the younger sons to find work. The oldest son, Gundars, earned $25 a month from his early morning paper route in Westmount for the Montreal *Gazette.* Sons Agnars and Vidvuds had also applied but had not been assigned jobs yet. These paper routes would give them the only money they were capable of earning. Valdmanis wanted Bloomfield to use his close contact with the chief editor of the *Gazette* to help them get the jobs. 'Please, please keep in mind,' Valdmanis concluded, 'that the family are the dear ones who have not deserved the situation they are facing now.'[81] The social impact of his conviction on his children also troubled Valdmanis. His heart ached for his daughter, Mara, whose first boyfriend broke up with her, apparently when he learned of her father's conviction: 'She is so good, trusting, and clever. So little fun she has had since as a small girl she left our country to go to foreign schools. She didn't have any friends or wasn't close to anybody, and suddenly she fell in love with Ansis ... My heart aches about that news and if that horrible misfortune would not have hit us, maybe everything would have been different.'[82]

A pervasive acceptance of his dismal future and the uncertainty about the meaning of life characterized Valdmanis's mood on the first anniversary of his prison term. Although he had had sufficient time to reflect, read, and again reflect, he had been unable to make any sense of life. 'Life is an enigma whose purpose and meaning are not known,' he confessed to Valdis Mateus. He had often been overcome by the feeling of injustice done to him: 'Then I try to remember everything back from childhood, all that I have been doing bad and then I say to myself – all that had already been refunded with interest. Sometimes I even get the desire for revenge, bad for the bad. But then I understand my inability to do anything now and that everything is being rearranged so that I will never be in a position to do anything ... Never again will I be able to rise again, regardless of what would happen and what I would do.'

Reading, information from home, and correspondence with a few friends is what he lived for. The Newfoundland government, as far as Valdmanis could determine, was tightening the noose more and more instead of granting the promised release. 'I have to remain silent even though the little one [Smallwood] has become so bold that he is talking about eight years for me.' Nor could Valdmanis expect or demand anything from Bloomfield. He suspected a continued effort to use damaging or detrimental information to sink him.[83]

By Christmas 1955 Valdmanis became so depressed that for the first time he even lost interest in writing letters. But he did not want his wife to lose hope and that thought alone restrained him from open despair. Everything around him was darkening. 'It feels like a net around me that is being continuously tightened so that I do not see any way out.' Gordon Higgins, whom he claimed not to have seen since 17 September 1954, appeared to be working for both sides. 'So I slowly suffocate.' In his youth Valdmanis had read the Norwegian novel *Emigrants.* He could not remember its author, but the tragedy of that story had seeped deeply into him. Valdmanis's life was shrinking more and more. 'More and more I am dropping behind the happenings in the world and I am afraid all of it will no longer make any sense to me if I drop too far behind.'[84]

Convict

The indictment and imprisonment of Valdmanis, whether viewed from his personal or the public perspective, did not end the aura of mystery surrounding his case. On the contrary, it has remained a source of rumours and speculation to this day. Valdmanis himself, despite his guilty plea, never accepted his conviction as punishment for a true crime, as his letters from prison repeatedly reveal. Even Irma's sincere apology to Smallwood in October 1954 for her husband's actions left questions unanswered. Alfred, she explained, 'went through so much in Europe that he swore, if he ever got the chance to make a lot of money, he would make it.'[85]

To Valdis, however, Alfred maintained in the letter on 23 December 1955 that his side of the story had not yet become known. He was confident it would eventually leak out, despite Smallwood's efforts to suppress it and no matter how long he was kept jailed. In his opinion, a recent newspaper article by a well-informed former Smallwood friend confirmed that others knew at least part of that story. The article in question appears to have been Harold Horwood's 'Political Notebook' column, in the *Evening Telegram* of 18 October 1955, suggesting that 'the inside facts of the Valdmanis case are still being hugged close to the breasts of the PC Leaders. These inside facts include copies of affidavits made at the preliminary hearings. The PC's may never get the opportunity to publish the affidavits in full, but they are determined by hook or by crook to get their sum and substance before the public in the hope that Liberal heads will roll.' A publication entitled 'The Facts Behind Valdmanis' might be a best-seller on the black market, the column suggested.

Indeed, as early as 1 October 1954 the *Evening Telegram* rated 'Dr Valdmanis' still top news: 'The Latvian, partially due to the government's handling of the case, has been newsworthy since his arrest on an international level.' The premier's desire to censor news about the convict was seen as another reason for continued media attention to every aspect of his life. It was rather wishful thinking, observed the German consul general to Bonn, on 4 October 1954, to assume that public interest in the Alfred Valdmanis case and its linkage to the German industries had vanished 'with one blow' after the sentencing.[86]

The first news update after the sentencing appeared on 14 October 1954. Valdmanis was reportedly resting well and being relatively serene in the penitentiary. He was doing a great deal of reading, mostly of religious literature, but for the time being declined a copy of *The Life of Billy Graham* offered by a friend. He wanted to catch up on the books he already had before touching another one.[87] From an *Evening Telegram* article of 8 December 1954, the public could learn that 'Dr Alfred Valdmanis, sentenced to four years hard labour, is in charge of stores at the penitentiary ... [and] seems contented, too. He eats well, likes the food, the accommodations, and reportedly is looking better than he has for some months.' He appeared 'much pleasanter than he used to be,' had regular contact with his wife in Montreal, but did not have many visitors. Although getting along well with his fellow prisoners, he had no close connections with them.

Edgar Pike, a teacher at the penitentiary, recalled years later Valdmanis's time there. His work assignment in the penitentiary's storeroom had been a privileged position giving access to contraband and the kitchen. In the storeroom, according to Pike, Valdmanis used to have three open books strategically placed in different corners. He would be reading these whenever he had a few minutes to spare while working. When Valdmanis found out that Pike had subscriptions to the *Times Literary Supplement* and *Listener* (published by the BBC), he had requested all the back copies and eagerly read them with his 'eyes lit up like a child being taught.' Valdmanis had impressed Pike with his insight into the value of education and the superiority of private institutions on the mainland.[88]

Indeed, to Newfoundlanders like Pike everything about Valdmanis continued to be as unconventional and mysterious as ever – his remarkably organized mind, multiple skills, tremendous sense of the value of time, and his foreign contacts. Most of his visitors used to speak in some foreign language, so no one understood the conversation. Pike found talking with him rather peculiar; like a computer Valdmanis seemed to take information from the speaker and file it away in his head. During dinner time Valdmanis managed to get access to the school building in order to play the Hammond organ. Concern about his physical condition made him eager to play volleyball, the only sport prisoners were allowed. Valdmanis played so intensely, Pike noticed, that 'his eyes popped out like organ stops.' He was also observed doing push-ups in his cell. Occasionally he had big meals with Latvian or German people.[89] At times he worked in the kitchen and his fellow inmates thought highly of his cooking.[90]

Even among Newfoundland's German industrialists, fantastic stories made the rounds. Terra Nova Textiles manager Fritz Stobbe claimed that 'Valdmanis practically turned the old jail inside out':

> Everything was cleaned up, they built a volleyball yard, they put a library in. The first time I saw the chief warden there – we used to make the uniforms for the guards and we also made the denims for the inmates – he said, 'Would you like to see Dr Valdmanis?' I said 'yes' and I got a guard to take me down. We went through a few clicking doors and I thought I would see Valdmanis in irons in a cell. The guard knocked at the door and said: 'Dr Valdmanis, can we come in?' 'Yes!' So I came in and Dr Valdmanis was sitting in an office, in an office! And he said, 'Hello, come in, sit down, how are you doing?' and all this and he said to the guard, 'Could you get me Max, please, and get me some coffee and cookies.' Max was something. He did twenty years for murder ... and he was a resident genius in the St John's jail. He ran the sewing machine and when there was anything wrong Max could fix it. He was also a certified pipefitter, and he was the chief cook. Max came with a cup of coffee and some cookies and we had quite a friendly chat.[91]

Not surprisingly, the Opposition, press, and radio repeatedly maintained that Valdmanis was receiving privileged treatment, that he had been permitted to leave the penitentiary and to visit homes and offices in the city, and that he was wined and dined in private homes. It was even alleged that in September 1955 he had been driven in a private car to Salmonier Line for salmon and trout fishing. In response, Attorney General Curtis did confirm that Valdmanis had been transferred for one month to the Salmonier prison camp in connection with his storekeeping duties. From there he had been taken in the prison warden's private car to fish. All prisoners were allowed to fish in their off moments, so Valdmanis was receiving no special consideration, Curtis insisted. Other than that, Valdmanis had been brought under guard to the office of the attorney general only once to investigate his assets and find out if anything could be recovered. He was being treated as all other prisoners, so the media and others should forget about him.[92]

The political opposition ensured that Valdmanis would not be forgotten. Fired up by an aggressive press campaign led by Smallwood's former friend-turned-critic, Harold Horwood, they campaigned to discredit the faltering new industries program. Throughout 1955 and 1956 they bombarded Smallwood with embarrassing evidence brought to light in 1954 and with excerpts from Valdmanis's unpublished defence. Put on the defensive, Smallwood blamed Valdmanis, or allowed him to be blamed, for the worst scandals and flaws associated with his new industries. Valdmanis, claimed Smallwood, was the culprit in various shady connections: He had given Max Braun-Wogau money to intercept Sennewald in November 1951, had helped Ludwig Grube get away with his illegal transfer of Newfoundland funds to Germany, had arranged for MIAG to buy the cement plant with the help of a government loan, had made the Newfoundland government pay $50,000 for breach of contract to the New York group, and had appointed Olga Leikucs a director of Atlantic Hardboards.[93]

By the end of 1955 the media expressed satisfaction that Smallwood was beginning to recognize 'incompetence on the part of foreign personnel entrusted with management of the projects' and was capable of 'cleaning up the mess.' An *Evening Telegram* editorial took this as an admission of the

> indiscretion of accepting for appointments the recommendations of such a type of individual as Valdmanis, of whose true record he could know little or nothing and whose dishonesty is attested by the prison sentence imposed

> upon him by the court of justice. It was a major blunder to entrust the important responsibilities of Director General of Economic Development to this refugee, whose story of his qualifications could not be confirmed, and it was a further indiscretion to accept from that individual recommendations of other foreign nationals to direct the establishment of new industrial schemes. The circumstances of their dismissal have not been given full publicity, but sufficient is known to show that they were unworthy of the responsibilities entrusted to them or of the princely salaries which they with Valdmanis were paid.[94]

As early as 22 September 1954 it was 'beyond all question' for Canada's national German-language paper *Der Nordwesten* that Alfred Valdmanis had caused great damage to the reputation of all Latvian, if not all European, immigrants. He was a disgrace they might have to fear for many years. During a visit to St John's in June 1955, Hubertus Herz confirmed that the exposure of financial manipulations in connection with the Valdmanis trial had discredited virtually all of Newfoundland's German new industries so that Germans in general no longer had a good press in the province.[95] West Germany could see trouble ahead for their expatriates because of developments in Newfoundland in the spring of 1955, the *Montreal Times* commented. In Ottawa a member of the House of Commons claimed to have learned from Smallwood that German immigrants employed in two government-backed industries would get 'the bum's rush' and be deported for saying certain things.[96]

Even more worried was Newfoundland's small and now divided Latvian community. Its members were suspected by the public and the political opposition of being in collusion with Valdmanis, even if, as in the case of Ernest Leja, they had cooperated with the prosecution to clear their names. In late 1954 an Atlantic Films and Electronics employee was shocked to hear a deputy minister in her store exclaim, 'Ah, you are one of those,' when she identified herself as a Latvian immigrant. Local Latvians remained generally convinced that Valdmanis's refusal to plead guilty on the first of the charges against him was proof that Smallwood had indeed pocketed the $270,000 in question.[97]

Starting in September 1955 Smallwood began to 'boot out' the foreign management of several of his new industries, in part for their close association with Valdmanis. The first to go was Max Braun-Wogau. By March 1955 fifteen other foreign managerial personnel had shared this fate, followed by a growing stream of skilled immigrant workers recruited by these industries. Signing an affidavit containing false information doomed Braun-Wogau in a clear-cut case. He had stated in it for his friend Valdmanis that Grube had bribed Smallwood with prefabricated German military barracks for hen-houses. In fact, Smallwood produced documentation showing he had paid for them. Braun-Wogau also used to 'go back and forth' to see Valdmanis in 1954, and they became very friendly with the Opposition, Smallwood charged.[98] The purge of industries caused one local German to remark in December 1955 that 'soon none of the Germans and Latvians who came here during the Valdmanis era would be left.'[99]

If Premier Smallwood was serious about cleaning up the Valdmanis mess, why was the second charge left hanging, why was it not dropped or proceeded with? Opposition member Malcolm Hollett wanted to know in September 1955. This drew the disclosure from Smallwood that he was indeed dragging out the case. Smallwood was looking for restitution and did not want Valdmanis to get away with anything. If Smallwood had his way, the Latvian would get eight years in jail instead of four.[100] This was exactly what Valdmanis had feared. But when rumours resurfaced in 1955 that Valdmanis had been a 'Jew baiter,' that he had 'shot two thousand Jews,' Smallwood discarded these as 'a filthy lie.' Joey Smallwood never changed his 1956 public portrayal of Valdmanis as 'a man of towering ability even if he is a great crook' who 'took me in. He took the Newfoundland Government in. He took Newfoundland in. He took in hundreds of people he met.'[101]

chapter twelve

'Maybe My Luck Is Used Up Already, Maybe Not': Epilogue, 1956–1970, and Conclusions

Alfred Valdmanis, a brilliant financier, planner and builder of industries, a dreamer who abruptly turns into a cold mathematician when his budget or economic development plans require so, he belongs to Old Europe at its best.

A thinker of the highest calibre, a trainee in his youth by the English and German economists and financiers like Montague and Dr Schacht, he soon proved that he can do more than just copy or duplicate. There is no doubt that he is one of the world's most enlightened and most powerful economic thinkers, and therefore respected, loved, and also feared. Official recognition, honours, and medals have been showered upon him; admiration, envy, and hatred have followed him too. – His mission lies in the fields of planning and directing industrialization, and the economic and social emancipation of peoples and countries still underdeveloped, divided, or asleep; and there is no doubt that we shall hear of him again – he simply is too big to get lost even on the big American continent.

Alfred Valdmanis, excerpt from Résumé, May 1963[1]

Alfred Valdmanis served just over two years of 'hard labour' in Newfoundland that ended on 1 January 1957. Released without fanfare, he was immediately hustled on board a Trans Canada Airlines plane for Montreal under the alias of A. Smith. However, he was noticed at the St John's airport by two *Evening Telegram* reporters who had obtained advance information of his parole and flight plans. Fellow passengers aboard his plane observed that Valdmanis did not leave the aircraft on any of its five stops. Picked up at Montreal airport by his wife and two male friends, Valdmanis refused to talk to reporters except to say that he had no plans.

His release had not been ordered in Newfoundland – the province had no parole board then – but in Ottawa by the director of remission services following investigation into the application on behalf of the prisoner. Having served slightly more than half his four-year sentence, he was required to report monthly to the parole authorities for the rest of his term.[2]

The fourteen years remaining in the life of Alfred Valdmanis were filled with futile searches for a new career, battling constant income tax reassessments, and attempts to rescue his pre-1954 reputation from what his family came to label 'the scandal.' Lost forever were most of the social and professional connections and such old and trusted friends as Friedrich Kreyser. Valdis Mateus, his closest friend and confidant remained loyal, although financially ruined and demoralized. Valdis had hoped in vain to augment his relatively meagre fortunes as a building superintendent in New Jersey through joint ventures with Alfred and his brother Osvald, especially the St Andrews enterprise. In New York Valdis used to devote a large portion of his time to Latvian exile politics on behalf of Alfred's political interests. This now earned him derision. Valdis died in 1973 of cancer.[3]

Home and Citizenship Endangered

For Valdmanis, returning to Montreal meant, above all, facing an impoverished family in a hostile world. All the family's assets except their home at 274 Roslyn Avenue had been surrendered to the Newfoundland government. Two-thirds of the mortgage on that house had been paid for with the $10,000 the family had brought with them from Europe. Thanks to efforts of his lawyer Major Louis Bloomfield, the mortgage payments had been stayed while Valdmanis was in prison. Valdmanis's son Gundars recalled that 'we kept the house afloat by everybody working (even the two 14-year-olds had summer jobs away from home), we three boys delivered 700 papers per day, and Mother – in addition to working – ran a virtual boarding-house.' There were fourteen people (all relatives) in a five-bedroom house. Mara's education was terminated. While in college, Gundars worked night shifts on construction projects until the St Lawrence would freeze over. They also relied on charity.[4]

While his family struggled to survive, Alfred Valdmanis was subjected to a review of his citizenship status by the Department of Citizenship and Immigration. A request for revocation of his citizenship and deportation from Canada was initiated by one F.H. Whitley of Montreal. Whitley wrote the minister in 1954 that immigrants having been granted Canadian citizenship and found guilty of less serious crimes used to be deported back 'whence they came':

> He [Valdmanis] came here with nothing and for years he has been living like a prince. Where did the money come from? How many private firms have been defrauded (or welched) we do not yet know ... Everyone knows that in East Europe as soon as a man gets a government job he sets to work to amass as much as he can at the country's expense to feather his nest for the future. They are all tarred with the same brush. Mr Smallwood should have been intelligent enough to know that. And no Provincial government can afford to pay a man $30,000 a year. Anyway, our friend Smallwood must feel pretty small now ... A poor unemployed man will steal to feed himself or his family. That can be understood, but an intelligent person capable of caring for himself, and given every opportunity in the world, has no excuse whatsoever for wrongdoing. Throw him out and good riddance to such of his ilk.[5]

In August 1956 William Hamilton, Progressive Conservative MP for the Montreal constituency of Notre Dame de Grâce, contacted Minister Jack Pickersgill to enquire whether any consideration had been given to revoking the citizenship of his constituent Valdmanis. Hamilton was concerned that the deportation of Valdmanis to his native country would amount to a death sentence in view of his known record of anti-communism. The matter was referred to the legal division of the Department of Citizenship and Immigration, which advised that, since his citizenship had not been obtained by false representations or fraud, the only possible prima facie grounds for revocation would be conviction of an offence involving disaffection or disloyalty to Her Majesty. In November 1956 Pickersgill informed Hamilton that there were no legal grounds to justify revocation of Alfred Valdmanis's Canadian citizenship.[6]

Tax Problems

Income tax problems for Valdmanis proved to be virtually intractable. These arose from the reassessment by the Department of National Revenue of Valdmanis's tax returns for the years 1950 to 1954. In 1956 the department's taxation division listed as undeclared income for those years a total of some $94,000. Excluded from this amount were restitutions to the government of Newfoundland of assets connected with MIAG and Benno Schilde. Despite the help of several lawyers, particularly Claude S. Richardson, requests for a much lower assessment were denied, allegedly because Valdmanis's former solicitor Gordon Higgins had missed the January 1955 deadline for filing an official notice of appeal.[7]

Valdmanis argued that during 1950–4 his entire income had consisted of his Canadian salary. To refute the claim that he should have reported on his tax returns salaries of $50,000 from Port Clyde Packing Company and interest amounting to almost $5,000 on loans, Valdmanis presented an affidavit from Samuel Zwecker, president of Port Clyde Packing. It stated that during the years 1951–3 Valdmanis 'did not receive any salaries, remuneration, bonuses, interest or any payments whatever.'[8]

Contrary to the taxation division's claim that commission payments of $25,000 and $3,997.56 through Elja Lurje were not accounted for, Valdmanis 'emphatically' stated that he had never received or possessed any such monies from Lurje. He insisted that all that he had received from Lurje were St Andrews Packers Ltd shares, Lurje's endorsement of his claim against St Andrews Packers, and the renovated St Andrews plant. Any property received from Lurje, Valdmanis declared, had had its origins with either MIAG or Benno Schilde and hence had to be transferred to the Newfoundland government. About one point Valdmanis wanted to leave no doubt: 'Lurje had acquired St Andrews Packers, and the claim against it, and had attempted to revitalize it, at an aggregate investment on his part which must have by far exceeded the amounts of $25,000 and $3,997.50.'[9]

To convince the director of appeals in Ottawa of what he considered the most plausible explanation for the fate of the money, Valdmanis disclosed a convoluted story. He maintained that he himself trusted Lurje and could only suspect what happened when Lurje came in possession of money. Painting a mysterious scenario, Valdmanis asserted that Lurje was 'certainly' also trusted by 'his lifetime German friends who testified [at Valdmanis's preliminary inquiry] that they "never knew him" though they still are in partnership with him in Bodenwerder, Germany.'[10] Unfortunately, Valdmanis did not elaborate further on this implication.

As proof of Lurje's close ties with these German friends, Valdmanis produced a written agreement of December 1949 between Lurje in New York and Friedrich Kreyser and Max Braun-Wogau in Bodenwerder, Germany. In this, the latter two (as co-owners of a share of Ur-Weser Gypsum Quarries Ltd and co-managers of that company and of United Building Industries Bodenwerder) confirmed to Lurje that they would endeavour to settle all their accounts either through direct transfers or through transfers to Mrs Katrina Mateus. Final accounting was to be made with the advice of Valdmanis or by his arbitration, if necessary. The document concluded that 'under present transfer regulations of Germany requiring transfer-permits, the actual transfer may require a long time; therefore we must regulate our deals on the basis of "trust and confidence," and final settlement can be arrived at, only when – in the unforeseeable future – all of us should be able to get together in the USA or in Germany.' Valdmanis explained that co-ownership of a share meant that, although Lurje owned one-third, Lurje's part was technically in the names of Kreyser and Braun-Wogau because persons of Jewish origin could not own property in Nazi Germany. Valdmanis acknowledged that the reference to Mrs K. Mateus meant, in fact, him. Nonetheless, he thought it should also be clear that he was not directly and personally interested; otherwise, he could not have been chosen as arbiter. Valdmanis maintained adamantly that no funds or anything else were ever transferred to him (or K. Mateus) from Kreyser, Braun-Wogau, or Lurje.[11]

Even though Valdmanis filed his current taxes regularly, he eventually claimed inability to pay his 'huge re-assessment.' On 26 March 1969 the government attached and seized all of his assets. The Montreal branch of the taxation division had become 'indignant at my flouting of my tax obligations and had decided to teach me a lesson,' he wrote his solicitor J. Claude Couture of Montreal, hoping that an acceptable settlement was still possible.[12] By September 1969, however, that hope had evaporated, and Valdmanis decided to declare bankruptcy claiming as his sole creditor the National Revenue Department for $118,000. On that occasion he listed total assets of $5,603.75, shares valued at $5,500, a car at $100, and earnings as an economic consultant in 1968 of $3,613. The media reported that Valdmanis was living in Edmonton, separated from his wife, who was self-supporting from her work, and that their four children were grown.[13]

Search for Employment

After his release from prison, Valdmanis had received good wishes from a number of old friends, including William Stephenson, Claude Richardson, and Bloomfield associate Murray G. Ballantyne. But no one could help him find a satisfactory career. His last résumé showed the following chequered employment record: 1956–8, senior sales officer, Brock Steel Corporation, Montreal; 1958–63, general manager, CARA

Development Corporation, Montreal; 1963–5, general manager, Cartonage du Quebec, Quebec City; 1965–7, chief economist, Loram Limited, Calgary; 1967–8, owner, Western Consultants, Edmonton; 1969–70, partner, Nash and Associates, Edmonton.[14] Although some of these titles appear impressive, the reality behind them has been difficult to ascertain and seems disappointing.

According to Gundars Valdmanis, the first two offers his father received after his release from prison were a senior position with the Jesuit order and a job with the Central Intelligence Agency (CIA), but on Gundars's advice he turned both of them down to look for a more appropriate career in private business. He eventually decided to revive an import–export business (CARA) with capital of $40,000 brought together by several Latvians. It started out selling such items as Japanese shirts and army surplus, but in 1962 was forced into receivership by lack of payment from defence construction work.[15]

In his 1963 search for work, Valdmanis used the Very Reverend Alfreds Skrodelis; Ray N. Bryson (consul for Denmark in Toronto); Gaston Pratte, chairman of the executive committee of the Banque Provinciale du Canada; and Edgars Andersons, professor of history at California State University in San Jose, as references. Skrodelis vouched for Valdmanis's 'personal integrity and high moral standards.' Bryson praised his devotion to a cause and 'quiet contempt for a certain type of political activity' he had had to encounter. Pratte asked his personal and business friends to extend to his friend of 'a good many years' the same consideration they would extend to him. Pratte, like former NALCO director Claude Richardson, was believed to belong to a group of well-connected Liberals who felt that Valdmanis deserved to be rehabilitated.[16]

Andersons permitted his own name to be associated with sworn statements including alleged extracts from Andersons's personal correspondence and references to his research on Baltic history from 1914 to 1945. In one extract Andersons is quoted as mentioning Valdmanis's name in connection with the 'outstandingly great role you filled in the history of Northeastern Europe.' Another extract, referring to Andersons's access to confidential German records and reports by American diplomats formerly stationed in the Baltic area, asserts that 'all these reports, without exception, show unconcealed admiration and respect of your abilities and dedicated work.' According to a concluding sworn statement, Andersons is alleged to have repeatedly praised Valdmanis, whom he 'quite obviously regards ... as the outstanding hero in European economics, industry and trade and something like a wonderchild in European economics and politics before the Second World War, and as a legendary Latvian national hero during the war.'[17]

Documented among the employment opportunities Valdmanis pursued are his approaches to the Royal Paper Box Company in Montreal, to the Lockheed–Georgia Company in Atlanta, and to Professor John Carancis, MD, in Cincinnati. His job application to the Royal Paper Box Company listed among his credentials the degree of doctor of jurisprudence from the University of Frankfurt and his positions as director general of economic development in Newfoundland and chairman of NALCO. This application admitted his incarceration. Although 'internationally known for his economic planning and industrial development,' according to his résumé, 'as a result of his employment and the political climate at the time, Dr Valdmanis was imprisoned in Newfoundland in 1954.'

To the Lockheed–Georgia Company, in response to an advertisement in *Time* magazine, Valdmanis presented himself as an economic planner with 'the best possible academic education ... which old Europe could give. I am a deep and clear economic thinker and analyst who does not shrink from coming to clear and unequivocal conclusions.' As additional assets, he noted his positions as '"Director General" and even "Cabinet Minister" without ever belonging to any political party or group.' For his activities he had earned official recognition and honours:

> In 1948 the Davis Foundation cited me, in economics and industrial development, as one of Europe's 'most outstanding scholars and scientists.' I have been an above-average professor of economics (product and market research management), Government researcher and advisor on industrial development and foreign trade, and a very successful chief policy officer and Executive in the exploration and development of natural resources, steel, and transportation and its problems. My income is over $25,000 per annum, which is about the senior level in Canada, but my family are desirous of migrating to the USA, and ... it seemed to me that I could so perfectly answer your needs.[18]

'With humility and even with some feeling of shame' Valdmanis approached Professor John Carancis at the University of Cincinnati, as a fellow Latvian, on the recommendation of the latter's sister-in-law. All his life he had not been forced to ask for help but had been in a position to help others. Now his applications did not even get him on the short lists, so he could not present himself in person for a job in the United States. 'I have to be seen to be judged,' he pleaded. Although fifty-five years old, he had no grey hair, still 'ranked' as a tennis player for singles, and had been considered as 'exceptionally gifted and, maybe, some kind of a *Wunderkind*.' He was looking for work in the United States, but he suspected that on paper his extensive theoretical and practical qualifications appeared confusing to Americans. How could one explain by mail that in Europe a 'general director' was 'a very rare bird, a person required to have exceptional abilities, trustworthiness and natural talent to direct and coordinate matters and people,' and to be 'capable of research and administration'? Valdmanis claimed expertise in both as well as in international marketing.

Could Carancis arrange for Valdmanis to be invited somewhere for a personal interview? His somewhat confusing resumé might not convey a clear picture of his abilities. However, his expertise would ideally qualify him for a position as general manager or assistant to the president. He would also be satisfied as an administrator or market researcher and would not be deterred by a relatively low salary because his entire family was eager to relocate and willing to work. Since his qualifications were 'way above average,' he would not cause his sponsors any embarrassment. Any pharmaceutical company considering him might find it interesting to know about his 'good personal contact with the higher leadership of IG Farben in Germany, Canada, and the United States.' He concluded by asking if it would be possible or beneficial for him to meet Carancis in Toronto or in Cincinnati?[19]

All was to no avail. In fact, among all the jobs he applied for in the United States, only W.R. Grace and Company in New York granted Valdmanis an interview. Since no opening for relocation to the United States materialized, Valdmanis had to content himself with two short-term positions in Canada, but away from Montreal. Upon his dismissal from Loram Limited of Calgary in 1967, along with his boss W.F. Sharon, Valdmanis wrote his son Gundars that very much in life depended simply on luck. 'Maybe mine is used up already, maybe not.' Few of the companies in Montreal to whom he had sent applications ever replied. Disappointingly, they had been 'all polite, but negative.'

Initially with the help of Claude Richardson, the search began for what would be Alfred Valdmanis's last job. Under consideration were a position in Zambia, an association as junior partner with Colonel John Holt Stethem's company of Executive Personnel Consultants in Montreal, and two of Richardson's contacts in Edmonton. A letter of reference that

W.F. Sharon addressed to Preston Manning, who was about to launch a management consulting firm called Manning Consultants Limited in Edmonton, heaped high praise on Valdmanis's qualifications and concluded that 'his greatest weakness lies in his tendency to wear his heart on his sleeve, and his readiness to accept personal situations at face value.'[20]

Quest for Rehabilitation

George H. Steer, Valdmanis's new solicitor after Claude Richardson's death in February 1969, tried a new stance in the continued efforts to rehabilitate Valdmanis's career. To a Vancouver law firm approached for assistance, Steer introduced his client as 'prominent in the news a few years ago in connection with his employment by the Government of Newfoundland,' but 'very highly regarded by many prominent people in the field.' These people believed, and Steer wanted it known that he agreed with them, that Valdmanis 'was pretty badly used in the Newfoundland affair.'[21]

Steer's openly revisionist position with regard to the 1954 conviction in Newfoundland supports Gundars's claim that in his last years Valdmanis, together with Claude Richardson, had been planning various undertakings to bring about a reversal of the publicly accepted verdict. Their plan was for Richardson to reopen the case by appealing directly to the Privy Council in England. Valdmanis, although he admitted to his children that he had wrongly taken some money, appears to have intended to clear his name by referring to other Canadian kickback cases.[22] Starting with the financial scandals that drove Quebec Premier Honoré Mercier from office in 1891, Valdmanis had collected information showing that 'for decades in Quebec, the payment of kickbacks by government suppliers to the party in power was known as *le système*, and no one fought it' until 1960. Even so, when in 1964 former Union Nationale Cabinet Minister Antonio Talbot became the first convicted for fraud, he was fined only $1,300 on thirteen counts of defrauding the government. He was spared a jail sentence, 'since none of the money went to Talbot personally,' and since his political and professional life would 'suffer' from a guilty verdict.[23]

Continued involvement in local Latvian events – in 1967–8 Valdmanis helped organize Alberta's Baltic Folk Festival – and contacts with Latvian expatriates also encouraged him to relegate the so-called scandal to what he believed was its proper context. But, while barely managing to cope with this one, another alleged scandal resurfaced from the past. Despite his apparent innocence, this one was beyond his ability to eliminate.

A 1962 KGB-sponsored publication, entitled *Kas ir Daugavas Vanagi?* and issued under the imprimatur of the Soviet Latvian State publishing house in Riga (translated into English in 1963 as *Daugavas Vanagi: Who Are They?*), identified Alfred Valdmanis as a close associate of a number of Latvian war criminals whose crimes had gone unpunished in the West. The book's allegations of Latvian war criminals hiding in the West triggered police searches and a wave of arrests. Prosecutions continue to this day in Germany, Britain, the United States, Australia, and Canada. Among those charged have been Viktors Arājs, Konrāts Kalējs, Boleslavs Maikovskis, and Alberts Eichelis. (Viktors Arājs was tried and convicted in Hamburg, Germany, where he died in prison in the 1970s.)

The book names Valdmanis as a longtime associate of Oskars Dankers. The latter, according to the postwar testimony of SS chief Friedrich Jeckeln, informed the SS in Riga regularly about internal communications within the Latvian self-administration. After the war Dankers found sanctuary in Canada. The Daugavas Vanagi association, founded by ex-legionnaires in 1946, awarded Dankers honourary membership. At its 13 May 1961 gathering in Toronto, Dankers was quoted as being most indignant about the prosecution and conviction of nine Latvian war criminals from the 18th Latvian Police Battalion. In his Canadian sanctuary, the book states, Dankers found the company of former minister Valdmanis and Colonel Arthur Silgailis, who were frequent guests at major gatherings of the organization.

The book tries to establish the complicity of Valdmanis by exhibiting two potentially incriminating documents unavailable elsewhere – the minutes of a meeting held on 11 July 1941 in Riga and a telegram to Hitler from Valdmanis as leader of the delegation. The telegram addressed to 'Adolf Hitler, Führer and Reichskanzler, Headquarters' offers 'special thanks to the great and victorious champion of the German people and of all indo-Germanic peoples – Adolf Hitler. We submit to his decision the hope of the entire Latvian people to be able to take part in the struggle for the liberation of Europe. The Latvian people are ready to participate in the rebuilding of Europe and are looking forward responsibly to an appropriate decision by Adolf Hitler.'[24]

This seemingly authentic document presents Valdmanis as a member of a clique of fascist Latvians who grovelled before the Führer for the privilege of introducing his new order, solving the Jewish question in Latvia, and preparing the country for German colonization. At the time, the *Daugavas Vanagi* book contends, those young Latvians did their utmost to prove their racial credentials so that they would qualify for official postwar adoption into the Germanic race. Although the book does not implicate Valdmanis directly in war crimes, it accuses Valdmanis of guilt by association.[25]

In 1962, shortly before the book's appearance, Professor Edgars Andersons had implored Valdmanis to record for the benefit of posterity his historic experiences as a member of the Ulmanis cabinet. In response, Valdmanis sent four letters in the following year that were intended as comments to those interested in his life's work. The overall tenor is set in the introduction:

> I loved Latvia, particularly in the period of reconstruction. I believed in the ideas and goals of the regime at the time and I gave all of what could be given by a young man offering his whole life for a certain goal. I was ready to give my life and I was ready to end it when the independence of Latvia ended. For the good of Latvia, however, I was able to continue living and working in foreign countries, even when I was on a lonely island (Newfoundland), sold and buried, mainly because of the fact that something had happened and a culprit had to be found. I was all alone without friends and without roots in a foreign land where I had done so much good. I saw that a human being is so little that he cannot die even if he wanted to. I have seen the sense of life collapsing. By comparison, the squabbles among the immigrants seemed to shrink in importance.

Published, starting in 1982, in issue numbers 95 to 98 of the American Latvian journal *Treji Vārti* (Three Gates), the edited letters to Andersons deal with Valdmanis's political career up to his arrest and deportation to Germany in 1943. They supplement the description of his political role and ambitions contained in *Dienas baltas nebaltas* and correct the somewhat slanted and apologetic perspective characterizing the presumably autobiographical account published under the name of Boriss Zemgals in 1948. In addition, they provide a reflective reappraisal of the years 1938 to 1943 which Valdmanis considered as the culmination of his career. His recurrent theme is that he always intended to do what he felt was best for Latvia despite unfortunately not always succeeding.

Meanwhile, in Canada Valdmanis wondered if he could ever hope to be employed by a management consulting firm like John Holt Stethem in Montreal and with his expertise enable it to expand from executive personnel placement to management consulting. Confiding at age fifty-eight to his friend and solicitor Claude Richardson,[26] he longed for such a positive turn of events. It would reunite him with his family and friends in Montreal and eliminate his worry about what to do when he is sixty-five 'and not yet rust-eaten by a long shot.' At age sixty-one, part of his wish came true. He was invited to join Nash and Associates Limited in Edmonton, a new chartered accountant firm, as consultant and partner. In March 1970 president Hugh G. Nash announced that Alfred Valdmanis's association was enabling his company to start a new management consulting service. Nash's new partner was introduced to the staff as

> a nationally and internationally noted economist and business administrator. He has had wide experience in government, industry and commerce, teaching and management consulting. He has, at one time or another, been a Cabinet Minister (Finance, Industry and Trade) of the Republic of Latvia, Foreign Trade Advisor to the Late Right Hon. C.D. Howe, Chief Executive Officer of or Consultant to a number of large private and government enterprises and is now the Managing Director and Chief Counsellor of Nash and Associates Ltd.[27]

Life seemed to be worth living again for Valdmanis. He acquired $20,000 worth of stock in oil companies. On 11 August 1970 Valdmanis even won a tennis championship. On the way home from that event, fifteen miles west of Edmonton, the Corvair Valdmanis was driving collided head-on with a car driven by Blanche Watson of Colinton, Alberta. The accident gave Watson chest injuries, but killed Valdmanis. He was sixty-two. At his burial in Montreal, the tennis racket found in his car was put into the grave with him.[28]

According to some Edmonton acquaintances, Valdmanis had changed lodgings frequently and without warning shortly before his death. His explanation was always that he feared from Newfoundland an attempt on his life, now that the tax reassessment time bomb had been defused.[29] But other friends told Gundars after the funeral that his father had been talking about clearing his name in connection with indications that Joey Smallwood was losing control of Newfoundland. Years later Edmonton friends were still considering initiatives to clear Valdmanis's name, rectify injustices caused to him, and 'illuminate his personality from the right perspective.'[30]

Obituaries

Smallwood, after hearing of Valdmanis's death, remarked that he was 'a brilliant but tragic figure.' Premier Smallwood's former finance minister Greg Power went even further in clearing the name of the Latvian, whom he had always disliked and distrusted, by portraying him as 'a talented, brilliant man, an accomplished musician, athlete, and linguist': 'Dr Valdmanis wasn't all bad. I feel if there had been good management for the Valdmanis industries they would have worked. They were the kind of industries, small industries, that we should be introducing that would have had a chance of succeeding in Newfoundland. At first the foreign businessmen came here with the thought of getting a foothold in the New World, but when they discovered what the local situation was, they obviously decided to make a fast buck and get out.' According to Power, Valdmanis had lost his money to two 'fast talking Jewish promoters in New York.' Had he selected a jury trial, Power believed, Valdmanis would have been acquitted because of the political atmosphere of the time.[31]

In obituaries Valdmanis remained 'a mystery man' to the end, 'brilliant' (*Evening Telegram*), a 'financial wizard' (*Globe and Mail*), who experienced 'meteoric rise, then prison' (Montreal *Gazette*). Most papers sketched him as 'a small, sharp man with a quick temper,' whose wartime record was clouded in secrecy, who promised Smallwood one new industry a year, and whose earnings had risen from $10,000 in 1950 to $30,000 in 1953 and then dropped to $3,613 in 1968. The *Daily News* editor credited Valdmanis, although an 'adventurer' whose promotions cost the province millions, with having established a profitable cement industry. He attributed Valdmanis's behaviour in Newfoundland to adversities that had shaped his career.[32]

One Newfoundland paper, the weekly *Sunday Herald*, on 16 August 1970, went so far as to allow Latvian reporter Tonija Krūka to clear Valdmanis's name. She had never accepted his guilt and had always been a staunch defender of his innocence. To prove that 'he was not the kind of man who would give away for money his good name' and high reputation among Latvians and friends all over the world, she reviewed some of the highlights of his life in Latvia from 1938 to 1943. In particular, she explained his award of the Swedish order of the North Star, his suffering under the first Soviet occupation, and the courage with which he criticized the Nazi occupation regime. 'Valdmanis came to Newfoundland with a glorious reputation,' the editor wrote in his summary of Krūka's article. 'He will long be remembered by Newfoundlanders and Latvians, but for different reasons.'

Albert Perlin had helped Joey Smallwood recruit this Latvian in Ottawa and came to know him well. In four *Daily News* articles Perlin had the final word on the significance of Newfoundland's Valdmanis era. Even for him, this 'little man with the square forehead and brushed-back hair that used to be characterized as Prussian,' had always remained a mystery. His appointment in Newfoundland was a by-product of the fear gripping Smallwood that Newfoundlanders would abandon the island for the mainland unless jobs could be created through a revolutionary expansion of the Newfoundland economy. On the eve of his appointment, Valdmanis had repeated to Perlin and other friends of Smallwood his 'well-rehearsed' life story. All the listeners found it so remarkable 'that it was hard to suspect that it had been invented.' However, mystery surrounded Valdmanis's somewhat contradictory claims of his German appointment to recruit a Latvian Legion, imprisonment to be executed, rescue by the king of Sweden, and then German employment as senior administrator in the wartime production of cement and gypsum. 'He told me he had no choice and was always under the eyes of a guard.'[33]

According to Perlin, Valdmanis came to Canada because Hugh Keenleyside 'took a liking to the intense little Latvian' in Geneva and tried to help him. As a consultant in Ottawa for the Department of Trade and Commerce, Perlin had learned, Valdmanis would 'toil' at a task 'day and night and then badger the life out of the officials who had given him the job, demanding insistently and impatiently that they take prompt action on his submission.' The head of the department, C.D. Howe, was therefore anxious to get the persistent Latvian 'out of his hair.' The government-financed cement and gypsum industries launched in Newfoundland became 'his opportunity to make a quick fortune and were to prove his ultimate undoing.'[34]

In Newfoundland, Perlin explained, these industries seemed to bear the promise of an economic revolution. The lure of transforming the poorhouse of North America into a rich, industrial province dulled perception of the realities behind the glamorous facade of the new industries. But little went according to plan. 'The weakness of the whole scheme lay in the failure to employ a consultant engineering firm to evaluate each operation, control its costs, and inspect the machinery and its capacity.' Perlin doubted whether anyone could be held responsible for this. 'Perhaps because of the impetuosity' with which the industrial development scheme was approached, it attracted adventurers. Such ventures as Ludwig Grube's rubber plant were not his doing, Valdmanis had told Perlin. Working 'day and night' on a complicated plan to procure financiers for NALCO's development plans, Valdmanis was critical of

Smallwood's idea of replacing NALCO with BRINCO, Perlin remembered. Valdmanis moved the NALCO office to Montreal only with the premier's permission.[35]

Perlin recalled that Valdmanis was rapidly losing favour in late 1953 when the new industries no longer looked promising. The government had spent $20 million and had little to show for it. The new industries were losing money and providing little employment for Smallwood's electorate: 'He came to see me one day in the summer of 1953, a depressed little man, his face tortured with anxiety, and most of the fire gone from him. He talked for hours, but it was a rambling conversation of which I recall very little ... He was concerned that he was out of favour and told me he was about to leave Newfoundland, the Premier having agreed that he could have the Nalco office moved to Montreal.'[36]

When Valdmanis was asked to resign in February 1954, Smallwood did not inform him that having charged personal luxuries to NALCO's account was one of the reasons. Valdmanis was allowed to remain a director of NALCO and receive a salary until his arrest, but it was only a third of his former salary as director general. Perlin found it curious that most of the extorted money traced by the RCMP had gone to two European refugees in New York, one of whom Perlin identified as Latvian and the other as Romanian. 'There was a scent of blackmail about the whole business, evidently associated with the past of Valdmanis.' Perlin did not think that the mystery surrounding this man could ever be unravelled.[37]

Conclusions

By the time of his death, it had become a public stock-in-trade that 'Alfred Valdmanis's life had more zigzags than the contours of Newfoundland, which he bestrode.'[38] From the time of his first major portrayal, on 25 May 1950 in the St John's *Daily News*, as the director general of economic development, the repetition of the embellished highlights of Valdmanis's fantastic career as originally presented to the Canadian Senate in 1949 became a regular identification mark: He was one of seven hundred boys specially selected to be trained for leadership in Latvia, at age twenty-three he was a doctor of jurisprudence at the University of Frankfurt, as a 'foe of the nation' he endured severe ordeals under Soviet and Nazi occupation but the king of Sweden intervened to save him, he rescued eight hundred people in the bombing of a Berlin public building and thus was a sure bet for a high decoration for bravery, he was a top planner with the International Refugee Organization in

Geneva, he was in high demand in Ottawa when Smallwood hired him, and so on.

The constant officially unquestioned dissemination of this 'story-book career' was tantamount to the systematic cultivation of a myth. Continuing for years, it coloured perception of Valdmanis's work in Newfoundland and refused to die even with exposure to reality. Indeed, the ambiguities surrounding his arrest, preliminary inquiry, and confession merely served to reinforce the *Wunderkind* story by adding the enigmas of scapegoat or con man. Instead of clearing the air, Valdmanis's conviction thus gave rise to an enduring legend.

Indeed, several versions of the Valdmanis legend gained currency upon the forced termination of his career in 1954 and have survived his death. Among family and friends, Valdmanis remained the great Latvian patriot whose promising career was destroyed by the need for a foreign scapegoat on a remote island. According to his native country's official Soviet line, he belonged to a clique of fascist Latvians worshipping the Führer, abetting in war crimes, and preparing Latvia for germanization. Among Latvian Social Democrats, and in post-communist Latvia, he came to be viewed as the ambitious fortune hunter who miraculously surmounted all odds by conspiring with Latvia's most powerful enemies – Soviet Russia and Nazi Germany.[39] In Canada and Britain his name became associated with the protection of war criminals.[40] And in Newfoundland he has come to embody the enigmatic carpetbagger leaving a legacy of fraud and costly failure.[41]

The legacy of Alfred Valdmanis's politics of survival haunts Latvians, Canadians, and Newfoundlanders to this day. Having barely reclaimed independence of their country from the former Soviet Union, Latvians are still trying to come to terms with his historical role in those fateful prewar and wartime years. Some consider Valdmanis 'very successful,' judged by what he accomplished as finance minister during his short term. They credit him with restoring good Swedish–Latvian relations, reorganizing the Ministry of Finance, activating foreign trade, establishing an Institute of Rationalization and a Research Institute for National Resources, and clearing up the matter of the Swedish match monopoly.[42] Others consider him a traitor, conspiring with the totalitarian powers about to occupy his country.[43] Under the wartime occupation regimes, the debate continues, did Valdmanis head a de facto government 'entirely' without German approval,[44] or was he the 'most prominent Latvian collaborator willingly serving Stalin and Hitler'?[45] In Newfoundland, his name is invoked to reinforce two equally one-sided and negative connotations – that of the 'murky,' 'shadowy,' 'Rasputin-like' foreign economist whose chief ambition was fraud,[46] and the more sinister one of the 'skilled international criminal' with an assumed record of war crimes.[47] In local lore, moreover, Newfoundland humour and mistrust of foreigners have combined to portray Valdmanis as a cunning comedian audaciously outsmarting the master politician J.R. Smallwood. One example is the enduring local legend, related by Alan Phillips in 1954 and retold as fact as late as 1998 by John Crosbie, about how Valdmanis negotiated his 10 per cent commission. On visits to Germany Valdmanis allegedly made these deals in German in the very presence of Smallwood. While negotiating with Valdmanis the German industrialists would bow politely towards the premier whenever the name 'Smallwood' was mentioned, and he would smile back not understanding a word being said.[48]

Valdmanis, of course, was much too circumspect to take such brazen risks. Nor do the images of comedian, international criminal, Rasputin-like economist, conspirator, traitor, head of a shadow government, and successful finance minister capture the essence of his life's work and aspirations. These images isolate episodes of his career and ignore the overall historical framework. Although his ultimate accomplishments came to virtually nothing, the secret of his fascinating life story is buried in his uncanny ability to survive almost unbelievable odds and surface atop the most diverse situations from 1934 to 1954. Part of his destiny is attributable to circumstance, but most of it to his own manipulations and ambitions. His tendencies to egomania as well as depression, although sometimes unduly magnified, do not unravel the mystery of the man's survival. A political chameleon and careerist, Alfred Valdmanis relied on his exceptional talents, antennae keenly attuned to changing situations, carefully cultivated network of contacts, charisma, and plain hard work. Within this larger context, and in view of the unrelenting endeavours of numerous opponents to bring him down, the survival of Alfred Valdmanis appears as an extraordinary, if not admirable, feat rather than a manifestation of deviant behaviour or criminal motives.

Seemingly born for the top, Valdmanis admitted more than once that he became President Ulmanis's finance minister too fast. He owed this promotion entirely to Ulmanis, whom he had impressed with his authoritarian political stance, professional competence, and strong work ethic. At the time his ambition to prove himself qualified for leadership seemed to fuel his unusual capacity for hard work. His career in Latvia's Ministry of Finance confirmed the value of competence and hard work for leadership and advancement. Reading the signs of the times, Valdmanis resigned from the cabinet at a time and in a manner that enabled him to prepare for the alternate possibilities of Soviet or German occupation. In addition to having persuasively projected the appropriate image to the diplomatic representatives of each future occupying power – alleged state secrets that he confided to the Soviet envoy were lies – previously nurtured contacts rescued him. From July 1941 to January 1943 Valdmanis settled on collaboration as the most expedient strategy to promote his own career while neutralizing hostile German officials, foiling policies detrimental to Latvians, and ameliorating daily life under the occupation regime. Terminating collaboration in 1943 was dangerous, and without the intercession of a German banker, an old acquaintance from prewar days and now a high-ranking Nazi official, his life story might have ended right there.

In the pursuit of his two-pronged postwar quest for both democratic credentials and leadership of the Latvian exile cause, Valdmanis's survival strategy began to backfire. While passing British, American, and United Nations security screenings with flying colours, in part thanks to his old network of contacts and affidavits prepared by himself under the alias of Boriss Zemgals, some of the Latvian refugee community in western Europe rebuffed his aspirations and exposed his alias. Luckily for him, influential Canadian contacts at his IRO workplace facilitated his migration to Canada. Omitting politically embarrassing aspects of his past from his new Canadian image, Valdmanis moved from short-term appointments with Carleton College and with the federal government to economic consulting with the governments of Nova Scotia and finally Newfoundland. Nova Scotia's failure to adopt his development scheme drove home the fundamental insecurity of his financial situation. That experience convinced him to ensure his economic survival, by whatever means necessary, as soon as the next opportunity arose.

There is no evidence that Valdmanis committed serious transgressions before he came to Newfoundland. Alfreds Bērziņš's accusation that Valdmanis was fired by President Ulmanis for mixing official with personal business appears as unfounded as his insinuation that in 1940 Valdmanis denounced Ulmanis and Andrejs Bērziņš to the NKVD. Nor is there verification of his involvement in any war crimes – his intransigent opponents would certainly have wasted no time to publicize any available evidence. The only guilt he could be rightly accused of was association with war criminals through his indiscriminate defence of the legionnaires' interests. In fact, war criminals among the legionnaires were admitted to Canada and remained unidentified for some time thereafter, thanks in part to the persuasive and persistent cover-up efforts by such leading Latvian spokesmen as Valdmanis.

Nor would it appear that Valdmanis's manipulation of his *curriculum vitae* was an extraordinary transgression. A 1996 job-hunters' guide has estimated that 'one-third to one-half of all job hunters lie on their resumes. They lie by: inflating their title or responsibilities, omitting their firings or failures, inflating their results, inflating their credentials, hiding jobs where they did terribly, and a lot of other subterfuges.'[49]

Dedication to Newfoundland's challenges would establish his reputation as a successful economist, Valdmanis assumed, ensure his financial survival, and serve as a launching pad for a more rewarding career elsewhere. On that basis, Alfred Valdmanis did his utmost – in terms of working excessive overtime and utilizing all his connections – to make Joey Smallwood's new industries' program a success. In their symbiotic relationship Smallwood was clearly the inspiring and driving force and Valdmanis at first the enthusiastic and then the increasingly reluctant executor of Smallwood's will.

In the end, though, personal failings overshadowed and obscured his professional potential and achievements. 'What baffling motive, what failure of moral or spiritual fibre, forced him on a career of crime, to not only theft, but to betrayal of confidence and position?' Canadians speculated after Valdmanis's conviction. The sad irony of the situation, as articulated by the *Globe and Mail*, was that 'this man was young, brilliant; before him stretched a dazzling future. And he did not need money. A man may steal because he has come to desperate financial straits, but while his crime is still a crime, it is understandable. Alfred Valdmanis, by most men's standards, had fortune as well as fame. He had a position of trust and high adventure, the acclaim of his fellow men, enjoyed a salary of $25,000 a year; the country of his adoption had been good to him ... What a tragedy is here!'[50] Indeed, his real tragedy was his mistaken belief that his compromise of ethics would enable his long-term survival at the height of success. Instead, it brought him down with a crash.

In the environment of postwar Canada, Valdmanis found it increasingly difficult to deal with his past in an acceptable manner. Valdmanis was vulnerable to the agendas of Latvia's postwar Soviet regime, the Latvian Social Democrats in Sweden, the legionnaires in North America, the revived Tālavija fraternity in exile, and the local and international refugee community at large that periodically exposed, queried, and attacked his record. Yet in the end his past only indirectly triggered his downfall, namely, through his quest for lasting economic prosperity.

With the duration of his Newfoundland job initially elusive, material security for himself and his family assumed top priority. Alfred Valdmanis equated material security with a lifestyle befitting him as a former cabinet minister and the aspiring leader of Latvians everywhere. In his zeal to lay the appropriate foundations for economic independence, he relied on a network of relatives and shady New York-based wheeler–dealer refugees. His plan to obtain investment funds fraudulently for this venture – by keeping commission payments – was hatched in April 1950 when he was unemployed and his prospects looked dismal.

Investigators have never been able to locate most of the $430,000 in commission funds that Valdmanis presumably diverted into unprofitable business ventures. After his arrest, some of the commission funds were found invested in a defunct fish plant in New Brunswick. Meanwhile, his New York associates had disappeared with the remaining liquid assets. Despite rumours of the money being swallowed by political opponents' blackmail, no proof of this exists. Nor has any evidence been uncovered that the Valdmanis family benefited in any way from monies that might have been concealed by him or his associates. Indeed, sitting in his mother's modest Montreal home, Gundars exclaimed with eloquent simplicity, 'Just look at how we live!'[51]

Various incriminating innuendos dogged Alfred Valdmanis throughout his career. But the only charge that haunted him until he confessed in the court room in St John's on 15 September 1954 was the diversion into his own New York investment account of the commission payments extorted in the name of the premier of Newfoundland. Valdmanis agonized over the subsequent devastation wrought to him and his family by the revelations. But while confessing to these 'transactions,' Valdmanis never did consider it a morally serious crime to enrich himself in office – in view of his circumstances and what he believed and, in part, observed to be well-established practices in his host society. At the time it was still widely held, as analysts of the local scene have disclosed, that '"a person who got something out of the government" was not really doing anything wrong; and if he was actually *in* the government, but did not gain financially from it, then "there must be something wrong with him." The notion of "to the victor the spoils," was generally accepted as right and just by politicians and people alike.'[52]

'Graft was rampant,' Smallwood biographer Richard Gwyn stressed and added: 'Smallwood knew of everything that happened and was supremely unconcerned.'[53] Never concealing his admiration for the corrupt Newfoundland leader Richard Squires, Joey Smallwood 'didn't object to people using their positions to gain special privilege,' Harold Horwood recalled. 'They were all doing it. Newfoundland had no conflict-of-interest legislation.'[54] John Crosbie's memoirs accuse even Smallwood of frequent conflicts of interest. In one case Smallwood hid for years his secret co-ownership of seven liquor stores leased to the Newfoundland government until an exposé by a royal commission. Crosbie also confirms Valdmanis's charge that Smallwood's elaborate residence on Roache's line 'was paid for and furnished by friends and associates who did business with the provincial government, including the swimming pool, which was constructed without charge by one of the Crosbie companies ... While claiming that he lived solely on his modest salary as premier, he enjoyed all the trappings of a wealthy man. He lacked for nothing.'[55] Not surprisingly, Valdmanis found it difficult to consider his transgression as the serious crime Smallwood and the public came to view it. And some of his Latvian followers have been wondering whether Smallwood did not seize upon this paper crime committed by a foreigner as a convenient excuse to divert attention from his own problems.

Even his opponents conceded that Alfred Valdmanis was an extraordinary, charismatic individual with a promising and premature, though controversial career. In his world of changing identities, Valdmanis nonetheless retained unchanged his patriotic commitment to the independence and welfare of Latvia as well as to the quest for unity among Latvians. As finance minister under President Kārlis Ulmanis, shrewd collaborator in Nazi-occupied Latvia, spokesman for Latvian POWs and displaced persons, advocate of Baltic immigration in Canada, and economic developer in Newfoundland, he defended Latvian interests consistently and under difficult circumstances. Valdmanis manoeuvred his survival through the chaos of the Second World War and a rootless immigrant life – until his odyssey demanded its price. His white-collar crime, though perhaps an understandable *faux pas* from a survivor's perspective, was by North American standards a serious moral and legal delinquency.

The purpose of life was not to pursue happiness, but to carry out a God-ordained task, Alfred Valdmanis had once written to his friend Friedrich Kreyser. Those recognizing their mission were usually driven to follow it 'like madmen.' Such humans were consumed by their own inner fire. In relation to that, Valdmanis philosophized, 'What is "happiness?"'

Valdmanis believed that everyone had to follow one's own 'star' on a path increasingly lonely and filled with mental anguish. Whether one collapsed physically or 'got run over, denounced, and stoned by the majority of the normal ones,' the bottom line remained accountability to one's conscience: 'Have I done good and created something? The honest answer to this question will "redeem eternally" or "damn eternally."' The purpose of life was 'to help – the smaller, the weaker, the poorer one ... to fan the fire in the soul again and again so that it burns – without worrying that it burns down – if only a little brother feels a bit of the warmth.'[56]

Never able to relax and enjoy life, Alfred Valdmanis believed himself driven by some uncontrollable force. His own admissions of his inner unrest and faults put in question the appropriateness of a blanket condemnation of him solely on the basis of his failings. To the end of his life Valdmanis remained tortured by his conscience, albeit a conscience whose sense of ethics was skewed by egomania and the traumas inflicted by a very turbulent past.

Notes

For identification of the abbreviations used below, see Abbreviations and Glossary (p. xiii), and References (p. 445).

Introduction

1 John Bemrose, 'The Biography Battleground,' *Maclean's*, 31 Oct. 1994, 61f.
2 *Daily News* (St John's), 18 Aug. 1970.
3 Agnis Balodis, *Latvijas un latviešu tautas vēsture* [History of Latvia and the Latvian Nation] (Riga, 1991).
4 For example, Alfred Bilmanis, *Latvia as an Independent State* (Washington, 1947), and *A History of Latvia* (Westport, 1951); Arnolds Spekke, *History of Latvia: An Outline* (Stockholm, 1951); and Igor I. Kavass and Adolph Sprudzs, eds., *Baltic States: A Study of Their Origin and National Development; Their Seizure and Incorporation into the USSR*, U.S. Congress. House Select Committee on Communist Aggression (Washington, 1954); A. Schwabe, *The Story of Latvia: A Historical Survey* (Stockholm, 1949).
5 Royal Institute of International Affairs, ed., *The Baltic States: A Survey of the Political and Economic Structure and the Foreign Relations of Estonia, Latvia, and Lithuania* (London, 1938); Georg von Rauch, *The Baltic States, the Years of Independence: Estonia, Latvia, Lithuania, 1917–1940* (Berkeley and Los Angeles, 1974); Jürgen von Hehn, *Lettland zwischen Demokratie und Diktatur: Zur Geschichte des lettländischen Staatsstreichs vom 15. Mai 1934*, Beiheft 3, Jahrbücher für Geschichte Osteuropas (Munich, 1957).

6 Nicholas Balabkins and Arnolds Aizsilnieks, *Entrepreneur in a Small Country: A Case Study against the Background of the Latvian Economy, 1919–1940* (Hicksville, 1975); Arnolds Aizsilnieks, *Latvijas saimniecības vēsture, 1914–1945* [Economic History of Latvia, 1914–1945] (Stockholm, 1968).

7 Seppo Myllyniemi, *Die Neuordnung der baltischen Länder, 1941–1944: Zum nationalsozialistischen Inhalt der deutschen Besatzungspolitik* (Helsinki, 1973); H.D. Handrack, *Das Reichskommissariat Ostland: Die Kulturpolitik der deutschen Verwaltung zwischen Autonomie und Gleichschaltung, 1941–1944* (Hann Minden, 1981); Helmut Krausnick and Hans-Heinrich Wilhelm, *Die Truppe des Weltanschauungskrieges: Die Einsatzgruppen der Sicherheitspolizei und des SD, 1938–1942* (Stuttgart, 1981); Timothy Patrick Mulligan, *The Politics of Illusion and Empire: German Occupation Policy in the Soviet Union, 1942–1943* (New York, 1988); Romuald Misiunas and Rein Taagepera, *The Baltic States: Years of Dependence, 1940–1990* (Berkeley and Los Angeles, 1983, 1993).

8 Myllyniemi, *Neuordnung.*

9 Rosenberg draft instructions of 8 May 1941, as quoted in IMT, vol. 26, p. 574.

10 In addition to Bilmanis and Spekke, see, e.g. Heinrihs Strods, *Zem melnbrūnā zobena: Vācijas politika Latvijā 1939–1945* [Under the Black-Brown Sword: Germany's Politics in Latvia, 1939–1945] (Riga, 1994), and Andrew Ezergailis, *The Holocaust in Latvia, 1941–1944: The Missing Centre* (Washington and Riga, 1996).

11 Leonīds Siliņš and Edgars Andersons, *Latvijas Centrālā Padome – LCP: Latviešu nacionalā pretestības kustība 1943–1945* [Central Council of Latvia – LCP: The Latvian National Resistance Movement, 1943–1945] (Uppsala, 1994).

12 Gregory Meiksins, *The Baltic Riddle: Finland, Estonia, Lithuania – Key Points of European Peace* (New York, 1943), 205; Latvian Legation, Washington, *Latvia under German Occupation, 1941–1943* (Washington, 1943), 111.

13 Haralds Biezais, *Latvija kāškrusta varā: Sveši kungi – pašu ļaudis* [Latvia under the Might of the Swastika: Foreign Rulers – Own People] (East Lansing, 1992), 150; Aivars Stranga, 'Starp Hitleru un Staļinu [Between Hitler and Stalin],' *Tēvzemes Avīze* [The Fatherland's Newspaper], 13 March 1992; P. Dravelis, 'Ministra vīzītkartes vietā [In lieu of the Minister's Business Card],' *Tēvzemes Avıze,* 13 March 1992; Haralds Biezais, 'Pateicībā Hitleram [In Gratitude to Hitler],' *Treji Vārti* [Three Gates], 95 (1982), 8–10.

14 Margot Blank, *Nationalsozialistische Hochschulpolitik in Riga (1941 bis 1944): Konzeption und Realität eines Bereiches deutscher Besatzungspolitik* (Lüneburg, 1991), 97–103.

15 M.R.D. Foot, 'What Good Did Resistance Do?' in Stephen Hawes and Ralph White, eds., *Resistance in Europe, 1939–1945* (London, 1975), 219.

16 *Der Spiegel*, 13 Sept. 1994, 157ff; *Globe and Mail*, 29 Sept. 1994, A16.

17 *Der Spiegel*, 6 and 13 Sept. 1993, 26 Sept. and 21 Nov. 1994.

18 Mark Wyman, *DP: Europe's Displaced Persons, 1945–1951* (Philadelphia, 1989); Haim Genizi, *America's Fair Share: The Admission and Resettlement of Displaced Persons, 1945–1952* (Detroit, 1993). John Alexander Swettenham, *The Tragedy of the Baltic States: A Report Compiled from Official Documents and Eyewitnesses' Stories* (London, 1952); Kathryn Hulme, *The Wild Place* (Boston and Toronto, 1953); E.F. Penrose, 'Negotiating on Refugees and Displaced Persons, 1946,' in R. Dennett and J.E. Johnson, eds., *Negotiating with the Russians* (Boston, 1951), 139–70.

19 Edgars Andersons, 'Latvians,' in Stephen Thernstrom, ed., *Harvard Encyclopedia of American Ethnic Groups* (Cambridge, Mass, 1980), 638–41; Edgars Andersons, ed., *Cross Road Country Latvia* (Waverly, 1953), 343–57.

20 Ilgvars Veigners, *Latvieši ārzemēs* [Latvians abroad] (Riga, 1993).

21 For example, J. Rutkis, ed., *Latvia, Country and People* (Stockholm, 1967), 318–27; Vito Vitauts Simanis, ed., *Latvia* (St Charles, Ill, 1984), 234–47; Central Board Daugavas Vanagi, *Latvia and Latvians* (London, 1978), 40–5.

22 Alti Rodal,'Nazi War Criminals in Canada: The Historical and Policy Setting from the 1940s to the Present,' prepared for the Commission of Inquiry on War Criminals (Ottawa, 1986).

23 Hans-Heinrich Wilhelm, 'Offene Fragen der Holocaust-Forschung: Das Beispiel des Baltikums,' in U. Backes et al., eds., *Die Schatten der Vergangenheit: Impulse zur Historisierung des Nationalsozialismus* (Frankfurt/M-Berlin, 1992), 403–25; and H.-H. Wilhelm, *Die Einsatzgruppe A der Sicherheitspolizei und des SD* (Frankfurt/M, 1996); Krausnick and Wilhelm, *Truppe*.

24 Marģers Vestermanis, 'Der lettische Anteil an der Endlösung: Versuch einer Antwort,' in Backes, *Die Schatten der Vergangenheit*, 426–49; Vestermanis, 'Der Holocaust in Lettland: Zur "postkommunistischen" Aufarbeitung des Themas in Osteuropa,' in Arno Herzig et al., eds., *Verdrängung und Vernichtung der Juden unter dem Nationalsozialismus* (Hamburg, 1992), 101–30.

25 Bernhard Press, *Judenmord in Lettland, 1941–1945* (Berlin, 1992).

26 Ezergailis, *Holocaust in Latvia*.

27 Richard Gwyn, *Smallwood: The Unlikely Revolutionary* (Toronto, 1968).

28 J.R. Smallwood, *I Chose Canada: The Memoirs of the Honourable Joseph R. 'Joey' Smallwood* (Toronto, 1973).

29 Herbert L. Pottle, *Newfoundland Dawn without Light: Politics, Power and the People in the Smallwood Era* (St John's, 1979).

30 Don Jamieson, *No Place for Fools: The Political Memoirs of Don Jamieson, vol. 1* (St John's, 1989).

31 William J. Brown, *And now ... Eighty-seven Years a Newfoundlander: Memoirs of William J. Browne, PC, QC, LLD, vol. 2, 1949–1965* (St John's, 1981).
32 Harold Horwood, *Joey: The Life and Political Times of Joey Smallwood* (Toronto, 1989).
33 Frederick C. Rowe, *The Smallwood Era* (Toronto, 1985).
34 See Hubert Cole, *Fouché: The Unprincipled Patriot* (New York, 1971).
35 Bernard Wasserstein, *The Secret Lives of Trebitsch Lincoln* (New Haven, 1988).
36 Hansjakob Stehle, 'Frommer Faschist von Stalin's Gnaden: Wie ein Abenteurer Polens Tragödien überlebte,' *Die Zeit*, 29 Sept. 1995.

Chapter 1: *Wunderkind* in Reborn Latvia

1 Smallwood, *I Chose Canada*, 346; Jamieson, 169f; Albert Perlin in the *Daily News* (St John's), 2 Sept. 1954 and 18 Aug. 1970.
2 Baxter Morgan, personal interview, 25 Apr. 1985.
3 Fritz W. Stobbe, personal interview, 3 Apr. 1986.
4 J.R. Smallwood interviewed about A. Valdmanis on CBC Radio, St John's, 27 May 1984; Smallwood, *I Chose Canada*, 357.
5 Osvald Valdmanis to author, 28 Jan. 1986; Gundars Valdmanis to author, 21 Feb. 1986; Irma Valdmanis, personal interview, 4 Apr. 1986.
6 Gundars Valdmanis to author, 9 Apr. 1986.
7 BA, R6/200, von Grundherr to Kleist, 28 Apr. 1942. Personal interviews in Riga: Irma Losis, 18 June 1993; Samuel Levitan, 18 June 1993; and Ingrid Trautmanis, 6 Nov. 1993.
8 Letter to the editor of *Newsweek* magazine as reprinted in the *Evening Telegram* (St John's,), 18 Dec. 1951.
9 Horwood, *Joey*, 184.
10 Personal interviews in Riga of Marģers Vestermanis, 19 June 1993; Samuel Levitan, 18 June 1993; and Jānis Strādinš, 15 June 1995.
11 Gwyn, 143f.
12 *Treji Vārti*, 95 (1982), 6.
13 Dagnija Surgovte to Tonya Bassler and Sofija Lucis, Riga, 16 June 1993.
14 Sir Ian Hamilton, *The Friends of England* (London, 1923), 141f.
15 Gisbert Mrozek and Jürgen Reiter, *Riga: Stadt an der Daugava* (Bremen, 1989), 15.
16 Jürgen Ernst Kroeger, *So war es: Ein Bericht* (Michelstadt, 1989), 9–12.
17 Spricis Paegle, as quoted in von Hehn, *Lettland*, 7f.
18 See Sigmar Stopinski, 'Das Baltikum im Patt der Mächte: Zur Entstehung der Staaten Estland, Lettland, und Litauen im Gefolge des Ersten Weltkriegs,' PhD thesis, Free University of Berlin, 1994; Alexander Schmidt,

Geschichte des Baltikums (Munich, 1992); Jürgen von Hehn et al., eds., *Von den baltischen Provinzen zu den baltischen Staaten: Beiträge zur Entstehungsgeschichte der Republiken Estland und Lettland 1917–1918* (Marburg/Lahn, 1971); and S.W. Page, *The Formation of the Baltic States* (Cambridge, Mass, 1959).

19 Spekke, 347–51; Bilmanis, *History*, 314, 316; Visvaldis Mangulis, *Latvia in the Wars of the 20th Century* (Princeton Junction, 1983), 46, 49; Simanis, 115–23.

20 A. Bļodnieks, as quoted in John Hiden and Patrick Salmon, *The Baltic Nations and Europe: Estonia, Latvia and Lithuania in the Twentieth Century* (London and New York, 1991), 77.

21 *Financial Times*, 18 Nov. 1938.

22 Hiden and Salmon, 86.

23 G.P. Bassler, 'Latvia and Democracy in International Historical Perspective,' paper presented at the Transition to Democracy conference, Riga, 1992. See summary of proceedings by University of Latvia, *The Transition to Democracy: Experience in Latvia and in the World, Riga, November 12th–14th, 1992* (Riga 1994), 111–17.

24 Spekke, 362.

25 For example, in 1919 Latvia introduced a state monopoly for flax, to be followed by state monopolies for alcohol (1920), matches (1928), wheat trade, sugar, and electrotechnical articles (1932), bacon (1933), iron and steel, as well as butter, eggs, and cheese (1934), etc. There was also a state monopoly for timber, since 84 per cent of the nation's forest lands were publicly owned. See Balabkins and Aizsilnieks, 39–43, 51.

26 'Staatskapitalistische Tendenzen in der Wirtschaft Lettlands,' *Der Wirtschafts-Ring* (Berlin), 16 (1939).

27 See Balabkins and Aizsilnieks, 64.

28 Maynard Owen Williams, 'Latvia, Home of the Letts,' *National Geographic Magazine*, vol. 46, no. 4 (1924), 414.

29 Marģers Vestermanis, personal interviews, Riga, 13 Nov. 1992 and 19 June 1993.

30 Ezergailis, *Holocaust in Latvia*, 82.

31 Miķelis Valters, *No sabrukuma uz plānveidotu saimniecību: Latvijas atjaunošanas problēmas, Latvijas nākotne* [From Collapse to Planned Economy: Problems of Latvia's Renewal, Latvia's Future] (Riga, 1933).

32 Bassler, 'Latvia and Democracy,' 111–17.

33 Royal Institute of International Affairs, 33ff.

34 Quoted in von Hehn, *Lettland*, 17.

35 Premier Margers Skujenieks, as quoted in *Baltische Monatshefte*, 1932, p. 684.

36 Jürgen von Hehn, *Die Umsiedlung der baltischen Deutschen – das letzte Kapitel baltisch–deutscher Geschichte* (Marburg/Lahn, 1982), 35.

37 Samuel Leviton, personal interview, Riga, 18 June 1993; Press, 10.

38 The *Aizsargi* or Home Guard organization (Aizsargu organizācija) originated in the war of Latvian independence 1918–20 to support the police in maintaining order and safeguard against subversive elements. Between 1920 and 1940 it remained organized on a voluntary and territorial principle. The commander of the regiment from each county was the county's chief of police. His assistant was an army officer responsible for training. There were twenty-one regiments, to be taken over by the army in the event of war. Until its dissolution by the Soviets in June 1940, the organization reported to the minister of public affairs. See Arthur Silgailis, *Latvian Legion* (San Jose, 1986), 7f.

39 See von Hehn, *Lettland*, 40–50.

40 'Trouble in Latvia,' *Evening Telegram*, 17 May 1934.

41 Manifesto of 16 May 1934, as reprinted in von Hehn, *Lettland*, 64.

42 Boriss Zemgals, *Dienas baltas nebaltas: Stāsts par Alfreda Valdmaņa darbu tautai un Tēvzemei* [Days of happiness and distress: the story of Alfred Valdmanis's work on behalf of his nation and fatherland] (Geneva, 1949), 15.

43 Pavolini gave the following reasons: (1) Premier Ulmanis was elevated to the status of a 'duce'; (2) the entire official press publicized the need for a strong, viable government; (3) demands were made for a totalitarian type of concord of all citizens above and outside political parties; (4) anti-parliamentarianism was encouraged; (5) nationalistic sentiments were stimulated; (6) propaganda was stepped up for creating a militarized nation, and incentives were provided for launching voluntary, sports, and youth organizations. Archivio Centrale dello Stato, Roma, Ministero della Cultura Popolare, MCP, parte VI, b. 301, as quoted in Stein Ugelvik Larsen, et al., eds., *Who Were the Fascists: Social Roots of European Fascism* (Oslo, 1980), 360.

44 Juris Silenieks, 'Kārlis Ulmanis,' in Simanis, *Latvia*, 148. LVVA, 2570/14/1597/5–7, Dienesta gaitas apraksts, 1936. LVVA, 2570/14/1597/74-77, Kārlis Ulmanis.

45 Georg von Rauch, *Geschichte der baltischen Staaten* (Munich, 1977), 150.

46 Von Hehn, *Lettland*, 56f.

47 Ibid., 54–61, 71.

48 See ibid., 60f.

49 AA, Ha Pol Vb Lettland/Wirtschaft 1, Nr. 1, Bd. 1, Jahresübersicht 1936, 3f.

50 See note 31. Balabkins and Aizsilnieks, 74f.

51 A. Kroders, in *Latvijas kareivis* [Latvia's Soldier], 78 (9 Apr. 1937).

52 L. Eķis's and A. Bērziņš's speeches, as published in English in *Latvian Economic Review* (Riga), vol. 1 (Jan. 1938), 6–10, 14–17.
53 For example, Bilmanis, *History*, 366; Simanis, *Latvia*, 129ff.
54 Balabkins and Aizsilnieks, 73–85.
55 'Latvia: An Authoritarian Economy,' *Economist*, 134 (1939), 503.
56 AVP, undated, untitled typescript, 25 pages, p. xxi.
57 *Münchener Neueste Nachrichten*, 4 July 1938.
58 Anna Jansone and Līna Iesalniece, personal interview interpreted by Sofija and Arnis Lucis, Ziemupe, 12 June 1993.
59 Marģers Vestermanis, personal interview, Riga, 19 June 1993. See also, Andrejs Plakans, *The Latvians: A Short History* (Stanford, 1995), 83–104. The 1920 census found that 70 per cent of Latvians could read and 63 per cent could both read and write. Latvia attributed this to the existence on its prewar territory of a larger number of secondary schools in proportion to population than in any other country.
60 Gundars Valdmanis to author, 21 Feb. 1986.
61 Ibid.
62 Osvald Valdmanis to author, 28 Jan. 1986.
63 Irma Losis, personal interview, Riga, 18 June 1993.
64 Karl Heinz Janssen, 'Die baltische Okkupationspolitik des Deutschen Reiches,' in Jürgen von Hehn et al., eds., *Von den baltischen Provinzen zu den baltischen Staaten* (Marburg/Lahn, 1971), 222–7.
65 AVP, résumé of Alfred Arthur Alexander Valdmanis, dated Weilburg, Germany, Mar. 1947.
66 LVVA, 2415/1/206/30.
67 AVP, unidentified contemporary Latvian newspaper clipping showing 'A. Waldmanis' in a photograph of the 1932 graduating class of 'Jaunee juristi,' 1932. Latvian thesis title: 'Nekustamas mantas piespiedu publiska pārdošana tiesas ceļā [Compulsory Public Sale of Real Estate Seized by the Courts].' Copy of certificate no. 772 issued by the University of Latvia, 28 August 1940, and signed by the secretary of the university, coincidentally also named A. Valdmanis.
68 Canada, Senate, *Proceedings of the Standing Committee on Immigration and Labour: On the Operation and Administration of the Immigration Act, etc., no. 4, Wednesday 27 April 1949* (Ottawa, 1949), 56.
69 Edgars Andersons to author, 18 Nov. 1985 and 20 Jan. 1986. There are no references to Valdmanis's alleged elite education and stint as von Schacht's special assistant in Zemgals, *Dienas baltas*.
70 Marģers Vestermanis, personal interview, Riga, 19 June 1993.
71 Zemgals, *Dienas baltas*, 9.

72 LVVA, 2886/1/4/2; von Hehn, *Lettland*, 19f; Ezergailis, *Holocaust in Latvia*, 80.
73 LVVA, 1307/3/56/19.
74 Ibid.
75 Zemgals, *Dienas baltas*, 9.
76 Ibid., 12. According to Valdmanis's official record of employment, prepared by the Chancellery of the State, he was promoted to this position on 12 Apr. 1934. LVVA, 1307/3/56/17.
77 Irma Valdmanis, personal interview, 4 Apr. 1986. Gundars Valdmanis, 21 Feb. 1986.
78 AVP, J. Sakars, Bescheinigung, Riga, 14 Oct. 1943.
79 See LVVA, 3235/1/22/731, 4377/1/1185, 6824/1/354.
80 Zemgals, *Dienas baltas*, 14.
81 Zenta Maurina, 'Cetri liktenīgi motīvi latviešu kulturā' [Four Fateful Motifs in Latvian Culture] in *Domu varavīksnē* [Within a Rainbow of Thoughts] (Riga, 1992); Vestermanis, 'Der Holocaust in Lettland,' 102f.
82 Zemgals, *Dienas baltas*, 18.
83 Ibid., 12. Valdmanis's assignment in Ghent is not confirmed in his official record of employment for 1933. However, for 1936 it contains an entry that 'with instructions from the minister of finance [he was] sent to Belgium to settle a dispute between the Ministry of Finance and the owner of a Belgian firm "Vercoutere" pertaining to a distrained shipment of Latvian flax in 1927.' Concerning Estonia, another entry in the official record indicates that in November 1937 Valdmanis was decorated with the Estonian White Star Order II Rank. LVVA, 1307/3/56/16–17.
84 Zemgals, *Dienas baltas*, 16; LVVA, 1307/3/56/17.
85 In 1932 Mussolini, as quoted in Denis Mack Smith, 'The Theory and Practice of Fascism,' in N. Greene, ed., *Fascism: An Anthology* (New York, 1968), 82, is reported to have remarked to Emil Ludwig: 'When the masses are like wax in my hands, when I stir their faith, or when I mingle with them and am almost crushed by them, I feel myself to be a part of them. All the same there persists in me a certain feeling of aversion, like that which the modeller feels for the clay he is moulding. Does not the sculptor sometimes smash his block of marble into fragments because he cannot shape it to represent the vision he has conceived?' Valdmanis mentioned this metaphor of the clay three times in his autobiographic essays of 1962–63: *Treji Vārti*, 95 (1982), 5, 6, and 96 (1983), 18.
86 *Treji Vārti*, 95 (1982), 5.
87 Ibid.
88 For details see Royal Institute of International Affairs, 182.

89 Zemgals, *Dienas baltas,* 16f.
90 LVVA, 1307/3/56/17.
91 Zemgals, *Dienas baltas,* 17, gives (probably erroneously) the date of July 1935 as the beginning of construction.
92 Bilmanis, *History,* 363.
93 *Treji Vārti,* 95 (1982), 5.
94 *Rīts* [Morning], 30 June 1937.
95 Allegedly because he had refused to accept special (monetary) compensation. Zemgals, *Dienas baltas,* 16f. Valdmanis's awards and decorations are listed in his record of employment, LVVA, 1307/3/56/16.
96 Zemgals, *Dienas baltas,* 18. Eķis's characterization of Valdmanis as a satellite of Bērziņš (see beginning of Chapter 2) casts doubts on Valdmanis assertions of defying the powerful Andrejs Bērziņš.
97 *Treji Vārti,* 95 (1982), 6.
98 AA, HaPol Vb Lettland/Wirtschaft 9, Bd. 1. *Rigasche Rundschau,* 18 Jan. 1938.
99 One of the chambers was responsible for literature and art and the other for science. Its members would be appointed by the respective ministries for three years. The chambers were to reserve cultural activity for persons and associations authorized by them. The council, created on 5 May 1938, was to ensure that Latvia would have only one culture, namely, the Latvian one, Ulmanis explained. See AA, Ha Pol Wiehl/Lettland, Bd. 2, Werner von Grundherr, 'Aufzeichnung,' 17 May 1938.

Chapter 2: 'The Most Active and Influential Member of the Cabinet'

1 Excerpt from 'Testimonium,' Geneva, 25 Nov. 1947.
2 AA, Deutsche Gesandtschaft Riga/Handakten/Allg. Geheimakten, Bd. I, Paket 121.
3 Zemgals, *Dienas baltas,* 19; *Treji Vārti,* 95 (1982), 6.
4 The letter reads: 'In compliance with your directive No. 3038 dated 14 June I feel honoured to report that today I have taken over from the former minister of finance, Mr Ludvigs Eķis, the leadership of the Ministry of Finance. With truly high esteem. A. Valdmanis.' LVVA, 1307/3/56/2.
5 *Treji Vārti,* 95 (1982), 5ff.
6 LVVA, 6824/1/26/6, Cabinet Protocol no. 39 of 21 June 1938.
7 AA, R 113305, Bericht über die Wirtschaftslage Lettlands im I. Halbjahr 1938.
8 *Rīts,* no. 165, and *Rigasche Rundschau,* 16 June 1938.
9 AA, Deutsche Gesandtschaft Riga/Handakten/Allg. Geheimakten, Bd. 1, Paket 121. AA, Riga/Wi4, Heft 3.

10 Zemgals, *Dienas baltas*, 21f.
11 LVVA, 6824/1/12/156, A. Valdmanis interview with V. Bandrēvičs, 14 Aug. 1938. LVVA, 6824/1/26/4, Cabinet Protocol no. 46 of 25 Aug. 1938.
12 *Treji Vārti*, 95 (1982), 5; n.a., 'Latvijas Banka 15 Years,' *Latvian Economic Review* (Riga), Jan. 1938, 23ff.
13 LVVA, 6824/1/38/26. The directive was issued on 7 June 1939.
14 LVVA, 6824/1/9/14–15. This directive (no. 376) was issued on 9 June 1939.
15 LVVA, 6824/1/38/13–14.
16 Zemgals, *Dienas baltas*, 24f.
17 LVVA, 6824/1/271/7.
18 *Rigasche Rundschau*, 29 Mar. 1939.
19 LVVA, 6824/1/26/5, Cabinet Protocol, 21 June 1938.
20 LVVA, 6824/1/12/229–31.
21 *Rigasche Rundschau*, 7 July 1938.
22 *Treji Vārti*, 96 (1983), 15.
23 AA, Ha Pol Vb, Lettland, Meyer to Rheinmetall-Borsig, 20 July 1938.
24 Ibid., Wiehl to Wessig, 13 Aug. 1938.
25 AA, R 113169.
26 *Treji Vārti*, 95 (1982), 6f.
27 Ibid., 96 (1983), 15.
28 Ibid., 16.
29 *Rigasche Rundschau*, 21 Sept. and 15 Oct. 1938.
30 AA, R 113169, von Kotze to AA, 23 Sept. 1938.
31 'Lettlands Aussenhandel im Oktober,' *Deutscher Handelsdienst*, 19 Nov. 1938.
32 AA, Ha Pol Wiehl/Lettland, Bd. 2, Schnurre, Berlin, to German Legation, Riga, 23 Jan. 1939.
33 AA, R 113166, von Kotze to AA, 22 June 1939.
34 Ibid., von Kotze to AA, 24 Jan. 1940.
35 Spekke, 368; Bilmanis, *History*, 368; Royal Institute of International Affairs, 165.
36 LVVA, 6824/1/75/32–35.
37 Bilmanis, *History*, 368.
38 Royal Institute of International Affairs, 165; Bilmanis, *History*, 368.
39 LVVA, 6824/1/75/33.
40 AA, R 113305, Bericht über die Wirtschaft Lettlands im Jahre 1938; R 113190, Lettisch–Sowjetische Wirtschaftsbeziehungen.
41 AA, Ha Pol Vb, 'Handelsbeziehungen zwischen fremden Staaten: Lettland–Schweden,' Bd. 1.
42 *Treji Vārti*, 96 (1983), 16.
43 AA, Ha Pol Vb, Elektrische Industrie und Wasserkraft (Lettland), Bd. 1.

44 AA, Ha Pol Vb, 'Handelsbeziehungen zwischen fremden Staaten: Lettland–Schweden,' Bd. 1, von Schack to AA, 21 Oct. 1938.
45 Ibid. AA, R 1131919. *Treji Vārti*, 96 (1983), 16.
46 LVVA, 6824/1/154/10.
47 *Jaunākās ziņas* [The Latest News], 7 Oct. 1938.
48 LVVA, 6824/1/35/41-6.
49 LVVA, 6824/1/35/23–8.
50 *Jaunākās ziņas*, 10 and 12 Oct. 1938.
51 Valdmanis and his group shot several animals but did not manage to kill them. A one-day dog chase failed to turn up any traces of them. LVVA, 6824/1/354/52.
52 LVVA, 6824/1/354/50, Kreyser to Valdmanis 21 Oct. 1938, and Valdmanis to Kreyser, 22 Oct. 1938.
53 *Jaunākās ziņas*, 17 Oct. 1938.
54 LVVA, 6824/1/75/33–35.
55 Ibid.
56 AA, Ha Pol Vb, Handelsbeziehungen zwischen fremden Staaten: Lettland–Schweden, Bd. 1.
57 AA, R 113191, German Legation, Stockholm, to German Foreign Office, Berlin, 25 Apr. 1939.
58 AA, Ha Pol Vb, Elektrische Industrie und Wasserkraft: Lettland, Bd. 1.
59 AA, R 113191. LVVA, 6824/1/12/215–19.
60 AA, Ha Pol Vb, Handelsbeziehungen zwischen fremden Staaten: Lettland–Schweden, Bd. 1.
61 *Rigasche Rundschau*, 12 May and 9 June 1939; *Baltic Times*, 25 May 1939.
62 *Treji Vārti*, 96 (1983), 16.
63 Ibid., 17.
64 AA, Ha Pol Vb, Elektrische Industrie und Wasserkraft: Lettland, Bd. 1.
65 *Treji Vārti*, 96 (1983), 15.
66 *Rīts*, 4 Oct. 1938; *Latvijas Kareivis*, 6 Oct. 1938.
67 AA, R 113305; LVVA, 6824/1/161/33.
68 AA, Riga/Handakten/Allg. Geheimakten.
69 LVVA, 6824/1/262/33.
70 AA, Riga/Handakten/Allg. Geheimakten. See report attached to memorandum by von Schack, 29 Oct. 1938.
71 *Treji Vārti*, 95 (1982), 8; *Rigasche Rundschau*, 12 May 1939.
72 *Treji Vārti*, 95 (1982), 6.
73 Ibid.; AA, Ha Pol Vb, Handelsbeziehungen zwischen fremden Staaten: Lettland–Schweden, Bd. 1.
74 AA, Riga/Handakten/Allgemeine Geheimakten.

75 *Treji Vārti*, 95 (1982), 7.
76 AA, Ha Pol Clodius, Lettland, Bd. 2, Stand der Handelsbeziehungen zwischen Deutschland und Lettland, 6 June 1939.
77 AA, Ha Pol Clodius, Akten betreffend Lettland, Bd. 3, von Schack to Berlin, 31 Oct. 1938.
78 AA, Ha Pol Wiehl/Lettland, Bd. 2, Stand der Handelsbeziehungen zwischen Deutschland und Lettland.
79 AA, Ha Pol Vb, Handelsbeziehungen zwischen fremden Staaten: Lettland–Schweden, Bd. 1.
80 AA, Riga, Gg 18, Dr Leckzyck.
81 BA, R6, vol. 200, A. Leckzyck to Pg. Malletke, 25 June 1941.
82 BA, R6, vol. 200, von Grundherr to Kleist, 28 Apr. 1942.
83 The original law had made joint-stock companies and cooperatives issuing shares subject to government review and required them to apply within six months to the Ministry of Finance for permission to continue operations. The amendment extended the period by another month to 31 July. *Rigasche Rundschau*, 22 June 1938.
84 LVVA, 6824/1/12/237–59; *Rigasche Rundschau*, 24 Nov. 1938.
85 Ibid.
86 Ibid.
87 AA, R 113166, and Riga/Wi65a, Heft 2.
88 As reported in *Rigasche Rundschau*, of 29 Dec. 1938.
89 *Rigasche Rundschau*, 9 Dec. 1938.
90 The sources for the fund would be (1) a single government payment of 500,000 lats to be transferred from the 1938–39 budget surplus, (2) annual contributions of 1.5 million lats from the Ministry of Finance, (3) contributions from industries according to Article 28 of the Law on Industrial and Trades' Cartels, and (4) donations and foundations. The disbursement of the fund would be decided by the cabinet on the basis of recommendations from the minister of finance. LVVA, 6824/1/315/53. *Zemgales Balss* [The Voice of Zemgale], 3 May 1939.
91 *Rigasche Rundschau*, 6 Feb. 1939.
92 *Preussische Zeitung* (Königsberg), 7 June 1939.
93 *Rigasche Rundschau*, 6 Feb. 1939.
94 Ibid.
95 *Rigasche Rundschau*, 29 Mar. 1939.
96 LVVA, 6824/1/76/100–102.
97 LVVA, 6824/1/38/13.
98 *Rigasche Rundschau*, 12 May 1939.
99 LVVA, 6824/1/315/16–101.

100 'Erste Maßnahmen zur Rationalisierung,' *Revalsche Zeitung*, 17 Jan. 1939. Dr Auler, 'Die deutsche Rationalisierung als Mittel der Leistungssteigerung,' *Betriebswirtschaftliche Praxis*, 24 Oct. 1939.
101 *Bergwerks Zeitung*, 24 Jan. 1939.
102 *Frankfurter Zeitung*, 19 Jan. 1939.
103 Ibid., 6 July 1939.
104 Ibid., 5 Feb. 1939.
105 See Valdmanis's speeches on the state of the economy of 28 Mar. 12 May, and 19 June 1939, as published in *Rigasche Rundschau*, 29 Mar., 12 May 1939, and 20 June 1939.
106 AA, R 113305, Deutsche Gesandtschaft Riga, Bericht über die Wirtschaft Lettlands im Jahre 1938, 1 Aug. 1939.
107 Aizsilnieks, *Latvijas saimniecības vēsture*, 829ff.
108 AA, R 113305, von Kotze, Bericht über die Wirtschaft Lettlands im Jahre 1938, 1 Aug. 1939; Arnold Bonwetsch, 'Lettlands Wirtschaft zur Jahreswende,' *Der Ostexpress*, 21 (3) (Jan. 1940), 1–3.
109 *Economist*, 11 Mar. 1939.
110 'Die Wirtschaftsnachbarn: Lettland. Staatskapitalistische Tendenzen in der Wirtschaft Lettlands,' *Der Wirtschafts-Ring* (Berlin), 16 (1939).
111 'Entwicklung zum Staatskapitalismus in Lettland,' *Nachrichten für Außenhandel*, 14 Jan. 1939.
112 'Lettland geht eigene Wege,' *Frankfurter Zeitung*, 14 Mar. 1939.
113 LVVA, 6824/1/13/62–3.
114 LVVA, 6894/1/76/90–1, Valdmanis to Kaminskis, 26 July 1939.
115 *Rigasche Rundschau*, 12 May 1939.
116 LVVA, 6824/1/38/26: Directive no. 375 of 7 June 1939 with note appended by J. Sakars of 27 Nov. 1939.
117 LVVA, 6824/1/38/1–3.
118 LVVA, 6824/1/38/12.
119 LVVA, 6824/1/13/88–9.
120 *Rigasche Rundschau*, 20 June 1939.
121 AA, R 113166, von Kotze to AA, 1 Mar. 1939.
122 LVVA, 2824/1/14/41–5.
123 AA, Deutsche Gesandtschaft Riga/Handakten/Allg. Geheimakten, von Kotze to Dr Schnurre, July 1939.
124 Aizsilnieks, *Latvijas saimniecības vēsture*, 829–46.
125 *Treji Vārti*, 95 (1983), 7.
126 LVVA, 6824/1/39/24, Minister President to A. Valdmanis, 9 Aug. 1939.
127 Zemgals, *Dienas baltas*, 26. There is no corroborating reference to Ulmanis's offer of the justice portfolio to Valdmanis.

128 See, e.g., AVP, 'Testimonium' by B. Zemgals, Geneva, 25 Nov. 1947.

129 Zemgals, *Dienas baltas*, 25f.

130 Edgars Andersons, ed., 'Alfreds Valdmanis – Kavējoties atmiņas' [Alfred Valdmanis – Reflections], *Treji Vārti*, 95 (1982), 4–8; 96 (1983), 15–19; 97 (1984), 11–14; 98 (1985), 17–18.

131 P. Drāvelis, 'Ministra vizītkartes vietā,' *Tēvzemes Avīze*, 13 Mar. 1992.

Chapter 3: 'Better to Die Standing Up Than to Keep on Living on Your Knees'

1 Zemgals, *Dienas baltas*, 15, cited from M. Braun-Wogau translation, *Days of Happiness and Distress* (St John's, 1957).

2 Edgars Andersons, 'The Pact of Mutual Assistance between the USSR and the Baltic States,' in A. Ziedonis, Jr, et al., eds., *Baltic History* (Columbus, 1974), 239, 249f; I. Grava-Kreituse, et al., *The Occupation and Annexation of Latvia, 1939–1940: Documents and Materials* (Riga, 1995), 98–104; M. Duhanovs, I. Feldmanis, and A. Stranga, *1939: Latvia and the Year of Fateful Decisions* (Riga, 1994).

3 LVVA, 6824/1/271/7; USSR, Department of External Affairs, *Polipedy Soobshchaiut ...: Sbornik Dokumentov ob Otnoshcheniiach CCCR c Latviei, Litvoi i Estoniei, Avgust 1939g – Avgust 1940g* [Accredited Representatives Reporting ...: Collection of Documents about Relationships of the USSR with Latvia, Lithuania, and Estonia, August 1939 – August 1940] (Moscow, 1990), 23.

4 AA, R 113305, von Kotze to AA, 4 and 9 Sept. 1939. Ha Pol Vb, Bd. 1, Materialsammlung für die deutsch-lettischen Wirtschaftsverhandlungen, Oct. 1939–40.

5 Ibid.

6 LVVA, 6824/1/50/236–8.

7 LVVA, 6824/1/50/50–73.

8 AA, R 113305, von Kotze to AA, 9 and 19 Sept. 1939.

9 AA, Ha Pol Wiehl/Lettland Bd. 2.

10 LVVA, 6824/1/27/132, Protocol no. 54, the sitting of the Cabinet of Ministers on 1 Oct. 1939, Valdmanis not attending. LVVA, 1307/2/1/98–9, handwritten minutes of the 3 Oct. 1939 cabinet meeting, Valdmanis attending. AA, Deutsche Gesandtschaft in Riga, Geheim 26, Paket 189/9, von Kotze to AA, 6 Oct. 1939; LVVA, 6824/1/50/341–5: Latvian and Russian text of the pact.

11 Alfreds Bērziņš, *1939: Lielo notikumu priekšvakarā* [1939: On the Eve of the Great Events] (New York, 1976), 220.

12 Andersons, ed., 'Alfreds Valdmanis,' *Treji Vārti*, 97 (1984), 11.

13 AA, Deutsche Gesandtschaft in Riga, Geheim 26, Paket 198/9, von Kotze to AA, 6 Oct. 1939.

14 Ibid.
15 Ibid.; LVVA, 5969/1/291/10; Zemgals, *Dienas baltas*, 28f.
16 *Treji Vārti*, 97 (1984), 11.
17 A. Bilmanis, ed., *Latvian–Russian Relations: Documents* (Washington, 1944), 193.
18 AA, Deutsche Gesandtschaft in Riga, Geheim 26, Paket 189/9, von Kotze to AA, 6 Oct. 1939. AA, R 29670, von Kotze to AA, 4 Oct. 1939.
19 See I.A. Chichaev to V.M. Molotov, 10 Oct. 1939, in USSR, Department of External Affairs, 99.
20 AA, R 113305, Dr Karl Rasche zu Staatssekretär W. Keppler, 25 Sept. 1939.
21 Dietrich Loeber, *Diktierte Option: Die Umsiedlung der Deutsch–Balten aus Estland und Lettland, 1939–1941* (Neumünster, 1972), 25f, 46.
22 The report is published in Loeber, 69–73.
23 AA, R 29670, Vorschlag für die Aktion zur Rettung der Volks- und Reichsdeutschen aus dem Baltikum, undated. See also Loeber, 76.
24 Zemgals, *Dienas baltas*, 28.
25 AA, R 29670, Kotze to AA, 13 Oct. 1939.
26 Von Hehn, *Umsiedlung*, 111–16.
27 LVVA, 6824/1/296/119–21; Loeber, 342–5, 515–26; Von Hehn, *Umsiedlung*, 105–16, 136ff.
28 BA, R6, vol. 200, Leckzyck Akte.
29 For example, LVVA, 6824/1/296/119–21 and 132, personal memorandum from the secretary general of the Chamber of Trade and Industry to Minister of Finance A. Valdmanis, 19 Oct. 1939, and statistics on real estate left behind. The transcript of a telephone conversation by von Kotze with German Foreign Office official F. von Twardowski, dated 20 Oct. 1939, indicates that there was rapid progress in German–Latvian negotiations towards a repatriation agreement from the moment Valdmanis had tendered his resignation to Ulmanis. See AA, R 29670, p. 076.
30 Zemgals, *Dienas baltas*, 29–32.
31 Ibid., 32.
32 See Aivars Stranga, 'Starp Hitleru un Staliņu (Between Hitler and Stalin),' *Tēvzemes Avīze* (Riga), 13 Mar. 1992.
33 *Treji Vārti*, 97 (1984), 11.
34 *Brīvā Zeme* [The Free Country], 21 Oct. 1939.
35 LVVA, 1307/3/56/14, and 6824/1/27/153–4.
36 LVVA, 1307/3/56/18.
37 LVVA, 6824/1/9/154–5. Also published in *Rigasche Rundschau*, 25 Oct. 1939.
38 *Neues Wiener Tagblatt*, 26 Oct. 1939.
39 See Stranga, 'Starp Hitleru un Staliņu.'

40 AVP, A. Bērziņš to A. Bilmanis, 28 Oct. 1947.
41 Bērziņš, *1939*, 264.
42 AA, R 113166, von Kotze to AA, 25 Oct. 1939.
43 USSR, Department of External Affairs, 177ff.
44 Seppo Myllyniemi, 'Die Folgen des Hitler–Stalin Paktes für die baltischen Republiken und Finland,' in B. Wegner, ed., *Zwei Wege nach Moskau: Vom Hitler–Stalin Pakt zum Unternehmen Barbarossa* (Munich, 1991), 77.
45 *Treji Vārti*, 97 (1984), 12.
46 Stranga, 'Starp Hitleru un Staļīņu'; see also Biezais, *Latvija Kāškrusta varā*, 107 ff.
47 *Treji Vārti*, 97 (1984), 12.
48 Ibid.
49 Ibid., 12ff.
50 AA, Deutsche Gesandtschaft in Riga, Po 2, Äussere Politik Lettlands, Paket 126/5.
51 Ibid.
52 Zemgals, *Dienas baltas*, 39f.
53 AA, Riga, Po 3, Bd. 8.
54 *Treji Vārti*, 96 (1983), 17f.
55 Zemgals, *Dienas baltas*, 32.
56 LVVA, 6824/1/27/210, 6824/1/163/51–2, and 1307/3/56/18.
57 Zemgals, *Dienas baltas*, 32.
58 LVVA, 6824/1/38/52–4.
59 LVVA, 6824/1/38/81.
60 LVVA, 6824/1/38.
61 LVVA, 6824/1/38/100–1.
62 Grava-Kreituse, *Occupation*, 53, 295–9; *Treji Vārti*, 96 (1983), 17.
63 Von Hehn, *Umsiedlung*, 179.
64 Kārlis Kangeris, 'Kollaboration vor der Kollaboration? Die baltischen Emigranten und ihre "Befreiungskomitees" in Deutschland 1940–41,' in W. Röhr, ed., *Okkupation und Kollaboration (1938–1945)* (Berlin, 1995), 170.
65 AA, R 29670.
66 BA, R6, vol. 200, Leckzyck Akte.
67 *Treji Vārti*, 97 (1984), 14.
68 Irma Valdmanis, personal interview, 4 Apr. 1986.
69 Zemgals, *Dienas baltas*, chapters 14–17.
70 AVP, report of speech by citizen Valdmanis, dated 23 Mar. 1941.
71 Personal interviews: Gundars Valdmanis, Montreal, 21 Feb. 1986; Irma Valdmanis, Montreal, 4 Apr. 1986; Irma Losis, Riga, 13 Nov. 1992. Helen Matheson, 'Thrown Off Train to Escape Reds, Latvian DP Boy's a Visitor Here,' *Wisconsin State Journal*, 3 Aug. 1949.

72 Plakāns, 147.
73 BA, R6, vol. 200, A. Leckzyck to Pg. Malletke, 25 June 1941.
74 Jānis Strādiņš, personal interview, Riga, 15 June 1995. Strādiņš, whose father Paul was the director of the TB sanatorium in which Valdmanis found refuge, is vice-president of the Latvian Academy of Sciences. He remembered well the 'hide and seek game' of Valdmanis during the Soviet occupation.
75 Marģers Vestermanis, personal interview, Riga, 19 June 1993. His father was a successful textile entrepreneur under Ulmanis; he was expropriated in 1940 but continued as manager of his firm. In early 1941 he was surprised to rediscover Valdmanis as chief administrator of the textile trust.
76 Zemgals, *Dienas baltas*, 40–7.
77 AVP, A. Bērziņš to A. Bilmanis, 28 Oct. 1947.
78 For example, Indulis Ronis, personal interview, Riga, 14 June 1993. Stranga, 'Starp Hitleru un Staļiņu.'
79 BA, R6, vol. 200, Leckzyck to Malletke, 25 June 1941.
80 Gundars Valdmanis to author, 21 Feb. 1986.
81 USSR, Department of External Affairs, 8–180.

Chapter 4: 'Elected to Lead and Manage Latvian National Affairs'

1 Bilmanis, *History*, 403f; Mangulis, 93ff; Shtromas, 189; Zemgals, *Dienas baltas*, 51ff.
2 BA, R90/265.
3 Silgailis, 10.
4 BA, R58/214, SD Ereignismeldung of 14 July 1941.
5 Report of Einsatzgruppe A, 15 Oct. 1941, in *IMT*, vol. 37, p. 676.
6 Wilhelm, *Die Einsatzgruppe A*, 137f.
7 Myllyniemi, *Neuordnung*, 105.
8 Zemgals, *Dienas baltas*, 56.
9 Biezais, *Latvija kāškrusta varā*, 32.
10 BA, R58/214 and 215; Silgailis, 12ff.
11 BA, R58/216, SD Ereignismeldung of 15 Aug. 1941.
12 BA, R58/215, SD Ereignismeldung of 1 Aug. 1941.
13 Kangeris, 'Kollaboration vor der Kollaboration?' 182, 187.
14 BA, R90/115, no. 1112–26, Trampedach report of 16/08/1941.
15 Vestermanis, 'Der Holocaust in Lettland,' 101–30; 'Der lettische Anteil an der Endlösung,' 426–49; and Ezergailis, *Holocaust in Latvia*, 175, 178.
16 Press, 137.
17 A. Ezergailis, 'Arājs kommanda,' *LPSR Zinātņu Akadēmijas Vēstis* [Bulletin of the Academy of Sciences of the Latvian SSR], 10 (495) (1988), 113–30, and

Holocaust in Latvia, 173, 178, 191f. See also Christopher H. Browning's review in *Journal of Baltic Studies* 28 (2) (1997), 185.

18 Andrew Ezergailis attributes the widespread involvement of Latvians in the destruction of Latvia's Jews almost solely to an assumed *Führerbefehl*. See, e.g. Ezergailis's 'Anti-Semitism and the Killing of the Jews of Latvia,' in Sander L. Gilman and S.T. Katz, eds., *Anti-Semitism in Times of Crisis* (New York, 1991); '"Vadoņa Pavēle" un SS Brigadenfīrera Dr Valtera Stalekera 1941. gada 6. augusta memorands' [The 'Führer's Order' and SS Major General Dr Walter Stahlecker's Memorandum of 6 August 1941] *Latvijas Vēstures Institūta Žurnāls* [Journal of the Latvian Historical Institute], 1 (1993), 108–14, 126–30; 'Holokausta pētīšanas problēmas' [Problems in Researching the Holocaust] ibid., 130–8; and Ezergailis's 1996 monograph *The Holocaust in Latvia*.

19 Frank Gordon, *Latvians and Jews between Germany and Russia* (Stockholm, 1990), 22–36.

20 Ibid., Sofija and Arnis Lucis, personal interview, 5 Mar. 1997.

21 See H. Voldemars and K. Vīcis, eds., *We Accuse the East – We Warn the West*; (n.p.[Germany], 1948), 22.

22 Alfreds Bērziņš, *Latvia* (Washington, 1968), 53f; Gordon, 26ff; Handrack, 127, 143.

23 In October 1941 Stahlecker reported (*IMT*, vol. 37, p. 683) that the first spontaneous executions of Jews and communists were carried out by Latvians themselves. This Stahlecker statement, though questioned by critics, has been confirmed by testimonies of Holocaust survivors and Latvian war criminals prosecuted in Germany. See following note.

24 Zentrale Stelle der Landesjustizverwaltungen Ludwigsburg, II 207 AR-Nr. 751/1964, Albert Eichelis, 7.1.12–20.7.84, Audrini Anklage vom 27.6.1977, pp. 848ff; and Staatsanwaltschaft Landau i.d. Pf., 7 Js 585/76, Anklage in der Strafsache gegen Albert Eichelis wegen Mordes. See also Press, 34; Vestermanis, 'Der lettische Anteil,' and Hans-Heinrich Wilhelm, 'Offene Fragen der Holocaust-Forschung,' 403–49; Krausnick and Wilhelm, *Truppe*, 596f; and Gertrude Schneider, 'The Two Ghettos in Riga, Latvia, 1941–1943,' in L. Dobroszycki and J.S. Gurock, eds., *The Holocaust in the Soviet Union* (Armonk and London, 1993), 182f.

25 LVVA, 97/1/4/33. In a personal interview on 3 June 1985, Jekste asserted that his actions and proclamations were not directed by anyone from Germany.

26 Sofija Lucis, personal interview, St John's, 17 Feb. 1993.

27 Ezergailis, 'Arājs kommanda,' 113–30. IMT, vol. 37, p. 702; David Cesarani, *Justice Delayed* (London, 1992) 17.

28 In 1941 von Roques is reported to have termed the war *militärischen Wahnsinn* (military madness) and the SS commandos *Kopfjäger* (head hunters). Kriegsheim denounced the mass killing of Jews and declared Germany unfit to rule over non-German peoples. He was dismissed from the army in May 1942. See Myllyniemi, *Neuordnung*, 75.

29 Kleist, 156. See also Myllyniemi, *Neuordnung*, 75.

30 Wagner committed suicide after the failed attempt on Hitler's life of 20 July 1944. See Handrack, 51.

31 Rosenberg draft instructions of May 1941, as quoted in IMT, vol. 26, 574.

32 Joachim Fest, 'Alfred Rosenberg – The Forgotten Disciple,' in *The Face of the Third Reich* (New York, 1970), 163–74.

33 Werner Hasselblatt (1890–1958) studied law in Dorpat, was a member of the Estonian Parliament (1923–32), and was internationally known for his advocacy of the rights of national minorities. See Myllyniemi, *Neuordnung*, 57ff. On the proposed expulsion of Latvian intelligentsia to Russia, see also *IMT*, vol. 26, p. 550.

34 Handrack, 38, 94f, 128.

35 Gerald Reitlinger, *The House Built on Sand: The Conflicts of German Policy in Russia, 1939–1945* (New York, 1960), 136.

36 Peter Kleist, *Zwischen Hitler und Stalin, 1939–45: Aufzeichnungen von Dr Peter Kleist* (Bonn, 1950), 164.

37 Harry Marnitz, *Nordlicht über der Düna: Kritische Betrachtungen und Erinnerungen an die deutsche Besatzungszeit in Lettland 1941–1943* (Michelstadt, 1991), 17, 33. Mulligan, 80f.

38 Myllyniemi, *Neuordnung*, 96, 114f.

39 Kleist, 148; Myllyniemi, *Neuordnung*, 67.

40 Mulligan, 82; Myllyniemi, *Neuordnung*, 67.

41 Silgailis, 17, 21.

42 German civil administration replaced German military government in the territories south of the Daugava, in Lithuania, and in Kurzeme on 25 July 1941, in the rest of Latvia and Belorussia on 1 September 1941, and in Estonia on 5 December 1941. See Myllyniemi, *Neuordnung*, 78ff.

43 Lohse had to stay in a hotel south of Riga on territory which since 25 July 1941 had been placed under civil administration. See BA, R6/13, Lohse to Rosenberg, 13 Aug. 1941.

44 Myllyniemi, *Neuordnung*, 66, 76.

45 BA, R6/75, no. 25.

46 Zemgals, *Dienas baltas*, 57f.

47 E. Avotiņš, J. Dzirkalis, V. Pētersons, *Daugavas Vanagi: Wer sind sie?* (Riga, 1963), 147ff.

48 Kangeris, 'Kollaboration vor der Kollaboration?' 183. There is, surprisingly, no reference to this memorandum in the minutes of the meeting of 11 July 1941, published in Avotiņš et al., *Daugavas Vanagi: Wer sind sie?*, 144–50.
49 Krausnick, 352. For the text of the telegram see Chapter 12.
50 There is some evidence that Deglavs was executed, possibly by or on behalf of Plensners. See Biezais, *Latvija kāškrusta varā*, 192ff.
51 Zemgals, *Dienas baltas*, 68.
52 Balodis, 305f.
53 BA, R58/216, SD report of 15 Aug. 1941. See also Misiunas and Taagepera, 48.
54 BA, R6/75, reports of 30 July and 22 Aug. 1941.
55 Handrack, 143f; Blank, 14ff; Misiunas and Taagepera, 48.
56 BA, R90/265.
57 LVVA, P-252/1/26/239. Sicherheitspolizei Riga, Vernehmung vom 16. März 1944.
58 Zemgals, *Dienas baltas*, 57–61.
59 BA, R6/200, A. Leckzyck to Parteigenosse Malletke, 25 June 1941. Leckzyck had recommended himself to Rosenberg's special adviser Malletke as an expert on the Soviet economy with intimate knowledge of 'Waldmann' from his prewar stint in Riga. Rosenberg, who on 10 July 1941 got wind of Leckzyck's appearance in Riga and his recruiting of 'highly questionable co-workers,' judged him 'completely unsuitable.' Characterizing Leckzyck as 'an unreliable rumour-monger' with a wife who 'cultivated friendships in Russian circles,' Rosenberg depicted Leckzyck as a 'highly undesirable and outright dangerous' adviser in Riga.
60 BA, R90/265, 'Die Gestaltung der lettischen Behörden'; and BA, R58/216, report of 15 Aug. 1941.
61 A. Jekste, personal interview, Montreal, 3 June 1985.
62 Marģers Vestermanis, personal interviews, Riga, 13 Nov. 1992 and 16 June 1993. See also Ezergailis, *Holocaust in Latvia.*
63 BA, R6/200, Leckzyck to Malletke, dated 25 June 1941 (but according to a marginal note not sent to Malletke until 29 Aug. 1941).
64 BA, R58/216; R90/265; R6/75.
65 BA, R90/265, 'Die Gestaltung der lettischen Behörden,' 4.
66 Ibid.
67 BA, R6/75 Kleist Bericht no. 4 of 30 July 1941.
68 Copies in AVP. The original text in German read: 'Einen anderen Weg haben wir nicht, und nach so vielen Irrtümern sagen wir ruhig und doch flammend: einen anderen Weg wollen wir nicht mehr und werden ihn uns auch nie mehr wünschen.'

69 BA, R 92/485, Memorandum by E. Bönner, 3 Oct. 1941.
70 Biezais, *Latvija kāškrusta varā*, 13–37.
71 BA, R58/215, Ereignismeldung of 1 Aug. 1941.
72 BA, R6/75, Bericht no. 4.
73 BA, R58/216, SD Ereignismeldung no. 53 of 15 Aug. 1941.
74 BA, R58/214.
75 BA, R58/216, Report no. 57.
76 BA, R6/75, Reports of 30 July and 22 Aug. 1941.
77 BA, R90/115.
78 BA, R58/216.
79 Handrack, 80.
80 BA, R6/75, Kleist report of 22 Aug. 1941.
81 Zemgals's account is confirmed by German records: BA, R90/265, 'Die Gestaltung der lettischen Behörden nach der Vertreibung der Bolschewisten,' 10. BA, R6/279, Kleist memo of 25 Apr. 1942, 1–3.
82 BA, R92/485, Bönner memo of 3 Oct. 1941.
83 Marnitz, 25, 42ff.
84 BA, R92/158, Sitzungsbericht of 23 Oct. 1942.
85 Hugo Wittrock, *Erinnerungen: Kommissarischer Oberbürgermeister von Riga, 1941–1944* (Lüneburg, 1979), 61f, 75.
86 Zemgals, *Dienas baltas*, 73. SD Ereignismeldung of 12 Jan. 1942 reported that effective 1 Feb. 1942, Weiss, Freimanis, Sanders, and Andersons were officially relieved of their duties in the self- administration. The political situation had been consolidated, the report stated, and the *Vertrauensrat* to which they belonged was no longer necessary. See BA, R58/220, 96f.
87 BA, R6/279, Kleist memo of 25 Apr. 1942.
88 LVVA, 1307/3/56, 'Tieslietu Generāldirekcija, Apliecība, 17 May 1944. AVP, memorandum by Valdmanis entitled 'Latvia in 1941,' Weilburg, Feb. 1946, 4.
89 BA, R58/220, SD Ereignismeldung, 9 Jan. 1942.
90 For example, Jānis Strādiņš, vice-president of the Latvian Academy of Sciences, recalled that Drechsler was well disposed towards Latvians. Jānis Strādiņš, personal interview, Riga, 15 June 1995.
91 BA, R6/13, Drechsler to Rosenberg, 29 Dec. 1942.
92 Marnitz, 17, 24f.
93 AVP, statement in defence of Egon Bönner, Weilheim, 7 Mar. 1947.
94 BA, R58/220, SD Ereignismeldung of 16 Jan. 1942, 36.
95 BA, R58/221, SD Ereignismeldung of 24 Apr. 1942.
96 BA, R6/279, Drechsler to Lohse, 25 Mar. 1942.
97 BA, R6/279, Kleist's report of 25 Apr. 1942. Myllyniemi, *Neuordnung*, 107.

98 BA, R6/200.

99 LVVA, P-69/1a/18, Gebietskommissar in Wolmar to Generalkommissar in Riga, Monatsbericht Mar. 1942.

100 BA, R6/279, Entwurf einer Anordnung über die Führung der Verwaltung im Generalbezirk Lettland, 10 Feb. 1942.

101 BA, R6/279, Burmeister to Rosenberg, 25 Mar. 1942.

102 BA, R6/246, Rosenberg to Lohse, 7 Mar. 1942.

103 BA, R6/279, Rosenberg to Lohse, 25 Apr. 1942.

104 AVP, statement by A. Kirs to Headquarters Command EUCOM APO 757, Hanau, 22 Oct. 1947, 3.

105 BA, R58/221, SD Ereignismeldung of 25 Mar. 1942.

106 Latvian Legation (1943), 13–18.

107 Zemgals, *Dienas baltas*, 76f.

108 BA, R92/485, 'Memorandum über aktuelle Fragen in Lettland,' Nov. 1941.

109 AVP, B. Zemgals, affidavit in support of A. Valdmanis, 25 Nov. 1947.

110 AVP, Valdmanis affidavit in support of Egon Bönner, 7 Mar. 1947.

111 Zemgals, *Dienas baltas*, 77.

112 *Treji Vārti*, 98 (1985), 17.

113 BA, R92/158, nos. 388, 392, 393.

114 BA, R92/485, Valdmanis to Generalkommissar in Riga, 19 Feb. 1943.

115 BA, R92/485, nos. 5–7, Dec. 1942.

116 BA, R58/221, SD Ereignismeldung of 8 Apr. 1942.

117 BA, R58/224, SD Ereignismeldung no. 51 of 23 Apr. 1943.

118 BA, Z42 IV/8B/7202, affidavit by A. Valdmanis in support of Hinrich Lohse, 29–30 July, 1947.

119 BA, R58/224, SD Ereignismeldung no. 51 of 23 Apr. 1943.

120 BA, R58/221, SD Ereignismeldung of 2 Mar. 1942.

121 BA, R92/158, Sitzungsbericht of 3 Dec. 1942.

122 BA, R6/39, Drechsler to Rosenberg, 29 Dec. 1942.

123 BA, R58/225, SD Mitteilungsblatt of 11 Aug. 1942.

124 Zemgals, *Dienas baltas*, 67f.

125 BA, R51/221, SD Ereignismeldung of 27 and 30 Mar., 8 and 24 Apr. 1942. Zemgals, *Dienas baltas*, 72.

126 AVP, untitled, six-page typed statement by A. Nepārts, Detmold, 23 Mar. 1946.

127 As quoted in Biezais, *Latvija kāškrusta varā*, 110f.

128 *IMT*, vol. 37, p. 697.

129 BA, R6/13, Reichskommissar für das Ostland to Reichsminister für die besetzten Ostgebiete, Riga, 13 Sept. 1941.

130 BA, R6/200.
131 BA, R6/279, note by Kleist, 25 Apr. 1942.
132 BA, R6/279, Trampedach memo, 10 Feb. 1942.
133 BA, R92/158; *Tēvija*, no. 136, 15 June 1942.
134 Silgailis, 14.
135 BA, R92/158, 30 Oct. 1942.
136 Zemgals, *Dienas baltas*, 69.
137 BA, R6/13, 'Einschaltung des Generaldirektors Waldmanis in die Jugendarbeit.'
138 BA, R6/13:142–3, 149–54, Siewert vs Simm, 5 Nov. 1942.
139 BA, R6/183, Lüer, Aktenvermerk Betr: Lettische Jugendorganisation, Riga, 15 Oct. 1942.
140 Lohse's memorandum of Mar. 1942 'Zur Neugestaltung des Verwaltungsaufbaus des Ostlandes,' as summarized in Myllyniemi, *Neuordnung*, 189 n175.
141 BA, R58/222, no. 282, Petersen to Werchan, 13 July 1942.
142 BA, R6/279, Rosenberg to Lohse, 12 Oct. 1942.
143 BA, R6/39, Drechsler to Rosenberg, 29 Dec. 1942.
144 BA, R91 Mitau/7, 'Bericht über die Abschlußtagung der lettischen Jugendführer in Riga am 25. und 26. Februar 1943.'
145 BA, R 09/19 Riga-Stadt, 'Bericht über den Verlauf der Studienfahrt der lettischen Jugendführer in das Reich vom 28.10.1942 – 22.11.1942.'
146 BA, R 91 Mitau/7, Vertraulich: 'Bericht über die Abschlußtagung der lettischen Jugendführer in Riga am 25. und 26. Februar 1943.'
147 BA, R90/160, 15 July 1942.

Chapter 5: 'Made No Bones about His Antipathy to the German Regime'

1 David Littlejohn, *The Patriotic Traitors: A History of Collaboration in German-Occupied Europe, 1940–45* (London, 1972), 337.
2 *Der Spiegel*, 13 Sept. 1994, 157f; *Globe and Mail*, 29 Sept. 1994, A16.
3 Myllyniemi, *Neuordnung*, 227f.
4 Silgailis, 15.
5 Zemgals, *Dienas baltas*, 79f.
6 Ibid., 7f. 80; Myllyniemi, *Neuordnung*, 229f.
7 Silgailis, 13ff.
8 Zemgals, *Dienas baltas*, 74, 81; Myllyniemi, *Neuordnung*, 210, 230.
9 BA, R6/24:94, Drechsler to Lohse, 20 Apr. 1943.
10 BA, R6/5:3–13, 'Das lettische Problem,' Nov. 1942.

11 Zemgals, *Dienas baltas*, 83, 86.
12 BA, R6/5:1–2, Landeseigene Verwaltung to Generalkommissar, Dec. 1942.
13 Zemgals, *Dienas baltas*, 86; translation by Max Braun-Wogau.
14 Ibid.; BA, R6/5:1, Dec. 1942, and R6/24:94, Drechsler to Lohse, 20 April 1943.
15 BA, R6/280:4–9, Stellungnahme, 5 Jan. 1943.
16 BA, R6/24:94, Drechsler to Lohse, 20 Apr. 1943.
17 Myllyniemi, *Neuordnung*, 218, 230.
18 Silgailis, 21.
19 This is translated from 'Protokols Nr. 1' circulated in Riga in 1943 and displayed as part of an exhibition by the Latvian War Museum (Latvijas Kara Muzējs) in Riga in 1993. A German translation of this document is among Valdmanis's personal papers (AVP).
20 Zemgals, *Dienas baltas*, 90. The original Latvian transcripts of this meeting, subsequently circulated in Riga as 'Protokols Nr. 1' and exhibited by Latvian War Museum in 1993 do not include Schröder's invitation to dinner and Valdmanis's response.
21 BA, R6/5:20–7, Protokoll der Sitzung der Lettischen Selbstverwaltung und der Führung des Generalkommissariats, n.d. [29 Jan 1943].
22 AVP, Memorandum by E. Nepārts, 23 Mar. 1946, 6.
23 Biezais, *Latvija kāškrusta varā*, 118, 133.
24 Zemgals, *Dienas baltas*, 99.
25 AVP, Valdmanis's curriculum vitae, written in Weilburg, Germany, Mar. 1947; and 'Latvia in 1941,' Weilburg, Germany, Feb. 1946.
26 Wittrock, 75.
27 BA, R58/224:8-9. AVP, untitled six-page typescript by A. Nepārts, 23 Mar. 1946.
28 BA, R 58/224, SD Ereignismeldung nos. 40 and 44 of 5 Feb. and 5 Mar. 1943.
29 BA, R6/24, Drechsler to Lohse, 24 Apr. 1943. Nuremberg Trial Records, NG-2721, Windecker to Foreign Office, 19 Apr. 1943, as quoted in Myllyniemi, *Neuordnung*, 243f.
30 BA, R6/24:122, Rosenberg to Lohse, 23 July 1943.
31 AVP, A. Kirs to Headquarters Command EUCOM, 22 Oct. 1947; Valdmanis's memorandum 'Latvia in 1941,' Feb. 1946.
32 LVVA, 1307/3/56, Valdmanis's curriculum vitae, 17 May 1944. Myllyniemi, *Neuordnung*, 243.
33 LVVA, P-252/1/26, Lange an Müller, 25 Jan. 1944, 7.
34 Wilhelm von Rüdiger, *Die 'Deutsch-Baltische Volksgruppe': Ausklang* (Hannover-Wülfel, 1957), 11.

35 Silgailis, 23.
36 BA, R6/84:61, Drechsler to Lohse, 19 June 1943; Myllyniemi, *Neuordnung*, 230–3; Silgailis, 22f., 239.
37 BA, R6/29:65, Schmutzler to Gebietskommissar Riga, 28 Apr. 1943; R6/29:106–10, Schmutzler to Generalinspektion der lettischen SS-Freiw. Legion, 8 Oct. 1943.
38 BA, R6/249, Trampedach to Rosenberg, 15 Mar. 1943.
39 BA, R58/224, SD Ereignismeldung of 2 Apr. 1943.
40 Mangulis, 120.
41 BA, R58/224, SD Ereignismeldung no. 51 of 23 Apr. 1943.
42 Spekke, 408.
43 BA, R58/224, SD Ereignismeldung no. 51 of 23 Apr. 1943.
44 Ibid., SD Ereignismeldung no. 48 of 2 Apr. 1943.
45 Ibid., SD Ereignismeldung no. 51 of 23 Apr. 1943.
46 BA, R6/5:28, Rosenberg to Hitler, 20 Mar. 1943; Myllyniemi, *Neuordnung*, 223f.
47 BA, R58/224, SD Ereignismeldung of 5 Mar. 1943.
48 Myllyniemi, *Neuordnung*, 218, 230ff.
49 Zemgals, *Dienas baltas*, 82.
50 BA, R6/246:54, Lohse to Rosenberg, 2 Dec. 1943.
51 BA, R6/29:11, 121–5; Wittrock, 75.
52 BA, R6/29:27–49.
53 W. von Rüdiger, 24–32.
54 BA, R6/24:24–96, Drechsler to Lohse, 20 Apr. 1943.
55 BA, R6/84, Drechsler to Rosenberg, 4 Aug. 1943.
56 BA, R6/84:60–8.
57 Myllyniemi, *Neuordnung*, 210f.
58 BA, R6/249:4–14; R6/67:12–14. Myllyniemi, *Neuordnung*, 215f, 242–6.
59 BA, R6/24:151–3, Lohse to Rosenberg, 4 Oct. 1943.
60 BA, R6/24:126–8, 29 July 1943.
61 BA, R6/29:62–3, Wittrock to Marquart, 29 Apr. 1943.
62 BA, R6/24:117–23, Rosenberg to Lohse, 23 July 1943.
63 BA, R6/24:136–9, Rosenberg to Lohse, 9 Sept. 1943.
64 BA, R6/5:33–6, Latvian directors general to Drechsler, 16 Nov. 1943.
65 BA, R6/5:103–10, Rosenberg to Hitler, 23 Nov. 1943.
66 BA, R6/246, Niederschrift, 10 Dec. 1943; and Rosenberg to Himmler, 17 Dec. 1943.
67 BA, R6/75, Gelegenheitsbericht, 18 Jan. 1944.

68 BA, R6/189:23–8, Aktenvermerk, 31 May 1944. R6/14, Rosenberg to Drechsler, betr: 'Lettische Denkschrift mit den 160 Unterschriften,' 3 July 1944.
69 Zemgals, *Dienas baltas*, 99f.
70 BA, R6/76; Myllyniemi, *Neuordnung*, 212.
71 AVP, statement by S. Suziedelis, Hanau, 19 Dec. 1945.
72 Latvian Legation, Washington, *Latvia under German Occupation 1941–1943*, with a preface by Alfred Bilmanis (Washington, 1943), 111.
73 He treated the June 1941 Soviet invasion as popularly acclaimed liberation from fascism and advocated a return of the Baltic republics into the Soviet fold.
74 Introduction by Prof. Frederic L. Schuman to G. Meiksins, *The Baltic Soviet Republics*, published by the National Council of Soviet-American Friendship (New York, 1944), 6.
75 Gregory Meiksins, *The Baltic Riddle: Finland, Estonia, Latvia, Lithuania – Key Points of European Peace* (New York, 1943), 198ff.
76 Ibid., 104, 193, 205–8, 216f.
77 Meiksins, *Baltic Soviet Republics*, 43.
78 Latvian Legation, *Latvia under German Occupation, 1941–1943*, 4–11.
79 Latvian Legation, Washington, *Latvia under German Occupation in 1943* (Washington, 1944), 24f.
80 Siliņš and Andersons, *Latvijas Centrālā Padome*, 38, 64f.
81 Biezais, *Latvija kāškrusta varā*, 123.
82 Letter to the editor of *Newsweek*, as reprinted in *Evening Telegram* (St John's), 18 Dec. 1951.
83 AVP, Erklärung, by Dr A. Windecker, 13 Dec. 1947.
84 AVP, Copy of a report about Dr Alfred Valdmanis, by Lt Col Graebe, undated.
85 'Wer marschiert hinter dem ersten Tank? Das ist der Dr Rasche von der Dresdner Bank!' See OMGUS, *Ermittlungen gegen die Dresdner Bank, 1946* (Nördlingen, 1986), VII, 255ff, 309.
86 Ibid., 167–74. AVP, U.S. Army Headquarters, Interrogation of Karl Rasche, 11 June 1947. Roswitha Czollek, *Faschismus und Okkupation: Wirtschaftliche Zielsetzung und Praxis des faschistischen deutschen Besatzungsregimes in den baltischen Sowjetrepubliken während des zweiten Weltkriegs* (Berlin, 1974), 87ff. Latvian Legation, *Latvia under German Occupation 1941–1943*, 28.
87 *Treji Vārti*, 98 (1985), 17.
88 Ibid., 18.
89 AVP, Interrogation of Dr Karl Rasche, Headquarters, War Crimes Enclosure CI Screening Staff APO 407, U.S. Army, 11 June 1947.

90 Irma Valdmanis, personal interview, 4 Apr. 1986.
91 AVP, 'Bescheinigung,' by J. Šakars, Hauptabteilungsleiter, Gerichte, dated Riga, 14 Oct. 1943.
92 AVP, statements by Wilhelm Burmeister, 6 July 1954; Dr Seehusen, 9 July 1953; and Jānis Krūmiņš, 16 July 1954. Certificate of award of Magister Jurisprudence by University of Latvia, 28 Aug. 1940.
93 Myllyniemi, *Neuordnung*, 250.
94 Heinz Höhne, *Der Orden unter dem Totenkopf: Die Geschichte der SS* (Hamburg, 1967), 385.
95 See Robert Wistrich, *Wer war wer im Dritten Reich? Ein biografisches Lexikon* (FrankfurtM, 1987), 230, and Reitlinger, 186. The official records pertaining to Lohse's treatment of Jews, deposited in LVVA, P-1026/1/3, as well as the evidence accumulated by Krausnick and Wilhelm, *Truppe*, 546f, 566f, 570, 573, 588, 600f, 603f, 613f, show that Lohse ensured the smooth functioning of the killing machinery in the RKO.
96 BA, Z 42 IV, 8 B, vol. 7202. Sworn deposit by Dr Alfred A. Valdmanis of 29/30 July 1947, with regard to the denazification and Soviet request for extradition of Hinrich Lohse. I am grateful to Marģers Vestermanis for drawing my attention to this document.
97 Bērziņš, *Tāls ir ceļš atpakaļ uz dzimteni*, 12, 26f.
98 AAS, no.44, A. Bērziņš to A. Bilmanis, 28 Oct. 1947. The evidence Bērziņš presents in this letter of his encounter with Valdmanis (as well as of Valdmanis's resignation from the Ulmanis cabinet in October 1939) deviates in a number of respects from the account in his 1971 memoirs *Tāls ir ceļš atpakaļ uz dzimteni.*
99 AVP, affidavit by Wilhelm Burmeister, 7 July 1953.
100 Zemgals, *Dienas baltas*, 105.
101 Information received from Gundars Valdmanis, 28 Jan. 1986.
102 AVP, Joan Münninghoff to Valdmanis, Voorburg, 17 July 1943.
103 AVP, Joan Münninghoff to Valdmanis, Voorburg, 24 Mar. 1944.
104 Supreme Court of Newfoundland, no. 533/1954, file 'The Queen v Valdmanis.' A less detailed version of the story is in Zemgals, *Dienas baltas*, 104.
105 AVP, U.S. Army Headquarters, Interrogation of Karl Rasche, 11 June 1947.
106 K. Čakste to V. Salnais, Feb. 1944, in: Siliņš and Andersons, *Latvijas Centrālā Padome*, 64.
107 *Treji Vārti*, 98 (1985), 18.
108 AVP, members of the council of the Latvian camp in Esslingen to the presidium of LCP, 7 Mar. 1947; rebuttal by Valdmanis, chairman of LCP, to memorandum of Esslingen committee, dated 7 Mar. 1947.

109 Zemgals, *Dienas baltas*, 106.

110 Canada, Senate, *Proceedings*, 55.

Chapter 6: 'I Had Committed All My Heart and My Efforts to Latvian Exiles'

1 AVP, typescript 'Estimated Number of Latvian Refugees in Germany,' undated. No reliable figures are available. Plakāns, 223, quotes an estimate by A. Svabe of 200,000 Latvians living in occupied postwar Germany. Bērziņš, *Tāls ir ceļš atpakaļ uz dzimteni*, 116, counted 82,000 Latvians in DP camps in the summer of 1945, and mentions the enumeration of 111,495 Latvians (62,486 males and 49,027 females) by the Latvian Central Committee in 1947. The Institut für Besatzungsfragen, ed., *Das DP-Problem: Eine Studie über die ausländischen Flüchtlinge in Deutschland* (Tübingen, 1950), 19, found 90,000 Latvian refugees in Germany in 1945. According to George Woodbridge, *UNRRA: The History of the United Nations Relief and Rehabilitation Administration* (New York, 1950), vol. 3, 423, nearly 100,000 displaced persons of Latvian nationality were receiving UNRRA assistance in June 1946. Malcolm J. Proudfoot, *European Refugees, 1939–52: A Study in Forced Population Movement* (London, 1957), 238n1, gives 72,922 as the number DPs claiming Latvian nationality in western Europe as of 30 September 1945.

2 Proudfoot, 207–20.

3 Zemgals, *Dienas baltas*, 109.

4 Lucius D. Clay, *Decision in Germany* (New York, 1950), 25.

5 Zemgals, *Dienas baltas*, 109f.

6 AVP, A. Dancauskis, 'Vai tas bija vajadzīgs [Was That Necessary?],' typescript submitted to *Tēvzeme* editor, Feb./Mar. 1946.

7 AVP, 'Estimated Number of Latvian Refugees in Germany.' n.d.

8 Zemgals, *Dienas baltas*, 110.

9 Ibid., refers to Col. Kramer who, according to Christoph Weisz, ed., *Omgus Handbuch: Die amerikanische Militärregierung in Deutschland, 1945–1949* (Munich, 1995), 813, was Maj. Abe Kramer, Acting Chief, Manpower Allocations Branch.

10 Zemgals, *Dienas baltas*, 111.

11 AVP, petition signed by representatives of 9 refugee committees, drawn up in Kempten, 9 July 1945.

12 Zemgals, *Dienas baltas*, 112.

13 Ibid., 112f.

14 AVP, Protocol of the Wildflecken National Committee, 17 July 1945.

15 AVP, Valdmanis to Bilmanis, Zariņš and B. Balūtis, 7 Aug. 1945; Zariņš to Valdmanis, 13 Aug., 7 and 21 Sept. 1945.
16 Zemgals, *Dienas baltas*, 114f.
17 AVP, Valdmanis to Mateus, 26 Sept. 1946; Valdmanis to Zariņš, 14 Oct. 1945.
18 AVP, Valdmanis to Zariņš, 14 Oct. 1945.
19 AVP, Valdmanis to Gulbis, 29 Aug. 1945.
20 Bērziņš, *Tāls ir ceļš atpakaļ uz dzimteni*, 128.
21 AVP, certificate by Public Safety Officer, 30 Oct. 1945.
22 AVP, Valdmanis to Zariņš, 14 Dec. 1945.
23 Zemgals, *Dienas baltas*, 112; Silgailis, 49, 182–8.
24 Voldemars and Vicis, *We Accuse the East*, 49; n.a., 'Das ist eine offene Wunde,' *Der Spiegel*, 51 (1991), 171.
25 Cesarani, 48f, 50, 65; Ezergailis, *Holocaust in Latvia*, 195.
26 PRO, FO 371/47051; Cesarani, 46f.
27 Cesarani, 46; Canada, Senate, *Proceedings*, 56; Zemgals, *Dienas baltas*, 121.
28 Zemgals, *Dienas baltas*, 122f.
29 AVP, Report no. 1399 by unidentified official of the Latvian Red Cross from Esslingen (probably R. Liepiņš), 17 Jan. 1946.
30 AVP, Valdmanis to Zariņš, 14 Oct. 1945.
31 Cesarani, 57–62.
32 Quoted in AVP, Council of Latvian colony Esslingen to LCK, 26 Jan. 1946.
33 AVP, Zariņš to Anna Bērziņa, 26 Oct. 1945.
34 Zemgals, *Dienas baltas*, 123.
35 AVP, Council of Latvian colony in Esslingen to LCK, 26 Jan. 1946.
36 Cesarani, 49f.
37 Zemgals, *Dienas baltas*, 128. AVP, A. Dancauskis, 'Vai tas bija vajadzīgs?' ms. for publication in *Tēvzeme*.
38 As quoted in Cesarani, 56f, 65.
39 Cesarani, 52f, 56.
40 AVP, 'Latvians in the Ranks of the German Army,' typescript (double-spaced), 4 pp. Whether and to whom it was submitted cannot be determined.
41 AVP, Public Safety Officer Gerald Ziskind to Interested American Authorities, Weilburg, 20 Mar. 1946.
42 AVP, minutes of the 1 December 1945 meeting of the Latvian colony in Esslingen. They also objected that several former Latvian officials of the German occupation period had been elected as members of the LCK.
43 Zemgals, *Dienas baltas*, 124f.

44 AVP, Valdmanis to Zariņš, 14 Dec. 1945.
45 AVP, K. Kundziņš and F. Gulbis on behalf of LCK to the chairman of the Latvian colony in Esslingen, K. Kalniņš, 22 Dec. 1945.
46 AVP, Zariņš to Valdmanis, 11 Jan. 1946.
47 AVP, Council of the Latvian colony in Esslingen to LCK, 26 Jan. 1946.
48 Ibid.
49 AVP, 'Tautietes un Tautieši! [Citizens! (male and female)]' LCP, 2nd session, Hanau, 23 Feb. 1946.
50 AVP, Dancauskis, 'Vai tas bija vajadzīgs?'
51 AVP, 'LCP Prezidiju Maiņa [The LCP Presidium Change],' LCP, 2nd session, Hanau, 23 Feb. 1946.
52 Zemgals, *Dienas baltas*, 125f.
53 Ibid., 130. AVP, Public Safety Officer Gerald Ziskind to Interested American Authorities, Weilburg, 20 Mar. 1946.
54 AVP, 'Latvia in 1941 (Occupied and Annected [*sic*] by Russia),' six-page (double-spaced) typescript, dated Weilburg, Feb. 1946.
55 AVP, A. Klīve and V. Bastjānis to P. Sterste, 13 July 1946.
56 AVP, Letter dated Stockholm, 22 Nov. 1946.
57 AVP, Zariņš to Klīve and Bastjānis, 7 Nov. 1946.
58 AVP, Zariņš to Valdmanis, 26 Nov. 1946.
59 AVP, LCP, 6th session, 2nd general meeting, 14 Feb. 1947.
60 AVP, 'Ne ārdīt un šķelt, bet vienot un celt! [Not to Unravel and Split, but to Unite and Build!]' six-page (double-spaced) typescript, undated.
61 AVP, Zariņš to Valdmanis, 8 Apr. 1947.
62 AVP, Identity card issued to Alfred Valdmanis by Anthony Biddle, Chief, Allied Contact Section, Headquarters U.S. Forces, European Theater, Allied Contact Section, 22 May 1947.
63 These documents are in the AVP.
64 Zemgals, *Dienas baltas*, 140f.
65 AVP, A. Klīve, V. Bastjānis, B. Krūka, and V. Slakāns on behalf of the Central Council of Latvia in Esslingen to K. Zariņš, 5 Mar. 1947.
66 AVP, A. Kacēns and K. Krievs, on behalf of 34 members of the Council of the Latvian Colony of Esslingen, to the presidium and members of the LCP and LCK, 7 Mar. 1947.
67 AVP, Valdmanis's response to the memorandum of 7 Mar. 1947 issued by the Esslingen committee, undated.
68 AVP, Bishop J. Rancāns, 'Paskaidrojums [Explanation],' *Latviešu Ziņas* [Latvian News], Apr. 1947; Zemgals, *Dienas baltas*, 137f.
69 Judged by the excerpts Bilmanis quoted, one of these presentations was Valdmanis's 'Latvia in 1941,' dated Weilburg, Feb. 1946.

70 AVP, Declaration by Ambassador A. Bilmanis, Washington, 21 June 1947. An almost identical version entitled 'Mans viedoklis [My Point of View'] was published by Bilmanis in *Latvijas Ziņas*, no. 48, 28 June 1947.
71 AAS, Bilmanis to Feldmanis, 8 July 1947.
72 AVP, cabled messages by Bilmanis of 24 and 25 July 1947.
73 AAS, Bilmanis to Feldmanis, 8 July 1947, forwarded by LCP of Stockholm, 15 Aug. 1947; a copy is also in AVP.
74 AVP, Zemgals to Bilmanis, 15 Sept. 1947.
75 AVP, Bilmanis to Zemgals, 23 Sept. 1947.
76 AVP, Zemgals to Bilmanis, 6 Oct. 1947.
77 AVP, Zemgals to Bilmanis, 20 Oct. 1947.
78 AAS, Bērziņš to Bilmanis, 28 Oct. 1947.
79 AVP, L. Zemgals to A. Āboliņš, 23 May 1949.
80 No one with an active life made no mistakes, Bērziņš mused in 1971. And he conceded that 'laudable as the often-heard claim may be that the truth should be known and told, those who demand the truth often end up projecting the past through their political view of the world.' Bērziņš, *Tāls ir ceļš atpakaļ uz dzimteni*, 128–37, 326.
81 AVP, J. Arājs, 'Taisnības uzvara [The Victory of Truth],' typed for publication, undated, probably late 1947.
82 AVP, Alfreds Gulbis, 'Vīrus, ne amatus [Men, Not Offices],' Fischbach, 3 Aug. 1947.
83 Zemgals, *Dienas baltas*, 143.
84 NAC, J. Pickersgill Papers, MG32 B34, vol. 37, file I-2-502, Series C-I, H.L. Keenleyside to Minister of Mines and Resources, 25 Nov. 1948.
85 Canada, Senate, 57, 62f; Zemgals, *Dienas baltas*, 143, 148.
86 AVP, Dr Alfreds A. Valdmanis, 'Liecība [Testimony],' PCIRO, 27 Feb. 1948.
87 AVP, Valdmanis to Valdis Mateus, 21 Nov. 1947.
88 AVP, Zariņš to Valdmanis, 19 Nov. 1947.
89 AVP, A. Valdmanis, 'Intelligence Division Frankfurtē. Izraksts [Report],' 25 Nov. and 26 Dec. 1947.
90 AVP, Valdmanis to Nepārts, 10 Jan. 1948.
91 AVP, Valdmanis to Valdis Mateus, 24 Jan. 1948.
92 AVP, 'To Headquarters Command EUCOM APO 757 from Latvian DP Camp Hanau,' 22 Oct. 1947.
93 AVP, Dr Alfred A. Valdmanis, 'Eidestattliche Erklärung,' Frankfurt, 26 Aug. 1947; Dr A. Windecker, 'Erklärung,' Nuremberg, 13 Dec. 1947.
94 AVP, 'Testimonium,' typescript in German with the certified signature of B. Zemgals, Geneva, 25 Nov. 1947.
95 AVP, Zariņš to Valdmanis, 10 Mar. 1948.

96 AAS, no. 425, Valdmanis to friends, 8 Jan. 1948.
97 AVP, 'To Intelligence Division, HQ EUCOM, APO 757, U.S. Army,' undated.
98 AVP, Dr Alfreds A. Valdmanis, 'Liecība,' PCIRO, 27 Feb. 1948.
99 AVP, Valdmanis to Valdis Mateus, 30 Mar. 1948; Canada, Senate, *Proceedings*, 57.
100 AVP, Valdmanis to Valdis Mateus, 24 Jan. 1948.
101 AAS, no. 428, Valdmanis to a friend, 22 Apr. 1948.
102 AVP, Valdmanis to Valdis Mateus, 21 and 25 Feb. 1948.
103 AVP, 'Projekts: Latvju Tautas Padomes pamatnoteikumi [Project: The Latvian National Council's Ground Rules],' undated (27 Feb. 1948).
104 AVP, A., 'Projekts par Tautas Padomi [The National Council Project],' *Latvju Ziņas*, no. 12, 14 Feb. 1948.
105 Zemgals, *Dienas baltas*, 153; AAS, no. 428, Valdmanis to a friend, 22 Apr. 1948.
106 Ibid., no. 425, Valdmanis to a friend, 8 Jan. 1948.
107 AVP, Valdmanis to Valdis Mateus, 20 Apr. 1948.
108 AAS, no. 428, Valdmanis to a friend, 22 Apr. 1948.
109 *Treji Vārti*, nos. 95–98 (1983–6).
110 AVP, Zariņš to Valdmanis, 10 Mar. 1948.
111 AVP, L. Zemgals to A. Āboliņš, Geneva, 23 May 1949. Leonīds Zemgals lived in Newfoundland while Valdmanis was there, then moved to Ottawa, and died in 1985. Gundars Valdmanis to author, 21 Feb. 1986.
112 AVP, August J. Osis to Gundars Valdmanis, 11 Dec. 1977.

Chapter 7: 'Starting Anew Like Our Fathers Did after the First World War'

1 SC, 6.01.012, Valdmanis: Corr. with banking houses, Amex agent to Valdmanis, 30 Aug. 1948.
2 Irma Valdmanis, personal interview, 4 Apr. 1986.
3 NAC, RG76, vol. 646, file 999888, pt. 1.
4 Rodal, 186–201; Matas, 22f.
5 Rodal, 201f. Sol Littman, *War Criminal on Trial: The Rauca Case* (Markham, 1983), 174f; Ezergailis, *Holocaust in Latvia*, 284.
6 NAC, RG76, vol. 824, file 552-1-582, H.L. Keenleyside to R.N. Bryson, 1 Sept. 1948.
7 AVP, Zariņš to Valdmanis, 19 Nov. 1947.
8 AVP, Zariņš to Valdmanis, 10 Mar. 1948.
9 AVP, Protocols no. 36/3. LCP, 10th session, 3rd general meeting, 5 Mar. 1948, Latvian camp at Babenhausen.

10 AVP, Valdmanis to V. Mateus, 30 Mar. 1948.
11 NAC, RG76, vol. 824, file 552-1-582, Estonian, Latvian and Lithuanian Refugee Committees in Germany to J.A. Glen, Minister of Mines and Resources, 9 Sept. 1948.
12 AVP, Protocol no. 40/2. LCP, 13 session, 2nd general meeting, Fulda, 6 Oct. 1948.
13 AVP, Protocol no. 38, LCP, 12th session, 8–9 July, 1948, Hanau.
14 Canada, *Report of the Department of Mines and Resources for the Fiscal Year Ended March 31, 1949* (Ottawa, 1949), 228.
15 NAC, RG76, vol. 824, file 552-1-582, Keenleyside to H. Klarks, Chairman, Latvian Central Committee, 10 Nov. 1948.
16 H.L. Keenleyside, *Memoirs of Hugh L. Keenleyside*, vol. 2, *On the Bridge of Time* (Toronto, 1982), 301f.
17 SC, Lady Davis Foundation, *Report Nineteen Forty-Nine* (Montreal, 1949), 1–5.
18 'Valuable immigrants,' *Winnipeg Free Press*, 18 Feb. 1949.
19 NAC, MG32 B34, vol. 37, file I-2-502, series C-I.
20 Ibid.; Secretary of the Lady Davis Foundation to Valdmanis, 2 July 1948.
21 *Evening Citizen*, Ottawa, 10 Feb. 1949.
22 AVP, 'The Middle Way,' by Harold Macmillan, MP, London 1938. Reflections on finance, foreign trade, and coordination are followed by the postulate of a minimum wage as a stabilizing factor in the reconstituted economy.
23 *Evening Citizen*, Ottawa, 10 Feb. 1949.
24 NAC, MG32 B34, vol. 37, file I-2-502, series C-I.
25 NAC, RG76, vol. 824, file 552-1-582, Charles Zariņš (as Kārlis Zariņš often signed himself in English) to Frederich Hudd, 12 May 1949.
26 Ibid., 'Memorandum,' signed by J. Feldmanis, Minister Plenipotentiary, former Permanent Latvian Delegate to the League of Nations, Representative of the Latvian refugee organization, Geneva, 24 Feb., 1949.
27 Following a request from the Premier of Newfoundland in December 1951, Valdmanis through European acquaintances tried in vain to obtain some kind of official statement from Swedish officials verifying his account of the Swedish intervention. See SC, 6.02.011, Kreyser and Braun-Wogau to Valdmanis, Dec. 1951 to Feb. 1952.
28 Canada, Senate, *Proceedings of the Standing Committee on Immigration and Labour: On the Operation and Administration of the Immigration Act, etc.*, no. 4, Wed., 27 Apr. 1949. The Hon. Cairine R. Wilson, Chairman. Witness Dr. Alfred A. Valdmanis, Professor of Economics, adviser to the Immigration Branch, Department of Mines and Resources (Ottawa, 1949).
29 *Review of Foreign Language Press in Canada*, May 1949.

30 Z. Udrovskij, 'Cynki latyshchkoi burshuazii v kachectve Di-Pi v Kanade [The Sons of the Latvian Bourgeoisie as DPs in Canada],' *Vestnik*, 1 Feb. 1950, 3. Translated by Dr Arnis Duks, Riga, and Arnis Lucis, St John's.
31 AVP, manuscript articles with the following titles: (1) 'Trimdinieka pardomas [Reflections of an Exile]'; (2) 'Taisnības tiesa [The Court of Truth]'; (3) 'Kāda neizdevusies "kontrrevolucija" [An Unsuccessful "Counter revolution"]'; (4) 'Cik viņu ir un ko viņi grib? [How Many of Them Are There and What Do They Want?]' (5) 'Kas darits lidz šim? [What's Been Done 'Til Now?]' (6) 'Ko tālāk? [Now What?]' (7) 'Reģionālas un lokālas latviešu organizācijas [Regional and Local Latvian Organizations].'
32 AVP, Helen Matheson, 'Thrown Off Train to Escape Reds, Latvian DP Boy's a Visitor Here,' *Wisconsin State Journal*, 3 Aug. 1949.
33 AVP, 24-page typescript, untitled and undated.
34 AVP, A.L. Jolliffe to Dr A.Valdmanis, 28 Aug. 1949.
35 SC [originally in file 'gypsum'], typescript by Nova Scotia Research Foundation, 'Gypsum Project: Second Memorandum for Discussion,' 21 Dec. 1949.
36 Ernest Leja papers (in family possession), vitae of Ernest Albert Leja (1896–1982). *Who's Who in the East: United States of America and Canada*, 12th ed. (Chicago, 1969), 654.
37 Herbert Matschen Papers (in private possession), collection of RIGIPS advertising materials from the 1980s. 'Rigips' stands for *Rigaer Gips*, i.e., Riga-type plaster.
38 SC, 6.01.015, E. Leja to B.J. Bachand, 18 Jan. 1950.
39 CNS Archive, C-165, Alfred A. Valdmanis Papers, 'A Valdmanis Statement: Neue Technik.' undated [1954].
40 Letter A. Jekste, Montreal, to author, 15 Apr. 1985.
41 Herbert and Gerda Matschen, personal interview, 6 Apr. 1986.
42 SC, 6.01.015, Kaulbach to Research Foundation, Halifax, 28 Feb. 1950.
43 SC, 6.02.014, Kreyser to Valdmanis, 23 May 1950.
44 SC, 6.01.015, Leja to Bachand, 18 Jan. 1950.
45 Ibid., Leja to Valdmanis, 9 Nov. 1949.
46 SC, 'File Gypsum,' undated (identifiable by its contents as the first memorandum for discussion, prepared by the Nova Scotia Research Foundation, 28 Nov. 1949).
47 SC, 6.01.008, Valdmanis to Howland, 17 Dec. 1949.
48 SC, 6.01.015, Draft Agreement: Conference held on Feb. 5, 6, and 7, 1950, between the 'Neue Technik GmbH' ... and Professor Dr Alfred A. Valdmanis, Canada.
49 SC, 6.01.008, Dr Valdmanis to Dr R.D. Howland, 18 Mar. 1950.

50 Ibid., attached personal notes summarizing five points of a discussion by Valdmanis with Col. MacKeen.
51 AOP, Valdmanis to Mateus, 20 Mar. 1950.
52 SC, 6.01.015, Leja to Valdmanis, 15 Apr. 1950.
53 SC, 6.01.008, MacKeen to Leja, 7 June 1950; Leja to MacKeen, 14 June 1950; Howland to Valdmanis, 15 June 1950; Valdmanis to Howland, 13 July 1950.
54 SC, 6.01.015, Leja to Valdmanis, 18 May 1950.
55 CS, 6.02.014, Kreyser to Valdmanis, 23 May 1950.
56 AVP, Valdmanis to Mateus, 24 Aug. 1954; Gundars Valdmanis, letter to the author, 9 Apr. 1986.

Chapter 8: 'Develop or Perish'

1 *Evening Telegram* (St John's), 5 May, 14 June 1953.
2 See G.P. Bassler, '"Develop or Perish": Joseph R. Smallwood and Newfoundland's Quest for German Industry, 1949–1953,' *Acadiensis*, 16(2) (1986), 96–101.
3 Ibid., 101f.
4 SC, Richardson Wood to Stacey May, 9 Feb. 1950, with 'Notes on Trip to Newfoundland February 6–7–8, 1950.'
5 David Alexander, 'Newfoundland's Traditional Economy and Development to 1934,' *Acadiensis*, 5(2) (1976), 76.
6 Bassler, '"Develop or Perish",' 104f.
7 SC, A. Perlin to J.R. Smallwood, 10 Nov. 1949.
8 Despite C.D. Howe's later refusal to accept credit for Valdmanis's appointment in Newfoundland, as believed by Gwyn, 142, there is irrefutable evidence that Howe was asked to and did play a major role in bringing Valdmanis and Smallwood together. See Horwood, *Joey*, 170; Smallwood, *I Chose Canada*, 346; Wayfarer [A. Perlin] in *Daily News*, 19 Aug. 1970. SC, J.R. Smallwood to C.D. Howe, 22 Mar. 1951; J.R. Chalker, personal interview, 2 May 1985.
9 Smallwood, *I Chose Canada*, 346f.
10 James R. Chalker, personal interview, 2 May 1985. Chalker was a Newfoundland cabinet minister who had accompanied Smallwood to Ottawa when he interviewed Valdmanis.
11 Smallwood, *I Chose Canada*, 346f.
12 SC, 6.01.015, Leja to Valdmanis, 18 May 1950; Kreyser to Valdmanis, 23 May 1950.
13 Wayfarer, *Daily News*, 19 Aug. 1970.

14 Smallwood, *I Chose Canada*, 347. CNS, 'Proceedings of the Ninth Sitting of the Second Session of the National Convention, Friday, Feb. 7, 1947,' 3.
15 Irma Valdmanis, personal interview, 4 Apr. 1986.
16 AVP, Valdmanis to Prof. Dr John C. Carancis, 10 Nov. 1963.
17 CNS Archives, C-165, 'A Valdmanis Statement – 1950,' 3.
18 SC, 2.02.002, Minutes of Meeting of Committee of Council, 23 May 1950.
19 Bobbie Robertson, personal interview, 13 June 1985.
20 Wayfarer, *Daily News*, 24 Sept. 1969. Jamieson, 169f.
21 Horwood, *Joey*, 173.
22 Smallwood, *I Chose Canada*, 347.
23 SC, 6.02.011, G.P. Porter to Valdmanis, 6 June 1950.
24 SC, 6.01.001, Alex Berzinsh to Valdmanis, 25 May 1950.
25 SC, Leja to Valdmanis, 18 May 1950, and Kreyser to Valdmanis, 23 May 1950.
26 CNS Archives, C-165, 'A Valdmanis Statement – 1950.'
27 CNS, 'Report on the Proposal in Relation to the Establishment of a Portland Cement Factory in Newfoundland,' July 1950.
28 SC, 6.02.014, Leja to Valdmanis, 18 May 1950; Kreyser to Valdmanis, 8 July 1950.
29 CNS Archives, C-165, 'A Valdmanis Statement: My Education on Newfoundland Matters,' 8.
30 SC, 6.01.005, Valdmanis to Smallwood, 12 Dec. 1950, Note no. 1.
31 SC, file 20/54/D7, Valdmanis to Deputy Minister of Economic Development N. Short, 31 Oct. 1950.
32 SC, 3.08.210. See text of agreements and correspondence in 'Cement and General Development Corporation' file. The 1 November 1950 Memorandum of Agreement provided for the formation of a company issuing $4 million worth of bonds – $3 million of these to the Newfoundland government as payment for the cement plant – to be redeemed by the sale of shares of the company's stock. A successful public stock issue, however, was to be delayed until after the cement plant began operating, because of 'certain machinations' of the Canadian cement monopoly.
33 SC, 6.01.005, Valdmanis to Smallwood, 12 Dec. 1950.
34 SC, 6.01.021, Valdmanis to Paul G. Kronacker, 19 Feb. 1951. On the options of selling the cement mill by May 1951, see Valdmanis's four-page memorandum to the cabinet, in SC, file 'North Star Cement Plant,' Valdmanis to Smallwood, 10 May 1951.
35 SC, file 'North Star Cement Ltd. – minutes of meetings,' Valdmanis to Smallwood, 16 Aug. 1951.
36 SC, 2.01.004, Executive Council, draft minutes of meeting of 8 Aug. 1952; *Daily News*, 11 Aug. 1952; *Evening Telegram*, 12 Aug. 1952.

37 NHA, *Proceedings*, 29 Mar. 1955, 174. See also CNS Archives, C-165, 'A Valdmanis Statement: Transfer of the Cement Hill to Its Present Site,' 29.
38 SC, 6.01.015, Howland to Valdmanis, 26 June 1950. SC, 3.10.005, G.D. Mallory to Valdmanis, 21 June 1950.
39 CNS, 'Report on the Establishment of a Gypsum Industry in Newfoundland,' Aug. 1950.
40 SC, 3.08.282, 'Notes to Ches and Premier,' (undated).
41 CNS, Coverdale and Colpitts, 'Preliminary Report on North Star Cement Company, Limited, Atlantic Gypsum Limited, Newfoundland Hardwoods Limited,' 20 Mar. 1952, 21.
42 Its terms make for an interesting comparison: The government agreed to finance the building of the plant, supplied working capital, and leased the enterprise to Chester Dawe as operator for 15 years at an annual rent equal to the depreciation on the plant, plus 3.5 per cent per annum on the working capital advanced and half the annual net profits. In March 1952 the Coverdale and Colpitts consulting engineering firm preparing a survey of the three government-owned industries was not permitted to examine the 'unusual agreement' with Chester Dawe nor obtain data for reliable estimates as to the total capital requirements or earning expectancies of this project. See ibid., 27, 35.
43 AVP, Valdmanis to Valdis Mateus, 9 Aug. 1950.
44 SC, 3.08.210, Valdmanis to T. Reed Vreeland, 22 June 1950, with 'Memorandum of Discussions'; T.W. Hill to Valdmanis, 25 July 1950; Valdmanis to Michael Lewin, 16 Aug. 1950.
45 SC, ibid., Valdmanis to Lewin, 16 Aug. 1950.
46 SC, file '20/45/D7,' Valdmanis to N. Short, 9 Sept. and 31 Oct. 1950.
47 SC, ibid., T.W. Hill to Smallwood, 27 Sept. 1950; Hill to Baisley Sheridan, 18 Dec. 1950.
48 CNS Archives, C-165, 'A Valdmanis Statement – NALCO,' 11; SC, 3.20.061, Harriman Ripley & Co., 'Draft Preliminary Memorandum Jan. 20, 1951, Re: Newfoundland and Labrador Corporation, Limited.'
49 James R. Chalker, personal interview, 2 May 1985.
50 *Hersfelder Zeitung*, 2 Dec. 1950.
51 *Diplomatisches Bulletin* (Cologne), 2 Oct. 1950, 130.
52 *Maclean's*, 1 July 1952.
53 *Frankfurter Allgemeine*, 18 Oct. 1950.
54 *Evening Telegram*, 26 Oct. 1950.
55 SC, 3.14.025, Valdmanis to Siegheim, 12 Dec. 1950.
56 Ibid., Valdmanis to Mr Premier, undated note attached to Valdmanis's letter to Siegheim.
57 SC, 3.20.100, Hassenbach and Aureden to Valdmanis, 19 Oct. 1950.

58 Ibid., Max Laufer to Valdmanis, 8 Dec. 1950. One of Valdmanis's contacts there happened to be an old school friend writing him in Latvian. See SC, 3.0.043, S. Malamet to Valdmanis, 13 Dec. 1950.

59 Ibid., Siegheim to Valdmanis, 20 Dec. 1950.

60 SC, 3.14.025-26, Pulpwood, Siegheim-Valdmanis, 1951–52. *Neue Züricher Zeitung*, 18 Sept. 1951.

61 NHA, *Proceedings*, 14 June 1951, 1220.

62 Drover went on visualizing Santa 'with his massive white beard handing out a thousand dollars and now I find we won't even get a million cents.' NHA, *Proceedings*, 24 Oct. 1951, 11.

63 SC, 6.01.005, Valdmanis to My dear Mr Premier, 12 Dec. 1950.

64 Ibid., Note no. 1.

65 Horwood, *Joey*, 171; Gwyn, 170f; 'Political Notebook,' *Evening Telegram*, 31 Dec. 1954.

66 SC, file 'Valdmanis personal,' Valdmanis to Smallwood, 12 Dec. 1950, Note no. 4.

67 SC, 6.01.005, Smallwood to Valdmanis, undated.

68 NHA, *Proceedings*, 12 Mar., and 3 and 16 May 1951.

69 A. Skrodelis, 'A Meeting with Premier E.R. Smallwood,' *Latvija*, 11 Mar. 1953.

70 Smallwood, *I Chose Canada*, 347.

71 CNS Archives, C-165, 'A Valdmanis Statement – 150,' 5; 'A Valdmanis Statement: My Education on Newfoundland Matters,' p. 3.

72 Ibid., 3f.

73 Alfred A. Valdmanis, 'Give the Island a Chance!' *Atlantic Guardian*, Apr. 1951, 11–17.

74 Rupert Jackson, 'Man of the Month: Industry Builder,' *Atlantic Guardian*, Apr. 1951, 17–21.

75 SC, Valdmanis to Nelson O. Man, 24 Jan. 1951.

76 J.R. Smallwood, personal interview, 24 Nov. 1983.

77 *Der Bund*, 2 May 1952.

78 SC, file 'General Finance,' 'To Whom It May Concern,' 21 Feb. 1951.

79 SC, file 'New Industries,' Valdmanis to Smallwood, 11 May 1951.

80 SC, 6.01.021, Graudins to M. Green, 21 Mar. 1952.

81 J.R. Smallwood, *Newfoundland is on the March* (St John's, 1952), 13.

82 SC, 6.01.006, Werner Hinneberg to Valdmanis, 13 Mar. 1951.

83 SC, 3.31.003, documents relating to Bleiindustrie, Oct. 1950 to Nov. 1952.

84 SC, 3.31.005, Valdmanis to Doctor and Walter J. Hinneberg, 'Nordmeer' Reederei GmbH, Hamburg, 24 Oct. 1950; W.J. Hinneberg to Valdmanis, 9 Nov. 1950. SC, 3.08.318, Dr Hinneberg to D.L. Graudins, 5 Jan. 1951;

Dr Hinneberg to Province of Newfoundland, 8 Jan. 1951. SC, 3.31.002, W.J. Hinneberg to Valdmanis, 10 Jan. 1951.

85 SC, 3.08.318, Dr Hinneberg to Province of Newfoundland, Department of Economic Development, 8 Jan. 1951.

86 SC, 3.31.005, typescripts titled 'Fischmehl,' 'Bekleidungsfabrik,' 'Farbenfabrik,' etc., Feb. 1951.

87 SC, 3.08.318, Dr W. Hinneberg to Valdmanis, 2 Mar. 1951. SC, 3.31.005, Valdmanis to Dr W. Hinneberg, 3 Mar. 1952.

88 SC, 3.31.005, Hinneberg to Valdmanis, 30 Mar. and 11 Apr. 1951, and to Graudins, 10 Apr. 1951. SC, 3.08.318, Hinneberg to Graudins, 31 Mar. 1951. SC, 6.01.006, Hinneberg to Valdmanis, 13 Mar. 1951.

89 SC, 3.08.318, Valdmanis to Hinneberg, 1 May 1951.

90 SC, 3.08.068, Atlantic Films and Electronics, 1951–54.

91 SC, 3.31.005, Hinneberg to Valdmanis, 5 and 15 June 1951.

92 SC, 2.19.003, Valdmanis to Smallwood, 31 May 1951.

93 SC, 2.02.003, cabinet minutes, 23 June and 5, 7, and 10 July 1951.

94 SC, 3.08.075, Valdmanis to Dr Ernst Leitz and Günther Leitz, 1 Nov. 1951; G. Leitz to Valdmanis, 9 Nov. 1951.

95 SC, 6.01.005, Valdmanis to My dear Mr Premier, 16 May 1951.

96 BA, B 102, Bd. 6081 Heft 2, Dr Kaulbach to Herr Lehmann, 17 Oct. 1951. SC, 6.01.021, Valdmanis to Kreyser, 2 Aug. 1951.

97 *Daily News* and *Evening Telegram*, 13 Oct. 1951; *Western Star* (Corner Brook), 25 Oct. 1951.

98 SC, 3.08.087, file 'Rieker & Co.'

99 SC, 2.02.003, cabinet minutes, 12 Oct. 1951.

100 SC, 6.02.011, Kreyser to Valdmanis, 25 Dec. 1951.

101 SC, 6.01.022, Smallwood to E. Zippmann, 10 Dec. 1951.

102 Ludwig Erhard, *Germany's Comeback in the World Market* (London, 1954), 180ff. The original German edition was published in 1953.

103 SC, 3.14.019, undated memorandum (Oct. 1951) by Valdmanis, 'Labrador Timber Development.'

104 SC, 6.02.011, unsigned draft letter (by Braun-Wogau) to Siegheim, 28 Jan. 1951; Kreyser to Valdmanis, 4 Feb. 1952.

105 SC, 6.01.022, Valdmanis to Siegheim, 13 Oct. 1951.

106 See, e.g., SC, 3.08.318 and 3.31.005, Hinneberg to Valdmanis, 1 Feb. 1952; Brinkmann and Mergell to Hinneberg, 22 Mar. 1951; Valdmanis to Hinneberg, 1 May 1951; also files 'A. Werner: Leather, Hides, Skins,' K. Thomas to A. Werner, 4 July 1951; and 'Knitting Mill,' Hans Bosse to Department of Economic Development, 21 Dec. 1951.

107 See, e.g., SC, 3.31.005, Hinneberg to Graudins, 10 Apr. 1952.

108 SC, 3.31.005, Hinneberg to Valdmanis, 11 Apr. 1951. SC, file 'Blocked DM,' K. Hirschfeld, 'Neufundländisch/schweizer/deutsche Zusammenarbeit zwischen der Regierung von Neufundland and ITC zur Verwendung blockierter DM Guthaben zur Errichtung von Industrie-Unternehmungen in Neufundland,' 6 Apr. 1951.

109 CNS Archives, C-165, Valdmanis, 'Fishing in Troubled Waters,' 9.

110 Ibid., 10.

111 AA, 414/302-02/40, Reifferscheidt and Dankwort to AA, 24 Sept. and 2 Oct. 1953, 16 Mar. and 27 Apr. 1954; J.H. Lerch to Staatssekretär Hallstein, 11 Mar. 1954.

112 SC, 2.02.003, cabinet minutes, 8 Dec. 1951.

113 SC, 6.01.021, Valdmanis to Hinneberg, 7 July 1951, and to Smallwood, 23 Nov. 1951. SC, 3.31.005, Hinneberg to Valdmanis, 28 July and 13 Aug. 1951; Hinneberg, 'Auskunft über Dr Lothar Sennewald, Augenarzt,' 23 July 1951. SC, 3.08.07, Valdmanis to Smallwood, 6 July 1951, and Valdmanis memorandum 'A New Industry for Newfoundland,' 21 June 1951.

114 SC, 3.08.074, Atlantic Optical Company Ltd 1951–54, and 3.08.07, Sennewald Scientific Equipment, 1951–52.

115 SC, 6.01.022, Valdmanis to Smallwood, 23 Nov. 1951.

116 NHA, *Proceedings*, 15 Apr. 1952.

117 According to Gordon F. Pushie (personal interviews of 18 Nov. 1983, 6 May 1985, and 16 Sept. 1991), Sennewald was arrested in 1954 to prevent his departure from the country. He was compelled to work in a St John's hospital until he had repaid his loan to the government. For confirmation, see BSA, report by H. Herz, 'Reise nach Neufundland vom 5. bis 21. April 1954,' 22 Apr. 1954.

118SC, file 'Consolidated Files Re: Finance,' Valdmanis to Smallwood, 8 Dec. 1951.

119 SC, 6.01.005, Valdmanis to G.D. Mallory, 4 and 14 Nov. 1951. SC, 6.01.006, Valdmanis memorandum, 10 Mar. 1952.

120 See SC, 3.10.013-7, St Laurent to Smallwood, 8 Dec. 1951.

121 SC, 6.02.011, Valdmanis to Kreyser, 30 June 1952.

122 SC, 3.31.005, Hinneberg to Valdmanis, 12 Jan. 1952; Valdmanis to Hinneberg, 4 Feb. 1952.

123 Philip Smith, *The Story of Churchill Falls* (Toronto, 1975), 15ff. Smallwood, *I Chose Canada*, 444–52.

124 *Latvija*, 8 Nov. 1951.

125 Gregory Power, personal interview, 27 Feb. 1984.

126 SC, 3.08.176-9, Superior Rubber Company 1951–71. SC, C-165, 'A Valdmanis Statement on Superior Rubber Company.' BSA, Dr Herz, 'Reise nach Neufundland vom 5. bis 21. April 1954.' BA, B 102, vol. 6846, Hefte 2 and 3.

127 CNS Archives, C-165, 'A Valdmanis Statement: Nalco.'
128 SC, 6.01.005, Valdmanis to Smallwood, 5 Feb. 1953.
129 SC, 6.02.011, Valdmanis to Kreyser, 6 Mar. 1953.
130 Ibid., Kreyser to Valdmanis, 7 and 25 Feb., and 7 Mar. 1953; Valdmanis to Kreyser, 16 Feb. and 6 Mar. 1953.

Chapter 9: 'The Past, Instead of Helping to Rebuild, Denies Itself'

1 See G.P. Bassler, *Sanctuary Denied: Refugees from the Third Reich and Newfoundland Immigration Policy, 1906–1949* (St John's, 1992), 202.
2 Memorial University of Newfoundland Archives (St John's), Board of Governors, box 1, files of Vincent P. Burke, Chairman, subfile, Memorial University College. I am grateful to Dr Melvin Baker for directing me to this information.
3 SC, 6.01.001, A. Berzinsh to Valdmanis, 25 May, 5 and 14 July, and 16 Sept. 1950; Valdmanis to Berzinsh, 28 Nov. 1950, 20 Mar. 1952.
4 List of German, Baltic German, and Latvian mill operators, prepared by Herbert Matschen for G.P. Bassler, 25 May 1986. SC, file 'Cement Plant,' Visas for German erectors, etc., VI, 1951.
5 SC, 6.01.001, Olga Leikucs to E. Ancoca un I. Endziņa kundzēm, 31 Oct. 1952. *Star* (Windsor, Ontario), 9 Nov. 1950.
6 SC, file 20/45/D7, Valdmanis to N. Short, 9 Sept. 1950.
7 Sigurds Mikelsons, personal interview, 3 June 1985. In their office correspondence, O.L. until her resignation at the end of August 1953 always carefully addressed him as 'Mr Valdmanis' and he addressed O.L. as 'Miss Leikucs.' Only once, on 13 May 1952, he scribbled on the margin of a file: 'Would my little girl take care of this by saying that Valdmanis is not in Newfoundland and will be absent for a long time?' SC, 6.01.001, letter by V. Muskrats to Valdmanis.
8 Dr V. Mikelsons, personal interview, 3 June 1985.
9 SC, file 'Appointments and Salaries,' Graudins to Valdmanis, 5 July 1950; Valdmanis to Smallwood, 24 Aug. 1950 and to Graudins, 29 Sept. 1950; Valdmanis to W.M. Marshall, 20 Dec. 1951; Olga Leikucs to Valdmanis, 6 July 1950; Cabinet minutes of 7 July 1950.
10 SC, 6.01.021, Graudins to Ray Manning and Dave Butler, 26 July 1951. SC, file 'German Technicians,' vitae of 12 Latvian specialists recommended for Newfoundland government positions. Those who did not arrive were: Arnolds Spūrmanis, Roberts Lapsiņš, Ilgvars Krastiņš, Georgs Odiņš, Oskars Krause, and Voldemārs Rameika.
11 SC, 6.01.001, certificate for Mrs Anna Dzinejs de Raimonds, signed by A.A. Valdmanis and E.J. Jacobsons, 4 Mar. 1952.

12 Personal interviews: Alberts Jekste, 28 Mar. and 8 June 1985; Arnis Lucis, 8 Feb. 1985; Zenta and Ralph Balodis, 2 Dec. 1983.
13 SC, 6.01.001, Hinneberg to Valdmanis, 5 June 1951; Valdmanis to Hinneberg, 18 June 1951.
14 SC, file 'Miscellaneous Correspondence,' V. Janums, Chairman, Latvian Central Committee to Whom It May Concern, 8 Oct. 1951; cable Smallwood to Hon. W.E. Harris, 23 Oct. 1951.
15 SC, file 'Re: Film Documentary,' Smallwood to Jekste, 23 Oct. 1951.
16 SC, file 'Miscellaneous Letters,' Jekste to Smallwood, 31 Oct. 1951.
17 SC, 'The Latvian Role in Newfoundland's Economic Development,' an interview with J.R. Smallwood for the Latvian paper *Latvija Amērikā*, 5 Nov. 1952. 'Woman Dentist of Europe Makes New Home in Newfoundland,' *Evening Telegram*, 2 Nov. 1951. 'European Dentist Does Not Qualify,' *Evening Telegram*, 30 May 1953.
18 SC, 6.01.001, Ernests Snikeris to Valdmanis, 7 Mar. 1952, and Aleksandrs Osītis to Valdmanis, 16 Sept. 1951.
19 Ellen Ploetner, Erika Treibergs, and Ingrid Tode, personal interviews, 22 July and 12 Aug. 1985, and 4 June 1986.
20 Herbert and Gerda Matschen, personal interview, 6 Apr. 1986, and H. Matschen, 'Beziehungen der Neueinwanderer untereinander, sowie gegenüber den Neufundländern in Corner Brook,' manuscript, 1986.
21 Georg and Hanna Dlugosch, personal interview, 28 Mar. 1984.
22 SC, 6.01.006, A.F. Conrad to Valdmanis, 23 June 1952. G.P. Bassler, 'Lutheran Congregation,' *Encyclopedia of Newfoundland and Labrador*, vol. 3 (St John's, 1991), 394f.
23 M.F. Kuester, *Where Birch Trees Grow ...: A History of Baltic German Immigration to Canada after World War II* (Edmonton, 1979), 78–81. Canadian Baltic Immigrant Aid Society Inc., *20 Jahre Baltischer Hilfsverein in Kanada* (Montreal, 1968), 24f.
24 For some striking comments on the passion Latvians have brought to the cause of national liberation and their difficulty to assimilate in a host society see, e.g., Neil Bissoondath, *Selling Illusions: The Cult of Multiculturalism in Canada* (Toronto, 1994), 126ff.
25 Arnis Lucis, personal interviews, 20 Feb. 1984 and 12 June 1985.
26 Arnis Lucis, personal interview, 24 July 1985.
27 Arnis and Sofija Lucis, personal interview, 20 Feb. 1984.
28 NHA, *Proceedings*, 30 Mar. 1951.
29 Ibid., 7, 15, and 27 Mar. 1951.
30 SC, 6.01.001, E. Pērkons to Valdmanis, 10 Nov. 1950.

31 SC, 'The Latvian Role in Newfoundland's Economic Development,' an interview with J.R. Smallwood for the Latvian paper *Latvija Amērikā*, 5 Nov. 1952.
32 See the article 'Evaluation of Dr Valdmanis in the Press of New Zealand,' *Latvija*, 12 Nov. 1952.
33 SC, 6.01.018, E.B. Warriner to Valdmanis, 21 Aug. 1950.
34 *Latvija*, 3 Nov. and 31 Dec. 1952.
35 *Latvija*, 11 Mar. 1953.
36 SC, 6.01.001, Aleksandrs Ositis to Valdmanis, 27 Oct. 1950; ed. Strazdins to Valdmanis, undated.
37 SC, 6.01.001, Lote Švābe to Valdmanis, 7 Sept. [1950?]; Olga Leikucs to E. Strazdins, 10 Oct. 1950; Vilis Lapinieks to Valdmanis, 10 Nov. and 5 Dec. 1950; E. Kerve to Valdmanis, 7 Sept. 1951.
38 Ibid., M. Puhris to Valdmanis, 21 July and 9 Sept. 1950; Valdmanis to Manu mīļo Rittmeister, 22 Aug., to Dr M. Puhris, 24 Oct. 1950, and to Mikelis Puhris, 26 Oct. 1950; Richard Rösner to Valdmanis, 8 Dec. 1950; Olga Leikucs to W. Gautier, 20 Feb. 1951.
39 Ibid., L.A. Darzins to Valdmanis, 23 Feb. and undated 1951; O. Leikucs to Darzins, 24 Apr. 1951.
40 Ibid., A. Bankins to Valdmanis, 8 Oct. 1952.
41 Ibid., Janis Brezinskis to Valdmanis, 17 July 1952.
42 Ibid., unidentified to Valdmanis, 9 Sept. 1952.
43 Ibid., J. Dombrovskis to Valdmanis, 20 Nov. 1951; A.L. Graudins to J. Dombrovskis, 3 Dec. 1951.
44 Ibid., M. Valters to Valdmanis, 21 July 1951; Valdmanis to Valters, 11 and 26 Aug. 1951.
45 Ibid., Teodors Reiters to Valdmanis, 21 June 1951.
46 Ibid., J. Inveiss to Mr General Director, 2 Oct. 1951.
47 Ibid., Ruta Viskers to Valdmanis, 28 Feb. 1952.
48 Ibid., Pēteris Ķikauka to Valdmanis, 4 Aug. and 25 Oct. 1951; Leikucs to Ķikauka, 31 Aug. 1951.
49 Ibid., W. Neimanis to Valdmanis, 13 Jan. 1952.
50 Ibid., Muskats to Valdmanis, 13 and 28 May 1952; Leikucs to Muskats, 22 May 1952.
51 Ibid., Ž. Leimanis to Valdmanis, 1 Sept. 1252.
52 Ibid., V. Vuškalns to Valdmanis, 15 July 1952; P. Avotiņš to Valdmanis, 5 Nov. 1952.
53 Ibid., Valdmanis to V. Dale, 22 June 1950.
54 Ibid., Valdmanis to Jānis Celms, 29 Jan. 1951.

55 Ibid., Valdmanis to Whom It May Concern, 5 Dec. 1952.
56 Ibid., Edgars Ozols to Valdmanis, 23 Sept. 1951; Pēteris Ozols to Valdmanis, 28 Aug. and 15 Sept. 1950; Valdmanis to P. Ozols, 6 Sept. 1950, and E. Ozols, 10 Oct. 1951; A. Stīpnieks to Valdmanis, 25 July and 2 Oct. 1951; Valdmanis to Whom It May Concern, 29 Sept. 1951; Leikucs to A. Stīpnieks, 11 Oct. 1951.
57 Ibid., K. Treilons to Valdmanis, 13 Feb. 1952, and B. Berziņš to Valdmanis, 16 Feb. 1952; Leikucs to Berziņš, 29 Feb. 1952.
58 Ibid., E. Pērkons to Valdmanis, 21 July 1950; Leikucs to E. Pērkons, 22 Nov. 1950.
59 Ibid., N. Zvirbulis to Valdmanis, 10 June 1952, to Leikucs, 15 Aug. 1952, to A. Āboliņš, July 1952, and to J. Arajs, 3 Sept. and 1 Oct. 1952; A. Āboliņš to J. Arajs, 3 Sept. 1952; A. Arajs to N. Zvirbulis, 17 Oct. 1952.
60 Ibid., M. Seja to Valdmanis, 8 June 1951; Leikucs to M. Seja, 22 June 1951.
61 Ibid., Ansis Jansons to Valdmanis, 5 Dec. 1951; Valdmanis to Tonija Krūka, 8 Dec. 1951; Krūka to Valdmanis, 12 Dec. 1951; I. Viksna to Valdmanis, 14 Dec. 1951.
62 Ibid., E.G. Grīnbergs to Mr Minister, 16 Feb. 1952; Leikucs to Grīnbergs, 19 Feb. 1952.
63 Ibid., J. Siliņš to Valdmanis, 22 Sept. 1952 and 28 Mar. 1953.
64 Ibid., Leikucs to J. Siliņš, 11 Mar. 1953; Siliņš to 'the Guard,' 4 Apr. 1953.
65 Ibid., Augusts Lūkiņš to Valdmanis, 22 Mar. 1953; Jānis Roziņš to Valdmanis, 16 June 1953; F. Richters to Valdmanis, undated; A. Immers to Valdmanis, 22 Apr. 1953; Leikucs to Lūkiņš, 9 Apr. and 19 May 1953, to Roziņš, 25 June 1953, to Richter, 30 June 1953; to Immers, 25 Apr. 1953.
66 Ibid., Ritums to Valdmanis, 22 Aug. 1950; Leikucs to Ritums, 7 Oct. 1950.
67 Ibid., J. Pusbarņieks to Valdmanis, 13 Sept. 1952.
68 SC, 6.01.004, A. Pētersons to Valdmanis, 6 July 1952.
69 SC, 6.01.001, H. Luters to Valdmanis, 15 Nov. 1952; Leikucs to H. Luters, 10 Jan. 1953.
70 Ibid., J. Radziņš to Valdmanis, 24 Jan. 1952.
71 SC, 6.1.004, A. Mednis to Valdmanis, 27 Dec. 1951; Valdmanis to A. Mednis, 7 Feb. 1952.
72 Ibid., Albiņš Sietiņsons to Valdmanis, 21 Aug. 1951, 5 Sept. 1952, and 8 Mar. 1953.
73 AVP, J. Blusanovičs to Valdmanis, undated.
74 *Sunday Herald* (St John's), 9 Oct. 1951.
75 *Sunday Herald*, 21 Oct. 1951; *Evening Telegram*, 25 Oct. 1951.
76 NHA, *Proceedings*, 24 Oct. 1951. *Evening Telegram*, 27 Oct. 1951. According to a personal interview with Mr S. Mikelsons (brother-in-law of Irma

Valdmanis) of 3 June 1985 in Montreal, Lurje had left Latvia before 1940 and transferred all his capital to New York.

77 *Evening Telegram*, 30 Oct. 1951.

78 NAC, MG 32 B 34, vol. 37, series I-2-502.

79 Ibid.

80 AVP, A. Slavitt to Valdmanis, 8 Nov. 1951.

81 Ibid.

82 Canada, House of Commons, *Debates*, 31 Oct. 1951, 566, and 7 Nov. 1951, 792f.

83 Leon von Bruemmer, as reprinted in *Evening Telegram*, 18 Dec. 1951.

84 SC, 3.24.001-10, Ron Gostick to Smallwood, 1 Nov. 1951.

85 SC, 6.02.011, George C. McNamara to Valdmanis, 12 Dec. 1951.

86 SC, 6.01.018, V. Antiņš to Valdmanis, and to Smallwood, 19 Dec. 1951; John Purens to Smallwood, 19 Dec. 1951; Dr Konstantins Jakobsons to Smallwood, 29 Jan. 1952; V. Kaliņš to Valdmanis, 19 Nov. 1951; Z. Zentiņš to Valdmanis, 8 Dec. 1951.

87 AAS, Brūno Kalniņš Archive, no. 409; Emīls Ogriņš to Cooperative Commonwealth Federation, Ottawa, 4 June 1952.

88 AVP, Valdmanis to Saul Hayes, 2 Nov., 18 Dec. 1951; S. Hayes to Valdmanis, 30 Oct., 16 Nov. 1951, 21 Jan. 1952; Silvia Welik to Valdmanis, 8 Nov. 1951; Claude Richardson to S. Hayes, 18 Dec. 1951.

89 SC, 6.02.011, J. Levenson to Valdmanis, 25 June and 11 Aug. 1952; Levenson to J. Arajs, 22 Oct. 1952; Valdmanis to Levenson, 4 July 1952.

90 SC, 6.01.001, Valdmanis to P. Kikauka, 29 Oct. 1951.

91 SC, 6.02.011, Kreyser to Valdmanis, 13 Dec. 1951; Valdmanis to Kreyser, 19 Dec. 1951.

92 SC, 6.01.011, Valdmanis to Burmeister, 22 June 1953, to H. Seehusen, 6 May 1953, to Kreyser, 11 Dec. 1950.

93 BSA, F. Kreyser to Dr Graf Posadowski, 14 Dec. 1950.

94 SC, 6.02.011, Max Braun-Wogau to Milo Alf, 20 Dec. 1951.

95 Ibid.

96 SC, 6.02.011, Braun-Wogau to Valdmanis, 11 Feb. 1952.

97 Ibid.

98 SC, 6.02.011, Valdmanis to Braun-Wogau, 27 Jan. 1952, and to Kreyser, 8 Feb. 1952; Kreyser to Valdmanis, 31 Jan. 1952.

99 SC, 6.02.011, Kreyser to Valdmanis, 4 Feb. 1952.

100 SC, box 129, file 'Official Confidential Correspondence and Semi-Official Personal Correspondence, 1952.'

101 *Sunday Herald*, 14 Oct. 1951.

102 'Latviešu loma Nūfaundlendas parveidošana [The Latvian Role in Newfoundland's Development],' *Latvija*, 5 Nov. 1952.

103 SC, 6.02.011, Valdmanis to Leon von Bruemmer, 6 May 1953.

Chapter 10: 'Only One Could Topple Him from His Height – Himself'

1 Ralph Matthews, *The Creation of Regional Dependency* (Toronto, 1983), 189.

2 'Valdmanis Transfers from Department of Economic Development to Nalco,' *Daily News*, 18 Feb. 1953; 'Valdmanis Becomes Chairman of NALCO and Quits Position of Director Economic Development,' *Evening Telegram*, 18 Feb. 1953.

3 SC, 3.31.003, Valdmanis to Georg E.R. Plange, 24 Feb. 1953.

4 SC, file 'NALCO #3,' NALCO Personnel, 31 Dec. 1953.

5 Gundars Valdmanis, personal interview, 5 Apr. 1986.

6 See, e.g., Arthur Blakely in the Montreal *Gazette*, 27 Apr. 1954, and A. Reifferscheidt to AA, Bonn, 27 Apr. 1954, in AA, vol. 414/331-01/40.

7 SC, box 134, file 'Official Secret – Re: Department of Economic Development.' A covering note by Valdmanis dated 3 Nov. 1953 and attached to the proofs instructed Rupert Jackson to send in the entry for publication without any corrections.

8 *Daily News*, 20 Aug. 1970; H. Montgomery Hyde, *The Quiet Canadian: The Secret Service Story of Sir William Stephenson* (London, 1962).

9 SC, 6.01.005, Valdmanis to My dear Mr Premier, 16 May 1951, and Valdmanis to Smallwood, 18 May 1951.

10 L.J. Jackman in the Montreal *Gazette*, 26 Nov. 1952.

11 SC, 6.02.011, Valdmanis to Kreyser, 30 June 1952.

12 SC, C-165, 'Valdmanis Statement Re Superior Rubber Company,' 10f.

13 SC, file 'NALCO #4,' C. Wallis to Smallwood, 2 Apr. 1954.

14 SC, 6.02.011, Valdmanis to Kreyser, 6 Mar. 1953.

15 SC, file 'NALCO #3,' A.A. Valdmanis, 'Confidential comments on Mackintosh's letter to the President of NALCO dated Mar. 13, 1953,' 15 May 1953.

16 SC, 6.01.023, Valdmanis to M. Lewin, 18 June 1953.

17 SC, 6.01.023, Valdmanis to Ewald Zippmann, 21 Sept. 1953.

18 SC, file 'NALCO #3,' NALCO Personnel, 31 Dec. 1953. SC, 6.02.011, Valdmanis to Kreyser, 21 Sept. 1953; minutes of board of directors meeting 3 Sept. 1953.

19 BA, B 102, Bd. 6847, Heft 1, Reifferscheidt to AA, Bonn, 13 Aug. 1953.

20 SC, 6.02.011, Valdmanis to Leon von Bruemmer, 5 May 1953.

21 NHA, *Proceedings*, 22 Mar. 1955.

22 SC, file 'NALCO #3,' Wallis to Valdmanis, 13 Jan. 1954.

23 Ibid., Wallis to Valdmanis, 14 Jan. 1954.

24 CNS Archives, C-165, 'A Valdmanis Statement: NALCO.'
25 Ibid.; SC, file 'NALCO #3,' V.P. Geffine to Smallwood, 19 Mar. 1954; Smallwood to Doyle, 10 Feb. 1954; Doyle to Smallwood, 27 Jan. 1954.
26 Gwyn, 157.
27 SC, 3.31.005, Valdmanis to R. Hanhart, 30 Nov. 1953, 8 and 29 Jan. 1954. SC, file 'NALCO #3,' Valdmanis to Smallwood, 26 Feb. 1954; cables Valdmanis to Smallwood, 29 and 30 Dec. 1953.
28 Arnis Lucis, personal interview, 27 Nov. 1985.
29 Jamieson, 200.
30 BA, B 102, Bd. 6848, Heft 1, Dr Schaller to Bundesministerium für Wirtschaft, 7 May 1954.
31 Jamieson, 199f.
32 SC, 3.31.005, Valdmanis to R. Hanhart, 29 Jan. 1954.
33 NHA, *Proceedings*, 29 Mar. and 23 Sept. 1955, 1386.
34 Personal interviews, Gundars Valdmanis, 21 Feb. and 5 Apr., 1986.
35 Gregory Power, personal interview, 27 Feb. 1984.
36 See SC, file 'Valdmanis Personal,' Valdmanis to Department of Finance, 10 Feb. 1954; Valdmanis to Smallwood, 10 Feb. 1954.
37 BSA, Reisebericht von Dr Herz, 22 Apr. 1954.
38 'To soften the shock to the public,' according to Gwyn, 160.
39 *Daily News*, 11 Feb. 1954; SC, file 'Valdmanis Personal,' Valdmanis to Smallwood, 10 Feb. 1954.
40 SC, file 'NALCO #3,' Valdmanis to Smallwood, 26 Feb. 1954.
41 NHA, *Proceedings*, 29 Mar. 1955. AA, 444/303-02/40, Reifferscheidt to AA, 24 Sept. 1953. CNS Archives, C-165, 'A Valdmanis Statement: The Rubber Plant Affidavit'; BSA, Dr Herz, 'Reise nach Neufundland vom 5. bis 21. April 1954,' 2f.
42 SC, file 'NALCO #3,' Valdmanis to Smallwood, 26 Feb. 1954.
43 BA, B 102, Bd. 6848, Heft 1, Adolph Reifferscheidt to AA, Bonn, 25 Feb. 1954.
44 SC, 6.01.006, Irma and Alfred Valdmanis to Smallwood, 5 Mar. 1954.
45 *Evening Telegram*, 12 Feb. 1954.
46 SC, file 'NALCO #3,' news release re: Valdmanis resignation, undated.
47 *Evening Telegram*, 12 and 13 Feb. 1954.
48 *Daily News*, 11 Feb. 1954.
49 *Daily News*, 21 Feb. 1953.
50 *Sunday Herald*, 28 June 1953.
51 'Doctor Valdmanis Had Distinguished Career in His Native Latvia,' *Daily News*, 25 May 1950.
52 Rupert Jackson, 'Newfoundland Poised for the Biggest Drive Yet,' *Financial Post*, 6 June 1953.

53 Reprinted in the *Evening Telegram*, 12 Aug. 1953.
54 *Evening Telegram*, 31 Mar. and 6 Apr. 1954.
55 *Evening Telegram*, 13 Mar. and 7 Apr. 1954.

Chapter 11: 'Something Had Happened and a Culprit Had to Be Found'

1 *Treji Vārti*, 95 (1982), 6.
2 *Evening Telegram*, 24 Apr. 1954.
3 NHA, *Proceedings*, 29 Mar. 1955, night session.
4 BSA, Bericht über das Ergebnis der Reise von Herrn Römer und Dr Herz nach Neufundland im März 1953.
5 CNS, SC, file 'Machine Plant Bay Roberts,' Smallwood to Leja, 28 Jan. 1954; file 'Eastern Machinery and Equipment Company Ltd,' Leja to Smallwood, 15 Feb. 1954; NHA, *Proceedings*, 29 Mar. 1955.
6 HHA, Herz to Smallwood, 8 Apr. 1954; Joseph R. Smallwood, personal interview, 24 Nov. 1983.
7 BSA, Herz, report 'Reise nach Neufundland vom 5. bis 21. April 1954,' 22 Apr. 1954.
8 *Daily News*, 26 Apr. 1954.
9 D.W.K. Dawe refused the request. Louise Dawe, personal interview, 4 June 1992.
10 *Evening Telegram*, 28 and 29 Apr. 1954; *Daily News*, 29 Apr. 1954.
11 *Evening Telegram*, 26 and 27 Apr. and 1 May 1954.
12 *Evening Telegram*, 26 Apr.; 1, 3, 5, and 7 May 1954; *Daily News*, 30 Apr. 1954.
13 *Evening Telegram*, 15 and 16 May 1954.
14 *Daily News*, 17 and 18 May 1954.
15 CNS Archives, C-165, A Valdmanis Statement – The Rubber Plant Affidavit, [1954].
16 *Evening Telegram*, 15 June 1954.
17 *Daily News* and *Evening Telegram*, 17 and 18 May 1954.
18 *Evening Telegram*, 22 May 1954.
19 *Daily News*, 19 May 1954.
20 *Daily News*, 3 Aug. 1954; *Evening Telegram*, 9 Aug. 1954.
21 *Evening Telegram*, 15 and 16 Sept. 1954.
22 *Evening Telegram*, 21 Sept. 1954.
23 *Evening Telegram*, 15 and 17 Sept. 1954; *Montreal Star*, 17 Sept. 1954; Montreal *Gazette*, 18 Sept. 1954.
24 NHA, *Proceedings*, 31 Mar. 1955, 279.
25 *Daily News*, 20 and 21 Sept. 1954.
26 *Evening Telegram*, 23 Sept. 1954.

27 AAS, Brūno Kalniņš Archive, Laimonis Ešenvalds to the *New York Times*, 29 Apr. 1954.
28 Ibid., Ešenvalds to Co-operative Commonwealth Federation, 29 Apr. 1954; Latvian Social Democratic Workers Party, 'A Few Facts about Alfreds Valdmanis,' undated.
29 Bobbie Robertson, personal interview, 13 June 1985.
30 AVP, A. Skrodelis to Gordon Higgins, 25 May 1954.
31 SC, file 'Valdmanis Affair,' O. Gobins to Premier Joseph Smallwood, 2 May 1954.
32 AVP, Emīls to Alfred, 30 June 1954.
33 NHA, *Proceedings*, 29 Mar. 1955, 188, and 31 Mar. 1955, 275f.
34 CNS Archives, C-165.
35 AVP, Wilhelm Burmeister to Gordon F. Higgins, 6 July 1954; notarized sworn statement by Jānis Krūmiņš, 16 July 1954.
36 CNS Archives, C-165, Alfred A. Valdmanis Papers.
37 Ibid., A Valdmanis Statement – My Education on Newfoundland Matters.
38 Ibid.
39 Ibid.
40 Supreme Court of Newfoundland, no. 533/1954, file 'The Queen v Valdmanis,' typed statement 'Benno Schilde,' undated, four pages.
41 CNS Archives, C-165, A Valdmanis Statement – Account 'Katrina Mateus' and Revolving (Party) Fund; NHA, *Proceedings*, 31 Mar. 1955, 273.
42 SC, 6.02.011, Lurje to Waldmanis, 8 Aug., 1 and 24 Sept. 1950; L. Viasmensky to Valdmanis, 13 and 17 Nov. 1950.
43 SC, 6.01.016, A. Malagodi to Valdmanis, 13 Feb. 1952; Valdmanis to Malagodi, 4 Mar. 1952.
44 SC, file 'Fish and Fish Products,' Project St Andrews North N.B.; Valdmanis to Malagodi, 4 Mar. 1952; Malagodi to Valdmanis, 13 Feb. 1952; Viasmensky to Dr A.A. Waldmanis, 13 Nov. and 28 Sept. 1950; Viasmensky to Elias Sourasky, 10, 11, and 17 Nov. 1950; Viasmensky to Dr Arnulfo Arias, 8 Nov. 1950; Valdmanis to Lurje, 28 Sept. 1950; Lurje to Valdmanis, 8 Aug. 1950 and 1 and 24 Sept. 1950; Leikucs to Lurje, 16 Aug. 1950.
45 AVP, Minutes of the Meetings of the Board of Directors of St Andrews Packers, Ltd, 1952–54; 'Statement and Designation by St Andrews Packers Ltd Pursuant to Section 210 of the General Corporation Law,' New York, 11 Jan. 1954.
46 SC, file 'Valdmanis Personal,' Valdmanis to Richard Kajaks, 26 Feb. 1954.
47 CNS Archives, C-156, Henhouses for the Farm; Jeep for Smallwood's Son. The former general manager of CMIC verified the Jeep story in June 1998.
48 Ibid., A Valdmanis Statement – The Rubber Plant Affidavit.

49 Ibid.

50 Ibid.

51 SC, file 'Valdmanis affair,' Smallwood to Lerch in Montreal, 14 July 1954.

52 AA, Ref. 414/301-01/40 and vol. 414/303-02/40. BA, B102, Bd. 6846, no. 3.

53 Supreme Court of Newfoundland, no. 533/1954, 'The Queen v Valdmanis.'

54 HHA, Kreyser to Herz, 25 May 1954.

55 HHA, Herz to Kreyser, 4 June 1954; Benno Schilde Archives, Herz to Kreyser, and Herz to Leja, 26 May 1954.

56 NHA, *Proceedings*, 29 Mar. 1955, 201.

57 In March 1955 Curtis quoted Valdmanis in the legislature writing to his wife from the penitentiary that 'Lurje lost all the money I gave him, and occasionally even threatened, threatened to get more.' See NHA, *Proceedings*, 31 Mar. 1955, 274f.

58 BA, B102, Bd. 6848, no. 1, Reifferscheidt to AA, Bonn, 19 Aug. 1954.

59 Ibid.

60 Ibid. AA, vol. 414/331-01/40, Reifferscheidt to AA, Bonn, 17 and 20 Sept. 1954.

61 AVP, Valdmanis to Valdis Mateus, 30 July 1954.

62 AVP, Valdmanis to Kiki [Katrina Mateus], Valdis, both Winters and Karl Sk., 8 Aug. 1954.

63 AVP, Valdmanis to Valdis [Mateus], 14 Aug. 1954.

64 Gundars Valdmanis to author, 9 Apr. 1986.

65 Ibid.

66 Ibid.

67 AVP, Valdmanis to Valdis and Kiki [Mateus], 24 Aug. 1954.

68 Ibid.

69 AVP, Valdmanis to Valdis and Kiki Mateus, 24 Aug. 1954, and to Mulītis (Irma Valdmanis), 25 Aug. 1954.

70 AVP, Valdmanis to Valdis Mateus, date illegible (possibly 3 Sept. 1954).

71 AVP, Valdmanis to Valdis Mateus, 3 Oct. 1954.

72 Ibid.

73 AVP, Valdmanis to Valdis Mateus, 31 Oct. 1954.

74 Ibid.

75 Ibid.

76 AVP, Valdmanis to Valdis Mateus, 9 and 31 Oct. (1954).

77 AVP, Valdmanis to Valdis Mateus, 11 Dec. 1954.

78 Ibid.

79 Ibid.

80 AVP, Valdmanis to unidentified, undated (approx. Jan.–Feb. 1955).

81 Ibid.

82 AVP, Valdmanis to Valdis Mateus, 7 Oct. 1955.
83 Ibid.
84 AVP, Valdmanis to Valdis Mateus, 23 Dec. 1955.
85 NHA, *Proceedings*, 29 Mar. 1955, 203. Irma Valdmanis verified the apology (personal interview, 4 Apr. 1986).
86 On a visit to St John's, in Oct. 1954, this German official was amazed at Smallwood's undiminished appetite for additional German industries. He promised prospective industrialists would now receive from Newfoundland 100 instead of 50 per cent of their starting capital to facilitate German authorization. See AA, 414/331-01/40, Reifferscheidt to AA, Bonn, 4 Oct. 1954.
87 *Evening Telegram*, 14 Oct. 1954.
88 Edgar Pike, personal interview, 21 Aug. 1992.
89 Ibid.
90 Wayfarer, *Daily News*, 21 Aug. 1970.
91 Fritz W. Stobbe, personal interview, 3 Apr. 1986.
92 NHA, *Proceedings*, 22 Sept. 1955, 1303f; 19 Mar. 1956, 58f.
93 Harold Horwood, 'Political Notebook,' *Evening Telegram*, 29 Sept. 1955; NHA, *Proceedings*, 26 Sept. 1955, 1438ff.; 19 Mar. 1956, 75; Apr. 1956, 246.
94 *Evening Telegram*, 30 Sept. 1955.
95 BSA, Herz to Schilde, Abt.231/Cz, 4 July 1955.
96 Quoted in NHA, *Proceedings*, 29 Mar. 1955, 180.
97 Sofija Lucis, personal interview, 1 Apr. 1985.
98 NHA, *Proceedings*, 19 Mar. 1956, 77, and 9 May 1956, 1129, 1142f.
99 *Evening Telegram*, 14 Dec. 1955.
100 Horwood, *Evening Telegram*, 29 Sept. 1955.
101 NHA, *Proceedings*, 29 Mar. 1955, 169; 26 Sept. 1955, 1433; 6 Apr. 1956, 344.

Chapter 12: 'Maybe My Luck Is Used Up Already, Maybe Not'

1 AVP, 'Sworn translations, extracts, and resumés,' Montreal, 7 May 1963.
2 *Evening Telegram*, 2 Jan. 1957; AVP, unidentified clipping from a Montreal paper of 3 Jan. 1957, entitled '"Mr Smith" Sidesteps Reporters' Questions.'
3 Gundars Valdmanis, personal interviews, 21 Feb. and 5 Apr. 1986.
4 Gundars Valdmanis to author, 9 Apr. 1986; Personal interview, Gundars Valdmanis, 16 Oct. 1985.
5 NAC, MG 32 B 34, F.H. Whitley to Minister of Immigration, 27 Apr. 1954. On 27 April 1954 Whitley had berated Smallwood in a similar vein for squandering the people's money by engaging 'such fellows as Valdmanis ... He lives in Westmount like a prince ... [and] had no thought for his fellow

men in the country, only for himself ... He really deserves to be deported. Any other immigrant would be deported for far less than what he has done!' SC, file 'Valdmanis Affair.'

6 NAC, MG 32 B 34, Hamilton to Pickersgill, 15 Aug. 1956; Memorandum for the Minister by L.A. Couture, 5 Sept. 1956; Pickersgill to Hamilton, 6 Nov. 1956.
7 AVP, D.J. McClellan, Director of Appeals, Department of National Revenue, to Messrs Emerson, Stirling, and Higgins, 20 Feb. 1956, with personal notes and documents attached re 'Adjustment to Assessments' dated 26 May 1954.
8 AVP, Samuel Zwecker to Whom It May Concern, 17 July 1957.
9 AVP, Valdmanis to Director of Appeals, Taxation Division, 4 Mar. 1956.
10 Ibid.
11 AVP, Kreyser and Braun-Wogau to Elja Lurje, 10 Dec. 1949, with remarks attached by A. Valdmanis, dated Feb. 1956.
12 AVP, Valdmanis to Claude Couture, QC, 30 Mar. 1969.
13 *Evening Telegram*, 19 and 22 Sept. 1969.
14 AVP, assorted documents and 1957 correspondence.
15 Gundars Valdmanis, personal interview, 16 Oct. 1985.
16 Gundars Valdmanis to author, 9 Apr. 1986.
17 AVP, 'Sworn translation, extracts and resumes,' Montreal, 7 May 1963.
18 AVP, Valdmanis to Dr C.J. Austin, Director of Marketing Planning, Lockheed-Georgia Company, Atlanta, 30 Oct. 1963.
19 AVP, Valdmanis to Prof. Dr John C. Carancis, 10 Nov. 1963.
20 AVP, Tētis (Dad) to Gundars, Alfred [Valdmanis] to Claude [Richardson], 21 Sept. 1966. W.F. Sharon to Preston Manning, 5 Aug. 1967.
21 AV, G.H. Steer to D.W.H. Tupper, 12 May 1969.
22 Gundars Valdmanis to author, 21 Feb. 1986; Gundars Valdmanis, personal interview, 16 Oct. 1985.
23 AVP, notes with comments by Gundars Valdmanis; G. Valdmanis to Ms Fleming, 10 Oct. 1970; clipping 'Beating *Le Système*' from *Time Magazine*, 22 May 1964.
24 Author's translation of the telegram's original German text from the German edition of E. Avotiņš, J. Dzirkalis, V. Pētersons, *Daugavas Vanagi: Wer sind sie?* (Riga, 1963), 150.
25 E. Avotiņš, J. Dzirkalis, V. Pētersons, *Daugavas Vanagi: Who Are They?* (Riga, 1963).
26 AVP, Alfred [Valdmanis] to Claude [Richardson], 21 Sept. 1966.
27 AVP, Hugh K. Nash to Office Staff, 6 Mar. 1970.
28 Gundars Valdmanis, personal interview, 16 Oct. 1985.

29 AVP, Gundars Valdmanis to Miss Fleming, Milner and Steer Ltd, Edmonton, 10 Oct. 1970.
30 AVP, August J. Osis to Gundars Valdmanis, 26 Feb. 1978.
31 *Evening Telegram*, 16 Aug. 1970.
32 *Evening Telegram*, 13 and 16 Aug. 1970; Montreal *Gazette*, 13 Aug. 1970; *Globe and Mail*, 13 Aug. 1970; *Daily News*, 13 and 14 Aug. 1970.
33 Wayfarer, 'The Valdmanis Era (1),' *Daily News*, 18 Aug. 1970.
34 Wayfarer, 'The Valdmanis Era (2),' *Daily News*, 19 Aug. 1970.
35 Wayfarer, 'The Valdmanis Era (3),' *Daily News*, 20 Aug. 1970.
36 Wayfarer, 'The Valdmanis Era (4),' *Daily News*, 21 Aug. 1970.
37 Ibid.
38 Canadian Press staff writer John LeBlanc, *Evening Telegram*, 16 Aug. 1967.
39 See Stranga, 'Starp Hitleru un Staliņu'; Biezais, *Latvija kāškrusta varā*, 150.
40 Rodal, 172ff; Cesarani, 46f, 146.
41 For the most recent restatements, see Bob Benson, 'Public Money Down the Drain,' *Evening Telegram*, 31 May 1998, and Crosbie, 43f. Gwyn, 168, summed up the prevailing view of Valdmanis's legacy thus: 'Had Smallwood literally taken $10–15 million and burnt it in a bonfire atop Signal Hill, the end result, in terms of Newfoundland's progress, would not have been greatly different.'
42 Balodis, 264f; P. Drāvelis, in *Tēvzemes Avīze*, 13 Mar. 1992.
43 Biezais, 'Pateicībā Hitleram,' *Treji Vārti*, 95 (1983), 8–10, and, *Latvija kāškrusta varā*, 150; Stranga, 'Starp Hitleru un Staliņu'; Kangeris, 'Opposition gegen das Ulmanis Regime oder Landesverrat,' 7f, 16.
44 Balodis, 305f.
45 Biezais, *Latvija kāškrusta varā*, 147.
46 Noel, 276; Rowe, 18f; Crosbie, 43.
47 Horwood, *Joey*, 189; Bob Benson, in *Evening Telegram*, 31 May 1998.
48 Alan Phillips, *The Living Legend: The Story of the Royal Canadian Mounted Police* (Boston and Toronto, 1954), 203; Gwyn, 164; Crosbie, 43f.
49 'The trend is not restricted to the young. People in high places – executives, superintendents of schools, and the like – have falsely claimed doctorates, and otherwise lied on their resumes. And have been caught.' See Richard Nelson Bolles, *What Color Is Your Parachute? A Practical Manual for Job-Hunters and Career Changers* Part 2: *The Parachute Workbook and Resource Guide* (Berkeley, 1996), 169.
50 'Fall of a Titan,' *Globe and Mail*, 28 Sept. 1954.
51 Irma and Gundars Valdmanis, personal interview, Montreal, 4–5 Apr. 1986.
52 Richard Gwyn as quoted in Noel, 275.

53 Gwyn, 135.
54 Horwood, *Joey*, 186.
55 Crosbie, 48–51.
56 SC, 6.02.011, Valdmanis to Kreyser, 19 Dec. 1951.

References

Manuscript Sources

Latvijas Centrālais Valsts Vēstures Arhīvs, Riga
Fonds 1303, 1307, 1314, 1710, 2415, 2570, 2886, 3235, 4377, 4597, 6209, 68247318, 7319
P-69, P-252, P-1026

Latvijas Centrālais valsts Oktobra revolūcijas un sociālistiskas celtniecības arhīvs, Riga
Fonds 75, 97, 174, 754, 822, 1019
P-69, P-70

Bundesarchiv, Koblenz
R 6 Reichsministerium für die besetzten Ostgebiete
R 58 Reichssicherheitshauptamt, Ereignismeldungen
R 90 Reichskommissar für das Ostland
R 91 Gebietskommissare im Geschäftsbereich des Reichskommissars für das Ostland
R 92 Generalkommissar in Riga
Z 42 Spruchgericht Bielefeld, Ermittlungssache gegen Hinrich Lohse
B 102, Bd. 6081 Wirtschaftsberichte Kanada, 1951–53

Bundesarchiv, Abteilungen Potsdam
62 DAF 3, Bd. 11, Lettland, 1930–40

Politisches Archiv des Auswärtigen Amts, Bonn
Deutsche Gesandtschaft Riga
Pol I, V, Länderakte Lettland
HaPol Vb, Lettland, Wirtschaft
HaPol Vb, Ostland, Wirtschaft
HaPol Clodius, Lettland
HaPol Wiehl, Lettland
R27206, R27207, R29670,
R113166, R113168, R113169, R113174, R113190, R113191, R113199, R113200, R113228, R113305
Ref. 414/302-3 Wirtschaftliche Beziehungen (Kanadas) zu Deutschland

National Archives of Canada, Ottawa
RG 26 Latvian Immigration, 1947–57
RG 27 Immigration (Belgium) – Latvians, 1950–52
RG 49 Defence Production, 1950–57
RG 76 Baltic Immigration, 1948–57
RG 76 Immigration from the Republic of Latvia, 1948–61
MG 26 Louis St Laurent Papers
MG 32 J.W. Pickersgill Papers

Centre for Newfoundland Studies Archives, St John's
J.R. Smallwood Collection
C-165 Alfred A. Valdmanis Papers

Alfred A. Valdmanis Papers, Montreal
Personal papers, 1934–70

August Osis Papers, Edmonton
Select personal papers of Alfred Valdmanis

Supreme Court of Newfoundland, St John's
The Queen vs Valdmanis

Benno Schilde Archives, Bad Hersfeld, Germany
Reports and correspondence re erection of gypsum plant in Newfoundland, 1950–55

Hubertus Herz Archives, Kirchseeon, Germany
Personal correspondence re Alfred Valdmanis and Benno Schilde contract with Newfoundland, 1950–55

Arbetarrörelsens Arkiv, Stockholm
Dr Brūno Kalniņš Papers

Zentrale Stelle der Landesjustizverwaltungen Ludwigsburg, Germany
II 207 AR-Nr. 751/1964, Albert Eichelis, 7.1.12-20.7.84, Audrini Anklage vom 27.6.1977

Interviews

Andersons, Edgars
Balodis, Ralph and Zenta
Browne, W.J.
Chalker, James R.
Crosbie, Gertrude
Dawe, Louise
Dlugosch, Georg and Hanna
Herz, Hubertus
Iesalniece, Līna
Jamieson, Don
Jansone, Anna
Jekste, Alberts
Kuester, Matthias F.
Leja, Gunar
Levitan, Samuel
Losis, Irma
Lucis, Arnis
Lucis Sofija
Matschen, Herbert and Gerda
Mikelsons, Sigurds
Morgan, Baxter
Pike, Edgar
Ploetner, Ellen
Power, Gregory
Pushie, Gordon F.
Robertson, Bobbie
Ronis, Indulis
Sann, Günther K.
Smallwood, Joseph R.
Stobbe, Fritz W.
Strādiņš, Jānis
Strods, Heinrihs

Surgovte, Dagnija
Tode, Ingrid
Trautmanis, Ingrid
Treibergs, Erika
Valdmanis, Gundars
Valdmanis, Irma
Vestermanis, Margers
Žagars, Eriks

Published Primary Sources

Newspapers and Periodicals

Atlantic Guardian (Halifax), 1951
Baltische Monatshefte (Riga), 1932
Daily News (St John's), 1949–70
Economist (London), 1939
Evening Telegram (St John's), 1950–70
Evening Citizen (Ottawa), 1949
Financial Times (London), 1938
Frankfurter Allgemeine, 1950
Frankfurter Zeitung, 1939
Gazette (Montreal), 1951–54
Hersfelder Zeitung, 1950
Jaunākās ziņas [The Latest News] (Riga), 1938
Laiks [Time] (New York and Montreal), 1950–54
Latvija–Brīvā Balss [Latvia–Free Voice] (Toronto), 1951
Latvija Amerika [Latvia in America] (Toronto), 1951–54
Latvijas Kareivis [Latvia's Warrior] (Riga), 1937–1938
Maclean's, 1951–54
Münchener Neueste Nachrichten, 1938
Newsweek, 1951
Der Nordwesten (Winnipeg), 1951–56
Rigasche Rundschau, 1934–39
Rīts [Morning] (Riga), 1937–39
Tēvzemes Avīze [The Fatherland's Newspaper] (Riga), 1992–97
Treji Vārti [Three Gates] (East Lansing), 1982–85
Western Star (Corner Brook), 1951
Winnipeg Free Press, 1949–70

Der Wirtschafts-Ring (Berlin), 1938–39
Die Zeit (Hamburg), 1970–97

Government Documents

Bilmanis, A., ed. *Latvian–Russian Relations: Documents.* Washington, 1944.

Canada, House of Commons. *Debates,* 1951.

Canada, Senate. *Proceedings of the Standing Committee on Immigration and Labour, No. 4, Wednesday 27 April 1949.* Ottawa, 1948.

Canada. *Report of the Department of Mines and Resources for the Fiscal Year Ended March 31, 1949.* Ottawa, 1949.

Freivalds, O., et al., eds. *Latviešu karavīrs otrā pasaules kara laikā: Dokumentu un atmiņu krājums* [The Latvian Warrior in the Time of the Second World War: A Collection of Documents and Memories], 11 vols. Toronto, 1970–84.

Grava-Kreituse, I., Feldmanis, I., Loeber, D.A., Goldmanis, J., and A. Stranga, *The Occupation and Annexation of Latvia, 1939–1940: Documents and Materials.* Riga, 1995.

Institut für Besatzungsfragen, ed. *Das DP-Problem: Eine Studie über die ausländischen Flüchtlinge in Deutschland.* Tübingen, 1950.

International Military Tribunal, Nuremberg. *Trial of the Major War Criminals before the International Military Tribunal Nuremberg, 14 November 1945 – 1 October 1946,* vols. 26, 37. Nuremberg, 1947.

Latvian Legation, Washington. *Latvia under German Occupation, 1941–1943,* with a preface by Alfred Bilmanis. Washington, 1943.

– *Latvia under German Occupation in 1943.* Washington, 1944.

Loeber, Dietrich. *Diktierte Option: Die Umsiedlung der Deutsch-Balten aus Estland und Lettland, 1939–1941.* Neumünster, 1972.

Newfoundland, House of Assembly, *Proceedings,* 1950–55.

OMGUS (Office of the Military Government for Germany, United States). *Ermittlungen gegen die Dresdner Bank, 1946.* Nördlingen, 1986.

Rodal, Alti. 'Nazi War Criminals in Canada: The Historical and Policy Setting from the 1940s to the Present.' Prepared for the Commission of Inquiry on War Criminals. Ottawa, 1986.

USSR, Department of External Affairs, ed. *Polipedy Soobshchaiut ...: Sbornik Dokumentov ob Otnoshcheniiach CCCR c Latviei, Litvoi i Estoniei, Avgust 1939g – Avgust 1940g* [Accredited Representatives Reporting ...: Collection of Documents about Relationships of the USSR with Latvia, Lithuania, and Estonia, August 1939 – August 1940]. Moscow, 1990.

Weisz, Christoph, ed. *Omgus Handbuch: Die amerikanische Militärregierung in Deutschland, 1945–1949.* Munich, 1995.

Autobiographical Literature

Andersons, Edgars, ed. 'Alfreds Valdmanis – Kavējoties atmiņās.' *Treji Vārti,* 95 (1982), 4–8; 96 (1983), 15–19; 97 (1984), 11–14; 98 (1985), 17–18.

Bērziņš, Alfreds. *1939: Lielo notikumu priekšvakarā* [On the Eve of the Great Events]. New York, 1976.

– *Tāļš ir ceļš atpakaļ uz dzimteni* [Long Is the Road back to the Land of One's Birth]. New York, 1971.

Browne, W.J. *And now ... Eighty-seven Years a Newfoundlander: Memoirs of William J. Browne, PC, QC, LLD. vol. 2, 1949–1965.* St John's, 1981.

Clay, Lucius D. *Decision in Germany.* New York, 1950.

Crosbie, John C. *No Holds Barred: My Life in Politics.* Toronto, 1997.

Horwood, Harold. *Joey: The Life and Times of Joey Smallwood.* Toronto, 1989.

Hulme, Kathryn. *The Wild Place.* Boston and Toronto, 1953.

Jamieson, Don. *No Place for Fools: The Political Memoirs of Don Jamieson,* vol. 1. St John's, 1989.

Keenleyside, H.L. *Memoirs of Hugh L. Keenleyside,* vol. 2, *On the Bridge of Time.* Toronto, 1982.

Kleist, Peter. *Zwischen Hitler und Stalin, 1939–45: Aufzeichnungen von Dr Peter Kleist.* Bonn, 1950.

Kroeger, Jürgen Ernst. *So war es: Ein Bericht.* Michelstadt, 1989.

Marnitz, Harry. *Nordlicht über der Düna: Kritische Betrachtungen und Erinnerungen an die deutsche Besatzungszeit in Lettland, 1941–1943.* Michelstadt, 1991.

Penrose, E.F. 'Negotiating on Refugees and Displaced Persons, 1946,' in R. Dennett and J.E. Johnson, eds., *Negotiating with the Russians.* Boston, 1951, 139–70.

Pottle, Herbert L. *Newfoundland Dawn without Light: Politics, Power and the People in the Smallwood Era.* St John's, 1979.

Rowe, Frederick C. *The Smallwood Era.* Toronto, 1985.

Siliņš, Leonīds, and Edgars Andersons, eds. *Latvijas Centrālā Padome – LCP: Latviešu nacionālā pretestības kustība, 1943–1945* [The Latvian Central Council – LCP: The Latvian National Resistance Movement, 1943–1945]. Uppsala, 1994.

Smallwood, Joseph R. *I Chose Canada: The Memoirs of the Honourable Joseph R. 'Joey' Smallwood.* Toronto, 1973.

– *Newfoundland in on the March.* St John's, 1952.

Wittrock, Hugo. *Erinnerungen: Kommissarischer Oberbürgermeister von Riga, 1941-1944.* Lüneburg, 1979.

Zemgals, Boriss. *Days of Happiness and Distress,* which is a report of the work of Dr Alfred Valdmanis in the interests of the Latvian Republic and its people, written by Boriss Zemgals and published by Leonīds Zemgals at Geneva, Switzerland, 1949. (Notarized translation by Max Braun-Wogau of extracts. St John's, 1951.)

Zemgals, Boriss. *Dienas baltas nebaltas: Stāsts par Alfreda Valdmaņa darbu Tautai un Tēvzemei.* Geneva, 1949.

Secondary Sources

Aizsilnieks, Arnolds. *Latvijas saimniecības vēsture 1914–1945* [The Economic History of Latvia, 1914–1945]. Stockholm, 1986.

Alexander, David. 'Newfoundland's Traditional Economy and Development to 1934.' *Acadiensis* 5, 2 (1976), 56–78.

Andersons, Edgars. *Cross Road Country Latvia.* Waverly, 1953.

– 'Latvians.' In Stephen Thernstrom, ed. *Harvard Encyclopedia of American Ethnic Groups.* Cambridge, Mass, 1980, 638–41.

– 'The Pacts of Mutual Assistance between the USSR and the Baltic States,' in A. Ziedonis, Jr, W.L. Winter, and M. Valgemäe, eds., *Baltic History.* Columbus, Ohio, 1974, 239–55.

Avotiņš, E., Dzirkalis, J., and V. Pētersons. *Daugavas Vanagi: Wer sind sie?* Riga, 1963.

– *Daugavas Vanagi: Who Are They?* Riga, 1963.

Baker, Melvin. 'Smallwood, Joseph Roberts (1900–1991),' in *Encyclopedia of Newfoundland and Labrador,* vol. 5. St John's, 1994, 208–15.

Balabkins, Nicholas, and Arnolds Aizsilnieks, eds. *Entrepreneur in a Small Country: A Case Study against the Background of the Latvian Economy, 1919–1940.* Hicksville, 1975.

Balodis, Agnis. *Latvijas un latviešu tautas vēsture* [The History of Latvia and the Latvian Nation]. Riga, 1991.

Bassler, Gerhard P. '"Develop or Perish": Joseph R. Smallwood and Newfoundland's Quest for German Industry, 1949–1953.' *Acadiensis* 15, 2 (1986), 93–119.

– 'Latvia and Democracy in International Historical Perspective,' in University of Latvia, ed., *The Transition to Democracy: Experience in Latvia and in the World, Riga, November 12th–14th, 1992.* Riga 1994, 111–17.

– 'Lutheran Congregation,' *Encyclopedia of Newfoundland and Labrador,* vol. 3. St John's, 1991.

– *Sanctuary Denied: Refugees from the Third Reich and Newfoundland Immigration Policy, 1906–1949.* St John's, 1992.

Benz, Wolfgang, Johannes Houwink ten Cate, and Gerhard Otto, eds. *Anpassung, Kollaboration, Widerstand: Kollektive Reaktionen auf die Okkupation.* Berlin, 1996.

Bērziņš, Alfreds. *Latvia.* Washington, 1968.

Biezais, Haralds. *Latvija kāškrusta varā: Sveši kungi – pašu laudis* [Latvia under the Might of the Swastika: Foreign Rulers – Own People]. East Lansing, 1992.

– 'Pateicība Hitleram [In Gratitude to Hitler]' *Treji Vārti* 95 (1983), 8–10.

Bilmanis, Alfred. *A History of Latvia.* Princeton, 1951.

– *Latvia as an Independent State.* Washington, 1947.

Bissoondath, Neil. *Selling Illusions: The Cult of Multiculturalism in Canada.* Toronto, 1994.

Blank, Margot. *Nationalsozialistische Hochschulpolitik in Riga (1941 bis 1944): Konzeption und Realität eines Bereiches deutscher Besatzungspolitik.* Lüneburg, 1991.

Bolles, Richard Nelson. *What Color Is Your Parachute? A Practical Manual for Job-Hunters and Career Changers.* Berkeley, 1996.

Cesarani, David. *Justice Delayed.* London, 1992.

Cole, Hubert. *Fouché: The Unprincipled Patriot.* New York, 1971.

Czollek, Roswitha. *Faschismus und Okkupation: Wirtschaftliche Zielsetzung und Praxis des faschistischen deutschen Besatzungsregimes in den baltischen Sowjetrepubliken während des zweiten Weltkriegs.* Berlin, 1974.

Dallin, Alexander. *German Rule in Russia, 1941–1945.* London, 1957.

Daugavas Vanagi, Central Board. *Latvia and Latvians.* London, 1978.

Drāvelis, P. 'Ministra vizītkartes vietā [In Lieu of the Minister's Business Card].' *Tēvzemes Avīze,* 13 March 1992.

Duhanovs, M., Feldmanis, I., and A. Stranga, *1939: Latvia and the Year of Fateful Decisions.* Riga, 1994.

Erhard, Ludwig. *Germany's Comeback in the World Market.* London, 1954.

Ezergailis, Andrew. 'Anti-Semitism and the Killing of the Jews of Latvia,' in Sander L. Gilman and S.T. Katz, eds., *Anti-Semitism in Times of Crisis.* New York, 1991.

– 'Arājs kommanda.' *LPSR Zinatņu Akademijas Vēstis* [Bulletin of the Academy of Sciences of the Latvian SSR] 10(495) (1988), 113–13.

– *The Holocaust in Latvia, 1941–1944: The Missing Center.* Washington and Riga, 1996.

– 'Holocausta petīšanas problēmas.' *Latvijas Vēstures Institūta Žurnals* [Journal of the Latvian Historical Institute] 1 (1993), 130–8.

– '"Vadoņa pavēle" un SS Brigadenfirera Dr Valtera Stalekera 1941. gada 6. augusta memorands ["The Führer's Order" and SS Major Walter Stahlecker's Memorandum of 6 August 1941]' *Latvijas Vēstures Institūta Žurnāls* 1 (1993), 108–14, 126–30.

Fest, Joachim. 'Alfred Rosenberg – The Forgotten Disciple,' in *The Face of the Third Reich.* New York, 1970, 163–74.

Foot, M.R.D. 'What Good Did Resistance Do?' in Stephen Hawes and Ralph White, eds., *Resistance in Europe, 1939–1945.* London, 1975.

Genizi, Haim. *America's Fair Share: The Admission and Resettlement of Displaced Persons, 1945–1952.* Detroit, 1993.

Gordon, Frank. *Latvians and Jews between Germany and Russia.* Stockholm, 1990.

Gwyn, Richard *Smallwood: The Unlikely Revolutionary.* Toronto, 1972.

Handrack, H.D. *Das Reichskommissariat Ostland: Die Kulturpolitik der deutschen Verwaltung zwischen Autonomie und Gleichschaltung, 1941–1944.* Hann. Münden, 1981.

Harris, Michael. *Rare Ambition: The Crosbies of Newfoundland.* Toronto, 1992.

Hehn, Jürgen von. *Lettland zwischen Demokratie und Diktatur: Zur Geschichte des lettländischen Staatsstreichs vom 15. Mai 1934.* Beiheft 3, Jahrbücher für Geschichte Osteuropas. Munich, 1957.

– *Die Umsiedlung der baltischen Deutschen – das letzte Kapitel baltisch–deutscher Geschichte.* Marburg/Lahn, 1982.

Hehn, Jürgen von, Rimscha, Hans von, and Hellmuth Weiss, eds. *Von den baltischen Provinzen zu den baltischen Staaten: Beiträge zur Entstehungsgeschichte der Republiken Estland und Lettland, 1917–1918.* Marburg/Lahn, 1971.

Hiden, John, and Patrick Salmon. *The Baltic Nations and Europe: Estonia, Latvia and Lithuania in the Twentieth Century.* London and New York, 1991.

Höhne, Heinz. *Der Orden unter dem Totenkopf: Die Geschichte der SS.* Hamburg, 1967.

Holborn, Louise W. *The International Refugee Organization, a Specialized Agency of the United Nations: Its History and Work, 1946–1952.* London, 1956.

Hyde, H. Montgomery. *The Quiet Canadian: The Secret Service Story of Sir William Stephenson.* London, 1962.

Janssen, Karl Heinz. 'Die baltische Okkupationspolitik des Deutschen Reiches,' in J. von Hehn, H. von Rimscha, and H. Weiss, eds, *Von den baltischen Provinzen zu den baltischen Staaten,* 222–7.

Kangeris, Karlis. 'Kollaboration vor der Kollaboration? Die baltischen Emigranten und ihre "Befreiungskomitees" in Deutschland 1940–41,' in W. Röhr, ed., *Okkupation und Kollaboration (1938–1945).* Berlin, 1995, 165–90.

– 'Opposition gegen das Ulmanis Regime oder Landesverrat? Geheime Kontakte lettischer Kreise mit Deutschland 1934–1940.' Paper presented to the 14th Conference of the Association for the Advancement of Baltic Studies, Chicago, June 1994.

Kavass, Igor I., and Adolph Sprudzs, eds. *Baltic States: A Study of Their Origin and National Development; their Seizure and Incorporation into the USSR.* U.S. Congress. House Select Committee on Communist Aggression. Washington, 1954.

Krausnick, Helmut, and Hans-Heinrich Wilhelm. *Die Truppe des Weltanschauungskrieges: Die Einsatzgruppen der Sicherheitspolizei und des SD, 1938–1942.* Stuttgart, 1981.

Kuester, M.F. *Where Birch Trees Grow ...: A History of Baltic German Immigration to Canada after World War II.* Edmonton, 1979.

Lady Davis Foundation. *Report Nineteen Forty-Nine.* Montreal, 1949.

Larsen, Stein Ugelvik, Hagtvet, B., and J.P. Myklebush, eds. *Who Were the Fascists: Social Roots of European Fascism.* Oslo, 1980.

Letto, Doug. *Chocolate Bars and Rubber Boots: The Smallwood Industrialization Plan.* Paradise, NF, 1998.

Littlejohn. David. *The Patriotic Traitors: A History of Collaboration in German-Occupied Europe, 1940–45.* London, 1972.

Littman, Sol. *War Criminal on Trial: The Rauca Case.* Markham, 1983.

Mangulis, Visvaldis. *Latvia in the Wars of the 20th Century.* Princeton Junction, NJ, 1983.

Matthews, Ralph. *The Creation of Regional Dependency.* Toronto, 1983.

Mauriņa, Zenta. 'Četri liktenīgi motīvi latviešu kultūrā [Four Fateful Motifs in Latvian Culture]' in *Domu varavīksnē* [Within the Rainbow of Thoughts]. Riga, 1992.

Meiksins, Gregory. *The Baltic Soviet Republics.* New York, 1944.

– *The Baltic Riddle: Finland, Estonia, Latvia, Lithuania – Key Points of European Peace.* New York, 1943.

Misiunas, R.J., and R. Taagepera. *The Baltic States: Years of Dependence, 1940–1990.* Berkeley, 1993.

Mrozek, Gisbert, and Jürgen Reiter. *Riga: Stadt an der Daugava.* Bremen, 1989.

Mulligan, Timothy Patrick. *The Politics of Illusion and Empire: German Occupation Policy in the Soviet Union, 1942–1943.* New York, 1988.

Myllyniemi, Seppo. 'Die Folgen des Hitler–Stalin Paktes für die baltischen Republiken und Finland,' in Bernd Wegner, ed., *Zwei Wege nach Moskau: Vom Hitler–Stalin Pakt zum Unternehmen Barbarossa.* Munich, 1991, 75–92.

– *Die Neuordnung der baltischen Länder 1941–1944: Zum nationalsozialistischen Inhalt der deutschen Besatzungspolitik.* Helsinki, 1973.

Nies, Susanne. *Lettland in der internationalen Politik: Aspekte seiner Aussenpolitik (1918–95).* Münster, 1997.

Noel, S.J.R. *Politics in Newfoundland.* Toronto, 1971.

Page, Stanley W. *The Formation of the Baltic States.* Cambridge, Mass, 1959.

Phillips, Alan. *The Living Legend: The Story of the Royal Canadian Mounted Police.* Boston and Toronto, 1954.

Plakans, Andrejs. *The Latvians: A Short History.* Stanford, 1995.

Press, Bernhard. *Judenmord in Lettland, 1941–1945.* Berlin, 1992.

Proudfoot, Malcolm J. *European Refugees, 1939–52: A Study in Forced Population Movement.* London, 1957.

Rauch, Georg von. *Geschichte der baltischen Staaten.* Munich, 1977.

– *The Baltic States: The Years of Independence – Estonia, Latvia, Lithuania, 1917–1940.* Berkeley and Los Angeles, 1974.

Reitlinger, Gerald. *The House Built on Sand: The Conflicts of German Policy in Russia, 1939–1945.* New York, 1960.

– *The SS: Alibi of a Nation, 1922–1945.* New York, 1968.

Royal Institute of International Affairs, ed. *The Baltic States: A Survey of the Political and Economic Structure and the Foreign Relations of Estonia, Latvia, and Lithuania.* London, 1938.

Rüdiger, Wilhelm von. *Die 'Deutsch-Baltische Volksgruppe': Ausklang.* Hannover-Wülfel, 1957.

Rutkis, J., ed. *Latvia, Country and People.* Stockholm, 1967.

Schechtman, Joseph B. *European Population Transfers 1939–1945.* New York, 1946.

Schmidt, Alexander. *Geschichte des Baltikums.* Munich, 1992.

Schneider, Gertrude, 'The Two Ghettos in Riga, Latvia, 1941–1943,' in Lucian Dobroszycki and Jeffrey S. Gurock, eds. *The Holocaust in the Soviet Union: Studies and Sources on the Destruction of the Jews in the Nazi-Occupied Territories of the USSR, 1941–1945.* Armonk and London, 1993, 181–93.

Schwabe, A. *The Story of Latvia: A Historical Survey.* Stockholm, 1949.

Shtromas, Alexander. 'The Baltic States,' in R. Conquest, ed., *The Last Empire: Nationality and the Soviet Future.* Stanford, 1986, 181–217.

Silenieks, Juris. 'Karlis Ulmanis,' in Vito Vitauts Simanis, ed., *Latvia,* 148.

Silgailis, Arthur. *Latvian Legion.* San Jose, 1986.

Simanis, Vito Vitauts, ed. *Latvia.* St Charles, Ill, 1984.

Smallwood, J.R. *Newfoundland Is on the March.* St John's, 1952.

Smith, Denis Mack. 'The Theory and Practice of Fascism,' in N. Greene, ed., *Fascism: An Anthology.* New York, 1968.

Smith, Philip, *The Story of Churchill Falls.* Toronto, 1975.

Spekke, Arnolds. *History of Latvia: An Outline.* Stockholm, 1951.

Stehle, Hansjakob. 'Frommer Faschist von Stalin's Gnaden: Wie ein Abenteurer Polens Tragödien überlebte.' *Die Zeit,* 29 September 1995.

Stopinski, Sigmar. 'Das Baltikum im Patt der Mächte: Zur Entstehung der Staaten Estland, Lettland, und Litauen im Gefolge des Ersten Weltkriegs.' PhD thesis, Free University of Berlin, 1994.

Stranga, Aivars. 'Starp Hitleru un Staliņū [Between Hitler and Stalin].' *Tēvzemes Avīze* (Riga), 13 March 1992.

Strods, Heinrihs. *Zem melnbrūnā zobena: Vācijas politika Latvijā 1939–1945* [Under the Black-Brown Sword: Germany's Politics in Latvia, 1939–1945]. Riga, 1994.

Swettenham, John Alexander. *The Tragedy of the Baltic States: A Report Compiled from Official Documents and Eyewitnesses' Stories.* London, 1952.

Valters, Miķelis. *No sabrukuma uz plānveidotu saimniecību: Latvijas atjaunošanas problēmas, Latvijas nākotne* [From Collapse to a Planned Economy: The Problems of Latvia's Renewal, Latvia's Future]. Riga, 1933.

Vardys, V. Stanley, and R.J. Misiunas, eds. *The Baltic States in Peace and War, 1917–1945.* University Park and London, 1978.

Veigners, Ilgvars. *Latvieši ārzemes* [Latvians Abroad]. Riga, 1993.

Vernant, Jacques. *The Refugee in the Post-War World.* New Haven, 1953.

Vestermanis, Marģers. 'Der Holocaust in Lettland: Zur "postkommunistischen" Aufarbeitung des Themas in Osteuropa,' in A. Herzig and I. Lorenz, eds., *Verdrängung und Vernichtung der Juden unter dem Nationalsozialismus.* Hamburg, 1992, 101–30.

– 'Der lettische Anteil an der Endlösung: Versuch einer Antwort,' in Uwe Backes, Eckhard Jesse, and Rainer Zitelmann, eds., *Die Schatten der Vergangenheit: Impulse zur Historisierung des Nationalsozialismus.* Frankfurt/M.–Berlin, 1992, 426–49.

Voldemars, H., and K. Vicis, eds. *We Accuse the East – We Warn the West.* N.p.[Germany], 1948.

Wasserstein, Bernard. *The Secret Lives of Trebitsch Lincoln.* New Haven and London, 1988.

Whitaker, Reg. *Double Standard: The Secret History of Canadian Immigration.* Toronto, 1987.

Who's Who in the East: United States of America and Canada, 12th ed. Chicago, 1969.

Wilhelm, Hans-Heinrich. *Die Einsatzgruppe A der Sicherheitspolizei und des SD.* Frankfurt/M, 1996.

– 'Offene Fragen der Holocaust-Forschung: Das Beispiel des Baltikums,' in U. Backes, E. Jesse, and R. Zitelmann, eds., *Die Schatten der Vergangenheit,* (Frankfurt/M-Berlin, 1992), 403–49.

Williams, Maynard Owen. 'Latvia, Home of the Letts.' *National Geographic Magazine* 46, 4 (1924), 399–443.

Wistrich, Robert. *Wer war wer im Dritten Reich? Ein biografisches Lexikon.* Frankfurt/M, 1987.

Woodbridge, George. *UNRRA: The History of the United Nations Relief and Rehabilitation Administration.* New York, 1950.

Wyman, Mark. *DP: Europe's Displaced Persons, 1945–1951.* Philadelphia, 1989.

Index

Ābolinš, Aleksandrs (Alexander), 43, 217, 290, 315, 343, 357, 421n79, 422n111, 434n59,
Abwehr, 106, 110, 148, 161, 166, 211
Adlon Hotel, 170
Africa, 143, 358, 359
Aguathuna (NF), 247, 250, 253
Aizsargi, 20, 102, 106, 107, 131, 196n38
Aizsilnieks, Arnolds, 5, 67, 71, 392n6, 395n27, 396n50, 397n54, 403n107, 403n24
Aldaris, A/S, 36
Alexander of Tunis, Field Marshal Harold Earl, 184, 221, 232
American Express Co, 220, 329, 348, 349, 351
Anderson(s), Edgar(s), vii, 7, 29, 217, 373, 378, 392n11, 393n19, 397n69, 404n130, 404n12, 416n80, 417n106
Andersons, Evalds, 118, 119
Angelus, Oscar, 162
Anhalt, Istvan, 226
Apsītis, Hermanis, 98
Arājs, J., 207, 421n81
Arajs, Jekabs T., 280, 290, 434n59, 435n89
Arājs, Viktors, 106, 107, 114, 115, 186, 187, 207, 377, 407n17, 408n27
Argentina, 49, 223, 285
Armstrong, O.K., 284
Arvida (Quebec), 293
Atlantic Films and Electronics Ltd, 267, 281, 366, 429n90
Atlantic Hardboard Industries Ltd, 344, 348, 365
Atlantic Jewellery and Watch Company, 344
Augustdorf, 285
Auskapš, Jūlijs, 88
Australia, 232, 246, 284, 359, 377
Austria, 59, 176, 195, 196, 223, 229, 232, 265, 270
Avotiņš, P., 288
Aylmer (Quebec), 227

Baker, Hyman, 354, 357
Balabkins, Nicholas, 5, 392n6, 395n25, 395n27, 396n50, 397n54
Ballantyne, Murray G., 372
Balodis, Agnis, 113, 391n3, 410n52, 432n12, 443n42, 443n44
Balodis, Jānis, 16, 20, 37, 58, 60, 71, 77, 78, 82, 88, 91, 92, 96, 202

Balodis, Ralph, 281, 432n12
Bandera, Stepan, 6
Bandrēvičs, Vilis, 43, 400n11
Bangerskis, Rūdolfs, 128, 151, 173f, 178, 183, 187
Bank of Latvia, 17, 41, 43, 45, 48, 65, 95, 120
Bankiņš, Aleksandrs, 286, 433n40
Bastjānis, Voldemārs, 179, 188, 190, 192, 197f, 203, 206, 210, 212f, 218, 420n55, 420n57, 420n65
Bay City (Michigan), 294
Bay D'Espoir (NF), 257, 259, 261, 268
Belgium, Belgian, 29, 34, 50, 157, 183f, 185, 190, 213, 235, 254, 265, 275, 287, 293, 398n83
Bell Island, 258, 269
Belorussia, 15, 106, 108f, 163, 409n42
Benninghaus, 134
Benno Schilde, 255f, 258, 267, 269, 329f, 340, 342f, 348–51, 356, 371, 439n40, 440n55, 441n95
Berend, Fritz, 305f
Bergs, Arveds, 30
Berķis, Krišjānis, 83, 89f
Berlin, viii, 8, 9, 22, 42, 45, 46, 48, 55, 57, 59, 60, 64, 76, 78, 79, 86, 91, 97, 106, 109–13, 115–20, 143, 154, 157, 161, 167, 170–3, 176, 183, 206, 222, 231, 305, 326, 335, 338, 382
Bernewitz, Pastor, 306
Bērziņš, Alfreds, 21, 24, 52, 54, 72, 81f, 83–6, 88, 97f, 100–2, 165, 170f, 179, 195, 199, 204–8, 218, 340, 353, 355, 360, 385, 397n52, 404n11, 406n40, 407n77, 408n22, 417n97f, 418n1, 419n20, 421n78, 421n80
Bērziņš, Andrejs, 23f, 35, 37, 39f, 46, 52, 60, 64, 71, 101, 204, 385, 399n96
Bērziņš, Bruno, 289, 434n57
Berzinsh, Alex, 251f, 279, 281, 426n24, 431n3
Biebrich on the Rhein, 173
Biķernieki (Bickern), 163
Bilmanis, Alfred, 84, 163f, 171, 179–81, 185, 188–92, 196–208, 210, 218, 391n4, 392n10, 395n19, 397n53, 399n92, 400n35, 400nn37–8, 405n17, 406n40, 407n1, 407n77, 416n72, 417n98, 419n15, 420nn69–78
Birznieks, Jānis, 49, 54
Black, W., 333
Blāzma, V., 203
Bloomfield, Louis M., 332, 354f, 357, 359–62, 369, 372
Blumbergs, J., 83f, 95f
Blumbergs, VEF technician, 170f
Bodenwerder, 239f, 371
Bofors, A.-B., 56
Bolšteins, Ludvigs, 90
Bonn, 5, 258, 315, 320f, 324, 352, 363
Bönner, Egon, 119, 121, 127f, 411n69, 411n82, 411n93, 412n110
Borries, Claus, 167, 168, 171
Boston, 222, 300, 345f
Braemer, Friedrich, 306
Braun-Wogau, Max, 53, 240, 270, 304–6, 319, 331, 333, 346, 354, 365–7, 371f, 404n1, 414n13, 423n27, 429n104, 435nn94–8, 442n11
Braun-Wogau, Trudi, 319, 346
Brazil, 223, 286, 288, 344
Breikšs, Leonīds, 30, 306
Brigus, 270
Brimelow, Thomas, 183f
BRINCO, 275, 314, 382
Brock Steel Corp, 372
Browne, William J., 298f
Bryson, Ray N., 373, 422n6

Bruemmer, Leon von, 12, 166f, 278, 299, 208, 435n83, 436n103, 436n20
Buchenwald concentration camp, 281
Buenos Aires, 288
Building Products Ltd, 245
Bulgaria, 226
Bulins, Karlis, 281, 289
Burmeister, Wilhelm, 124, 129, 157, 168f, 171, 304, 340, 412n101, 417n92, 417n99, 435n92, 439n35

Cadbury, George, 249
Čakste, Konstantīns, 161, 165, 417n106
Čakste, Mintauts, 180
Canada Cement Co, 254
Canadian Anti-Communist League, 299f
Canadian Council of Laymen, 284
Canadian Imperial Bank of Commerce, 349
Canadian Industries Construction Holding Trust, 330
Canadian Javelin, 314–17, 320–2, 327
Canadian Jewish Congress, 302
Canadian Machinery Holding Trust, 254
Canadian Promoting and Trading Ltd, 270
Canaris, Wilhelm, 306
CARA Development Corp, 372f
Carancis, John, 374f, 426n16, 442n19
Carbonear, 267, 270
Carleton College, 227f, 238, 270
Cartonage du Québec, 373
Case, Superintendent, 335
CCF (Co-operative Commonwealth Federation), 301, 338
Celmiņš, Augusts, 43
Celmiņš, Gustavs, 112–14, 116, 141, 149, 165, 202
Celms, Jānis, 130f, 288f, 433n54
Cement and General Development Corp, 252, 312, 426n32
Central Council of Latvia (see LCP)
Cēsis sanatorium, 98
Chalker, James, 258, 425n8, 425n10, 427n49
Chicago, 290
Chichaev, Ivan A., 78, 405n19
Christian Union, 29
Churchill, Winston, 212, 301
Churchill Falls, 275, 430n123
Cielēns, Feliks, 162
Claudius Peters, 258
Clay, Lucius, 177, 418n4
CMIC, 346, 351, 439n47
Communist Party, 6, 20, 21, 96, 98f, 101, 108, 131f, 162, 183, 192, 221, 229, 230, 233, 298, 383
Communists (see Communist Party)
Connors Brothers, 345
Copenhagen, 286, 290
Corner Brook, 251, 279, 281f, 286, 289, 298, 304, 349
Council of American–Latvian Organizations, 300
Couture, Claude S., 372, 442n6, 442n12
Credit Bank of Latvia, 21, 23f, 29, 35–8, 39, 54, 65, 85, 100f
Crosbie, John, 384, 388, 443n41, 443n46, 443n48, 443n55
Cuba, 344
Curtis, Leslie R., 255, 269, 275, 316, 320, 332, 334, 336, 340, 343, 346f, 350, 352, 354, 365, 440n57
Czech(oslovakia), 17, 57, 58, 226

Dālbergs, Artūrs, 56, 90
Dāle, Viktors, 31, 288, 433n53
Dancauskis, A., 178, 186, 418n6, 419n37
Dāniels, Viktors, 131f, 137, 148
Dankers, Oskars, 106, 116, 118–22, 141, 143f, 146f, 150f, 157, 161, 163, 164, 166, 192, 377
Dannenbergs, P(ēteris), Steamship Co, 288
Dārziņš, Luiz Ansis, 286, 433n39
Daugavas Vanagi, 213, 215, 236, 295, 300, 377f
Daugavpils, 304
Davis, Mortimer, 226
Dawe, Chester, 256, 427n42
Dawe, Donald W.K., 329, 332, 346, 438n9
Deglavs, Viktors, 106, 112f, 114f, 410n50
Degviela, A/S, 36, 59
Delvigs, A., 43
Democratic Centre, 19
Denmark, 50, 127, 195, 269, 285, 288, 290, 373
Department of National Revenue, 335, 372, 442n7
Detmold, 179, 181, 193, 195, 197, 201, 285, 290, 412n126
Detroit, 229, 293f
Dinsbergs, Aleksandrs, 43, 48, 59, 60, 76
Dombrovskis, Johans, 287, 433n43
Dorn, Wilhelm, 266–8
Douay Import and Export (see Duane Import and Export Corp)
Doyle, John C., 314–17, 346, 437n25
Dravnieks, Arvīds, 131, 176, 178f
Drechsler, Heinrich, 110, 119–22, 125, 128–30, 134–6, 142–4, 146–50, 152, 155–61, 169, 411n90f, 411n96, 412n122, 413n9, 413n143, 414n16, 414n29, 415n36, 415n54f, 415n64, 416n68
Dresdner Bank, 166f, 170, 416n85
Droschiba, A/S, 36
Duane Import and Export Corp, 327, 343
Duparquet (Quebec), 293
Dyckerhoff Cement Works, 173

Eckart Strickwarenfabrik, 270
Edmonton, 5, 219, 327, 373, 375f, 379
Eichelis, Alberts, 377, 408n24
Einbergs, Bernhards, 60, 78, 90, 92, 105, 165, 202
Eisenach, 174
Eisenhower, Dwight D., 177, 181, 232, 296
Eķis, Ludvigs, 35–7, 39f, 397n52, 399n96
Elpers, Arnolds, 76
Eltermanis, Alfonss, 43, 294
Eltermans (see Eltermanis)
EMENCO (Eastern Machinery and Engineering Co), 329f, 342, 349f
Endziņš, Lieut, 131
Enskilda Bank, 56
Erhard, Ludwig, 258, 271, 429n102
Eriksson, Hermann, 52, 56
Esenvalds, Laimonis, 338, 439n27f
Esslingen, 184, 188–90, 192f, 194–8, 210f, 215, 218, 221, 417n108, 419n29, 419n32, 419n35, 419n42, 420n45, 420n47, 420nn65–7
Estonia, 7, 15, 19, 22, 34, 37, 76, 90, 120, 132, 141, 157, 161f, 168, 173, 176, 178, 222, 226, 229, 391n5, 398n83, 409n33, 409n42
Eupen and Malmedy, 229

Farmers Union, 21, 32, 106, 120, 131, 293
Feldmanis, Jūlijs, 200–3, 209, 229f, 421n71, 421n73, 423n26
Ferryland, 275
Fibre Engineering and Machinery Co, 244
Finland, 47, 50, 56, 87, 89, 97, 162, 188, 198, 260
Flensburg, 179, 279
Ford Motor Co, 229
Fouché, Joseph, 7
France, French, 29, 139, 185, 287
Frankfurt am Main, 176, 195, 210, 212, 239, 241, 269, 296
Frankfurt an der Oder, 225–7, 298, 326, 374, 382
Freimanis, Arturs, 118f, 411n86
Fridrichsons, J., 100
Fromme, Mr, 168
Funk, Walther, 76

Gailītis, A., 293
Garmisch-Partenkirchen, 269, 348
Geffine, Victor, 315–17, 437n25
Geneva, 185, 200–2, 208f, 211, 216f, 224, 226, 229f, 282, 326, 381, 383
Gestapo, 12, 148, 165, 169–71, 173f, 206
Glen, J. Allison, 223, 423n11
Gobiņš, Ojārs, 339, 439n31
Goodrich, Noel, 352
Göring, Hermann, 76, 108, 111
Gostik, Ron, 300, 435n84
Gotha, 174, 176f
Graebe, Kurt, 148, 166f, 211, 416n84
Graudins, Arnolds L., 280, 326, 428n80, 428n84, 429n88, 429n107, 431n9f, 433n43
Grīnbergs, Ernests Gunars, 290, 434n62
Grīnbergs, Teodors (see Gruenbergs)
Grobins, Wolf, 279, 281
Grube, Ludwig, 272, 275f, 319, 346, 365, 367, 381
Gruenbergs, Teodors, 112, 211
Grundherr, Werner von, 12, 81, 97, 394n7, 399n99, 402n82
Grüne Mappe, 111
Gulbis, Alfreds, 208, 421n82
Gulbis, Fricis, 178f, 181, 189, 419n19, 420n45
Gwyn, Richard, 7, 13, 387, 393n27, 394n11, 425n8, 428n65, 437n26, 437n38, 443n41, 443n52, 444n53

Haguma GmbH, 270, 272, 275, 424n42, 429n96
Hahlbrock, G., and Co, 270, 273
Hahn, Baron, 282
Hahn, Joseph H., 343
Haiti, 344
Halifax, 241, 246, 356
Hamburg, 258, 265, 266, 267, 271, 377
Hamelin, 270
Hamilton, William, 370, 442n6
Hamilton River, 259, 275, 314
Hanhart, Rudolf, 317, 437n27, 437n32
Hanning und Kahl, 270, 275
Hanover, 270, 275f
Harbour Breton, 251
Harriman-Ripley, 254, 258, 260, 268, 312, 314, 427n48
Harris, Walter E., 297f, 303, 432n14
Hasselblatt, Werner, 109, 409n33
Hayes, Saul, 302f, 435n88
Hehn, Jürgen von, 21, 391n5
Heidelberg, 269

Herz, Hubertus, vii, 329f, 342, 348, 349–52, 366, 430n117, 430n126, 437n37, 437n41, 438n4, 438nn6–7, 440n54f, 441n95
Higgins, Gordon, 297f, 299, 303, 332f, 335, 339, 340, 350, 352–4, 358f, 362, 371, 439n30, 439n35, 442n7
Hill, Thomas, 252, 427n44, 427n47
Hilpert, Hanna, 270
Himmler, Heinrich, 79, 140, 144, 152, 160, 169, 415n66
Hinneberg, Walter J., 265
Hinneberg, Werner, 265–7, 269f, 273–5, 344, 428n82, 428n84, 429n85, 429nn87–9, 429n91, 429n106f, 430n108, 430n113, 430n122, 432n13
Hitler, Adolf, 6, 10, 21, 57, 79f, 102, 107, 109, 111, 112, 115f, 118, 132, 134, 136, 140f, 144, 146, 147, 153, 160, 163, 166, 169, 173, 202, 230f, 233, 282, 295f, 337f, 377, 383
Hitler–Stalin Pact, 73f
Hochseefischerei Kiel AG, 345
Hoechst AG, 269
Hoffmann, A.C., 266
Holland (see Netherlands)
Hollet, Malcolm, 327, 367
Holyrood, 270, 333, 346
Honderich, Beland, 360
Horthy, Miklos von, 6
Horwood, Harold, 7, 12f, 251, 261, 323, 324, 327, 337f, 363, 365, 388, 494n32
Howe, C.D., 249, 251, 379, 381, 425n8
Howland, Robert D., 238, 242, 245, 424n47, 424n49, 425n53, 427n38
Huhn, Karl, 288
Hunt, Emerson, Stirling, and Higgins, 332

IBEC, 248
Iesalniece, Lina, 26, 397n58
IG Farben, 258, 269, 277, 375
Immers, Arvīds, 293, 434n65
Innes, Robert, 213, 223, 226
Innsbruck, 178
International Refugee Organization (see IRO)
International Women's Association, 44
Inveiss, J., 287f
IRC (see Red Cross)
IRO, 9, 176, 208f, 213, 222f, 224, 226, 228–30, 232, 239, 246, 280, 282, 284, 289, 297, 326, 382, 385
Italy, 17, 18, 35, 185, 275

Jablonskis, Andrejs, 100
Jackson, Rupert, 263, 326, 428n74, 436n7, 437n52
Jacobsons, Eduard, 280, 358, 431n11
Jagars, A., 100, 203
Jamieson, Don, 7, 10f, 251, 317f, 393n30
Jansone, Anna, 25, 397n58
Jansons, Ansis, 290, 434n61
Janums, Vilis, 183, 185, 196, 234f, 283, 290, 432n14
Jaunlatvieši, 131
Jeckeln, Friedrich, 109, 110, 140f, 145, 150, 152, 377
Jekste, Alberts, viii, 108, 267, 280f, 297, 353, 355, 358, 408n25, 410n61, 424n40, 432n12, 432n15, 432n16
Jelgava (Mitau), 126, 127, 131, 136, 153, 171, 289
Jenny, William, 266
Jews, 3, 7f, 12f, 15, 17–20, 104f, 113, 126, 279, 293, 296–8, 304–7, 380; anti-Semitism, 13, 20, 33, 37, 70, 85,

104, 166, 230, 293, 300, 302f, 323, 367, 372; Aryanization, 68, 166; Holocaust, 3, 7, 13, 107–9, 114, 122, 132, 163, 169, 183, 121f, 295–8, 306, 367, 377f, 408n18, 408n23, 409n28, 417n95; Mischlinge, 126
Jodrey, Roy, 238
Johannson, Agnar, 32, 99f
Johannson, Elizabeth, 70, 99f
Johansson, B., 52
John Cabot Textiles, 344
Johnson, Robert, 325
Jugendheim, 267f
Jung und Lindig, 266

Kācens, A., 188, 197, 420n66
Kalējs, Konrāts, 377
Kalniņš, Bruno, 197
Kalniņš, Pauls, 179f, 181, 196, 210
Kalniņš, Siegrid, 306
Kalpakieši, 16, 105
Kalpaks, Oskars, 16, 155
Kameras (chambers), 22, 37, 61, 399n99
Kaminskis, Jānis, 69, 83f, 93, 403n114
Kampe, Andrejs, 76
Karčevskis, 100, 293
Kārkliņš, 100
Kassel, 184,
Kattowitz, 253
Kaulbach, Herbert, 270
Kaunas, 162
Kavanagh, Margaret, 333
Keenleyside, Hugh, 222, 223, 226–9, 381, 421n84, 422n6, 423n15f
Ķegums, viii, 24, 35f, 48, 51f, 55, 71, 90, 93f, 96, 289
Ķēniņš, Atis, 19, 96
Ķerve, Ernests, 286, 433n37
Keyserlingk, Robert W. von, 282, 296
Kiegelmeier, A/S, 94
Ķikauka, Pēteris, 288, 433n48, 435n90
Kipling, Rudyard, 224
Kirchensteins, Augusts, 96, 202, 204
Kirmse, Erich, 334, 348, 349
Ķirš, Mazpulki inspector, 132
Kīsle, Dr, 178
Kleist, Peter, 81, 97, 111, 113, 115, 116–19, 122f, 125, 144, 158, 250, 394n7, 402n82, 409n29, 409n36, 409n39, 410n67, 411n80f, 411n87, 411n97, 413n131
Klīve, Ādolfs, 43, 120, 165, 179
Klumberg, W., 115
Koch, Egon, 275
Koch, Fritz, 305
Korea, 288
Kotze, Ulrich von, 60, 70, 76–80, 86, 90, 92, 97, 103, 167, 400n30, 400n33, 400n34, 403n108, 403n121, 403n123, 404n4, 404n8, 405n18, 405n25, 405n29, 406n42
Kramer, Abe, 177, 418n9
Krastiņš, Ilgvars, 431n10
Krāstiņš, J., 149
Kreišmanis, Ernests, 105, 114
Kreuger match trust, 52, 55f
Kreyser, Friedrich, 32, 52f, 167, 240, 242f, 246, 250, 252f, 255, 258, 259, 265, 267, 270, 274, 276f, 303f, 306, 313f, 343, 344, 348–51, 369, 371f, 388f, 401n52, 423n27, 424n43, 425n12, 425n55, 426n25, 426n28, 429n96, 429n100, 429n104, 430n121, 431n129f, 435nn91–3, 435n98f, 436n11, 436n14, 436n18, 440n55, 442n11, 444n56
Kriegsheim, Arno, 109, 409n28

Kripēns, Arvīds, 141, 178, 183, 185f
Kristīga apvienība (see Christian Union)
Kroeger, Jürgen Ernst, 15, 394n16
Kronacker, Paul, 254, 426n34
Kruger, Captain, 359, 360
Krūka, Tonīja, 290, 360, 380, 434n61
Krūmiņš, G., 43, 50
Krumins, Janis, 280, 281, 340, 417n92, 439n35
Krupp firm, 258
Kudra, A/S, 94
Küchler, Georg von, 111
Kundziņš, Kārlis, 179, 182, 186, 189, 199, 420n45
Kunetz (Kunečs), Anna, 43, 97, 102, 115
Kurzeme (Kurland), 14, 15, 25, 27, 280, 287
Kviesis, Alberts, 20, 120, 161, 173, 204

Labrador, 248, 254, 258–61, 263, 268, 271, 275, 311–14, 316f, 324
Lady Davis Foundation, 226, 238, 282, 332, 354f, 361, 423n17, 423n20
Laiviņš, J., 178
Landau, Julius, 268
Langins, E., 281, 358
Langins, Junija, 281, 358
Lapenieks, Vilis, 286
Lapins, Karl, 280
Lapsiņš, Roberts, 431n10
Latgallians, 123
LATUCO, 259f, 268
Latvian Central Committee (see LCK)
Latvian Central Council (see LCP)
Latvian Chamber of Trade and Industry (see LTRK)
Latvian National Centre, 284
Latvian National Federation in Canada (see LNAK)
Latvian Social Democratic Workers Party, 301, 338, 439n28
Latvian Society of Tennessee, 300
Latvian–Soviet Mutual Assistance Pact, 76, 80, 83, 87, 404n2
Latvijas Kokvilna, A/S, 37f
Latvijas Kokvilnas Ražojumi (LKR), 37f, 59
Latviešu Nacionālā Apvienība (Latvian National Federation), 30
Latviešu Nacionālā Partija, 131
Lavenieks, LCP chairman, 211
LCK, 179, 181f, 184–6, 188–97, 200, 213f, 223, 283, 290, 419n32, 419n35, 419n42, 420n45, 420n45, 420n47, 420n66
LCP (Latvijas Centrālā Padome, founded 1943), 6, 162, 164f, 180, 191, 193, 421n73
LCP (Latviešu Centrālā Padome, founded 1945), 179, 182, 186, 188f, 191–7, 200f, 206–8, 211, 213, 223, 234f, 417n108, 420n49, 420n51, 420n59, 420n66, 423n12f
Leckzyck, Adolf, 46f, 60f, 74, 81, 86, 91f, 102f, 114f, 123, 133f, 155, 160, 306, 402n80f, 405n28, 406n66, 407n73, 407n79, 410n59, 410n63
Legion, Royal Canadian, 32
Legion (Latvian), 13, 109, 139f, 141, 144, 146, 150–3, 158, 160, 173, 218, 221, 230, 281, 289, 291, 381, 415n37
Legionnaires (Latvian), 7, 9, 178, 182–7, 189, 205, 208, 209, 213, 221, 229f, 232, 234f, 286, 289–91, 295, 300f, 377, 385, 386

Leikucs, Olga, 279f, 288, 290–3, 308, 326, 333f, 365, 431n5, 431n7, 431n9, 433nn37–9, 431n48, 431n50, 434nn56–61f, 434nn64–6, 434n69, 439n44
Leimane, Ilona, 30
Leimanis, Žanis, 288, 433n51
Leitz, 268, 269, 273, 429n94
Leja, Ernest, 239–46, 250, 252–5, 279, 281, 329–31, 340, 341f, 348–51, 353–6, 358, 366, 424n36, 424n38, 424n44f, 425nn52–4, 425n12, 426n25, 426n28, 438n5, 440n55
Lejiņš, J., 178f
Lerch, Johannes, 269, 272, 330f, 348, 430n111, 440n51
Lettonia, 29, 107
Levenson, Jeannot, 303, 435n89
Levitan, Samuel, 12, 394n7
Lewin, Michael, 252, 257, 314, 427n44f, 436n16
Libau (see Liepāja)
Libauer Bank, 167
Liepāja, viii, 3, 25, 27–32, 74, 103, 180, 280, 305
Liepiņš, Roberts, 173, 180, 184, 197, 206, 209, 210, 212f, 218, 419n29
Lincoln, Trebitsch, 7f
Lithuania, 15, 19, 50, 57, 60, 68, 95, 99, 102, 105, 111, 120, 132, 133, 150, 158, 162, 176, 178, 222
Livland, 14, 15
LNA (Lavijas Nacionālā Apvienība), 214f
LNAK (Latviešu Nacionālā Apvienība Kanādā), 290, 301
LNC (Latvian National Committee), 359–61
LNK (Latvijas Nacionālā Komiteja), 178f
LNP (Latviešu Nacionālā Padome), 214f, 234, 236
LOC (Latvijas Organizācijas Centrs), 105f, 112f, 115
Lockheed-Georgia Co, 374
Lohse, Hinrich, 110
Loram Ltd, 373, 375
Losis, Irma, 12, 397n63, 406n71
LSCO (Latvijas Skautu Centrālā Organizācija), 28
LTA (Latvju Tautas Apvienība), 215
LTP (Latvju Tautas Padome), 213f
LTRK (Latvian Chamber of Trade and Industry), 37, 41, 61–5, 71
Lūbeck, 110, 178f
Lucis, Arnis, vi, viii, xi, 281, 397n58, 408n20, 424n30, 432n12, 432nn25–7, 437n28
Lucis, Sofija, vi, 394n13, 397n58, 408n20, 408n26, 432n12, 432n27, 441n97
Lūkiņš, Augusts, 293, 434n65
Lurje, Elja, 296–8, 342–5, 351, 355, 357, 371f, 435n76, 439n42, 439n44, 440n57, 442n11
Lūsis, Mazpulki leader, 132, 134
Luters, Hermans, 293, 434n69
Luxemburg, 229

MacKeen, J.C., 238, 242, 243, 245, 425n50, 425n53
Mackintosh, George M., 307f, 314, 436n15
Macmillan, Harold, 227, 423n22
MacNeill, R.J., 315
Madison (Wisconsin), 237
Maikovskis, Boleslavs, 377
Malagodi, Alfred, 345, 439n43f

Malletke, Ostministerium official, 172, 402n81, 410n59, 410n63
Mallory, G.D., 238, 427n38, 430n119
Malmanis, 106
Mannheim, 178
Manning, Preston, 376, 442n20
Marx, Herbert, 272, 319, 348f
Mateass, Aleksandrs, 135, 155
Mateus, Katrina (Kiki), 32, 318, 329, 330f, 343f, 349, 350f, 353f, 356f, 372
Mateus, Valdis, 32, 180, 210, 211, 213, 215, 244, 256, 284, 318, 343–5, 353–62, 369
Mauriņa, Zenta, 33, 398n81
Maurins, Janis, 360
Mazpulki, 22, 132, 134–7, 159
McGill University, 220, 226f
McNamara, George, 300, 435n85
Mednis, Arturs, 294, 434n71
Mednis, J., 100
Meiksins, Gregory, 162f, 190, 298f, 416nn74–5
Melliņš, A., 118f
Mercier, Honoré, 376
Mertens, Michael, 268
Mexico, 344
MIAG, 253–5, 258, 267, 268, 269, 270, 272, 319, 329–34, 340–2, 348–51, 352, 356, 365, 370f
Mickelsen, S.R., 177
Miezis, J., 179
Mikelsons, Professor, 203
Miķelsons, Sigurds, vii, 280, 431n7f, 434n76
Mikelsons, Velta, 281, 333
Milwaukee, 287
Mitterand, François, 6, 139
Molotov, Viacheslav, 76f, 79, 95, 405n19
Montagnes, James, 325
Montgomery, Sir Bernard, 184, 186, 232
Montreal, viii, 5, 100, 220, 227, 238, 250, 272, 282, 299, 301, 303, 315f, 318, 320, 321, 322, 331, 332, 335f, 340, 342, 344, 348f, 351, 352, 354, 355, 357, 358, 360f, 363, 366, 368–70, 372, 373, 374, 375, 379, 380, 382, 387
Morgan, Baxter, viii, 11, 394n2
Mortgage Bank of Latvia, 35, 65, 69
Moscow, 56, 76, 78, 79, 83, 87, 90, 99, 103, 201, 211, 281,
Moser and Sons, 270, 273
Münninghoff, Joan, 171f, 417n102f
Munske, German youth leader, 135
Munters, Vilhelms, 37, 50f, 58, 60f, 72, 76–8, 80–3, 86–9, 91f, 97f
Murdock, John, 317, 318
Murray, Miles, 335f, 340
Muskats, V., 288, 433n50
Mussolini, Benito, 18, 21f, 34, 398n85

Nagel, Colonel, 115
NALCO, 9, 258, 276f, 285, 292, 311–23, 327, 328, 330, 338, 342, 346f, 350, 373f, 381f, 427n48, 436n2, 436n4, 436n13, 436n15, 436n18, 436n22, 437n24f, 437n27, 437n40, 437n42, 437n46
Nash and Associates, 373
Nash, Hugh G., 379
Naudīte, 85
Neimanis, Welta, 288, 433n49
Nelson, Donald, 249
Nepārts, A., 131f, 148, 149, 412n126, 414n22, 414n27, 421n90
Netherlands, 29, 50, 130, 171f, 177, 269, 275

Neue Technik GmbH, 240, 242–6, 253, 255, 265, 279, 304, 348f, 351, 424n39, 424n48
Neustadt, 293
New Jersey, 293, 369
New York, 49f, 162f, 220, 244, 252, 254, 256–8, 260, 262, 268, 280, 284, 289, 295, 296, 298, 301, 302, 305, 312, 313, 314, 318, 319, 329, 338, 339, 340, 342–6, 349, 351, 358, 365, 369, 371, 375, 380, 382, 387
New York group, 252, 254–8, 260, 268, 312, 365
New Zealand, 25, 284, 359, 433n32
Nickel, 137
NKVD, 97, 101, 102, 205, 206, 291, 385
Noltein, Oberlandesrichter, 306
Nordmeer shipping company, 266, 428n84
North Star Cement Ltd, 254, 426n34f, 427n41
North Star Development Corp, 320f, 344
North Sydney, 247, 250
Nova Scotia Research Foundation, 238, 240, 242f, 424n35, 424n42, 424n46
Nuremberg, 166, 178, 185, 210
Nylander, Lennard, 305

Ogle, A/S, 36
Osis, August J., 219, 422n112, 443n30
Osis, Roberts, 141, 173, 178, 186, 189
Ositis, Aleksandrs, 278, 285, 432n18, 433n36
Osoling, Pastor, 306
Ozols, Edgars, 289, 434n56
Ozols, Peteris, 289, 434n56

Pāts, Konstantin, 90
Palin, Eduard, 89
Panama, 344
Pārups, 131, 149
Pavelic, Ante, 6
Pavolini, Alessandro, 21, 396n43
PCIRO (see IRO)
Pērkonkrusts, Pērkonkrustieši, 6, 18, 21, 29, 30, 105–7, 112–14, 118, 129, 131f, 135, 138
Pērkons, E., 289f, 432n30
Perlin, Albert, 4, 10f, 139, 247, 249, 251, 310, 323, 326f, 381f
Pētersons, Armands, 293, 434n68
Petten, Ray, 249, 298, 330
PHD (Polizeihilfsdienst), 106
Phillips, Alan, 384, 443n48
Phillips, Bloomfield, Vineberg, and Goodman, 332
Piasecki, Boleslaw, 7f
Pickersgill, Jack W., viii, 370, 441n5, 442n6
Pike, Edgar, 363f, 441n88
Pippy, Chesley A., 311, 315, 347
Plange, Georg E.R., 266, 436n3
Plensners, Aleksandrs, 106, 112–16, 129, 143, 179, 206, 218, 410n50
Plūme, Roberts, 144
Poland, 8, 14, 57, 74, 79, 133
Poles, 7f, 15, 113, 133, 212
Poorthsdyk, 172
Port Clyde Packing Co, 343, 371
Potsdam, 5, 178
Power, Gregory, viii, 275, 347, 380, 430n125
Prague, 168, 170f, 174
Pratte, Gaston, 373
Priede, J., 221
Prīmanis, Mārtiņš, 52, 77, 131, 142, 144, 147, 164
Puhris, Mikelis, 286, 433n38

Puntulis, Haralds, 221f
Pusbarņieks, Jānis, 293, 434n67
Pushie, Gordon F., viii, 319, 324, 346, 352, 430n117

Quebec City, 220, 373
Quinton, Herman, 254, 258

Radziņš, Jānis, 293, 434n70
Raimonds, Anna Dzinejs de, 280, 431n11
Rainis, Jānis, 11
Rancāns, Jāzeps, 100, 179f, 188, 197–201, 203, 206–13, 420n63
Rasche, Karl, 166–8, 304, 405n20, 416n85f, 416n89
Rationalization, Institute of, 43, 48, 62, 64f, 70, 383
Rattermann, E.E., and Brothers, 70
Raudziņš, D., 149
Rawe and Company, 270
Red Cross, 32, 184; International (IRC), 184, 185, 200; Latvian, 179, 180, 200, 209, 218, 419n29
Reifferscheidt, Adolph, 315, 320f, 352, 430n111, 436n6, 436n19, 437n41, 437n43, 440nn58–60, 441n86
Reiters, Teodors, 287, 433n45
Rēzekne, 221
Rheinmetall-Borsig AG, 46, 44n23
Ribbentrop, Joachim von, 79, 166, 231
Richardson, Claude S., 371, 372, 375, 376, 379, 442n20, 442n26
Richters, F., 293, 434n65
Rickert, Swedish ambassador, 305
Rieker, Roland, 270
Riga Film, 108, 267, 281
Rigaer Vereinigte Portland-Zementwerke und Baustoff GmbH, 167
Rīgas Cementa Fabrikas, 32, 52
Rigips, 239
Ripley, J.P., 254, 258, 260, 268, 307, 312, 314, 427n48
Ritums, Eriks, 293, 434n66
Robertson, Bobbie, viii, 251, 339, 426n19, 439n29
Rockefeller, Nelson, 248
Roemer, August, 348
Roethe, Eberhard Hermann, 267, 346, 350
Rogers, Texas oil millionaire, 254, 298
Roosevelt, Franklin D., 301
Roques, Karl von, 109, 114, 115, 118, 145, 409n28
Rosenberg, Alfred, 109–11, 113, 115–19, 121–5, 128, 134, 136f, 144, 149, 152–5, 157–61, 168f, 392n9, 409n32, 409n43, 410n59, 411n92, 412nn101–3, 412n122, 412n129, 413n142f, 414n30, 415n38, 415n50, 415n55, 415n59, 415n62f, 415n65f, 416n68
Rothschild, Anthony de, 275, 314
Royal Paper Box Co, 374
Rozenšteins, H., 90
Roziņš, Jānis, 293, 434n65
Rozītis, E., 211
Rüdiger, Wilhelm von, 154f, 306, 415n34
Rullis, former scout leader, 135
Runte, Dr, 172
Rūsis, attorney, 173
Russia (see USSR)

Sachsenhausen concentration camp, 170
Saeima, 16f, 19–21, 29f, 165, 179f, 196, 204, 293
Saint John (New Brunswick), 331f

Šakars, Jānis, 43, 100, 168, 398n78, 403n116, 417n91
Salcmanis, Jānis, 43, 50
Saldnieks, Lavīze, 26f
Salnais, Voldemars, 52, 165, 417n106
Sanders, Visvaldis, 29, 118f
Sandler, Richard, 52, 56
Saulite, Voldemar, 280
Schacht, Hjalmar, 10, 28f, 45, 232f, 299, 331, 368, 397n69
Schack, Eckhard von, 22, 39, 42, 57, 60, 64, 401n44, 401n70, 402n77
Schieferit, 239
Schmidt, C.Ch., 32, 240
Schmorda, 174
Schröder, Walther, 110, 119, 140f, 144–7, 152, 414n20
Schulze, Johannes, 268
Schuma (Schutzmannschaft), 106, 140f, 156
Schuman, Frederic L., 416n74
Schwartz, E., 306
Schweizerischer Bankenverein, 166
Sclanders, Ian, 325
Seehusen, Harald, 304, 417n92, 435n92
Seja, M., 290, 434n60
Selonija, 29
Senate (Canada), 28, 228, 231–3, 299, 326, 331, 382, 397n68
Senate (Latvia), 34, 120, 125f
Sennewald, Lothar, 268, 273, 276, 331, 365, 430n113f, 430n117
Sentab, A.-B., 51
Sharon, W.F., 375f, 442n20
Sharpe, E.L., 333
Short, N., 257, 280
Siberia, 14, 99–101, 108, 238, 239, 281
Siebert, Walter E., 313
Siegheim, Arthur, 259f, 267, 268f, 271, 317, 427nn55–6, 428n59f, 429n104f
Sietiņsons, Albiņš, 294, 434n72
Silgailis, Arturs, 143, 144, 218, 377
Siliņš, Jānis, 290–2, 434n63f
Simm, GK adviser, 135, 146, 158
Skaistlauks, Voldemars, 183, 221
Skanska Cement, 52, 305
Skirpa, Kazys, 105
Skrodelis, Alfreds, 282, 284, 339, 359, 373, 428n69, 439n30
Slakāns, V., 210, 420n65
Slavitt, Arthur, 298, 343, 345, 435n80
Šlessers, Anna Irma Elvira (see Valdmanis, Irma)
Šlessers, Jānis, 32
Šlessers, Kiki (see Mateus, Katrina)
Sloka, 279
Slovakia, 6, 107, 123, 142, 144, 152, 153, 157, 159, 162, 197, 199, 202
Smallwood, Joseph R., ix, 3, 7, 10f, 13, 248–55, 258–64, 268–70, 272f, 275–7, 283f, 296–8, 300, 307f, 310–20, 323–5, 328–32, 336–43, 346–51, 359, 362f, 365, 367, 370, 379, 380–2, 384, 386–8, 394n4, 425n7f, 426nn30–5, 427n40, 427n47, 427n56, 428n67, 428n69f, 428n76, 428n79, 429n92, 429n101, 430n115, 430n118, 430n120, 431n9, 431n128, 436n9, 436n13, 437n25, 437n39f, 437n42, 437n44, 438n5f, 441n86, 441n5
Smetona, Antanas, 95
Smith, A., 368
Smith, H.D., 242
Snikeris, Ernests and Ruta, 281, 432n18
Social Democrats, 13, 20f, 53f, 123, 179, 180, 301, 338, 383, 386
Soviet Union (see USSR)

Speer, Albert, 173
Speich, Rudolf, 166
Spencer, Edward, 275
Springers, 355, 360
Squires, Richard, 341, 387
St Andrews (New Brunswick), 327, 331, 343–6, 351, 357, 369, 371, 439n44
St Andrews Packers, 343, 345, 371, 439n45
Stadtoldendorf, 239f, 265
Stahlbau Rheinhausen, 259
Stahlecker, Walter, 105f, 109, 132, 408n23
Staks, Feliks, 203
Stalin, Josef, 6, 74, 78, 87, 104, 141, 163, 176, 238, 383
Stamford (Connecticut), 285
Steer, George H., 376, 442n21
Šteinbriks, Olģerts, 132, 137
Steinbrück, Kurt, 254, 348
Stephenson, Sir William, 248, 311–13, 372, 436n8
Sterste, P., 191f, 420n55
Stethem, John Holt, 375, 378
Stewart, J.M., 238
Sthamer, G., 91
Stinnes, Hugo, 267, 268
Stīpnieks, Aleksandrs, 289, 434n56
Stobbe, Fritz, viii, 11, 364, 394n3
Stockholm, viii, 5, 51–6, 164, 201, 207, 287, 301, 305, 306, 338f
Storch, Gillel, 305f
Straus, Nikolajs, 280
Strazdiņš, Ed, 285, 433n36
Strēlnieki, 16
Stutthof concentration camp, 303
Sudbury, 293
Suerbier, Werner, 267f
Suks (possibly identical with Eduards Suksis), 294
Suksis, Eduards, 43, 100, 203
Superior Rubber Co Ltd, 276, 319, 333, 346, 430n126, 436n12
Suziedelis, J., 162, 176, 416n71
Švābe, Arveds, 179, 196, 418n1
Švābe, Lote, 285, 433n37
Svenska Diamantberg-Borrings A/B, 306
Sweden, 15, 36, 46, 51–6, 59, 97, 139, 162, 164f, 183, 191–4, 203, 207, 214, 231, 234, 254, 259, 269, 274, 285, 289, 293, 301, 306, 325f, 337f, 340, 381, 382, 386
Switzerland, 17, 21, 50, 259, 265, 269, 274f, 287, 324, 344

Tālavija, 29, 82, 293, 294, 295, 386
Talbot, Antonio, 376
Tanner, Väinö, 359
Tauriņš, Alfred, 226
Tērauds, A/S, 59
Terra Nova Textiles Ltd, 364
Thuringia, 174, 176, 177, 208
Tiso, Josef, 6
Tonningen, Rost van, 130
Topsail, 270
Toronto, 222, 233, 258, 276, 280, 284, 287, 288, 290, 295, 297, 298, 301f, 312, 318, 333, 338, 360, 373, 375, 377
Trampedach, Friedrich, 117, 123f, 134, 138, 150f, 157, 407n14, 413n132, 415n38
Trautmanis, Ingrid, 12
Treilons, Klandis, 289, 434n57
Tuck, W.H., 213, 223
Turība, A/S, 59

Turta, Ronald, 315f, 318, 321
Twardowski, F. von, 405n29

Ukrainians, 295
Ulmanis, Kārlis, viii, 5, 8, 12, 16, 20–5, 30, 34f, 36–8, 39–41, 43–7, 54, 56f, 59, 61, 64, 66f, 71f, 73f, 76, 80–93, 95–8, 100–3, 105, 107, 112f, 116, 120, 123, 125, 131–3, 154, 162, 171, 180f, 191, 196, 200, 202–6, 225, 227, 234, 240, 260, 277, 290f, 293, 302, 378, 384f, 388, 396n43, 396n44, 399n99, 403n27
Ungurs, A., 203, 294
United Cotton Mills Ltd, 344, 346
United Nations, 176, 200, 209, 214, 221, 230, 236, 289, 354, 385
United States, 21, 49f, 58, 59, 80, 162f, 177, 190, 195, 222, 229, 232, 237f, 243, 246, 274, 276, 281, 285, 290, 301, 312, 319, 343f, 351, 359, 375, 377
UNRRA, 208, 239
Ur-Weser Gypsum Quarries Ltd, 371
USSR (Soviets, Russia), viii, 8, 13, 16, 20, 24–7, 46f, 48, 50, 57, 60, 73f, 76–82, 86–90, 92, 95–105, 107f, 111, 113–15, 131, 133, 151, 154, 162f, 175–8, 183–7, 192, 202, 205f, 208, 234f, 237–40, 249f, 264, 280f, 288f, 326, 359, 377, 380, 382f, 385, 386
UTAG, 80f, 97

Vainode, 29
Vairogs, A/S, 36, 56, 59
Valdmanis, Ansis, 26
Valdmanis, Emīls, 27, 339f
Valdmanis, Gundars, vii, 11f, 32
Valdmanis, Irma, vii, 11, 31f, 98, 99f, 168, 171, 220, 318, 322, 332, 351, 354f, 357, 361, 362, 386, 394n5, 398n77, 437n44
Valdmanis, Osvald, 11, 26–8, 29, 331, 343, 345, 369, 394n5
Valdmanis, Vaiva Mara, 31, 355, 361, 369
Valdmanis, Videvuds, 32
Valmiera, 123, 412n99
Valters, Miķelis, 18, 23, 185, 190, 193, 287, 395n31, 433n44
Vanags, Pēteris, 118f, 173
Veitnieks (Veitmanis), Kornelijs, 60, 88
VEF (Valsts Elektrotehniska Fabrika), 58, 170, 280
Veiss, Voldemars, 106, 118, 119–21, 122, 141, 144, 411n86
Venezuela, 222, 280, 288, 303
Vereinigte Baustoffwerke Bodenwerder, 240, 371
Vestermanis, Marģers, viii, 7, 13, 33, 393n24, 394n10, 395n29, 407n15, 407n75, 417n96
Vētra, N., 179, 183
Vīgants, Marta, 101, 203
Vīksna, P., 131
Vīksne, Ingrīda, 290, 434n61
Vilners, E., 43
Viskers, Ruta, 288, 433n47
Vītols, Pāvels, 98
Vītols, Teodors, 58
Voits, attorney, 173
Volkshilfe, 129, 153
Volonts, Jānis, 88
Vreeland, T. Reed, 252, 427n44
Vuškalns, Vilis, 288, 433n52
Vyshinskii, Andrei, 96, 293

Wabush (Labrador), 314, 316
Waffen-SS, 7, 13, 140, 160, 182–6, 209, 213, 220, 221, 228, 230, 232, 299, 337
Wagner, Eduard, 109, 409n30
Wallenberg, Jacob, 52
Wallis, Cedric, 315f, 318, 426n13, 426n22f
Walsh, Sir Albert, 334, 335, 336
Washington, 84, 163, 179, 211, 218, 237, 256, 288
Watson, Blanche, 379
Wehtje, Ernst, 305
Weis, Gustav Karl, 344
Weltner, C.H., 251
Westerburg, 186
Westermann, 306
Western Consultants, 373
Whitley, F.H., 369f, 441n5
Wiesbaden, 173, 231, 283
Wigforss, Erik, 52
Wilke, Heinz-Joachim, 334, 348f
Windecker, Adolf von, 110, 148, 149, 165–8, 211, 304, 414n29, 416n83, 421n93
Windsor Plaster Co, 244
Wittrock, Hugo von, 110, 119, 128, 148, 153, 159, 306, 411n85, 415n61
Wolfsberger, General, 150
Wolmar (see Valmiera)
Wood Gundy, 258, 260, 268, 312, 314
World Jewish Congress, 305
Würzburg, 178, 214
Žagars, Voldemārs, 43
Zāmuels, Valdemārs, 31, 34
Zariņš, Kārlis, 179f, 182f, 185f, 188–90, 192f, 194f, 197, 201, 203, 210, 212, 217, 222, 229f, 235f, 419n15f, 419n22, 419n30, 419n33, 420n44, 420n46, 420n57f, 420n61, 420n65, 421n88, 421n95, 422n110, 422n7f, 423n25
Zedelghem, POW camp, 83, 185, 190
Zemgale, 85, 95
Zemgalis, Mr, 288
Zemgals, Boriss, 29, 31–5, 39f, 71f, 73, 81f, 92, 94, 96–8, 100f 119f, 127f, 130, 141, 145f, 148, 165, 171, 179, 186, 201–5, 211, 216–19, 249, 305, 378, 385, 396n42, 397n69, 404n128, 411n81, 421nn74–7, 421n79
Zemgals, Gustavs, 217
Zemgals, Leonīds, 217f, 422n111
Zhukov, V., 186
Zībarts, Jānis, 43
Ziemupe (Seemuppen), viii, 15, 25f, 397n58
Zionism, 297
Zionist Federation of Latvia, 296
Zippmann, Ewald, 317, 344, 351, 429n101, 436n17
Ziskind, Gerald, 182, 187, 419n41, 420n53
Zotov, Ivan S., 74, 87–9
Zvirbulis, Nikolājs, 290, 434n59
Zwecker, Samuel, 343, 351, 371, 442n8

www.ingramcontent.com/pod-product-compliance
Lightning Source LLC
LaVergne TN
LVHW090757070826
844660LV00022B/1012

* 9 7 8 1 4 8 7 5 9 8 1 5 0 *